The Writer's Sourcebook

The Writer's Sourcebook

Strategies for Reading and Writing in the Disciplines

Laurie G. Kirszner
Philadelphia College of Pharmacy and Science

Stephen R. Mandell
Drexel University

Holt, Rinehart and Winston
New York   Chicago   San Francisco   Philadelphia
Montreal   Toronto   London   Sydney   Tokyo   Mexico City
Rio de Janeiro   Madrid

This book is dedicated to our mothers,
Mimi B. Gertz and Stella G. Mandell,
and to the memory of our fathers,
Abraham L. Gertz and Harry A. Mandell

Library of Congress Cataloging-in-Publication Data

The writer's sourcebook.

Includes index.
1. English language — Rhetoric.   2. College readers.
I. Kirszner, Laurie G.   II. Mandell, Stephen R.
PE1408.W7717   1987   808'.0427   86-24716

ISBN 0-03-002593-1

CBS COLLEGE PUBLISHING
Holt, Rinehart and Winston
The Dryden Press
Saunders College Publishing

Acknowledgments are on page 637

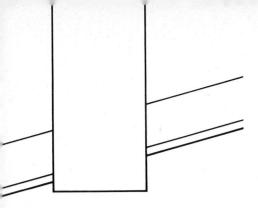

To the Instructor

By now the link between reading and writing has been well established, and research into the cognitive processes of student writers has clarified the important role that reading plays in the writing process. *The Writer's Sourcebook: Strategies for Reading and Writing in the Disciplines* developed out of the conviction that in order to be effective writers, students must be effective readers. Much of the writing students will be called upon to do in college and in their lives beyond college begins with close reading of material from a variety of sources — and from diverse subject areas — and focuses on gathering ideas from those sources and integrating them into original, unified essays. Consequently, being able to read, understand, interpret, and synthesize information are basic skills which all students must master if they are to become effective writers.

The Writer's Sourcebook is not a "research paper book"; that is, it does not show students all aspects of how to write a major library research paper. It does, however, prepare them to write such a paper by introducing research skills like analytical reading; source evaluation; using quotation, paraphrase, summary, synthesis, and critique; and using documentation. In other words, the text acquaints students with the strategies they need to read, judge, and use sources in a paper.

The Writer's Sourcebook combines a diverse collection of sixty-eight provocative reading selections with an instructional component that shows students how to read purposefully and analytically and write essays that use readings as source material. The connection between the processes of reading and writing is emphasized in every chapter.

Part I, "Reading and Writing from Sources," consists of three chapters designed to introduce students to the basic strategies they need to write source-based essays. Chapter 1, "Reading Sources," emphasizes active reading as preparation for writing, focusing first on comprehension skills such as how to survey a source, how to recognize cues to structure and emphasis and identify main ideas, and how to develop a system of selective highlighting that will bring a writer's key strategies and ideas into focus. The chapter then turns to analytical reading skills, explaining and illustrating the process of marginal annotation and encouraging students to expand annotations into outlines or into entries in a brainstorming journal.

Chapter 2, "Working with Source Material" treats quotation, paraphrase, summary, synthesis, and critique, five strategies critical to students writing essays that require them to make connections among sources and assimilate ideas from sources into their own writing. Each of these strategies is explained carefully, and the process of applying each is fully illustrated in examples and exercises drawn from sources similar to those with which students actually work.

Chapter 3, "Writing with Sources: A Case Study," traces the writing process of one student from instructor's assignment through finished paper, applying the strategies covered in Chapters 1 and 2. The student plans, organizes, writes, and revises a source-based paper, reading and evaluating her sources, highlighting and annotating them, reacting further to their ideas in her brainstorming journal, and synthesizing material from her sources with her own ideas. Three drafts of her paper (following MLA documentation style) illustrate her writing process, and a series of exercises takes students through the process of writing a source-based essay of their own. Throughout Part I, frequent exercises allow students to practice each skill that is introduced.

Part II, "Thematic Anthology for Reading and Writing," a thematically arranged collection of reading selections ranging across the disciplines, consists of eight chapters: "The American Dream," "The Dawning of the Atomic Age," "The Legacy of the Fifties," "The Changing Image of the Hero," "Issues in Education," "Religion and Society," "Working," and "The Impact of Technology." Many of the selections in these chapters are not just sources of information but are also models for the kinds of writing that students do in other disciplines. Within each chapter are six or seven reading selections, each accompanied by extensive apparatus keyed to the active reading strategies presented in Chapters 1 and 2. Three question sets follow each selection. "Reading Sources" questions focus on comprehension, typically asking students to identify key ideas, structural cues, and other features. "Reacting to Sources" questions ask students to respond actively and analytically to a text's ideas, writing marginal annotations or making brief outlines or entries in a brainstorming journal. These two question sets differ from those found in most college readers and rhetorics in that in most cases they require students to mark their texts, actually beginning the process of writing a paper. In the third and final question set, "Working with Sources," students are given assignments that require them to integrate two or three selected quotations from the source into an original paragraph; to write a paraphrase, a summary, and a critique of a portion of the source; and to write a synthesis that integrates ideas from a section of the source with material from another source. These three question sets are arranged so that students move from relatively simple tasks, such as highlighting or single-word responses; to sentence- and paragraph-length responses; to writing more complex, structured paragraphs. Then, in "Writing with Sources: Using a Single Source," students are given a choice of paper topics on the reading selection. At the end of each chapter is "Writing with Sources: Using Multiple Sources," suggestions for paper topics that combine ideas from two or more of the chapter's selections.

Part III, "Essays for Further Reading," consists of three chapters (eighteen reading selections) on the topics "Coming of Age," "The Nature of Violence," and "Life in America." Working on the assumption that when students master active reading skills they will need less structured guidance, the essays in Part III are followed only by suggested paper topics.

The text concludes with two appendices. Appendix A, "Plagiarism," defines and illustrates plagiarism and gives advice on how to avoid it. Appendix B, "Documentation," presents a concise yet thorough guide that explains and illustrates MLA, APA, and number-reference documentation formats.

The advantages of *The Writer's Sourcebook* are numerous. The text is able, in one volume, to demonstrate an interactive, analytical approach to writing; to trace the process of writing source-based essays; and to supply readings and accompanying questions, exercises, and paper topics that enable students to practice these skills immediately.

An *Instructor's Manual* is available upon adoption of the text by writing to: English Editor, 383 Madison Avenue, New York, N.Y. 10017.

We wish to thank the following colleagues for their comments and sound advice: Jane Parks Clifford, University of Missouri at St. Louis; Gretchen Flesher, University of Utah; Mary Helen Halloran, University of Wisconsin at Milwaukee; Nevin Laib, Northern Arizona University; Patricia Murray, DePaul University; Jean Reynolds, Polk Community College; and Mary Soliday, University of Illinois. In addition, we would like to acknowledge our debt to Susan McDougall, our research assistant.

At Holt, Rinehart and Winston we are grateful to Françoise Bartlett, Gloria Gentile, Kate Morgan, Nancy Myers, and especially to our extraordinary editor, Charlyce Jones Owen.

Finally, again and always, we thank our families: Mark, Adam, and Rebecca Kirszner and Demi, David, and Sarah Mandell.

Philadelphia
December 1986

L. G. K.
S. R. M.

To the Student

During your years as a college student, as writing becomes more and more important to you, you will find that you will often be called upon to write papers that draw on other writers' ideas. The goal of *The Writer's Sourcebook* is to prepare you to write such papers by showing you how to read your sources.

The importance of reading cannot be emphasized strongly enough. Reading can provide access to new ideas and experiences, unlocking doors and broadening horizons. Learning to become a critical reader, one who actively questions and interprets and evaluates what you read, will strengthen your ability to interact with people and ideas in the world around you.

In addition to its importance in itself, mastering critical reading skills is an important first step toward writing effective papers. In this sense, reading sources can be seen as the first stage of the writing process, a stage you begin even before you start to plan, organize, write, and revise a paper. As you move through the writing process, you may return to your sources again and again. Each time, you may see additional points, make new connections among ideas, notice contradictions, interpret the text differently, or develop different insights — and these changing perceptions will affect the paper you are writing.

First, though, you will need to learn how to approach a source so that it will yield the most helpful material to you as a writer. To this end, *The Writer's Sourcebook* encourages you to become an *active reader* — one who interacts with the text instead of reading passively to accumulate data — and to see reading, like writing, as a dynamic, give-and-take process.

The first section of *The Writer's Sourcebook* introduces you to the skills you will need when you read in preparation for writing. In this section we show you how to *highlight* material to aid your comprehension; how to *annotate* sources with your own marginal questions and comments; and then how to prepare longer, more structured responses to what you read. We also explain how to integrate *quotation, paraphrase,* and *summary* of material from your sources into papers of your own and how to assimilate source material into your paper by using the techniques of *critique* and *synthesis.* In addition, we trace the writing process of a student in an English composition course as she writes a paper based on several sources. The next two sections of the book contain a varied collection of readings drawn from subjects that represent all areas of the college curriculum. These readings are accompanied by questions and writing topics designed to reinforce the skills introduced in Part I and to allow you to practice responding actively to ideas in sources and integrating them effectively into your papers. The book closes with two appendices offering information that will help you to avoid plagiarism and to use proper documentation formats.

It is our hope that *The Writer's Sourcebook* will help you to approach both reading and writing in a positive way—and that it will make you more skilled, more effective, and more confident at both.

Philadelphia
December 1986

L. G. K.
S. R. M.

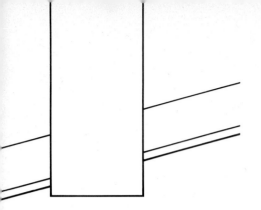

Contents

Reading and Writing from Sources

1

Reading Sources

Reading is a rich and complex activity, a give-and-take process of assimilating, interpreting, and reacting to the ideas of others. In order to integrate source material effectively into your own writing, you must first understand your sources. To do this, you must learn to bring words to life by interacting with them: asking questions, making inferences, seeing connections, developing insights, making judgments, and drawing conclusions. In other words, you must become an *active reader*. Only then will you be able to generate ideas for source-based essays of your own.

The process of reading is *interactive;* reading is an ongoing dialogue between a reader and the text. Any time you are reading to understand — whether you are mastering material for an examination or preparing to write a paper — you will need to read and reread, selectively highlight key ideas, and make careful annotations. Sometimes, especially when planning a paper, you will also need to expand your annotations into more complete, detailed notes.

Reading for Comprehension

In order to use source material effectively in a paper, you must understand the author's meaning, purpose, and emphasis. Several strategies can help you to do this. Identifying key ideas and obvious visual cues in your text and learning to recognize more subtle signals can be extremely helpful, but identification of these elements is only the first step. You must also develop the habit of selectively highlighting important ideas and essential signals so that as you read and reread you will be able to understand and interpret material and take meaningful notes.

Reading and Rereading

To comprehend a reading selection fully, you will have to read it not once but several times. In many ways your first reading of a selection is comparable to your first draft in writing. When you write a first draft, you write quickly. Your goal is to get ideas down on paper without paying much attention to sentence style, grammar, mechanics, or the like. Your first reading is a similar exploration: at this point you do not read to understand the subtleties of language or to identify complex rhetorical strategies; you read for general ideas. As you return to a text again and again, however, your focus changes.

Like writing, reading is a *recursive* rather than a *linear* process. In other words, when you read to understand a work, you do not simply begin at the beginning and proceed in a straight line to the end. As you read and reread a work, meaning changes and expands with each reading. As we read we wander, stumble, make missteps, backtrack, and retrace our steps as we move from uncertainty, from a tentative idea of how things will turn out (or what an author is "getting at"), to greater certainty. As we reread, we notice additional details, clarify points, and make new associations, confirming or correcting our first impressions as we increase our understanding of the material. As we read and reread, then, what we are actually engaged in is a process of *revision*—we revise our impressions and judgments and form less tentative, more definite conclusions.

Because this constant process of revision helps us as we move toward an understanding of our source material, it is an essential part of how we learn to incorporate what we read into our writing. For this reason, it is important that all writers take an active role in reading, interacting with the text by highlighting and annotating, asking questions and drawing conclusions.

Surveying Your Source

Before you read a source even once, survey it quickly to see whether you can find clues to the writer's purpose and meaning in the source's approach or emphasis. Sometimes you will notice nothing that can be of help to you, but frequently visual stress is placed on certain ideas. For instance, certain terms may be set in *italic* or **bold-face** type or, in a textbook or periodical article, they may be boxed, underscored, or printed in color. Prominent headings may reinforce certain words or phrases in the text, and key concepts may be set off in numbered lists. Finally, a preview or summary paragraph may identify the most important points in an article or a book chapter. Recognizing such obvious visual cues, if they are present, can give you a valuable head start as you prepare to read.

In the following paragraph from an anthropology textbook, a number of readily apparent visual cues send signals to the reader.

Patterns of Marital Residence

In societies in which newly married couples customarily live with or close to their kin, there are several residence patterns that may be established. Since children in all societies are required to marry outside the nuclear family (because of the incest taboo), and since couples in almost all societies live together after they are married (with a few exceptions),[2] it is not possible for an entire society to practice a system in which all married offspring reside with their own parents. Some children, then, have to leave home when they marry. But which children remain at home and which reside elsewhere? Societies vary in the way they typically deal with the problem of which married children stay near their kin and which leave. Actually, there are only four societal patterns which occur with any sizable frequency. They are:

1. *Patrilocal residence:* the son stays and the daughter leaves, so that the married couple lives with or near the husband's parents (67 percent of all societies).[3]
2. *Matrilocal residence:* the daughter stays and the son leaves, so that the married couple lives with or near the wife's parents (15 percent of all societies).
3. *Bilocal residence:* either the son or the daughter leaves, so that the married couple lives with or near either the husband's parents or the wife's parents (7 percent of all societies).
4. *Avunculocal residence:* both son and daughter normally leave, but the son and his wife settle with or near his mother's brother (4 percent of all societies).

A fifth pattern of residence, of course, is neolocal, in which the newly married couple does not live with or near kin.

5. *Neolocal residence:* both son and daughter leave; married couples live apart from the relatives of either spouse (5 percent).

Carol R. Ember and Melvin Ember, *Cultural Anthropology*

Notice that the heading *Patterns of Marital Residence,* set in large type, is given the greatest prominence. The patterns themselves are set off in a numbered list introduced by "They are" and a colon, with the name of each pattern set in italic type for further emphasis. These visual signals, obvious to anyone surveying the page, can tell the reader immediately which ideas the text's authors consider most important.

Recognizing Key Words

Every source depends on certain key words and phrases to convey its meaning, and writers place particular emphasis on those terms in a variety of ways that are a bit more subtle than the obvious visual signals discussed above. For instance, a word or phrase may be placed in a prominent *position* — in the source's title, introduction, or conclusion, or in the opening or closing sentence of a paragraph. Alterna-

---

[2] In the very few societies in which married couples live apart, each with his or her own kin, we speak of a *duolocal* (two-place) pattern of residence. The Nayar of southern India, referred to in the last chapter, had such a pattern.

[3] Percentages calculated from Coult and Habenstein, *Cross Tabulations of Murdock's World Ethnographic Sample.*

tively, a key term may be stressed through effective use of *repetition*. Obviously, repeating a word — regardless of its importance to the piece of writing — simply because no appropriate equivalent comes to mind will not strengthen or clarify a writer's emphasis. But if a word or phrase is repeated throughout an essay, attention will be called to it. If the writer wishes to emphasize this word or phrase, then, repetition can be extremely effective. This technique is even more effective when repetition is enhanced by a grammatically parallel structure. (*Parallel* sequences use corresponding parts of speech and sentence structure in paired elements, where they may be introduced by phrases like *not only . . . but also* or *either . . . or,* or in a series.) Finally, a writer may call attention to a particular term by using it in a section of the source in which a central point is being made.

The selection that follows is the opening paragraph of a book-length study called *Native American Humor*. The writer, Walter Blair, appropriately places emphasis on the words *American* and *humor*.

The term, "American humor," like many another term in general use, is more easily understood than defined. As it is usually employed, it does not mean all humor produced in America, since much humor orginating in this country is not in any way marked by its place of origin. Nor does it mean humor with characteristics discoverable in the comedy of no other land, since apparently there is no such humor. It means humor which is *American* in that it has an emphatic "native quality"[1] — a quality imparted by its subject matter and its technique. Its subject matter is national in the sense indicated in 1838 by a writer who was hailing the beginnings of this type of writing. Said this writer, an English critic:

Humour is national when it is impregnated with the convictions, customs, and associations of a nation. . . . National American humour must be all this transferred into shapes which produce laughter. The humour of a people is their institutions, laws, customs, manners, habits, characters, convictions, — their scenery whether of the sea, the city, or the hills, — expressed in the language of the ludicrous. . . .[2]

Its technique, which will be characterized hereafter, is of a sort which develops effectively such subject matter. The phrase, "native American humor," suggests as well as any the usual implication of the term.

Walter Blair, *Native American Humor*

In this passage the writer uses all three of the strategies identified above. First, he presents his key terms in a critical section of the book (the opening

---

[1] The phrase is that of Will D. Howe, in *The Cambridge History of American Literature* (New York, 1918), II, 150.
[2] H.W., "Slick, Downing, Crockett, Etc.," *The London and Westminster Review*, XXXII, 138 – 139 (December, 1838).

paragraph), where he defines the phrase *American humor.* Second, he repeats the words *American* (four times) and *humor* (ten times) frequently, using them together in the phrase *American humor* three times in the course of the paragraph. In addition, he places the key words in prominent positions in his paragraph, using them together in the first and last sentences, where he adds further emphasis by placing them within quotation marks. The writer also uses parallelism to call attention to the word *humor* ("it does not mean all humor . . . "; "Nor does it mean humor . . . "; "It means humor . . . "). As a result of these strategies, the reader can easily understand the writer's emphasis.

Recognizing Cues to Structure and Emphasis

To follow the logic and sequence of a writer's ideas, you must be able to identify words and expressions that introduce key points, distinguish main ideas from supporting details, show the path of a line of reasoning, or signal how the direction of an argument might be shifting. As you read, such words and expressions aid comprehension by signaling and reinforcing the structure of the source or revealing the writer's emphasis.

Many of the words and phrases that signal logic and sequence are commonly used *transitional* expressions. For instance, narrative material — material that tells what happened — will frequently include signals like *then, next, after that,* and *now;* a selection that explains a process might include similar transitions, plus cues like *the first (second, third)* step; and a source that compares and contrasts will use expressions like *however, although, but, in contrast,* or *similarly.* If a section of your source traces causes or effects, you can expect to encounter words and phrases like *as a result, therefore, consequently,* and *because,* which can help point you to important causes or effects. If a source presents examples in support of a point, phrases like *for instance* and *for example* can direct you to those examples.

Other techniques also aid comprehension by revealing the underlying structure or emphasis of a passage. For example, pronouns that refer to nouns in previous sentences keep a passage's ideas in order and keep readers on track. Parallelism can also clarify the logic of an argument by calling attention to corresponding or contrasting ideas. And phrases that include intensifiers or deemphasizers — phrases like "the *most* compelling reason" or "a *less* commonly observed reaction" — can tell careful readers a lot about the relative importance of a writer's ideas.

Longer essays may have sentences ("Now we will turn to the analysis. . . .") or even entire paragraphs devoted to clarifying structure or emphasis, and these too may be viewed as signals that can tell you that one train of thought has been completed and another is about to begin or that one idea is subordinate to another. When you fail to pay attention to these cues — whether they are words, phrases, sentences, or entire paragraphs — you can easily misinterpret your sources.

The following paragraph makes effective use of words and expressions to reveal its structure and emphasis.

> The origin of the American war lay in the mercantilist policy of the day, especially as applied by mother countries to their colonies. The Americans had to import either English-made goods, or foreign goods by way of England; and had to export their own goods either to England (when they were not competing with the English market) or nowhere at all. As a result, the colonists had successfully resorted to contraband trade, which — no doubt more because it was successful than because it was contraband — angered the mother country. After 1759 the strongest tie that bound the colonies to Great Britain — their fear of a French invasion from Canada — was severed, and the remaining ties were imponderable ones. It was only, however, after the Peace of Paris — which left England's finances shaky — that a first real crisis arose. Grenville decided on a colonial stamp tax to defray part of the cost of maintaining defensive troops in America. The idea may have been reasonable enough, since the colonists, not England, were to benefit most from what was paid out; but the method was incredibly foolhardy. To tax people without their consent was a menace to their liberties; but, worse yet, it was a slap at their pride. A quarter of a century before, when the colonists were much less powerful, Walpole had seen the folly of adopting such tactics. Now there was downright danger in doing so. But Grenville pushed his Stamp Act through Parliament. The colonies ignored it, stormed and rioted, boycotted English goods; and even though the Stamp Act was soon revoked, the stage was set for trouble.

Louis Kronenberger, *Kings and Desperate Men: Life in Eighteenth-Century England.*

In the preceding paragraph, words and phrases like *As a result, After 1759, however, since, A quarter of a century before, Now, But,* and *even though* help readers follow the logic and sequence of the writer's argument. Clear pronoun references and skillful parallelism ("the strongest tie . . . the remaining ties"; "a menace to their liberties . . . a slap at their pride") also help signal the sequence of the paragraph's ideas. In addition, expressions like *especially, the strongest tie, a first real crisis,* and *worse yet* communicate the relative importance of various ideas.

Identifying Important Ideas

When you learn to write paragraphs and essays, you are often told to present the most important idea of each paragraph in a *topic sentence* (frequently the paragraph's opening sentence), which the paragraph will go on to support with specific details. Professional writers sometimes do the same thing, using an explicit topic sentence to give focus and unity to a paragraph and the rest of the paragraph to provide specific support for that topic sentence.

You also learn to summarize the central idea of an entire essay in a clearly worded *thesis statement* (see Chapter 3). Professional writers often do this too.

Moreover, they may also provide a one- or two-sentence summary of a *paragraph cluster,* a group of related paragraphs that develops a single idea.

In the following paragraph cluster, each paragraph has its own topic sentence, but the sentence "There are three common justifications for incomes in the doctors' range" presents a main idea that summarizes the three-paragraph cluster.

Trying to explain doctors' incomes is a bit more puzzling. There are three common justifications for incomes in the doctors' range. First, they might be necessary to entice people into taking socially necessary risks. But this argument, while it may apply to oil drilling or starting silicon-chip factories, will not wash for medicine. It is not easy to get into medical school, but once there, a budding young doctor has as close to a sure thing as our society offers. Few people flunk out of med school these days, and even if one despises patients or faints at the sight of blood, one can always go into radiology or pathology and pull down an easy $100,000 a year. Risk is all but eliminated from the picture.

High salaries are also justified as compensation for bearing heavy responsibilities. This argument clearly has some validity when applied to physicians. Doctors do make life-and-death decisions, and surely that calls for some incentive. But nurses also bear a burden of responsibility. Does the difference really justify a four-to-one income ratio? The argument seems to fall flat when one realizes that two of the highest-paid medical specialties are those with the least responsibility for patients. They are radiology (in which one makes diagnoses for other doctors' patients with X rays, ultrasound, CAT scanners, and the like) and pathology (in which one examines cell specimens in a laboratory). Both specialties have median incomes well above those of even surgeons and obstetricians.

Finally, there is the justification you will most often hear from doctors themselves: the long and expensive period of education and training necessary to enter medicine. Most American doctors have put in eight hard years of higher education, followed by three to five years of residency. In recent years most have racked up $20,000, $30,000, or even $50,000 in debts, depending on family finances and tuition levels. For most aspiring doctors, deferred gratification has become a way of life, often well into their thirties.

David Osborne, "Rich Doctors, Poor Nurses"

In each of the three paragraphs above, a topic sentence explicitly states the central idea of the paragraph; therefore, readers skimming for important ideas will be able to locate them easily. Moreover, the three topic sentences in the cluster form a parallel sequence:

First, they might be necessary to entice people into taking socially necessary risks.
High salaries are *also* justified as compensation for bearing heavy responsibilities.
Finally, there is the justification you will most often hear from doctors themselves: the long and expensive period of education and training necessary to enter medicine.

This use of parallelism aids comprehension and places additional emphasis on the three possible justifications for doctors' high salaries, each of which the writer will go on to refute.

Selective Highlighting

Recognizing an author's most important ideas and the strategies used to communicate them is important. To be an active reader, however, you must also develop the habit of selectively highlighting those key points and essential signals. As you become experienced in reacting to your reading, you will learn how to highlight important terms and signals so that they will be most meaningful to you.

Highlighting is the process of marking elements in the text. Above all, it is a process of careful selection. Highlighting too much is just as useless as highlighting too little, or highlighting irrelevant or unimportant information.

There are many methods of highlighting material. The most widely used is probably underlining, but you can also place stress on material by using asterisks or check marks, by placing vertical lines in the margin alongside important sections of text, by bracketing phrases or circling words, or by using arrows to indicate possible connections between points.

Naturally, you cannot highlight information if the source you are using is borrowed from the library, or if it is a book or article you do not want to mark up. When you are using a library book, you may have no choice but to take notes on separate pages or on index cards. But highlighting directly on a source is so helpful that you should make every effort to do so. If you are working with a relatively brief portion of a source, you can duplicate it so that you can highlight and annotate the copy. (See pages 18 – 22 for information on making marginal notes.)

Begin highlighting only after you have read your source through once or twice. Start by underlining your source's central idea and topic sentences or summary statements. Then box or circle key words and phrases and particularly apt examples or crucial statistics; bracket or underline distinctive phrases you might want to quote in your paper. Feel free to devise your own set of shorthand symbols and to modify them regularly so they continue to meet your needs.

Do your highlighting with a marker that will let you correct any tendency to highlight too much. Using pencil allows you to revise what — and how much — you highlight as your rereading encourages you to revise your reactions to your source. As you develop a clear picture of your writing task, you will want to shift the focus of your reading, and your highlighting should reflect this shift. Using pencil rather than pen keeps your highlighting flexible.

In the following passage, a student's judicious use of highlighting stresses the source's main points.

Name-shifting is especially frequent, and probably always has been, when we must come face to face with the less happy facts of our existence, for life holds even for the most fortunate of men experiences which are inartistic, violent, and hence shocking to contemplate in the full light of day — for instance, the first and last facts of human existence, birth and death, despite the sentimentality with which we have surrounded them. And it is certainly true that the sting of the latter is somewhat alleviated – for the survivors, anyway – by calling it by some other name, such as "the Great Adventure," "the flight to glory," and "the final sleep," which are among the many terms cited by Miss Pound in the article just alluded to. Mortician is a much flossier word than undertaker (which is itself a euphemism with the earlier meanings 'helper,' 'contractor,' 'publisher,' and 'baptismal sponsor,' among others), but the loved one whom he prepares for public view and subsequent interment in a casket (earlier a jewel-box, as in *The Merchant of Venice*) is just as dead as a corpse in a coffin. But such verbal subterfuges are apparently thought to rob the grave of some of its victory; the notion of death is made more tolerable to the human consciousness than it would otherwise be. Birth is much more plainly alluded to nowadays than it used to be, particularly by young married people, who seem to be strangely fascinated by the unpleasant clinical details attendant upon it. The free use of *pregnant* is not much older than World War II. A woman *with child, going to have a baby,* or *enceinte* used to terminate her condition by her *confinement,* or, if one wanted to be really fancy about it, her *accouchement.*

Ideas of decency likewise profoundly affect language. All during the Victorian era, ladies and gentlemen were very sensitive about using the word *leg, limb* being almost invariably substituted, sometimes even if only the legs of a piano were being referred to. In the very year which marks the beginning of Queen Victoria's long reign, Captain Frederick Marryat noted in his *Diary in America* (1837) the American taboo on this word, when, having asked a young American lady who had taken a spill whether she had hurt her leg, she turned from him, "evidently much shocked, or much offended," later explaining to him that in America the word *leg* was never used in the presence of ladies. Later, the captain visited a school for young ladies where he saw, according to his own testimony, "a square pianoforte with four limbs," all dressed in little frilled pantalettes. For reasons which it would be difficult to analyze, a similar taboo was placed upon belly, *stomach* being usually substituted for it, along with such nursery terms as *tummy* and *breadbasket* and the advertising copy writer's *midriff. Toilet,* a diminutive of French *toile* 'cloth,' in its earliest English uses meant a piece of cloth in which to wrap clothes, subsequently coming to be used for a cloth cover for a dressing table, and then the table itself, as when Lydia Languish in Sheridan's *The Rivals* says, "Here, my dear Lucy, hide these books. Quick, quick! Fling *Peregrine Pickle* under the toilet — throw *Roderick Random* into the closet. . . ."[20] There are other related meanings. The word came to be used in America as a euphemism for privy — itself in turn a euphemism, as are *latrine* (ultimately derived from Lat. *lavāre* 'to wash') and lavatory (note the euphemistic phrase "to wash one's hands"). But *toilet* is now frequently replaced by *rest room, comfort station, powder room,* or the intolerably coy *little boys'* (or *girls'*) *room.* It is safe to predict that

---

[20] It should be pointed out that about fifty years ago the direction for the disposal of *Roderick Random* would have been as risible as that for *Peregrine Pickle,* when *closet* was frequently used for *water closet,* now practically obsolete in American English.

these evasions will in their turn come to be regarded as indecorous, and other expressions substituted for them.

Euphemism is likewise resorted to in reference to certain diseases. Like that which attempts to prettify, or at least to mollify birth, death, and excretion, this type of verbal subterfuge is doubtless deeply rooted in fear and superstition. An ailment of almost any sort, for instance, is nowadays often referred to as a *condition* (*heart condition, kidney condition,* *malignant condition,* and so forth), so that *condition,* hitherto a more or less neutral word, has thus had a pejorative development, coming to mean 'bad condition.'[21] *Leprosy* is no longer used by the American Medical Association because of its repulsive connotations; it is nowadays replaced by the colorless *Hansen's Disease. Cancer* may be openly referred to, though it is notable that in the syndicated horoscopes of Carroll Righter, a well-known Hollywood astrologer, the term is no longer used as a sign of the zodiac; those born under Cancer are now designated "Moon Children." The taboo has been removed from reference to the various specific venereal diseases, formerly *blood diseases* or *social diseases.*

Old age and its attendant decay have probably been made more bearable for many elderly and decrepit people by calling them *senior citizens.* A similar verbal humanitarianism is responsible for *underprivileged* 'poor,' the previously mentioned *sick* 'insane,' *social justice* 'charity,' *exceptional child* 'a pupil of subnormal mentality,'[22] and a good many other voguish euphemisms, some of which have been cited in another connection. In the last cited example, pejoration has also operated — unless it can be conceived generally that being below par intellectually is a desirable thing, as the schools would seem to have supposed. One wonders whether to the next generation an "exceptional man" will be thought of as a dull and stupid man, that is, an exceptional child grown to maturity, and whether the "exceptional bargains" offered by the stores had not better be passed up in favor of merely average ones. Sentimental equalitarianism has led us to attempt to dignify humble occupations by giving them high-sounding titles: thus a *janitor* (originally a doorkeeper, from *Janus,* the doorkeeper of heaven in Roman mythology) has in many parts of America become a *custodian* and there are many engineers who would not know the difference between a slide rule and a cantilever. H. L. Mencken cites, among a good many others, *demolition engineer* 'house-wrecker,' *sanitary engineer* 'garbage man,' and *extermination engineer* 'rat-catcher.'[23] The meaning of *profession* has been generalized to such an extent that it may include practically any trade or vocation. The writer of a letter to the editor of *Life* comments as follows on the publication of a picture of a plumber in a previous issue: "I think you have done an injustice to the plumbing profession" (August 6, 1951); and a regional chairman of the Wage Stabilization Board informed a waitress who complained of the smallness of her tips, according to an Associated Press item of June 19, 1952, that "if tipping were viewed by your profession as a true

[21] Note that, although *to have a condition* means 'to be in bad health,' *to be in condition* continues, confusingly enough, to mean 'to be in good health.'

[22] Note that the child who exceeds expectations has been stigmatized by the schools as an *over-achiever.*

[23] *The American Language,* 4th ed. (New York, 1936), pp. 289–91.

incentive for better, faster and more agreeable service, this might go a long way toward relieving the situation.'' Long ago James Fenimore Cooper in *The American Democrat* (1838) denounced such democratic subterfuges as *boss* for *master* and *help* for *servant,* but these seem very mild nowadays. One of the great concerns of the democratic and progressive age in which we live would seem to be to ensure that nobody's feelings shall ever be hurt — at least, not by words.

Thomas Pyles, *The Origins and Development of the English Language*

Highlighting in the preceding passage focuses on only the most important ideas; notice that the reader does *not* highlight digressions, literary references, stylistic embellishments, or any but the most pertinent and memorable examples. Topic sentences, summary statements, and distinctively worded phrases are underlined; key terms (in this case, the word *euphemism,* the focus of the passage, and its synonyms) are circled; helpful examples are boxed; and arrows connect related words. The system is a simple one, but the selective highlighting reduces the passage to a core of information that can be easily understood and interpreted.

Exercise 1

— Survey the following passage and note the visual cues the authors use. What signals do these cues give the reader about the authors' purpose, meaning, and emphasis?
— As you read, identify the stylistic cues to structure and emphasis; if necessary, use them to help you identify key words and important ideas.
— Circle the key words in the passage.
— Underline the passage's central idea and each paragraph's topic sentence.

Nonverbal Communcation Serves Many Functions   Just because this chapter deals with nonverbal communication, don't get the idea that our words and our actions are unrelated. Quite the opposite is true: Verbal and nonverbal communication are interconnected elements in every act of communication. Nonverbal behaviors can operate in several relationships to verbal messages.

First, nonverbal behaviors can *repeat* what is said verbally. If someone asked you for directions to the nearest drugstore, you could say, "North of here about two blocks," and then repeat your instructions nonverbally by pointing north.

Nonverbal messages may also *substitute* for verbal ones. When you see a familiar friend wearing a certain facial expression, you don't need to ask, "How's it going?" In the same way, experience has probably shown you that other kinds of looks, gestures, and other clues say, "I'm angry at you" or "I feel great" far better than words.

A third way in which verbal and nonverbal messages can relate is called *complementing*. If you saw a student talking to a teacher, and his head was bowed slightly, his voice was low and hesitating, and he shuffled slowly from foot to foot, you might conclude that he felt inferior to the teacher, possibly embarrassed about something he did. The nonverbal behaviors you observed provided the context for the verbal behaviors — they conveyed the relationship between the teacher and student. Complementing nonverbal behaviors signal the attitudes the interactants have for one another.

Nonverbal behaviors can also *accent* verbal messages. Just as we can use *italics* in print to underline an idea, we can emphasize some part of a face-to-face message in various ways. Pointing an accusing finger adds emphasis to criticism (as well as probably creating defensiveness in the receiver). Shrugging shoulders accent confusion, and hugs can highlight excitement or affection. As you'll see later in this chapter, the voice plays a big role in accenting verbal messages.

Nonverbal behavior also serves to *regulate* verbal behavior. By lowering your voice at the end of a sentence, "trailing off," you indicate that the other person may speak. You can also convey this information through the use of eye contact and by the way you position your body.

Finally—and often most significantly—nonverbal behavior can often *contradict* the spoken word. People often simultaneously express different and even contradictory messages in their verbal and nonverbal behaviors. A common example of this sort of "double message" is the experience we've all had of hearing someone with a red face and bulging veins yelling, "Angry? No, *I'm not angry!*"

Usually, however, the contradiction between words and nonverbal clues isn't this obvious. At times we all try to seem different than we are. There are many reasons for this contradictory behavior: to cover nervousness when giving a speech or in a job interview, to keep someone from worrying about us, or to appear more attractive than we believe we really are.

Even though some of the ways in which people contradict themselves are subtle, double messages have a strong impact. Research suggests that when a receiver perceives an inconsistency between verbal and nonverbal messages, the unspoken one carries more weight.

As we discuss the different kinds of nonverbal communication throughout this chapter, we'll point out a number of ways in which people contradict themselves by either conscious or unconscious behaviors. Thus, by the end of this chapter you should have a better idea of how others feel, even when they can't or won't tell you with their words.

Ronald B. Adler and Neil Towne, *Looking Out/Looking In,* **3rd. ed.**

Exercise 2

Read each of the following passages carefully and evaluate the reader's highlighting. In each case, consider whether the reader has set off too much or too little and whether the material highlighted is well chosen.

1   While Rubens was executing his murals for the Festival Hall, an obscure French painter named Nicolas Poussin, who had been working on minor decorations, left the Luxembourg Palace for the less confining atmosphere of Rome. There he soon built a solid reputation that came to the attention of Cardinal Richelieu, who bought many of Poussin's paintings and determined to bring the artist back to Paris. In 1640, Poussin did return to decorate the Grand Gallery of the Louvre—and receive from Louis XIII a shower of favors and the much desired title of First Painter to the King. The inevitable courtly intrigues that followed such marked attention made Poussin so miserable that after two years he returned to Rome. There he acted as the artistic ambassador of France and supervised the French painters sent under government subsidies to study and copy Italian masterpieces for the decoration of the Louvre. And there, for the rest of his life,

Poussin had the <u>freedom to pursue his classical studies</u>, the independence to <u>work out his own principles and ideals</u>, and the time to paint pictures ranging from <u>mythological</u> ✳ and <u>religious subjects</u> to <u>historical canvases and architectural landscapes</u>.

William Fleming, *Arts and Ideas,* 6th ed.

2   The whole process of button making was nicely contained and comprehensible. It started at the bottom of the factory and rose, machine by machine, to the top. On the first floor, the <u>liquid plastic was poured into an oil drum, mixed with dye and hardener, and slopped into a centrifuge</u> like a big spin-dryer, where it was whirled around <u>until it formed an even, translucent sheet of soft rubbery stuff</u>. <u>The sheet was passed into a machine that punched it into a thousand or so round button blanks</u>; the blanks were fed <u>on a conveyor belt into an oven where they were baked hard</u>; then they were cooled and sent on up to the next floor. Here more <u>machines drilled needle holes in them and carved patterns on their fronts and backs</u>. They were <u>polished</u> in a tumbling vat of wooden shoe pegs, and on the top floor they were <u>sorted</u> into cardboard boxes. <u>They looked like pretty trinkets, colored rose, shot pearl, smoke, primrose, cornflower blue, amber and scarlet</u>. I would never have guessed that such a quantity of <u>technology</u> and <u>expertise</u> had gone into the making of every button on my shirtfront.

Jonathan Raban, *Old Glory: An American Voyage*

Exercise 3

Use underlining, circles, boxes, arrows, and any other symbols you like to high-light this brief article. Be sure to highlight all essential information — but *only* essential information.

Kitty Genovese is set upon by a maniac as she returns home from work at 3 A.M. Thirty-eight of her neighbors in Kew Gardens, N.Y., come to their windows when she cries out in terror; not one comes to her assistance, even though her assailant takes half an hour to murder her. No one so much as calls the police. She dies.

Andrew Mormille is stabbed in the head and neck as he rides in a New York City subway train. Eleven other riders flee to another car as the 17-year-old boy bleeds to death; not one comes to his assistance, even though his attackers have left the car. He dies.

Eleanor Bradley trips and breaks her leg while shopping on New York City's Fifth Avenue. Dazed and in shock, she calls for help, but the hurrying stream of people simply parts and flows past. Finally, after 40 minutes, a taxi driver stops and helps her to a doctor.

How can so many people watch another human being in distress and do nothing? Why don't they help?

Since we started research on bystander responses to emergencies, we have heard many explanations for the lack of intervention in such cases. "The megalopolis in which we live makes closeness difficult and leads to the alienation of the individual from the group," says the psychoanalyst. "This sort of disaster," says the sociologist, "shakes the sense of safety and sureness of the individuals involved and causes psychological withdrawal." "Apathy," say others. "Indifference."

All of these analyses share one characteristic: they set the indifferent witness apart from the rest of us. Certainly not one of us who reads about these incidents in horror is apathetic, alienated or depersonalized. Certainly these terrifying cases have no personal implications for us. We needn't feel guilty, or re-examine ourselves, or anything like that. Or should we?

If we look closely at the behavior of witnesses to these incidents, the people involved begin to seem a little less inhuman and a lot more like the rest of us. They were not indifferent. The 38 witnesses of Kitty Genovese's murder, for example, did not merely look at the scene once and then ignore it. They continued to stare out of their windows, caught, fascinated, distressed, unwilling to act but unable to turn away.

Why, then, didn't they act?

There are three things the bystander must do if he is to intervene in an emergency: *notice* that something is happening; *interpret* that event as an emergency; and decide that he has *personal responsibility* for intervention. As we shall show, the presence of other bystanders may at each stage inhibit his action.

The unseeing eye

Suppose that a man has a heart attack. He clutches his chest, staggers to the nearest building and slumps sitting to the sidewalk. Will a passerby come to his assistance? First, the bystander has to notice that something is happening. He must tear himself away from his private thoughts and pay attention. But Americans consider it bad manners to look closely at other people in public. We are taught to respect the privacy of others, and when among strangers we close our ears and avoid staring. In a crowd, then, each person is less likely to notice a potential emergency than when alone.

Experimental evidence corroborates this. We asked college students to an interview about their reactions to urban living. As the students waited to see the interviewer, either by themselves or with two other students, they filled out a questionnaire. Solitary students often glanced idly about while filling out their questionnaires; those in groups kept their eyes on their own papers.

As part of the study, we staged an emergency: smoke was released into the waiting room through a vent. Two thirds of the subjects who were alone noticed the smoke immediately, but only 25 percent of those waiting in groups saw it as quickly. Although eventually all the subjects did become aware of the smoke — when the atmosphere grew so smoky as to make them cough and rub their eyes — this study indicates that the more people present, the slower an individual may be to perceive an emergency and the more likely he is not to see it at all.

Seeing is not necessarily believing

Once an event is noticed, an onlooker must decide if it is truly an emergency. Emergencies are not always clearly labeled as such; "smoke" pouring into a waiting room may be caused by fire, or it may merely indicate a leak in a steam pipe. Screams in the street may signal an assault or a family quarrel. A man lying in a doorway may be having a coronary — or he may simply be sleeping off a drunk.

A person trying to interpret a situation often looks at those around him to see how he should react. If everyone else is calm and indifferent, he will tend to remain so; if everyone else is reacting strongly, he is likely to become aroused. This tendency is not merely slavish conformity; ordinarily we derive much valuable information about new situations from how others around us behave. It's a rare traveler who, in picking a roadside restaurant, chooses to stop at one where no other cars appear in the parking lot.

But occasionally the reactions of others provide false information. The studied nonchalance of patients in a dentist's waiting room is a poor indication of their inner anxiety. It is considered embarrassing to "lose your cool" in public. In a potentially acute situation, then, everyone present will appear more unconcerned than he is in fact. A crowd can thus force inaction on its members by implying, through its passivity, that an event is not an emergency. Any individual in such a crowd fears that he may appear a fool if he behaves as though it were.

To determine how the presence of other people affects a person's interpretation of an emergency, Latané and Judith Rodin set up another experiment. Subjects were paid $2 to participate in a survey of game and puzzle preferences conducted at Columbia University by the Consumer Testing Bureau. An attractive young market researcher met them at the door and took them to the testing room, where they were given questionnaires to fill out. Before leaving, she told them that she would be working next door in her office, which was separated from the room by a folding room-divider. She then entered her office, where she shuffled papers, opened drawers and made enough noise to remind the subjects of her presence. After four minutes she turned on a high-fidelity tape recorder.

On it, the subjects heard the researcher climb up on a chair, perhaps to reach for a stack of papers on the bookcase. They heard a loud crash and a scream as the chair collapsed and she fell, and they heard her moan, "Oh, my foot . . . I . . . I . . . can't move it. Oh, I . . . can't get this . . . thing . . . off me." Her cries gradually got more subdued and controlled.

Twenty-six people were alone in the waiting room when the "accident" occurred. Seventy percent of them offered to help the victim. Many pushed back the divider to offer their assistance; others called out to offer their help.

Among those waiting in pairs, only 20 percent — 8 out of 40 — offered to help. The other 32 remained unresponsive. In defining the situation as a nonemergency, they explained to themselves why the other member of the pair did not leave the room; they also removed any reason for action themselves. Whatever had happened, it was believed to be not serious. "A mild sprain," some said. "I didn't want to embarrass her." In a "real" emergency, they assured us, they would be among the first to help.

The lonely crowd

Even if a person defines an event as an emergency, the presence of other bystanders may still make him less likely to intervene. He feels that his responsibility is diffused and diluted. Thus, if your car breaks down on a busy highway, hundreds of drivers whiz by without anyone's stopping to help — but if you are stuck on a nearly deserted country road, whoever passes you first is likely to stop.

To test this diffusion-of-responsibility theory, we simulated an emergency in which people overheard a victim calling for help. Some thought they were the only person to hear the cries; the rest believed that others heard them, too. As with the witnesses to Kitty Genoveses's murder, the subjects could not *see* one another or know what others were doing. The kind of direct group inhibition found in the other two studies could not operate.

For the stimulation, we recruited 72 students at New York University to particpate in what was referred to as a "group discussion" of personal problems in an urban university. Each student was put in an individual room equipped with a set of headphones and a microphone. It was explained that this precaution had been taken because participants might feel embarrassed about discussing their problems publicly. Also, the experimenter said that he would not listen to the initial discussion, but would only ask for reactions later. Each person was to talk in turn.

The first to talk reported that he found it difficult to adjust to New York and his studies. Then, hesitantly and with obvious embarrassment, he mentioned that he was prone to nervous seizures when he was under stress. Other students then talked about their own problems in turn. The number of people in the "discussion" varied. But whatever the apparent size of the group — two, three or six people — only the subject was actually present; the others, as well as the instructions and the speeches of the victim-to-be, were present only on a pre-recorded tape.

When it was the first person's turn to talk again, he launched into the following performance, becoming louder and having increasing speech difficulties: "I can see a lot of er of er how other people's problems are similar to mine because er I mean er they're not er e-easy to handle sometimes and er I er um I think I I need er if if could er er somebody er er er give me give me a little er give me a little help here because er I er *uh* I've got a one of the er seiz-er er things coming *on* and and er uh uh (choking sounds) . . . "

Eighty-five percent of the people who believed themselves to be alone with the victim came out of their room to help. Sixty-two percent of the people who believed there was *one* other bystander did so. Of those who believed there were four other bystanders, only 31 percent reported the fit. The responsibility-diluting effect of other people was so strong that single individuals were more than twice as likely to report the emergency as those who thought other people also knew about it.

The lesson learned

People who failed to report the emergency showed few signs of the apathy and indifference thought to characterize "unresponsive bystanders." When the experimenter entered the room to end the situation, the subject often asked if the victim was "all right." Many of them showed physical signs of nervousness; they often had trembling hands and sweating palms. If anything, they seemed more emotionally aroused than did those who reported the emergency. Their emotional behavior was a sign of their continuing conflict concerning whether to respond or not.

Thus, the stereotype of the unconcerned, depersonalized *homo urbanus,* blandly watching the misfortunes of others, proves inaccurate. Instead, we find that a bystander to an emergency is an anguished individual in genuine doubt, wanting to do the right thing but compelled to make complex decisions under pressure of stress and fear. His reactions are shaped by the actions of others — and all too frequently by their inaction.

And we are that bystander. Caught up by the apparent indifference of others, we may pass by an emergency without helping or even realizing that help is needed. Once we are aware of the influence of those around us, however, we can resist it. We can choose to see distress and step forward to relieve it.

John M. Darley and Bibb Latané, "Why People Don't Help in a Crisis"

Making Marginal Notes

Being an active reader also involves making notes in the margins of your text. Selective highlighting records your reactions to your source by showing you which ideas you consider most important. But to explore *why* certain ideas are important and *how* they relate to other ideas, you must annotate your text.

When you *annotate,* you record your reactions in brief marginal and interlinear notes (notes written in between lines of text). You may also write longer comments at the top or bottom of a page, perhaps summarizing a difficult passage in your own words, or you may arrange your notes in lists, charts, or other graphic forms. Do not be afraid to make these notes — talk back to your text. Annotation is an important part of the writing process, and the comments and queries you note at this point can be invaluable in helping you uncover material to write about later. Remember, though, that the notes you take are tentative; your annotations can be supplemented, revised, or deleted as you reread and reassess them, and they can be expanded or disregarded as you write.

You may jot down important ideas in the margins, or between the lines, for any of several purposes: to record first impressions, to place emphasis, to question, summarize, evaluate, compare, contrast, debunk, interpret, clarify, concur, or disagree. Or you can make notes to direct your further research. The important thing is to let go and react.

If you are unable (or unwilling) to write in your sources, you will have to devise a system to keep notes and text connected. Some writers clip index cards or pieces of paper beside the appropriate portions of their sources. Others use sheets of paper in various sizes and colors with a sticky edge that attaches firmly to a page. These pieces of paper may be moved and reattached over and over again, and this makes them ideal for annotating borrowed material that cannot be photocopied. It is most efficient, however, to annotate directly on your source whenever possible.

Probably the most important annotations you do are the kind designed to help you understand your source's meaning. You may take such notes at any time you have challenging material to master, whether or not you expect to write a paper that draws on your source. When you do this kind of annotation, you may use a variety of tactics. For instance, if your source has placed great weight on a particular idea, you should remind yourself of this; an exclamation point or a marginal note that says "Very important" or "Central point" is more emphatic than underlining alone. As you read, you may encounter ideas that are obscure, confusing, or contradictory. If so, you should place question marks — or write questions — in the margins; finding the answers will help you understand your source. If you come upon an unfamilar word or phrase, look it up and write the definition in the margin. Better yet, supply a synonym for a word; "translate" an expression, rephrasing it in more accessible terms or briefly summarize a complicated argument. Used freely, such annotations can aid comprehension.

Annotations can also help you to make a preliminary evaluation of your source's potential usefulness. (See "Critiquing Sources" in Chapter 2 for information for evaluating the accuracy, currency, and reliability of a source and determining its purpose.) For instance, you can record your initial assessment of the author's purpose (Does he or she seem biased or fair? Does he or she have an ax to grind?) or qualifications (Is the writer well-known and respected or unknown? Is the writer writing outside his or her area of expertise?) or gauge the nature of the author's target audience (Is this audience an educated or even scholarly group? Does the author expect readers to possess specialized or technical knowledge about the subject? Is the target audience likely to be neutral to the writer's position, or might readers react favorably — or with hostility?). Your marginal comments might read "Check background" or "Other works on this topic?" or "Popular or scholarly periodical?" Any notes you make at this point can suggest ideas to write about later.

Additionally, annotations can serve as general stimuli for your writing. If you agree with a writer's point, you might jot down "Yes" or "Right" in the margin; if you disagree, "No" or "Not true" will do. If you can think of an example to support a generalization in your source, add "e.g." or "ex." and the relevant example in the margin. If you want to compare or contrast a point with an idea expressed elsewhere in the source, "But see par. 2" or "Vs. above argument" might be helpful. If you think of an exception to your source's argument, your comment could be "But not . . . " or "Except . . . . " As you read and reread, you will notice links between your source and other sources — other readings, your own experiences and observations, and perhaps nonprint sources like films, lectures, and the like. Recording these links is very important, for such connections can be valuable stimuli as you move from reading to writing, and you cannot assume that you will remember them unless you write them down as they occur to you. It is important that you jot down *any* links you notice — parallels, discrepancies, contradictions — so that you can explore them in writing if your paper warrants such investigation. To record connections with other print sources, for instance, you might include annotations like "McGuire disagrees" or "Also see Madison text" or "Check against *Times* article." To call up your own experiences, you could use notes like "Bring in traineeship experience" or "Like Brad's father's illness." To remind you of relevant nonprint sources, comments like "Compare soc. film on family structure" or "Documentary on oncogenes contradicts this point" or "Prof. Bradley's lecture supports this" can be very helpful.

Good annotations can do more than help you understand a source's meaning, evaluate its usefulness, and remember your initial reactions to its ideas; they can also give you a real start on a piece of writing of your own. As you read and reread, let yourself make associations, follow hunches, consider possibilities. Some — even most — of these explorations will probably turn out to be dead ends. But the few that do not can enrich your writing with a provocative aside, a new direction for part of your paper, or even a central idea for your entire piece of writing.

The passage below, excerpted from an essay that appears in full on pages 354–363, supplements careful highlighting with full annotations — questions as well as statements — designed to aid the reader's comprehension, record the reader's reactions to the passage, make connections with other sources, and explore tentative ideas for writing.

The "Threat" of Creationism

Isaac Asimov

A noted author argues against a small but vocal group of Fundamentalists whose campaign to legalize teaching the biblical version of how life was created has been surprisingly successful.

Isaac Asimov, a professor of biochemistry at Boston University School of Medicine, is the author of 232 books, including science fiction, books on literature, history, science, mathematics and the Bible. *well qualified—but biased?*

Scientists thought it was settled.

The universe, they had decided, is about 20 billion years old, and Earth itself is 4.5 billion years old. Simple forms of life came into being more than three billion years ago, having formed spontaneously from nonliving matter. *= group of primates of which man is* They grew more complex through slow evolutionary processes and the first hominid ancestors of humanity appeared *only remaining species* more than four million years ago. Homo sapiens itself — the present human species, people like you and me — has walked the earth for at least 50,000 years.

But apparently it isn't settled. There are Americans who believe that the earth is only about 6,000 years old; that human beings and all other species were brought into existence by a divine Creator as eternally separate varieties of beings, and that there has been no evolutionary process. *shows Asimov disagrees—purpose could be to discredit creationists*

They are creationists — they call themselves "scientific" creationists — and they are a growing power in the land, demanding that schools be forced to teach their views. *any passed?* State legislatures, mindful of votes, are beginning to succumb to the pressure. In perhaps 15 states, bills have been *Did this bill* introduced, putting forth the creationist point of view, and in *actually go into effect?* others, strong movements are gaining momentum. In Arkansas, a law requiring that the teaching of creationism receive equal time was passed this spring and is scheduled *also active against* to go into effect in September 1982, though the American *prayer in schools?* Civil Liberties Union has filed suit on behalf of a group of *any common ground?* clergymen, teachers and parents to overturn it. And a California father named Kelly Segraves, the director of the *Check bio text* Creation-Science Research Center, sued to have public- *and lecture* school science classes taught that there are other theories of *notes* creation besides evolution, and that one of them was the Biblical version. The suit came to trial in March, and the judge ruled that educators must distribute a policy statement *Does this apply* to schools and textbook publishers explaining that the *only to California?* theory of evolution should not be seen as "the ultimate *Has statement been* cause of origins." Even in New York, the Board of Education *prepared?* has delayed since January in making a final decision, expected this month, on whether schools will be required to include the teaching of creationism in their curriculums. *What was decision?*

The Rev. Jerry Falwell the head of the Moral Majority, who supports the creationist view from his television pulpit, claims that he has 17 million to 25 million viewers (though

Arbitron places the figure at a much more modest 1.6 million). But there are 66 electronic ministries which have a total audience of about 20 million. And in parts of the country where the Fundamentalists predominate — in the so-called Bible Belt — creationists are in the majority. *sections of the South and Midwest*

They make up a fervid and dedicated group, convicted beyond argument of both their rightness and righteousness. *hostile tone!* Faced with an apathetic and falsely secure majority, smaller groups have used intense pressure and forceful campaigning — as the creationists do — and have succeeded in disrupting and taking over whole societies.

Yet, though creationists seem to accept the literal truth of the Biblical story of creation, this does not mean that all religious people are creationists. There are millions of Catholics, Protestants and Jews who think of the Bible as a source of spiritual truth and accept much of it as symbolically rather than literally true. They do not consider the Bible to be a textbook of science, even in intent, and have no problem teaching evolution in their secular institutions. *important distinction — grants that many religious people take Bible symbolically, not literally*

To those who are trained in science, creationism seems like a bad dream, a sudden reliving of a nightmare, a renewed march of an army of the night risen to challenge free thought and enlightenment. *Overkill? Language is emotional, not scientific*

The scientific evidence for the age of the earth and for the evolutionary development of life seems overwhelming to scientists. How can anyone question it? What are the arguments the creationists use? What is the "science" that makes their views "scientific"? Here are some of them: *will use scientific data to refute creationists' arguments*

New York Times Magazine

Exercise 4

Read these two passages about the early days of television. When you have finished, reread them slowly, highlighting and annotating them. Your annotations should be designed to aid comprehension, make connections between the two sources, and explore ideas for a paper.

1   Reared on television, records, and movies, the boom generation became our first Media Generation. Along with the new modes of thinking . . . came a new idea: entertainment as a natural and necessary part of life. Entertainment was joining, and even replacing, work and education as an expectation of every young person. Most entertainment was communicated through the electronic media — whether on records

or TV sets or movie screens — and more and more people were spending more and more of their time with the media. According to a 1976 study by Cleveland State University, the number of hours devoted to media by the 18–24 age group rose from 13.9 in 1965, when only a few baby boomers were in that category, to 18.5 in 1975, when it was composed entirely of that generation.

The medium that shaped the boom generation most profoundly was television. It is rivaled only by the automobile and perhaps the long-playing record as the technological innovation which has set the baby boom apart from previous generations. In one four-year stretch from 1948 until 1952, the number of television sets in use in the United States jumped from a few thousand to 15 million. After that, childhood was forever altered. Parents of boom babies who at first looked to television as their helper, an electronic baby-sitter, found that instead it was their foe, an implacable competitor that was winning the battle for their children's minds. Urie Bronfenbrenner of Cornell has reported a forty-year decline in the amount of time children spend with their parents, much of the recent loss due to television. The earliest and most affectionately recalled memories of many Americans born after 1946 often consist not of interactions with their parents and families but of shows watched on television. In the 1950s, as historian Eric Goldman has observed, a workable definition of a home could be the place where the television set was. Now we know further that the "family room" in American homes is not necessarily where the family eats or plays but rather is where the television set is located.

If their parents owned a TV set, and most of them did, the children of the boom started using it when they were about 2. At 6, they had watched up to 5000 hours in their short lives and were dedicated TV consumers, with regular viewing times and favorite programs. They watched more and more as they grew older, reaching an early peak in sixth grade when the average child watched 4½ hours daily and upward of 6½ on Sundays. During the sixties, when most boom children were forming their TV habits, average viewing time rose a total of about an hour a day. By the time an average child of the baby boom reached the age of 18, he or she would have been under television's hypnotic influence an average of 4 hours a day for 16 years. The total of roughly 24,000 hours — one-quarter of a person's waking life — is more than children spend in classrooms or with their parents. The only activity that consumes more of a child's time is sleeping. In just six years, from 1960 to 1966, the proportion of Americans who named television as their favorite leisure activity doubled to 46 percent.

This prodigious investment of time came with a cost. Of all the machines that have entered our lives in this century, television was the most ravenous of time. When television entered the home, for instance, the amount of time individuals spent with all media combined rose by only fifty-eight minutes. But television itself was eating up time in three- and four-hour chunks. That meant that it was robbing time from every other endeavor. We read fewer magazines and books and newspapers. We spent less time going to movies, socializing, conversing, traveling, thinking, daydreaming, and even sleeping. When the television entered the home, children began going to bed later and were less likely to be read to by their parents. When — or if — they did learn to read, children with television spent less time reading than children without television.

The glowing blue light also plunged the boom children into an environment that was as alien to their parents' experience as if they'd moved to never-never land. It was an alternate reality that was absorbing but strangely discombobulating. In the new world inhabited by children three or four hours a day — call it Televisionland — there was violence but rarely blood or pain. There was death but never emptiness. People did not work regularly but were rarely hungry or in need. In fact, economic realities were not present at all. There was little unemployment in Televisionland and no food stamps. Fathers were not wage earners but hapless buffoons, outwitted by both their children and their wives. There was desire in Televisionland, but lust and greed were somehow mixed up with cravings for prettier hair and whiter laundry.

Landon Y. Jones, *Great Expectations: America and the Baby Boom Generation*

2   Observers of the contemporary scene were well aware of television's initial impact on American society; some were less sanguine than others about the result. Bishop Fulton Sheen, who enjoyed a wide reputation as a radio speaker, saw it as "a blessing. Radio is like the Old Testament . . . , hearing wisdom without seeing; television is like the New Testament, because in it the wisdom becomes flesh and dwells among us." Gilbert Seldes, long a skeptical critic of radio and film, saw it as "a golden hope, away from the fallacy of mass entertainment and toward a great communications and entertainment medium in a democratic society." Others were not so certain, but all agreed that, as John Houseman wrote in 1950, television would soon be "the dominant medium of mass communication in the world . . . because of its incontestable technical superiority over all other existing means of communication."

There was much to support Houseman's view. Television was radio with eyes, a newspaper without print, movies individualized. It involved its audience totally and instantaneously with a compelling combination of sight, sound, and motion that no other medium provided. Television fostered the illusion of intimacy—seen at home, individually or in a small group, positing a one-to-one relationship between the figure on the screen and the viewer at the set. Television also fostered the illusion of realism (like radio but more completely) because it showed what happened *when* it happened, visibly and audibly, with neither time-lag nor intervening agency. Films, newspapers, and the phonograph always involved intermediaries—a cameraman, a cutter or editor, a reporter, a selection of events, a choice of information—which television barely inferred. What appeared on the television screen (despite the fact that it was edited) appeared to be "the real thing." As philosopher-critic Marshall McLuhan pointed out, television is a "cool" medium in that as part of a new communications system (as opposed to "hot" or "linear" media like print) it makes the viewer a participant rather than a spectator. It is television's "all inclusive *nowness,"* McLuhan wrote in *Understanding Media,* which makes it very nearly the ultimate "instantaneous electronic environment . . . a total field of instantaneous data in which . . . involvement is mandatory."

Television's most overwhelming characteristic is the size of its audience, always measured in millions, which makes it the greatest shared popular experience in history. Its life blood from the first was advertising, designed to sell products to a mass audience which in turn (as in other mass media) forced it toward conformity and standardization. Television is primarily a selling machine of great efficiency if properly handled. NBC's two-year study of its impact on the buying habits of a Midwestern town showed that advertising could increase sales from 48 per cent to 200 per cent (depending on the type of product) within a few weeks. (One recipe, presented on the Kraft Music Hall, almost immediately brought a half-million requests.) Television's grasp of its audience is all-encompassing. In 1967 95 per cent of all households owned at least one set while 25 per cent had two or more. During the peak viewing season (January and February) the average set is on forty-four hours a week; the potential audience for any single program is calculated at eighty-three – eighty-five million. (The "TV Dinner," that most McLuhanesque of culinary innovations, appeared in 1954.) The average American

male at age sixty-five has spent three thousand days, or nearly nine years, watching
television; a five-year-old American child has spent more hours before the set than a
student spends in class during four years of college.

Russel Nye, *The Unembarrassed Muse: The Popular Arts in America*

Expanding Annotations

If you have annotated carefully, reviewing your notes should help you understand
your source. Perhaps you will also have gained a sense of how it relates to other
sources you have read and how you can use your ideas and your sources in an essay
of your own.

But brief annotations that summarize or interpret your source may not give
you the depth of understanding or the amount of original material you need to
begin writing. You may need to use more elaborate, and more time-consuming,
strategies to analyze and interpret your sources and develop original ideas. For
instance, some writers *outline* their sources, or parts of sources, on a separate page
as an aid to comprehension. Others write expanded notes in a *brainstorming
journal,* continuing their dialogue with their sources over several pages.

Outlining Your Sources

Outlining a source, or a portion of a source, can help you understand your material.
When you outline, you identify your source's central ideas and clarify the relationships among main ideas, subordinate ideas, and supporting details. The process
of constructing an outline of a source is a systematic one. It should begin after you
have highlighted your source. If you have room, you can construct a brief outline
in the margin of your source; if not, use a separate sheet of paper.

An outline assigns number and letter designations to each piece of information, indenting each item to show its relative importance. Major divisions of your
source, such as material summarized in topic sentences, are listed flush with the
left margin and assigned Roman numerals (I, II, III, and so on). Divisions of
secondary importance are indented slightly and preceded by capital letters (A, B,
C); major supporting examples, indented further, are designated 1, 2, 3, and so on;
more specific supporting details, indented still further, are introduced by lower-
case letters (a, b, c, and so on).

Although an outline can consist of words, phrases, or complete sentences, it
must be consistent: all entries on the same level must be in the same form (phrases
or sentences). Outlining a source will be most helpful as a comprehension strategy if you paraphrase your information in short parallel phrases or sentences. This
technique will help you to see correspondences. Besides, you will master your
material more easily if you put your source's information into your own words
instead of copying from it.

The passage that appears on pages 10–13 may be outlined as follows.

Euphemisms

Main idea: Euphemisms, sometimes "rooted in fear and superstition," have commonly been used to disguise unpleasant facts of life.

  I. Birth and Death
      A. Use of euphemisms for birth
          1. Pre-World War II use of euphemisms
              a. "with child"
              b. "going to have a baby"
          2. Post-World War II use of "pregnant"
      B. Use of euphemisms for death
          1. "mortician" for "undertaker"
          2. "casket" for "coffin"
          3. "loved one" for "corpse"
 II. Body Parts
      A. Victorian use of euphemisms
          1. "limb" for "leg"
          2. "stomach" for "belly"
      B. Modern use of euphemisms
          1. "toilet" for "privy"
          2. "rest room" for "toilet"
III. Diseases
      A. Use of "condition" for various ailments
      B. Use of "Moon Children" for "Cancer" in horoscopes
 IV. Old Age and Handicaps
      A. Use of "senior citizens" for "elderly"
      B. Use of various euphemisms for handicapped
          1. "underpriviledged" for "poor"
          2. "sick" for "insane"
          3. "exceptional" for "retarded children"
  V. Occupations
      A. Euphemization of job titles
          1. "custodian" for "janitor"
          2. "sanitary engineer" for "garbage man"
      B. Generalization of term "profession"

Notice that the preceding outline is clear and logical and that it presents an accurate summary of the passage's main points and their relationships to one another. Notice, too, that all topics on the same level of the outline are expressed in parallel terms and that no heading contains only one subheading. (Keep in mind that you cannot subdivide a heading into one part. If you have a heading with a single subdivision, you must either delete the subdivision — perhaps revising the larger category to include it — or add another one.)

Exercise 5

Prepare an outline for the essay "Why People Don't Help in a Crisis" in Exercise 3 (pp. 15–18), showing the relationships between its main ideas and its supporting points.

Keeping a Brainstorming Journal

A *brainstorming journal* is an account of your reactions to your readings, a place to test your ideas. Your journal entries need not have a set format or style; use whatever technique works for you. To get into the habit of exploring in some depth the ideas you encounter in your sources, use a separate notebook as your journal. Here you will expand your annotations, using the journal as an extension of your source's margins. You will have space to let your thoughts wander freely, unrestricted by the confines of the margins. In your journal you have room to probe your own mind for fresh ideas, or search for links with other sources or with your own experiences.

Your journal can help you pin down a source's meaning, find material to write about, fight writer's block, make associations, make tentative interpretations, form judgments, or find a fresh perspective from which to view your topic. It can also help you decide to change your mind or to move in a new direction.

Here is an entry a student wrote in her brainstorming journal after reading and annotating the passage by Landon Y. Jones in Exercise 4 (pp. 23–24).

> Jones recognizes the tremendous impact TV had on the "baby boom" generation, but he stops short of seeing the full effect it continues to have, and not just on them but on my generation too. He's right when he says "childhood was forever altered," but it goes beyond childhood. Our whole lives are affected. It isn't just that TV takes up time (which it does) or that it cuts down on family interaction. I've heard all this before, from my parents and in that article "TV: The Plug-in Drug" we read in soc. It's more overwhelming. I plan my time around the *TV Guide* listings. I get dressed and eat breakfast watching TV, and I run out between classes to watch my soaps, even though nothing new ever happens. When my parents work late, my sisters and I eat on trays in front of the TV. I watch TV while I read or talk on the phone—I even watch while I study. Half the time I don't even pay much attention to it. In fact, I don't *watch* TV—I *look at* TV. And I'm not a critical viewer, either—I watch anything. There's something wrong here. It's almost as if the more I see, the less discriminating I become.

Notice that this entry goes well beyond the scope of the typical marginal annotations, exploring the writer's reactions to the passage.

Exercise 6

Write a journal entry in response to the short essay "Why People Don't Help in a Crisis" in Exercise 3 (pp. 15–18).

2

Working with Source Material

In Chapter 1 you learned how to react to reading, to make the connection between the ideas on a page and the responses you make as you read. To write about reading, however, you must do more than react to it; you must put the writer's ideas into your own words, compare the writer's ideas to the ideas of other writers, or analyze the effectiveness of the writer's argument. In this chapter we will examine the basic techniques that you use when reading serves as the basis of your writing: *quotation, paraphrase, summary, synthesis,* and *critique.*

Keep in mind that outside of an assignment to help you practice these skills, you almost never use quotation, paraphrase, summary, synthesis, or critique in isolation or without a specific purpose in mind. These forms are the building blocks of the more complex forms of discourse that you use in much of your college writing. In combination they are central to short essays, midterm and final examinations, technical reports, and long research papers. Even so, at this beginning stage it makes sense to present each of these skills in isolation. Once you have mastered them, you will be able to use these techniques in almost all the writing that you do both in and out of college.

Quoting Sources

You *quote* when you copy an author's remarks just as they appear in your source, word for word, including all punctuation, capitalization, and spelling. When recording quotations, enclose all words that are not your own within quotation marks and identify your source with appropriate documentation (see Appendix B). Check carefully to make sure that you have not inadvertently left out quotation marks or miscopied material from your source.

When used effectively, quotations can enrich your writing by adding the distinctive word choice or tone of your source. You should quote when you believe that an author's exact words will enhance your paper. When used indiscriminately, however, quotations break the flow of your discussion and give the impression that your paper is just a collection of other people's words.

As a rule, use only those quotations that support your point and contribute to the overall effectiveness of your discussion. Before including any quotation in your paper, ask yourself if a summary or paraphrase of the source would offer you more flexibility or serve your purpose better.

The following guidelines can help you decide whether or not to use a quotation.

Quote when the words of a source are so distinctive that to put them into your own words would lessen their impact. In these cases it is best to let the sources speak for themselves.

"Fourscore and seven years ago our fathers brought forth on this continent a new nation, conceived in liberty and dedicated to the proposition that all men are created equal." (Abraham Lincoln, Gettysburg Address)

"An unjust law is a code that a numerical or power majority group compels a minority group to obey but does not make binding on itself. This is *difference* made legal." (Martin Luther King, Jr., "Letter from Birmingham Jail")

Quote when the words of a source lend authority to your discussion. An author who is a recognized expert on your subject is as convincing as an expert witness at a trial.

According to Charles Darwin, "Natural selection acts only by the preservation and accumulation of small inherited characteristics. . . . " (Charles Darwin, *Origin of Species*)

To the writer and critic Henry James, Hawthorne's simplicity "has helped him appear complete and homogeneous." (Henry James, *The Life of Hawthorne*)

Quote when the words of an author are so concise that a paraphrase would create a long, clumsy, or incoherent phrase or would change the meaning of the original.

"Impressions like these," says Henry Adams, "are not reasoned or catalogued in the mind." (Henry Adams, *The Education of Henry Adams*)

As Rousseau says, "The oldest form of society — and the only natural one — is the family." (Jean Jacques Rousseau, *The Social Contract*)

Like every other element, quotations must be smoothly integrated into your discussion. Too often students just drop quotations into their papers without introducing them with identifying phrases, embedding them into sentences, or commenting upon them afterward. In short, to be effective quotations should be placed in context.

Consider this passage.

> For Gustave Eiffel designing the interior support for the Statue of Liberty was a problem. "Her fragile skin needed support not only against gravity but against the high winds of New York harbor that would buffet the great surface, far larger than any sail" (Trachtenberg 131).

The quotation is awkwardly dropped into the discussion. You could weave it into the sentence this way.

> Gustave Eiffel wanted to design a support for the Statue of Liberty that would protect her skin "not only against gravity but against the high winds of New York harbor" (Trachtenberg 131).

Or you could use a *running acknowledgment* in which you include in the text of your paper the author's name and sometimes the name of the source.

> Marvin Trachtenberg points out that Gustave Eiffel wanted to design an interior pylon that would support the Status of Liberty despite "the high winds of New York harbor that would buffet the great surface, far larger than any sail" (131).

You could also combine quotation and your own words, using only a significant word or two from your source.

> According to Marvin Trachtenberg Gustave Eiffel wanted to design a support system that would stand up to the winds that would "buffet" the Statue of Liberty (131).

Just as you should vary your use of quotation, summary, and paraphrase, you should also try different ways of working quotations into your paper. In general, the running acknowledgment is most effective when you want to call attention to the author's name because his or her expertise in the subject you are discussing strengthens your paper's credibility. You should vary the verbs that you use to acknowlege your sources; for example, you can use *suggests, observes, notes, concludes, believes,* or any of several more precise alternatives to *says.* You can also vary the placement of the identifying phrase, putting it at the beginning, at the end, or in the middle.

> "Her fragile skin needed support," notes Trachtenberg, "not only against gravity but against the high winds of New York harbor that would buffet the great surface, far larger than any sail" (131).

If the quotation does not fit with the verb tense or the construction of your sentence, you may need to change the quotation somewhat. You can alter words in the quotation if you acknowledge your changes by enclosing them in brackets.

> *Awkward:* Because of its size and its simplicity of form, the statue is often dismissed as a bad example of public sculpture. Still, "its particulars and drapery details — like its thematic attributes — were thoughtfully devised" (Trachtenberg 104).

Revised: Even though it is often dismissed as a bad example of public sculpture, the particulars of the Statue of Liberty show it to be "thoughtfully devised" (Trachtenberg 104). [words omitted from the original quotation]

Revised: Because of its size and its simplicity of form, the Statue of Liberty is often dismissed as a bad example of public sculpture. Still, "its particulars and drapery details — like its thematic attributes — [are] thoughtfully devised" (Trachtenberg 104). [verb tenses changed to match the paper's tense]

You can reduce the length of quotations by substituting an ellipsis mark (three equally spaced periods) for the deleted words.

Original: "The most widely appealing aspect of the Statue of Liberty — after the thrill of her sheer scale and grandeur of her site — is the triumph of technique and skill involved in her construction" (Trachtenberg 119).

Revised: "The most widely appealing aspect of the Statue of Liberty . . . is the triumph of technique and skill involved in her construction" (Trachtenberg 119).

When reducing the length of a quotation, make sure that you delete only words that are incidental to the meaning of a passage and that you do not change or misrepresent your source.

Occasionally, you may want to use a quotation consisting of more than four lines of text. Set off such a quotation by indenting it ten spaces from the margin. Double space, and do not use quotation marks. Usually you introduce a long quotation with a colon, but sometimes the context may require different punctuation. If you are quoting a single paragraph or less of text, do not indent the first paragraph. If you are quoting two or more paragraphs, indent each one three additional spaces.

> According to Trachtenberg, the campaign to raise money in America to construct the Statue's base ran into trouble almost immediately:
>
> > The most abiding misunderstanding was that the gift was not so much to the nation, but to New York. Thus, it was generally felt that, if anyone, the residents of New York should pay. When they balked, the newspapers of several cities — including Milwaukee, Boston, and particularly Philadelphia, home of the Liberty Bell and where the arm was first exhibited — seriously proposed that the site be transferred to their more deserving city, whose patriotic citizens would immediately put up the funds. (182).

Use long quotations when you want to present a block of information while at the same time conveying a sense of an author's style or thought process. Keep in mind, however, that long quotations can be extremely distracting.

Exercise 1

Using your own words, put an identifying phrase at the beginning, in the middle, and at the end of each of the following quotations. Be sure to vary the verbs that you use to identify the speaker.

Example: "In our time it is broadly true that political writing is bad writing." (George Orwell, "Politics and the English Language")

> In his essay "Politics and the English Language" George Orwell remarks, "In our time it is broadly true that political writing is bad writing."
> "In our time," remarks George Orwell in his essay "Politics and the English Language," "it is broadly true that political writing is bad writing."
> "In our time it is broadly true that political writing is bad writing," remarks George Orwell in his essay "Politics and the English Language."
> 1. "One night I was allowed to stay up until the stars were in full command of the sky." (Russell Baker, "Summer Beyond Wish")
> 2. "Scientists are wedded to reason, to the meticulous working out of consequences from assumptions to the careful organization of experiments designed to check those consequences." (Isaac Asimov, *The Left Hand of the Electron*)
> 3. "And above all other things a prince must guard himself against being despised and hated; and generosity leads you to both one and the other." (Niccolò Machiavelli, *The Prince*)
> 4. "Wealth is clearly not the good that we have been seeking, for it is merely useful as a means to something else." (Aristotole, *The Nichomachean Ethics*)
> 5. "Childhood was invented, and when it was, children's literature followed quite naturally." (Roger Sale, *Fairy Tales and After: From Snow White to E. B. White*)

Paraphrasing Sources

A *paraphrase* is a detailed restatement, in your own words, of the content of a passage. In it you not only present the main points of your source, but retain their order and emphasis as well. A paraphrase will often include brief phrases quoted from the original to convey its tone or viewpoint. When you write a paraphrase, you should present only the author's ideas and keep your own interpretations, conclusions, and evaluations separate.

You paraphrase when you need detailed information from specific passages of a source but not the author's exact language. For this reason paraphrase is especially useful when you are presenting technical material to a general audience. It can also be helpful for reporting complex material or a particularly intricate discussion in easily understood terms. Although the author's concepts may be essential, the terms in which they are described could be far too difficult for your readers to follow. In such cases paraphrase enables you to give a complete sense of the author's ideas without using his or her words. Paraphrase is also useful when you want to convey the sense of a section of a work of literature or a segment of dialogue.

Before you write a paraphrase, review your highlighting and annotations carefully. If the subject of your paraphrase is fairly long, outlining the source before you begin can help you determine the direction of an argument as well as the points that you want to emphasize. In the Declaration of Independence, for example, Jefferson's premises form the center of the document, and a list of grievances against George III act as supporting evidence. In a paraphrase of the Declaration of Independence, you would not want to place more emphasis on one of the many abuses committed by George III than on Jefferson's "self-evident" truths. In fact, you would not even want to give these two points equal weight. An outline of the Declaration of Independence would quickly clarify the author's emphasis and indicate the relative importance of these ideas.

Because a paraphrase closely follows the ideas of a source, you should go through a source sentence by sentence, selecting synonyms for important terms. A useful tool for this task is a thesaurus that lists synonyms and occasionally antonyms for a great number of words. Keep in mind, however, that to reflect an author's meaning accurately, a synonym should reflect as closely as possible the meaning and the associations of the original word. In order to select accurate synonyms, you must take the time to read a source carefully, paying particular attention to the nuances of language that the author employs. For instance, in the Declaration of Independence Jefferson uses the phrase, "We hold these truths to be *self-evident*. . . . " To substitute *overt* for *self-evident* would ignore the fact that *self-evident* means "requiring no proof" while *overt* means "not hidden." A more accurate synonym would be either *apparent* or *obvious,* both having connotations approximating those of the original term. If, however, you find that no synonym precisely corresponds to a key term in your source, include the original term enclosed in quotation marks in your paraphrase.

As you write your paraphrase, follow your source closely. Rearrange and condense sentences, substituting synonyms for key terms and enclosing within quotation marks words and phrases that cannot be paraphrased. As you proceed, eliminate all material that is not essential for your meaning. Make certain, however, that you retain the meaning and emphasis of your source. Because you are using synonyms and rearranging sentences, you must be especially careful to stay true to your source. It is extremely easy at this stage to distort meaning by unintentionally changing the context of an author's remarks or by letting your own ideas and judgments intrude.

How long a paraphrase is depends upon the complexity of the ideas you are trying to communicate. A paraphrase of a simple passage or of a discussion that is characterized by frequent repetitions will usually be briefer than the original. Complicated paraphrases of material containing a great deal of technical terminology can be as long as or even longer than the original source. For example, consider the term *mass* in the following passage.

In order to describe the mechanics of the physical universe, three quantities are required: time, distance, and *mass.* Since time and distance are relative quantities one might guess that the *mass* of a body also varies with its state of motion. And indeed the most important practical results of Relativity have arisen from this principle — the relativity of *mass.*

Lincoln Barnett, *The Universe and Doctor Einstein*

In its everyday sense *mass* means "weight," but in its technical sense it refers to a body's resistance to acceleration. To paraphrase the source's discussion of

Einstein's theory of relativity for a general audience, you would have to explain *mass* to readers who probably have no knowledge of physics. Doing so would require you to use several words — and possibly even several sentences — for the single term of the source. Even so, be certain that you include only explanations that are needed by your audience and that those explanations are clear and accurate.

Read the following passage by the noted historian William Appleman Williams from his book *The Contours of American History.* As you do so try to identify the main ideas and any technical terms that you feel will need to be explained to a general audience.

Inner city

As railroads played an increasing role in northern logistics and troop movements, they also announced the coming of a new order. They extended and integrated the market place and so made it possible to specialize and consequentially accelerate other economic activities. This was a tremendous boost for cities, and by the 1870's the pattern of industrial urbanism was firmly established. Railroads symbolized the steady rise of the corporation as a form and way of organizing economic activity, and revealed the depersonalizing of labor that went with this institution. By the 1870's, for example, 520 of 10,395 businesses in Massachusetts were incorporated. But the 520 held $131,182,090 of the $135,892,712 total capital and employed 101,337 of 166,588 workers.

The accumulation of capital for such corporations being a major task, the financier became more important both as an active entrepreneur and as a supplier of commercial services. Railroads not only developed close connections with such investment firms, but generally reintroduced the idea of thinking about the economic life of the country as a system. Yet they did so, not as public leaders as in the days of mercantilism, but as private leaders of one of the functional groups and institutions that were becoming the competing units of laissez faire. Hence the individual began losing his effective power and sense of relevance at an increasing rate. Yet at the same time the wide powers of private leaders began to create a kind of harmony in the system which tended to reinforce the ideology of laissez faire even though it ultimately became irrelevant to the reality of the system.

Clearly enough, these aspects of the railroad did not mature immediately. It is vital to recognize, however, that they did have an immediate impact. Given a national transportation system, for example, general advertising became feasible. A New York firm promptly responded and in 1879 began making market analyses and supplying plans, writers, and artists for advertising campaigns. Functional groups — such as the American National Steel manufacturers, the Iron Founders Association, the National Board of Trade — formed their own organizations. The basic pattern is well exemplified in the American Bar Association, organized in 1878.

The organization of the passage is straightforward: Its three paragraphs examine the effects of railroads on northern cities during the second half of the nineteenth century. The first sentence of paragraph 1 signals this structure by saying that the railroads announced the coming of a new order. The second sentence states the central idea of the paragraph, that railroads helped to speed up other economic activities. Listing the main ideas of each paragraph makes clear the progression of the author's thoughts and shows how the material in one paragraph is connected to the material in another:

— Railroads made it possible to accelerate other economic activities such as the rise of corporations.
— The increase of capital for these corporations made the financier more important.
— Although the different characteristics of the railroad did not fully develop all at once, they did have an immediate effect.

Three technical terms — *urbanism, mercantilism,* and *laissez faire* — are central to this passage. If your paraphrase were intended for a general audience, you would have to explain them in simpler terms. For example, instead of *industrial urbanism* you could say *factories located in the cities.* A paraphrase that was part of a short paper for your history instructor, however, could contain these terms within quotation marks.

The following paraphrase accurately reflects the order and the relative importance of the ideas in the original passage.

Railroads proclaimed the arrival of great changes in northern cities. They expanded and consolidated the buying and selling of goods and as a result stimulated other business dealings. The cities benefited from these activities, and by the later part of the nineteenth century, many factories were located in the cities, confirming the rise of "urban industrialism." The railroads, with their way of doing business and their use of workers, reflected the growth of the corporate system. For example, soon after the Civil War corporations in Massachusetts held most of the capital and employed most of the workers.

Because of this consolidation of money, those who supplied money became influential figures. Railroads did business with them and revived the concept that all business functions in the country were interconnected. This way of doing business was different from the previous system, called "mercantilism," that saw the accumulation of capital and colonial expansion as a national policy. The railroads considered themselves distinct from national policy and felt that they should be able to compete with other corporations without government interference. Even though this "laissez faire" policy resulted in a decrease in the power of the individual, the strength of those who ran private industry did tend to create a balance that seemed to support the corporate system.

Although these characteristics of the railroad developed over a period of time, they did have an effect at once. A transcontinental railroad made possible advertising on a national scale. In addition, individuals with similar economic interests banded together to further their own ends. Typical of such groups was the American Bar Association.

[handwritten note: Note: In a paraphrase you must always consider the reader]

Notice that this paraphrase closely follows the organization of the original. Even so, some information is deleted — the dollar figures in paragraph 1, for example. All three technical terms — *urban industrialism, mercantilism,* and *laissez faire* — are distinctive and therefore difficult to paraphrase accurately, so they, along with their definitions, are included in the paraphrase. Word choice and sentence structure are particularly important in capturing the subtlety of the author's points. For example, in paragraph 1, it is not enough to say that the railroads consolidated the buying and selling of goods. You must also say that *as a result* the railroads stimulated other business dealings. Finally, even though the argument contained in the original passage is complex, some material can be deleted. The transitional clause that begins paragraph 1, the dollar figures that end the same paragraph, and the many examples of self-interest groups can all be eliminated without loss of meaning.

Before you can consider your paraphrase finished, you should compare it to the original, making sure that you have followed the order and emphasis of the original and that you have not unwittingly misrepresented any of the author's ideas. Read your paraphrase one more time to see if you can condense it further and to make sure your ideas are clearly and logically connected. If your sentences seem choppy, insert appropriate transitional words and phrases. Finally, check your grammar, punctuation, and spelling.

Writing a Paraphrase: A Review

1. Read your source several times, highlighting and annotating it until you are sure you understand it.

2. If necessary, outline the section of your source you intend to paraphrase, or list all key points.

3. Select synonyms for important terms.

4. Draft your paraphrase, following the order and emphasis of the original. Proceed sentence by sentence, rearranging sentences and substituting synonyms for key terms.

5. Revise your paraphrase, making sure that it is consistent with the meaning of your source. Check for coherence, grammar, punctuation, and spelling. Include transitions to clarify the relationships among your ideas, and enclose all distinctive words and phrases from your source in quotation marks.

Exercise 2

Assume that in preparation for a paper on the general topic "The Effects of One Kind of Technology on Society" you read the following passage from the article "Cycling Eighty Years Ago: A Change in Social Habits When the New Bicycle Replaced the Penny-Farthing," by David Rubinstein, which appeared in the magazine *History Today.* Paraphrase the passage, including a quotation to convey the tone and phrasing of the original.

To middle-class women cycling held even more attractions than to men. It allowed women to take part in active recreation far more than ever before, and in some cases it allowed them to escape their chaperons, although the Chaperon Cyclists' Association was set up in 1896 for the benefit of timid or conventional parents. But, most important, cycling helped women to liberate themselves by defeating conservative opinion. It was in the 1890s that writers and journalists drew attention to the New Woman, the direct ancestor of the liberated woman of our own day. Independent in speech and action, the New Woman insisted on freedom from the trammels of convention, and the bicycle was her symbol. The aging writer Mrs. Eliza Lynn Linton, the best known of the anti-feminists of the day, made quite clear her main objection to cycling by girls in an article written in 1896: 'Chief of all dangers attending this new development of feminine freedom is the intoxication which comes with unfettered liberty.' Within limits of time and space the bicycle was indeed a means of achieving unfettered liberty, and its use gave a powerful fillip to the women's movement at an important stage.

Cycling in long skirts was a dangerous pastime, and a handful of daring women resorted to rational dress, a kind of knickerbocker outfit which exposed them to hostility and sometimes to violence. Popular in France, rational dress was blighted in England by use of the powerful weapon of ridicule. Among the brave group of women who supported the Rational Dress League, founded in 1898, was Alys, wife of Bertrand Russell. The League's leader was the redoubtable Florence, Viscountess Harberton, whose clash in October 1898 with Martha Jane Sprague, landlady of the Hautboy Hotel in Ockham, Surrey, was a *cause célèbre* of the day. How many of the trousered women who use the Hautboy today have ever heard of Lady Harberton?

Refused admittance to the coffee room of the Hautboy while wearing rational dress, Lady Harberton persuaded the somewhat reluctant Cyclists' Touring Club to bring Mrs Sprague before Surrey Quarter Sessions. The landlady was acquitted on a technicality, but the publicity that surrounded the case and the strong feelings on both sides gave Lady Harberton an honoured place among the pioneers of women's freedom. As to rational dress, she noted a dilemma in a letter to a supporter: 'It looks best on the young and slim (everything does!),' but at that time young middle-class women normally could not control their own wardrobes, and their fear of ridicule also tended to prevent them from wearing knickerbockers.

Rational dress failed in its day; but its adherents played a part in the shift of opinion which, after 1914, brought about sweeping changes in women's clothes. More generally the step towards emancipation represented by the bicycle was noted in 1897 by the *Sketch*, a fashionable illustrated weekly, which commented that the bicycle achieved more for women than all the activities of politicians and journalists. 'Evolution has hitherto worked in cycles, but to-day the cycle is making evolution hurry up.'

Summarizing Sources

Unlike a paraphrase, which is a detailed restatement of a source, a *summary* is a general restatement, in your own words, of the meaning of a passage. Always much shorter than the original, a summary provides an overview of a piece of writing, focusing on the main idea. Because of its brevity, a summary usually eliminates the illustrations, secondary details, and asides that characterize the original. Like a paraphrase, a summary contains only the essence of a passage, not your interpretations or conclusions.

You summarize when you want to convey a general sense of an author's ideas to your readers. Summary is a useful technique when you want to record the main idea, but not the specific points or the exact words, of something that you have read. Because it need not follow the order or emphasis of a source, summary enables you to relate an author's ideas to your topic in a way that paraphrase and quotation do not.

Before you begin to write a summary, determine your purpose. Are you summarizing a passage so that you will remember it later, or are you gathering specific information to support a point you are making? In the first case you will want to summarize the entire passage; in the second, you will want to focus on just the information that you need.

You should also be sure that you understand the passage that you are going to summarize. Skim the passage, and then read it carefully, identifying its main idea and supporting points. Then highlight and annotate your text. Be certain that you know the definitions of all key terms, especially technical terms. Do not assume that just because you know the everyday meaning of a word, you also know its definition as it applies to a particular discipline. *Class,* for example, has one set of meanings in daily conversation, but it has entirely different meanings in a sociology text or in an article having to do with mathematics. Names of literary and philosophical movements also present problems. *Romanticism* and *Structuralism,* for instance, denote concepts that have nothing to do with the colloquial meaning of *romance* or *structure.* To attempt to summarize the following passage without knowing the technical meaning of *Romanticism* would be difficult, if not impossible.

Romanticism, in the form of *"pre-Romanticism,"* started some fifty years before the Bastille was stormed. But the hands which razed the ancient fortress to the ground were directed by hearts and minds which had been formed gradually and for a long time before they rose in revolt. The [French] Revolution had been well on the way before the waters rose in revolt. The same impulse — in different guises — was at work in the mounting spirit of Revolution as in the *Romantic* current.

J. L. Talmon, *Romanticism and Revolt: Europe 1815 – 1848*

Once you are sure that you understand the passage that you want to summarize, write a one-sentence restatement of its main idea. Next, decide what material to include and what to delete. One way of deciding what is or is not essential material is to underline the topic sentences and the supporting points of each paragraph. Having done this, cross out excess words and phrases, unnecessary examples, and asides that are contained in the original. In the process, consolidate the key ideas to create a summary statement that contains only the essence of the writer's ideas. Begin writing your summary with this one-sentence restatement of your source. This statement will act as a guide and ensure coherence as you write.

The rest of your summary should include the ideas of your source, but should not use the exact words of the source or its sentence structure. As you write, make sure that your summary is consistent with the central idea at the beginning of your summary.

Consider the following passage about Egyptian art by E. H. Gombrich from his book *The Story of Art.*

The combination of geometric regularity and keen observation of nature is characteristic of all Egyptian art. We can study it best in the reliefs and paintings that adorned the walls of tombs. The word "adorned," it is true, may hardly fit an art which was meant to be seen by no one but the dead man's soul. In fact, these works were not intended to be enjoyed. They, too, were meant to "keep alive." Once, in a grim past, it had been the custom when a powerful man died to let his servants and slaves accompany him into the grave. Later these horrors were considered either too cruel or too costly, and art came to the rescue. Instead of real servants, the great ones of this earth were given images as substitutes. The pictures and models found in Egyptian tombs were connected with the idea of providing the soul with helpmates in the other world.

To us these reliefs and wall-paintings provide an extraordinarily vivid picture of life as it was lived in Egypt thousands of years ago. And yet, looking at them for the first time, one may find them rather bewildering. The reason is that the Egyptian painters had quite a different way from ours of representing real life. Perhaps this is connected with the different purpose their painting had to serve. What mattered most was not prettiness but completeness. It was the artists' task to preserve everything as clearly and permanently as possible. So they did not set out to sketch nature as it appeared to them from any fortuitous angle. They drew from memory, according to strict rules which ensured that everything that had to go into the picture would stand out in perfect clarity. Their method, in fact, resembled that of the map-maker rather than that of the painter. Fig. 3 shows it in a simple example, representing a garden with a pond. If we had to draw such a motif we might wonder from which angle to approach it. The shape and character of the trees could be seen clearly only from the sides, the shape of the pond would be visible only if seen from above. The Egyptians had no compunction about this problem. They would simply draw the pond as if it were seen from above, and the trees from the side. The fishes and birds in the pond, on the other hand, would hardly look recognizable as seen from above, so they were drawn in profile.

Before summarizing this passage, you should first isolate its central concepts and write a one-sentence summary of its main idea. The first paragraph concerns the significance of Egyptian art and explains how art provided the wealthy Egyptians with helpmates in the next life. The second paragraph expands this discussion, focusing on the Egyptian painters' unique way of representing real life. The main idea that extends through both paragraphs can be stated as follows: "Despite its use of basic shapes and its fidelity to nature, Egyptian tomb art was not meant for decoration.''

Once you have isolated the main ideas of the passage, you can proceed to cross out information that you do not need to convey the author's key points. Here is the same passage with all excess material deleted.

~~The combination~~ of geometric regularity and keen observation of nature is characteristic of all Egyptian art. ~~We can study it best in the~~ reliefs and paintings that adorned the walls of tombs. ~~The word "adorned," it is true, may hardly fit~~ an art which was meant to be seen by no one but the dead man's soul. ~~In fact, these works were not intended to be enjoyed.~~ They, ~~too~~ were meant to "keep alive." ~~Once, in a grim past, it~~ had been the custom when a powerful man died to let his servants and slaves accompany him into the grave. Later ~~these horrors were considered either too cruel or too costly, and art came to the rescue.~~ Instead of real servants, ~~the great ones of this earth~~ were given images as substitutes. The pictures ~~and models found in Egyptian tombs were connected with the idea~~ of providing the soul with helpmates in the other world.

To us these reliefs and wall-paintings provide ~~an extraordinarily~~ vivid picture of life ~~as it was lived~~ in Egypt thousands of years ago. ~~And yet, looking at them for the first time, one may find them rather bewildering. The reason is that~~ the Egyptian painters had quite a different way from ours of representing real life. ~~Perhaps~~ this is connected with the different purpose ~~their painting had to serve~~. What mattered most was not prettiness but completeness. ~~It was the artists' task~~ to preserve everything as clearly and permanently as possible. So ~~they did not set out~~ to sketch nature as it appeared to them ~~from any fortuitous angle~~. They drew from memory, ~~according to strict rules which ensured that everything that had to go into the picture would stand out in perfect clarity~~. Their method, in fact, resembled that of the map-maker rather than that of the painter. ~~Fig. 3 shows it in a simple example, representing a garden with a pond. If we had to draw such a motif we might wonder from which angle to approach it. The shape and character of the trees could be seen clearly only from the sides, the shape of the pond would be visible only if seen from above. The Egyptians had no compunction about this problem. They would simply draw the pond as if it were seen from above, and the trees from the side. The fishes and birds in the pond, on the other hand, would hardly look recognizable as seen from above, so they were drawn in profile.~~

Notice that transitional words and phrases associated with crossed-out material, stylistic niceties, and unimportant ideas are deleted from the passage above. The long example —a discussion of a specific picture —at the end of the second paragraph, for instance, has been eliminated entirely.

The following summary begins with a sentence that expresses the central idea of the passage. The summary then consolidates the material that remains into sentences which use almost none of the words from the original source.

Despite its use of basic shapes and its fidelity to nature, Egyptian tomb art was not meant for decoration. Found on the walls of tombs and in relief, these images took the place of the servants and slaves that at one time were buried along with rich people to help them in the afterlife. It is this function that explains the difference between Egyptian art and the art that we are used to. Egyptian artists were not interested in how beautiful a picture was but in how accurately it preserved individual items of value to the dead person. Because the items of value themselves, not their relationships to one another, were their central concern, the pictures created by Egyptian artists were more like maps than paintings (Gombrich 231).

Using fewer words, this summary conveys the most important points of the original. It consolidates sentences and, in so doing, clarifies the relationships among ideas. For instance, the first paragraph is condensed into two sentences. Although not as stylistically pleasing as the original these sentences still emphasize that for all its beauty and attention to detail, Egyptian art was not meant to be viewed. Except for essential terms such as *tomb art* and *Egyptian,* this summary uses synonyms instead of the exact words of the source. Occasionally, this results in diction that is not as precise as the original (*basic shapes* instead of *geometric,* for example), but on the whole, the summary effectively conveys key points. By varying sentence structure and by using transitions, the writer is able not only to construct a smooth paragraph, but also to indicate the relationships among important ideas.

Once you have written your summary, you should make sure that its format is consistent with your purpose. The summary can be a *restatement,* like the one above, duplicating the tone of the original and presenting information in an abbreviated form. In this case you identify yourself with the author and try to assume his or her point of view. A summary can also be a *description.* In this case, you establish distance between yourself and your source, assuming your own perspective. You not only present ideas from your source but you also describe the progression of the writer's ideas and mention the author's name in a running acknowledgment. Here is an example:

In *The Story of Art,* E. H. Gombrich opens his discussion of Egyptian art by observing that despite its use of basic shapes and its fidelity to nature Egyptian tomb art was not meant for decoration. He goes on to say that the images found on the walls of tombs and in relief took the place of the servants and slaves that at one time were buried along with rich people to help them in the afterlife. It is this function, Gombrich believes, that explains the difference between Egyptian art and the art that we take for granted. He notes that the Egyptian artist was not interested in how beautiful a picture was but in how accurately it preserved the things of value to the dead person. For this reason the Egyptian artist did not feel bound to a single perspective when rendering a scene.

A descriptive summary is useful in research papers where you want to include bibliographic information in the text in order to eliminate information from footnotes or parenthetical documentation (see Appendix A). By bringing the author of your source to the forefront, you remove yourself from the discussion and give readers the impression of objectivity. Because this technique can increase the credibility of your discussion, it is especially useful when you are arguing a point or trying to convince your readers of something.

As you look over your summary, make certain that it contains the level of detail necessary to carry out your purpose. You should anticipate the needs of those who will read your summary and understand the level of complexity of the ideas that you are trying to convey. In general your summary should be about one quarter to one-fifth the length of your original source. Keep in mind, though, that although brevity is desirable in a summary, it should not be achieved at the expense of clarity or accuracy.

Make certain that your sentences are clear and carefully formed and that your words communicate precisely the meanings that you want them to. Transitional words and phrases should smoothly connect your sentences to one another to make the progression of your ideas apparent to your readers. Finally, be sure to include the source of your summary so that both you and your audience will know that the ideas that you are presenting are someone else's, not yours.

Writing a Summary: A Review

1. Determine your purpose.
2. Read the passage carefully, identifying its main idea and supporting points.
3. Highlight and annotate your source.
4. Write a one-sentence statement of the main idea of your source.
5. Decide what material from your source you will include.
6. Write a draft of your summary beginning with the one-sentence statement of your source's main idea.
7. Revise your summary for coherence, grammar, punctuation, and spelling. Make sure that your summary is consistent with your purpose.

Exercise 3

Reread the passage about bicycles in Exercise 2 (p. 37). Write a one-paragraph summary of the passage.

Critiquing Sources

In a paraphrase or a summary you present only the ideas contained in your sources. Often, however, you have to do more than put an author's ideas into your own words.

A *critique* is a systematic evaluation of a source. In it you put source material into perspective, discuss its purpose, or explain what it means. Critiquing is a broad process. You can write critiques of art exhibits, plays, movies, lectures, concerts, magazine articles, books, and so on. A critique does more than say that a work is "interesting" or that a particular remark "helps a person understand the subject"; to be effective, a critique must clearly present the standards by which you judge materials. When reading your critique, your readers must be able to determine the criteria you used to judge your source and the thought processes that led you to your conclusions.

Before you can determine the usefulness or importance of a source, you must first evaluate it — assess its accuracy, its currency, and its reliability — and determine the writer's purpose. Sometimes an expert — your instructor or librarian, for instance — may be able to help you with this assessment, but more often you will have to draw your own conclusions.

Before you read a source, check its date of publication to see whether the information is likely to be current or outdated. This is especially important in the case of scientific or technological subjects, which usually require up-to-date treatment. However, in the social sciences or the humanities as well, research is always shedding new light on old subjects. Keep in mind that your purpose will determine how current your information must be. If, for example, you plan to use a source for historical background, the latest material on the subject may not be necessary. But if you plan to rely on a source for current information — a paper on recent critical evaluations of *Hamlet* or new developments in research for a chicken pox vaccine — your source itself must be up-to-date.

Before you use a source, consider its reliability. Is the source a scholarly journal or a popular magazine? Who are its readers, and how do their expectations affect its content? Does the treatment seem full and objective or superficial, biased, or sensational? Consider, too, what you can determine about the writer's background, reputation, credentials, education, or other published works. Is the author writing outside of his or her area of expertise or on a familiar subject? Perhaps the book you are using has information about the author on the dust jacket or in a biographical note. You can also find information about a book and its author by going to the reference desk of your college library and consulting a biographical dictionary, *Contemporary Authors,* or *Book Review Digest.* In the course of your other reading you may uncover other information about an author or a source that can help you assess reliability. For instance, do other writers find this author or this source reliable? fair? You can also compare the factual information in your source with an objective source, such as an encyclopedia or a textbook, to see whether a writer is distorting information. A disagreement in fact does not automatically mean that your source is incorrect, but it alerts you to the possibility that you should check further.

Finally, determine the author's purpose. A knowledge of why a work was written can help you understand what a writer is suggesting as well as what he or she seems to be explicitly saying. A writer may be writing to offer new information to the scholarly community, to convey information to the general public, to instruct, to carry out business, to present his or her beliefs, to attempt to change the audience's beliefs, to stimulate thought, or simply to entertain. Whatever the case, a knowledge of the author's purpose can help you determine how useful a source is for your writing.

You may gain some idea of the writer's purpose in a particular source from reading other works by the same author or a critical article about the source. You may even learn about a writer's purpose from your instructor or from your other reading. A periodical article may have an editor's headnote that identifies the writer's purpose, and a book may have a preface in which a writer outlines his or her intentions. Or the writer may make his or her purpose known in an explicit purpose statement or in a title. At other times, however, you will have to infer the writer's purpose from the source itself, extracting meaning and nuances beyond what the words alone can communicate. The author's tone, his or her selective use of facts, and the overall focus of the piece should give you clues to the author's intent. The annotations that you make as you read should indicate your sense of the author's purpose, so be sure to take these notes into account when you consider how to use a source in your writing.

Sometimes you will be able to make critical judgments based on your own knowledge of a subject. Often, however, you will have to do research to find information on which to base your critique. As you read you begin to make basic assumptions about your source, and you record these interpretations as marginal notes or entries in your brainstorming journal. As you read further, you may discover that several sources disagree or that some of your authors share a common set of ideas. These observations also should be recorded. The more you read, the more you will begin to see the boundaries of your subject and how particular authors fit into the landscape.

Once you feel that you understand your source, establish the critical yardstick that you will use to measure and evaluate it. Develop a definite set of criteria, and determine how these criteria affect your judgment of your source. The basis on which you judge a source will vary according to the source itself. You could judge a source on the basis of its logic, biases, technique, or grasp of the facts. Whatever the case, the criteria of your criticism should be clear to both you and your readers.

Begin writing your critique by stating your subject. By doing so, you let your readers know your focus and prepare them for the discussion to follow. Next, summarize the main points of your source, and give your readers the background information that they need to understand the context of your discussion. Then state the major point of your criticism and the criteria that you will use to evaluate your source. Then analyze your source with respect to your criticism, supporting your assertions with references to your source. Some of your critical assumptions will be your own; others will come from your reading. Be certain that all your points relate to your criteria. Conclude by summing up your points and reminding readers of the reasons for your conclusions.

Keep in mind that writing a good critique takes time, practice, and risk. It requires you to respond to an author's work and, in the process, to judge ideas and consider varying points of view. You must isolate specific points in your source and decide how valid you think they are. Having arrived at your conclusions, you must support your judgments with references to the author's words, with personal insights, or with material that others have written about your subject. The result is a critique that presents your unique view of a subject. Just as two people witnessing an accident may have different opinions concerning who was at fault, two people writing a critique may reach very different conclusions about the same source. What matters is that your judgments are sound and that you follow a carefully thought-out set of standards.

Following are several paragraphs from an essay about rock videos that appeared in *Newsweek*. As you read, consider the strengths and weaknesses of the author's argument.

What we're really talking about here is the wholesale substitution of common, shared memories for individual memories; a substitution that ends up robbing us of pieces of our own lives. The personal side of music is steadily being replaced by the corporate side, so that the associations and mental pictures that go along with songs for the MTV generation don't relate to *their* lives, but to the lives of the people who conceived the videos.

We're left with popular music that has the same distant, antiseptic feel as network television: you may enjoy it, but you must admit that it doesn't, in any meaningful way, feel as though it *belongs* to you. The combination of sight and sound not only promotes passive viewing, but serves to depersonalize the entertainment offered.

Young lovers today, I suspect, do not elbow each other excitedly when an old Duran Duran clip comes on the TV screen and coo, "Look, darling, they're showing our video."

And that's depressing news: future generations will be locked into the prefabricated memories of a false musical experience, restricted by monolithic visual interpretations of songs that pre-empt and defy the exercise of individual experience, motion and memory.

Videos will not be the death of pop music, radio or the old rock groups that never thought to film themselves moving their lips to the words. But ultimately the insidious combination of film and song will sap away some of the great power of music and change how we feel about it in a very fundamental way.

Eric Zorn, "Memories Aren't Made of This"

In this passage, Eric Zorn attempts to convince his audience that rock videos take the place of the imaginative associations that people have as they listen to popular music. The nature of the topic makes it possible for you to critique this passage using your personal knowledge of the subject. The following student critique of the passage was written as part of a longer paper on the current status of popular music.

Another criticism of rock videos is offered by Eric Zorn in his *Newsweek* article "Memories Aren't Made of This." Zorn seems to feel that combining music with video images will cause people to "see" music rather than hear it. His point is based on the assumption that the visual medium of film substitutes prepackaged images for original individual ones (32). It is here that Zorn is guilty of overstating his case. Certainly popular music will carry the associations that the rock videos provide, but they will also carry the personal associations that individuals develop when they listen to it. Zorn provides no evidence that one kind of association cancels out the other. This weakness in Zorn's argument can be seen when you apply it to other art forms that combine one medium with another. Does seeing a live concert destroy the audience's ability to personalize the music that they hear? Does attending a ballet provide "shared memories" that "[rob] us of pieces of our own lives" (32) and prevent us from personalizing the music? Of course not. And, far from being the death of popular music, as Zorn asserts, rock videos have given popular music new life and enriched the experience of listening to popular music.

The student who wrote this evaluation begins by stating the subject of his critique. He then goes on to summarize the main points of his source and to state the major point of his criticism — that the author overstates his case. The rest of the paragraph analyzes the sources's argument in light of this criticism. Especially effective are the student's use of quoted material and his application of the source's argument to live concerts and ballet. Notice that transitional phrases — *another criticism* and *This weakness in Zorn's argument* — signal the progression of the critique and establish the student writer's position. The student ends his critique by stating his conclusion and reminding readers of his judgments and his reasons for making them.

After writing your critique, make sure that you have clearly defined your reasons for criticizing your source and that you have stated your major point in a sentence, preferably at the beginning of your discussion. Be certain that you have summarized your source in enough detail so that your readers can follow your analysis and that all your points relate to your central idea. Be sure that your assertions are supported with references to your source and that your readers can distinguish your ideas from those of your source. Finally, make certain that you have included quotation marks where needed and that you have included all necessary documentation (see Appendix A).

Writing a Critique: A Review

1. Read your source several times, highlighting and annotating it until you are certain you understand it.

2. Evaluate your source and arrive at the criteria that you will use to judge it.

3. Identify the subject of your critique.

4. Summarize the main points of your source. Give readers the background material they need to understand your discussion.

5. State your evaluation and the criteria that you used to arrive at it.

6. Analyze your source's points with respect to your criticism. Use references to your source to support your points.

7. Conclude by reinforcing your judgments and the criteria that you applied.

8. Revise your critique making sure that all your points relate to your criteria and that you have distiguished your ideas from the ideas of your source. Check spelling, punctuation, and grammar.

Exercise 4

Read the following article and write a critique, describing what you believe to be the author's attitude toward her subject. Use material from the source to support your assertions, and document all material that is not your own.

I'm a Junk-Food Junkie

I'm tired of pretending to like raw cauliflower, yogurt shakes or macrobiotic rice. I won't mask my penchant for Mars Bars and Charleston Chews, and, quite frankly, I make a concerted effort to avoid cracked wheat, tofu or anything that sprouts. I admit it: I'm a junk-food junkie.

Junk food is connected to my very being. I made it from kindergarten through high school without ever hearing of soy beans. In college, I thrived on Spaghetti-Os and candy corn until that cold day, junior year, when my roommate bought our dorm's very first loaf of whole-grain bread. That was only the beginning. Natural Trail Mix and sesame treats (marvelous gourmet snacks — for parakeets) replaced corn chips and pretzels; carrot juice won out over colas, the vegetarian burger eclipsed the Big Mac. I found myself bowing to peer pressure and denouncing the very foods I adored.

But invariably I would come to my senses by remembering one very important fact of life: In grade school it was always the kid with the red Delicious apple who wanted to trade with the one who had the Twinkies — never the other way around.

What's so great about junk food? It's fun. You don't eat it because your body needs it; it will make neither your nails nor hair grow faster, nor supply you with vitamins B_3, B_6, B_{12} or any other nutrients that sound like a bingo call.

Junk foods even have fun names. How can you resist anything called Cheez Doodles, Peanut Butter Cup, Crunch Bar or Chunky? Even generically speaking, is there a soul among us who doesn't find the word "cookie" irresistibly cute?

Junk food makes or breaks a holiday. Who would honestly prefer a hard-boiled Easter egg to one of solid chocolate? Imagine trick-or-treating for mung sprouts.

Junk food is also often cheaper than its healthier counterparts. For the price of a half pound of raw cashews (tasteless!) or sundried apricots (yech!), you can buy enough Double Stuf Oreos to see you through even the most trying of times. And unlike healthful snacks that contain no preservatives, junk food endures.

Finally, junk food can be your friend. In recent years, I've spent some of the best Saturday nights of my life with the Messrs. Baskin and Robbins.

Unfortunately, it is considered neither chic nor mature to admit loving junk food. While one is encouraged to rave about salade Nicoise and ratatouille, which usually sound better than they taste, one is frowned upon for showing equal enthusiasm for double-fudge brownies, which always taste even better than they sound. It's acceptable to eat heaps of three-bean salad without shame, but one must sneak a maraschino cherry while everyone's out of the room. And, except for melon, no one dares to order dessert anymore unless they're willing to accept a raised eyebrow, not to mention a "Do you *really* need that?" from the killjoy in your company.

But as frank as I am in proclaiming my addiction, social disapproval makes me uncomfortable eating many junk foods in public. At business lunches, I find myself saying "baked" when I long to say "French fried." I can't seem to order dessert without announcing, "I'll work this off at the gym," or "This is the first dessert I've had since the Bicentennial." At birthday parties, I always ask the cake cutter for "just a sliver," though I secretly wish she'd divide the sliver among the other nineteen guests and hand the rest over to me.

If taste buds mature as we reach adulthood, I should have turned the corner on junk food many years ago, but I just can't muster up the same zest for fruit juice as I can for fruit pie. And I *know* I'm not alone. I couldn't have been the sole inspiration for the slogan "Nobody doesn't like Sara Lee."

Fellow junkies: I know you're out there. Come forth. Come out of the pantry and snack in solidarity.

Mollie Fermaglich, *Glamour*

Synthesizing Sources

So far we have discussed quotation, a technique for using an author's exact words in your paper; paraphrase and summary, methods that allow you to take an author's ideas and put them into your own words; and critique, a way of evaluating a source. Often, however, writing a paper involves taking material from several sources and combining it with your own ideas to reach new and interesting conclusions. A *synthesis* joins material from two or more sources to achieve a coherent view of a subject. In doing so it relies on all the methods that we have discussed so far in this chapter. For example, you could read three newspaper accounts of negotiations to avoid a baseball players' strike and, after considering the differences, similarities, and biases of each account, arrive at a balanced view of the subject. The synthesis you write would contain a main idea that demonstrates your understanding of the negotiations and might also include quotations and summaries and paraphrases of material from your sources that supports your assertions. Although your ideas about the negotiations would be drawn from the articles that you read, your conclusions would be your own.

You begin to synthesize material by comparing your sources, taking note of their similarities and differences and their respective viewpoints. Naturally, before you compare your sources you must make sure that you understand them individually. The techniques discussed in Chapter 1 can help you with this. Your marginal annotations and your journal entries can be of great help at this stage, isolating areas of agreement and disagreement.

As you compare your sources, note the areas where your sources agree. All your sources may be on the same topic—the admission of women to medical school, for instance—but they may have different viewpoints or emphases. Do all the authors feel, for example, that women have made gains in being admitted to medical schools? Do they agree about the extent of these gains and that the 1980s have been very good years for admissions? Do these authors offer statistical evidence to back up their claims, and is this evidence consistent among your sources?

You should also record the points on which your sources disagree. Does one of your sources say that despite recent gains, women physicians still have a difficult time getting into male-dominated specialties such as surgery and urology? In addition, does another source say that although admission of women to medical schools has been increasing, the total number of women applying to medical schools has been decreasing? When you write down these points, remember to note the data that your sources include to support their assertions.

Finally, see if your sources all reach the same conclusions. Keep in mind that even if two sources contain substantially the same facts, their authors can reach quite different conclusions. Pay special attention to the thought processes that led the authors to their conclusions, and be sure to make note of any slips in logic or unwarranted assumptions that you find.

As you review the items that you have recorded, determine whether or not they follow a pattern. Grouping the pieces of information that you have located can help you draw your ideas together and uncover relationships you may have missed. Keep in mind that there are many different ways to group information. Be sure to experiment to find the different connections that exist. The similarities and differences you uncover should not only shed light on your sources and their conclusions but should also help you understand the ideas that you intend to write about.

As you write your synthesis, remember that *your* ideas, not those of your sources, form the center of your discussion. Begin your synthesis with a statement of your main idea. Then state your points, one at a time, using material from your sources to support your assertions. Sometimes you will support your points with quotations; at other times you will use summaries or paraphrases. Make certain that you use documentation to keep your ideas and the ideas of your sources separate. Introduce your points with strong topic sentences and include the transitional words and phrases your readers need to follow your ideas. End your synthesis by restating your main idea and reenforcing the point of your discussion.

Following is a synthesis written by a student as part of a research paper on computer anxiety. Notice how she uses summary, paraphrase, and quotation to support her points and how she uses documentation to give credit to her sources.

Even though some of what people fear about computers is legitimate, many concerns have no basis in fact. Certainly it is true that the new generation of computers can perform some sophisticated functions. New ''smart'' computers that are in the experimental stage can talk to one another and can understand spoken commands. One can already see the day when typists and stenographers will be outmoded by their computer counterparts. Office computers will be able to communicate with one another, storing information and correlating data without any intervention from human beings (Sheils 72).

In his book *Gödel, Escher, Bach,* Douglas R. Hofstadter says that someday a computer will have both "will . . . and consciousness" (423). Even so, these computers will not be running out of control. What these computers will be able to do will be limited by their programmers. Thus the control of and the responsibility for these computers will ultimately rest with their human creators.

What, then, is the role of computers in our lives? To be sure, computers carry out at incredible speed many of the mundane tasks that make our way of life possible. Computer billing — with all its faults — makes modern business possible, and without computers we could not get the telephone service or television reception that we have come to take for granted. But computers are more than fast calculators. They are well on their way to being capable of learning, creating, and someday even thinking (Raphael 21). It goes without saying then, that as a result of the computer, both we and our culture will change profoundly (Turkle 15). These changes need not be negative, however. Naturally there will be dislocations, but human beings have weathered other challenges — consider industrialization in the last century — and there is no indication that we cannot do the same now.

Notice that the student who wrote this synthesis uses her sources to support her ideas about the topic. The passage contains the student's assertions supported by material from her sources. Never losing sight of her purpose, the student marshals her arguments and does not give in to the temptation to let her sources carry the weight of the discussion. Instead, the sources illustrate examples or expand points that the student herself makes. Because of this, the student takes control of her sources, weaving them together into a unified and persuasive discussion. Notice that the student begins her synthesis by stating her main idea and ends by restating her point and bringing the various lines of her discussion together.

Once you have finished writing your synthesis, read it to make sure that it accurately expresses your viewpoint. Keep in mind that a synthesis is more than a compilation of other people's ideas, and make certain that it presents your perspective on your subject. Next, check to see that you have convincingly supported your points and that the information you have included is relevant to your topic. Make certain that you have identified your assertions in topic sentences and that they clearly express your ideas. Be sure that you have supplied all the transitional words and phrases that you need to ensure that your synthesis is smooth and coherent. Finally, make certain that you have documented all material that you borrowed from your sources.

Writing a Synthesis: A Review

1. Compare your sources, noting areas where they agree and disagree. Group information to uncover relationships.

2. State the main idea of your synthesis.

3. Present your points, supporting them with quotations, paraphrases, sum-

maries, and critiques. Make certain that you use documentation to give credit to your sources.

4. Conclude by restating your main point and by drawing the various lines of your thought together.

5. Revise to make sure that your viewpoint controls your synthesis and that you have clearly identified your sources. Make sure that your points are fully supported by material from your sources. Check grammar, punctuation, and spelling.

Exercise 5

Read the following passages about the increasing use of part-time instructors by colleges and universities, and write a one-paragraph synthesis combining your ideas with the ideas of your sources. Make certain that your ideas give the paragraph its focus, and document all material that you borrow from your sources.

1 Richard P. Chait, a professor at Case Western Reserve University in Cleveland and author of the book *Beyond Traditional Tenure,* maintains that . . . adjunct [nontenure-track] appointments serve the needs of institutions that are already too heavily tenured, while providing positions for young academicians who might otherwise find no place within the professoriate.

But the part-time and temporary appointments have also caused considerable controversy. For example, according to Dr. Chait, aside from its positive aspects the adjunct approach tends to undermine institutions by reducing the portion of the faculty available to serve on committees, advise students and carry on the life of the college, since temporary and part-time faculty usually have no obligation to the institution beyond showing up to teach courses.

"Most part-timers are poorly paid, have marginal job security at best and get little institutional support for their teaching efforts," stated the 1984 report "Part-Time Faculty: Higher Education at a Crossroads," written by Judith M. Gappa of San Francisco State University, who is in charge of part-time faculty there. "Nearly all to some extent resent the uncollegial treatment they receive and are frustrated by the impediments to good teaching performance they must put up with." (Gene I. Maeroff, "A Changing World for Professors")

2 There is also a perceived threat from part-time teachers. More than half the [full-time] faculty surveyed believed that part-timers are taking positions away from full-time teachers. The notion of a lifetime commitment to the professoriate appears to be declining, often leaving today's college student less secure. In their darker moments, faculty members wonder if the campus of the future will be staffed by specialists who pop in and out.

From a management view, flexibility is welcomed. Last-minute appointments can be made, lower salaries can be paid and long-term benefits denied. Educationally, part-time teachers can, in fact, enrich the campus by giving special knowledge and experience to their students. Still, the impact of such staffing arrangements on the full-time faculty and the erosion of a sense of community on campus is real. (Ernest L. Boyer, "How Professors See Their Future")

3 At the end of each academic year more than a third of the professors at Illinois State

University . . . lose their jobs. They are not dismissed; the contracts for their one-year temporary positions simply run out. And for them the end of the summer marks the beginning of a scramble to reserve new teaching positions.

In the late 1960's, before the university nearly doubled in size from 13,000 students in 1968 to 28,000 last year, a fifth of its professors — even then a large number — were in temporary or so-called "nontenure-track" positions. But as the university has grown, its governing board has urged the administration to keep costs down, keep course offerings flexible and avoid becoming "overtenured," according to Richard Godfrey, its director of institutional advancement.

Temporary faculty members, hired semester by semester or year by year to teach mostly full course loads, provide the answer. They are told when applying for the job that they are expected only to teach students — often large introductory courses or required courses like writing — and they are not reviewed by a tenure committee because they are never considered for such life-time appointments. (William R. Greer, "Temporaries Also Grow")

3

Writing with Sources:
A Case Study

This chapter traces the process of writing a paper that integrates material gathered from one or more sources with your own experiences, observations, and critical judgments. As you read the chapter, you will be asked to review all the skills introduced in Chapters 1 and 2. Read carefully and actively, selectively highlighting and annotating your sources. Then, as your paper takes shape, go on to take more detailed notes, quoting, paraphrasing, and summarizing ideas in your sources and writing sections of synthesis or critique that weave source material in with your own ideas. Finally, shape, write, and revise your essay, tailoring it for your intended audience. The writing that you do will not progress in neat steps; rather, different concerns will emerge as you write. Your essay-in-progress will constantly be growing and changing as you bring your audience and purpose into focus and as you learn more about your topic from reading, thinking, writing, and rewriting.

Starting Your Paper

Choosing a Topic

Your first concern when writing a source-based essay is deciding on a topic. This focus is essential if you are going to select and evaluate source material for your paper. Often you are assigned a particular topic for a paper: "Analyze the potential impact of prefabricated homes on the United States construction industry," "Trace the influence of the abolition movement on the women's suffrage movement," or "Compare the exploitation of children in Dickens's *Oliver Twist* and Sinclair's *The Jungle,*" for instance. If your topic is assigned, you can proceed at once to look for

53

pertinent source material. Sometimes, however, you will have to develop a topic on your own, but even then you do not usually have to start from scratch. Most likely, you will be given a choice of topics or at least a general subject area ("the rise of technology," for example) with which to start.

To select a topic, you must take into account a number of factors. First, consider your *preferences* and your *familiarity* with various subjects. For instance, would you rather limit the general topic "the rise of technology" to "the space program," "medical advances," or "computers"? You might also consider the *availability* of suitable source material, especially in light of the time limit for your paper. For example, you cannot reasonably expect to complete in two weeks a paper on Japanese import quotas if you decide that you must first consult a book that is only available through interlibrary loan or review a press release from a company based in Tokyo.

Remember that any topic that you choose at this point will have to be narrowed until it is suitable for the *scope* of the paper you are writing. Even if you know you can locate many valuable sources for a paper on prejudice, you will not possibly be able to treat such a broad, unfocused topic effectively. In fact, without narrowing this topic you would not even know where to begin looking for material, what to look for first, or how to sort material out when you had collected it. You will be able to write a more intelligent paper if you focus on a narrower topic, such as the effects of prejudice on female students admitted under court order to a previously all-male high school.

One useful technique you can use to narrow your topic is *freewriting*. When you freewrite, you write for a fixed period of time — say, five or ten minutes — concentrating on your topic. You write whatever comes into your mind, not bothering about grammar, sentence structure, or spelling. The only thing that you should care about is generating ideas that you can use to develop a narrow topic. At first, you may have trouble thinking of things to write about your subject, but keep writing anyway. Eventually your ideas will begin to flow. Once you complete your freewriting exercise, read what you have written and see if any of your ideas suggest possible topics. Sometimes you will find that something that you have written suggests an interesting or novel line of thought. If this is the case, use this idea as the center of a new exercise and freewrite on it. This new line of inquiry may yield some interesting narrow topics.

Another way to narrow your subject is to *brainstorm*. Like freewriting, brainstorming relies on the free association of ideas to help you unlock your mind and make connections. With brainstorming, however, you list ideas rather than write them in sentences. Brainstorming is a more focused activity than freewriting and works best when you already know something about your subject. Using your general subject as your guide, write down everything that you know about your subject. By reviewing your list, you often discover patterns that you did not know even existed.

Finally, you can narrow your subject by asking *questions* that can help you systematically search a topic. One such group of questions — the *journalistic questions* — can help you discover a number of useful narrow topics from a single general subject. At one time beginning reporters were told to answer the questions *who, what, why, where, when,* and *how* when they wrote a news story. This formula is not applied as universally as it once was in news writing, but you can use it to help you find things to write about. Begin with your subject and ask each question in turn. Although some questions will not apply, others will yield good results.

Who, for example, proposed the 1964 Voting Rights Act?
What were some forms of prejudice experienced by young adults before the 1964 Voting Rights Act?
Why was it passed?
Where did some of the early support for such an act originate?
When was the bill first proposed?
How was this law enacted?

You can also ask other, more specific questions to help you narrow your topic further. Later, these questions can help you to arrive at a possible arrangement for your essay (see p. 65).

How does a *narrative* account of one person's experiences show the need for the Voting Rights Act?
How could the public's reaction to the bill be *described?*
What were some *examples* of objections to the Voting Rights Act?
What did the *process* of passing the 1964 Voting Rights Act entail?
What were the *effects* of the 1964 Voting Rights Act?
How did this legislation *compare* to other laws concerning racial discrimination that were passed at the same time?
How could the provisions of the bill be *classified?*
How did the bill's supporters *define* "voting rights"?

By asking questions such as these, you will be able to arrive at a workable topic for your paper. With a narrow topic to guide you as you proceed to develop your paper, it will be easier for you to find source material that is pertinent to the points you are trying to make.

Keeping a Brainstorming Journal

If you make entries in a *brainstorming journal* from the day a paper is assigned, you will create a useful record of your ideas and reactions. You can begin your entries in this journal by assessing the relative merits of different topics, freewriting and brainstorming, and making lists of questions to help you narrow your focus. Later, you can explore connections between sources, consider possible angles for your paper, analyze the strengths and weaknesses of an argument, or develop support for ideas of your own. Eventually, you may summarize or paraphrase key sections of your sources or copy down interesting quotations along with your reactions to them, Finally, you can begin to draft sections of your paper in which you synthesize and critique material. Thus a brainstorming journal can become an extremely valuable resource for you throughout the writing process.

Understanding Your Purpose

Your concept of your paper's purpose — what you want to accomplish by writing your paper — is an important factor guiding your choice of source material and, at various stages in the writing process, your paper's content, arrangement, and style. For instance, do you expect to inform your readers? to evaluate your sources? to analyze an author's style? to compare two sources' viewpoints? to change your readers' minds? to criticize? speculate? debunk? persuade? amuse? Your purpose or combination of purposes may change as you narrow your topic and the focus of your paper becomes sharper.

College papers that rely on sources usually carry out a particular purpose — for instance, to *argue* in favor of or against a political system; to *evaluate* a work of art or literature or a government or educational program; to *analyze* a social or economic policy; to *assess* the relative merits of two methods of testing for the presence of a toxic substance; or to *analyze* a writer's style or a musician's technique. In addition, students writing such papers are usually expected to take a stand, balancing their personal responses with information culled from reputable sources to support that stand — to state, for example, *why* a work of art falls short of what the artist hoped to accomplish, or *why* one of two testing methods is more effective. A clear understanding of your paper's purpose will help you choose the best source material, arrange it effectively, and support your thesis convincingly.

Understanding Your Audience

As you plan, shape, write, and revise your paper, you should also be thinking about who your audience is and what your attitude to that audience should be. When you write a college paper, you have the advantage right from the outset of knowing a good deal about your audience. You can assume, for instance, that your readers are educated and well read — although not necessarily experts outside their areas of specialization. You can also assume that this audience expects certain minimum standards from a source-based paper, and this knowledge should guide you as you select, arrange, and present your material. For example, your readers expect your paper to be clearly written and organized, with effective transitions and other stylistic cues that will enable them to follow the logic and sequence of your ideas. They expect standard diction, grammatical correctness, some measure of stylistic fluency, and reasonably varied sentence structure and word choice. In addition, they expect your assertions to be well supported, and they expect you to acknowledge all borrowed material, clearly distinguishing your own ideas from those of your sources, and to draw your own conclusions.

As you write, your assessment of your audience's possible reactions to your ideas can help you make decisions about factors like how to phrase your thesis, how to arrange your ideas, and how much explanation to provide. If you believe your readers may be hostile to your thesis, you should phrase it very tactfully. If, however, you think your readers will readily accept your ideas, you can be more straightforward. Similarly, your suspicion that your audience will be likely to challenge your ideas may lead you to save a particularly controversial idea for later into your paper—after you have presented your rationale and supported your position in greater detail than you would for an audience you perceive as sympathetic to your thesis. Therefore, as you work your way through the writing process, it makes good sense to keep in mind how your readers are likely to respond to your writing.

Assembling Source Material

Once you settle on a topic and have a clear idea of your essay's purpose and audience, your next task is to find sources that you can use as you write your paper. Your instructor will probably give you some help here, either by suggesting how much and what kind of material is appropriate for your assignment, or by giving you specific sources to use in your essay. As you consider what sources to use, you should ask yourself some basic questions. How many sources should you consult? What proportion of your paper should be based on sources? How wide a range of sources are you required to read? Must your treatment consider a full range of viewpoints or just a single one? Should your sources take a neutral stance, or can they be subjective? Will popular or journalistic sources like newspapers and news magazines be acceptable, or will your instructor expect you to consult only scholarly journals?

As you assess the value of potential source material, you must consider—and reconsider—your paper's purpose and audience. Both will shift as your paper becomes more focused and your goals become clearer, but you should still allow them to help guide your choice of source material. For example, if you suspect your audience knows little about a technical topic that is the focus of your paper, you might want to include a simple definition from one of your sources. If your purpose is to debunk a popularly held misconception that you believe your audience shares, you might consult a wider variety of sources by highly respected authors than you would if you believed that your audience already accepted your main idea. Keep in mind that the more you know about your readers, and about your own goals, the easier it will be to select appropriate source material.

A Student Writes with Sources

Throughout this chapter, we will follow the progress of Amy King, a student in a freshman composition class, as she plans, writes, and revises a paper that incorporates source material.

Amy's instructor gave the class the following assignment: "Write a two- to three-page essay in which you assess the current state of patriotism in our country." In addition, Amy's instructor handed out copies of the following articles, telling students to select several to use as source material for their papers.

Apple, R. W., Jr. "New Stirrings of Patriotism." *New York Times Magazine* 5 Aug. 1985: 48.

Fleischaker, David. "Different Drummers." *Newsweek* 11 Dec. 1983: 38–39.

Greenfield, Meg. "Patriotism and Disappointment." *Newsweek* 14 Nov. 1983: 124.

Keeley, Joseph C. "A Few Kind Words for Uncle Sam." *The American Legion Magazine* Sept. 1984: 20–21.
Lapham, Lewis H. "The New Patriotism." *Harper's* June 1984: 7–8.
"School Spirit. . . ." *The New Republic* 1 Oct. 1984: 12.
Witkin, Gordon. "Patriotism Is Back in Style." *U.S. News and World Report* 9 July 1984: 58–59.

Since Amy had been given a general topic, her task had been simplified somewhat. Even so, she still had to read the articles that her instructor had distributed and decide which ones she would use for her paper. As she went on to explore the amount and quality of the source material she had, she would have to narrow her topic further, deciding on which aspects of this still fairly broad topic to focus.

Amy's instructor had advised the class to be careful not to overload their papers with borrowed ideas, so Amy knew that she would have to select only the most pertinent sources and only essential information from her sources. Before she could select those sources, though, she had to do some reading—and some thinking.

As she flipped through the articles, Amy realized that she had more than enough material for her paper. Her task now would be to skim and evaluate the articles, taking the time later to read them more carefully and to highlight and annotate points that looked useful.

Exercise 1

Select a topic for a short paper and narrow it to a workable size. Then, with your instructor's help, locate five to seven sources for your paper.

Moving Toward a Hypothesis

Once you have decided on a topic and have located source material about it, you begin in earnest the dual process of making the topic narrower and more focused and selecting the sources most pertinent to your increasingly narrower topic. Your goal is to shape the topic into a *hypothesis*—a tentative main idea for your paper—that your source material and your own ideas can support.

Considering Your Own Experiences

As you explore your source material, reconsider what you know about your topic in light of the emerging focus of your paper. Your own life experience alone cannot "prove" a point, but it can shed light on a topic, add interest, or suggest new directions for your reading and writing. Likewise, although you cannot expect your audience to accept your opinions and judgments as indisputably true just because you say they are ("I feel that patriotism is not what it used to be"), your personal beliefs can be convincing if they are supported by fact or by the opinions of others who know a great deal about your topic.

A Student Writes with Sources

One of the reasons that Amy was anxious to write about patriotism was that she had strong personal convictions about what patriotism was and was not. She considered herself a patriotic person, but she was disturbed by friends who equated patriotism with complete and uncritical acceptance of whatever the government did. Moreover, she had begun to notice that print and television advertisements were exploiting the theme of patriotism in ways that she considered deceptive. Neither of these formless ideas was enough to give Amy a hypothesis for her paper, but each was important enough to warrant future consideration.

Highlighting and Annotating Your Sources

At the same time your ideas are starting to take shape, you are beginning to highlight and annotate your sources, keeping in mind possible directions for your paper as you read. The annotations you make at this point are naturally unfocused, more often uncovering questions and tentative links than drawing conclusions. Still, these notes are a valuable form of brainstorming because they suggest ideas to write about and possible new directions for research.

A Student Writes with Sources

When Amy skimmed the *U.S. News and World Report* article "Patriotism Is Back in Style," by Gordon Witkin, she saw at once that it included a good deal of interesting information. Because of this she decided to read it more closely, searching for ideas that would lead her to a hypothesis for her paper. Here is a highlighted and annotated section of this article.

applications up at military academies —

Far from being just a fad, the patriotic stirrings and the popularity of things military have strategic significance for the nation. Military careers are finding favor among achievement-minded American youth. The Naval Academy, says its public affairs officer, Cmdr. Kendell Pease, has had "the highest number of applicants since we started keeping records. . . . We're projecting the highest combined Scholastic Achievement Test scores in the last 19 years."

z = first year students

Col. Manley Rodgers, director of admissions at the Military Acadamy at West Point, N.Y., reports 12,700 youths applied for 1,443 spaces as plebes last year. "Once again," says the colonel, "young men and women feel it is not only a challenge but an honor to serve our country. The wounds and agony this nation endured in the late 1960s and early 1970s during the Vietnam War have healed." (Witkin 59)

but is this just because of patriotism, or could it have something to do with the economy— or the unemployment rate? or the fact that we're not at war?

Notice that Amy's notes at this point in her research are fairly brief and tentative. She has underlined the key points, defined an unfamiliar term, and included a short summary to aid her comprehension. She also asks questions, challenging one of her source's points. As her paper's direction becomes clearer, her notes will become nore detailed and more focused.

Exploring Your Reactions

As you read your sources more and more carefully, you will find that your reactions are outgrowing the margins of your text. When this happens, you can turn to your *brainstorming journal.* Here you can think on paper, exploring in depth your responses to your sources and to your own emerging ideas.

A Student Writes with Sources

After reading two of her sources carefully, Amy made the following entry in her brainstorming journal.

> Witkin seems to feel that patriotism is on the rise, but I don't agree with his definition of patriotism. I'm not sure that what he calls patriotism is what I would call patriotism. Maybe he's referring to nationalism or even a kind of chauvinism. (Check terms in political science text.) Witkin says Americans are "displaying a patriotic fervor," and his examples seem to support this: Fourth of July celebrations, sales of American flags, "Buy American" campaigns, and sales of GI Joe and other military toys are strong. But do these, as Witkin says, really show "love of country," or do they show something else? The pictures in the article — fireworks, ceremonies in honor of the Vietnam War's unknown soldier, and the Olympic torch being carried through the streets of Salt Lake City — certainly symbolize what most of us call "patriotism," but Witkin's definition seems too confident, too simple. On the other hand, the article in the *New Republic* seems to be too negative. It comes close to ridiculing people who consider themselves to be patriotic, saying that much of what we see in America now is not "the best" kind of patriotism ("worship of a nation's ideals"), but rather "raw, vainglorious nationalism" or "exclusionary" patriotism ("the worst kind"). I think that this author is just using the issue of patriotism to attack the President and his foreign policy. Actually, neither of these sources gets to the heart of the matter — just what *is* the current state of patriotism in America today? Maybe my first problem is to decide what we all mean by the term patriotism.

In this journal entry Amy explores the validity of the ideas contained in two of her sources. Notice that she uses summary, paraphrase, and selected brief quotations in her journal entry and that she draws no definite conclusions. Although Amy's initial speculations are tentative, they eventually will help her arrive at a hypothesis.

Reviewing Your Notes

At some point — when you feel your paper's ideas are coming together, when you decide you have enough source material, or simply when you get bogged down — you will want to take stock of your progress. At this time you should carefully review your marginal annotations and journal entries to see whether they lead you to a hypothesis that your source material can support. You should try to identify your most interesting and provocative points and begin to draw tentative conclusions based on them. In the process you should consider how your own ideas and the ideas of your sources work together to suggest a hypothesis.

When you have reviewed your notes, you may find gaps in your material or questions that you still cannot answer. If so, you may have to go back to your sources and read them again, this time looking for specific information. For instance, you may have to locate material that will provide a specific viewpoint or focus that you need for balance, or you may need to look for examples to support a particular point that you want to make. Remember that as your reading becomes more and more focused, you may decide to locate, read, and annotate additional source material at any time.

A Student Writes with Sources

After Amy had read her sources, she looked over the notes she had taken. One of her sources, the article in *U.S. News and World Report,* seemed to be celebrating a return to a new patriotism, but the examples it contained seemed to suggest that patriotism meant flag waving, Olympic victories, and popular support for shows of military might. Two other articles, in the *New Republic* and *Harper's,* disagreed with this interpretation, saying such interpretations of patriotism distorted and oversimplified the term's meaning. Amy felt that each of these articles was biased toward either a liberal or conservative viewpoint. Amy's instructor agreed with her assessment and pointed out examples of slanted language and unsupported generalizations.

What Amy found particularly unfair was that none of these authors even tried to maintain a neutral position or was able to resist attacking an opponent's viewpoint. She realized that she needed to find material that would help her put her ideas into perspective, so she went back to her brainstorming journal and reviewed the entries for the other articles that she had read. The article from the *New York Times Magazine* seemed to present a more balanced discussion of her subject. Amy hoped that with the help of this source, she could form a hypothesis.

Forming a Hypothesis

When you begin to see a clear direction for your paper, and when you are satisfied that you have accumulated enough information about your topic, you are ready to form your hypothesis. Although only tentative, and likely to change as your ideas crystallize, a hypothesis takes a firm stand, indicating not only what issue you will discuss but also how you will approach it and what position you will take.

Formulate your hypothesis on the basis of what you want to say and what your sources will support. Keep in mind that you must have a clear sense of purpose and audience before you put your hypothesis into words. You need to decide, for example, whether your purpose is to analyze, evaluate, compare, or something else, and whether your audience is likely to react to your ideas in a favorable, hostile, or neutral manner. This knowledge can help you to phrase your hypothesis in the most accurate and effective way.

A Student Writes with Sources

Forming a hypothesis was not easy for Amy. Even after reading all her sources she was still confused. After struggling with a number of different ideas, she finally decided to use her confusion to her advantage by writing an essay whose purpose would be to refute commonly held ideas about patriotism and explain to her audience what she felt patriotism really was. She worded her hypothesis in this way.

> **Patriotism as it is portrayed in the media and elsewhere is superficial and misleading.**

With this hypothesis, Amy could critique both the liberal and conservative points of view she found in her sources and perhaps also bring in advertising and her annoyance with the commercialization of certain patriotic themes.

Exercise 2

Read and annotate the sources for your paper, consulting additional sources if necessary. When you see a possible direction for your paper emerging, form your hypothesis.

Shaping Your Paper

With your hypothesis as your guide you can begin to develop a definite structure for your paper. The first step in this direction consists of reviewing your sources and taking additional, more focused notes so that you can refine your hypothesis into a *thesis,* a statement that will give more definite shape to your ideas.

Conducting a Focused Review of Your Sources

By this stage you have probably reviewed your highlighted sources, your annotations, and your journal entries several times, but now you can begin to see your material in light of your hypothesis. As you review, you continue to expand your annotations and journal entries, asking new questions or finding answers to old questions, adding new ideas or deleting irrelevant ones, identifying the information that will be central to your paper. You might also decide to look at an additional source or discard one that will not serve your purpose.

A Student Writes with Sources

As Amy reviewed her sources and her notes in light of her hypothesis, she found herself adding details, clarifying ideas, and identifying concepts that seemed worth pursuing. After she had gone through all her material and thought about it, she wrote a journal entry in which she attempted to clarify her feelings about patriotism.

> If patriotism is more than flag-waving or a spontaneous response, then what is it? As Apple says in the *New York Times Magazine,* "Who is a patriot, anyhow . . .?" Every product, every politician, claims to have a monopoly on patriotism, but isn't patriotism really a reflection of the highest ideals that our country stands for? Opportunity? Freedom? Human rights? The *New Republic* article seems to miss the point. The author acknowledges that the United States was founded on a set of noble ideals, but then he dwells on the various negative kinds of patriotism. The *Harper's* article talks about the tension between American ideals and commercialism. Again there is no detailed consideration of ideals that form the basis of this country. These ideals should form the center of my paper. What many people forget is that patriotism is more than symbols; there has to be something that the symbols stand for.

Using Note Cards

If you are generating a good deal of material in the form of notes, you will probably be having trouble sorting and grouping your ideas. If this is the case, you should recopy all the notes that you intend to use in your paper onto 3- by 5-inch index cards. Include only one note on each card, writing only on the front of the card, and take care to include a descriptive heading and the *exact* source (including the page number) of the note. This method may seem time consuming, but in the long run it will save you time by providing you with the flexibility to group and regroup ideas until you arrive at an organization that supports your hypothesis. Notes on loose leaf paper are unwieldy and can cause you to waste a great deal of time just trying to locate information.

If you are using only a very few sources, you may decide that you do not need to make note cards. In this case, you may decide to keep open books or photocopied articles in front of you as you write. Even so, you will still have to identify your paper's main ideas and arrange them in an effective order, tentatively grouping supporting points under main ideas.

A Student Writes with Sources

Amy's review of her sources and her notes not only revealed that she had a lot of material but also suggested one possible way of organizing that material. She copied her notes onto note cards, being careful to put only one note on each card. She realized that including more than one note on each card would limit her ability to reorganize her notes as she changed her ideas about her paper. Next, she grouped main ideas and supporting points into the following tentative organization.

Concept of patriotism distorted
   In popular press
      liberal
      conservative
   In advertising
      print ads
      television ads
   By people
      ordinary people
      famous people
Patriotism should reflect the country's ideals
      opportunity
      equality
      freedom

With the help of this tentative arrangement, Amy was now able to refine her hypothesis into a thesis.

Deciding on a Thesis

With your ideas sorted into a tentative arrangement, you are ready to develop your thesis. Whereas your hypothesis is a working idea that guides the early stages of your research, your *thesis* is a specific, clearly worded, arguable statement of the main idea of your essay. A thesis statement is more than a topic ("The current state of patriotism in America"), a statement of fact ("Patriotic toys are selling in record quantities"), or an announcement of your paper's subject ("In this paper I will discuss patriotism"). A thesis statement not only takes a stand, it also reflects the shape of the paper ("On the wane during the 1960s, patriotism is about to make a dramatic comeback among college students.").

It may take several attempts before you arrive at a thesis that actually conveys your main idea. You may have to reread some of your notes as well as certain portions of your sources. Once you have arrived at a thesis, make sure that it is accurate and that your sources can support it. Remember: At this point, your thesis is tentative. As you write and revise, you will probably change or sharpen your thesis to make it consistent with your purpose.

A Student Writes with Sources

After several attempts at rewording her hypothesis until it conveyed her main idea and reflected her emphasis, Amy arrived at this thesis statement.

> As it is portrayed in the media and in advertising, "patriotism" is superfi-
> cial and seems to have little relationship to the principles upon which this
> country was originally founded.

Not only does this thesis state Amy's position accurately and succinctly, it also helps
to bring the emerging structure of her essay into focus.

Deciding on a Tentative Structure

A college essay includes a thesis, or central idea, and supporting material—
reasons, facts, examples, and so on—that demonstrate the thesis is valid. But
"thesis and support" is just a general structure. Within this pattern there are many
different ways to organize material, and knowing that your paragraphs, or even
whole essays, may be structured according to these patterns of development may
help you as you plan, draft, and revise.

The most commonly used patterns of development suggest the following
different directions for papers on the subject of patriotism.

Narration: "How I Learned I Loved My Country"
Description: "The American Flag—Symbol of Patriotism"
Exemplification: "Why Patriotism Is on the Upswing"
Process: "How to Teach Patriotism in the Schools"
Cause and Effect: "The Effect of the Vietnam War on Patriotism"
Comparison and Contrast: "Patriotism vs. Jingoism"
Classification and Division: "Three Kinds of Patriotism"
Definition: "What Is Patriotism?"

As you review your thesis statement and your supporting material and consider
ways of ordering your points, your notes will suggest one or more of these patterns
of development that can help you shape your material.

If you have more material than you can organize easily, you might need to
make an outline. You can make an informal *scratch outline* that lists the main
points and supporting material. Although not highly detailed, it shows the relationship of one main point to another and the relative importance of each. It also
helps you decide on a tentative order in which to present the points in your paper.

If you have time, and if you feel you need a detailed plan for your essay, you
can prepare a *formal outline* (see Chapter 1). Unlike a scratch outline, a formal
outline lists the main points and all the supporting ideas of your paper, using
letters and numbers to indicate the sequential and logical relationships among the
ideas. Because it is so detailed, a formal outline is a guide that you can rely on and
follow closely as you write. (However, do not hesitate to depart from your outline
if you find it no longer reflects your ideas.) If you have made note cards, your
descriptive headings can serve as the main headings on your formal outline. If you
have not made note cards, you will have to determine the major points and then
organize supporting material under each category and subcategory.

A Student Writes with Sources

When Amy reviewed her thesis and the supporting material in her sources and her notes, she saw two different patterns of development emerging. She saw that in the first half of her paper she could possibly use *exemplification,* presenting a series of illustrations to support her claims; in the rest of the essay, she could formulate her own *definition* of "real patriotism." When she recognized these emerging patterns, she was able to visualize a shape for her developing essay.

At this point, Amy made the following scratch outline, putting the points she planned to treat into a definite order.

Patrotism treated as an empty symbol
    Advertising
        print ads
        television ads
    Popular Press
        liberal
        conservative
Patriotism as a reflection of the country's ideals
    The Original American Dream
        freedom
        opportunity
        equality
    Materialism
    Definition of Patriotism
        responsibility to country
        responsibility for country

With her thesis and this scratch outline, Amy was ready to write her first draft.

Exercise 3

After reviewing your sources and your notes, decide on a thesis and make a scratch outline for your paper. Keep in mind that both your thesis and your arrangement are tentative and could change as you write and revise your essay.

Writing Your First Draft

At this stage of your writing your main concern is to get your ideas down on paper so that you can react to them. Only by writing can you determine what you have to say about your topic and clarify the exact relationships among the points you included on your outline. Because your first draft is a discovery draft, you should not spend a lot of time worrying about spelling and sentence structure or crafting the perfect introduction or conclusion. In subsequent drafts you will add, delete, and change a good deal of what you write now.

If you find that you are having a difficult time getting started, try freewriting for a while. If ideas still do not flow, review your notes and your outline and then try freewriting again. As you write your first draft, follow your outline and your note cards. Be sure to get down all the ideas that you can think of about your topic. Do not be afraid of being repetitious or wordy; after you finish writing, you can sort out your ideas and choose the best ones to develop in your next draft.

The Parts of Your Paper

Most papers that you write will contain three general sections: an introduction, a body, and a conclusion. Before you begin to write, you should understand the overlapping functions of each of these sections.

Introduction   Because you cannot arrive at an introduction before you have discovered the basic structure of your ideas, you will almost never plan out this section in advance on your outline. Even so, you should sketch out an introduction on your rough draft so that you can develop it in subsequent drafts of your essay.

Often ending with your thesis, your introduction brings your readers from their world to the world of your essay. Contrary to what many beginning writers think, an effective introduction is an integral part of an essay, agreeing with it in purpose, tone, and style. It defines the issues discussed in your paper and sets forth your purpose in writing. In a paper based on sources, your introduction will frequently identify your sources or summarize a source's point of view. Thus, your introduction prepares your readers for what is to follow—sometimes by signaling the content of the essay or by establishing the critical background of the problem you are going to discuss.

Depending on your purpose and audience, you can employ any of a number of different strategies when constructing an introduction. You can, for example, begin with a *question* or an *anecdote* if you want to create interest in your topic or establish a context for your discussion. If your topic is unfamiliar to your readers, you can begin with a *definition* or with an *overview* of your subject. You can also begin your essay with a *refutation* of an assertion made by one of your sources. By doing so, you strengthen your position by addressing an objection to your argument that your audience may make. Finally, you can begin your essay with a *direct announcement* of your thesis or a *survey of critical opinion* pertaining to your topic. You can use these strategies when you are addressing an academic audience that already has interest in your topic

Body   The body of your essay, mapped out in your outline, contains your explanation or analysis of the issues that you have defined in your introduction. In addition, it usually includes your reasons for agreeing or disagreeing with your sources. Combining summary, paraphrase, quotation, and critique, the body paragraphs will present your sources and use them to further your argument. You might give a point-by-point analysis of an author's position, or you might identify specific points of disagreement and present counterarguments and evidence.

Whatever strategy you decide upon, you should include as much supporting information from your sources as you can. Specific examples will help you maintain the focus of your paper and keep your discussion from wandering. Not only will your readers be able to understand points that are supported by specific details, but strong support will help you convey your points more effectively.

As you write your rough draft, make sure that you keep an accurate record of material that you get from your sources. Be especially careful to include references and page numbers for all ideas that are from your sources and to enclose all direct quotations within quotation marks. Experienced writers often circle all quotation marks that they include in their rough drafts so that they will not mistake someone else's words for their own as they write and revise subsequent drafts.

Conclusion   Most writers do not concentrate on writing a conclusion until after they have completed several drafts of their essay and determined exactly what they want to say. Knowing what functions an effective conclusion performs, however, will help you to develop one as you move from draft to draft.

A good conclusion refers to the points that you have made and sums them up for your readers. Because readers remember best what they encounter last, you should conclude your essay in a way that is calculated to make certain that your points stay with your readers. For example, you could end a paper with an apt *quotation* from one of your sources, with a *prediction* of future events, with a *recommendation* for action, or with an *answer* to a question posed earlier in your essay. Often, however, all an academic audience needs is a simple *restatement* of the important elements of your argument; any attempt to be unduly novel or provocative could undercut your purpose. Regardless of your strategy, the conclusion should reflect your essay's purpose and be consistent with the rest of your essay in tone and style.

A Student Writes with Sources

After reviewing her note cards, Amy began to write her first draft. Because she knew her subject and was familiar with her sources, her writing moved smoothly. She completed a single section of her outline at one sitting and made sure that she identified her sources whenever she used them. Amy wrote as much as she could and did not worry when she departed slightly from her outline. She knew that she was writing a discovery draft and that she would draw her essay together in subsequent drafts. At this point, she wanted to write down all she could about her subject so she could find out what she had to say about her topic.

Here is a typed version of Amy's first draft. Notice that even at this stage she includes parenthetical documentation after all material from her sources and that she circles all quotation marks so that she will not mistake an author's words for her own.

Recently, a surge of national pride seems to have taken place. Almost immediately the national press dubbed this phenomenon "The New Patriotism." As it is portrayed by Madison Avenue and the popular press, this type of patriotism has little relationship to the principles to which this country is dedicated.

The Bay of Pigs invasion in the early 1960s created problems for Americans. Then in quick succession came the assassinations of John and Robert Kennedy and Martin Luther King, Jr. The ten-year conflict in Vietnam ending in a hasty withdrawal, the taking of American hostages by Iran along with an abortive rescue operation, and the killing of over two hundred Marines in Beirut all challenged American's view of itself. Recently, however, the election of Ronald Reagan, a President who talks about a new spirit in America; the successful invasion of Grenada; and America's performance in the 1984 Los Angeles Olympics have sparked a rekindling of patriotic fervor (Witkin 58).

Lee Iacocca, the president of Chrysler Corporation, encourages consumers to buy American-made goods. So does Victor Kiam, the president of Remington products. Several large department stores are running "Buy American" displays. The manufacturers of American textile products have adopted a large "Made in U.S.A." label for their products. One clothing designer has launched an "American Look" line of sportswear. Products with a military theme are also gaining acceptance. Out of favor since the Vietnam era, toys such as GI Joe showed impressive sales figures in recent years (Witkin 58). Perhaps most interesting is the popularity of movies like *Red Dawn* (which, incidentally, was described in its ads as "America's movie") and *Rambo.*

In an article in *U.S. News and World Report,* Gordon Witkin announces, with all the depth of a television situation comedy, that at last ⟨"⟩Americans feel good about America⟨"⟩ (58). The liberal *New Republic* is also not above bending the definition of *patriotism.* ⟨"⟩But the dominant form of exclusionary patriotism is political, and the main purveyor is the Republican Party ⟨"⟩ ("School Spirit . . ."). The author then goes on to say that some Republicans have taken to accusing those who disagree with them of being unpatriotic. Joseph C. Keeley, the author of an article in the conservative *The American Legion Magazine* asks if the foreign criticism that has been aimed at America is warranted. After saying that the answer is ⟨"⟩a resounding no,⟨"⟩ he adds that we should not hesitate to reply to America's detractors, for at last ⟨"⟩patriotism seems to be returning to favor in this country ⟨"⟩ (20).

For many Americans, patriotism refers to the freedoms that are guaranteed by the Bill of Rights and the Constitution. To people around the world these basic freedoms remain real; this is the reason why so many Europeans, Asians, and Africans leave their native lands and risk their lives and property to come to America (Apple 85). Unlike most nations in the world, the United States was founded on a set of democratic and intellectual ideals that has defined its sense of nationhood since its inception. The practice of these ideals, as well as the celebration of the democratic vision that is central to our way of life, form the basis for a constructive form of patriotism. This kind of patriotism stands against the forms of patriotism that exclude others who do not support a narrow set of political, intellectual, or religious values ("School Spirit . . .").

American patriotism does not refer to any government or any institution of government. Woodrow Wilson summed up this phenomenon.

Allegiance to America means 😐 allegiance to a great ideal, to a great body of principles, to a great hope of the human race 😐 (qtd. in Apple 87). Unfortunately, the current discovery of patriotism by the media has more to do with advertising and with creating news copy than with the highest ideals of our founders. It confuses conformity and stereotyping with the idealistic impulses that still characterize much of the American spirit (Lapham 8). A patriotism that limits our ability to offer constructive criticism to the government or that defines the views that should be shared by the majority is not in line with the values for which America stands.

A mature definition of patriotism takes into consideration the ideals to which we as a nation are dedicated. The patriotism portrayed by Madison Avenue and the media does little to enhance the principles that define the American character.

Exercise 4

Using your outline and your note cards, write a rough draft for a two- to three-page essay. Follow the suggestions presented above and be prepared to submit your note cards, outline, and brainstorming journal along with your rough draft. Be prepared to discuss how you moved from your outline to your thesis and how you chose specific parts of your sources to use in your paper.

Revising Your Drafts

When you revise a draft of your paper, you literally "re-see" it. Revision — unlike editing, in which you check grammar, punctuation, and spelling — can involve a radical restructuring of your ideas and your paper. Often it is best to carry out your revision in stages, concentrating first on global issues such as organization, and later on paragraphs, sentences, and words. This technique helps you keep your concerns straight and makes it easier for you to follow an orderly process as you revise. For this reason, experienced writers routinely make large-scale structural revisions on the first draft of their papers and concentrate on revising sentences and words on later drafts.

Revising the First Draft

Begin to revise your first draft by reassessing your audience and considering whether or not your statements fairly and convincingly communicate your message. Decide whether your paper fulfills your readers' expectations and whether your discussion carries out the promises made by your introduction and, more specifically, by your thesis. Does your thesis imply, for example, that you will discuss several causes of World War I when you actually intend to examine only the role of French nationalism? If so, change your thesis to signal your intentions.

Leaving your thesis as it is would cause readers to expect something more than you intend to deliver. Does your introduction set the tone for your discussion and does it give readers enough background material about your subject? Does your conclusion accurately sum up the points that you make in your paper? Or do you introduce new ideas or reach a conclusion that is not justified by your discussion? Do you restate your thesis and bring your paper to a definite and satisfying end?

The body of your paper — especially its content and general organization — deserves special attention when you write a paper based on sources. The paragraphs in the body of your essay should not only relate to one another, they should also relate to the thesis of your essay. As you write an essay, it is easy to lose sight of the underlying structure of your ideas and to include material that strays from the direction that your thesis defines. Of course unexpected turns in your discussion are not necessarily bad; sometimes your best ideas will come as the result of a "wrong" turn or an unexpected shift in thought. Even so, your readers will expect the statements in your finished essay to be explicitly connected to one another and to your thesis.

One way to check the content and organization of your paper is to outline your first draft after you have finished writing it. Outlining allows you to see at a glance if you have a thesis-and-support structure and if the points in an individual paragraph relate to the main idea of the paragraph. You can, for instance, see if you have enough information about an individual point or if a single point should be broken into two separate points. You can also decide if your points are presented in the most effective order or if you should add points to your discussion. If your outline shows that a section of your essay looks weak, you can easily add information or rewrite this section to fit in with the rest of your discussion.

You can check the underlying structure of your ideas by isolating your thesis statement and the topic sentence of each body paragraph. (Often occurring as the first sentence of a paragraph, a *topic sentence* states its main idea.) This technique helps you see if the topic sentences of your essay relate to the thesis and to each other. Checking the structure in this way can reveal, for example, that the link between one of your body paragraphs and your thesis is not apparent, or that the connection between two body paragraphs is unclear. Often you can correct these problems by supplying the appropriate transitional words and phrases or by rewording the topic sentences, but sometimes you may have to rework the entire paragraph.

You should also make sure that you have integrated your source material smoothly into your paper. See if you have made effective use of quotation, summary, and paraphrase. Be certain that you have supplied appropriate lead-ins for all quotations. To be effective a lead-in should do more than simply identify a quotation. It should make clear why you are using the quotation and how it fits into the discussion. "Wittgenstein says," for example, does little to clarify the progression of your thought. "Unlike Kant, Wittgenstein says," enables readers to follow the movement of your discussion.

Reread all summaries and paraphrases, making sure that they are accurate and that they do not include the exact language of your sources. Keep in mind that all words and phrases from your sources should be enclosed in quotation marks and documented. Be certain that your source material supports your points or illustrates your ideas — and that *your* points form the basis of your discussion. Your voice, not the voices of your sources, should form the center of your paper. For this reason it is important that you use paragraphs of summary, transitional sentences, and transitional words and phrases to direct the course of the essay and to show readers that you have control over your sources.

A Student Writes with Sources

After completing her first draft, Amy put it aside for a few hours. This "cooling off" period gave her the distance that would enable her to see any inconsistencies in her presentation.

When Amy outlined her paper, she saw that her points followed a logical order. Even so, she decided that she could add more material clarifying the ideals for which America stood. She also realized that she had included much material with which her audience might not be familiar. Her references to the Bay of Pigs invasion and to the movie *Red Dawn,* for example, would need some clarification. Even though the Bay of Pigs invasion was an important event during John Kennedy's administration, many people today know nothing about it. Similarly, because *Red Dawn* had been released in 1985, she could not assume that her audience would remember it, despite the fact that the movie had received a great deal of publicity and had been shown on television. Other events, such as the Los Angeles Olympics, might be better known, but their significance to her discussion might not be apparent to her readers.

Next, Amy checked the relationship between her thesis and her topic sentences. By isolating her thesis and the topic sentence of each of her body paragraphs, Amy assembled the following outline.

> As it is portrayed by Madison Avenue and the popular press, this type of patriotism has little relationship to the principles to which this country is dedicated. (thesis)
>
> The Bay of Pigs invasion in the early 1960s created problems for Americans.
> Lee Iacocca, the president of Chrysler Corporation, encourages consumers to buy American-made goods.
> In an article in *U.S. News and World Report,* Gordon Witkin announces, with all the depth of a television situation comedy, that at last "Americans feel good about America" (58).
> For many Americans patriotism refers to the freedoms that are guaranteed by the Bill of Rights and the Constitution.
> American patriotism does not refer to any government or any institution of government.

Looking at this outline, Amy realized that her topic sentences did not clearly relate to her thesis. She knew that she would have to modify her topic sentences to clarify her emphasis and the progression of her ideas. For instance, she planned to change paragraph 3's topic sentence; in her second draft, this sentence would state explicitly that advertising exploits patriotism. With these changes, Amy's new outline looked like this:

As it is portrayed by Madison Avenue and the popular press, this type of patriotism has little relationship to the principles to which this country is dedicated. (thesis)

Until the advent of the new patriotism, pride in America had been declining for nearly twenty-five years.
Madison Avenue has been quick to recognize the potential of the return of patriotism and has not hesitated to use it to sell products.
Like Madison Avenue, the popular press employs patriotism in an oversimplified and often emotionally charged way.
For many Americans, however, patriotism is more than a celebration of materialism or an exercise of political rhetoric.
What is truly unique about American patriotism is that it does not refer to any government or any institution of government.

Amy also saw that not all her source material was effectively integrated into her paper. She felt that one of her paraphrases contained words that were too close to the original. In addition, not all of her quotations were introduced effectively. For example, the following quotation was just dropped into her paper and therefore seemed to have no obvious relationship to the sentence that preceded it.

The liberal *New Republic* is also not above using patriotism for its own ends. "But the dominant form of exclusionary patriotism is political, and the main purveyor is the Republican Party" ("School Spirit . . .").

Adding the proper introductory phrase, however, established the source of the quotation and made clear her reason for including it.

The liberal *New Republic* is also not above bending the definition of *patriotism*. For example, the author of a recent column states, "the dominant form of exclusionary patriotism is political, and the main purveyor is the Republican Party" ("School Spirit . . .").

After reviewing her changes, Amy wrote this draft of her essay.

Recently a surge of national pride seems to have taken place. Almost immediately the national press dubbed this phenomenon "The New Patriotism." As it is portrayed by Madison Avenue and the popular press, this type of patriotism has little relationship to the principles to which this country is dedicated.

Until the advent of the new patriotism, pride in America had been declining for nearly twenty-five years. The abortive Bay of Pigs invasion of Cuba in the early 1960s was one of the first events to challenge American self-confidence. Then in quick succession came the assassinations of John and Robert Kennedy and Martin Luther King, Jr. The ten-year conflict in Vietnam, ending in a hasty withdrawal; the taking of American hostages by Iran along with a failed rescue operation; and the killing of over two hundred Marines in Beirut all contributed to the national malaise. A rekindling of patriotism came, however, with the election of Ronald Reagan, a President whose campaign speeches spoke of "a new pride in America." Further escalating this trend were the successful invasion of the Caribbean island of Grenada; the success of American athletes in the 1984 Los Angeles Olympics; and an improving economic climate.

Madison Avenue has been quick to recognize the potential of the return to patriotism and has not hesitated to use it to sell products. Lee Iacocca, the president of Chrysler Corporation, encourages consumers to buy American-made goods. So does Victor Kiam, the president of Remington products. Several large department stores are running "Buy American" displays. The manufacturers of American textile products have adopted a large "Made in U.S.A." label for their products. One clothing designer has launched an "American Look" line of sportswear. Products with a military theme are also gaining acceptance. Out of favor since the Vietnam era, toys such as GI Joe have shown impressive sales figures in recent years (Witkin 58). Perhaps most interesting is the popularity of war movies like *Red Dawn* (which, incidentally, was described in its ads as "America's movie") and *Rambo,* movies that show Americans facing and surmounting overwhelming odds. The problem with both these films is that they seem to offer simple and unrealistic military solutions to the complex problems that face America in the world.

Like Madison Avenue, the popular press employs patriotism in an oversimplified and often emotionally charged way. In an article in *U.S. News and World Report,* Gordon Witkin announces, with all the depth of a television situation comedy, that at last ⁽ᶜ⁾ Americans feel good about America ⁽ᵔ⁾ (58). The liberal *New Republic* is also not above bending the definition of *patriotism.* For example, the author of a recent column states, ⁽ᶜ⁾ the dominant form of exclusionary patriotism is political, and the main purveyor is the Republican Party ⁽ᵔ⁾ ("School Spirit . . ."). He then goes on to say that some Republicans have taken to accusing those who disagree with them of being unpatriotic. Joseph C. Keeley, the author of an article in the conservative *The American Legion Magazine,* asks if the foreign criticism that has been aimed at America is warranted. After saying that the answer is ⁽ᶜ⁾ a resounding no, ⁽ᵔ⁾ he adds that we should not hesitate to reply to America's detractors, for at last ⁽ᶜ⁾ patriotism seems to be returning to favor in this country ⁽ᵔ⁾ (20).

For many Americans, however, patriotism is more than a celebration of materialism or an exercise of political rhetoric. It refers to the freedoms that are guaranteed by the Bill of Rights and the Constitution, not the trendy appeals put forward by advertising agencies and the popular press. To people around the world, the basic freedoms that we take so much for granted remain real; this explains why so many Europeans, Asians, and Africans leave their native lands and risk their lives and property to come to America (Apple 85). Unlike most nations in the world, the United States was founded on a set of democratic and intellectual ideals that has defined its sense of nationhood since its beginnings. These ideals, as well as the democratic vision that is central to our way of life, form the basis of a constructive form of patriotism. This kind of patriotism stands against the forms of patriotism that exclude others who do not support a narrowly defined set of political, intellectual, or religious values ("School Spirit . . .").

What is truly unique about American patriotism is that it does not refer to any government or any institution of government. Woodrow Wilson summed up this phenomenon when he said allegiance to America means ⁽ᶜ⁾ allegiance to a great ideal, to a great body of principles, to a great hope of the human race⊙ (qtd. in Apple 87). Unfortunately, the current discovery of patriotism by the media has more to do with advertising and with creating news copy than with the highest ideals of our founders. It confuses conformity and stereotyping with the idealistic impulses that still characterize much of the American spirit (Lapham 8). For this reason, a patriotism that limits our ability to offer constructive criticism to the government or that defines the views that should be shared by the majority is not in line with the values for which America stands.

A mature definition of patriotism takes into consideration the ideals to which we as a nation are dedicated. The patriotism portrayed by Madison Avenue and the media does little to enhance the principles that define the American character.

Exercise 5

Using the guidelines discussed above, revise the first draft of your essay. Keep a record of the changes you made, and be prepared to explain the reasons for your revisions.

Revising the Second Draft

When you revised your first draft, you carried out a general structural revision. After you complete your second draft, you should check your paper's general structure again. First, review the paragraphs of your essay. Make sure that your introduction creates interest and leads smoothly to your thesis. Check again to see that your thesis accurately defines your essay. Rewrite it to reflect any changes that you made when you revised your draft. Then look once more at each of the body paragraphs and determine if all the topic sentences address the same thesis. In addition, make sure that your body paragraphs contain enough examples or information to support their topic sentences. If they do not, freewrite, brainstorm, or reread your sources to find more material. Be sure that your conclusion restates your thesis and that it brings your essay to a definite end.

Now you should turn your attention to the smaller elements of your paper. Begin by checking the sentences and words of your essay. Make certain that the sentences within each paragraph relate to one another. Often only a word or two —*first, next, then, in addition, on the one hand,* or *on the other hand,* for example — is all that is necessary to clarify logical connections between the points in your sentences and to indicate the direction that your discussion is taking. Read your sentences carefully, making sure that they accurately express your ideas. Recast sentences that seem awkward, wordy, or unclear. Use coordinating conjunctions (*and, but, or, nor, for, yet,* and *so*) to combine short sentences that contain ideas that have the same weight; use subordinating conjunctions (such as *because, while, if,* and *before*) and relative pronouns (such as *who, which, whom,* and *that*) to combine two sentences that contain ideas of unequal importance. Be certain that your word choice is accurate and that you say exactly what you mean to say. Sharpen your use of words to capture the ideas that you want to express. Eliminate words and phrases that contribute nothing to the meaning of your sentence (words and phrases like *nice, really, sure, very, there are,* and *there is* are often good candidates). Whenever you can, substitute *concrete* words — words that refer to things — for *abstract* words — words that refer to qualities.

After revising your sentences and words, check your documentation. If you are using parenthetical references, make certain that they contain the correct source and page number. Be certain that you have documented all ideas — except those based on general knowledge — that have influenced your thinking and that you have documented all quotations, summaries, and paraphrases. Keep in mind that references must clearly indicate what information comes from your sources and should appear immediately after the borrowed material. If you are using endnotes, make sure that your numbers are in sequence and that you have not left out or repeated any numbers. Make certain that the note or parenthetical reference conforms exactly — especially regarding the use of italics, punctuation, and capitalization — to the format that your instructor has prescribed.

Next, assemble your List of Works Cited or your Bibliography (see Appendix B for a discussion of these items). As you gathered your material, you assembled a preliminary list of your sources. Now you must put the individual entries on this list into the appropriate form for inclusion in your paper. Make sure that your entries are arranged in alphabetical order (a number-reference List of Works Cited may be arranged differently) and that each entry contains the author's full name (last name first), the full title of the source, and complete publication information. Be certain that your use of commas, periods, capitalization, italics, and quotation marks conforms exactly to the requirements of the format you are using. Keep in mind that the page numbers you include for articles must refer to the *complete* article, not just to the pages that you use in your paper.

Finally, choose an appropriate title for your paper. When chosen carefully, titles will prepare readers for the information that you are going to present. Titles are usually more than straightforward announcements of your subject (although for some formal academic presentations that is all that is appropriate); by creating interest they can draw readers into your discussion. Like your introduction, an effective title should agree in tone and purpose with the rest of your paper. When you evaluate your title, consider that a title establishes certain expectations in your readers, and that the rest of your paper must deliver exactly what your title leads your readers to expect. If your paper is a comparison of two eighteenth-century views of the monarchy, a title such as "The Effects of the Monarchy on Eighteenth Century England" would be misleading. More accurate would be "A Comparison of the Views of John Locke and Thomas Hobbes on the Monarchy."

A Student Writes with Sources

When Amy looked at her second draft, she realized that her introduction contributed little to the effectiveness of her essay. It stated her thesis but did not provide much insight into her subject. Amy thought that she could give her readers a sense of the new patriotism by beginning her introduction with references to advertisements that she had seen recently. These quotations would illustrate the way that advertisers tried to convert the patriotic feelings of Americans into sales. This strategy would establish the framework of her discussion and would draw her readers into the rest of her discussion.

Amy felt that although her thesis stated her position, it did not provide the emphasis that she wanted. She realized that her thesis focused on the misuse of patriotism by Madison Avenue and the popular press but did not indicate that the rise of national fervor signaled a basic change in American attitudes. A more accurate thesis statement would be "But although a return of national pride has occurred, the type of patriotism that is portrayed by Madison Avenue and the popular press seems to have little to do with the principles upon which this country was founded."

After rereading the body paragraphs, Amy felt that although she could probably add more material, the examples that she included adequately supported her points. Not all her points, however, were clearly related to the points that she was making. Amy thought that her discussion of military toys and war movies, for example, did not illustrate the point of her second paragraph—that Madison Avenue was quick to recognize the potential of the return to patriotism. She knew that she would have to rewrite this discussion to make it consistent with her purpose.

Amy also saw that her conclusion was weak. She felt that she could sum up her discussion better than she had, and perhaps end with a statement that would stay with her audience after they had finished reading. After looking through one of her sources that contained some interesting and insightful statements, she located an idea that she felt she could use in her conclusion. She thought that this reference would allow her to end with a flourish and to reinforce some ideas that were central to her discussion.

Next, Amy concentrated on the sentences and words of her essay. She saw that some of her sentences needed better transitions. For example, the connection between the following sentences from her last body paragraph is weak.

> It confuses conformity and stereotyping with the idealistic impulses that still characterize much of the American spirit (Lapham 8). A patriotism that limits our ability to offer constructive criticism to the government or that defines the views that should be shared by the majority is not in line with the values for which America stands.

Adding the phrase "for this reason" to the second sentence, she realized, would clarify the relationship between the two ideas and enable one sentence to flow smoothly into the next.

Amy also felt that the following sentences in her first body paragraph were choppy and could be combined.

> Lee Iacocca, the president of Chrysler Corporation, encourages consumers to buy American-made goods. So does Victor Kiam, the president of Remington products. Several large department stores are running "Buy American" displays. The manufacturers of American textile products have adopted a large "Made in U.S.A." label for their products.

She used coordinating conjunctions to combine some sentences, clarifying the relationship among her ideas.

> Lee Iacocca, the president of Chrysler Corporation, and Victor Kiam, the president of Remington products, encourage consumers to buy American-made goods. Several large department stores are running "Buy American" displays, and the manufacturers of American textile products have adopted a large "Made in U.S.A." label for their products.

Amy deleted awkward words and phrases and any words that did not contribute to her discussion. For example, in the following sentence *kind of* is vague and adds little information. By eliminating this phrase she lost no meaning and stated her point more concisely.

> This [kind of] patriotism stands against the forms of patriotism that exclude others who do not support a narrowly defined set of political, intellectual, or religious values ("School Spirit . . .").

Amy also felt that she could delete the phrase "with all the depth of a television situation comedy," from the following sentence.

> In an article in *U.S. News and World Report,* Gordon Witkin announces [,with all the depth of a television situation comedy,] that at last "Americans feel good about America" (58).

This phrase was not consistent with the objective tone of her discussion and could strike some of her readers as being fresh or glib.

Next Amy checked her references to make sure they were consistent with the Modern Language Association documentation style, which her instructor required. When she was sure that she had correctly inserted all page numbers and punctuation, she assembled her List of Works Cited. Because she had made her preliminary bibliography by recording individual entries on 3- by 5-inch cards, all she had to do was arrange her cards alphabetically and type them on a separate sheet following her last page of text.

Finally, Amy chose a title for her paper. After brainstorming for about ten minutes, she arrived at the following list of possibilities.

> Feeling Good About America
> The New Patriotism
> Patriotism and the American Character
> New vs. Old Patriotism: A Study in Contrasts
> A Mature Definition of Patriotism

Amy wanted her title to convey the main idea of her paper. Because she felt that it misrepresented her thesis, she eliminated "A Mature Definition of Patriotism." She also decided against "Feeling Good About America" and "Patriotism and the American Character" because they were too vague and did not communicate her exact meaning. For a while she seriously considered "The New Patriotism," but she eventually decided that it was not original enough and that it would not cause her reader to want to read further. Eventually she decided on "New vs. Old Patriotism: A Study in Contrasts" because it gave her readers a clear sense of her intentions and it agreed in tone and purpose with the rest of her paper.

After revising her paper, Amy edited carefully for grammar, spelling, and punctuation. She realized that although she could continue revising her paper, given her time limit and the restrictions of her assignment, she had done a good job. When she was ready to submit her final draft, she read it one final time to make certain that she had not missed anything and that she had not made any errors when typing.

Here is the final draft of Amy's paper.

New vs. Old Patriotism: A Study in Contrasts

A commercial for Budweiser beer begins with quick cuts of city skylines, wheat fields, and people enjoying themselves. In the background is a song that begins, "Where I come from, people stand tall and proud." Sears and Lord and Taylor run "Buy America" campaigns, and a Diet Pepsi ad features former vice-presidential candidate Geraldine Ferraro. It seems that advertisers have discovered that a change has taken place in America— patriotism is now back in style. But although a return of national pride has occurred, the type of patriotism that is portrayed by Madison Avenue and the popular press seems to have little to do with the principles upon which this country was founded.

Until the advent of the new patriotism, pride in America had been declining for nearly twenty-five years. The abortive Bay of Pigs invasion of Cuba in the early 1960s was one of the first events to challenge American self-confidence. Then in quick succession came the assassinations of John and Robert Kennedy and Martin Luther King, Jr. The ten-year conflict in Vietnam, ending in a hasty withdrawal; the taking of American hostages by Iran along with a failed rescue operation; and the killing of over two hundred Marines in Beirut contributed to the national malaise. A rekindling of patriotism came, however, with the election of Ronald Reagan, a President whose campaign speeches spoke of "a new pride in America." Further escalating this trend were the successful invasion of the Caribbean island of Grenada; the success of American athletes in the Los Angeles Olympics; and an improving economic climate.

Madison Avenue has been quick to recognize the potential of the return to patriotism and has not hesitated to use it to sell products. Lee Iacocca, the president of Chrysler Corporation, and Victor Kiam, the president of Remington products, encourage consumers to buy American-made goods. Several large department stores are running displays designed to capitalize on patriotism. The manufacturers of American textile products have adopted a large "Made in U.S.A." label for their products. One clothing designer has launched an "American Look" line of sportswear. Advertisers have also had remarkable success with toys that have a military theme. Aggressive television advertising campaigns have given toys such as GI Joe impressive gains in sales last year (Witkin 58). Perhaps most interesting is the success that advertising has had with war movies like *Red Dawn* (which, incidentally, was described in its ads as "America's movie") and *Rambo*.

Like Madison Avenue, the popular press employs patriotism in an oversimplified and often emotionally charged way. In an article in *U.S. News and World Report*, Gordon Witkin uses clichés like "Americans feel good about America" (58). The liberal *New Republic* is also not above bending the definition of patriotism to its own use. For example, although the author of a recent column criticizes some Republicans for misusing the term "patriotism," he uses the term to serve his own ends when he says, "the dominant form of exclusionary patriotism is political, and the main purveyor is the Republican Party" ("School Spirit . . ."). Similarly, Joseph C. Keeley, the author of an article in the conservative *The American Legion Magazine,* has his own definition of patriotism in mind when he says that we should not hesitate to reply to America's detractors, for at last "patriotism seems to be returning to favor in this country" (20). In his article he makes it clear that for him patriotism means an unquestioning loyalty to American foreign policy.

    For many Americans, however, patriotism is more than a celebration of materialism or an exercise of political rhetoric. It refers to the freedoms that are guaranteed by the Bill of Rights and the rest of the Constitution, not the trendy appeals put forward by advertising agencies and the popular press. To people around the world the basic freedoms that we take so much for granted remain real; this explains why so many Europeans, Asians, and Africans leave their native lands and risk their lives and property to come to America (Apple 85). Unlike most nations in the world, the United States was founded on a set of democratic and intellectual ideals that has defined its sense of nationhood since its beginnings. These ideals, as well as the democratic vision that is central to our way of life, form the basis of a constructive form of patriotism. This patriotism stands in contrast to the forms of patriotism that exclude those who do not support a narrowly defined set of political, intellectual, or religious values ("School Spirit . . .").

    What is truly unique about American patriotism is that it does not refer to any government or any institution of government. Woodrow Wilson summed up this phenomenon when he said allegiance to America means "allegiance to a great ideal, to a great body of principles, to a great hope of the human race" (qtd. in Apple 87). Unfortunately, the current discovery of patriotism by the media has more to do with advertising and with creating news copy than with the highest ideals of our founders. The media's use of patriotism confuses stereotypical images of patriotism with the idealistic impulses that still characterize much of the American spirit (Lapham 8). For this reason, an expression of patriotism that expresses just our materialistic aspirations or that defines the views that should be shared by the majority is not in line with the values for which America stands.

    An accurate definition of patriotism should take into account all the ideals to which we as a nation are dedicated. It should emphasize the resourcefulness of the American character, the freedoms that we all too often take for granted, and the healthy diversity of our culture. Far from doing these things, the patriotism portrayed by Madison Avenue and the media does little more than encourage our chauvinistic impulses. Perhaps if those who celebrate the new patriotism would bother to look around they would agree with Lewis H. Lapham when he says that regardless of what the media say about the emergence of a "new patriotism," the majority of Americans have always been patriotic and have cared for the values that have characterized this country since its beginnings (8).

Works Cited

Apple, R. W., Jr. "New Stirrings of Patriotism." *New York Times Magazine* 5 Aug. 1985: 48+.

Keeley, Joseph C. "A Few Kind Words for Uncle Sam." *The American Legion Magazine* Sept. 1984: 20–21.

Lapham, Lewis H. "The New Patriotism." *Harper's* June 1984: 7–8.

"School Spirit. . . ." *The New Republic* 1 Oct. 1984: 12.

Witkin, Gordon. "Patriotism Is Back in Style." *U.S. News and World Report* 9 July 1984: 58–59.

Exercise 6

Using the guidelines discussed above, revise the second draft of your essay. Just as you did with your first draft, keep a record of the changes you made and be prepared to discuss the reasons for your revisions.

Thematic Anthology for Reading and Writing

The chapters that follow put the concepts introduced in Chapters 1 through 3 into practice. Each chapter presents a group of readings on a common theme: The American Dream; The Dawning of the Atomic Age; The Legacy of the Fifties; The Changing Image of the Hero; Issues in Education, Religion, and Society; Working; the Impact of Technology; Coming of Age; The Nature of Violence; and Life in America. Focusing on a single issue, each group of essays enables you to examine the ways different selections relate to one another and to consider these relationships in writing.

Each reading selection is introduced by a headnote that includes biographical and bibliographical information designed to help you evaluate both the author and the essay itself. Throughout the first eight chapters, each essay is followed by questions designed to help you practice active reading and integrating source material into your writing. Following this section is Essays for Further Reading, a three-chapter sequence that enables you to apply the principles of active reading according to strategies you design on your own.

As you read through the text, you will be asked to write two kinds of essays. After each reading selection, you will find questions encouraging you to give your opinions and interpretations of the ideas you have encountered in it. At the end of each chapter, you will be asked to draw together ideas from more than one reading.

All of the readings that follow present you with a cross section of ideas that will, we hope, interest you and make writing with sources what it should be — an adventure in which you explore territory mapped by others and perhaps in the process discover new territories of your own.

4

The American Dream

Unlike many other countries, the United States was founded on a set of principles that expressed the ideals of those who lived here. It was — and to a great extent still is — a great experiment in democracy. Many of the immigrants who fled the class-bound societies of Europe and Asia dreamed of achieving political and religious freedom and a better standard of living for themselves and for their families. Often, however, life in America was harder than these immigrants expected. The periodic depressions and recessions that characterized the late nineteenth and early twentieth centuries made finding employment difficult. In addition, the fear and prejudice of older immigrant groups as well as increasing isolationist sentiments made life difficult. Today not just immigrants but many groups are struggling to make the American dream come true.

In the Declaration of Independence Thomas Jefferson expresses the ideals that were central to the creation of America. Next, in "The Laws," Maxine Hong Kingston illustrates how these ideals were often overlooked when restrictive legislation was passed to limit Chinese immigrants. Marvin Trachtenberg, in "America and the Statue of Liberty," shows how the statue reflects the ever-changing image of the United States and for this reason has come to hold a special place in our culture. In "Choosing a Dream: Italians in Hell's Kitchen," Mario Puzo describes the hopes and dreams of Italian immigrants during the 1930s in New York City's Lower East Side. Finally, Martin Luther King, Jr., in "I Have a Dream" and Betty Friedan in "Feminism's Next Step" discuss the aspirations of two groups that have yet to realize their full potential in America.

The Declaration of Independence

Thomas Jefferson

Born in Virginia in 1743 and trained as a lawyer, Thomas Jefferson was a prominent patriot in prerevolutionary America. As a delegate to the Continental Congress, he was selected to draft the Declaration of Independence, the document that formally proclaimed the separation of the thirteen American colonies from Great Britain. Although Benjamin Franklin, John Adams, and the Congress made some revisions, Jefferson is credited with the distinctive wording of the Declaration as well as the spirit of its ideas. In the years after the American Revolution, Jefferson served as governor of Virginia, as secretary of state under George Washington, as John Adams's vice-president, and finally as the third president of the United States (1801 – 09). In his public life as well as in his writings, Jefferson strove to be consistent with the ideals of the Declaration of Independence, opposing in principle any laws that gave power to the wealthy classes or to an established church. For Jefferson, the purpose of government was to guarantee the "unalienable rights" with which all people are endowed—among them, "life, liberty and the pursuit of happiness." The Declaration of Independence he created sets forth the ideals and philosophical principles upon which the United States of America was founded. In this sense it expresses the dreams of those who come to this country from other lands.

In Congress, July 4, 1776
The unanimous Declaration of the thirteen
United States of America

1   When in the course of human events, it becomes necessary for one people to dissolve the political bands which have connected them with another, and to assume among the powers of the earth, the separate and equal station to which the Laws of Nature and of Nature's God entitle them, a decent respect to the opinions of mankind requires that they should declare the causes which impel them to the separation.

2   We hold these truths to be self-evident, that all men are created equal, that they are endowed by their Creator with certain unalienable rights, that among these are life, liberty and the pursuit of happiness. That to secure these rights, governments are instituted among men, deriving their just powers from the consent of the governed. That whenever any form of government becomes destructive of these ends, it is the right of the people to alter or to abolish it, and to institute new government, laying its foundation on such principles and organizing its powers in such form, as to them shall seem most likely to effect their safety and happiness. Prudence, indeed, will dictate that governments long established should not be changed for light and transient causes; and accordingly all experience hath shown, that mankind are more disposed to suffer, while evils are sufferable, than to right themselves by abolishing the forms to which they are accustomed. But when a long train of abuses and usurpations, pursuing invariably the same object evinces a design to reduce them under absolute despotism, it is their right, it is their duty, to throw off such

Parallelism

government, and to provide new guards for their future security. Such has been the patient sufferance of these Colonies; and such is now the necessity which constrains them to alter their former systems of government. The history of the present King of Great Britain is a history of repeated injuries and usurpations, all having in direct object the establishment of an absolute tyranny over these States. To prove this, let facts be submitted to a candid world.

3   He has refused his assent to laws, the most wholesome and necessary for the public good.

4   He has forbidden his Governors to pass laws of immediate and pressing importance, unless suspended in their operation till his assent should be obtained; and when so suspended, he has utterly neglected to attend to them.

5   He has refused to pass other laws for the accommodation of large districts of people, unless those people would relinquish the right of representation in the Legislature, a right inestimable to them and formidable to tyrants only.

6   He has called together legislative bodies at places unusual, uncomfortable, and distant from the depository of their public records, for the sole purpose of fatiguing them into compliance with his measures.

7   He has dissolved representative houses repeatedly, for opposing with manly firmness his invasions on the rights of the people.

8   He has refused for a long time, after such dissolutions, to cause others to be elected; whereby the legislative powers, incapable of annihilation, have returned to the people at large for their exercise; the State remaining in the meantime exposed to all the dangers of invasion from without and convulsions within.

9   He has endeavoured to prevent the population of these states; for that purpose obstructing the laws of naturalization of foreigners; refusing to pass others to encourage their migration hither, and raising the conditions of new appropriations of lands.

10   He has obstructed the administration of justice, by refusing his assent to laws for establishing judiciary powers.

11   He has made judges dependent on his will alone, for the tenure of their offices, and the amount and payment of their salaries.

12   He has erected a multitude of new offices, and sent hither swarms of officers to harass our people, and eat out their substance.

13   He has kept among us, in times of peace, standing armies without the consent of our legislatures.

14   He has affected to render the military independent of and superior to the civil power.

15   He has combined with others to subject us to a jurisdiction foreign to our constitution, and unacknowledged by our laws; giving his assent to their acts of pretended legislation:

16   For quartering large bodies of armed troops among us:

17   For protecting them, by a mock trial, from punishment for any murders which they should commit on the inhabitants of these States:

18   For cutting off our trade with all parts of the world:

19   For imposing taxes on us without our consent:

20   For depriving us in many cases, of the benefits of trial by jury:

21   For transporting us beyond seas to be tried for pretended offences:

22   For abolishing the free system of English laws in a neighbouring Province, establishing therein an arbitrary government, and enlarging its boundaries so as to render it at once an example and fit instrument for introducing the same absolute rule into these Colonies:

23   For taking away our Charters, abolishing our most valuable laws, and altering fundamentally the forms of our governments:

24   For suspending our own Legislatures, and declaring themselves invested with power to legislate for us in all cases whatsoever.

25   He has abdicated government here, by declaring us out of his protection and waging war against us.

26   He has plundered our seas, ravaged our coasts, burnt our towns, and destroyed the lives of our people.

27   He is at this time transporting large armies of foreign mercenaries to complete the works of death, desolation and tyranny, already begun with circumstances of cruelty and perfidy scarcely paralleled in the most barbarous ages, and totally unworthy the head of a civilized nation.

28   He has constrained our fellow citizens taken captive on the high seas to bear arms against their country, to become the executioners of their friends and brethren, or to fall themselves by their hands.

29   He has excited domestic insurrections amongst us, and has endeavoured to bring on the inhabitants of our frontiers, the merciless Indian savages, whose known rule of warfare, is an undistinguished destruction of all ages, sexes, and conditions.

30   In every stage of these oppressions we have petitioned for redress in the most humble terms: our repeated petitions have been answered only by repeated injury. A prince whose character is thus marked by every act which may define a tyrant is unfit to be the ruler of a free people. ← the British thought of themselves as free

31   Nor have we been wanting in attention to our British brethren. We have warned them from time to time of attempts by their legislature to extend an unwarrantable jurisdiction over us. We have reminded them of the circumstances of our emigration and settlement here. We have appealed to their native justice and magnanimity, and we have conjured them by the ties of our common kindred to disavow these usurpations, which would inevitably interrupt our connections and correspondence. They too have been deaf to the voice of justice and of consanguinity. We must, therefore, acquiesce in the necessity, which denounces our separation, and hold them, as we hold the rest of mankind, enemies in war, in peace friends.

32   We, therefore, the Representatives of the United States of America, in General Congress assembled, appealing to the Supreme Judge of the world for the rectitude of our intentions, do, in the name, and by authority of the good people of these Colonies, solemnly publish and declare, That these United Colonies are, and of right ought to be Free and Independent States; that they are absolved from all allegiance to the British Crown, and that all political connection between them and the State of Great Britain, is and ought to be

totally dissolved; and that as Free and Independent States, they have full power to levy war, conclude peace, contract alliances, establish commerce, and to do all other acts and things which Independent States may of right do. And for the support of this declaration, with a firm reliance on the protection of Divine Providence, we mutually pledge to each other our lives, our fortunes, and our sacred honor.

Reading Sources: The Declaration of Independence

Read this document, surveying it to identify key terms and important concepts. Highlight these phrases and ideas, and then answer these questions.

1. Where does Jefferson emphasize ideas through parallel sentence structure? through paragraph length?
2. What is the effect of the repetition of *He* in paragraphs 3 – 15?
3. How does Jefferson link paragraph 15 to the rest of the Declaration?
4. Identify the words and phrases Jefferson uses to convey the contrast between freedom and tyranny.
5. After reviewing Jefferson's arguments, sum up the main idea of the Declaration of Independence in one sentence.

Reacting to Sources

Reread the selection carefully, making marginal notes to aid your comprehension and reinforce connections. Then further annotate the selection if you need to do so in order to answer any of these questions. (You may already have addressed some of the questions in your marginal notes.)

1. Using a dictionary if necessary, supply brief marginal definitions of these words as they are used in this selection: *impel* (1), *unalienable* (2), *transient* (2), *disposed* (2), *usurpations* (2), *despotism* (2), *hither* (9), *tenure* (9), *standing* (13), *plundered* (26), *ravaged* (26), *perfidy* (27), *excited* (29), *redress* (30), *consanguinity* (31).
2. The word *brethren* (31) is considered archaic and is seldom used today. Find other examples of such words, and clarify their meanings with synonyms, using a dictionary if necessary. What would be the effect of updating Jefferson's language?
3. Explain the following statement in a marginal note: "A prince whose character is thus marked by every act which may define a tyrant is unfit to be the ruler of a free people" (30).
4. What is Jefferson's purpose in paragraphs 30 and 31?
5. Formulate two questions you might ask to clarify your understanding of paragraphs 30 and 31.
6. In paragraph 2, Jefferson says, "whenever any form of government becomes

destructive of these ends, it is the right of the people to alter or to abolish it, and to institute new government, . . ." Do you agree or disagree? Write a journal entry explaining your position.

Working with Sources

1. Write a one-hundred-word summary of the Declaration of Independence.
2. Write a critique of the ideas in paragraph 2.
3. In a journal entry, comment on the potential impact of the following phrases on the selection's intended audience: "We hold these truths to be self-evident" (2); "let facts be submitted to a candid world" (2). Be sure to integrate the quotations smoothly into your writing.
4. Paraphrase paragraphs 27–29, trying to capture the sense and impact of Jefferson's ideas without using his language.
5. Write a brief synthesis that blends the ideas in paragraphs 30 and 31 of this selection with the ideas in paragraph 6 of "I Have a Dream" (pp. 115–119).

Writing with Sources: Using a Single Source

Integrating information from the Declaration of Independence with your own ideas, write an essay on one of these topics. Be sure to acknowledge all ideas that are not your own.

1. In paragraph 3 of "I Have a Dream" (pp. 115–119), King says, "When the architects of our republic wrote the magnificent words of the Constitution and the Declaration of Independence, they were signing a promissory note to which every American was to fall heir." Write an essay in which you consider in what sense the Declaration of Independence is a "promissory note" to all Americans.
2. Although the Declaration of Independence was written in response to a very specific situation—one that existed over two hundred years ago—and although it does not use modern language, it is nevertheless a relevant document that addresses issues faced by Americans today. Write an essay in which you support this statement.
3. Write an essay in which you argue for or against the need for a new, modernized Declaration of Independence.

The Laws

Maxine Hong Kingston

Maxine Hong Kingston, the child of immigrant Chinese parents, was born in the United States and grew up in Stockton, California, where her family settled. She graduated from the University of California at Berkeley in 1962 and taught high school and college in California and Hawaii. Today she lives with her husband, who is an actor, and her child in Honolulu, Hawaii. Her first book, *The Woman Warrior: Memoirs of a Girlhood Among Ghosts* (1976), examines the author's girlhood in California. Her second book, *China Men* (1980), deals with the men in her family and how they entered the American mainstream. "The Laws," excerpted from *China Men,* focuses on American immigration laws and how they have affected Chinese immigrants. Although the Chinese were the only nationality explicitly singled out for exclusion from the United States by Congress, all immigrants faced increasingly restrictive immigration laws from 1917 on. More than merely a list, "The Laws" illustrates the nativist prejudice and discrimination that the Chinese immigrants struggled against to gain a foothold in America.

The United States of America and the Emperor of China cordially recognize the inherent and inalienable right of man to change his home and allegiance, and also the mutual advantage of the free migration and emigration of their citizens and subjects respectively from the one country to the other for purposes of curiosity, of trade, or as permanent residents. —Article V of the Burlingame Treaty, signed in Washington, D.C., July 28, 1868, and in Peking, November 23, 1869

1   **The First Years**   1868, the year of the Burlingame Treaty, was the year 40,000 miners of Chinese ancestry were Driven Out. The Fourteenth Amendment, adopted in that same year, said that naturalized Americans have the same rights as native-born Americans, but in 1870 the Nationality Act specified that only "free whites" and "African aliens" were allowed to apply for naturalization. Chinese were not white; this had been established legally in 1854 when Chan Young unsuccessfully applied for citizenship in Federal District Court in San Francisco and was turned down on grounds of race. (He would have been illegal one way or another anyway; the Emperor of China did not give permission for any of his subjects to leave China until 1859.) Debating the Nationality Act, Congressmen declared that America would be a nation of "Nordic fiber."

2   1878   California held a Constitutional Convention to settle "the Chinese problem." Of the 152 delegates, 35 were not American citizens but Europeans. The resulting constitution, voted into existence by a majority party of Working Men and Grangers, prohibited Chinese from entering California. New state laws empowered cities and counties to confine them within specified areas or to throw them out completely. Shipowners and captains were to be fined and jailed for hiring or transporting them. (This provision was so little respected that the American merchant marine relied heavily on Chinese seamen from the

Civil War years to World War I.) "Mongolians, Indians, and Negroes" were
barred from attending public schools. The only California fishermen forced to
pay fishing and shellfish taxes were the Chinese, who had brought shrimp nets
from China and started the shrimp, abalone, and lobster industries. (The taxes
were payable monthly.) Those Chinese over eighteen who were not already
paying a miner's tax had to pay a "police tax," to cover the extra policing their
presence required. Though the Chinese were filling and leveeing the San
Joaquin Delta for thirteen cents a square yard, building the richest agricultural
land in the world, they were prohibited from owning land or real estate. They
could not apply for business licenses. Employers could be fined and jailed for
hiring them. No Chinese could be hired by state, county, or municipal governments for public works. No "Chinese or Mongolian or Indian" could testify in
court "either for or against a white man."

3   At this time San Francisco supplemented the anti-Chinese state laws with
some of its own: a queue tax, a "cubic air ordinance" requiring that every
residence have so many cubic feet of air per inhabitant, a pole law prohibiting
the use of carrying baskets on poles, cigar taxes, shoe taxes, and laundry taxes.

4   Federal courts declared some of the state and city laws unconstitutional,
and occasionally citizens of a county or city repealed an especially punitive
ordinance on the grounds that it was wrong to invite the Chinese to come to
the United States and then deny them a livelihood. The repealed laws were
often reenacted in another form.

5   1880   The Burlingame Treaty was modified. Instead of being free, the
immigration of Chinese laborers to the United States would be "reasonably
limited." In return (so as not to bring about limits on American entry into
China), the American government promised to protect Chinese from lynchings.

6   1881   The Burlingame Treaty was suspended for a period of twenty
years. (Since 1881 there has been no freedom of travel between China and the
United States.) In protest against this suspension and against the refusal to
admit Chinese boys to U.S. Army and Naval academies, China ordered scholars
studying in the United States to return home. The act suspending the treaty did
have two favorable provisions: all Chinese already resident in the United States
in 1882 could stay; and they were permitted to leave and re-enter with a
Certificate of Return.

7   1882   Encouraged by fanatical lobbying from California, the U.S. Congress passed the first Chinese Exclusion Act. It banned the entrance of Chinese
laborers, both skilled and unskilled, for ten years. Anyone unqualified for
citizenship could not come in—and by the terms of the Nationality Act of
1870, Chinese were not qualified for citizenship. Some merchants and scholars
were granted temporary visas.

8   1884   Congress refined the Exclusion Act with An Act to Amend an Act.
This raised fines and sentences and further defined "merchants" to exclude

"hucksters, peddlers, or those engaged in taking, draying, or otherwise preserving shell or other fish for home consumption or exportation."

9   **1888**   The Scott Act, passed by Congress, again forbade the entry of Chinese laborers. It also declared that Certificates of Return were void. Twenty thousand Chinese were trapped outside the United States with now-useless re-entry permits. Six hundred returning travelers were turned back at American ports. A Chinese ambassador, humiliated by immigration officers, killed himself. The law decreed that Certificates of Residence had to be shown on demand; any Chinese caught without one was deported.

10   **1889**   Chinese pooled money to fight the various Exclusion Acts in the courts. They rarely won. In *Chae Chan Ping* v. *The United States,* Chae Chan Ping argued for the validity of his Certificate of Return. The Supreme Court ruled against him, saying that "regardless of the existence of a prior treaty," a race "that will not assimilate with us" could be excluded when deemed "dangerous to . . . peace and security. . . . It matters not in what form aggression and encroachment come, whether from the foreign nation acting in its national character or from vast hordes of its people crowding in upon us." Moreover, said the Court, "sojourners" should not "claim surprise" that any Certificates of Return obtained prior to 1882 were "held at the will of the government, revocable at any time, at its pleasure."

11   **1892**   The Geary Act extended the 1882 Exclusion Act for another ten years. It also decreed that Chinese caught illegally in the United States be deported after one year of hard labor.

12   Chinese Americans formed the Equal Rights League and the Native Sons of the Golden State in order to fight disenfranchisement bills. Chinese Americans demanded the right to have their citizenship confirmed before traveling abroad.

13   **1893**   In *Yue Ting* v. *The United States,* the U.S. Supreme Court ruled that Congress had the right to expel members of a race who "continue to be aliens, having taken no steps toward becoming citizens, and incapable of becoming such under the naturalization laws." This applied only to Chinese; no other race or nationality was excluded from applying for citizenship.

14   **1896**   A victory. In *Yick Wo* v. *Hopkins,* the U.S. Supreme Court overturned San Francisco safety ordinances, saying that they were indeed designed to harass laundrymen of Chinese ancestry.

15   **1898**   Another victory. The Supreme Court decision in *The United States* v. *Wong Kim Ark* stated that a person born in the United States to Chinese parents is an American. This decision has never been reversed or changed, and it is the law on which most Americans of Chinese ancestry base their citizenship today.

16   1900   Deciding *The United States* v. *Mrs. Cue Lim,* the Supreme Court ruled that wives and children of treaty merchants — citizens of China, aliens traveling on visas — were allowed to come to the United States.

17   1904   The Chinese Exclusion Acts were extended indefinitely, and made to cover Hawaii and the Philippines as well as the continental United States. The question of exclusion was not debated in Congress; instead, the measure passed as a <u>rider</u> on a routine appropriations bill. China boycotted American goods in protest.

18   1906   The San Francisco Board of Education ordered that all Chinese, Japanese, and Korean children be segregated in an Oriental school. President Roosevelt, responding to a protest from the Japanese government, persuaded the Board of Education to allow Japanese to attend white schools.

19   1917   Congress voted that immigrants over sixteen years of age be required to pass an English reading test.

20   1924   An Immigration Act passed by Congress specifically excluded ''Chinese women, wives, and prostitutes.'' Any American who married a Chinese woman lost his citizenship; any Chinese man who married an American woman caused her to lose her citizenship. Many states had also instituted <u>antimiscegenation</u> laws. A Supreme Court case called *Chang Chan et al.* v. *John D. Nagle* tested the law against wives; Chang Chan et al. lost. For the first time, the 1924 Immigration Act distinguished between two kinds of ''aliens'': ''immigrants'' were admitted as permanent residents with the opportunity to become citizens eventually; the rest — scholars, merchants, ministers, and tourists — were admitted on a temporary basis and were not eligible for citizenship. The number of persons allowed in the category of immigrant was set by law at one-sixth of one percent of the total population of that ancestry in the United States as of the 1920 census. The 1920 census had the lowest count of ethnic Chinese in this country since 1860. As a result, only 105 Chinese immigrants were permitted each year.

21   In *Cheuno Sumchee* v. *Nagle,* the Supreme Court once again confirmed the right of treaty merchants to bring their wives to the United States. This was a right that continued to be denied to Chinese Americans.

22   1938   A Presidential proclamation lifted restriction on immigration for Chinese and nationals of a few other Asian countries. The Chinese were still ineligible for citizenship, and the quota was ''100.''

23   1943   The United States and China signed a treaty of alliance against the Japanese, and Congress repealed the Exclusion Act of 1882. Immigration continued to be limited to the 1924 quota of 105, however, and the Immigration and Nationalization Service claimed to be unable to find even that many qualified Chinese. A ''Chinese'' was defined as anyone with more than 50

percent Chinese blood, regardless of citizenship or country of residence. At this time Japanese invaders were killing Chinese civilians in vast numbers; it is estimated that more than 10 million died. Chinese immigration into the United States did not rise.

24   1946   Congress passed the War Bride Act, enabling soldiers to bring Japanese and European wives home, then enacted a separate law allowing the wives and children of Chinese Americans to apply for entry as "non-quota immigrants." Only now did the ethnic Chinese population in the United States begin to approach the level of seventy years previous. (When the first Exclusion Act was passed in 1882, there were some 107,000 Chinese here; the Acts and the Driving Out steadily reduced the number to fewer than 70,000 in the 1920s.)

25   1948   The Refugee Act passed by Congress this year applied only to Europeans. A separate Displaced Persons Act provided that for a limited time — 1948 to 1954 — ethnic Chinese already living in the United States could apply for citizenship. During the post-war period, about 10,000 Chinese were permitted to enter the country under individual private bills passed by Congress. Confidence men, like the Citizenship Judges of old, defrauded hopeful Chinese for promising to acquire one of these bills for $1,500.

26   1950   After the Chinese Communist government took over in 1949, the United States passed a series of Refugee Relief Acts and a Refugee Escapee Act expanding the number of "non-quota immigrants" allowed in. As a condition of entry, the Internal Security Act provided that these refugees swear they were not Communists. (Several hundred "subversives or anarchists" of various races were subsequently deported; some were naturalized citizens who were "denaturalized" beforehand.)

27   1952   The Immigration and Nationality Act denied admission to "subversive and undesirable aliens" and made it simpler to deport "those already in the country." Another provision of this act was that for the first time Chinese women were allowed to immigrate under the same conditions as men.

28   1954   Ruling on *Mao* v. *Brownell,* the Supreme Court upheld laws forbidding Chinese Americans to send money to relatives in China. Before the Communist Revolution, there were no such restrictions in effect; Chinese Americans sent $70 million during World War II. Nor could they send money or gifts through CARE, UNESCO, or church organizations, which provided only for non-Communist countries.

29   1957   The Refugee Relief Act of 1953 expired in 1956 and was followed by the Act of 1957, which provided for the distribution of 18,000 visas that had remained unused.

30   1959   Close relatives, including parents, were allowed to enter.

31   1960   A "Fair Share Refugee Act" allowed certain refugees from Communist and Middle Eastern countries to enter. Close to 20,000 people who were "persecuted because of race, religion, or political beliefs" immigrated before this act was repealed in 1965, when a new act allowed the conditional entry of 10,200 refugees annually.

32   1962   A Presidential directive allowed several thousand "parolees" to enter the United States from Hong Kong. Relatives of citizens and resident aliens were eligible. President Kennedy gave Congress a special message on immigration, saying, "It is time to correct the mistakes of the past."

33   1965   A new Immigration and Nationality Act changed the old quota system so that "national origin" no longer means "race" but "country of birth." Instead of being based on a percentage of existing ethnic populations in the United States, quotas were reallocated to countries — 20,000 each. But this did not mean that 20,000 Chinese immediately could or did come to the United States. Most prospective immigrants were in Hong Kong, a British colony. Colonies received 1 percent of the mother country's allotment: only 200. "Immediate relatives," the children, spouses, and parents of citizens, however, could enter without numerical limitations. Also not reckoned within the quota limitations were legal residents returning from a visit abroad.

34   1968   Amendments to the Immigration and Nationality Act provided that immigrants not be allocated by race or nation but by hemispheres, with 120,000 permitted to enter from the Western Hemisphere and 170,000 from the Eastern Hemisphere. This act limits immigration from the Western Hemisphere for the first time in history. The 20,000-per-country quota remained in effect for the Eastern Hemisphere, no per-country limitation for the Western Hemisphere.

35   1976   The Immigration and Nationality Act Amendments, also called the Western Hemisphere Bill, equalized the provisions of law regulating immigration from the two hemispheres. The House Committee on the Judiciary in its report on this legislation stated, "This constitutes an essential first step in a projected long-term reform of U.S. Immigration law." The 20,000-per-country limit was extended to the Western Hemisphere. The limitation on colonies was raised from 200 to 600.

36   1978   The separate quotas for the two hemispheres were replaced by a worldwide numerical limitation on immigration of 290,000 annually. On the basis of the "immediate relatives" clause, about 22,000 Chinese enter legally each year, and the rate is increasing. There are also special quotas in effect for Southeast Asian refugees, most of whom are of Chinese ancestry. In the last

decade, the ethnic Chinese population of the United States has doubled. The 1980 census may show a million or more.

Reading Sources: "The Laws"

Read the selection, surveying it to identify key terms and important concepts. Highlight these phrases and ideas, and then answer these questions.

1. What visual cues are used in "The Laws"? Are they used to clarify emphasis, to enhance comprehension, or for both purposes? Explain.
2. Many of the key pieces of information in this selection are the names of laws, acts, and treaties. What other kinds of information have you identified as important?
3. How does Kingston generally link ideas between paragraphs? Why is this technique effective?
4. What device does Kingston use to connect the paragraphs providing information about the years 1896 and 1898?
5. How does the use of direct quotations from laws and court decisions add to this selection?
6. After reviewing your highlighted material and the answers to questions 1–5, write a sentence that sums up the main idea of this selection. Why do you think Kingston does not state this idea directly? Do you think her strategy is a wise one?

Reacting to Sources

Reread the selection carefully, making marginal notes to aid your comprehension and reinforce connections. Then, further annotate the essay if you need to do so in order to answer any of these questions. (You may already have addressed some of the questions in your marginal notes.)

1. Using a dictionary if necessary, supply brief marginal definitions of these words as they are used in this selection: *naturalized* (1), *leveeing* (3), *queue* (3), *deported* (11), *disenfranchisement* (12), *rider* (17), *antimiscegenation* (20), *confidence* (25), *reckoned* (33).
2. In a brief marginal note, explain what you think the following phrases meant in their original contexts: "Nordic fiber" (1), "the Chinese problem" (2), "subversive and undesirable aliens" (27). Why do you think Kingston chose to place them within quotation marks?
3. Identify: the Internal Security Act (26); CARE (28); UNESCO (28).
4. Explain the significance of this statement in a brief marginal comment: "The repealed laws were often reenacted in another form" (4). Find an example in the selection to support this statement.

5. What does the word *fanatical* (7) reveal about Kingston's feelings? Where else does her language reveal her feelings?
6. In a marginal note, briefly summarize the distinction between the two kinds of aliens covered by the 1924 Immigration Act (20).
7. In the last three sentences of paragraph 20, Kingston presents an injustice in objective, understated language. Where else does she do this? What does she accomplish by using this technique?
8. In a brief marginal note, explain the significance of this statement: "This act limits immigration from the Western Hemisphere for the first time in history" (34).
9. Read the selection's headnote. In your brainstorming journal, comment on how Kingston's life or work might have influenced her purpose when she wrote her essay. How does this information influence your response to her writing? Explain.
10. In paragraph 32, Kingston quotes President Kennedy's speech to Congress. In a journal entry, explore your reactions to Kennedy's statement. How is your reaction similar to or different from Kingston's?
11. Outline the ideas in paragraph 2.

Working with Sources

1. Using the outline you prepared in response to Reacting to Sources, question 11, write a fifty-word summary of paragraph 2.
2. Write a critique of the ideas expressed in the excerpt from the Burlingame Treaty, which Kingston uses to introduce her selection. Include a discussion of why Kingston chooses to begin with this material.
3. In a journal entry, discuss how Kingston uses the following quotations to support her central idea.

    "'Mongolians, Negroes, and Indians' were barred from attending public schools" (2).
    "The Scott Act . . . again forbade the entry of Chinese laborers" (9).
    "A Chinese ambassador, humiliated by immigration officers, killed himself" (9).
    Be sure to integrate the quotations smoothly into your writing.
4. Paraphrase the ideas in paragraph 23.
5. Write a brief synthesis blending the ideas in paragraph 1 of this selection with the ideas in paragraph 2 of the Declaration of Independence (pp. 86–89).

Writing with Sources: Using a Single Source

Integrating information from "The Laws" with your own ideas, write an essay on one of these topics. Be sure to acknowledge all ideas that are not your own.

1. If you know family members who immigrated to this country, ask them whether United States immigration laws helped or hindered their entry into the United States. In a short essay, compare and contrast their experiences with the problems of the Chinese as described by Kingston.
2. It could be argued that despite the discrimination suffered by the Chinese, changes in the laws in the past twenty-five years have more than compensated for past inequities. Write an essay in which you support or refute this argument.
3. Review the laws Kingston presents in her essay, and try to define the changes that have taken place over the years. How do these changes reflect a shift in attitude on the part of other Americans toward Chinese immigrants?

America and the Statue of Liberty

Marvin Trachtenberg

Marvin Trachtenberg attended Yale University and then the Institute of Fine Arts of New York University. A respected scholar and teacher, he is the author of a number of academic works, including *The Statue of Liberty* (1977), the book from which the following essay was excerpted. In this essay, Trachtenberg traces the many identities that the Statue of Liberty has assumed over the years. Intended by the French as a memorial to French independence and described by one contemporary critic as "a bag of potatoes with a stick projecting from it," the Statue of Liberty has come to stand for America. No longer the "Mother of Exiles" who stands ready to receive the "wretched refuse" of many nations, the statue now symbolizes America as "the richest and mightiest nation on earth." The recent refurbishing of the statue has given new vitality to the "Lady of the Harbor" and may signal yet another shift in identity for Bartholdi's creation.

1   In the end, everybody finally joined in acclamation of the *Statue of Liberty* (or at least refrained from cavil). Members of New York society fell over one another to participate in the dedication ceremonies at Bedloe's Island on 28 October 1886, from which the public that had sponsored the construction was naturally excluded, although allowed to watch from the shore. All the world seemed to be there — certainly all New York, which had boisterously accompanied the colorful parade down to preliminary ceremonies at City Hall and the Battery, for it was a day to remember. On the island speech after speech was heard in the rain — but not that of Senator Evarts addressing the President. For, before he had finished, Bartholdi, responding to a false cue, unveiled the face of his goddess and triggered off a chorus of foghorns and a twenty-one-gun salute. The sculptor, lionized already on his visit of 1876, was the man of the hour — it was officially, in fact 'Bartholdi Day' ('You are the greatest man in America today!' said President Cleveland). Given golden keys to the city and later fêted at Delmonico's by all the notables, it was his proud-

est moment. He could consider himself fortunate; his only regret was that his aged mother could not be alongside him, and that Laboulaye, who had led him to the vision of the promised land, could not join him there, having died at a ripe age in 1883.

2   But soon all *Liberty*'s creators were to pass from the scene, like ripples in water spreading from the center of a disturbance and subsiding. Several decades passed, and the old historical realities were displaced by new. Like an adopted child, the statue retained the hereditary physical form of its natural parents, but took its mature character from its foster home. The gesture and diffuse collection of attributes of the statue received much of their meaning from the historical context. When this was gone, the political allusion intended by Laboulaye and his colleagues was largely lost (not to mention the more shadowy, personal meaning it had for Bartholdi). For the Americans, there was no profit in maintaining the symbolism of international revolution (even on the intended moderate terms of the 'conservative republicans'). Few among the American public wished to be reminded of the frailty of the thirteen colonies in 1776, and how they had welcomed aid from a mighty nation that had since grown soft. And certainly whatever was sensed of the imperialist French undertones of the statue was felt as abhorrent. The purging of cumbersome allusion has been observed in the eventual shift of the statue's popular name: at the time of its appearance often called 'the Bartholdi statue,' *Liberty Enlightening the World* became simply *The Statue of Liberty,* the embodiment of the universal ideal in a particular work instead of the old incorporeal image. But this neutralization of meaning was equally valid for all the world. Had it been the only transformation of meaning *Liberty* would have been a statue without a country, as it were, and would have involved no special significance for the United States. What came to pass, however, was that *Liberty* acquired, simultaneously with her becoming a new universal icon, a close identification with her home, for she was not only neutralized, but naturalized as well. She gradually assumed something of deep American appeal.

3   As early as 1883 the French meanings were lost on Emma Lazarus. In her famous poem 'The New Colossus,' the beacon of liberty seen across the sea was not intended to serve France or any other nation, but rather to guide those Europeans eager for a new life *away* from Europe entirely, to the 'golden door' of America, where an uplifted torch was symbolic not of 'enlightenment' but simply of 'welcome'. Most Americans today are far removed from their immigrant ancestors' state of mind, so many of whom *were,* to one degree or another, Lazarus's 'wretched refuse', particularly during the closing decades of the nineteenth century and the early years of the twentieth. Moreover, most travelers now come to the country not by ship, but by airplane. The sentiment that the statue carried for the millions of European immigrants who arrived before the 'golden door' all but closed in the 1920s has dwindled, although surviving as a pervasive folkloric theme. But in 1903, at the height of immigration, this sentiment was so widely accepted as expressing the statue's meaning that a plaque bearing the poem was affixed to the pedestal as an *ex post facto* inscription.

4   The experience of the immigrants involved crucial implications for *Liberty.* Their vision of America as political and economic liberation reinforced a natural tendency to perceive *Liberty* 'welcoming' as 'America welcoming'. The statue was becoming the image not so much of America the protagonist of Liberty, but simply America itself.

5   This new identity was facilitated by the absence of competitors. Of course, Liberty, early identified with America, became a catchword of the new American republic. But as a personification of America it was by no means alone, or even the first. An Indian Princess, deriving from Renaissance 'Allegories of the Four Continents', was the earliest. She was later transformed, during the Revolutionary era, into a plumed Greek Goddess, Hercules and Minerva also being associated with America at this time. Finally there arrived the indigenous characters of Brother Jonathan and Uncle Sam who survived in vernacular iconography while most of the other figures soon fell from fashion. As the nineteenth century drew on to Bartholdi's day, it becomes clear that *Liberty* had only one true competitor as the American icon — Columbia. This figure was a vaguely defined, synthetic personage whose name derived from Columbus. Its use is first recorded in the 1690s and it became increasingly popular after the Revolution — *Hail Columbia* (1798), Joel Barlow's *Columbiad* (1807). But Bartholdi — by choosing Liberty — effectively pre-empted a monumental realization of Columbia. For his statue subsumed Columbia's vague image as a grand lady in white. Thus, in the end, there could be no successful competitor to Bartholdi's personification of a principal American idea.

6   The tide of immigration subsided, and at the same time the new American image was diffused deeply into the national consciousness. Its force was carried considerably by the immigrants. But it was during the Great War of 1914 – 18 that the statue attained potent meaning for all American groups. Ships that had brought the diverse immigrant masses 'welcomed' by *Liberty* now sailed out under her militant gaze carrying united, armed Americans. 'Make the world safe for democracy' was now the cry, and 'Liberty bonds' one of the means. Emma Lazarus's poem had been isolationist in sentiment: 'Liberty' had withdrawn into America and become one with her. When the statue, with her new lighting of 1916, turned to face the world again (and this time not just France) it was as America, Light of the World — America, not only as the embodiment of liberty, but as a land which had become a symbol itself and less of a refuge for the world's 'wretched refuse' against whom a wall of restrictions was being raised. Bartholdi's name for his statue — indeed, even its new abbreviated, universalist popular title — was now a euphemism: what he had unwittingly wrought was the Statue of America.

7   In retrospect, now, it is possible to reconsider the factors that have granted *Liberty* such longevity and unrivalled celebrity. In our time, what seems to be a deep human urge to allegorical expression — especially at the collective level — has not been rooted out by modernism, but only suppressed. As the greatest survival in the West of the tradition of allegorical personification, *Liberty* has been a recipient of this bottled-up energy. But, obviously, her awesome potency as a symbol is also due to what she has come to symbolize:

the richest and mightiest nation on earth, and the one traditionally believed to have a special destiny in the liberation and realization of the spirit of man. It is a belief not always in harmony with the turn of events, but it is an abiding idea, and channels a tremendous force to *Liberty* as allegorical survival.

8   *Liberty*'s vitality centers on her personification of America, but it also involves her extraordinary fluidity as a symbolic image. The statue's definitive symbolism was not exclusive. It dimmed, but it did not extinguish the earlier 'French' and 'immigrant' meanings. The statue still, in fact, thrives as Bartholdi's Goddess of Liberty and as Lazarus' 'Mother of Exiles' (the latter role now aggrandized in the Museum of American Immigration at the statue's feet). Yet *Liberty*'s variability of meaning comprehends not only the persistence of her iconographic history, but also an ongoing relationship to manifold aspects of actuality. Such a famous symbol begs reinterpretation, and *Liberty* has proved to be a Protean source of public imagery. This has been much abetted by her site, posture, expression, and especially her attributes, which are open to seemingly unlimited possibilities of reinterpretation through changes of every conceivable kind — exaggeration and distortion, deletion and supplementation, fragmentation and duplication. Particularly common is the process of abbreviation (already by, and for, Bartholdi) in which the mere presence of the torch or radiant crown suffices to establish as *Liberty* an allegory that may range from the outrageous to the banal, or from the sublime to the simply vulgar.

9   But the reinterpretations and uses of the *Statue of Liberty* have been so numerous and various as to defy compilation. Even before the statue was completed it was worked into popular iconography for private gain (for example, as the masthead for Pulitzer's *The World*), and it appeared as sensationalist allegory, most notably in Thomas Nast's grisly 1881 woodcut protesting a witches' brew of crime, epidemics, and political corruption. It has since been the subject of every conceivable commercial and ideological exploitation, among which its use as a head-piece for wigs in advertising copy, or with tears streaming at some political outrage, represent the average level of imagination (although there has been some comic relief in this process, notably Claes Oldenburg's 'project' for the total substitution of a giant electric fan). *Liberty* has naturally appeared — even 'starred'— in the cinema: as a heroine in Hitchcock's memorable *Saboteur* of 1942 — a time when *Liberty*'s lights were extinguished to make the same point as when they went on in 1916; as the universally understood means of the 'shattering' revelation of nuclear holocaust at the end of the science-fiction spectacular, *Planet of the Apes,* 1967; or, in a more crassly exploitative way, in a dismal Hollywood product starring a rejuvenated, septuagenarian Mae West posing in advertisements in the statue's guise (referring also to a famous studio that has adopted a disguised *Liberty* as *its* symbol). This latter tendency, which seems to be intensifying of late (perhaps a collective expression of the degraded state of American morale), was practiced by Bartholdi himself, who patented the form of *Liberty* in 1876 in hopes of ultimately being able to compensate financially his years of unpaid labor with royalties from copies, a scheme that came to practically nothing because

of a faulty contract in which the inattentive sculptor signed away his legal rights to a shady manufacturer.

10   Perhaps the most unthinking attempt to exploit the statue has been by the feminist movement, which was drawn towards *Liberty* at an early date. The most recent factions have tended to make of the statue a symbol of woman 'liberated' and a firebrand of feminist revolution. The irony is, of course, that in the feminist context she is as much martyr as heroine, for she stands immobilized and most heavily draped — like any presentable lady of the nineteenth century — idealized on a high pedestal and put there by a whole crew of firm believers in the traditional arrangement between the sexes. Furthermore, not as we see her, but as we know her, this decent woman takes on an altogether different character — for a fee she is open to all for entry and exploration from below.

11   Despite iconographic assault and degradation Bartholdi's colossus remains, for good or ill, the image of America. As such the question of its meaning has been truly deepened, to my knowledge, only by — of all writers — Franz Kafka. The opening paragraph of one of his major novels, *Amerika*, written in 1913, depicts the protagonist, a poor immigrant boy, standing 'on the liner slowly entering the harbor of New York, [when] a sudden burst of sunshine seemed to illumine the *Statue of Liberty*, so that he saw it in a new light, although he had sighted it long before. The arm with the sword rose up as if newly stretched aloft, and round the figure blew the free winds of heaven. "So high," he said to himself . . .' Kafka may have been thinking of the upraised sword of the *Arminius*.* But even in faraway Prague, he was not one senselessly or unwittingly to confuse such things (and such phrases as 'saw it in a new light' and especially 'as if newly stretched aloft' hint that he knew what he was about). The matter-of-fact tone in which the misrepresentation is expressed is entirely characteristic of Kafka, whose supreme importance as a writer lies in the haunting, final truth of his nightmare world. It seems neither melodramatic nor out of place to note that now there is every reason to believe that the resolution of the question — whose image of America is real, Bartholdi's or Kafka's? — could touch the fate of the world.

Reading Sources: "America and the Statue of Liberty"

Read the selection, surveying it to identify key terms and important concepts. Highlight these phrases and ideas, and then answer these questions.

1. How do the first two paragraphs of Trachtenberg's essay provide clues to the structure of the essay?
2. How do Trachtenberg's topic sentences help readers follow the sequence of his discussion?

---

* Leader of the ancient Germans who, in A.D. 9, utterly defeated the Roman legions.

3. Circle each use of the words *allusion, personification,* and *enlightenment* in Trachtenberg's essay. What concepts does Trachtenberg emphasize by repeating these terms?
4. Underline the thesis of Trachtenberg's essay.
5. Outline the major points that Trachtenberg makes in his essay. Why does he choose to order his points as he does?
6. Underline the transitional words and phrases that Trachtenberg uses in paragraph 8. How do these elements help readers follow the logic of the paragraph?

Reacting to Sources

Reread the selection, carefully, making marginal notes to aid your comprehension and reinforce connections. Then further annotate the selection if you need to do so in order to answer any of these questions. (You may already have addressed some of the questions in your marginal notes.)

1. In a marginal note, sum up the meaning of paragraph 5.
2. Provide marginal definitions of the following words as they are used in this selection: *diffuse* (2), *naturalized* (2), *protagonist* (4), *facilitated* (5), *iconographic* (8), *manifold* (8), *Protean* (8), *abetted* (8). Use a dictionary if necessary.
3. Do you agree with Trachtenberg's comment in paragraph 10 that feminists have "unthinkingly" exploited the statue? Write a marginal note in which you explain your opinion.
4. Write three marginal questions to help clarify the statements in paragraph 3.
5. Find two examples to support Trachtenberg's statement that the Statue of Liberty "gradually assumed something of deep American appeal" (2).
6. Find a statement in the essay for which your own knowledge or experience provides either support or contradictory evidence. Write a brief marginal note that presents your material.
7. Identify Trachtenberg's purpose in paragraph 6. What is his purpose in the entire essay? Record your observations in a journal entry.
8. In a journal entry, consider the implications of Trachtenberg's conclusion. Look up both Bartholdi and Kafka in an encyclopedia and comment on the implications of Trachtenberg's statement that "the resolution of the question — whose image of America is real, Bartholdi's or Kafka's? — could touch the fate of the world."
9. In a journal entry, discuss how Trachtenberg's comments in paragraph 3 shed light on the sentiments expressed by Mario Puzo in paragraphs 38 through 40 of "Choosing a Dream: Italians in Hell's Kitchen" (pp. 106–113).
10. List the various identities that the Statue of Liberty has assumed over the years. In a journal entry analyze how the public currently interprets the Statue of Liberty. What factors do you believe have affected this interpretation? Does your analysis support or contradict Trachtenberg's ideas?

Working with Sources

1. Write a fifty-word summary of paragraph 6.
2. Write a critique of the ideas in paragraph 7.
3. Use the following two quotations from Trachtenberg's essay in a journal entry in which you express your reactions to the essay.

   "What came to pass, however, was that *Liberty* acquired, simultaneously with her becoming a new universal icon, a close identification with her home, for she was not only neutralized, but naturalized as well" (2).

   "But the reinterpretations and uses of the *Statue of Liberty* have been so numerous and various as to defy compilation" (9).

   Be sure to integrate the quotations smoothly into your writing.
4. Write a paraphrase of paragraph 5.
5. Write a one-paragraph synthesis that blends ideas in paragraph 10 of this essay and ideas in paragraph 44 of "Feminism's Next Step," by Betty Friedan (pp. 121–131).

Writing with Sources

Integrating information from "America and the Statue of Liberty" with your own ideas, write an essay on one of these topics. Be sure to acknowledge all ideas that are not your own.

1. Write an essay in which you compare your view of the Statue of Liberty with Trachtenberg's view. Be specific in your comparison, making references to Trachtenberg's essay whenever possible.
2. Look through some magazines at your college library, and find several advertisements that feature the Statue of Liberty. Write an essay in which you discuss in what way the advertisement uses the image of the Statue of Liberty to make its point. In your essay make specific references to the section in which Trachtenberg discusses the exploitation of the Statue.
3. In his essay, Trachtenberg implies that the Statue of Liberty is no longer the vital symbol that it once was. After interviewing your parents and your grandparents (if possible) about their impressions of the statue, write an essay in which you discuss whether or not their perceptions of the Statue of Liberty support Trachtenberg's contention.

Immigrants in the inner city

Choosing a Dream: Italians in Hell's Kitchen

Mario Puzo

Mario Puzo grew up in Hell's Kitchen, the neighborhood on Manhattan's West Side that he writes about in "Choosing a Dream." After serving in the military during World War II, he attended New York's New School for Social Research and Columbia University. His first two novels, *The Fortunate Pilgrim* and *The Dark Arena,* were critically acclaimed but did not achieve popular success. *The Godfather,* a novel about an Italian-American crime family, became an instant success, selling more than 15 million copies in the United States alone. Since then Puzo has published *The Sicilian* (1984), authored six screenplays, and won Academy Awards for his two screen adaptations of *The Godfather.* In "Choosing a Dream: Italians in Hell's Kitchen" Puzo looks back at his childhood during the 1930s in New York City. Here he conveys his own aspirations as well as the dreams and hopes of the Italian immigrants who lived in his neighborhood.

1   As a child and in my adolescence, living in the heart of New York's Neapolitan ghetto, I never heard an Italian singing. None of the grown-ups I knew were charming or loving or understanding. Rather they seemed coarse, vulgar, and insulting. And so later in my life when I was exposed to all the clichés of lovable Italians, singing Italians, happy-go-lucky Italians, I wondered where the hell the moviemakers and story-writers got all their ideas from.

2   At a very early age I decided to escape these uncongenial folk by becoming an artist, a writer. It seemed then an impossible dream. My father and mother were illiterate, as were their parents before them. But practicing my art I tried to view the adults with a more charitable eye and so came to the conclusion that their only fault lay in their being foreigners; I was an American. This didn't really help because I was only half right. I was the foreigner. They were already more "American" than I could ever become.

3   But it did seem then that the Italian immigrants, all the fathers and mothers that I knew, were a grim lot; always shouting, always angry, quicker to quarrel than embrace. I did not understand that their lives were a long labor to earn their daily bread and that physical fatigue does not sweeten human natures.

4   And so even as a very small child I dreaded growing up to be like the adults around me. I heard them saying too many cruel things about their dearest friends, saw too many of their false embraces with those they had just maligned, observed with horror their paranoiac anger at some small slight or a fancied injury to their pride. They were, always, too unforgiving. In short, they did not have the careless magnanimity of children.

5   In my youth I was contemptuous of my elders, including a few under thirty. I thought my contempt special to their circumstances. Later when I wrote about these illiterate men and women, when I thought I understood them, I felt a condescending pity. After all, they had suffered, they had labored all the days of their lives. They had never tasted luxury, knew little more economic security than those ancient Roman slaves who might have been their

ancestors. And alas, I thought, with new-found artistic insight, they were cut off from their children because of the strange American tongue, alien to them, native to their sons and daughters.

6   Already an artist but not yet a husband or father, I pondered omnisciently on their tragedy, again thinking it special circumstance rather than a constant in the human condition. I did not yet understand why these men and women were willing to settle for less than they deserved in life and think that "less" quite a bargain. I did not understand that they simply could not afford to dream; I myself had a hundred dreams from which to choose. For I was already sure that I would make my escape, that I was one of the chosen. I would be rich, famous, happy. I would master my destiny.

7   And so it was perhaps natural that as a child, with my father gone, my mother the family chief, I, like all the children in all the ghettos of America, became locked in a bitter struggle with the adults responsible for me. It was in-evitable that my mother and I became enemies.

8   As a child I had the usual dreams. I wanted to be handsome, specifically as cowboy stars in movies were handsome. I wanted to be a killer hero in a world-wide war. Or if no wars came along (our teachers told us another was impossible), I wanted at the very least to be a footloose adventurer. Then I branched out and thought of being a great artist, and then, getting ever more sophisticated, a great criminal.

9   My mother, however, wanted me to be a railroad clerk. And that was her *highest* ambition; she would have settled for less. At the age of sixteen when I let everybody know that I was going to be a great writer, my friends and family took the news quite calmly, my mother included. She did not become angry. She quite simply assumed that I had gone off my nut. She was illiterate and her peasant life in Italy made her believe that only a son of the nobility could possibly be a writer. Artistic beauty after all could spring only from the seedbed of fine clothes, fine food, luxurious living. So then how was it possible for a son of hers to be an artist? She was not too convinced she was wrong even after my first two books were published many years later. It was only after the commercial success of my third novel that she gave me the title of poet.

10   My family and I grew up together on Tenth Avenue, between Thirtieth and Thirty-first streets, part of the area called Hell's Kitchen. This particular neighborhood could have been a movie set for one of the Dead End Kid flicks or for the social drama of the East Side in which John Garfield played the hero. Our tenements were the western wall of the city. Beneath our windows were the vast black iron gardens of the New York Central Railroad, absolutely blooming with stinking boxcars freshly unloaded of cattle and pigs for the city slaughterhouse. Steers sometimes escaped and loped through the heart of the neighborhood followed by astonished young boys who had never seen a live cow.

11   The railroad yards stretched down to the Hudson River, beyond whose garbagey waters rose the rocky Palisades of New Jersey. There were railroad tracks running downtown on Tenth Avenue itself to another freight station called St. Johns Park. Because of this, because these trains cut off one side of

the street from the other, there was a wooden bridge over Tenth Avenue, a romantic-looking bridge despite the fact that no sparkling water, no silver flying fish darted beneath it; only heavy dray carts drawn by tired horses, some flat-boarded trucks, tin lizzie automobiles and, of course, long strings of freight cars drawn by black, ugly engines.

12   What was really great, truly magical, was sitting on the bridge, feet dangling down, and letting the engine under you blow up clouds of steam that made you disappear, then reappear all damp and smelling of fresh ironing. When I was seven years old I fell in love for the first time with the tough little girl who held my hand and disappeared with me in that magical cloud of steam. This experience was probably more traumatic and damaging to my later relationships with women than one of those ugly childhood adventures Freudian novelists use to explain why their hero has gone bad.

13   My father supported his wife and seven children by working as a trackman laborer for the New York Central Railroad. My oldest brother worked for the railroad as a brakeman, another brother was a railroad shipping clerk in the freight office. Eventually I spent some of the worst months of my life as the railroad's worst messenger boy.

14   My oldest sister was just as unhappy as a dressmaker in the garment industry. She wanted to be a school teacher. At one time or another my other two brothers also worked for the railroad — it got all six males in the family. The two girls and my mother escaped, though my mother felt it her duty to send all our bosses a gallon of homemade wine on Christmas. But everybody hated their jobs except my oldest brother who had a night shift and spent most of his working hours sleeping in freight cars. My father finally got fired because the foreman told him to get a bucket of water for the crew and not to take all day. My father took the bucket and disappeared forever.

15   Nearly all the Italian men living on Tenth Avenue supported their large families by working on the railroad. Their children also earned pocket money by stealing ice from the refrigerator cars in summer and coal from the open stoking cars in the winter. Sometimes an older lad would break the seal of a freight car and take a look inside. But this usually brought down the "Bulls," the special railroad police. And usually the freight was "heavy" stuff, too much work to cart away and sell, something like fresh produce or boxes of cheap candy that nobody would buy.

16   The older boys, the ones just approaching voting age, made their easy money by hijacking silk trucks that loaded up at the garment factory on Thirty-first Street. They would then sell the expensive dresses door to door, at bargain prices no discount house could match. From this some graduated into organized crime, whose talent scouts alertly tapped young boys versed in strongarm. Yet despite all this, most of the kids grew up honest, content with fifty bucks a week as truck drivers, deliverymen, and white-collar clerks in the civil service.

17   I had every desire to go wrong but I never had a chance. The Italian family structure was too formidable.

18   I never came home to an empty house; there was always the smell of supper cooking. My mother was always there to greet me, sometimes with a policeman's club in her hand (nobody ever knew how she acquired it). But she

was always there, or her authorized deputy, my older sister, who preferred throwing empty milk bottles at the heads of her little brothers when they got bad marks on their report cards. During the great Depression of the 1930s, though we were the poorest of the poor, I never remember not dining well. Many years later as a guest of a millionaire's club, I realized that our poor family on home relief ate better than some of the richest people in America.

19   My mother would never dream of using anything but the finest imported olive oil, the best Italian cheeses. My father had access to the fruits coming off ships, the produce from railroad cars, all before it went through the stale process of middlemen; and my mother, like most Italian women, was a fine cook in the peasant style.

20   My mother was as formidable a personage as she was a cook. She was not to be treated cavalierly. My oldest brother at age sixteen had his own tin lizzie Ford and used it to further his career as the Don Juan of Tenth Avenue. One day my mother asked him to drive her to the market on Ninth Avenue and Fortieth Street, no more than a five-minute trip. My brother had other plans and claimed he was going to work on a new shift on the railroad. Work was an acceptable excuse even for funerals. But an hour later when my mother came out of the door of the tenement she saw the tin lizzie loaded with three pretty neighborhood girls, my Don Juan brother about to drive them off. Unfortunately there was a cobblestone lying loose in the gutter. My mother dropped her black leather shopping bag and picked up the stone with both hands. As we all watched in horror, she brought the boulder down on the nearest fender of the tin lizzie, demolishing it. Then she picked up her bag and marched off to Ninth Avenue to do her shopping. To this day, forty years later, my brother's voice still has a surprised horror and shock when he tells the story. He still doesn't understand how she could have done it.

21   My mother had her own legends and myths on how to amass a fortune. There was one of our uncles who worked as an assistant chef in a famous Italian-style restaurant. Every day, six days a week, this uncle brought home, under his shirt, six eggs, a stick of butter, and a small bag of flour. By doing this for thirty years he was able to save enough money to buy a fifteen-thou-sand-dollar house on Long Island and two smaller houses for his son and daughter. Another cousin, blessed with a college degree, worked as a chemist in a large manufacturing firm. By using the firm's raw materials and equipment he concocted a superior floor wax which he sold door to door in his spare time. It was a great floor wax and with his low overhead, the price was right. My mother and her friends did not think this stealing. They thought of it as being thrifty.

22   The wax-selling cousin eventually destroyed his reputation for thrift by buying a sailboat; this was roughly equivalent to the son of a Boston brahmin spending a hundred grand in a whorehouse.

23   As rich men escape their wives by going to their club, I finally escaped my mother by going to the Hudson Guild Settlement House. Most people do not know that a settlement house is really a club combined with social services.

The Hudson Guild, a five-story field of joy for slum kids, had ping pong rooms and billiard rooms, a shop in which to make lamps, a theater for putting on amateur plays, a gym to box and play basketball in. And then there were individual rooms where your particular club could meet in privacy. The Hudson Guild even suspended your membership for improper behavior or failure to pay the tiny dues. It was a heady experience for a slum kid to see his name posted on the billboard to the effect that he was suspended by the Board of Governors.

. . .

24   The Hudson Guild was also responsible for absolutely the happiest times of my childhood. When I was about nine or ten they sent me away as a Fresh Air Fund kid. This was a program where slum children were boarded on private families in places like New Hampshire for two weeks.

25   As a child I knew only the stone city. I had no conception of what the countryside could be. When I got to New Hampshire, when I smelled grass and flowers and trees, when I ran barefoot along the dirt country roads, when I drove the cows home from pasture, when I darted through fields of corn and waded through clear brooks, when I gathered warm brown speckled eggs in the henhouse, when I drove a hay wagon drawn by two great horses — when I did all these things — I nearly went crazy with the joy of it. It was quite simply a fairy tale come true.

26   The family that took me in, a middle-aged man and woman, childless, were Baptists and observed Sunday so religiously that even checker playing was not allowed on the Lord's day of rest. We went to church on Sunday for a good three hours, counting Bible class, then again at night. On Thursday evenings we went to prayer meetings. My guardians, out of religious scruple, had never seen a movie. They disapproved of dancing, they were no doubt political reactionaries; they were everything that I came later to fight against.

27   And yet they gave me those magical times children never forget. For two weeks every summer from the time I was nine to fifteen I was happier than I have ever been before or since. The man was good with tools and built me a little playground with swings, sliding ponds, seesaws. The woman had a beautiful flower and vegetable garden and let me pick from it. A cucumber or strawberry in the earth was a miracle. And then when they saw how much I loved picnics, the sizzling frankfurters on a stick over the wood fire, the yellow roasted corn, they drove me out on Sunday afternoons to a lovely green grass mountainside. Only on Sundays it was never called a picnic, it was called "taking our lunch outside." I found it then — and now — a sweet hypocrisy.

. . .

28   From this Paradise I was flung into Hell. That is, I had to help support my family by working on the railroad. After school hours of course. This was the same railroad that had supplied free coal and free ice to the whole Tenth Avenue when I was young enough to steal with impunity. After school finished at 3 P.M. I went to work in the freight office as a messenger. I also worked Saturdays and Sundays when there was work available.

29   I hated it. One of my first short stories was about how I hated that job. But of course what I really hated was entering the adult world. To me the adult world was a dark enchantment, unnatural. As unnatural to the human dream as death. And as inevitable.

30   The young are impatient about change because they cannot grasp the power of time itself; not only as the enemy of flesh, the very germ of death, but time as a benign cancer. As the young cannot grasp really that love must be a victim of time, so too they cannot grasp that injustices, the economic and family traps of living, can also fall victim to time.

. . .

31   America may be a fascistic, warmongering, racially prejudiced country today. It may deserve the hatred of its revolutionary young. But what a miracle it once was! What has happened here has never happened in any other country in any other time. The poor who had been poor for centuries — hell, since the beginning of Christ — whose children had inherited their poverty, their illiteracy, their hopelessness, achieved some economic dignity and freedom. You didn't get it for nothing, you had to pay a price in tears, in suffering, but why not? And some even became artists.

32   Not even my gift for retrospective falsification [remembering the good and not the bad] can make my eighteenth to twenty-first years seem like a happy time. I hated my life. I was being dragged into the trap I feared and had foreseen even as a child. It was all there, the steady job, the nice girl who would eventually get knocked up, and then the marriage and fighting over counting pennies to make ends meet. I noticed myself acting more unheroic all the time. I had to tell lies in pure self-defense, I did not forgive so easily.

33   But I was delivered. When World War II broke out I was delighted. There is no other word, terrible as it may sound. My country called. I was delivered from my mother, my family, the girl I was loving passionately but did not love. And delivered WITHOUT GUILT. Heroically. My country called, ordered me to defend it. I must have been one of millions, sons, husbands, fathers, lovers, making their innocent getaway from baffled loved ones. And what an escape it was. The war made all my dreams come true. I drove a jeep, toured Europe, had love affairs, found a wife, and lived the material for my first novel. But of course that was a just war as Vietnam is not, and so today it is perhaps for the best that the revolutionary young make their escape by attacking their own rulers.

34   Then why five years later did I walk back into the trap with a wife and child and a civil service job I was glad to get? After five years of the life I had dreamed about, plenty of women, plenty of booze, plenty of money, hardly any work, interesting companions, travel, etc., why did I walk back into that cage of family and duty and a steady job?

35   For the simple reason, of course, that I had never really escaped, not my mother, not my family, not the moral pressures of our society. Time again had done its work. I was back in my cage and I was, I think, happy. In the next twenty years I wrote three novels. Two of them were critical successes but I didn't make much money. The third novel, not as good as the others, made me rich. And free at last. Or so I thought.

36   Then why do I dream of those immigrant Italian peasants as having been happy? I remember how they spoke of their forebears, who spent all their lives farming the arid mountain slopes of Southern Italy. "He died in that house in which he was born," they say enviously. "He was never more than an hour from his village, not in all his life," they sigh. And what would they make of a phrase like "retrospective falsification"?

37   No, really, we are all happier now. It is a better life. And after all, as my mother always said, "Never mind about being happy. Be glad you're alive."

38   When I came to my "autobiographical novel," the one every writer does about himself, I planned to make myself the sensitive, misunderstood hero, much put upon by his mother and family. To my astonishment my mother took over the book and instead of my revenge I got another comeuppance. But it is, I think, my best book. And all those old-style grim conservative Italians whom I hated, then pitied so patronizingly, they also turned out to be heroes. Through no desire of mine. I was surprised. The thing that amazed me most was their courage. Where were their Congressional Medals of Honor? Their Distinguished Service Crosses? How did they ever have the balls to get married, have kids, go out to earn a living in a strange land, with no skills, not even knowing the language? They made it without tranquillizers, without sleeping pills, without psychiatrists, without even a dream. Heroes. Heroes all around me. I never saw them.

39   But how could I? They wore lumpy work clothes and handlebar moustaches, they blew their noses on their fingers and they were so short that their high-school children towered over them. They spoke a laughable broken English and the furthest limit of their horizon was their daily bread. Brave men, brave women, they fought to live their lives without dreams. Bent on survival, they narrowed their minds to the thinnest line of existence.

40   It is no wonder that in my youth I found them contemptible. And yet they had left Italy and sailed the ocean to come to a new land and leave their sweated bones in America. Illiterate Colombos, they dared to seek the promised land. And so they, too, dreamed a dream.

. . .

41   But maybe the young are on the right track this time. Maybe they know that the dreams of our fathers were malignant. Perhaps it is true that the only real escape is in the blood magic of drugs. All the Italians I knew and grew up with have escaped, have made their success. We are all Americans now, we are all successes now. And yet the most successful Italian man I know admits that though the one human act he never could understand was suicide, he understood it when he became a success. Not that he ever would do such a thing; no man with Italian blood ever commits suicide or becomes a homosexual in his belief. But suicide has crossed his mind. And so to what avail the finding of the dream? He went back to Italy and tried to live like a peasant again. But he can never again be unaware of more subtle traps than poverty and hunger.

42   There is a difference between having a good time in life and being happy. My mother's life was a terrible struggle and yet I think it was a happy life. One tentative proof is that at the age of eighty-two she is positively indignant at the thought that death dares approach her. But it's not for everybody that kind of life.

43   Thinking back I wonder why I became a writer. Was it the poverty or the books I read? Who traumatized me, my mother or the Brothers Karamazov? Being Italian? Or the girl sitting with me on the bridge as the engine steam deliciously made us vanish? Did it make any difference that I grew up Italian rather than Irish or black?

44   No matter. The good times are beginning, I am another Italian success story. Not as great as DiMaggio or Sinatra but quite enough. It will serve. Yet I can escape again. I have my retrospective falsification (how I love that phrase). I can dream now about how happy I was in my childhood, in my tenement, playing in those dirty but magical streets — living in the poverty that made my mother weep. True, I was a deposed dictator at fifteen but they never hanged me. And now I remember, all those impossible dreams strung out before me, waiting for me to choose, not knowing that the life I was living then, as a child, would become my final dream.

Reading Sources: "Choosing a Dream: Italians in Hell's Kitchen"

Read the selection, surveying it to identify key terms and important concepts. Highlight these phrases and ideas, and then answer these questions.

1. Notice how often Puzo repeats the words *child, adolescent,* and *immigrant.* What does he achieve with this repetition?
2. What words and phrases indicate the sequence of Puzo's ideas from paragraph to paragraph? How do these elements show the change in Puzo's thinking about the adults who lived in Hell's Kitchen?
3. Puzo uses not one but several paragraphs to introduce his essay. What does he accomplish in these paragraphs? At what point does he move into the body of his discussion?
4. What is the thesis of Puzo's essay?
5. Underline the topic sentences in paragraphs 8 to 19 of Puzo's essay and tell how they help readers follow the progression of his ideas. What points does Puzo make in this paragraph cluster, and how do they support his thesis?
6. Where does Puzo begin his conclusion? In what way does it reinforce the points that he has developed throughout the rest of the essay?

Reacting to Sources

Reread the selection carefully, making marginal notes to aid your comprehension and reinforce connections. Then further annotate the selection if you need to do so in order to answer any of these questions. (You may already have addressed some of the questions in your marginal notes.)

1. In a few sentences summarize the points that Puzo makes in his introductory paragraphs.
2. Write brief marginal definitions of these words as they are used in this essay: *magnanimity* (4), *condescending* (5), *omnisciently* (6), *traumatic* (12). Use a dictionary if necessary.
3. What does Puzo mean in paragraph 2 when he says, "I was the foreigner. They [adults] were already more 'American' than I could ever become."
4. Write a brief marginal comment in response to the ideas expressed in paragraph 39.
5. In paragraph 7 Puzo says, "It was inevitable that my mother and I became enemies." Write a marginal note explaining why you agree or disagree with this sentiment.
6. Write three marginal questions to help clarify the ideas expressed in paragraph 44.
7. What does Puzo mean by *retrospective falsification* (32 and 36)? Write a marginal comment explaining the use of this phrase in each paragraph.
8. Read paragraph 18 and write a journal entry in which you compare the importance of Puzo's mother with the role that your mother plays in your family life.
9. In paragraph 17 Puzo says, "I had every desire to go wrong but I never had the chance. The Italian family structure was too formidable." Explore this idea further in a journal entry.
10. Puzo wrote this essay while the war in Vietnam was still being fought. Go through the essay and underline the statements that seem dated or that no longer would be accepted as self-evident by many readers. Comment on how these statements influence your reactions to Puzo's ideas.
11. In a journal entry, compare and contrast the sentiments expressed in paragraph 18 of this essay with this statement:

    "Family" is not just a buzz word for reactionaries; for women, as for men, it is the symbol of that last area where one has any hope of control over one's destiny, of meeting one's most basic human needs, of nourishing that core of personhood threatened now by vast impersonal institutions and uncontrollable corporate and government bureaucracies."

    Betty Friedan, "Feminism's Next Step"

12. In paragraph 33 Puzo says that World War II "delivered" him. Explain this comment in a journal entry; then, making specific reference to your own experience and ideas, comment on whether you think a draft-age person today would feel the same way.

Working with Sources

1. Write a summary of paragraphs 8 and 9.
2. Write a critique of paragraph 31. As you plan your critique, consider whether Puzo was able to be objective about America or whether events at the time he was writing his essay colored his view.

3. Use the following two quotations in a journal entry in which you express a reaction to the essay.

   "To me the adult world was a dark enchantment, unnatural. As unnatural to the human dream as death" (29).

   "And all those old-style grim conservative Italians whom I hated, then pitied so patronizingly, they also turned out to be heroes" (38).

   Be sure to integrate the quotations smoothly into your writing.
4. Write a paraphrase of Puzo's introduction.
5. Write a one-paragraph synthesis that blends the ideas in paragraphs 39 and 40 of this essay with ideas in paragraph 1 in the Declaration of Independence (pp. 86–89).

Writing with Sources

Integrating information from "Choosing a Dream: Italians in Hell's Kitchen" with your own ideas, write an essay on one of these topics. Be sure to acknowledge all ideas that are not your own.

1. Compare your parents' ambitions for you with those of Puzo's mother. Consider to what extent your parents' ethnic identity or racial background has determined their aspirations.
2. Discuss the significance of the title of this essay, considering whether it accurately describes the point Puzo makes.
3. Compare Puzo's early view of Italian immigrants with the view he adopted after he matured. How do you account for this change of viewpoint?
4. Discuss the significance of Puzo's final remark: "And now I remember, all those impossible dreams strung out before me, waiting for me to choose, not knowing that the life I was living then, as a child, would become my final dream." Support your points with direct references to Puzo's essay.

A. Perfect example of Figuritive language.

I Have a Dream

Martin Luther King, Jr.

Born January 15, 1929, in Atlanta, Georgia, and killed by an assassin's bullet in Memphis, Tennessee, on April 4, 1968, Martin Luther King is for many Americans the symbol of the modern civil rights movement. Educated at Morehouse College, Crozer Theological Seminary, and Boston University (Ph.D., 1954), King became passionately involved with the struggle of black Americans to win the rights enjoyed by other Americans: equal access to education, housing, employment, and the ballot box. King did more than just speak out for what he believed—he led marches and sit-ins, went to jail for his beliefs, and even put his life in jeopardy.

Throughout his career as a civil rights leader, King continued to preach nonviolence and to set an example by working through acts of peaceful civil disobedience — even in the face of violence and hatred. He helped to organize the Montgomery, Alabama, bus boycott (1955–56), which brought about the end of segregated seating on public transportation in that city. In 1957, he became the first leader of the Southern Christian Leadership Conference, an organization dedicated to achieving equal rights through nonviolence. In 1963 he organized a series of demonstrations against racial discrimination in Birmingham, Alabama — peaceful protests that were broken up by police using fire hoses and dogs against protesters. Perhaps the highlight of King's career was the August 28, 1963 March on Washington. A quarter of a million people gathered at the Lincoln Memorial to hear his "I Have a Dream" speech, which expressed his version of the American Dream. The following year, King was awarded the Nobel Peace Prize.

1   Five score years ago, a great American, in whose symbolic shadow we stand, signed the Emancipation Proclamation. This momentous decree came as a great beacon light of hope to millions of Negro slaves who had been seared in the flames of withering injustice. It came as a joyous daybreak to end the long night of captivity.

2   But one hundred years later, we must face the tragic fact that the Negro is still not free. One hundred years later, the life of the Negro is still sadly crippled by the manacles of segregation and the chains of discrimination. One hundred years later, the Negro lives on a lonely island of poverty in the midst of a vast ocean of material prosperity. One hundred years later, the Negro is still languishing in the corners of American society and finds himself an exile in his own land. So we have come here today to dramatize an appalling condition.

3   In a sense we have come to our nation's capital to cash a check. When the architects of our republic wrote the magnificent words of the Constitution and the Declaration of Independence, they were signing a promissory note to which every American was to fall heir. This note was a promise that all men would be guaranteed the unalienable rights of life, liberty, and the pursuit of happiness.

4   It is obvious today that America has defaulted on this promissory note insofar as her citizens of color are concerned. Instead of honoring this sacred obligation, America has given the Negro people a bad check; a check which has come back marked "insufficient funds." But we refuse to believe that the bank of justice is bankrupt. We refuse to believe that there are insufficient funds in the great vaults of opportunity of this nation. So we have come to cash this check — a check that will give us upon demand the riches of freedom and the security of justice. We have also come to this hallowed spot to remind America of the fierce urgency of *now*. This is no time to engage in the luxury of cooling off or to take the tranquilizing drugs of gradualism. *Now* is the time to make real the promises of Democracy. *Now* is the time to rise from the dark and desolate valley of segregation to the sunlit path of racial justice. *Now* is the time to open the doors of opportunity to all of God's children. *Now* is the time

to lift our nation from the quicksands of racial injustice to the solid rock of brotherhood.

5   It would be fatal for the nation to overlook the urgency of the moment and to underestimate the determination of the Negro. This sweltering summer of the Negro's legitimate discontent will not pass until there is an invigorating autumn of freedom and equality. Nineteen sixty-three is not an end, but a beginning. Those who hope that the Negro needed to blow off steam and will now be content will have a rude awakening if the nation returns to business as usual. There will be neither rest nor tranquillity in America until the Negro is granted his citizenship rights. The whirlwinds of revolt will continue to shake the foundations of our nation until the bright day of justice emerges.

6   But there is something that I must say to my people who stand on the warm threshold which leads into the palace of justice. In the process of gaining our rightful place we must not be guilty of wrongful deeds. Let us not seek to satisfy our thirst for freedom by drinking from the cup of bitterness and hatred. We must forever conduct our struggle on the high plane of dignity and discipline. We must not allow our creative protest to degenerate into physical violence. Again and again we must rise to the majestic heights of meeting physical force with soul force. The marvelous new militancy which has engulfed the Negro community must not lead us to a distrust of all white people, for many of our white brothers, as evidenced by their presence here today, have come to realize that their destiny is tied up with our destiny and their freedom is inextricably bound to our freedom. We cannot walk alone.

7   And as we walk, we must make the pledge that we shall march ahead. We cannot turn back. There are those who are asking the devotees of civil rights, "When will you be satisfied?" We can never be satisfied as long as the Negro is the victim of the unspeakable horrors of police brutality. We can never be satisfied as long as our bodies, heavy with the fatigue of travel, cannot gain lodging in the motels of the highways and the hotels of the cities. We cannot be satisfied as long as the Negro's basic mobility is from a smaller ghetto to a larger one. We can never be satisfied as long as a Negro in Mississippi cannot vote and a Negro in New York believes he has nothing for which to vote. No, no, we are not satisfied, and we will not be satisfied until justice rolls down like waters and righteousness like a mighty stream.

8   I am not unmindful that some of you have come here out of great trials and tribulations. Some of you have come fresh from narrow jail cells. Some of you have come from areas where your quest for freedom left you battered by the storms of persecution and staggered by the winds of police brutality. You have been the veterans of creative suffering. Continue to work with the faith that unearned suffering is redemptive.

9   Go back to Mississippi, go back to Alabama, go back to South Carolina, go back to Georgia, go back to Louisiana, go back to the slums and ghettos of our northern cities, knowing that somehow this situation can and will be changed. Let us not wallow in the valley of despair.

10   I say to you today, my friends, that in spite of the difficulties and frustra-

tions of the moment I still have a dream. It is a dream deeply rooted in the American dream.

11   I have a dream that one day this nation will rise up and live out the true meaning of its creed: "We hold these truths to be self-evident; that all men are created equal."

12   I have a dream that one day on the red hills of Georgia the sons of former slaves and the sons of former slaveowners will be able to sit down together at the table of brotherhood.

13   I have a dream that one day even the state of Mississippi, a desert state sweltering with the heat of injustice and oppression, will be transformed into an oasis of freedom and justice.

14   I have a dream that my four little children will one day live in a nation where they will not be judged by the color of their skin but by the content of their character.

15   I have a dream today.

16   I have a dream that one day the state of Alabama, whose governor's lips are presently dripping with the words of interposition and nullification, will be transformed into a situation where little black boys and black girls will be able to join hands with little white boys and white girls and walk together as sisters and brothers.

17   I have a dream today.

18   I have a dream that one day every valley shall be exalted, every hill and mountain shall be made low, the rough places will be made plain, and the crooked places will be made straight, and the glory of the Lord shall be revealed, and all flesh shall see it together.

19   This is our hope. This is the faith with which I return to the South. With this faith we will be able to hew out of the mountain of despair a stone of hope. With this faith we will be able to transform the jangling discords of our nation into a beautiful symphony of brotherhood. With this faith we will be able to work together, to pray together, to struggle together, to go to jail together, to stand up for freedom together, knowing that we will be free one day.

20   This will be the day when all of God's children will be able to sing with new meaning

> My country, 'tis of thee,
> Sweet land of liberty,
>   Of thee I sing:
> Land where my fathers died,
> Land of the pilgrims' pride,
> From every mountain-side
> Let freedom ring.

21   And if America is to be a great nation this must become true. So let freedom ring from the prodigious hilltops of New Hampshire. Let freedom ring from the mighty mountains of New York. Let freedom ring from the heightening Alleghenies of Pennsylvania!

22   Let freedom ring from the snowcapped Rockies of Colorado!

23   Let freedom ring from the curvaceous peaks of California!
24   But not only that; let freedom ring from Stone Mountain of Georgia!
25   Let freedom ring from Lookout Mountain of Tennessee!
26   Let freedom ring from every hill and molehill of Mississippi. From every mountainside, let freedom ring.
27   When we let freedom ring, when we let it ring from every village and every hamlet, from every state and every city, we will be able to speed up that day when all of God's children, black men and white men, Jews and Gentiles, Protestants and Catholics, will be able to join hands and sing in the words of the old Negro spiritual, "Free at last! free at last! thank God almighty, we are free at last!"

Reading Sources: "I Have A Dream"

Read the selection, surveying it to identify key terms and important concepts. Highlight these phrases and ideas, and then answer these questions.

1. What key phrase is repeated for emphasis in paragraph 2? What two key words are repeated for emphasis in paragraph 4? What word in paragraph 7 is emphasized through repetition? What word in paragraph 9? Explain why King stresses each word or phrase.
2. King begins his speech with the image of the Emancipation Proclamation as a symbol of hope, and he ends it with a quotation from a spiritual. By placing references to these sources in key positions, he puts a great deal of emphasis on them. Why is such emphasis appropriate?
3. How does King use language to link paragraphs 10–18? paragraphs 20–27?
4. Identify each of King's allusions to historical leaders and documents. What is the effect of these allusions?

Reacting to Sources

Reread the selection carefully, making marginal notes to aid your comprehension and reinforce connections. Then further annotate the selection if you need to do so in order to answer any of these questions. (You may already have addressed some of the questions in your marginal notes.)

1. Using a dictionary if necessary, supply brief marginal definitions of these words as they are used in this selection: *manacles* (2), *languished* (2), *hallowed* (4), *gradualism* (4), *inextricably* (6), *redemptive* (8), *interposition* (16), *nullification* (16), *prodigious* (21).
2. What does King mean in paragraph 24 when he says, "But not only that"? Explain his point in a brief marginal note.
3. Do you agree or disagree with King's statement in paragraph 10 that his dream

is "deeply rooted in the American dream"? Explain your feelings in a journal entry.

4. Do some research to find out what King means in paragraph 16 when he says that the governor of Alabama's "lips are presently dripping with words of interposition and nullification." Explain King's words in a marginal note.

5. Read the selection's headnote carefully. Comment in your journal on how your knowledge of King's own life influences your reactions to his ideas.

6. Has King's dream come true? Is it a dream shared by most Americans? Explain your view in a journal entry.

Working with Sources

1. Summarize paragraph 27.
2. Write a critique of the ideas in paragraph 6.
3. Write a journal entry in which you explore your reactions to these quotations from "I Have a Dream."

   "Nineteen sixty-three is not an end, but a beginning" (5).
   "We cannot turn back" (7).
   "From every mountainside, let freedom ring" (26).

   Be sure to integrate the quotations smoothly into your writing.
4. Paraphrase the first five sentences of paragraph 4.
5. Write a paragraph synthesizing the ideas in paragraph 6 with the ideas in paragraph 2 of the Declaration of Independence (pp. 86 – 89).

Writing with Sources: Using a Single Source

Integrating information from "I Have a Dream" with your own ideas, write an essay on one of these topics. Be sure to acknowledge all ideas that are not your own.

1. Using King's essay as your guide, write an essay supporting or arguing against the assertion that black Americans have come a long way since 1963.
2. Write an essay in which you use King's speech — and the information about his life presented in the headnote — to argue for or against nonviolence as a means of achieving political and social change.
3. Write an essay in which you discuss how King's elaborate figurative language and his frequent use of balanced and parallel phrasing strengthen (or weaken) his speech.

Feminism's Next Step

Betty Friedan

Betty Friedan graduated from Smith College in 1942 and served as a research fellow at University of California at Berkeley. She married in 1947 and spent much of her time raising three children, although she found time to write for several women's magazines. In 1957, at the age of thirty-six, she carried out a survey of two hundred of her fellow Smith College alumnae and found that many of them felt bored and unhappy with their lives. When Friedan explored this problem, she discovered that many women in all walks of life experienced the same dissatisfaction. She summed up her findings in a magazine article and eventually in *The Feminine Mystique* (1963), a book that brought her instant fame. In *The Feminine Mystique* Friedan argued that advertisements, educators, and women's magazines present a narrow and empty view of women's lives and restrict them to the dual roles of mother and housekeeper. She claimed that these roles stifle the creativity and potential of women, causing them to be unhappy and frustrated. Friedan continued to write and lecture, and in 1966 she founded the National Organization for Women (NOW). After serving as president of NOW from 1966 to 1970, she organized the nationwide Women's Strike for Equality (1970) and founded the National Women's Political Caucus (1971). "Feminism's Next Step" is excerpted from Friedan's most recent book, *The Second Stage* (1981), in which she examines the future of feminism in light of past successes and failures. Friedan's criticism defines her version of the American Dream: a world in which both women and men can reach their true potential "by transcending the false polarization between feminism and the family."

1   "The women's movement is over," said my friend, a usually confident executive, who is also a wife and feminist. "At least," she continued in a grim tone, "it is in my shop. The men are making jokes about bimbos again, and the other woman in the executive group and I just look at each other. It doesn't matter if we get mad; they act as if we aren't there. When a new job opens up, all they look for now is men. It's as if the word has gone out that we've lost our case; there won't be any equal rights amendment, so they don't need to worry anymore about lawsuits over sex discrimination, even though laws against it are still on the books. They figure they can do what they want about women now, like the old days."

2   The women's movement in some form will never be over. But the rights that women have struggled to win in the last decade are in deadly danger, with right-wing groups in Congress determined to gut laws against sex discrimination and to abolish legal abortion and a conservative Supreme Court already backtracking on equality. We now have less than 365 days to pass the equal rights amendment, which is both the symbol and the substance of women's rights. If E.R.A. does not become part of the Constitution by June 30, 1982, it may not come up again in this century.

3   And there are other signs that we have reached, not the beginning of the end, but the end of the beginning.

4   Listening to my own daughter and others of her generation, I sense something off, out of focus, going wrong. From the daughters, working so hard at their new careers, determined not to be trapped as their mothers were, expecting so much and taking for granted the opportunities we fought for, I've begun to hear undertones of pain and puzzlement, almost a bitterness that they hardly dare admit. As if, with all those opportunities that we won for them, they are reluctant to speak out loud about certain other needs some of us rebelled against — needs for love, security, men, children, family, home.

5   I sense a frustration in women not so young, about those careers they're lucky to have, facing agonizing conflicts over having children. Can they have it all? How?

6   I sense a desperation in divorced women and men and an unspoken fear of divorce in those still married, which is being twisted into a backlash against equal rights that are more essential than ever for the divorced.

7   I sense a sullen impatience among some of those women who entered the work force in unprecedented millions over the last 10 years, who are in fact earning 59 cents for every dollar men earn because the only jobs available to most women are still in the low-paying clerical and service fields. Even among the few who have broken through to the executive suite, I sense the exhilaration of trying to be superwomen giving way to disillusionment with the tokens of power.

8   What is going wrong? Why this uneasy sense of battles won, only to be fought again, of battles that should have been won and yet are not, of battles that suddenly one does not really want to win, and the weariness of battle altogether — how many feel it?

9   I, and other feminists, dread to discuss these troubling symptoms because the women's movement has been the source and focus of so much of our energy, strength and security for so long. We cannot conceive that it will not go on forever the same way it has for nearly 20 years. But we cannot go on denying these puzzling symptoms of distress. If they mean something is seriously wrong, we had better find out and change direction yet again, before it is too late.

10   I believe it is over, the first stage. We must now move into the second stage of the sex-role revolution, which the women's movement set off.

11   In that first stage, our aim was full participation, power and voice in the mainstream — inside the party, the political process, the professions, the business world. But we were diverted from our dream by a sexual politics that cast man as enemy and seemed to repudiate the traditional values of the family. In reaction against the feminine mystique, which defined women solely in terms of their relation to men as wives, mothers and homemakers, we insidiously fell into a feminist mystique, which denied that core of women's personhood that is fulfilled through love, nurture, home. We seemed to create a polarization between feminists and those women who still looked to the family for their very identity, not only among the dwindling numbers who were still full-time housewives, but also among women who do not get as much sense of worth or security from their jobs as they get — or wish they could get — from being someone's wife or mother. The very terms in which we fought for

abortion, or against rape, or in opposition to pornography seemed to express a hate for men and a lack of reverence for childbearing that threatened those women profoundly. That focus on sexual battles also took energy away from the fight for the equal rights amendment and kept us from moving to restructure work and home so that women could have real choices. We fought for equality in terms of male power, without asking what equality really means between women and men.

12   I believe that we have to break through our own feminist mystique now and move into the second stage — no longer against, but with men. In the second stage we have to transcend that polarization between feminism and the family. We have to free ourselves from male power traps, understand the limits of women's power as a separate interest group and grasp the possibility of generating a new kind of power, which was the real promise of the women's movement. For the second stage is not so much a fixed agenda as it is a process, a mode that will put a new value on qualities once considered — and denigrated as — special to women, feminine qualities that will be liberated in men as they share experiences like child care. These qualities, used mainly in the private world of the family until now, were previewed for the first time publicly in the women's movement; now they will be used in a larger political sphere by both men and women.

13   We discovered the first-stage limits — and the potential — of women's power in the last election. After the momentous passage of the equal rights amendment by Congress in 1972 and approval by 35 of the 38 states needed to ratify a Constitutional amendment, E.R.A. had become deadlocked in the 15 unratified states. Despite majority popular support, as shown by the polls, E.R.A. was taken up as a target of right-wing political groups and became a focus for the reactionary political wave that was beginning to sweep the country. Discussion of it bogged down in hysterical claims that the amendment would eliminate privacy in bathrooms, encourage homosexual marriage, put women in the trenches and deprive housewives of their husbands' support.

14   What the equal rights amendment says is, "Equality of rights under the law shall not be denied or abridged by the United States or any state on account of sex." What it would do is put half the population under the full protection of the Constitution and the Bill of Rights for the first time, guaranteeing inalienable equal opportunity for women in employment, education and other spheres. It would also provide the basis for equality in social security, marriage and divorce law, pensions, and military service. . . .

15   It will take a miracle of political wisdom and survival skills for women to save the equal rights amendment by June 30, 1982. The women's movement has made such miracles happen before. The great march on Washington by thousands of women in the hot summer of 1979 made their real passion for equality clear enough to Congress to achieve extension of the traditional seven-year deadline for ratification of Constitutional amendments.

16   For a miracle like that, in the current reactionary political climate, the leaders of every woman's organization — from NOW and the League of Women Voters to the most career-oriented professional woman's caucuses and nonpoli-

tical college sororities — would have to put aside their separate agendas. They would have to give not only lip service priority to E.R.A., but they would have to summon an emergency mobilization of their members, their staffs and their own treasuries, even mortgaging their buildings, to put all possible woman power into states like Virginia, Georgia, Oklahoma, North Carolina, as well as Illinois, Missouri and Florida, dividing the command of different states among the different organizations, or agreeing to follow a combined command.

17   Republican politicians from President Reagan down would have to be made to understand that their responsibility for killing the equal rights amendment might be the margin for defeat for Republicans in 1984. And Democratic politicians would have to understand that our voting bloc — now larger than the traditional ethnic and blue-collar base — could be their only hope for power again in this century, but only if they mobilize their still considerable political muscle, expertise and flagging courage for equal rights for women as masterfully as they did to bring about the 96 – 0 defeat for cuts in old-age Social Security in the Senate.

18   And the seemingly apathetic "me" generation of students would have to be aroused, as they haven't been since the Vietnam War, the daughters to pay their dues and insure the opportunities they now take for granted, the sons to insure their own new dreams for more fulfilling lives. The women who have had assertiveness training and learned to dress for success would have to apply the hard skills and money from their own careers to insure that the doors the women's movement forced open don't close on them. The women afraid of divorce would have to see equal rights as the best insurance for themselves and their families against financial disaster.

19   Recently, a well-dressed woman in her 40's, facing a crisis in her own 25-year marriage, told me of her despair at the inability of women leaders to "get their act together" and truly mobilize to meet the crisis of E.R.A.

20   "They're not sure even now whether to ask women to go to Virginia or Georgia or Oklahoma. They say we might rock the boat," she said. "Don't they realize we have to rock the boat now? Who handed them or even President Reagan the right to give up our daughters' possibility to live lives of hope and equality for the rest of this century? It's not a matter of the specific details of the change E.R.A. will make in the laws of this state or that. If we lose the E.R.A., the rights we all take for granted now will be up to the whim of the individual judge again or the boss or husband. We won't have real control over our own lives without equal rights in the Constitution."

21   That woman had gotten her own suburban friends, who had never been near a NOW meeting or consciousness-raising group, to pool their money to hire a top professional political consultant to assess the chances of passing E.R.A. in the time left. One teen-ager contributed $800 she had raised baby-sitting for E.R.A. More valuable than the study itself — which showed that passage of E.R.A. was still politically possible — was the urgency of these women. If only that could be made visible.

22   That energy is out there, waiting for leadership. And the fact is, the most recent national poll conducted by Yankelovich, Skelly and White in May 1981,

confirming the conservative mood of the nation in support of Reagan on economic issues, recorded a substantial 61 percent majority for passage of E.R.A. as compared with 30 percent against.

23   Finally, I think we have to face the fact that on June 30, 1982, we may lose the battle to get equal rights for women into the Constitution — and consider the real consequences. Many women whose own power in the executive suite or political arena arose from the women's movement for equality in a sense they have forgotten or never acknowledged in their own careers — will most surely lose that power. Women who were persuaded that E.R.A. was against the family, and that all they needed was a man to take care of them the rest of their lives, will have reason to fear financial disaster in divorce. Leaders of special-interest groups — men or women whose concerns are for the rights of homosexuals, blacks, Jews, children, the aged — may realize too late that defeat of the E.R.A., which protects the rights of half the nation, may doom the already threatened rights of much smaller interest groups.

24   If we had not been diverted by sexual politics, we might not now be watching the dismantling of affirmative-action programs against sex discrimination in education and employment by conservative extremists in the Senate. The defeat of the Senators on the Moral Majority hit list (Birch Bayh, Frank Church, John C. Culver, George S. McGovern) cannot be attributed solely to disgust with Carter or to Reagan's coattails. The women's movement has to assume some responsibility. We underestimated the threat and did not mobilize ourselves in all-out defense of the men who were explicitly targeted for defeat by the National Conservative Political Action Committee supposedly because they supported equal rights for women, the right to abortion and homosexual rights.

25   Is a distorted sexual politics at work if the women's movement did not rise to the support of these men with the same passion as, for instance, it supported Bella Abzug or Elizabeth Holtzman in their Senate races? Is a distorted sexual politics responsible for the lumping of these three issues together in such an inflammable, sexually charged package? It is all very well for leaders of the women's movement today to insist, correctly, that the equal rights amendment has nothing to do with either abortion or homosexuality — in fact, it has nothing to do with sexual behavior at all. But the sexual politics that distorted the sense of priorities of the women's movement during the 1970s made it easy for the so-called Moral Majority to lump E.R.A. with homosexual rights and abortion into one explosive package of licentious, family-threatening sex.

26   There is no doubt that the radical right with its almost unlimited money is using abortion and homosexuality as a red herring. For surely, homosexuality and abortion are not the main problems in America today. But up through history to Hitler and the Ayatollah, and not exempting Stalinist Russia, control and manipulation of sexuality and the family and suppression of the rights and personhood of women have been key elements in authoritarian power. The emotions and repressions linked to sexuality are so powerful that it is also relatively easy to divert people's attention from their own basic economic inter-

ests and even from asking the tough political questions simply by manipulating sexual hysteria.

27   The Founding Fathers of this republic wrote into the Bill of Rights the protection of certain basic areas of privacy. Surely it is politically unwise to seem to threaten that area of inviolate sexual privacy now, as part of an effort to secure these basic rights for women. Tactics that smack of sexual exhibitionism, even slogans like "sexual preference," distort the basic principle; they seem to invade that very right of privacy for which we fight.

28   Maybe there was something slightly off in the way we handled abortion. Such slogans as "free abortion on demand" had connotations of sexual permissiveness, affronting not only the moral values of conservatives but implying a certain lack of reverence for life and the mysteries of conception and birth.

29   After all, why do feminists seem to be fighting "for abortion" against women who say they are fighting for "the right to life"? How can we fight the real battle in such terms? Who is really for abortion? That is like being for mastectomy. I, myself, am for life. I am for the choice to have children, which those who would ban access to safe, legal, medical abortion endanger.

30   The true potential of women's power can be realized only by transcending the false polarization between feminism and the family. It is an abstract polarization that does not exist in real life.

31   For instead of the polarization that has plagued the women's movement in the last few years and prevented the very possibility of political solutions, new research shows that virtually all women today share a basic core of commitment to the family and to their own equality within and beyond it, as long as family and equality are not seen to be in conflict.

32   One such study, "Juggling Contradictions: Women's Ideas About Families," was conducted by Nancy Bennett, Susan Harding, et al. of the Social Science Research Community at the University of Michigan in 1979. The 33 women in this study were between the ages of 28 and 45, white, with children, living in small and medium-size Michigan cities. A third of the women had some college education, most of the families had an income of between $15,000 and $30,000, and more than half the women were employed, most of them part time, at jobs ranging from selling real estate to nursing, hairdressing and cleaning houses.

33   The researchers admitted that their preconceptions and practically everything they had read had prepared them to put the women they interviewed into two categories — familial or individualistic. The "familial ideology" places a tremendous value on the family and on motherhood, both as an activity and as a source of identity. It holds that family — husband and children — should be the primary focus of a woman's life and that the needs of the family should be placed above all else. In contrast, the "individualistic ideology" places the individual on an equal level with the family — mothers have needs and goals to meet as persons apart from the family.

34   The researchers reported: "Instead of finding categories of women, we found categories of ideas . . . bits and pieces of two distinct belief systems —

familial and individualistic ideologies. None of the women we spoke with subscribed completely to one ideology or the other; they all expressed some combination of the two, in their words and in their lives. The ideologies are opposed in the political arena. . . . The women we spoke with, however, did not present these ideas as contradictory."

35   The researchers stressed: "We were not surprised to find conflicting ideas or ideologies expressed by the women we interviewed, but to find them combined in the views and behavior of each woman."

36   The tension between the two ideologies — woman-as-individual and woman-serving-her-family — looked irreconcilable in the abstract, but was, in fact, reconciled in the women's lives. They worked, usually part time or on different shifts from their husbands, shared child care with husbands or grand-mothers or others and approved of child-care centers, even if they were not yet ready to use them themselves.

37   Even those who themselves symbolize or preach one or the other ideology can be seen combining both in their own lives. When Rosabeth Moss Kanter, the eminent sociologist and author of "Men and Women in the Corporation," takes her 2-year-old son to a board meeting, her partner-husband, Barry, takes over with the child. They describe this arrangement in feminist terms. But when Marabel Morgan "saves" her marriage, not by decking her body in ostrich feathers but by enlisting her husband as partner-manager to keep track of and invest the money she earns lecturing on the "Total Woman," she describes this as "feminine," not feminist.

38   There are not two kinds of women in America. The political polarization between feminism and the family was preached and manipulated by extremists on the right — and colluded in, perhaps unconsciously, by feminist and liberal or radical leaders — to extend or defend their own political power. Now, as ideological polarization is being resolved in real life by juggling and rationaliz-ing new necessities in traditional terms and old necessities in feminist terms, women will strengthen the family in evolving ways.

39   Politically, for the women's movement to continue to promote issues like E.R.A., abortion and child care solely in individualistic terms subverts our own moral majority. Economic necessity and the very survival of the family now force the increasing majority of women to work and to make painful choices about having more children. And women who merely tolerated, or even disapproved of, these concerns, will now face them as matters of concrete personal urgency and the survival of their families. The women's movement has appealed to women as individualists; the Moral Majority has played to and elicited an explosive, defensive reaction on behalf of women as upholders of the family. Perhaps the reactionary preachers of the Moral Majority who decry women's moves to equality as threats to the family are merely using the family to limit women's real political power. In a similar vein, feminists intent on mobilizing women's political power are, in fact, defeating their own purpose by denying the importance of the family.

40   That Michigan study showed something very important. All the women believed in equality and all of them believed in the family — from the same or

converging needs for security, identity, and some control over their lives. Whether or not they supported a particular issue depended on how they perceived its affecting them. No appeal would be acceptable, even to the most individualistic, if it denied or conflicted with their commitment to the family, which they all shared.

41   "Family" is not just a buzz word for reactionaries; for women, as for men, it is the symbol of that last area where one has any hope of control over one's destiny, of meeting one's most basic human needs, of nourishing that core of personhood threatened now by vast impersonal institutions and uncontrollable corporate and government bureaucracies. Against these menaces, the family may be as crucial for survival as it used to be against the untamed wilderness and the raging elements, and the old, simple kinds of despotism.

42   For the family, all psychological science tells us, is the nutrient of our humanness, of all our individuality. The Michigan women, and all the others they exemplify, may show great political wisdom as well as personal survival skills in holding on to the family as the base of their identity and human control.

43   It is time to start thinking of the movement in new terms. It is very important indeed that the daughters — and the sons — hold on to the dream of equality in the years ahead and move consciously to the second stage of the sex-role revolution. If we cannot, at this moment, solve the new problems we can no longer deny, we must at least pass on the right questions. These second-stage questions reflect the most urgent problems now facing this nation.

44   There is a quiet movement of American men that is converging on the women's movement, though it is masked at the moment by a resurgence of *machismo.* This movement of men for self-fulfillment beyond the rat race for success and for a role in the family beyond breadwinner makes it seem that women are seeking power in terms men are leaving behind. Even those women who have made it on such terms are forfeiting the quality of life, exchanging their old martyred service of home and children for harassed, passive service of corporation.

45   In the second stage, women have to say "No" to standards of success on the job set in terms of men who had wives to take care of all the details of life, and standards at home set in terms of women whose whole sense of worth and power had to come from that perfectly run house, those perfectly controlled children. Instead of accepting that double burden, women will realize that they can and must give up some of that power in the home and the family when they are carrying part of the breadwinning burden and some beginnings of power on the job. Instead of those rigid contracts that seemed the feminist ideal in the first stage, there will be in the second stage an easy flow as man and woman share the chores of home and children — sometimes 50–50, sometimes 20–80 or 60–40, according to their abilities and needs. In the second stage, the woman will find and use her own strength and style at work, instead of trying so hard to do it man's way, and she will not feel she has to be more independent than any man for fear that she will fall back into that abject dependence that she sometimes secretly yearns for.

46   Politically, instead of focusing on woman as victim and on sexual battles that don't really change anything, like those marches against pornography, feminists in the second stage will forge new alliances with men from unions, church and corporation that are essential if we are to restructure jobs and home on a human basis.

47   Despite the recent Supreme Court decision, which ruled that women may be excluded from the draft, I feel that in the second stage, questions like "Should women be drafted?" will be obsolete, for it will be understood that for the nation's survival, women simply will have to be drafted if a major war threatens. With the dangers of nuclear holocaust, new questions need to be asked about the defense of the nation that demand a sensitivity to human values and to life on the part of both male and female military leaders.

48   Above all, the second stage involves not a retreat to the family, but embracing the family in new terms of equality and diversity. The choice to have children—and the joys and burdens of raising them—will be so costly and precious that it will have to be shared more equally by mother, father and others from, or in place of, the larger family. The trade-offs will be seen more clearly as both men and women become realistic about the values and the price. It will probably not be possible economically for most women to have a real choice to be just a housewife, full-time or lifelong. But men as well as women will be demanding parental leave or reduced schedules for those few years — or in early, middle or later life for their own rebirth. A voucher system, such as Milton Friedman and other conservatives have already proposed for different purposes, could be used to provide a "child allowance," payable perhaps as a tax rebate, to every man or woman who takes primary responsibility for care of a child or dependent parent at home. She or he would get equal credit in the wage-earning spouse's pension and old-age Social Security vestment; this credit would not be lost in case of divorce. If both parents returned to work and shared child-care responsibilities, they could use those vouchers to help pay for child care in the community. Many advanced nations have such a child or family allowance.

49   And in the second stage, unions and companies will begin to give priority to restructuring hours of work—flextime and flexible benefit packages—not just to help women but because men will be demanding them and because improved quality of work will not only cost less but yield greater results in terms of reduced absenteeism, increased productivity and profit than the conventional package.

50   But in the second stage when we talk about "family" we will no longer mean just Mom and Dad and the kids. We will be more keenly aware of how the needs of both women and men for love and intimacy and emotional and economic sharing and support change over time and of the new shapes family can take. In the second stage we will need new forms of homes and apartments that don't depend on the full-time service of the housewife, and new shared housing for single parents and people living alone — widowed, married and divorced—who are the largest new group in the population.

51   The only bright spot in the housing market this past year was the great

increase in sales of homes and condominiums to single women living alone. But since in fact it takes two incomes to buy housing today, banks and boards of condominiums and mortgage lending officers will increasingly be faced with requests for mortgages or leases by two, three or more persons unrelated by blood or marriage.

52   The common interests of all these kinds of families will create the basis for a new political alliance for the second stage that may not be a women's movement. Men may be — must be — at the cutting edge of the second stage. Women were reborn, in effect, merely by moving across into man's world. In the first stage, it almost seemed as if women and men were moving in opposite directions, reversing roles or exchanging one half-life for another. In the second stage, we will go beyond the either-or of "superwoman" or "total woman" and "house husband" or "urban cowboy" to a new wholeness: an integration, in our personal lives, of the masculine and feminine in each of us in all our infinite personal variety — not unisex but new human sex.

53   If we can move beyond the false polarities and single-issue battles, and appreciate the limits and true potential of women's power, we will be able to join with men — follow or lead — in the new human politics that must emerge beyond reaction. It will be a new, passionate volunteerism, an activism that comes out of living these new problems for which there may be no single answer. It must have the same kind of relevance to the vital interests in life of both men and women and meet the same needs for higher purpose and communality as did the women's movement.

54   Now, those whose roots are in the service of life must have the strength to ask, if no one else does, what should government be responsible for if not for the needs of people in life? And the strength to start from those real needs of life to take back government, for the people. The second stage may even now be evolving, out of or aside from what we have thought of as our battle.

55   I know that equality, the personhood we fought for, is truly necessary for women — and opens new life for men. But I hear now what I could not hear before — the fears and feelings of some who have fought against our movement. It is not just a conspiracy of reactionary forces, though such forces surely play upon and manipulate those fears.

56   There is no going back. The women's movement was necessary. But the liberation that began with the women's movement isn't finished. The equality we fought for isn't livable, isn't workable, isn't comfortable in the terms that structured our battle. The first stage, the women's movement, was fought within and against and defined by that old structure of unequal, polarized male and female sex roles. But to continue reacting against such structure is still to be defined and limited by its terms. What's needed now is to transcend those terms and transform the structure itself.

57   How do we surmount the reaction that threatens to destroy the very gains we thought we had already won in the first stage of the women's movement? How do we surmount our own reaction, which shadows our feminism and our femininity (we blush even to use that word now)? How do we transcend the

polarization between women and women and between women and men to achieve the new human wholeness that is the promise of feminism, and get on with solving the concrete, practical, everyday problems of living, working and loving as equal persons? This is the personal and political business of the second stage.

Reading Sources: "Feminism's Next Step"

Read the selection, surveying it to identify key terms and important concepts. Highlight these phrases and ideas, and then answer these questions.

1. What is Friedan's thesis? Where does she state it?
2. Friedan's introduction runs almost ten paragraphs. Why is it so long? What material does she present in it? Why does she feel the need to present this information before she states her thesis?
3. Friedan uses the terms *first stage* and *second stage* throughout her essay. What does she mean by these terms, and how do they help her structure her discussion?
4. Friedan spends much of her essay analyzing and discussing the first stage of the feminist movement. At what point does she turn her attention to the second stage? How does she signal this transition to her readers?
5. Where does Friedan begin her conclusion? What strategy does she use to end her essay? What points does she emphasize in her conclusion?

Reacting to Sources

Reread the selection carefully, making marginal notes to aid your comprehension and reinforce connections. Then further annotate the selection if you need to do so in order to answer any of these questions. (You may already have addressed some of the questions in your marginal notes.)

1. Rewrite paragraph 11, simplifying Friedan's analysis of the problems of the first stage.
2. Using a dictionary if necessary, supply brief marginal definitions of these words and phrases as they are used in this essay: *repudiate* (11), *polarization* (11), *transcend* (12), *denigrated* (12), *red herring* (26), *ideology* (33).
3. Write a journal entry defining the terms *sexual politics* and *feminist mystique*.
4. Do you agree with Friedan's comments in paragraph 4? Write a marginal comment in which you explain why or why not.
5. Write three marginal questions in response to the ideas expressed in paragraphs 33–35.
6. Give examples from the essay that support Friedan's general statement, "Above all, the second stage involves not a retreat to the family, but embracing the family in new terms of equality and diversity" (48).

7. In paragraphs 17–24 Friedan talks about the possibility of the Equal Rights Amendment's not passing. Write a journal entry in which you assess the accuracy of Friedan's warnings. Does the fact that some of her predictions did not come about after the amendment was rejected undermine her credibility?

8. Find a statement in Friedan's essay for which your own knowledge or experience provides contradictory evidence. Write a marginal note that presents your contradiction.

9. In paragraph 29 Friedan says, "After all, why do feminists seem to be fighting 'for abortion' against women who say they are fighting for 'the right to life'? How can we fight a real battle in such terms? Who is really for abortion?" Explore these ideas further in a journal entry.

11. When *The Feminine Mystique* first appeared, some feminists criticized Friedan for assuming that women should take part in an exploitative, male-dominated society. They also felt that Friedan addressed a white-middle-class audience and ignored the plight of minority women. Do these criticisms apply to "Feminism's Next Step"? How do they affect the usefulness of this source?

Working with Sources

1. Write a fifty-word summary of paragraph 25.
2. Write a critique of the ideas in paragraphs 36 to 38.
3. In a journal entry, compare the sentiments expressed in paragraph 50 of this essay with the following statement from Betty Friedan's early work *The Feminine Mystique* (1963): "Each suburban wife struggled with it alone. As she made the beds, shopped for groceries, matched slipcover material, ate peanut butter sandwiches with her children, chauffeured Cub Scouts and Brownies, lay beside her husband at night—she was afraid to ask even to herself the silent question—'Is this all?' "
4. Paraphrase paragraphs 43 to 47.
5. Write a synthesis that blends the ideas in paragraphs 52–54 of this essay with the ideas in paragraph 10 of Marvin Trachtenberg's "America and the Statue of Liberty" (pp. 99–103).

Writing with Sources: Using A Single Source

Integrating information from "Feminism's Next Step" with your own ideas, write an essay on one of these topics. Be sure to acknowledge all ideas that are not your own.

1. Write an essay in which you discuss why Friedan says that feminists have to "break through" the feminist mystique that characterized the first stage of their movement.

2. Write an essay in which you agree or disagree with Friedan's statement, "The women's movement is over."
3. Using the two ideologies (woman-as-individual and woman-serving-her-family) that Friedan discusses in paragraph 36, write an essay in which you examine the familial attitudes of two members of your family. (You may apply these categories to men as well as women.)

Writing with Sources: Using Multiple Sources

Integrating information from sources in this chapter with your own ideas, write an essay on one of the topics below. Be sure to acknowledge ideas that are not your own.

1. Using two of this chapter's selections as source material, write an essay in which you attempt to answer the question Langston Hughes asks in the first line of this short poem.

   Dream Deferred

   What happens to a dream deferred?

   Does it dry up
   like a raisin in the sun?
   Or fester like a sore —
   And then run?
   Does it stink like rotten meat?
   Or crust and sugar over —
   like a syrupy sweet?

   Maybe it just sags
   like a heavy load.

   Or does it explode?

2. Using as many of this chapter's sources as necessary, write an essay in which you formulate a definition of the American dream. You may use your own experiences to supplement your sources' information.
3. The Statue of Liberty is a symbol for many Americans. Using Trachtenberg's essay and one or two additional sources from this chapter, write an essay in which you discuss the different kinds of objects and ideas that symbolize America.
4. Is the American dream essentially the same for everyone, or does each generation (or each sex, or each racial or ethnic group) strive for something different? Write an essay in which you discuss the similarities and differences in the views of the American dream held by Jefferson, King, Puzo, and Friedan.
5. Write a paper in which you discuss your family's reasons for coming to America. Use the essays in this section, as well as interviews with family members, to develop a theory explaining what about America caused your family to immigrate.

5

The Dawning of the Atomic Age

On the morning of August 6, 1945, an atomic bomb with a force of 20,000 tons of TNT was dropped on Hiroshima, followed three days later by a second bomb on Nagasaki. The result was widespread death and destruction and the immediate and unconditional surrender of Japan. When the radiation levels subsided and the first Americans went in to survey the damage, even battle-hardened veterans were shocked by the devastation they saw. The decision to drop the bomb had engendered much debate within the limited circle of scientists and government officials who knew of its existence. Some argued that the bomb should be dropped on an unpopulated area as a demonstration of American power. Others argued that because the bomb could end the war, it might save hundreds of thousands of lives. One thing clear to those involved in this project, however, was that after the bomb, the world would never be the same again.

In "First Atomic Bomb Dropped on Japan," which appeared on the front page of the *New York Times* on August 7, 1945, reporter Sidney Shalett tells the American public what had taken place. Next, in "That Day at Hiroshima" Alexander H. Leighton gives a firsthand description of the devastation that he saw when he investigated the bomb site four months after the bomb was dropped. James West Davidson and Mark Hamilton Lytle in "The Decision to Drop the Bomb" construct an interpretive model to help explain the complex events that contributed to the decision to drop the atomic bomb. In "The U.S. Was Right"/"The U.S. Was Wrong," John Connor and Gar Alperovitz debate the decision to drop the bomb. Finally, Albert Einstein in "Atomic War or Peace" and Norman Cousins in "Modern Man Is Obsolete" consider the moral and ethical questions raised by the bombing and the implications of this event for the future.

134

First Atomic Bomb Dropped on Japan

Sidney Shalett

On Tuesday, August 7, 1945, households all over America learned that the United States had dropped the atomic bomb on the Japanese city of Hiroshima. Germany had already surrendered, and the war with Japan was in the forefront of Americans' minds. The front page of the *New York Times,* where this article appeared, was jammed with other stories about the development of atomic weapons and about the progress of the war in the Far East. In addition to several dramatic stories about Hiroshima, the front page reported on nuclear tests held three weeks earlier in New Mexico; a successful American air strike over Tarumisu in southern Kyushu (the southernmost of Japan's three major islands); the race between the United States and Germany for the secrets of the atomic bomb; and the "hidden cities" (Oak Ridge, Tennessee; Los Alamos, New Mexico; and Richland Village, Washington) where the atomic bomb project took shape.

New Age Ushered

1 The White House and War Department announced today that an atomic bomb, possessing more power than 20,000 tons of TNT, a destructive force equal to the load of 2,000 B-29's and more than 2,000 times the blast power of what previously was the world's most devastating bomb, had been dropped on Japan.

2   The announcement, first given to the world in utmost solemnity by President Truman, made it plain that one of the scientific landmarks of the century had been passed, and that the "age of atomic energy," which can be a tremendous force for the advancement of civilization as well as for destruction, was at hand.

3   At 10:45 o'clock, this morning, a statement by the President was issued at the White House that sixteen hours earlier — about the time that citizens on the Eastern seaboard were sitting down to their Sunday suppers — an American plane had dropped the single atomic bomb on the Japanese city of Hiroshima, an important army center.

Japanese Solemnly Warned

4 What happened at Hiroshima is not yet known. The War Department said it "as yet was unable to make an accurate report" because "an impenetrable cloud of dust and smoke" masked the target area from reconnaissance planes. The Secretary of War will release the story "as soon as accurate details of the results of the bombing become available."

5   But in a statement vividly describing the results of the first test of the atomic bomb in New Mexico, the War Department told how an immense steel tower had been "vaporized" by the tremendous explosion, how a 40,000-foot cloud rushed into the sky, and two observers were knocked down at a point 10,000 yards away. And President Truman solemnly warned:

6   "It was to spare the Japanese people from utter destruction that the ultimatum of July 26 was issued at Potsdam. Their leaders promptly rejected that ultimatum. If they do not now accept our terms, they may expect a rain of ruin from the air the like of which has never been seen on this earth."

Most Closely Guarded Secret

7 The President referred to the joint statement issued by the heads of the American, British and Chinese Governments, in which terms of surrender were outlined to the Japanese and warning given that rejection would mean complete destruction of Japan's power to make war.

8   [The atomic bomb weighs about 400 pounds and is capable of utterly destroying a town, a representative of the British Ministry of Aircraft production said in London, the United Press reported.]

9   What is this terrible new weapon, which the War Department also calls the "Cosmic Bomb"? It is the harnessing of the energy of the atom, which is the basic power of the universe. As President Truman said, "The force from which the sun draws its power has been loosed against those who brought war to the Far East."

10   "Atomic fission" — in other words, the scientists' long-held dream of splitting the atom — is the secret of the atomic bomb. Uranium, a rare, heavy metallic element, which is radioactive and akin to radium, is the source essential to its production. Secretary of War Henry L. Stimson, in a statement closely following that of the President, promised that "steps have been taken, and continue to be taken, to assure us of adequate supplies of this mineral."

11   The imagination-sweeping experiment in harnessing the power of the atom has been the most closely guarded secret of the war. America to date has spent nearly $2,000,000,000 in advancing its research. Since 1939, American, British and Canadian scientists have worked on it. The experiments have been conducted in the United States, both for reasons of achieving concentrated efficiency and for security; the consequences of having the material fall into the hands of the enemy, in case Great Britain should have been successfully invaded, were too awful for the Allies to risk.

12   All along, it has been a race with the enemy. Ironically enough, Germany started the experiments, but we finished them. Germany made the mistake of expelling, because she was a "non-Aryan," a woman scientist who held one of the keys to the mystery, and she made her knowledge available to those who brought it to the United States. Germany never quite mastered the riddle, and the United States, Secretary Stimson declared, is "convinced that Japan will not be in a position to use an atomic bomb in this war."

A Sobering Awareness of Power

13 Not the slightest spirit of braggadocio is discernable either in the wording of the official announcements or in the mien of the officials who gave out the

news. There was an element of elation in the realization that we had perfected this devastating weapon for employment against an enemy who started the war and has told us she would rather be destroyed than surrender, but it was grim elation. There was sobering awareness of the tremendous responsibility involved.

14   Secretary Stimson said that this new weapon "should prove a tremendous aid in the shortening of the war against Japan," and there were other responsible officials who privately thought that this was an extreme understatement, and that Japan might find herself unable to stay in the war under the coming rain of atom bombs.

15   It was obvious that officials at the highest levels made the important decision to release news of the atomic bomb because of the psychological effect it may have in forcing Japan to surrender. However, there are some officials who feel privately it might have been well to keep this completely secret. Their opinion can be summed up in the comment by one spokesman: "Why bother with psychological warfare against an enemy that already is beaten and hasn't sense enough to quit and save herself from utter doom?"

16   The first news came from President Truman's office. Newsmen were summoned and the historic statement from the Chief Executive, who still is on the high seas, was given to them.

17   "That bomb," Mr. Truman said, "had more power than 20,000 tons of TNT. It had more than 2,000 times the blast power of the British 'Grand Slam,' which is the largest bomb (22,000 pounds) ever yet used in the history of warfare."

Explosive Charge Is Small

18 No details were given on the plane that carried the bomb. Nor was it stated whether the bomb was large or small. The President, however, said the explosive charge was "exceedingly small." It is known that tremendous force is packed into tiny quantities of the element that constituted these bombs. Scientists, looking to the peacetime uses of atomic power, envisage submarines, ocean liners and planes traveling around the world on a few pounds of the element. Yet, for various reasons, the bomb used against Japan could have been extremely large.

19   Hiroshima, first city on earth to be the target of the "Cosmic Bomb," is a city of 318,000, which is — or was — a major quartermaster depot and port of embarkation for the Japanese. In addition to large military supply depots, it manufactured ordnance, mainly large guns and tanks, and machine tools and aircraft-ordnance parts.

20   President Truman grimly told the Japanese that "the end is not yet."

21   "In their present form these bombs are now in production," he said, "and even more powerful forms are in development."

22   He sketched the story of how the late President Roosevelt and Prime Minister Churchill agreed that it was wise to concentrate research in America, and how great secret cities sprang up in this country where at one time, 125,000

men and women labored to harness the atom. Even today more than 65,000 workers are employed.

23   "What has been done," he said, "is the greatest achievement of organized science in history.

24   "We are now prepared to obliterate more rapidly and completely every productive enterprise the Japanese have above ground in any city. We shall destroy their docks, their factories and their communications. Let there be no mistake; we shall completely destroy Japan's power to make war."

25   The President emphasized that the atomic discoveries were so important, both for the war and for the peace, that he would recommend to Congress that it consider promptly establishing "an appropriate commission to control the production and use of atomic power within the United States."

26   "I shall give further consideration and make further recommendations to the Congress as to how atomic power can become a powerful and forceful influence toward the maintenance of world peace," he said.

27   Secretary Stimson called the atomic bomb "the culmination of years of herculean effort on the part of science and industry, working in cooperation with the military authorities." He promised that "improvements will be forth-coming shortly which will increase by several fold the present effectiveness."

28   "But more important for the long-range implications of this new weapon," he said, "is the possibility that another scale of magnitude will be developed after considerable research and development. The scientists are confident that over a period of many years atomic bombs may well be developed which will be very much more powerful than these atomic bombs now at hand."

Investigation Started in 1939

29 It was late in 1939 that President Roosevelt appointed a commission to investi-gate use of atomic energy for military purposes. Until then only small-scale research with Navy funds had taken place. The program went into high gear.

30   By the end of 1941 the project was put under direction of a group of eminent American scientists in the Office of Scientific Research and Develop-ment, under Dr. Vannevar Bush, who reported directly to Mr. Roosevelt. The President who appointed a General Policy Group, consisting of former Vice President Henry A. Wallace, Secretary Stimson, Gen. George C. Marshall, Dr. James B. Conant, president of Harvard, and Dr. Bush. In June, 1942, this group recommended vast expansion of the work and transfer of the major part of the program to the War Department.

31   Maj. Gen. Leslie R. Groves, a native of Albany, N.Y., and a 48-year-old graduate of the 1918 class at West Point, was appointed by Mr. Stimson to take complete executive charge of the program. General Groves, an engineer, holding the permanent Army rank of lieutenant colonel, received the highest praise from the War Department for the way he "fitted together the multifarious pieces of the vast country-wide jigsaw," and, at the same time, organized the virtually air-tight security system that kept the project a secret.

32   A military policy committee also was appointed, consisting of Dr. Bush, chairman; Dr. Conant, Lieut. Gen. Wilhelm D. Styer and Rear Admiral William R. Purnell.

33   In December, 1942, the decision was made to proceed with construction of large-scale plants. Two are situated at the Clinton Engineer Works in Tennessee and a third at the Hanford Engineer Works in the State of Washington.

34   These plants were amazing phenonema in themselves. They grew into large, self-sustaining cities, employing thousands upon thousands of workers. Yet, so close was the secrecy that not only were the citizens of the area kept in darkness about the nature of the project, but the workers themselves had only the sketchiest ideas — if any — as to what they were doing. This was accomplished, Mr. Stimson said, by "compartmentalizing" the work so "that no one has been given more information than was absolutely necessary to his particular job."

35   The Tennessee reservation consists of 59,000 acres, eighteen miles west of Knoxville; it is known as Oak Ridge and has become a modern small city of 78,000, fifth largest in Tennessee.

36   In the State of Washington the Government has 430,000 acres in an isolated area, fifteen miles northwest of Pasco. The settlement there, which now has a population of 17,000, consisting of plant operators and their immediate families, is known as Richland.

37   A special laboratory also has been set up near Santa Fe, N.M., under direction of Dr. J. Robert Oppenheimer of the University of California. Dr. Oppenheimer also supervised the first test of the atomic bomb on July 16, 1945. This took place in a remote section of the New Mexico desert land, with a group of eminent scientists gathered, frankly fearful to witness the results of the invention, which might turn out to be either the salvation or the Frankenstein's monster of the world.

38   Mr. Stimson also gave full credit to the many industrial corporations and educational institutions which worked with the War Department in bringing this titanic undertaking to fruition.

39   In August, 1943, a combined policy committee was appointed, consisting of Secretary Stimson, Drs. Bush and Conant for the United States; the late Field Marshal Sir John Dill (now replaced by Field Marshal Sir Henry Maitland Wilson) and Col. J. J. Llewellin (since replaced by Sir Ronald Campbell), for the United Kingdom, and C. D. Howe for Canada.

40   "Atomic fission holds great promise for sweeping developments by which our civilization may be enriched when peace comes, but the overriding necessities of war have precluded the full exploration of peacetime applications of this new knowledge," Mr. Stimson said. "However, it appears inevitable that many useful contributions to the well-being of mankind will ultimately flow from these discoveries when the world situation makes it possible for science and industry to concentrate on these aspects."

41   Although warning that many economic factors will have to be considered "before we can say to what extent atomic energy will supplement coal, oil and

water as fundamental sources of power," Mr. Stimson acknowledged that "we are at the threshold of a new industrial art which will take many years and much expenditure of money to develop."

42   The Secretary of War disclosed that he had appointed an interim committee to study post-war control and development of atomic energy. Mr. Stimson is serving as chairman, and other members include James F. Byrnes, Secretary of State; Ralph A. Bard, former Under-Secretary of the Navy; William L. Clayton, Assistant Secretary of State; Dr. Bush, Dr. Conant, Dr. Carl T. Compton, chief of the Office of Field Service in OSRD and president of Massachusetts Institute of Technology, and George L. Harrison, special consultant to the Secretary of War and president of the New York Life Insurance Company. Mr. Harrison is alternate chairman of the committee.

43   The committee also has the assistance of an advisory group of some of the country's leading physicists, including Dr. Oppenheimer, Dr. E. O. Lawrence, Dr. A. H. Compton and Dr. Enrico Fermi.

44   The War Department gave this supplementary background on the development of the atomic bomb:

45   "The series of discoveries which led to development of the atomic bomb started at the turn of the century when radioactivity became known to science. Prior to 1939 the scientific work in this field was world-wide, but more particularly so in the United States, the United Kingdom, Germany, France, Italy and Denmark. One of Denmark's great scientists, Dr. Neils Bohr, a Nobel Prize winner, was whisked from the grasp of the Nazis in his occupied homeland and later assisted in developing the atomic bomb.

46   "It is known that Germany worked desperately to solve the problem of controlling atomic energy."

Reading Sources: "First Atomic Bomb Dropped on Japan"

Read this selection, surveying it to identify key terms and important concepts. Highlight these phrases and ideas, and then answer these questions.

1. What visual cues does this newspaper article use to highlight important points?
2. What key words are repeated over and over again in this article? Explain why each of these words is central to the article.
3. As a newspaper reporter, Shalett attempts to maintain objectivity about the government's decision to drop the bomb. What techniques does he use to keep his reporting objective? Does he reveal his attitude toward the subject anywhere? Explain.
4. Paragraph 9 begins with the sentence, "What is this terrible new weapon, which the War Department also calls the 'Cosmic Bomb'?" Identify the boundaries of the paragraph cluster this sentence introduces.
5. What technique does Shalett use to link the sentences in paragraph 12? How does he link the ideas in paragraph 32 with those in paragraph 33?

Reacting to Sources

Reread the selection carefully, making marginal notes to aid your comprehension and reinforce connections. Then further annotate the article if you need to do so in order to answer any of these questions. (You may already have addressed some of the questions in your marginal notes.)

1. Using a dictionary if necessary, supply brief marginal definitions for these words as they are used in the article: *harnessing* (9), *loosed* (9), *expelling* (12), *braggadocio* (13), *mien* (13), *quartermaster* (19), *ordnance* (19), *herculean* (27), *multifarious* (31), *sketchiest* (34), *compartmentalizing* (34), *precluded* (40).
2. The article's first paragraph consists of just one densely worded sentence. In a marginal note, comment on the appropriateness and effectiveness of this strategy.
3. In paragraph 3 Shalett mentions that at about the time the bomb was dropped, "citizens of the Eastern seaboard were sitting down to their Sunday suppers." What is his purpose in making such an observation?
4. List the kinds of information that the article states are "not yet known." How might knowledge of such information influence the newspaper's readers to take a stand for or against the government's decision to drop the bomb? Explore this idea in a journal entry.
5. Write a marginal comment expressing your response to Truman's warning to the Japanese in paragraph 6.
6. Write a marginal note in response to the ideas in paragraph 15. Make sure your note makes clear the conflict Shalett identifies between the two groups of officials.
7. What purpose does paragraph 16 serve in this essay?
8. Outline the paragraph cluster extending from paragraph 29 through paragraph 39.
9. Do you agree or disagree with the ideas expressed in paragraph 13? Using examples from the article to support your conclusion, write a journal entry explaining why you agree or disagree.
10. In paragraph 37, describing the first test of the atomic bomb, Shalett says scientists were "fearful," not sure whether the bomb would "turn out to be the salvation or the Frankenstein's monster of the world." Explain this comment in a marginal note.
11. Find a statement in the article which you believe is contradicted by your own knowledge about the aftermath of what happened at Hiroshima. Write a journal entry in which you present this contradiction.
12. Contrast the objective tone of the article itself with the subjective comments made by Truman and Stimson. What is the effect of this contrast?
13. This article, from a respected American newspaper, appeared the day after the bombing. What limitations do you believe were placed on this report by the time and place of its appearance? Explain your reasoning in a journal entry.

Working with Sources

1. Write a fifty-word summary of paragraphs 9–12.
2. Write a critique of the ideas expressed by Secretary of War Stimson in paragraph 40.
3. Use these quotations from the article in a journal entry in which you express your reaction to them.

   > Secretary of War Stimson's statement in paragraph 14 that the bomb "should prove a tremendous aid in the shortening of the war against Japan."

   > President Truman's comment in paragraph 26 that atomic power "can become a powerful and forceful influence toward the maintenance of world peace."

   Be sure to integrate the quotations smoothly into your writing.
4. Paraphrase paragraph 11.
5. Write a one-paragraph synthesis that blends ideas in paragraphs 27 and 28 of this article and paragraph 10 of "Modern Man is Obsolete" (pp. 175–178).

Writing with Sources: Using a Single Source

Integrating information from this selection with your own ideas, write an essay on one of these topics. Be sure to acknowledge all ideas that are not your own.

1. Write an essay in which you argue for or against Truman's statement (quoted in paragraph 23) that "what has been done is the greatest achievement of organized science in history."
2. Consider how the average Japanese citizen might have reacted to this news article. Taking the point of view of such a citizen, write an essay in which you use the information in the article to support the thesis "What happened at Hiroshima must never happen again."
3. Write an essay in which you explore the accuracy of the article's speculations about the future of atomic energy. For example, has atomic energy provided "fundamental sources of power" (41)?

That Day at Hiroshima

Alexander H. Leighton

Born in 1908, Alexander Leighton received his B.A. from Princeton, his M.A. from Cambridge University, and his M.D. from Johns Hopkins University. An Emeritus Professor of Social Psychiatry at the Harvard University School of Public Health and Professor of Psychiatry at Dalhousie University in Halifax, Nova Scotia, Leighton has had a distinguished career as a professor and researcher. His work has included field work among Navajos and Eskimos and advisory and consulting positions with organizations like the U.S. Department of the Interior, the Peace Corps, and the World Health Organization. In addition, he has been the recipient of numerous honorary degrees and awards in the fields of mental health, human relations, and public health. In December of 1945, as research leader of the U.S. Strategic Bombing Survey's Morale Division team, Leighton entered the city of Hiroshima to investigate the effects of the atomic bomb and to prepare a report on his team's findings. In a 1946 issue of the *Atlantic Monthly,* he reported his personal impressions of what he saw and his reactions to the survivors' stories.

1

1 We approached Hiroshima a little after daybreak on a winter day, driving in a jeep below a leaden sky and in the face of a cold, wet wind. On either side of the road, black flat fields were turning green under winter wheat. Here and there peasants worked, swinging spades or grubbing in mud and water with blue hands. Some in black split-toed shoes left tracks like cloven hoofs. To the north, looming close over the level land, mountains thrust heavy summits of pine darkly against the overcast. To the south and far away, the bay lay in dull brightness under fitful rain.

2   "Hiroshima," said the driver, a GI from a Kansas farm, who had been through the city many times, "don't look no different from any other bombed town. You soon get used to it. You'll see little old mud walls right in the middle of town that wasn't knocked down. They been exaggerating about that bomb."

3   Within a few miles the fields along the road were replaced by houses and shops that looked worn and dull yet intact. On the road itself people straggled to work, some on bicycles, most of them on foot — tattered and bandy-legged old men, girls with red cheeks and bright eyes, ancient women under towering bundles, middle-aged men looking stiff in Western business suits. In one place there were several Koreans together, the women easily distinguished from the Japanese by their white blouses and the full skirts that swung as they strode. At a bus stop a crowd stood waiting in a line long enough to fill a train. Half a mile farther on we passed the bus, small, battered, and gray, standing half obliterated by the cloud of smoke that came from the charcoal burner at the back while the driver stood working at its machinery.

4   Children of all ages waved, laughed, and shouted at us as had the children in other parts of Japan.

5   "Haro-goodabye! Haro-goodabye!"

6   "Jeepu! Jeeeepu!"

7   Like the children of Hamelin to the piper, they came rushing, at the sound of our approach, from doorways and alleyways and from behind houses, to line up by the road and cheer. One little fellow of about six threw himself into the air, his little body twisting and feet kicking in a fit of glee.

8   The adults gazed at us with solemn eyes or looked straight ahead. They were more subdued than those I had seen elsewhere in Japan. The children seemed different, possessed by some common animation denied their elders — an animation which impelled them toward the occupation forces, toward the strong and the new.

9   Presently a two-story trade school appeared, with boards instead of window glass, and then a factory in the same condition. Soon there were shops and houses all along the way with windows missing. A house came into view with its roof pressed down, tiles scattered, and walls bulging outward. A shop with no front, like an open mouth, showed its contents, public and private, clear to the rear window.

10   The road turned to the Ota River, where the tide was running out and boats lay heaved over on the beach. A bridge ended suddenly like a headless neck. Now every house and shop was damaged and lay with only one end or a corner standing.

11   Then all the buildings ceased and we came as if from a forest out on a plain, as if from tumult into silence. Imagine a city dump with its smells of wet ashes, mold, and things rotting, but one that runs from your feet almost to the limits of vision. As is often the case with level and desolate places on the earth, the sky seemed close above it. The predominant colors were red and yellow, crumbles of stone, bricks, red earth, and rust. Low walls made rectangles that marked where houses had stood, like sites of prehistoric villages. Here and there in the middle distance, a few large buildings stood about, buttes in the rubble of the plain.

12   "You see them?" said the driver, as if it were a triumph for his side. "The bomb didn't knock them down."

13   Running like ruler lines through the waste were black roads surprisingly dotted with people, some on foot and some in carts of all sizes drawn by man, woman, horse, or cow. Clothing was old and tattered and of every combination from full European to full Japanese. People looked as if they had grabbed what they could from a rummage sale.

14   Occasionally, blending like protective coloration with the rubble were shacks built out of fragments of boards and iron. Around them were vegetable gardens, for the most part full of *daikon,* Japanese radish. A few more pretentious sheds were going up, shining bright yellow with new boards.

15   We slowed down to go around a piece of cornice that lay partly across the road like a glacial boulder, and from somewhere in a band of children who cheered and called to us came the gift of a tangerine that landed on the floor of the jeep. Wondering at them, I picked it up and put it in my pocket.

16   When crossing a bridge, we could see down through the swiftly running water to the stones and shells on the bottom. This clearness gave a feeling of odd contrast to the disorder of the land. We passed a number of trees burned black but still holding up some leafless branches as if in perpetual winter.

17   The drive ended at a large building that was still standing, a former bank, now a police headquarters, where I had an appointment with the chief to arrange for office space and guides. The driver said, as he got out, "This is it."

2

18   One hears it said that, after all, Japanese cities were really a collection of tinderboxes, while American urban centers are made of stronger stuff. In Hiroshima there were many buildings of types common in the United States and some, prepared against earthquakes, far stronger. The engineers of the U.S. Strategic Bombing Survey concluded from their examination that "the overwhelming bulk of buildings in American cities would not stand up against an atomic bomb bursting at a mile or a mile and a half from them." To this must be added the realization that the bomb dropped at Hiroshima will be considered primitive by future standards.

19   The bank building which housed the police headquarters was a well-made structure of stone, three stories high. Through an imposing entrance my interpreter and I went past tall and solid metal doors that were bent inward like cardboard and no longer usable. The lobby was large and high, but dark because it had no window glass and the openings were boarded to keep out the wind. Through poor light there loomed the white face of a clock up on one wall, its hands pointing to 8.10 — the time it had stopped on August 6.

20   In the years when that clock had been going, Hiroshima had been a city, at first unknown to Europe and America, then a source of immigrants to the United States, and finally an enemy port. It lay on a delta between the seven mouths of the Ota and was traversed by canals and an ancient highway that connected Kyoto in the east with Shimonoseki in the west. Close around the city stood mountains covered with red pine, while before it stretched the bay, indented with headlands and spread with islands, in places narrow and steep like a fjord. In shallows near the shore, rows of poles stood as if in a bean patch, set in the sea to anchor oysters and to catch edible seaweed passing in the tide. In deeper water, fishing boats with hawkish prows and planked with red pine were tending nets. A few fishermen used cormorants to make their catch.

21   Hiroshima had expanses of park, residences, gardens, orange and persimmon trees. Since there had been much traveling back and forth by relatives of immigrants to California, the influence of the United States was marked. On main streets there were movies and restaurants with facades that would have fitted into shopping districts of Bakersfield or San Diego.

22   But Hiroshima was also ancient. Its feudal castle raised a five-story keep that could be seen a long distance over the level land of the delta. There were three large temples and many smaller ones and the tombs of the Asano family

and of the wife and son of the leader of the Forty-seven Ronin, Oishi-Yoshio. There were also Christian churches, whose bells mingled with the temple gongs and the honking of auto horns and the rattling of trolleys.

23   The people of the city had earned their living by buying and selling farm produce and fish, by making mountain pines into boats for the fishing fleet of the Inland Sea, by meat packing, rubber processing, and oil refining, by making textiles from the cocoons of wild silkworms, by brewing rice and grape wine, by manufacturing paper umbrellas, needles, *tabi* socks, small arms, metal castings, and by working in utilities and services such as electricity, transportation, schools, and hospitals.

24   During the war there was an increase of industrialization, and plants grew up, chiefly in the outskirts.

25   There was a famous gay district with little streets along which a person walking in the night could hear laughter, the twang of the *shamisen,* and geishas singing.

26   The university had been an active cultural center but also stressed athletics, particularly swimming. There were sometimes mass aquatic exercises when hundreds of students would swim for miles, strung out in the bay in a long line with boats attending.

27   Although not a fortified town, Hiroshima was a major military command station, supply depot, and staging area because of its protected position and because of Ujina Harbor with access to the Pacific, the Sea of Japan, and the East China Sea. More than a third of the city's land was taken up with military installations, and from the harbor troopships left for Korea, Manchuria, China, and the southern regions. However, toward the end of hostilities, most of the shipping had ceased because of sinkings in the Inland Sea.

28   The population of Hiroshima was given as well over 300,000 before the war, but this was reduced by evacuation, before the atomic bomb fell, probably to about 245,000. It is still not certain how many the bomb killed, but the best estimate is from 70,000 to 80,000.

3

29   About seven o'clock on the morning of August 6 there was an air-raid warning and three planes were reported in the vicinity. No one was much disturbed. For a long time B-29's flying over in small numbers had been a common sight. At some future date, Hiroshima might suffer an incendiary raid from masses of planes such as had devastated other Japanese cities. With this possibility in mind there had been evacuations, and firebreaks were being prepared. But on this particular morning there could be no disaster from just three planes.

30   By 7.30 the "all clear." had sounded and people were thinking again of the day's plans, looking forward to their affairs and engagements of the morning and afternoon. The castle keep stood in the sun. Children bathed in the river. Farmers labored in the fields and fishermen on the water. City stores and factories got under way with their businesses.

31   In the heart of the city near the buildings of the Prefectural Government

and at the intersection of the business streets, everybody had stopped and stood in a crowd gazing up at three parachutes floating down through the blue air.

32   The bomb exploded several hundred feet above their heads.

33   The people for miles around Hiroshima, in the fields, in the mountains, and on the bay, saw a light that was brilliant even in the sun, and felt heat. A countrywoman was going out to her farm when suddenly, "I saw a light reflected on the mountain and then a streak just like lightning came."

34   A town official was crossing a bridge on his bicycle about ten miles from the heart of the city when he felt the right side of his face seared, and thinking that he had sunstroke, he jumped to the ground.

35   A woman who was washing dishes noticed that she felt "very warm on the side of my face next to the wall. I looked out the window toward the city and saw something like a sun in bright color."

36   At a slower pace, after the flash, came the sound of the explosion, which some people have no recollection of hearing, while others described it as an earth-shaking roar, like thunder or a big wind. A black smoky mass, lit up with color, ascended into the sky and impressed beholders with its beauty. Red, gold, blue, orange, and many other shades mingled with the black.

37   Nearer to the city and at its edges, the explosion made a more direct and individual impact on people. Almost everyone thought that an ordinary bomb had landed very close to him, and only later realized the extent of the damage.

38   A man who was oiling the machinery in a factory saw the lights go out and thought that something must be wrong with the electricity. "But when the roof started crumbling down, I was in a daze, wondering what was happening. Then I noticed my hands and feet were bleeding. I don't know how I hurt myself."

39   Another, who was putting points on needles, was knocked unconscious, and when he came to, found "all my surroundings burned to the ground and flames raging here and there. I ran home for my family without knowing I was burned around my head. When I arrived home, our house was devastated and destroyed by flames. I ran to the neighbors and inquired about my family and learned that they had all been taken to safety across the river."

40   An invalid who was drinking tea said, "The tin roof sidings came swirling into my room and everything was black. Rubble and glass and everything you can think of was blasted into my house."

41   Said a woman, "I was in the back of the house doing the washing. All of a sudden, the bomb exploded. My clothes were burned off and I received burns on my legs, arms, and back. The skin was just hanging loose. The first thing I did was run in the air-raid shelter and lie there exhausted. Then I thought of my baby in the house and ran back to it. The whole house was knocked down and was burning. My mother and father came crawling out of the debris, their faces and arms just black. I heard the baby crying, and crawled in and dug it out from under the burning embers. It was pretty badly burned. My mother carried it to the shelter."

42   In the heart of the city death prevailed and few were left to tell us about it. That part of the picture has to be reconstructed, as in archeology, from the remains.

43   The crowd that stood gazing upward at the parachutes went down withered and black, like a burned-out patch of weeds. Flames shot out of the castle keep. Trolleys bulging with passengers stopped, and all died at once, leaving burned figures still standing supporting each other and fingers fused to the straps. The military at their barracks and officers were wiped out. So too were factories full of workers, including students from schools, volunteers from neighboring towns working on the firebreaks, children scavenging for wood, the Mayor's staff, and the units for air-raid precaution, fire, welfare, and relief. The larger war industries, since they were on the fringe of the city, were for the most part not seriously damaged. Most of the personnel in the Prefectural Government offices were killed, though the Governor himself happened to be in Tokyo. In hospitals and clinics, patients, doctors, and nurses all died together, as did the priests and pastors of the temples and churches. Of 1780 nurses, 1654 were killed, and 90 per cent of the doctors in Hiroshima were casualties.

44   People who were in buildings that sheltered them from the instantaneous effects that accompanied the flash were moments later decapitated or cut to ribbons by flying glass. Others were crushed as walls and floors gave way even in buildings that maintained their outer shells erect. In the thousands of houses that fell, people were pinned below the wreckage, not killed in many cases, but held there till the fire that swept the city caught up with them and put an end to their screams.

45   A police chief said that he was in his back yard when the bomb went off. He was knocked down and a concrete wall fell over him, but he was able to dig himself out and go at once toward the police station in the bank. "When I arrived at the office, I found ten policemen, some severely wounded. These were evacuated to a place of safety where they could get aid. We tried to clean up the glass from the windows, but fire was spreading and a hot southerly wind was blowing. We used a hose with water from a hydrant and also formed a bucket brigade. At noon the water in the hydrants gave out, but in this building we were lucky because we could pump water from a well. We carried buckets up from the basement to the roof and threw water down over the building. People on the road were fainting from the heat and we threw water on them too and carried them into the one room in the building that had not been affected by the bomb. We applied oil and ointment to those who had burns.

46   "About 1.00 P.M. we began to apply first aid to the people outside, since the fire seemed under control as far as this building was concerned. A doctor came to help. He himself was wounded in one leg. By night this place was covered by a mass of people. One doctor applied all the first aid."

47   A doctor who was at a military hospital outside Hiroshima said that about an hour after the bomb went off, "many, many people came rushing to my clinic. They were rushing in all directions of the compass from the city. Many were stretcher cases. Some had their hair burned off, were injured in the back, had broken legs, arms, and thighs. The majority of the cases were those injured from glass; many had glass imbedded in the body. Next to the glass injuries, the most frequent were those who had their faces and hands burned, and also

the chest and back. Most of the people arrived barefooted; many had their clothes burned off. Women were wearing men's clothing and men were wearing women's. They had put on anything they could pick up along the way.

48   "On the first day about 250 came, who were so injured they had to stay in the hospital, and we also attended about 500 others. Of all of these about 100 died."

49   A talkative man in a newspaper office said that the most severely burned people looked like red shrimps. Some had "skin which still burned sagging from the face and body with a reddish-white skin underneath showing."

50   A reporter who was outside the city at the time of the explosion, but came in immediately afterward, noticed among the dead a mother with a baby held tightly in her arms. He saw several women running around nude, red from burns, and without hair. Many people climbed into water tanks kept for putting out fires and there died. "The most pathetic cases were the small children looking for their parents. There was one child of about eleven with a four-year-old on his back, looking, looking for his mother in vain."

51   Shortly after the bomb fell, there was a high wind, or "fire storm" engendered by the heat, that tore up trees and, whirling over the river, made water-spouts. In some areas rain fell.

52   The severely burned woman who had been washing when the bomb fell said that she went down to the river, where "there were many people just dripping from their burns. Many of them were so badly burned that you could see the meat. By this time it was raining pretty badly. I could not walk or lie down or do anything. Water poured into the shelter and I received water blisters as well as blisters from the burns. It rained a lot right after the bomb."

53   Although the fire burned for days, the major destruction did not take very long. A fisherman out on the bay said, "I saw suddenly a flash of light. I thought something burned my face. I hid in the boat face down. When I looked up, later, Hiroshima was completely burned."

4

54 Hiroshima, of course, never had been prepared for a disaster of the magnitude which overtook it, but in addition the organized sources of aid that did exist were decimated along with everything else. As a result, rescue had to come from surrounding areas, and soon trucks and trains were picking up the wounded, while hospitals, schools, temples, assembly halls, and tents were preparing to receive them. However, the suburbs and surrounding areas were overwhelmed by the rush of immediate survivors out of the bombed region and so, for about a day, help did not penetrate far into the city. This, together with the fact that survivors who were physically uninjured were stunned and bewildered, resulted in great numbers of the wounded dying from lack of aid.

55   The vice-mayor of a neighboring town that began receiving the wounded about 11.30 in the morning said, "Everybody looked alike. The eyes appeared to be a mass of melted flesh. The lips were split up and also looked like a mass of molten flesh. Only the nose appeared the same as before. The death scene

was awful. The patient would turn blue and when we touched the body the skin would stick to our hands."

56   Those who ventured into Hiroshima were greeted by sights they were reluctant to describe. A businessman reported: "The bodies of half-dead people lay on the roadside, on the bridges, in the water, in the gardens, and everywhere. It was a sight no one wants to see. Practically all of these people were nude. Their color was brownish blackish and some of their bodies were dripping. There was a fellow whose head was half burned so that I thought he was wearing a hat." Another man said, "The bodies of the dead were so burned that we could not distinguish men from women."

57   In the public parks great numbers of both wounded and dead were congregated. There were cries for aid and cries for water and there were places where unidentifiable shapes merely stirred.

58   In the late afternoon, aid began to come farther into the city from the outer edges. Rice balls and other food were brought. From their mission up the valley a number of Jesuits came, and one of them, Father Siemes, gave a vivid and careful description of what he had seen, when he was later interviewed by members of the Bombing Survey in Tokyo. He said, "Beneath the wreckage of the houses along the way many had been trapped and they screamed to be rescued from the oncoming flames. They had to be left to their fate."

59   On a bridge, he encountered a procession of soldiers "dragging themselves along with the help of staves or carried by their less severely injured comrades. Abandoned on the bridge there stood with sunken heads a number of horses with large burns on their flanks.

60   "Fukai, the secretary of the mission, was completely out of his mind. He did not want to leave the house when the fires were burning closer, and explained that he did not want to survive the destruction of his fatherland." He had to be carried away by force.

61   After dark, the priests helped pull from the river two children who suffered chills and then died. There was a sand-spit in the river, covered with wounded, who cried for help and who were afraid that the rising tide would drown them. After midnight, "only occasionally did we hear calls for help."

62   Many patients were brought to an open field right behind Hiroshima station, and tents were set up for them. Doctors came in from the neighboring prefectures and from near-by towns such as Yamaguchi, Okayama, and Shimane. The Army also took part in relief measures, and all available military facilities and units were mobilized to that end.

63   A fisherman who came to Hiroshima to see what had happened said, "I cannot describe the situation in words, it was so pitiful. To see so many people dead was a terrible sight. Their clothes were shredded and their bodies puffed up, some with tongues hanging out. They were dead in all shapes."

64   As late as the second day the priests noted that among cadavers there were still many wounded alive. "Frightfully injured forms beckoned to us and then collapsed."

65   They carried some to the hospitals, but "we could not move everybody who lay exposed to the sun." It did not make much difference, anyway, for in

the hospitals there was little that could be done. They just lay in the corridors, row on row, and died.

66   A businessman came into Hiroshima on the third day. "I went to my brother's house in the suburbs and found that all were wounded but none killed. They were stunned and could hardly speak. The next day, one of the four children died. She got black and blue in the face, just as if you had mashed your finger, and had died fifteen minutes after that. In another half hour, her sister did the same thing and she died also."

67   The wife of a soldier who had been with the Hiroshima troops said, "My husband was a soldier and so he was to die, but when it actually happened, I wondered why we did not all go with him. They called me and I went to see. I was to find him in the heap, but I decided against looking at the bodies. I want to remember him as he was — big and healthy, not some horribly charred body. If I saw that, it would remain forever in my eyes."

68   A police chief told how the dead were collected and burned. "Many could not be identified. In cases where it was possible, the corpses or the ashes were given to the immediate family. Mostly, the cremation was done by the police or the soldiers, and the identified ashes were given to the family. The ashes of those not identified were turned over to the City Hall. There still are boxes in the City Hall. Occasionally even now one is identified, or is supposed to be identified, and is claimed."

69   The destroyed heart of Hiroshima consisted of 4.7 square miles, and the best estimates indicate that the mortality rate was 15,000 to the square mile. For many days funeral processions moved along the roads and through the towns and villages all around Hiroshima. The winds were pervaded by the smell of death and cremation. At night the skies were lit with the flames of funeral pyres.

5

70 Very few of the people we interviewed at Hiroshima attempted to make a play for sympathy or to make us feel guilty. The general manner was one which might be interpreted as due either to lingering apathy and absence of feeling consequent on shock, or to reserve which masked hate. It was probably a mixture of both, in varying degrees in different people. But on the surface everyone appeared willing to cooperate and oblige.

71   An official of a near-by small town thought that "if America had such a weapon, there was no use to go on. Many high school students in Hiroshima who were wounded in the raid spoke incoherently on their death-beds, saying, 'Please avenge that raid for us somehow.' However, most of the people felt that since it was war, it was just *shikata ga nai,* could not be helped. But we were unified in the idea that we had to win the war."

72   A newspaper reporter said that after the bomb fell, some felt that this was the end, while others wanted to go on regardless. "Those who had actually experienced the bomb were the ones who wanted to quit, while those who had not, wanted to go on."

73   The wife of a soldier killed in the blast said, "Though many are resentful against America, I feel no animosity. It was an understood war and the use of weapons was fair. I only wonder why they didn't let the people know about this bomb and give us a chance, before bombing us, to give up."

74   A police chief believed that the general reaction among the people was one of surprise and a feeling that "we have taken the worst beating, we have been the goats." He said, "They felt that America had done a terrible thing and were very bitter, but after the surrender they turned on the Japanese military. They felt they had been fooled, and wondered if the military knew that the bomb was coming and why they did not take steps. The bomb made no difference in the fighting spirit of the people: it drew them together and made them more cooperative. My eldest son was killed, but I felt it was destiny that ruled. When I see people who got away without any injury, I feel a little pang of envy naturally, but I don't feel bitter toward them."

75   Poking in the ruins one day, I came on the stone figure of a dog, one of that grinning type derived from China which commonly guards the entrances to temples. It was tilted on its pedestal but undamaged, and the grin gleamed out as if it were hailing me. Its rakish air and its look of fiendish satisfaction with all that lay around drew me on to inspect it more closely. It was then apparent that the look was not directed at me, but out somewhere beyond. It was, of course, only a piece of stone, and it displayed no particular artistic merit; yet in looking at it I felt that I was a clod, while it had a higher, sentient wisdom locked up within.

76   The look and the feeling it inspired were familiar and I groped to remember where I had seen it before other than on temple dogs. The eyes were creased in a fashion that did not exactly connotate mirth, and the lips were drawn far back in a smile that seemed to blend bitterness, glee, and compassion. The word "sardonic"came to mind, and this led to recognition and a realization of terrible appropriateness.

77   All who have acquaintance with the dead know the curious smile that may crop over the human face as *rigor mortis* sets in, a smile of special quality called by doctors *risus sardonicus.* The dog had this look, and it seemed to me probable that some ancient Oriental sculptor, in seeking an expression for temple guardians that would drive off evil spirits, had taken this death grin as his model, and thus it had come down through hundreds of years to this beast looking out on Hiroshima.

78   Many a soldier has seen this face looking up at him from the field of battle, before he himself was wearing it, and many a priest and doctor has found himself alone with it in a darkened room. As with the dog, at first the look seems at you, and then beyond you, as if there lay at last behind it knowledge of the huge joke of life which the rest of us feel vaguely but cannot comprehend. And there is that tinge of compassion that is as dreadful as it is unknowable.

79   As I continued to study this stone face, it began to appear that the grin was not directed at the waste and the destruction around, at the red and yellow and the smells, any more than it was at me. It was not so much a face looking

at Hiroshima as it was the face of Hiroshima. The carved eyes gazed beyond the rubble, beyond the gardens of radishes and fields of winter wheat, beyond the toiling adults and the rippling children with their tangerines and shouts of "Haro-goodabye!" surging up with new life like flowers and weeds spreading over devastation, beyond the mountains with red pines in the blue sky, beyond all these, over the whole broad shoulder of the world to where, in cities and towns, watches on wrists and clocks on towers still ticked and moved. The face seemed to be smiling and waiting for the harvest of the wind that had been sown.

80   There was one woman in Hiroshima who said, "If there are such things as ghosts, why don't they haunt the Americans?"

81   Perhaps they do.

Reading Sources: "That Day at Hiroshima"

Read this selection, surveying it to identify key words and important concepts. Highlight these phrases and ideas, and then answer these questions.

1. Are any visual cues used in this essay? Explain.
2. What are the central ideas Leighton tries to convey in his essay? Underline the sentences in the essay that communicate these ideas.
3. What techniques does Leighton use to achieve transition from sentence to sentence in paragraph 9? In paragraph 54? How does he link paragraphs 9, 10, and 11? How does he link paragraphs 72, 73, and 74?
4. How does Leighton place emphasis on the idea in paragraph 32? Is such emphasis necessary? Explain.
5. Where does Leighton use statistics to balance his largely subjective account? What is the effect of this use of statistics? Why do you think he does not use more such objective information?

Reacting to Sources

Reread the selection carefully, making marginal notes to aid your comprehension and reinforce connections. Then further annotate the selection if you need to do so in order to answer any of these questions. (You may already have addressed some of the questions in your marginal notes.)

1. Using a dictionary if necessary, supply marginal definitions of these words as they are used in this essay: *grubbing* (1), *cloven* (1), *bandy-legged* (3), *impelled* (8), *tumult* (11), *buttes* (11), *tinderboxes* (18), *traversed* (20), *fjord* (20), *cormorants* (20), *feudal* (22), *keep* (22), *gay* (25), *geishas* (25), *incendiary* (29), *firebreaks* (29), *engendered* (51), *decimated* (54), *prefectures* (62), *pyres* (69), *rakish* (75), *sentient* (75), *sardonic* (76).
2. In paragraph 2 a G.I. from Kansas is quoted as saying, "They been exaggerating about that bomb." In a journal entry, explain the effect this statement is

calculated to have on the reader, and then go on to consider the purpose the entire paragraph serves in the essay.

3. In a brief marginal note, identify this allusion: "Like the children of Hamelin to the piper . . ." (7). Use a dictionary or encyclopedia if necessary. What is the effect of this allusion? Why does the author use it?

4. In one sentence, summarize the differences between the children's reactions and the adults' (paragraphs 4 – 8). What does Leighton suggest through this contrast?

5. Write a journal entry in response to the background presented in paragraphs 20 – 28. What is Leighton's purpose in presenting this background?

6. In a marginal note, formulate three questions to clarify your understanding of the ideas in paragraph 18.

7. Comment in a journal entry on the intended impact on the essay's readers of the survivors' words in paragraphs 33 – 41.

8. In paragraph 42 Leighton says, "That part of the picture has to be reconstructed, as in archeology, from the remains." Explain this statement in a journal entry.

9. Comment on the purpose served by the vivid description in paragraphs 55 – 56 and 63 – 66. Is such graphic description gratuitous, or is it necessary? Explain in a journal entry.

10. Outline the paragraph cluster beginning with paragraph 75 and ending with paragraph 79.

11. How does your knowledge that Leighton actually visited Hiroshima affect your acceptance of his ideas? Would you be more or less likely to accept his impressions as accurate if his visit had occurred just a few days or weeks after the bomb was dropped? Explain.

12. Does Leighton show any conflicting feelings concerning the bomb? Explain in a journal entry.

Working with Sources

1. Write a one-sentence summary of paragraph 70.
2. Write a critique of the ideas in paragraphs 75 – 79.
3. Use these quotations from "That Day at Hiroshima" in a journal entry in which you assess the effectiveness of Leighton's descriptions.

   "Imagine a city dump with its smells of wet ashes, mold, and things rotting, but one that runs from your feet almost to the limits of vision" (11).

   "People looked as if they had grabbed what they could from a rummage sale" (13).

   "Trolleys bulging with passengers stopped, and all died at once, leaving burned figures still standing supporting each other and fingers fused to the straps" (43).

"A talkative man in a newspaper office said that the most severely burned people looked like red shrimps" (49).

Be sure to integrate the quotations smoothly into your writing.

4. Paraphrase paragraph 43.
5. Write a one-paragraph synthesis that blends ideas in paragraphs 73–74 with ideas in paragraphs 12–13 of "The U.S. Was Wrong" (pp. 165–167).

Writing with Sources: Using a Single Source

Integrating information from "That Day at Hiroshima" with your own ideas, write an essay on one of these topics. Be sure to acknowledge all ideas that are not your own.

1. Using information from Leighton's essay, write an essay in which you compare Hiroshima and its people before the bomb and afterwards.
2. In paragraph 79, Leighton comments that the face of the stone dog he finds in the ruins is "not so much a face looking at Hiroshima as . . . the face of Hiroshima." Write an essay explaining in what sense this is true.
3. The editor's note that introduces Leighton's article in the *Atlantic Monthly* comments, "Obviously the survivors were confused and not always strictly accurate in their recollection." Why do you feel the editor found it necessary to include such a statement? Do you believe the survivors' memories are "strictly accurate" or not? Explain your reasoning in an essay.

The Decision to Drop the Bomb

James West Davidson and Mark Hamilton Lytle

James West Davidson was educated at Haverford College and Yale University, where he received a Ph.D. He is a full-time writer and also teaches in the Department of History at Smith College. Mark Hamilton Lytle attended Cornell University and obtained a Ph.D. at Yale University. Along with Davidson, he coauthored *The United States: A History of the Republic* (1981) and *After the Fact: The Art of Historical Detection* (1982), from which this essay was excerpted. In "The Decision to Drop the Bomb" Davidson and Lytle show how the study of how large organizations work can help historians explain why the United States dropped the atomic bomb. Not intended to provide a simple solution for a complex problem, the organizational model that Davidson and Lytle develop supplements traditional explanations and allows historians to see "old" facts in a new light.

1   Why, many critics have asked, did the United States not make a greater effort to explore the peace initiatives? And why, when the United States was

eventually willing to compromise on "unconditional surrender," did it wait until 150,000 Japanese had died needlessly? Using rational actor analysis, those critics have argued that since Japan was clearly defeated before Hiroshima, the United States had another target—the Soviet Union. Had the Russians' declaration of war, rather than the bomb, forced a surrender, Truman feared that Stalin might demand a larger role in the Japanese peace negotiations. The most cynical critics charge that the second bomb was dropped to minimize the impact of the Russian declaration of war the day before.

2   Rational actor analysis alone cannot adequately answer the questions historians have raised about the decision to drop the bomb. Other models are needed to explain why the United States dropped the second bomb so soon, why policymakers ruled out a demonstration, why they failed to tell the Russians about the bomb, and how they chose the targets. We need a model that recognizes that governments are more than the leaders who determine policy on the basis of rational calculation. Decision makers stand atop a pyramid of organizations and political actors who participate in the formulation and application of government policies. Large actions at the center require a myriad of smaller activities at various levels of bureaucracy. If we looked at a government as a clock, rational actor analysis would define the telling of time as the visible movements of the hands controlled by a closed box. A model representing organizational processes, on the other hand, takes us inside the clock to observe the complex of gears and levers that move the hands. It allows the historian to analyze internal mechanisms that help determine external action.

3   Observation instructs us, however, that people in organizations are less predictable than gears in a clock and that government agencies seldom approach such a degree of coordinated activity. Often the organizations that comprise a government work at cross purposes or pursue conflicting objectives. While the Surgeon General's office warns that cigarette smoking "may be hazardous," the Department of Agriculture produces films on the virtues of American tobacco. To understand better the difference between rational actor and organizational process models, imagine yourself in the stands at a football game. We see the players moving in coordinated patterns in an effort to control the movement of the ball. Rational actor analysis suggests that the coach, or another centralized decision maker, has selected the strategies best suited to win the game. That larger strategy, in turn, determines the plays that the offense and defense will use.

4   After closer observation, we begin to sense that the play is not as centrally coordinated as we anticipated. Different groups of players move in patterns determined by their positions as well as the team strategy. Linemen block, ends run pass patterns, and quarterbacks hand off the ball. We come to understand that the team is made up of subunits that have regularly assigned tasks. In each situation, the players do not try to think of the best imaginable play, but rather they repeat those actions they have been trained to perform. Thus, a halfback will generally advance the ball by running and leave the passing to the quarterback. On many plays, we observe that some players' actions seem inappropriate. A halfback runs when he should be blocking. Where the rational

actor might attribute that move to some purposeful attempt at deception, an organizational process analysis might define it as a breakdown of coordination among subunits. What one model treats as planned, the other treats as a mistake.

5   Thus the organizational process model leads the historian to treat government behavior not as centralized acts and choices, but as the actions of bureaucracies functioning in relatively predictable patterns. Organizations begin by breaking problems into parts, which are parcelled out to the appropriate subunits. The subunits usually respond according to established procedures or routines without necessarily having any sense of the larger problem. A lineman, for example, does not need to know who will run the ball, only whether to block his opponent to the left or right. Standard operating procedures (SOP's) allow organizations to coordinate the independent activities of many groups and individuals. Each group contributes to the final outcome by doing those things it has been trained and assigned to do. Failure to perform any one task may undermine the entire operation. If just one of seven linemen misses his block, the runner may be tackled without advancing the ball.

6   While SOP's make coordination possible, they also define and limit the actions of organizations. Specialization both within and among organizations restricts the number of tasks they can perform. Available equipment, training, and information make it difficult to deviate from regular routines. The weather bureau could not easily shift from predicting rain to predicting fluctuations in the economy. And where the rational actor weighs all available choices to find the best one, SOP's determine the range and pattern of choices that organizations consider. They are generally content to choose standardized and previously determined policies rather than searching for the optimum one.

7   Since organizations are generally more preoccupied with avoiding failure than with gambling on success, they tend to be conservative. Where the rational actor might decide, after weighing the potential benefits against possible consequences, to make a bold new departure, organizations change in small, incremental steps. Corporations, for example, like to test market a product before they risk investing in expensive new plants, distribution networks, and advertising. Though such caution may cost several years of profitable sales, it reduces the risk of flooding the market with Edsels and electric forks.

8   Reward structures in organizations reinforce their conservatism. Those who do their jobs properly day after day continue to work. Those who make errors lose their jobs or fail to win promotions. Individuals have little incentive to take risks. Critical decisions are generally made in committees so that no individual assumes sole responsibility if a venture fails. But committees take much longer to act and often adopt unwieldy compromises. (An old adage defines a camel as a horse designed by a committee.) As a further hedge against failure, goals and responsibilities are set well within the individual or groups' performance capabilities. People are given eight hours to do four hours' work. Such practices stifle individual initiative and encourage inefficiency. Mountains of paperwork and miles of red tape are the ultimate symbol of organizational caution and conservatism.

9   By treating the decision to drop the bomb not as a single act but as the

outcome of many organizational routines, historians can gain new insight into old issues. An organizational process model helps explain why the United States bombed Japan and not Germany, why the Manhattan Project produced just two bombs by August 1945, and why Nagasaki was destroyed so soon after Hiroshima. The historian shifts his attention from such external factors as Soviet-American relations and Japan's military situation and focuses instead on the procedures, priorities, and outputs of the organizations which participated in the development and deployment of the bomb.

10   The decision to build a bomb first required the creation of new organizations and the reorientation of existing ones. Before the Manhattan Project no organization had ever applied scientific research to weapons development on such a giant scale. Had the emigré scientists approached the United States Government solely through normal organizational channels the bomb might not have been built during World War II. Navy bureaucrats did not even understand Fermi when he delivered his warning in 1939. Other scientific bureaus had neither the capacity nor the incentive to undertake such a large and risky venture. But by circumventing the standard organizational channels and going right to President Roosevelt, the scientists attracted the support needed to initiate atomic weapons research.

11   To get the project under way, Roosevelt had to create an *ad hoc* committee to investigate the military potential of nuclear fission. His decision to appoint Lyman Briggs, a government physicist, as head of the Uranium Committee may have delayed the project by at least a year. As the director of the Bureau of Standards, Briggs knew little about nuclear physics. He was by temperament "slow, conservative, methodical"—ideal bureaucratic qualities totally unsuited to the bold departure Roosevelt sought. Briggs's many other responsibilities distracted him from his new role, while his commitment to safer and more conventional areas of research led him to discount the potential of the new project. In addition, the traditional American prejudice against foreigners led Briggs and other bureaucrats to mistrust the emigré scientists who were best equipped to get the project underway quickly.

12   Not until Roosevelt created the National Defense Research Committee did nuclear physics gain adequate support. Roosevelt gave NDRC responsibility for applying science to the military demands of the impending war. As chairman of NDRC, Vannevar Bush made the far-sighted decision to keep his organization independent of the military bureaucracies. He knew generals and admirals would fight against civilian interference and that scientists would balk at military regulation of their research. Under Bush, scientists remained free to pursue the research they and not the military thought was important. Traditional definitions of missions and military needs would not cut off funds or new research projects.

13   But even under Bush, atomic research moved slowly until the Peierls and Frisch reports convinced him that a practical weapon of unparalleled power could be built. At that point Roosevelt replaced the ineffectual Uranium Committee with the S-1 Committee, which included Stimson, Marshall, Vice President Wallace, Conant, and Bush. The presence of the highest ranking

bureaucrats guaranteed a high priority for the project. Roosevelt's desire to keep abreast of its progress allowed the three top administrators, Bush, Conant, and General Groves, direct access to the White House. As Bush worked to organize the project, he decided to operate where necessary under the War Department rather than the Navy.*

14   The Navy had repeatedly shown either indifference or hostility to advice from civilian scientists. The Army and particularly its Air Corps branch proved far more receptive to new research. Consequently, the atom bomb was developed with the Army's mission and organizational routines in mind. Such skillful administrative negotiation of organizational minefields accounted in part for the project's success.

15   In other areas, administrative and organizational conflict delayed the project. President Roosevelt had established two incompatible priorities for Bush: speed and security. The scientists felt speed should come before security; military administrators like Groves opted for security over speed. As late as 1943, the scientists despaired at their lack of progress. They feared that the race against German physicists was already lost. Groves's security regulations struck them as an unnecessary, even fatal, impediment to their research. Military SOP demanded strict adherence to a chain of command and rigid compartmentalization of all tasks. A military officer who had taken Szilard's approach of going to the president over his superiors' heads might well find himself court-martialed or assigned to some remote Aleutian Island.

16   The conflict between speed and security became particularly acute at Los Alamos. To maximize security Groves tried to place the laboratory under military control. All the scientists would don uniforms and receive ranks based on their importance. Scientists, however, feared that military regulations would undermine their traditional autonomy to pursue research as they saw fit. Oppenheimer could not recruit many scientists to come to Los Alamos until he demilitarized the project.

17   Compartmentalization, another Groves scheme, seriously inhibited research. Physicists believed their work required open access to all relevant information. They thought best when they understood the wider ramifications of their work. Groves disdained their habit of engaging in freewheeling discussions that regularly drifted far afield of the topic at hand. He could not appreciate the creative dimension of scientific work. Scientists should stick to their jobs and receive information solely on a "need to know" basis. "Just as outfielders should not think about the manager's job of changing pitchers," Groves said to justify his system, ". . . each scientist had to be made to do his own work." While compartmentalization promoted security, it denied scientists vital information from other areas of the project. Some scientists, like Szilard, avoided the problem by violating security procedures. Oppenheimer eased the problem at Los Alamos by conducting seminars where his staff could

* At that time the Army and Navy had separate organizations. The head of each held a cabinet post. The Marines were a branch of the Navy, the Air Corps a branch of the Army. Congress created the unified defense structure under a single secretary in 1947.

exchange ideas and information, but information never flowed freely among the many research and production sites.

18   Security procedures indicate, too, that long before the war ended many policymakers saw the Soviet Union as their chief enemy. Few security precautions were designed against Japanese or even German agents. Military intelligence concentrated its counterespionage efforts against Soviet and communist spies. Known communists or scientists with communist associations were kept under constant surveillance. Had intelligence officers prevailed, they would have barred Oppenheimer from the project because of his previous involvement with communist front organizations. To his credit, Groves overruled the nearsighted sleuths in Army intelligence and saved the project's most valuable member. In the meantime, security precautions against a war-time ally continued to work to the advantage of the Nazis by delaying the project.

19   The military was not solely responsible for project bottlenecks. The procedures of organized science added to the difficulties as well. Scientists recruited from private industry did not share their academic colleagues' preoccupation with speed. Work in industry had conditioned them to move cautiously, with an eye toward efficiency, permanence, and low risk. Academic scientists felt such industrial values "led to a considerable retardation of the program." But the traditions of academic science also slowed the project. The bulk of research money had most often been directed to the celebrities in each field. Ernest Lawrence's reputation made him a magnet for grants and contributions. Manhattan Project administrators automatically turned to him as they sought methods to refine the pure U-235 needed for the bomb. Much of the money spent at Oak Ridge, Tennessee, went into Lawrence's electromagnetic process based on the Berkeley cyclotron.

20   Lawrence's program proved to be one of the most conspicuous failures of the Manhattan Project. By 1944, Oppenheimer had the design for a uranium bomb, but scarcely any U-235. In desperation he looked toward a process of gas-diffusion developed four years before by a young and relatively unknown physicist named John Dunning. Lawrence had been so persuaded of the superiority of his own method that he had steered attention and money away from Dunning. Compartmentalization prevented other physicists from learning more about Dunning's work. In 1944 Oppenheimer changed the priorities and the gas-diffusion process began to produce refined U-235 at a far greater rate than Lawrence's cyclotron. Physicists soon acknowledged that electromagnetic separation was obsolete, but in the meantime, the completion of the Uranium bomb, "Little Boy," was delayed until July 1945.

21   The organizational process model gives historians an even more startling insight into the choice of targets and the decision to bomb Nagasaki just three days after Hiroshima. To select the targets, Groves appointed a Target Committee comprised of scientists and ordnance specialists. Their priorities reflected both the military's desire to end the war quickly and the scientists' hope to transmit a dramatic warning to the world. They sought cities that included military installations and a larger concentration of structures subject to the blast in case the bomb missed its primary target. Kyoto, the ancient cultural and political center of Japan, topped their list.

22   Secretary of War Stimson vetoed that choice. As a former secretary of state and a man of broad cultural and political experience, he believed that the destruction of Kyoto would engender in the Japanese an undying bitterness toward the United States. Any hopes of integrating a revitalized and reformed Japan into a healthy postwar Asia might die with Kyoto. Stimson's position near the top of the organizational hierarchy gave him a different perspective from lower-level planners who weighed other issues. On the final target list Hiroshima ranked first, Nagasaki ranked fourth, and Kyoto not at all.

23   It was the weather, and not diplomatic or military strategy, that sealed Nagasaki's fate. After the bombing of Hiroshima and the Russian declaration of war, Japanese leaders had decided to sue for peace. Advocates of surrender just needed enough time to work out acceptable terms and to reconcile the military diehards to the inevitable. As the Japanese discussed policy, the Americans followed standard military procedure. Control shifted from the commander in Washington, President Truman, to the commander of the bomber squadron on the island of Tinian in the Pacific. Plans called for "Fat Man," a plutonium bomb, to be ready by August 11. Since work went faster than expected, the bomb crew advanced the date to the 10th. The forecast called for clear skies on the 9th, followed by five days of bad weather. Urged on by the squadron commander, the crew had "Fat Man" armed and loaded on the morning of the 9th. And again following military SOP, the pilot shifted his attack to Nagasaki, when clouds obscured his primary target.

24   The timing of that attack on Nagasaki could only be explained through the application of the organizational process model. Had the original plan been followed, Japan might well have surrendered before the weather cleared. Nagasaki would have been spared. The man who ordered the attack had little appreciation of the larger military picture that made Nagasaki a target or that made the Soviet Union a diplomatic problem connected with the atom bomb. He acted according to the SOP's of the organization that trained him and placed him in a position of authority. He weighed factors important to a bomb squadron commander, not to diplomats or political leaders.

Reading Sources: "The Decision to Drop the Bomb"

Read the selection, surveying it to identify key terms and important concepts. Highlight these phrases and ideas, and then answer these questions.

1. What concepts do the authors explain in their introduction? What does the introduction tell you about the authors' intended audience?
2. At what point do the authors state their thesis? How does the thesis provide transition between the introduction and the body of the essay?
3. Underline the transitional words and phrases in paragraph 8. How do these elements help readers follow the logic of the paragraph?
4. How do the terms *standard operating procedure* and *compartmentalization* help the authors to illustrate their model of organizational process?

5. Where do the authors state their conclusion? What points do they choose to emphasize there?

Reacting to Sources

Reread the selection carefully, making marginal notes to aid your comprehension and reinforce connections. Then further annotate the selection if you need to do so in order to answer any of these questions. (You may already have addressed some of the questions in your marginal notes.)

1. In a marginal note explain the difference between *rational actor* and *organizational process* models. In a journal entry indicate how these concepts help explain why the atomic bomb was dropped.
2. Using a dictionary if necessary, supply brief marginal definitions of the following words as they are used in the essay: *bureaucracies* (5), *fluctuations* (6), *incremental* (7), *emigré* (10), *ad hoc* (11), *autonomy* (16).
3. In a marginal note, explain how in paragraphs 2 and 4 the authors use analogy to explain an unfamiliar concept.
4. Do you agree or disagree with the thoughts expressed in paragraph 8? Make a marginal note explaining your answer.
5. Give three examples from the essay of how Standard Operating Procedures defined and limited the actions of those involved with making the atomic bomb.
6. Write a journal entry in which you explain how compartmentalization seriously inhibited research.
7. Read the introduction to the selection. Comment on how your knowledge of the authors' other writings and expertise influences your acceptance of their ideas.
8. Use an encyclopedia to find out more about the individuals mentioned in paragraph 13. In a journal entry, explain who they were and why the authors specifically mention them.
9. After looking up the following names and places in an encyclopedia, write a journal entry explaining their significance in the essay: *Enrico Fermi* (10), *Los Alamos* (16), *J. Robert Oppenheimer* (16).
10. In a journal entry, compare this essay's central idea with the ideas expressed in the *New York Times* article on pages 135–140.
11. Outline the ideas presented in paragraphs 21–24.

Working with Sources

1. Write a one-sentence summary of paragraph 17.
2. Write a critique of the ideas in paragraph 8.
3. Use the following two quotations from the selection in a journal entry in which you express a reaction to the essay.

"Thus the organizational process model leads the historian to treat government behavior not as centralized acts and choices, but as the actions of bureaucracies functioning in relatively predictable patterns" (5).

"By treating the decision to drop the bomb not as a single act but as the outcome of many organizational routines, historians can gain new insight into old issues" (9).

Be sure to integrate the quotations smoothly into your writing.

4. Guided by the outline you made in response to "Reacting to Sources," question 11, paraphrase paragraphs 21–24.

5. Write a one-paragraph synthesis that blends ideas contained in paragraph 24 of this essay with the ideas contained in paragraph 10 of "Modern Man Is Obsolete" (pp. 175–178).

Writing with Sources: Using a Single Source

Integrating information from "The Decision to Drop the Bomb" with your own ideas, write an essay on one of these topics. Be sure to acknowledge all ideas that are not your own.

1. Discuss the Standard Operating Procedure of an organization with which you are familiar. Be sure to point out how these procedures define and limit the actions of the organization.

2. Define *compartmentalization* and discuss how it delayed scientists in their efforts to develop the atomic bomb.

3. Develop your own analogies for explaining the *rational actor* and *organizational process* models. Be sure to review the models the authors use in paragraphs 2 and 4 of this selection.

The U.S. Was Right

John Connor

The U.S. Was Wrong

Gar Alperovitz

In August, 1985, the fortieth anniversary of the dropping of the atomic bomb on Hiroshima, the *New York Times* published these two opposing articles. Arguing in favor of the United States's action is John Connor, Professor of Anthropology at California State University in Sacramento. Connor, who feels the action was justified because it saved lives, was attached to General Douglas MacArthur's headquarters in Tokyo between 1949 and 1950. His article appears first. Taking the opposing viewpoint is Gar Alperovitz, a historian and political economist. Alperovitz, who argues that the action was unnecessary in view of the Japanese army's imminent defeat, is the author of *Atomic Diplomacy: Hiroshima and Potsdam.*

1 SACRAMENTO, Calif. — Forty years ago this week in Hiroshima: the dreadful flash, the wrist watches fused forever at 8:16 A.M. The question still persists: Should we have dropped the atomic bomb?

2 History seldom gives decisive answers, but recently declassified documents point to a clear judgment: Yes, it was necessary to drop the bomb. It was needed to end the war. It saved countless American and Japanese lives.

3 In the early summer of 1945, Japan, under tight control of the militarists, was an implacable, relentless adversary. The Japanese defended territory with a philosophy we had seldom encountered: Soldiers were taught that surrender was worse than death. There was savage resistance to the end in battle after battle.

4 Of the 5,000-man Japanese force at Tarawa in November 1943, only 17 remained alive when the island was taken. When Kwajalein was invaded in February 1944, Japanese officers slashed at American tanks with samurai swords; their men held grenades against the sides of tanks in an effort to disable them.

5 On Saipan, less than 1,000 of the 32,000 defending Japanese troops survived. Casualties among the Japanese-ruled civilians on the island numbered 10,000. Parents bashed their babies' brains out on rocky cliff sides, then leaped to their deaths. Others cut each other's throats; children threw grenades at each other. America suffered 17,000 casualties.

6 Just 660 miles southeast of Tokyo, Iwo Jima's garrison was told to defend the island as if it were Tokyo itself. They did. In the first day of fighting, there were more American casualties then during "D-Day" in Normandy. At Okinawa — only 350 miles south of Kyushu — more than 110,000 Japanese soldiers and 100,000 civilians were killed. Kamikaze attacks cost the Navy alone some 10,000 casualties. The Army and Marines lost more then 50,000 men.

7 In the early summer of 1945, the invasion of Japan was imminent and everyone in the Pacific was apprehensive. The apprehension was justified, because our intelligence was good: With a system code named "Magic," it had penetrated Japanese codes even before Pearl Harbor. "Magic" would play a crucial role in the closing days of the war.

8 Many have maintained that the bomb was unnecessary because in the closing days of the war intercepted Japanese diplomatic messages disclosed a passionate desire for peace. While that is true, it is irrelevant. The Japanese Government remained in the hands of the militarists: *Their* messages indicated a willingness to fight to the death.

9 Japanese planes, gasoline and ammunition had been hoarded for the coming invasion. More than 5,000 aircraft had been hidden everywhere to be used as suicide weapons, with only enough gas in their tanks for a one-way trip to the invasion beaches. More than two million men were moving into positions to defend the home islands.

10 The object was to inflict such appalling losses that the Americans would agree to a treaty more favorable than unconditional surrender. The Army Chief

of Staff, Gen. George C. Marshall, estimated potential American casualties as high as a million.

11   The willingness of the Japanese to die was more than empty bravado. Several of my colleagues at Kyushu University told me that as boys of 14 or 15, they were being trained to meet the Americans on the beaches with little more than sharpened bamboo spears. They had no illusions about their chances for survival.

12   The Potsdam declaration calling for unconditional surrender was beamed to Japan on July 27. On July 30, the Americans were informed that Japan would officially ignore the ultimatum. A week later, the bomb was dropped.

13   Could we not have warned the Japanese in advance, critics asked, and dropped a demonstration bomb? That alternative was vetoed on the grounds the bomb might not work, or that the plane carrying it might be shot down. Moreover, it is questionable how effective a demonstration bomb might have been. The militarists could have imposed a news blackout as complete as the one imposed after the disastrous battle of Midway and continued on their suicidal course. That is exactly what happened at Hiroshima. Within hours, the Japanese Government sent in a team of scientists to investigate the damage. Their report was immediately suppressed and was not made public until many years after the war.

14   After midnight on Aug. 10, a protracted debate took place in an air-raid shelter deep inside the Imperial Palace. The military insisted that Japan should hold out for terms far better than unconditional surrender. The peace faction favored accepting the Potsdam declaration, providing that the Emperor would be retained. The two factions remained at an impasse. At 2 A.M., Prime Minister Kantaro Suzuki asked the Emperor to decide. In a soft, deliberate voice, the Emperor expressed his great longing for peace. The war had ended.

15   It was impossible, in August 1945, to predict the awesome shadow the bomb would cast on humanity. The decision to drop it seemed both simple and obvious. Without it, the militarists might have prevailed, an invasion ordered. And the loss of both American and Japanese lives would have been awesome.

16   The atomic bomb accomplished what it had been designed to do. It ended the war.

1   WASHINGTON — Though it has not yet received broad public attention, there exists overwhelming historical evidence that President Harry S. Truman knew he could almost certainly end World War II without using the atomic bomb: The United States had cracked the Japanese code, and a stream of documents released over the last 40 years show that Mr. Truman had two other options.

2   The first option was to clarify America's surrender terms to assure the Japanese we would not remove their Emperor. The second was simply to await the expected Soviet declaration of war—which, United States intelligence advised, appeared likely to end the conflict on its own.

3   Instead, Hiroshima was bombed on Aug. 6, 1945, and Nagasaki on Aug. 9. The planned date for the Soviet Union's entry into the war against Japan was Aug. 8.

4   The big turning point was the Emperor's continuing June-July decision to open surrender negotiations through Moscow. Top American officials — and, most critically, the President — understood the move was extraordinary: Mr. Truman's secret diaries, lost until 1978, call the key intercepted message "the telegram from Jap Emperor asking for peace."

5   Other documents — among them newly discovered secret memorandums from William J. Donovan, director of the Office of Strategic Services — show that Mr. Truman was personally advised of Japanese peace initiatives through Swiss and Portuguese channels as early as three months before Hiroshima. Moreover, Mr. Truman told several officials he had no objection in principle to Japan's keeping the Emperor, which seemed the only sticking point.

6   American leaders were sure that if he so chose "the Mikado could stop the war with a royal word" —as one top Presidential aide put it. Having decided to use the bomb, however, Mr. Truman was urged by Secretary of State James F. Byrnes not to give assurances to the Emperor before the weapon had been demonstrated.

7   Additional official records, including minutes of top-level White House planning meetings, show the President was clearly advised of the importance of a Soviet declaration of war: It would pull the rug out from under Japanese military leaders who were desperately hoping the powerful Red Army would stay neutral.

8   Gen. George C. Marshall in mid-June told Mr. Truman that "the impact of Russian entry on the already hopeless Japanese may well be the decisive action levering them into capitulation at that time or shortly thereafter if we land."

9   A month later, the American-British Combined Intelligence Staffs advised their chiefs of the critical importance of a Red Army attack. As the top British general, Sir Hastings Ismay, summarized the conclusions for Prime Minister Winston Churchill: "If and when Russia came into the war against Japan, the Japanese would probably wish to get out on almost any terms short of the dethronement of the Emperor."

10   Mr. Truman's private diaries also record his understanding of the significance of this option. On July 17, 1945, when Stalin confirmed that the Red Army would march, Mr. Truman privately noted: "Fini Japs when that comes about."

11   There was plenty of time: The American invasion of Japan was not scheduled until the spring of 1946. Even a preliminary landing on the island Kyushu was still three months in the future.

12   Gen. Dwight D. Eisenhower, appalled that the bomb would be used in these circumstances, urged Mr. Truman and Secretary of War Henry L. Stimson not to drop it. In his memoirs, he observed that weeks before Hiroshima, Japan had been seeking a way to surrender. "It wasn't necessary," he said in a later interview, "to hit them with that awful thing."

13   The one man who presided over the Joint Chiefs of Staff, Adm. William D.

Leahy, was equally shocked: "The use of this barbarous weapon at Hiroshima and Nagasaki was of no material assistance in our war against Japan. The Japanese were already defeated and ready to surrender."

14   Why, then, was the bomb used?

15   American leaders rejected the most obvious option — simply waiting for the Red Army attack — out of political, not military, concerns.

16   As the diary of one official put it, they wanted to end the war before Moscow got "in so much on the kill." Secretary of the Navy James V. Forrestal's diaries record that Mr. Byrnes "was most anxious to get the Japanese affair over with before the Russians got in."

17   United States leaders had also begun to think of the atomic bomb as what Secretary Stimson termed the "master card" of diplomacy. President Truman postponed his Potsdam meeting with Stalin until July 17, 1945 — one day after the first successful nuclear test — to be sure the atomic bomb would strengthen his hand before confronting the Soviet leader on the shape of a postwar settlement.

18   To this day, we do not know with absolute certainty Mr. Truman's personal attitudes on several key issues. Yet we do know that his most important adviser, Secretary of State Byrnes, was convinced that dropping the bomb would serve crucial long-range diplomatic purposes.

19   As one atomic scientist, Leo Szilard, observed: "Mr. Byrnes did not argue that it was necessary to use the bomb against the cities of Japan in order to win the war. Mr. Byrnes' . . . view [was] that our possessing and demonstrating the bomb would make Russia more manageable."

Reading Sources: "The U.S. Was Right" and "The U.S. Was Wrong"

Read this pair of articles, surveying them to identify key terms and important concepts. Highlight these phrases and ideas, and then answer these questions.

1. What visual cues are used to highlight key ideas in these articles?
2. Outline the main points each writer uses to support his thesis.
3. What devices does Connor use to link sentences in paragraph 13? How does Alperovitz link paragraph 14 to the paragraphs that precede it?
4. Both authors make a point of saying that newly revealed information — "recently declassified documents" for Connor; "a stream of documents released over the last 40 years" and "newly discovered secret memorandums" for Alperovitz — supports their claims. Why do you think they do this?
5. What are the "two other options" Alperovitz believes were available to the United States?
6. How do Connor's comments about Japanese soldiers in paragraphs 3 – 6 support his thesis?
7. In paragraphs 8 and 13, Connor anticipates his readers' possible objections to

his thesis. How does he refute these objections? Does Alperovitz use this strategy in his article? If so, where? If not, why not?

8. To support his thesis, Alperovitz quotes a number of scientists and military leaders. What effect are these quotations calculated to have on his readers? Is Connor's essay weakened by his decision not to use this strategy, or is his use of statistics just as good a technique for his purposes? Explain.

9. Alperovitz never mentions Japanese soldiers' attitudes, and Connor does not mention the Soviets' imminent entry into the war. Why not?

Reacting to Sources

Reread both articles carefully, making marginal notes to aid your comprehension and reinforce connections. Then further annotate them if you need to do so in order to answer any of these questions. (You may already have addressed some of the questions in your marginal notes.)

1. Using a dictionary if necessary, supply brief marginal definitions of these words as they are used in the articles. Connor: *declassified* (2), *implacable* (3), *garrison* (6), *kamikaze* (6), *ultimatum* (12), *militarists* (13). Alperovitz: *intelligence* (2), *Mikado* (6), *levering* (8), *capitulation* (8).

2. In a journal entry, evaluate the two articles' introductions and conclusions. Which do you consider more effective? Why?

3. Review the headnote that introduces the articles. Do you think both men are equally qualified to write on this issue? Explain.

4. Find two examples in Connor's article to support his claim in paragraph 8 that the Japanese were willing "to fight to the death."

5. Formulate three questions to help you understand the ideas in paragraph 11 of Connor's article.

6. In paragraph 11 Alperovitz says, "There was plenty of time." Why would Connor disagree? Does this statement weaken or strengthen Alperovitz's case? Explain in a journal entry.

7. Write a marginal note explaining Alperovitz's point in paragraphs 12 and 13.

8. In a marginal note, explain what Alperovitz means when he says that the American leaders' decision not to wait for the Red Army attack was made "out of political, not military concerns" (15).

Working with Sources

1. Write a fifty-word summary of paragraphs 4 – 6 (Connor).

2. Write a critique of the ideas expressed in the last three sentences of paragraph 15 (Connor).

3. Select statements from three of the people Alperovitz quotes in his article, and explore your reactions to those statements in a journal entry. Be sure to integrate the quotations smoothly into your writing.

4. Paraphrase paragraph 6 (Alperovitz).
5. Write a one-paragraph synthesis that blends ideas in paragraph 2 of Connor's article with ideas in paragraph 15 of Alperovitz's.

Writing with Sources: Using a Single Source

Integrating information from this pair of articles with your own ideas, write an essay on one of these topics. Be sure to acknowledge all ideas that are not your own.

1. Drawing information from both articles, write an essay in which you attempt to answer the question Alperovitz poses in paragraph 14: "Why, then, was the bomb used?"
2. In paragraph 15 of "The U.S. Was Right" Connor says, "It was impossible, in August 1945, to predict the awesome shadow the bomb would cast on humanity." In an essay that draws on your own ideas and experiences as well as on Connor's and Alperovitz's articles, consider the effects of this "awesome shadow" on your life.
3. Which writer makes a more convincing case? Write an essay defending your choice.

Atomic War or Peace

Albert Einstein

Albert Einstein grew up in Munich and received his Ph.D. in physics from the University of Zurich in 1905. That year he published his special theory of relativity, which revolutionized physics. Einstein went on to publish his general theory of relativity in 1915, and in 1921, he won the Nobel Prize in physics. In 1933 Einstein came to the United States to escape Nazi anti-Semitism and accepted a professorship of theoretical physics at Princeton University. In 1939 Einstein wrote to President Franklin D. Roosevelt and advised him of the feasibility of developing atomic weapons. This, along with intelligence reports that Germany was developing an atomic bomb, caused the United States to embark on the Manhattan Project. It is interesting to note that the man who formulated the equation that made the atomic bomb possible, $E = mc^2$, possessed a deep social consciousness and supported pacifist causes throughout most of his life. Ironically, because of his pacifism, Einstein was considered a security risk and was not allowed to take part in this project. The dropping of the bomb on Japan caused Einstein personal anguish and led him to embrace world government as the one chance human beings had to save themselves from nuclear destruction. "Atomic War or Peace" appeared in the November 1945 *Atlantic Monthly,* only three months after the first atomic bomb was dropped on Hiroshima. Even though this essay is now more than forty years old, it expresses concerns that unfortunately are still with us today.

1   The release of atomic energy has not created a new problem. It has merely made more urgent the necessity of solving an existing one. One could say that it has affected us quantitatively, not qualitatively. As long as there are sovereign nations possessing great power, war is inevitable. This does not mean that one can know when war will come but only that one is sure that it will come. This was true even before the atomic bomb was made. What has changed is the destructiveness of war.

2   I do not believe that the secret of the bomb should be given to the United Nations Organization. I do not believe it should be given to the Soviet Union. Either course would be analogous to a man with capital who, wishing another individual to collaborate with him on an enterprise, starts by giving him half his money. The other man might choose to start a rival enterprise, when what is wanted is his co-operation. The secret of the bomb should be committed to a world government, and the United States should immediately announce its readiness to do so. Such a world government should be established by the United States, the Soviet Union and Great Britain, the only three powers which possess great military strength. The three of them should commit to this world government all of their military resources. The fact that there are only three nations with great military power should make it easier, rather than harder, to establish a world government.

3   Since the United States and Great Britain have the secret of the atomic bomb and the Soviet Union does not, they should invite the Soviet Union to prepare and present the first draft of a Constitution for the proposed world government. This would help dispel the distrust of the Russians, which they feel because they know the bomb is being kept a secret chiefly to prevent their having it. Obviously, the first draft would not be the final one, but the Russians should be made to feel that the world government will guarantee their security.

4   It would be wise if this Constitution were to be negotiated by one American, one Briton and one Russian. They would, of course, need advisers, but these advisers should serve only when asked. I believe three men can succeed in preparing a workable Constitution acceptable to all the powers. Were six or seven men, or more, to attempt to do so, they would probably fail. After the three great powers have drafted a Constitution and adopted it, the smaller nations should be invited to join the world government. They should also be free not to join and, though they should feel perfectly secure outside the world government, I am sure they will eventually wish to join. Naturally, they should be entitled to propose changes in the Constitution as drafted by the Big Three. But the Big Three should go ahead and organize the world government, whether or not the smaller nations decide to join.

5   Such a world government should have jurisdiction over all military matters, and it need have only one other power. That is the power to interfere in countries where a minority is oppressing the majority and, therefore, is creating the kind of instability that leads to war. For example, conditions such as exist today in Argentina and Spain should be dealt with. There must be an end to the concept of non-intervention, for to abandon non-intervention in certain circumstances is part of keeping the peace.

6   The establishment of a world government should not be delayed until similar conditions of freedom exist in each of the three great powers. While it is true that in the Soviet Union the minority rules, I do not believe that the internal conditions in that country constitute a threat to world peace. One must bear in mind that the people in Russia had not had a long tradition of political education; changes to improve conditions in Russia had to be effected by a minority for the reason that there was no majority capable of doing so. If I had been born a Russian, I believe I could have adjusted myself to this situation.

7   It should not be necessary, in establishing a world government with a monopoly of authority over military affairs, to change the internal structure of the three great powers. It would be for the three individuals who draft the Constitution to devise ways for collaboration despite the different structures of their countries.

8   Do I fear the tyranny of a world government? Of course I do. But I fear still more the coming of another war. Any government is certain to be evil to some extent. But a world government is preferable to the far greater evil of wars, particularly when viewed in the context of the intensified destructiveness of war. If such a world government is not established by a process of agreement among nations, I believe it will come anyway, and in a much more dangerous form; for war or wars can only result in one power being supreme and dominating the rest of the world by its overwhelming military supremacy.

9   Now that we have the atomic secret, we must not lose it, and that is what we would risk doing if we gave it to the United Nations Organization or to the Soviet Union. But, as soon as possible, we must make it clear that we are not keeping the bomb a secret for the sake of maintaining our power but in the hope of establishing peace through world government, and that we will do our utmost to bring this world government into being.

10   I appreciate that there are persons who approve of world government as the ultimate objective but favor a gradual approach to its establishment. The trouble with taking little steps, one at a time, in the hope of eventually reaching the ultimate goal, is that while such steps are being taken, we continue to keep the bomb without convincing those who do not have the bomb of our ultimate intentions. That of itself creates fear and suspicion, with the consequence that the relations between rival countries deteriorate to a dangerous extent. That is why people who advocate taking a step at a time may think they are approaching world peace, but they actually are contributing by their slow pace to the possibility of war. We have no time to waste in this way. If war is to be averted, it must be done quickly.

11   Further, we shall not have the secret of the bomb for very long. I know it is being argued that no other country has money enough to spend on the development of the atomic bomb and that, therefore, we are assured of the secret for a long time. But it is a common mistake in this country to measure things by the amount of money they cost. Other countries which have the raw materials and manpower and wish to apply them to the work of developing atomic power can do so; men and materials and the decision to use them, and not money, are all that is needed.

12   I do not consider myself the father of the release of atomic energy. My part in it was quite indirect. I did not, in fact, foresee that it would be released in my time. I only believed that it was theoretically possible. It became practical through the accidental discovery of chain reaction, and this was not something I could have predicted. It was discovered by Hahn in Berlin, and he himself at first misinterpreted what he discovered. It was Lise Meitner who provided the correct interpretation and escaped from Germany to place the information in the hands of Niels Bohr.

13   In my opinion, a great era of atomic science cannot be assured by organizing science in the way large corporations are organized. One can organize the application of a discovery already made, but one cannot organize the discovery itself. Only a free individual can make a discovery. However, there can be a kind of organization wherein the scientist is assured freedom and proper conditions of work. Professors of science in American universities, for instance, should be relieved of some of their teaching so as to have more time for research. Can you imagine an organization of scientists making the discoveries of Charles Darwin?

14   I do not believe that the vast private corporations of the United States are suitable to the needs of the times. If a visitor should come to this country from another planet, would he not find it strange that, in this country, private corporations are permitted to wield so much power without having to assume commensurate responsibility? I say this to stress my conviction that the American government must retain control of atomic energy, not because socialism is necessarily desirable but because atomic energy was developed by the government; it would be unthinkable to turn over this property of the people to any individual or group of individuals. As for socialism, unless it is international to the extent of producing a world government which controls all military power, it might lead to wars even more easily than capitalism because it represents an even greater concentration of power.

15   To give any estimate as to when atomic energy might be applied for peaceful, constructive purposes is impossible. All that we know now is how to use a fairly large quantity of uranium. The use of small quantities, sufficient, say, to operate a car or an airplane, is thus far impossible, and one cannot predict when it will be accomplished. No doubt, it will be achieved, but no one can say when. Nor can one predict when materials more common than uranium can be used to supply atomic energy. Presumably, such materials would be among the heavier elements of high atomic weight and would be relatively scarce due to their lesser stability. Most of these materials may already have disappeared through radioactive disintegration. So, though the release of atomic energy can be, and no doubt will be, a great boon to mankind, this may not come about for some time.

16   I myself do not have the gift of explanation which would be needed to persuade large numbers of people of the urgency of the problems that now face the human race. Hence, I should like to commend someone who has this gift of explanation: Emery Reves, whose book *The Anatomy of Peace* is intelligent, clear, brief, and, if I may use the absurd term, dynamic on the topic of war and need for world government.

17   Since I do not foresee that atomic energy will prove to be a boon within the near future, I have to say that, for the present, it is a menace. Perhaps it is well that it should be. It may intimidate the human race into bringing order to its international affairs, which, without the pressure of fear, undoubtedly would not happen.

Reading Sources: "Atomic War or Peace"

Read the selection, surveying it to identify key terms and important concepts. Highlight these phrases and ideas, and then answer these questions.

1. What is Einstein's thesis? Where does it appear?
2. Where does Einstein define what he means by *world government?*
3. Why does Einstein begin paragraph 8 with a question?
4. What techniques does Einstein use to link paragraphs 9 through 11?
5. Outline the major points that Einstein makes in paragraphs 13 and 14. How do these points further his argument?
6. Underline the transitional words and phrases that Einstein uses in paragraph 15. How do these elements help readers follow his discussion?

Reacting to Sources

Reread the selection carefully, making marginal notes to aid your comprehension and reinforce connections. Then further annotate the essay if you need to do so in order to answer any of these questions. (You may already have addressed some of the questions in your marginal notes.)

1. After looking up the terms *quantitatively* and *qualitatively,* write a sentence that sums up the main idea of paragraph 1.
2. Using a dictionary if necessary, supply brief marginal definitions of these words as they appear in the essay: *analogous* (2), *monopoly* (7), *commensurate* (14), *boon* (17).
3. What is Einstein's purpose in writing this essay? In a brief marginal note comment on how his purpose affects the essay's usefulness as a source.
4. Do you agree or disagree with the ideas expressed in paragraph 2? Write a marginal comment explaining why.
5. Is Einstein contradicting himself at the end of paragraph 5 when he says, "There must be an end to the concept of non-intervention, for to abandon non-intervention in certain circumstances is part of keeping the peace"? Explain in a marginal note.
6. Einstein begins paragraph 8 by saying that he fears the tyranny of world government. Explain this comment in a marginal note.
7. In view of what we know about the atomic age, what parts of Einstein's essay seem dated? How do these sections affect your response to the rest of the essay?

8. Using an encyclopedia, look up the three scientists that Einstein mentions in paragraph 12. Why does he mention them? Does he expect readers to be familiar with their work? Explain your answer in a journal entry.

9. Throughout his essay, Einstein uses the first person ("I") to make his points. Why do you think he chooses to use this technique?

10. Read the essay's headnote. Comment on how the author's life and other writings might have influenced his ideas. How does your knowledge of his life and work influence your acceptance of those ideas?

11. In paragraph 17 Einstein says, "Since I do not foresee that atomic energy will prove to be a boon within the near future, I have to say that for the present it is a menace." Using your own experience and reading explore this idea further in a journal entry.

12. In a journal entry, compare this essay's central idea with the following statement from paragraph 7 of Norman Cousins's "Modern Man Is Obsolete": "And since man's survival on earth is now absolutely dependent on his ability to avoid a new war, he is faced with the so-far insoluble problem of eliminating those causes" (pp. 175 – 178).

Working with Sources

1. Write a fifty-word summary of paragraphs 1 – 7.
2. Write a critique of the ideas in paragraphs 9 – 11.
3. Read the following two quotations from Einstein's essay and use them in a journal entry in which you express a reaction to the essay.

   "The secret of the bomb should be committed to a world government, and the United States should immediately announce its readiness to do so" (2).

   "But, as soon as possible, we must make it clear that we are not keeping the bomb a secret for the sake of maintaining our power but in the hope of establishing peace through world government, and that we will do our utmost to bring this world government into being" (9).

   Be sure to integrate the quotations smoothly into your writing.
4. Paraphrase paragraphs 13 and 14.
5. Write a one-paragraph synthesis that blends the ideas contained in paragraphs 3 and 4 of this essay with ideas contained in paragraph 13 of "Modern Man Is Obsolete" (pp. 175 – 178).

Writing with Sources: Using a Single Source

Integrating information from "Atomic War or Peace" with your own ideas, write an essay on one of these topics. Be sure to acknowledge all ideas that are not your own.

1. Knowing what you do about the direction in which the world has moved in the forty years since Einstein wrote "Atomic War or Peace," write an essay in which you comment on the accuracy of Einstein's assumptions. Be specific, using material from the essay as the basis for your discussion.
2. Write an essay in which you agree or disagree with the statement "Even though Einstein wrote his essay over forty years ago, his concerns for the future of atomic energy remain current."
3. Write an essay in which you agree or disagree with Einstein's assertion that world government is the only thing that can save the human race from itself.

Modern Man Is Obsolete

Norman Cousins

Norman Cousins was born in 1912 and was educated at Columbia University. An outstanding editor and an author of many books, Cousins has written widely on social and political issues. His most recent books are *Anatomy of an Illness* (1978) and *The Healing Heart* (1983), which examine his successful battle against cancer. "Modern Man Is Obsolete" was written in 1946 in response to the dropping of the atomic bomb. Philosophic in focus, it considers the arrival of the atomic age and the ability of human beings to cope with the challenges of this new era.

1   The beginning of the Atomic Age has brought less hope than fear. It is a primitive fear, the fear of the unknown, the fear of forces man can neither channel nor comprehend. This fear is not new; in its classical form it is the fear of irrational death. But overnight it has become intensified, magnified. It has burst out of the subconscious and into the conscious, filling the mind with primordial apprehensions. It is thus that man stumbles fitfully into a new era of atomic energy for which he is as ill equipped to accept its potential blessings as he is to control its present dangers.

2   Where man can find no answer, he will find fear. While the dust was still settling over Hiroshima, he was asking himself questions and finding no answers. The biggest question of these concerns himself. Is war inevitable because it is in the nature of man? If so, how much time has he left — five, ten, twenty years — before he employs the means now available to him for the ultimate in self-destruction — extinction? If not, then how is he to interpret his own experience, which tells him that in all recorded history there have been only three hundred years in the aggregate during which he was free of war?

3   Clearly following upon these are other questions, flowing out endlessly from his fears and without prospect of definitive answer. Even assuming that he could hold destructive science in check, what changes would the new age bring or demand in his everyday life? What changes would it bring or demand in his culture, his education, his philosophy, his religion, his relationships with other human beings?

4   In speculating upon these questions, it should not be necessary to prove that on August 6, 1945, a new age was born. When on that day a parachute containing a small object floated to earth over Japan, it marked the violent death of one stage in man's history and the beginning of another. Nor should it be necessary to prove the saturating effect of the new age, permeating every aspect of man's activities, from machines to morals, from physics to philosophy, from politics to poetry; in sum, an effect creating a blanket of obsolescence not only over the methods and the products of man but over man himself.

5   It is a curious phenomenon of nature that only two species practice the art of war — men and ants, both of which, significantly, maintain complex social organizations. This does not mean that only men and ants engage in the murder of their own kind. Many animals of the same species kill each other, but only men and ants have practiced the science of organized destruction, employing their massed numbers in violent combat and relying on strategy and tactics to meet developing situations or to capitalize on the weaknesses in the strategy and tactics of the other side. The longest continuous war ever fought between men lasted thirty years. The longest ant war ever recorded lasted six-and-a-half weeks, or whatever the corresponding units would be in ant reckoning.

6   While all entomologists are agreed that war is instinctive with ants, it is encouraging to note that not all anthropologists and biologists are agreed that war is instinctive with men. Those who lean on experience, of course, find everything in man's history to indicate that war is locked up within his nature. But a broader and more generous, certainly more philosophical, view is held by those scientists who claim that the evidence of a war instinct in men is incomplete and misleading, and that man *does* have within him the power of abolishing war. Julian Huxley, the English biologist, draws a sharp distinction between human nature and the *expression* of human nature. Thus war is not a reflection but an expression of man's nature. Moreover, the expression may change, as the factors which lead to war may change. "In man, as in ants, war in any serious sense is bound up with the existence of accumulations of property to fight about. . . . As for human nature, it contains no specific war instinct as does the nature of harvester ants. There is in man's makeup a general aggressive tendency, but this, like all other human urges, is not a specific and unvarying instinct; it can be molded into the most varied forms."

7   But even if this gives us a reassuring answer to the question — is war inevitable because of man's nature? — it still leaves unanswered the question concerning the causes leading up to war. The expression of man's nature will continue to be warlike if the same conditions are continued that have provoked warlike expressions in him in the past. And since man's survival on earth is now absolutely dependent on his ability to avoid a new war, he is faced with the so-far insoluble problem of eliminating those causes.

8   In the most primitive sense, war in man is an expression of his extreme competitive impulses. Like everything else in nature, he has had to fight for

existence; but the battle against other animals, once won, gave way in his evolution to battle against his own kind. Darwin called it natural selection; Spencer called it the survival of the fittest; and its most over-stretched interpretation is to be found in *Mein Kampf,* with the naked glorification of brute force and the complete worship of might makes right. In the political and national sense, it has been the attempt of the "have-nots" to take from the "haves," or the attempt of the "haves" to add further to their lot at the expense of the "have-nots." Not always was property at stake; comparative advantages were measured in terms of power, and in terms of tribal or national superiority. The good luck of one nation became the hard luck of another. The good fortune of the Western powers in obtaining "concessions" in China at the turn of the century was the ill fortune of the Chinese. The power that Germany stripped from Austria, Czechoslovakia, Poland, and France at the beginning of World War II she added to her own.

> *Man is but a reed, the most feeble thing in nature, but he is a thinking reed. The entire universe need not arm itself to crush him. A vapor, a drop of water suffices to kill him. . . . All our dignity, then, consists of thought. By it we must elevate ourselves, and not by space and time which we cannot fill. Let us endeavor then to think well: that is the principle of morality. By space the universe encompasses and swallows me up like an atom; by thought I comprehend the world.*
> —BLAISE PASCAL, "The Philosophers" (1670)

> *Let Earth unbalanced from her orbit fly,*
> *Planets and Suns run lawless through the sky;*
> *Let ruling angels from their spheres be hurled,*
> *Beings on Beings wrecked, and world on world . . .*
>   *So, wondrous creature, mount where Science guides;*
> *Go, measure Earth, weigh air, and state the tides;*
> *Instruct the planets in what orbs to run,*
> *Correct old Time, and regulate the Sun . . .*
>
>   . . .
>
> *Atoms or systems into ruin hurled,*
> *And now a bubble, burst, and now a world.*
> — ALEXANDER POPE, "An Essay on Man" (1733)

9   What does it matter, then, if war is not in the nature of man so long as man continues through the expression of his nature to be a viciously competitive animal? The effect is the same, and therefore the result must be as conclusive —war being the effect, and complete obliteration of the human species being the ultimate result.

10   If this reasoning is correct, then modern man is obsolete, a self-made anachronism becoming more incongruous by the minute. He has exalted change in everything but himself. He has leaped centuries ahead in inventing a new world to live in, but he knows little or nothing about his own part in that world. He has surrounded and confounded himself with gaps — gaps between revolutionary technology and evolutionary man, between cosmic gadgets and human wisdom, between intellect and conscience. The struggle between

science and morals that Henry Thomas Buckle foresaw a century ago has been all but won by science.

11   Given ample time, man might be expected eventually to span those gaps normally; but by his own hand, he is destroying even time. Decision and execution in the modern world are becoming virtually synchronous. Thus, whatever gaps man has to span he will have to span immediately.

12   This involves both biology and will. If he lacks the actual and potential biological equipment to build those bridges, then the birth certificate of the atomic age is in reality a *memento mori*. But even if he possesses the necessary biological equipment, he must still make the decision which says that he is to apply himself to the challenge. Capability without decision is inaction and inconsequence.

13   Man is left, then, with a crisis in decision. The main test before him involves his *will* to change rather than his *ability* to change. That he is capable of change is certain. For there is no more mutable or adaptable animal in the world. We have seen him migrate from one extreme clime to another. We have seen him step out of backward societies and join advanced groups within the space of a single generation. This is not to imply that the changes were necessarily always for the better; only that change was and is possible. But change requires stimulus; and mankind today need look no further for stimulus than its own desire to stay alive. The critical power of change, says Spengler, is directly linked to the survival drive. Once the instinct for survival is stimulated, the basic condition for change can be met.

14   That is why the power of total destruction as potentially represented by modern science must be dramatized and kept in the forefront of public opinion. The full dimensions of the peril must be seen and recognized. Only then will man realize that the first order of business is the question of continued existence. Only then will he be prepared to make the decisions necessary to assure that survival.

No man can rob us of our will. — EPICTETUS (c. 60)

Reading Sources: "Modern Man Is Obsolete"

Read the selection, surveying it to identify key terms and important concepts. Highlight these phrases and ideas, and then answer these questions.

1. What ideas does Cousins contrast in paragraph 1?
2. What is the importance of the terms *primitive, nature,* and *change* in this essay?
3. How does Cousins link the ideas in paragraph 6 with the ideas in paragraph 7? Identify any sentence whose primary purpose is to provide transition.
4. What is the thesis of this essay? What information does Cousins provide to support his thesis?

5. Where does Cousins begin his conclusion? What phrase does he use to introduce this section of his essay?

Reacting to Sources

Reread the selection carefully, making marginal notes to aid your comprehension and reinforce connections. Then further annotate the essay if you need to do so in order to answer any of these questions. (You may already have addressed some of the questions in your marginal notes.)

1. In a few sentences, rewrite paragraph 1 to simplify its ideas.
2. Using a dictionary if necessary, supply brief marginal definitions of these words as they are used in the essay: *primordial* (1), *saturating* (4), *permeating* (4), *obsolescence* (4), *anachronism* (10), *incongruous* (10).
3. What is the function of the quotations that Cousins includes with his essay? Write one or two sentences next to each one, explaining its relevance.
4. Do you agree or disagree with the following statement: "The expression of man's nature will continue to be warlike if the same conditions are continued that have provoked warlike expressions in him in the past" (7). Write a journal entry in which you explain why.
5. Write three marginal questions in response to the statements in paragraph 10.
6. Give two examples to support Cousins's assertion in paragraph 2: "Where man can find no answer, he will find fear."
7. "Given ample time, man might be expected eventually to span those gaps normally; but by his own hand he is destroying even time" (11). Do you agree or disagree with this statement? Write a journal entry explaining why.
8. Identify Cousins's purpose in writing this essay. Compose a journal entry in which you explain your answer.
9. In a journal entry comment on how the explosion of the atomic bomb in 1945 might have influenced the ideas that Cousins presents in his essay.
10. In marginal notes explain Cousins's reference to Darwin, Spencer, and the book *Mein Kampf* in paragraph 8 and to Oswald Spengler in paragraph 13. Use an encyclopedia to look up names that are unfamiliar to you.
11. In a journal entry compare Cousins's thesis in this essay to Einstein's in his essay. How do you account for the similarities and the differences?
12. Outline the ideas in paragraphs 8–12. How do these ideas set the stage for Cousins's conclusion in paragraphs 13 and 14?

Working with Sources

1. Write a summary of the ideas in paragraphs 5 and 6.
2. Write a critique of the ideas in paragraph 8.

3. Use the following two quotations from the essay in a journal entry in which you express a reaction to the essay:

   "If this reasoning is correct, then modern man is obsolete, a self-made anachronism becoming more incongruous by the minute" (10).

   "That is why the power of total destruction as potentially represented by modern science must be dramatized and kept in the forefront of public opinion" (14).

   Be sure to integrate the quotations smoothly into your writing.
4. Paraphrase paragraphs 10 through 12.
5. Write a one-paragraph synthesis that blends the ideas contained in paragraphs 9 and 13 of this essay with the ideas contained in paragraph 17 of "Atomic War or Peace" (pp. 169–173).

Writing with Sources: Using a Single Source

Integrating information from "Modern Man Is Obsolete" with your own ideas, write an essay on one of these topics. Be sure to acknowledge all ideas that are not your own.

1. Write an essay in which you respond to Cousins's assertion that modern man is obsolete. Use the essay and your own experience as your sources of information.
2. "The main test," says Cousins in paragraph 13, is man's "*will* to change rather than his *ability* to change." Write an essay in which you argue that in the years since the bomb was dropped, people have (or have not) demonstrated the will to change.
3. In paragraph 2 Cousins asks, "Is war inevitable because it is in the nature of man?" Write an essay in which you agree or disagree with the conclusion that he reaches.

Writing with Sources: Using Multiple Sources

Integrating information from sources in this chapter with your own ideas, write an essay on one of the following topics. Be sure to acknowledge ideas that are not your own.

1. In "That Day at Hiroshima" Leighton predicts that "the bomb dropped at Hiroshima will be considered primitive by future standards" (18). In "Atomic War or Peace," Einstein says, "Since I do not foresee that atomic energy will prove to be a boon within the near future, I have to say that, for the present, it is a menace" (17). Use these and several other predictions made in the readings in

this chapter to assess the accuracy of predictions made in 1945 about the atomic age.

2. Read a section of the revised (1985) edition of John Hersey's *Hiroshima,* and compare its descriptions with those in "That Day at Hiroshima."

3. Using information culled from all of the readings in this chapter, write your own essay entitled either "The U.S. Was Right" or "The U.S. Was Wrong."

4. The dropping of the bomb signaled the beginning of the nuclear age. In an essay compare the responses of Einstein and Cousins to this new age, and discuss how both men try to come to terms with the advent of nuclear power.

5. Write an essay in which you develop your own theory of why the United States dropped the atomic bomb. Use the essays in this section as source material, and include critiques of the ideas that disagree with your position.

6

The Legacy of the Fifties

Those who did not live through the fifties often tend to see it as an innocent, carefree decade—a time of hula hoops and poodle skirts, bobby socks and convertibles—and, most of all, as a decade dominated by the emergence of television and by the culture of the teenager. But many other forces contributed to shaping the decade. In politics, in music, in literature, in science and medicine, and even in the American family, it was a time when old assumptions and values were challenged and a time when new uncertainties and fears emerged. The events of the fifties changed the course of our lives both as individuals and as a nation and continue to have an impact on our society today.

In "The Big Barbecue" Landon Y. Jones chronicles the post-World War II migration to the suburbs and the adjustments this exodus necessitated in the lives of Americans. He also examines the growing influence of the postwar "baby boom" on U.S. social and economic institutions. In "The Summer Before Salk" Charles Mee, Jr., recreates the fearful climate of the tense and tragic summer that preceded the development of the first vaccine against polio. The Editors of Time/ Life Books trace the development of a different kind of fear: in "I Have Here in My Hand . . . " they follow the rise to power of Senator Joseph McCarthy and examine the impact of his accusations on the American people. Cultural changes that took place during the fifties are considered by Charlie Gillett in "The Rise of Rock and Roll" and by John Tytell in "The Beat Generation." Both selections explore the tension between the conservative mainstream and disturbing new influences. Finally, William Manchester's "Beep Beep" looks forward to the next several decades with an account of the impact of Sputnik, the first satellite to orbit the earth, on U.S. political and educational philosophy.

182

The Big Barbecue

Landon Y. Jones

Landon Jones, a frequent commentator on the baby boom phenomenon, has consulted at the White House and at the U.S. Congress and written articles for such publications as *The Atlantic, Esquire,* and *Saturday Review*. A native of St. Louis, Jones is presently the managing editor of *Money* magazine. "The Big Barbecue" is a chapter from his popular history *Great Expectations* published in 1980. Subtitled *America and the Baby Boom Generation,* the book sets out to show the tremendous impact on American social, cultural, and political life of this group of children, whom Jones calls "the largest and most influential generation America has ever produced."

1   In the early 1950s, the huge Census Clock in Washington was clicking like a runaway taxi meter. Every seven seconds the Birth Light blinked off a new baby. Boys were arriving with familiar names like Robert, John, James, Michael, William, Richard, Joseph, Thomas, Steven, and David, making a Top Ten of favorite names that was proudly all-American. Girls were named Linda, Mary, Barbara, Patricia, Susan, Kathleen, Carol, Nancy, Margaret, and Diane. And perhaps thanks to Debbie Reynolds, "Deborah" would have a run all of her own later in the decade.

2   Like the steel industry, mothering was running at close to 100 percent capacity, and it was harder and harder to keep up. In January of 1952, General Electric decided to celebrate its seventy-fifth anniversary by awarding five shares of common stock to any employee who had a baby on October 15. Some public-relations whiz tried to predict the eventual number of winners by dividing the total of 226,000 G.E. employees by the U.S. crude birthrate. Unfortunately, he forgot that G.E. workers as a population were considerably more fertile than the United States as a whole, since they contained no one under 17 nor over 65. In the end, the company's guess that thirteen G.E. babies would be born amounted to underestimation on a grand scale. The workers, true to the thriving surplus economy of the era, came through with no less than 189 new G.E. babies that day.

3   But General Electric was not about to complain. It was investing $650 million in new plants and assembly lines over seven postwar years to prepare for the boom in babies. As early as 1948, *Time* noted that the U.S. population had just increased by "2,800,000 more consumers" (*not* babies) the year before. Economists happily predicted that the new babies would set off a demand explosion for commodities such as homes, foodstuffs, clothing, furniture, appliances, and schools, to name only a few examples. *Fortune* pronounced the baby boom "exhilarating" and with an almost-audible sigh of relief concluded that the low birthrates of the 1930s were a "freakish interlude, rather than a trend." "We need not stew too much about a post-armament depression," the magazine wrote. "A civilian market growing by the size of Iowa every year ought to be able to absorb whatever production the military will eventually turn loose."

4   As the economic and baby booms surged on together, the cheerleading became almost feverish. Public-service signs went up in New York City subways reading, "Your future is great in a growing America. Every day 11,000 babies are born in America. This means new business, new jobs, new opportunities." After-dinner speakers began to talk about "Prosperity by Population" and lofted tantalizing guesses of up to five million new babies a year by 1975. Financial magazines editorialized about the joys of "this remarkable boom." "Gone, for the first time in history," announced *Time* in 1955, "is the worry over whether a society can produce enough goods to take care of its people. The lingering worry is whether it will have enough people to consume the goods."

5   The most euphoric article of all, perhaps, was a story *Life* printed in 1958, at the height of the boom. Three dozen children were crowded onto the cover along with the banner headline: KIDS: BUILT-IN RECESSION CURE — HOW 4,000,000 A YEAR MAKE MILLIONS IN BUSINESS. Inside, the article began with another headline — ROCKETING BIRTHS: BUSINESS BONANZA — and continued chockablock with statistics and photographs about new citizens who were "a brand-new market for food, clothing, and shelter." In its first year, *Life* calculated, a baby is not just a child but already a prodigious consumer, "a potential market for $800 worth of products." Even before returning from the hospital, an infant had "already rung up $450 in medical expenses." Four-year-olds are not just sugar and spice or puppy-dog tails but rather represent "a backlog of business orders that will take two decades to fulfill." A rhapsodic *Life* then clinched its case by visiting Joe Powers, a thirty-five-year-old salesman from Port Washington, New York. He and his wife, Carol, had produced ten children and were buying 77 quarts of milk and 28 loaves of bread a week, just for starters. Faced with examples like that of meritorious devotion to the Procreation Ethic, little wonder that some American mothers felt as if it were their *duty* to have children. Either they were pregnant or, if not, wondered whether they should be.

6   The baby-boom kids had kicked off in America a buccaneering orgy of buying and selling that carried all things before it. The only thing like it earlier was the Gilded Age of the post–Civil War 1870s, which the historian Vernon Louis Parrington so aptly dubbed "the Great Barbecue." Here was a feast spread out for an entire nation, and everyone scrambling for it. More food was spoiled than eaten, perhaps, and the revelry was a bit unseemly, but no one minded. Everywhere people were getting rich in a demographic debauch.

7   The spending boom started, literally, at the bottom. Diapers went from a $32-million industry in 1947 to $50 million in 1957. The diaper services (disposables had not yet arrived) also prospered. Mothers and fathers were paying $5 million annually (twice the preboom business) to have baby's shoes bronze-plated at L. E. Mason, Inc., in Boston. The under-5 appetite, which had grown from 13 million mouths to 20 million by 1960, more than one out of every ten Americans, was consuming baby food at a rate of 1.5 billion cans a year in 1953 (up from 270 million cans in 1940).

8   As the kids grew up, so did the markets. Throughout the 1950s, the 5–13 age group grew by an additional one million baby boomers every year. The toy

industry set sales records annually after 1940, growing from an $84-million-a-year stripling to a $1.25-billion giant. Sales of bicycles doubled to two million a year; cowboy outfits became a $75-million subindustry; space-science toys claimed another $60 million. Children's clothes became a boom market, and packaging researchers suddenly discovered the troika of "family" sizes — Giant, Economy, and Supereconomy. At its peak, the juvenile market was ringing up a staggering $33 billion annually.

9   The rain of spending did not fall evenly on society. Rather, it was both a cause and an effect of what amounted to the opening of a new American frontier: the suburbs. Historians had already suggested that America's expansiveness during the nineteenth century was built on the common goal of settling the West. Now there was a new impetus behind the conquering of the suburban frontier: babies. The suburbs were conceived for the baby boom — and vice versa. Here in green garlands around the cities, Americans were creating new child-oriented societies, "babyvilles" teeming with new appetites, new institutions, and new values. Families who were asked why they moved to the suburbs first mentioned better housing and leisure, as if they were conforming to the old goal of a country place that began with the French aristocracy. But then, invariably, they added that they thought suburbia was "a better place to bring up the kids." The common acceptance of this goal united the suburbs. "Instead of the wagon train, where people leaned on one another as they moved across the continent," historian Daniel Boorstin remarked, "Americans in suburbs leaned on one another as they moved rapidly about the country and up the ladder of consumption." Author William H. Whyte found the same communal spirit in his examination of the mythical suburb of Park Forest. Families shared baby-sitters, cribs, lawn mowers, tea services, and baseball equipment. "We laughed at first at how the Marxist society had finally arrived," one suburban executive told Whyte. "But I think the real analogy is to the pioneers."

10   As an internal migration, the settling of the suburbs was phenomenal. In the twenty years from 1950 to 1970, the population of the suburbs doubled from 36 million to 72 million. No less than 83 percent of the total population growth in the United States during the 1950s was in the suburbs, which were growing fifteen times faster than any other segment of the country. As people packed and moved, the national mobility rate leaped by 50 percent. The only other comparable influx was the wave of European immigrants to the United States around the turn of the century. But, as *Fortune* pointed out, more people moved to the suburbs every year than had ever arrived on Ellis Island.

11   By now, bulldozers were churning up dust storms as they cleared the land for housing developments. More than a million acres of farmland were plowed under every year during the 1950s. Millions of apartment-dwelling parents with two children were suddenly realizing that two children could be doubled up in a spare bedroom, but a third child cried loudly for something more. The proportion of new houses with three or more bedrooms, in fact, rose from one-third in 1947 to three-quarters by 1954. The necessary *Lebensraum* could only be found in the suburbs. There was a housing shortage, but young couples armed with VA and FHA loans built their dream homes with easy credit and

free spending habits that were unthinkable to the baby-boom grandparents, who shook their heads with the Depression still fresh in their memories. Of the 13 million homes built in the decade before 1958, 11 million of them—or 85 percent—were built in the suburbs. Home ownership rose 50 percent between 1940 and 1950, and another 50 percent by 1960. By then, one-fourth of *all* housing in the United States had been built in the fifties. For the first time, more Americans owned homes than rented them.

12   We were becoming a land of gigantic nurseries. The biggest were built by Abraham Levitt, the son of poor Russian-Jewish immigrants, who had originally built houses for the Navy during the war. The first of three East Coast Levittowns went up on the potato fields of Long Island. Exactly $7900—or $60 a month and no money down—bought you a Monopoly-board bungalow with four rooms, attic, washing machine, outdoor barbecue, and a television set built into the wall. The 17,447 units eventually became home to 82,000 people, many of whom were pregnant or wanted to be. In a typical story on the suburban explosion, one magazine breathlessly described a volleyball game of nine couples in which no less than five of the women were expecting.

13   Marketers were quick to spot what amounted to capitalism's Klondike Lode. "Anybody who wants to sell anything to Americans should take a long look at the New Suburbia," marveled *Fortune* in 1953. "It is big and lush and uniform—a combination made to order for the comprehending marketer." It went far beyond toys and diapers. In suburbia's servantless society, laborsaving devices were necessary adjuncts to having children. The number of washing machines sold in America went from 1.7 million in 1950 to 2.6 million in 1960. Sales of electric clothes dryers doubled during one two-year stretch. With a then-astonishing average family income of $6500 (compared to $3800 for everyone else), the suburbanites were creating an American way of spending organized around children and the needs they created. Retailers eagerly followed them to the suburbs, opening branch stores by the dozen and clearing the way for the later age of shopping malls.

14   The settlers of suburbia also brought with them beasts of burden. They had Fords in their future—and Chevys and De Sotos and Hudsons and Studebakers. The car, especially the second car, was the one indispensable suburban accessory. Car registrations soared along with the birthrate: from 26 million in 1945 to 40 million in 1950 to 60 million by the end of the decade. The number of two-car families rose 750,000 a year and doubled from 1951 to 1958. Station wagons, the housewife's version of the Willys Jeep, began crisscrossing the suburbs like water bugs, dropping off husbands, picking up children, stopping by the supermarket. "A suburban mother's role is to deliver children obstetrically once," said Peter De Vries, "and by car forever after." *Time* joked that "if the theory of evolution is still working, it may well one day transform the suburban housewife's right foot into a flared paddle, grooved for easy traction on the gas pedal and brake."

15   Even in those days, the automobile had seized its central place in the emotional life of the baby boom. It was the first entire generation to be driven before it walked. It was the first generation to grow up in cars, even to seek its

entertainment in cars. Back in 1933 a chemicals manufacturer named Richard Hollinshead had turned a parking lot in Camden, New Jersey, into the World's First Automobile Movie Theatre. Fifteen years later, there were only 480 drive-ins in the country. But between 1948 and 1958 the number zoomed to 4000, equipped with everything from playgrounds for the kids to Laundromats for Mom. For millions of baby-boom parents, a night at the drive-in neatly solved the suburban dilemma of what to do if you couldn't get a baby-sitter. Much later, the adolescent baby boomers would find their own use for the passion pits. Here is Lisa Alther in *Kinflicts:*

> Mixed with the dialogue were the various sighs and gasps and sucking sounds from the front seats and blasts from car horns throughout the parking area as, in keeping with Hullsport High tradition, couples signalled that they'd gone all the way.

16   Nowhere was the postwar baby-surburb-car symbiosis more symbolically apparent than during the gasoline shortage of July 1979 in the Philadelphia suburb of Levittown, Pennsylvania. There some 75,000 people live on 7000 acres of suburb. But, for a city of such density, it is served by little mass transportation. Threatened by the loss of their cars, angry young Levittowners staged the nation's first gas riot, burning cars, stoning ambulances, and battling police. Ironically, many of the 195 who were arrested belonged to the same families who had originally settled there during the baby-boom years and who, in 1960, won the Little League World Series for Levittown.

17   Meanwhile, the suburbs continued to grow and prosper and create a whole new sequence of bench marks for American Studies teachers. In 1956, white-collar workers outnumbered blue-collar workers for the first time. In 1970, the suburbs became the largest single sector of the nation's population, exceeding both central cities and the farms. By 1972, the suburbs were even offering more jobs than the central cities. Everyone was enthusiastically buying "on time" (as it was called then), and the number of Americans who thought installment financing was a good thing increased from 50 percent to 60 percent in ten years.

18   Sociologists began to pursue the suburbanites like doctors after a new virus. The baby-boom parents were poked and prodded and examined with the kind of fascination hitherto reserved for South Sea Islanders. They were, to be sure, pioneering a life-style (the dread word first came into currency then) that would be predominant in America. Often living in small houses filled with children, they moved outside to their patios and barbecue pits and created a new, rigorously informal style. Lawn and porch furniture sales went from $53 million in 1950 to $145 million in 1960. Hot dog production likewise zoomed from 750 million pounds to more than 2 billion pounds in the decade. Everyone first-named everyone and no one criticized the neighbor's kids (at least in front of a neighbor). Books of the time began to portray a strange netherworld of rathskellers and dens, of cheese dips and cocktails (the required icebreakers in a highly mobile society), or Kaffeeklatsches and card parties, and of outer-directed husbands and neurotic corporate wives.

19   Some of these studies no doubt revealed more of the anxieties of the

examiners than the examined. (Did ordinary citizens really have "identity crises"?) But, if there was a common message, it was of the *sameness* of suburbia. It was as if the same forces that produced prosperity and fertility also produced homogeneity. Parents had rediscovered the old verities — home, hearth, children, church. But they had also made a faith out of brand names, modular housing, and gray flannel suits. Everywhere were the same drugstores, the same franchises, the same music on the radio. The children, too, were being shaped by a world of repeatable experience. But they were not being molded by their parents or their teachers. Instead, there was another dominant presence in the early lives of the baby boomers. It was one that would forge their unity as a generation. It would mobilize them as a consumer force. It was television. In 1938, E. B. White prophesied that "television is going to be the test of the modern world and . . . in this new opportunity to see beyond the range of our vision we shall discover either a new and unbearable disturbance of the general peace or a saving radiance in the sky. We shall stand or fall by television — of that I am quite sure." In the year White wrote that, barely 2 percent of American families owned the small, flickering Philcos and DuMonts dwarfed in their elephantine cabinets. But in less than a decade, the age of television swept over us. From fewer than 6000 sets manufactured at the baby boom's outset in 1946, production leaped, almost impossibly, to 7 million a year by 1953. Eighty-six percent of American homes had television sets at the end of the decade and, by 1967, 98 percent of all homes had sets, effectively saturating the market. The exponential growth curve of television was steeper than that of any other technological innovation of the century — including the telephone, radio, and automobile.

20   It was also the most important new child-care development of the century, one that would redefine the environment in which Americans grew up. Some of the oldest baby boomers remember when the first sets were lugged into their homes. But, for most, television was not an intruder in the home but what Buckminster Fuller called "the third parent," practically a family member itself. These children treated the glowing box not with the awe due a mysterious and wonderful invention but with the unquestioned familiarty of an old armchair or the kitchen sink.

21   Families wanted to stay home in the 1950s, and television made it easier. Aside from the growth in drive-ins, movies almost withered away during the baby-boom years. In 1946, the first year of the boom, Hollywood had recorded its biggest year ever: 400 features were released and 90 million went to the movies every week. Then in 1947, movie attendance dropped 10 percent as parents stayed home with their babies. By January 1953, when a record 50 million of them watched another baby-boom mother, Lucy Ricardo, have her baby on *I Love Lucy,* movie attendance had been cut to one-half the 1946 level, despite such lures as 3-D movies. (The first was *Bwana Devil* in 1952.) With most of its screens located in emptying downtowns instead of expanding suburbs — in New York City alone, 55 theaters closed in 1951 — Hollywood lost an audience it would not even begin to reclaim until it squeezed theaters into suburban malls twenty years later.

22   Television, meanwhile, was giving the baby-boom children a series of vivid images that would color their memories forever. They all sang "M-I-C-K-E-Y M-O-U-S-E" with Karen and Doreen. (In those days, no one noticed that there were no black or Asian or Hispanic Mousketeers.) They grew up glued to *Howdy Doody,* part of a vast Peanut Gallery in a national Doodyville. Mr. Bluster was a faintly disguised Ike, and as author Jeff Greenfield has observed, Clarabell was the original Yippie. Two decades later, in the aftermath of the Vietnam antiwar strife, Buffalo Bob and Howdy put together a road show that offered a burned-out student generation a return to a childhood myth that somehow seemed more real, or at least comforting, than the 1960s had been.

23   The baby-boom parents themselves were mirrored in nuclear-family dramas like *The Adventures of Ozzie and Harriet, Father Knows Best,* and *The Life of Riley.* Yet, on TV at least, the birthrate remained surprisingly low — evidently the bumbling Ozzie Nelsons and Chester A. Rileys were a lot more savvy about some family matters than their children ever could have suspected. (*The Brady Bunch,* with its amalgram of six children by two different marriages, was more of a postboom family that arrived ahead of its time.) Perhaps the prototypical baby-boom family was the Cleavers in *Leave It To Beaver.* Beaver Cleaver could have been penned by Norman Rockwell as a sort of Tom Sawyer relocated in Pasadena. The rumor that the actor who played Beaver, Jerry Mathers, had been killed later in Vietnam seemed cruelly symbolic of the death of the generation's own innocence. (The reality was, if anything, even more appropriate: Mathers had actually gone from selling insurance to real estate, while his klutzy buddy, Eddie Haskell, had really become a cop with the Los Angeles Police Department.)

24   As the baby boomers grew out of diapers, advertisers looked at the figures and discovered that American mothers had created the biggest market in history. Now technology had produced the tool to move it: television. The earliest ads had been silly jingles about chlorophyll toothpaste and chlorophyll chewing gum. But then a marketing consultant named Eugene Gilbert stumbled on a galvanizing truth: "An advertiser who touches a responsive chord in youth can generally count on the parent to succumb finally to purchasing the product." It was the Relativity Theorem of television: a law that changed everything. Money for commercials flowed like a river as TV went about the business of turning toddlers into consumer trainees. Tests showed that children could recognize the word "detergent" before they could read. They sang "Pepsi-Cola hits the spot/Twelve full ounces, that's a lot" before they knew the national anthem. They were trained to buy. As Joyce Maynard wrote in her autobiographical memoir, published when she was all of 20, "We are, in the fullest sense, *consumers,* trained to salivate not at a bell but at the sight of a Kellogg's label or a Dunkin' Donuts box." This generation could not be organized socially or politically, Dwight Macdonald argued, because it had already been organized as a body of affluent consumers. Fittingly, the NBC program *Saturday Night Live,* which later drew its audience from the grown-up kids of the fifties, chose as one of its first satirical themes something they knew best: commercials.

25   Let's turn now to what was the most fruitful expression of the alliance between television and advertising and the boom generation: fads. Fads were so much intertwined with the social history of the fifties that it is easy to forget that they've always been a part of the American scene. This century had already given us everything from Mah-Jongg to marathon dancing to miniature golf. But there's one crucial difference between the earlier fads and the crazes of the fifties. Fads used to be started by young adults and then spread up and down to younger and older people. But the fads of the fifties, almost without exception, were creations of the children. They flowed *up*. Back in the twenties or thirties, for instance, it would have been impossible to imagine the under-ten group starting anything. They were just as demographically powerless then as they are now. But in the fifties, the critical mass of baby boomers entered the impressionable pre-school and elementary-school ages. And where the baby boom went was where the action would be.

26   Toy manufacturers have always gone straight for the jugular of childhood: imaginative play. What has always been the sustaining fantasy of American children? The West. In the suburbs, millions of pint-sized cowboys were riding the ranges. Hopalong Cassidy was their first hero, and by 1950 kids were wearing some $40 million worth of Hoppy's black outfits and six-shooters. Then Gene Autry, Roy Rogers, Wyatt Earp, and the Cisco Kid rounded up another $283 million on toy guns, boots, chaps, and lassos between 1955 and 1959. The generation that someday would passionately oppose a foreign war won its spurs early at home, acquiring a peacetime arsenal that rivaled the Pentagon's in firepower.

27   Television merchandised these Burbank cowpokes with enough success to make marketers look increasingly seriously at the young generation. Then, in 1955, the baby boom unleashed its economic clout once and for all in the biggest bonanza to date. The previous December, some 40 million Americans had watched as 29-year-old Fess Parker pulled on Davy Crockett's buckskins on *Disneyland* (ABC, Wednesday night). As director Steven Spielberg remembered it:

> I was in third grade at the time. Suddenly the next day, everybody in my class but me was Davy Crockett. And because I didn't have my coonskin cap and my powder horn, or Old Betsy, my rifle, and the chaps, I was deemed the Mexican leader, Santa Anna. And they chased me home from school until I got my parents to buy me a coonskin cap.

By May, Davy Crockett was whooping and hollering into a seven-month shopping spree that saw more than $100 million change hands. A record, "The Balled of Davy Crockett" by Bill Hayes, became one of the biggest hits of all time, with versions in sixteen languages, not to mention the "Davy Crockett Mambo." The wholesale price of raccoon skins jumped from 26 cents a pound to $8 a pound. More than 3000 different Crockett items were moving off the shelves, including sweat shirts, sleds, blankets, snowsuits, toothbrushes, and lunch boxes.

28   Then, at Christmas, Crockett collapsed. The kids had burned it out overnight. The price of Crocket T-shirts was slashed from $1.29 apiece to 33 cents and still were not moving. Crockett had "pancaked," *Variety* groaned in a headline. "He laid a bomb." Not exactly. Crockett turned out to be a different kind of pathfinder. The hold of Walt Disney on childhood imagination, building throughout the fifties, was stronger than ever. The "Frontierland" that Disney made a staple of his amusement parks owes it all to Fess Parker. More importantly, the baby-boom children had come into their own as consumers who could make or break entire product lines. The discovery was exhilarating. Surveying the thriving market of 1955, a Seattle banker announced, "Anybody who can't find cause for at least selective optimism is just congenitally morose." In its year-end review, *Time* concluded that "1955 showed the flowering of American capitalism."

29   For the rest of the decade, other fads swarmed like mayflies in the sun. In 1958, two Pasadena entrepreneurs imported an idea from another baby-boom country, Australia. Their Wham-O corporation began to manufacture simple plastic hoops at a cost of 50 cents each and sold them for $1.98. Hula-Hoops became a national infatuation. Upwards of 20,000 were manufactured daily and Wham-O and its imitators flooded the market with more than 20 million in a matter of months. (A loophole — or better, hoophole — in the patent law prevented Wham-O from cornering the market.) Then, like Davy Crockett, Hula-Hoops fizzled quickly in the winter. *The Wall Street Journal's* epitaph: HOOPS HAVE HAD IT. But the unconscious eroticism the fad had released found another expression just two years later when the same kids started a swivel-hipped dance craze called the Twist.

30   All of these fads had an effect on the baby boom that made them unlike children of the past. They were the first generation of children to be isolated by Madison Avenue as an identifiable market. That is the appropriate word: *isolated*. Marketing, and especially television, *isolated* their needs and wants from those of their parents. From the cradle, the baby boomers had been surrounded by products created especially for them, from Silly Putty to Slinkys to skateboards. New products, new toys, new commercials, new fads — the dictatorship of the new — was integral to the baby-boom experience. So prevalent was it that baby boomers themselves rarely realized how different it made them. They breathed it like air.

31   Joyce Maynard remembered how a typical new product, Barbie dolls, arrived in her world "like a cloudburst, without preparation. Barbie wasn't just a toy, but a way of living that moved us suddenly from tea parties to dates with Ken at the soda shoppe." In twenty years, Mattel sold 112 million copies of Barbie, Ken, little sister Skipper, cousin Francie, and dozens of others to Joyce Maynard and her peers. Barbie has worn one thousand outfits, enough to make Mattel one of the top manufacturers of women's clothing in the world. Barbie herself, gifted with a high-breasted, wasp-waisted look and a plastic personality, was born in 1959 and turned twenty-one in 1980. For that matter, the prototype Barbie — designer Bill Barton's daughter Barbie — is also a baby boomer.

That's the way it's always been for the baby boom. Products were made for the generation, and the generation was made for the products.

Reading Sources: "The Big Barbecue"

Read the selection, surveying it to identify key terms and important concepts. Highlight these phrases and ideas, and then answer these questions.

1. List some of the sources to which Jones attributes his information. Given the purpose and audience of the popular history from which this essay is drawn, are his sources appropriate? Explain.
2. Why does Jones call this selection "The Big Barbecue"?
3. What is the baby boom? List the most dramatic trends Jones associates with the baby boom.
4. In his own descriptions and in the quotations he selects, Jones stresses the close association between the baby boom and the accompanying economic boom. Give examples of the economic terms he applies to the fifties children to make this association explicit.
5. Jones relies heavily on statistical evidence and direct quotations in this essay. Cite some examples of his use of each. Would other types of evidence work as well in these contexts? Explain.
6. Identify the boundaries of the paragraph cluster introduced by the topic sentence of paragraph 10. What other paragraph clusters can you identify in the essay?
7. Is paragraph 16 merely a digression, or does it serve a useful purpose in the essay? Explain.
8. What, according to Jones, was the "one crucial difference between the earlier fads and the crazes of the fifties" (25)? Why is this difference so significant?
9. Does this essay have a thesis — a central statement to make about the baby boom children? Explain.

Reacting to Sources

Reread the selection carefully, making marginal notes to aid your comprehension and reinforce connections. Then further annotate the selection if you need to do so in order to answer any of these questions. (You may already have addressed some of the questions in your marginal notes.)

1. Using a dictionary if necessary, supply brief marginal definitions of these words as they are used in this selection: *euphoric* (5), *prodigious* (5), *rhapsodic* (5), *buccaneering* (6), *unseemly* (6), *debauch* (6), *stripling* (8), *troika* (8), *impetus* (9), *Lebensraum* (11), *symbiosis* (16), *netherworld* (18), *rathskellers* (18), *exponential* (19), *prototypical* (23), *klutzy* (23), *galvanizing* (24), *demographically* (25).

2. Explain in a brief marginal note what Jones means by each of the following: "capitalism's Klondike Lode" (13); "Clarabell was the original Yippie" (22); "It was the Relativity Theorem of television . . ." (24).
3. In a few sentences, rewrite paragraph 5 to simplify its ideas.
4. Outline the paragraph cluster beginning with paragraph 14 and extending through paragraph 16.
5. Write three questions to clarify your understanding of the ideas in paragraph 19.
6. In paragraph 20, Jones calls television "the most important new child-care development of the century, one that would redefine the environment in which Americans grew up." Give several examples from the essay to support this general statement.
7. In paragraph 22, Jones notes parenthetically, "In those days, no one noticed that there were no black or Asian or Hispanic Mousketeers." Write a journal entry in which you explore your reactions to this statement.
8. Do you agree or disagree with Dwight Macdonald's statement paraphrased by Jones in paragraph 24? Write a journal entry in which you explain why.
9. In a journal entry, explore your reactions to this statement: "The generation that someday would passionately oppose a foreign war won its spurs early at home, acquiring a peacetime arsenal that rivaled the Pentagon's in firepower" (26).
10. In a journal entry, consider possible similarities and differences between the fads of the fifties and those of your own childhood.

Working with Sources

1. Write a seventy-five-word summary of paragraph 9.
2. Write a critique of the ideas in paragraph 30.
3. Write a journal entry in which you explore your reactions to these quotations from "The Big Barbecue":

> "The baby-boom kids had kicked off in America a buccaneering orgy of buying and selling that carried all things before it" (6).

> ". . . the baby-boom children had come into their own as consumers who could make or break entire product lines. The discovery was exhilarating" (28).

> "Products were made for the generation, and the generation was made for the products" (31).

Be sure to integrate the quotations smoothly into your writing.
4. Paraphrase paragraph 20.
5. Write a one-paragraph synthesis that blends ideas in sentences 3–8 of paragraph 19 of "The Big Barbecue" and those in paragraph 9 of "The Beat Generation" (pp. 216–221).

Writing with Sources: Using a Single Source

Integrating information from "The Big Barbecue" with your own ideas, write an essay on one of these topics. Be sure to acknowledge ideas that are not your own.

1. Jones compares the settlers of the suburbs in the fifties both to the American pioneers during the nineteenth century (9) and to "the wave of European immigrants to the United States around the turn of the century" (10). In an essay, consider how the phenomenon of the move to the suburbs in the fifties was like and unlike the other two migrations.
2. Write an essay in which you consider how your own experiences have been similar to or different from those of a typical suburban child of the fifties. You may choose to focus on one aspect of life in the fifties — consumerism, the automobile, television, or fads, for instance — or on several.
3. Consider carefully the commercials on television today. At which age group or groups are most of them aimed? Are these the same groups targeted by advertisers in the fifties? Write an essay explaining your conclusion and accounting for the similarities or differences in target audiences.

The Summer Before Salk

Charles L. Mee, Jr.

Author of popular histories like *Meeting at Potsdam* (1975), *The End of Order: Versailles 1919* (1980), and *The Ohio Gang* (1981), Charles Mee grew up near Chicago and was educated at Harvard. He has written plays (some of which were produced off Broadway in the 1960s) and children's books. He has also worked at *American Heritage* magazine and has served as editor of *Horizon*. Recent projects include a book on the Marshall Plan and more plays. In "The Summer Before Salk" Mee recreates the oppressive atmosphere of the summer of 1953, when the nation, terrified by the threat of polio, waited for a cure to be found.

1   The first symptom was the ache and stiffness in the lower back and neck. Then general fatigue. A vaguely upset stomach. A sense of dissociation. Fog closing in. A ringing in the ears. Dull persistent aching in the legs. By then the doctor would have been called, the car backed out of the garage for the trip to the hospital; by then the symptoms would be vivid: fierce pain, as though the nerves in every part of the body were being probed by a dentist's device without Novocain. All this took a day, twenty-four hours.

2   At the hospital, nurses would command the wheelchair — crowds in the hallway backing against the walls as the group panic made its way down the hall to the examining room, where, amid a turmoil of interns, orderlies, and nurses, the head nurse would step up and pronounce instantly, with authority,

"This boy has polio," and the others would draw back, no longer eager to examine the boy, as he was laid out on a cart and wheeled off to the isolation ward while all who had touched him washed their hands.

3 Poliomyelitis is a disease caused by a viral agent that invades the body by way of the gastrointestinal tract, where it multiplies and, on rare occasions, travels via blood and/or nervous pathways to the central nervous system, where it attacks the motor neurons of the spinal cord and part of the brain. Motor neurons are destroyed. Muscle groups are weakened or destroyed. A healthy fifteen-year-old boy of 160 pounds might lose seventy or eighty pounds in a week.

4 As long ago as the turn of the century doctors agreed that it was a virus, but not everyone believed that the doctors knew. One magazine article had said it was related to diet. Another article said it was related to the color of your eyes. Kids at summer camp got it, and when a boy at a camp in upstate New York got it in the summer of 1953, a health officer said no one would be let out of the camp till the polio season was over. Someone said that public gatherings had been banned altogether in the Yukon. In Montgomery, Alabama, that summer the whole city broke out; more than eighty-five people caught it. An emergency was declared, and in Tampa, Florida, a twenty-month-old boy named Gregory died of it. Five days later, his eight-year-old sister, Sandra, died of it while their mother was in the delivery room giving birth to a new baby.

5 The newspaper published statistics every week. As of the Fourth of July, newspapers said there were 4,680 cases in 1953 — more than there had been to that date in 1952, reckoned to be the worst epidemic year in medical history, in which the final tally had been 57,628 cases. But none of the numbers were reliable; odd illnesses were added to the total, and mild cases went unreported. Nonetheless, the totals were not the most terrifying thing about polio. What was terrifying was that, like any plague, you never knew where or when it might strike. It was more random than roulette — only it did seem to strike children disproportionately, and so it was called infantile paralysis — and it made parents crazy with anguish.

6 The rules were: Don't play with new friends, stick with your old friends whose germs you already have; stay away from crowded beaches and pools, especially in August; wash hands before eating; never use another person's eating utensils or toothbrush or drink out of the same Coke bottle or glass; don't bite another person's hands or fingers while playing or (for small children) put another child's toys in your mouth; don't pick up anything from the ground, especially around a beach or pool; don't have any tooth extractions during the summer; don't get overtired or strained; if you get a headache, tell your mother.

7 Nevertheless, kids caught it. In the big city hospitals, kids were stacked like cordwood in the corridors. Carts and wheelchairs congested the aisles. The dominant odor was of disinfectant. The dominant taste was of alcohol-disinfected thermometers. In the Catholic hospitals, holy medals and scapulars covered the motionless arms and hands of the children. On the South Side of Chicago, a mother cried just to see the name above the door of the place where her child was taken: the Home for Destitute Crippled Children. In some

places, parents were allowed to visit their children only once a week — not because of any special fact about polio, only because that was how children's wards were run in 1953. A child in bed with polio never forgot the sound made in the corridor by his mother's high-heeled shoes.

8   Injections of gamma globulin were prescribed for those who had not yet caught it. Certain insurance against measles, gamma globulin did not prevent catching polio, but it did seem to minimize the crippling effects. It was in short supply. Injections were given only to pregnant women and those under the age of thirty who had had a case of polio in the immediate family — or to prevent the spread of an epidemic. The precious supplies were placed under the administration of the incorruptible Office of Defense Mobilization.

9   In Illinois, rumors spread of bootleg gamma globulin. If you were lucky enough to qualify for a shot, you had to endure the humiliation that went with it: you had to pull down your pants and say which buttock would take the inch-long needle. To buy off your pride, the doctor gave you a free lollipop.

10   When the epidemic broke out in Mongtomery, Alabama, the story was that 620 volunteer doctors, nurses, housewives, and military personnel administered sixty-seven gallons of gamma globulin (worth $625,000), thirty-three thousand inch-long needles, and thirty-three thousand lollipops. In New York, parents picketed the health department for twenty-seven hours to get it for their children. In some places people said that parents were bribing local officials for vials of gamma globulin. At the same time, an article in the June issue of *Scientific American* reported there was doubt that the stuff was worth a damn. *The New York Times* reported that one little girl came down with polio within forty-eight hours of getting a gamma globulin shot.

11   In the hospitals, meanwhile, children — shrouded in white gowns and white sheets, nursed by women in white surgical masks, white dresses starched to the smooth brittleness of communion wafers — lay in dreadful silence, listening to the faint whispers of medical conversations on the far side of the drawn white curtains, the quiet shush of soft-soled nurses' shoes, and the ever-present sound of water in a basin, the ceaseless washing of hands.

12   Parents stood at a distance — six feet from the bed — wearing white gowns and white masks.

13   One boy's uncle gave him a black plastic Hopalong Cassidy bank when he was in the isolation ward. After the customary two-to-three-week stay there, after the fevers passed, he was moved into the regular children's ward. On the way, the nurses discarded the contaminated bank along with its savings.

14   Some children were not told what they had (lest it be too dangerous a shock to them), and so they discovered for themselves. One boy acquired from his visitors the biggest collection of comic books he had ever had. When he dropped one, he jumped out of bed to pick it up, crumpled in a heap and found he couldn't get up off the floor again.

15   Some would recover almost entirely. Some would die. Some would come through unable to move their legs, or unable to move arms and legs; some could move nothing but an arm, or nothing but a few fingers and their eyes. Some would leave the hospital with a cane, some with crutches, crutches and

steel leg braces, or in wheelchairs — white-faced, shrunken, with frightened eyes, light blankets over their legs. Some would remain in an iron lung — a great, eighteen-hundred-pound, casketlike contraption, like the one in which the woman in the magic show (her head and feet sticking out of either end) is sawed in half. The iron lung hissed and sighed rhythmically, performing artificial respiration by way of air pressure.

16   Some moaned. Some cried. Some nurtured cynicism. Some grew detached. Some were swept away by ungovernable cheerfulness. Rarely did anyone scream in rage, however common the feeling. All were overpowered, all were taught respect — for the unseen powers of nature, the smallness of human aspiration, the capacity for sudden and irrevocable change, the potential of chance.

17   As it happened, in the spring of 1953, Dr. Jonas Salk, an insignificant-seeming fellow with big ears, a receding hairline, and a pale complexion, had published a paper in a scholarly journal, reporting that he had induced the formation of antibodies against three types of polio viruses. He hadn't quite fully tested it, he hastened to say, but he had tried it on 161 children and adults with no ill effects. When newspapers got hold of the story, parents phoned their family doctors. Those with medical connections tried to find a way to get to Salk. Salk became famous in an instant — and from the moment of his first announcement, such an outpouring of hope and gratitude attached to him that he came to stand, at once, as the doctor-benefactor of our times.

18   During the summer of 1953, reporters called him weekly for news of progress. His vaccine, he explained, was a dead-virus vaccine. He devastated the virus with formaldehyde and then whipped it up into an emulsion with mineral oil to fortify it, and in this way he thought he had something that, when it was injected into a person, would stimulate a person's natural defense mechanisms to produce antibodies. However, he was not able to hurry the testing process along. In May 1953, he expanded the test to include more than seven hundred children. And not until the spring of 1954 were more than a million children inoculated in a large field trial financed by the March of Dimes, and, as the papers said, the "total conquest of polio" was in sight. Within the next half dozen years, the Salk vaccine reduced the incidence of polio by perhaps 95 percent, preventing maybe as many as three thousand cases of polio in the United States.

19   Yet Salk's triumph did not last for long. The March of Dimes, in its own need for publicity and contributions, lionized Salk mercilessly — and his fellow doctors soon got tired of his fame. He was not — and never has been since — invited to join the National Academy of Sciences. And soon enough, Salk's colleagues began to point out that Salk, after all, had made no basic scientific discovery. Many people have been working on a preventive for polio. The basic discovery had been made by three fellows at Harvard — Doctors Enders, Weller, and Robbins — who had shown that a polio virus could be grown in certain tissue cultures of primate cells. Before the Harvard finding no one had been able to make a vaccine because no one had been able to cultivate the virus in test-tube cultures. After the Harvard finding, Salk's vaccine was mere

applied science. (The Harvard doctors got the Nobel; Salk did not.) Salk had just pulled together the work of others. And some of the others thought Salk had been premature in publishing his paper, that he was rushing his vaccine into the world incautiously. Then, in 1955, a batch with live virus slipped out, and 260 children came down with polio from having taken the Salk vaccine or having contact with persons who had taken it.

20   Meanwhile, even as Salk's vaccine was eliminating polio in the United States, it was already obsolescent. Dr. Albert Sabin, a researcher who told interviewers that work was his recreation, was coming up with a new vaccine. His vaccine used an attenuated (that is to say, live) virus with special properties to stimulate the production of antibodies, and it seemed to offer immunity for much longer than Salk's vaccine, possibly for many years. This virus retained the capacity to multiply in the intestinal tract, thus passing from someone who had received the vaccine to someone who hadn't and inoculating them as well. The Sabin vaccine could be stored indefinitely in deep-freeze units; it could be taken orally and produced cheaply. It was given extensive tests in 1958 and 1959. By 1962 it had replaced the Salk vaccine almost entirely in the United States and most of the rest of the industrialized world. Although Sabin never got the Nobel either, in the next two decades his vaccine prevented perhaps two to three million cases of polio.

21   But Sabin's happiness was not uncomplicated, either. Though no one likes to mention it—and it does not diminish the good of the vaccine, since the odds are only "one in six or seven million"—sometimes a Sabin inoculation would be, as one specialist in polio has said, "associated with" a case of polio: the attenutated vaccine can never be as absolutely safe as the dead-virus vaccine.

22   Moreover, while the Sabin vaccine has eliminated polio in most of the temperate-climate countries where it's been used, it has not done so well elsewhere: in the Third World, it turns out, polio has not been ended at all. There, uncertain conditions of refrigeration cause the Sabin vaccine to break down. For some reason, too — perhaps because people in parts of the Third World carry other viruses in their systems that interfere with the polio vaccine — some inoculations don't take. The Sabin vaccine does not work with just one dose but requires several doses, which involves massive vaccination of a community. This has been accomplished in Cuba and Brazil but the logistics are staggering in many Third World countries. Despite the inoculation programs of the past two decades, about 375,000 people come down with polio every year in the Third World: seven and a half million in the last twenty years.

23   Some highly refined ironies: At the moment, conditions of sanitation and hygiene are so bad in the Third World that many children come down with polio before the age of two. Fortunately, however, at that age polio comes and goes often without leaving a trace of paralysis. As physical standards of living improve, children will not get polio at such early ages: they will get it instead when they are teenagers, when the paralytic rate is higher. So as health conditions improve in the Third World polio may well increase, increasing the need for vaccination.

24   Some say now that the Salk vaccine will make a comeback, that it will work where the Sabin vaccine has not worked — that the Salk vaccine will hold up better under the conditions of Third World refrigeration, that there is even some indication that a more potent Salk-type vaccine might require only one or two inoculations. Recent tests by the Israeli government in the Gaza Strip seem to make a case for the Salk vaccine. A French pharmaceutical company is manufacturing a Salk-type vaccine that also vaccinates against diphtheria, tetanus, and whooping cough. It may be that Salk will become famous again.

25   These days, as polio continues to occur in the Third World, most of those who gather at the special conferences on the disease feel that the old Salk vaccine — which has continued to be used in some of the smaller European countries — ought to be brought back on a large scale. Most of them feel not that the Salk should replace the Sabin but rather, given everyone's doubts, that both vaccines are needed, in different circumstances, or perhaps in combination.

26   But when the two grand old men of the fight against polio, Salk and Sabin themselves, appear at these conferences, they disagree. Each man — as modest and thoughtful and impressive as he is in private — takes on a missionary zeal in public, strutting and scrapping for preeminence, each arguing for the ultimate superiority of his own vaccine. Sabin argues politics: the administration of his vaccine must be improved. Salk argues effectiveness is possible with fewer doses with his vaccine and warns of live-virus-vaccine-associated polio. At one such recent encounter, Salk tried everything, even charm and banter, to win over the audience; he and Sabin agreed on only one thing, he said with a skilled debater's smile, "that only one vaccine is necessary."

27   And so the two renowned old doctors go on grappling with each other and with themselves, speaking not only of the progress of science and the triumph of reason but also — like those of us who got polio in the summer of 1953 and have toted around a couple of canes ever since — of the equivocalness of greatness, the elusiveness of justice, the complexity of success, the persistence of chance.

Reading Sources: *"The Summer Before Salk"*

Read the selection, surveying it to identify key terms and important concepts. Highlight these phrases and ideas, and then answer these questions.

1. What key terms does Mee emphasize by repeating them throughout this essay?
2. The word *white* is repeated several times in paragraph 11. What is the effect of this repetition? In paragraphs 15 and 16, how do repetition and parallelism help get Mee's point across?
3. How does Mee place emphasis on the ideas in paragraph 6?
4. What techniques does Mee use to link ideas between paragraphs 2 and 3? paragraphs 6 and 7? What transitional devices connect paragraphs 18 and 19? paragraphs 19 and 20? paragraphs 20 and 21? What different strategies does Mee use to link the sentences in paragraph 4?

5. Paragraph 12 is only one sentence long. What effect is Mee trying to achieve with this brief paragraph?
6. What is the topic sentence of paragraph 17? paragraph 19?
7. The first sixteen paragraphs of this essay set the stage for the entrance of Jonas Salk and his confrontation with Albert Sabin. What is Mee's purpose in this long introduction? What is his purpose in the rest of the essay?
8. Identify the 5 or 6 sentences that you consider to be central to the essay's meaning. (You might, for instance, consider the last sentence of paragraph 16 and the final sentence of the essay.) When you have done this, try to sum up the essay's main idea in one sentence.
9. Would you characterize Mee's tone as generally objective or subjective? Explain.

Reacting to Sources

Reread the selection carefully, making marginal notes to aid your comprehension and reinforce connections. Then further annotate the essay if you need to do so in order to answer any of these questions. (You may already have addressed some of the questions in your marginal notes.)

1. Using a dictionary if necessary, supply brief marginal definitions of these words as they are used in this selection: *dissociation* (1), *gastrointestinal* (3), *neurons* (3), *destitute* (7), *incorruptible* (8), *bootleg* (9), *primate* (19), *obsolescent* (20), *logistics* (22), *grappling* (27), *equivocalness* (27).
2. In paragraph 7, Mee says, "A child in bed with polio never forgot the sound made in the corridor by his mother's high-heeled shoes." Explain the meaning of this statement in a marginal note.
3. Write three questions to clarify your understanding of the ideas in paragraph 10.
4. Identify Mee's purpose in paragraph 13, and write a brief marginal comment explaining it.
5. Outline the paragraph cluster beginning with paragraph 17 and extending through paragraph 19.
6. Give two examples from the essay to support Mee's general statement in paragraph 17 that Salk "became famous in an instant."
7. Explain this statement in a brief marginal comment: "After the Harvard finding, Salk's vaccine was mere applied science" (19). Do you agree or disagree? Explain.
8. In a journal entry, explain what Mee means when he says, in paragraph 26, "Each man — as modest and thoughtful and impressive as he is in private — takes on a missionary zeal in public. . . ."
9. In a journal entry, assess the relative merits of the Salk and Sabin vaccines.
10. Reread the introduction and paragraph 27. Comment on how Mee's own bout with polio might have influenced his purpose. Does your knowledge of his illness make you more or less receptive to his ideas? Explain.

11. In a journal entry, consider possible connections between this essay and your own experience with or knowledge of catastrophic illness. If you have no such experience or knowledge, try to relate Mee's ideas to those presented in a work of fiction that treats this topic.

Working with Sources

1. Write a fifty-word summary of paragraphs 26–27.
2. Write a critique of the ideas in paragraphs 26 and 27.
3. Write a journal entry in which you explore your reactions to these quotations from "The Summer Before Salk":

   "What was terrifying was that, like any plague, you never knew where or when it might strike" (5).

   "In the big city hospitals, kids were stacked like cordwood in the corridors" (7).

   "Some would remain in an iron lung—a great, eighteen-hundred-pound, casketlike contraption, like the one in which the woman in the magic show (her head and feet sticking out of either end) is sawed in half" (15).

   Be sure to integrate the quotations smoothly into your writing.
4. Paraphrase the ideas in paragraph 3.
5. Write a one-paragraph synthesis that blends ideas in paragraph 5 of "The Summer Before Salk" and those in paragraph 5 of "The Big Barbecue" (pp. 183–192).

Writing with Sources: Using a Single Source

Integrating information from "The Summer Before Salk" with your own ideas, write an essay on one of these topics. Be sure to acknowledge ideas that are not your own.

1. Write an essay in which you consider in what sense Jonas Salk was the ideal hero of the fifties. If you like, you may read brief encyclopedia articles on more traditional fifties heroes—such as Elvis Presley, Mickey Mantle, or James Dean—and compare and contrast Salk with them.
2. As described in Mee's essay, both Salk and polio are alternately simple facts of scientific history and larger-than-life, almost mythical elements. Write an essay in which you illustrate Mee's dual vision and present a rationale for it.
3. Contrast the polio threat with a modern health problem of the same dimensions. Compare and contrast our society's reactions to what you consider to be today's biggest medical nightmare with the way those in the fifties reacted to polio and to its victims.

"I Have Here in My Hand . . . "

The Editors of Time-Life Books

Frustrated by the war in Korea and by the Soviet Union's aggressive acts in Europe, Americans in the fifties felt increasingly angry and powerless. The Russians, who had been our allies in World War II, were suddenly a dangerous threat. With the Cold War at its height, the U.S. House of Representatives' Un-American Activities Committee (HUAC) set out to identify American Communists and Communist sympathizers. The committee pointed the finger of accusation at writers, actors, directors, university professors, and political leaders, asking suspected "traitors" not only to confess their own leftist leanings but also to incriminate others. In its zeal, HUAC hounded many who were innocent, destroying families, careers, and even lives in the process. In this climate, Senator Joseph McCarthy was able to capture the attention of the nation with his search for "Reds," eventually coming to be seen by many as "the second most powerful man in the country." For nearly four years McCarthy dominated U.S. politics, challenging the workings of the Senate, the State Department, the federal civil service, and even U.S. foreign policy. But when his investigation of the U.S. Army escalated into the Senate's Army–McCarthy hearings, McCarthy met his match in Joseph Welch, the Army's special counsel. For 36 days in 1954, 20 million Americans watched the televised hearings; when they were over, McCarthy's almost magical hold on the country had been broken. On December 2, 1954, the U.S. Senate voted 67 to 22 to condemn him. He died in 1957. "'I Have Here in My Hand . . . ,'" which outlines McCarthy's rise to power, appeared in *This Fabulous Century,* a Time-Life series covering each decade of American history in a separate volume.

1   The era of McCarthyism began the night of February 9, 1950, in the old McLure Hotel in Wheeling, West Virginia, where the Senator had flown to address the local Republican Lincoln Day dinner. In the four and a half previous years — since the end of World War II — Communism had changed from ally to menace; and the United States, an essentially insular nation, had suddenly been thrust into leadership of a complex, contentious world. Nothing seemed to go right for the new leaders. Communists had taken over Czechoslovakia and Hungary and had conquered China; they had exploded an A-bomb and encircled West Berlin with a blockade. Americans were angry and bewildered. What had gone wrong? Had the U.S. been sold out? There were those who thought so. "Traitors in the high councils in our own government," said an ambitious California Congressman named Richard Nixon, "have made sure that the deck is stacked on the Soviet side."

2   The House Un-American Activities Committee began to seek out the traitors. To the astonishment of some Americans and the dismay of all, it found some. A number of government employees who were Communists or Communist sympathizers apparently had fed highly confidential information to the Russians. Several of them were convicted of various crimes in the aftermath of the committee hearings — notably a one-time State Department offical named

Alger Hiss. There were not many such cases. But there were enough to lend a semblance of reasonableness to the growing Red scare.

3   It was at this moment that Joseph McCarthy stepped forward, claiming he had the names of live Reds, busy undermining the government right now. Holding aloft a document, he told his West Virginia audience: "I have here in my hand a list of 205 names known to the Secretary of State as being members of the Communist Party and who nevertheless are still working and shaping the policy of the State Department." Next day, when he spoke in Denver, the 205 Communists had become 205 "security risks"; the day after, in Salt Lake City, the 205 security risks changed to "57 card-carrying Communists"; 10 days later in the Senate the 57 Communists became "81 cases."

4   The fact was that there were no names at all. What McCarthy held in his hand that night was a three-year-old letter from former Secretary of State James Byrnes; it informed a Congressman that permanent tenure for 205 unnamed State employees might be denied on various grounds, including drunkenness. Six months after the Wheeling speech, a hastily convened Senate subcommittee concluded that the Senator had perpetrated a "fraud and a hoax." But no one was listening; an anxious nation was launched on a four-year binge of hysteria and character assassination. Americans needed to lay blame and Joseph McCarthy had offered them some simple, understandable targets.

5   In a later speech McCarthy conjured up more frightening arithmetic: "We've been losing to international Communism at the rate of 100 million people a year." Then, ominously: "Perhaps we should examine the background of the men who have done the planning, and let the American people decide whether . . . we've lost because of stumbling, fumbling idiocy, or because they planned it that way."

6   Millions of Americans listened as McCarthy, under protection of Senatorial immunity, then began naming names. He called Secretary of State Dean Acheson "The Red Dean." He described Far East expert Owen Lattimore as the "top Russian espionage agent in the U.S." and charged that U.S. Ambassador to the U.N. Philip Jessup was "preaching the Communist Party line." Besides name-calling McCarthy quickly proved that he could break people. Millard Tydings, a conservative Maryland Democrat who had chaired the 1950 Senate subcommittee that branded McCarthy's Wheeling charges a "hoax," ran for reelection later that year. McCarthy was waiting. He had a composite photograph put together purporting to show Tydings talking amibly with former U.S. Communist chief Earl Browder, saturated Maryland with copies and was widely credited with defeating the Senator's bid for a sure fifth term. He also took the scalps of other Senators who got in his way, among them Senate Democratic floor leader Scott Lucas of Illinois, Ernest MacFarland of Arizona and William Benton and Raymond Baldwin of Connecticut. He accused the Voice of America of deliberately constructing two radio transmitters where they would be ineffective; M.I.T. and RCA experts later disproved McCarthy but by then one engineer who had been involved had committed suicide. McCarthy encouraged fanatical anti-Communist government workers to leak confidential documents to him and grinned that he commanded a "Loyal American Underground."

7   This was McCarthyism, the exploitation of a nation's fears, a brutal attack on Americans with divergent views, and it became an overriding fact of American life. Although in four years McCarthy was unable to offer legal support for a single charge, nevertheless people were stampeded. "McCarthy may have something," said Massachusetts Congressman John F. Kennedy. Truman's Attorney General, J. Howard McGrath, in 1952 ordered six detention camps readied to incarcerate alleged spies and saboteurs.

8   Joseph McCarthy was that classic American figure, the poor farm boy battling to escape the harsh, sterile dirt farm of his youth, determined to get his share of the American dream. As a youth Joe had tried to make it chicken farming, then tried being a chain-grocery manager. At 20 he quit, crammed four years of high school into one and got into Marquette University, where he made ends meet by jockeying a gas pump, playing poker and coaching boxing. He moved ahead, twisting and turning. At college he switched from engineering to law, in politics he ran for local office as a Democrat and lost, then switched to Republican and won, becoming a Wisconsin circuit court judge. After World War II he made it to the United States Senate.

9   McCarthy's first three years in the Senate marked him as simply another ambitious young legislator—somewhat prone to use the knee and the elbow, but always with a smile, a wisecrack, the friendly, open look of the American boy playing the get-ahead game, certain everyone understood he meant nothing personal. Joe wasn't mad at anybody, he was just going places. He briefly supported the interests of the sugar and soft drink industries and acquired the Washington nickname of "The Pepsi-Cola Kid," then served the housing interests and got himself called "Water Boy of the Real Estate Lobby." To please his German-American constituents he intruded into a Senate investigation of 43 Nazi SS men who had confessed to murdering captured GIs during the Battle of the Bulge and so helped muddy the proceedings of the "Malmédy Massacre" hearings that the murderers were spared. It kept him busy, but it didn't seem to be getting him anywhere.

10   Then, in Wheeling that February evening as the '50s began, Joe finally caught hold of a star and started his meteoric climb. Within a few months he was describing President Truman and Acheson as "the Pied Pipers of the Politburo," adding of the President: "The son of a bitch ought to be impeached." He called General George C. Marshall, Chief of the U.S. General Staff in World War II and later Secretary of State, "a man steeped in falsehood," and "an instrument of the Soviet conspiracy." This was going a bit far, and Dwight Eisenhower bristled with rage at the slur on his former commander. Nevertheless, in July of 1952, the same Republican Presidential convention that nominated Ike invited McCarthy to address the delegates; convention chairman Walter Hallanan hailed the Senator, who had been a rear-echelon leatherneck in World War II, as "Wisconsin's Fighting Marine"; and Joe strode through the Chicago International Amphitheater, to be cheered as the band blared "From the Halls of Montezuma." Later, when Ike stumped Wisconsin, he dropped from his prepared speech a paragraph extolling Marshall.

11   By now Joseph McCarthy seemed to be the second most powerful man in

the country. "The Senate," said the *Christian Science Monitor,* "is afraid of him." So, apparently, was everyone else. One day in 1953 a U.S. diplomat just back from abroad was handed a note by a State Department colleague: "Let's get out of here. This place is wired." They walked and the Washington official said: "You just don't know what's happened here. People don't talk at staff meetings any more. They've discovered that an opinion which is nonconformist is reported." Even Eisenhower was reluctant to throw down any challenge. Privately Ike described McCarthy as "a lawless man." But when Ike's advisers pleaded that the President strike down this apparently ungovernable menace, Ike declined. "I just will not," he said. "I refuse to get into the gutter with that guy."

12   There seemed no stopping McCarthy. He boasted: "McCarthyism is Americanism with its sleeve rolled." He gloried in being himself: the poor kid from the wrong side of the tracks who had fought his way up, who was going to teach the snobs a thing or two. "McCarthyism," wrote critic Peter Viereck, "is the revenge of the noses that for 20 years of fancy parties were pressed against the outside window pane." The Wisconsin Senator had tapped into one of the universal, recurring themes in American life: the antagonism between the uppitty, dudish, big-city smart alecks and the rough and ready, independent, true-blue Americans from the backwoods. "It is not the less fortunate . . . who have been selling this nation out," he cried, "but rather those who have had all the benefits — the finest homes, the finest college educations, and the finest jobs in government. The bright young men who are born with silver spoons in their mouths are the worst."

13   As 1954 began, McCarthy took on the biggest game of all. He amended his slam at the Democrats, "Twenty years of treason," and charged "Twenty-one years of treason." The meaning was amply clear. A few months later, when a *New York Herald Tribune* reporter attempted to question Ike about McCarthy, the President "clenched his hands together and . . . declining to talk, and nearly speechless with emotion, . . . strode from the room. His eyes appeared moist." As of that moment, the Senator seemed to have the whole country in his pocket.

Reading Sources

Read the essay, surveying it to identify key terms and important concepts. Highlight these phrases and ideas, and then answer these questions.

1. What events made it possible for McCarthy to rise so quickly?
2. Why did Republicans at first see McCarthy as a "godsend"?
3. What was President Eisenhower's impression of McCarthy? What actions and events helped form this impression?
4. This selection chronicles only McCarthy's rise to power. Where, if anywhere, do the authors signal that this rise will be followed by a fall?

5. How do the authors link paragraphs 6 and 7? What techniques do they use to connect the sentences in paragraph 6?
6. This essay was published in 1970. How do you think its authors expected the brief references to Richard Nixon (1) and John Kennedy (7) to affect readers? How do these references affect you today?
7. Is this essay's purpose primarily persuasive or informative? Explain.

Reacting to Sources

Reread the essay carefully, making marginal notes to aid comprehension and reinforce connections. Then further annotate the essay if you need to do so in order to answer any of these questions. (You may already have addressed some of the questions in your marginal notes.)

1. Using a dictionary if necessary, supply brief marginal definitions of these words as they are used in this essay: *contentious* (1), *purporting* (6), *divergent* (7), *incarcerate* (7), *leatherneck* (10), *extolling* (10).
2. How much do the authors expect their readers to know about McCarthy and his era? How can you tell? Explain your impressions in a journal entry in which you analyze the essay's intended audience.
3. Throughout the essay, the authors describe McCarthy in very vivid language. Identify several examples of such language and, in marginal comments, note the likely effects of such description on the average reader's view of McCarthy.
4. While sharply condemning McCarthy's tactics, the authors also reveal some sympathy for him. Locate examples of both sympathetic and critical language, and write a journal entry analyzing the authors' attitude toward McCarthy.
5. What purpose do the authors hope to achieve in paragraph 8? Are they successful? Explain in a marginal comment.
6. Formulate three questions whose answers might clarify your understanding of the events the authors summarize in paragraph 2.
7. Give two examples from the essay to support the authors' general statement in paragraph 4 that "Americans needed to lay blame and Joseph McCarthy had offered them some simple, understandable targets."
8. Outline paragraph 6.
9. In paragraph 7 the authors say, "Although in four years McCarthy was unable to offer legal support for a single charge, nevertheless people were stampeded." Explore this idea further in a journal entry.
10. In one sentence, rewrite paragraph 10 to simplify its ideas.
11. In paragraph 13 the authors say, "As 1954 began, McCarthy took on the biggest game of all. He amended his slam at the Democrats, 'Twenty years of treason,' and charged 'Twenty-one years of treason.' The meaning was clear." Write a marginal note in which you explain the authors' point.
12. A *Chicago Tribune* editorial published after McCarthy's death stated, "Senator McCarthy was a Partiotic American and a determined opponent of Communists. And because of that every 'liberal' commentator lost no opportunity to

villify him. The White House palace guard plotted his ruin. The President singled him out for studied insults. No man in public life was ever persecuted and maligned because of his beliefs as was Senator McCarthy." Write a journal entry in which you consider the validity of this position.

Working with Sources

1. Following the outline you made in response to Reacting to Sources, question 8, write a fifty-word summary of paragraph 6.
2. Write a critique of Peter Viereck's ideas in paragraph 12.
3. Write a journal entry in which you explore your reactions to these quotations from "I Have Here in My Hand . . . ":

   "There were not many such cases. But there were enough to lend a semblance of reasonableness to the growing Red Scare" (2).

   "Millions of Americans listened as McCarthy, under protection of Senatorial immunity, . . . began naming names" (6).

   "This was McCarthyism, the exploitation of a nation's fears, a brutal attack on Americans with divergent views, and it became an overriding fact of American life" (7).

   Be sure to integrate the quotations smoothly into your writing.
4. Paraphrase paragraph 9.
5. Write a one-paragraph synthesis that blends ideas in paragraph 1 of this essay and paragraph 12 of "Beep Beep" (pp. 224–231).

Writing with Sources: Using a Single Source

Integrating information from "I Have Here in My Hand . . . " with your own ideas, write an essay on one of these topics. Be sure to acknowledge ideas that are not your own.

1. In one sense, McCarthy can be seen as a heroic figure, a "poor kid from the wrong side of the tracks" who took on the most powerful people of his time — and almost won. In what sense is this a reasonable characterization of the man and his career? Write an essay in which you evaluate the validity (and consider the limitations) of this view.
2. Elsewhere, the authors of this selection write, "All told, McCarthy had probably come as close to wrecking the U.S. political system as had any man in the previous century." Do you agree? Or, do you believe that, in the long run, it is possible that men like McCarthy might strengthen the U.S. political system? Write an essay explaining your position.
3. It could be argued that McCarthy, whether hero or villain, was most of all a typical product of his age. Write an essay in support of this position.

The Rise of Rock and Roll

Charlie Gillett

Charlie Gillett was born in England in 1942. He was educated at Cambridge and later at Columbia University. After working as a lecturer in social studies and filmmaking, as a television production assistant for the BBC, and as a radio disc jockey, he founded Oval records, an independent record company, which he continues to run. Gillett's books include *All in the Game* (1971), *Making Tracks: The Story of Atlantic Records* (1974), and *Rock Almanac* (1977). He has also contributed to *Rolling Stone, Creem,* the *Village Voice,* and other periodicals. Published in 1970 and revised and expanded in 1983, *The Sound of the City,* from which "The Rise of Rock and Roll" is excerpted, is considered a classic history of rock and roll. The book analyzes rock's social and musical origins and the influences of various performers during a twenty-five-year period, beginning with the roots of rock and roll in the music of black artists: rhythm and blues.

1   In almost every respect, the sounds of rhythm and blues contradicted those of popular music. The vocal styles were harsh, the songs explicit, the dominant instruments — saxophone, piano, guitar, drums — were played loudly and with an emphatic dance rhythm, the production of the records was crude. The prevailing emotion was excitement.

2   Only some Negro records were of this type, but they were played often enough on some radio programmes to encourage the listeners who found these programmes to stay tuned. The other records played were similar to the music already familiar in the white market. But as the white listeners began to understand the different conventions by which black audiences judged their music, they came to appreciate the differences between the sing-along way white singers handled ballads, and the personal way black groups handled them.

3   The early and fullest impression on the new white audience of these stations was made by the dance blues — whose singers included Amos Milburn, Roy Brown, Fats Domino, and Lloyd Price — which provided a rhythm and excitement not available in white popular music. At first the number of white people interested in this music was not enough to have much effect on the sales of popular music. This portion of the audience probably consisted at first of college and a few high school students who cultivated an "R & B cult" as most of their equivalents earlier (and even then) cultivated a jazz cult.

4   By a happy coincidence, we happen to have some observations of remarkable insight made by the sociologist David Riesman on the popular music audience in this period, which illuminate the character of the specialist audience. In an article, "Listening to Popular Music," Riesman noted that two groups could be identified: the majority audience, which accepted the range of choices offered by the music industry and made its selections from this range without considering anything outside it; and the minority audience, which he described with details that are relevant here.

5   The minority group is small. It comprises the more active listeners, who

are less interested in melody or tune than in arrangement or technical virtuosity. It has developed elaborate, even overelaborate, standards of music listening; hence its music listening is combined with much animated discussion of technical points and perhaps occasional reference to trade journals such as *Metronome* and *Downbeat*. The group tends to dislike name bands, most vocalists (except Negro blues singers), and radio commercials.

6   The rebelliousness of this minority group might be indicated in some of the following attitudes towards popular music: an insistence on rigorous standards of judgment and taste in a relativist culture; a preference for the uncommercialized, unadvertised small bands rather than name bands; the development of a private language and then a flight from it when the private language (the same is true of other aspects of private style) is taken over by the majority group; a profound resentment of the commercialization of radio and musicians. Dissident attitudes towards competition and cooperation in our culture might be represented in feelings about improvisation and small "combos"; an appreciation for idiosyncrasy of performance goes together with a dislike of "star" performers and an insistence that the improvisation be a group-generated phenomenon.

7   There are still other ways in which the minority may use popular music to polarize itself from the majority group, and thereby from American popular culture generally: a sympathetic attitude or even preference for Negro musicians; an egalitarian attitude towards the roles, in love and work, of the two sexes; a more international outlook, with or without awareness, for example, of French interest in American jazz; an identification with disadvantaged groups, not only Negroes, from which jazz springs, with or without a romantic cult of proletarianism; a dislike of romantic pseudo-sexuality in music, even without any articulate awareness of being exploited; similarly a reaction against the stylized body image and limitations of physical self-expression which "sweet" music and its lyrics are felt as conveying; a feeling that music is too important to serve as a backdrop for dancing, small talk, studying, and the like; a diffuse resentment of the image of the teenager provided by the mass media.

8   To carry matters beyond this descriptive suggestion of majority and minority patterns, requires an analysis of the social structure in which the teenager finds himself. When he listens to music, even if no one else is around, he listens in a context of imaginary "others" — his listening is indeed often an effort to establish connection with them. In general what he perceives in the mass media is framed by his perception of the peer-groups to which he belongs. These groups not only rate the tunes but select for their members in more subtle ways what is to be "heard" in each tune. It is the pressure of conformity with the group that invites and compels the individual to have recourse to the media both in order to learn from them what the group expects and to identify with the group by sharing a common focus for attention and talk.

. . .

9   Riesman's observation that no matter what the majority chooses, there will be a minority choosing something different explains how popular music

continues to change, no matter how good — or bad — the dominant types of music are at any particular period. And because the minority audience defines itself as being radical within the music audience, its taste is likely to favour, consciously or unconsciously, music with some element of social comment or criticism in it.

10   During the early fifties, young people like those described by Riesman turned in increasing numbers to rhythm and blues music, and to the radio stations that broadcast it. If the first listeners were those with relatively sophisticated standards for judging music, those that came later include many whose taste was more instinctive, who like the dance beat or the thrilling effect of a hard-blown saxophone, people who may have found the rough voices of the singers a bit quaint and appealing as novelties.

11   It was this second group of listeners who provided the inspiration and audience for Alan Freed, who, with Bill Haley, played a crucial role in popularizing rhythm and blues under the name "rock 'n' roll".

12   Alan Freed was a disc jockey on an evening quality music programme in Cleveland, Ohio, when he was invited, sometime in 1952, to visit a downtown record store by the owner, Leo Mintz. Mintz was intrigued by the musical taste of some of the white adolescents who bought records at his store, and Freed was amazed by it. He watched the excited reaction of the youths who danced energetically as they listened to music that Freed had previously considered alien to their culture — rhythm and blues. He recalled (in the British *New Musical Express,* September 23, 1956):

> I heard the tenor saxophones of Red Prysock and Big Al Sears. I heard the blues-singing, piano-playing Ivory Joe Hunter. I wondered. I wondered for about a week. Then I went to the station manager and talked him into permitting me to follow my classical programme with a rock 'n' roll party.

At Mintz's suggestion, Freed introduced a euphemism for rhythm and blues by calling his show "Moondog's Rock 'n' Roll Party", which started in June, 1951. By March, 1952 Freed was convinced he had enough listeners to justify promoting a concert featuring some of the artists whose records he had been playing. "Moondog's Coronation Ball" was to be staged at the Cleveland Arena, capacity 10,000; but according to firemen's estimates more than 21,000 people showed up, mostly black, causing such a panic that the show had to be called off (as reported in the *Cleveland Press*). Abandoning the idea of holding mammoth dances, Freed persevered with reserved-seat shows, and climaxed his career in Cleveland in August, 1953 with a bill that featured the Buddy Johnson Orchestra, Joe Turner, Fats Domino, the Moonglows, the Harptones, the Drifters, Ella Johnson, Dakota Staton, and Red Prysock.

13   Freed's success among white audiences with Negro music was widely reported in *Billboard,* and in 1954 he was signed by a New York station, WINS, which he quickly established as New York's leading popular music station. He continued to champion the original Negro performers of songs which were "covered" — recorded by someone else — for the white market by the major

companies, and in interviews he accused other disc jockeys of prejudice when they preferred to play the cover versions.

14   Once the new audience became apparent, juke-box distributors began putting rock 'n' roll records in juke boxes, which then provided a new channel of communication for white record buyers who did not yet tune in to the Negro radio stations. At the same time, in response to the new demand for uptempo dance tunes with a black beat from audiences at dance halls, a number of white groups were incorporating rhythm-and-blues-type material into the repertoires. It was with such a song, "Crazy Man Crazy", recorded for the independent Essex, that Bill Haley and His Comets made their first hit parade appearance in 1953 and pushed rock 'n' roll up another rung of popular attention.

15   By the end of 1953, at which point the Negro market comprised only 5.7 per cent of the total American record sales market, a number of people in the music industry were beginning to realize the potential of Negro music and styles for at least a segment of the white market. Decca took a chance and considerably outpaced its rival major companies by contracting Haley from Essex. At his first session with Decca, he recorded "Rock Around the Clock" and "Shake, Rattle and Roll", which between them were to transform throughout the world the conception of what popular music could be.

16   Haley's records were not straight copies of any particular black style or record. The singer's voice was unmistakably white, and the repetitive choral chants were a familiar part of many "swing" bands. In these respects the music was similar to a style known as "western swing" (and in particular a group called Bob Wills and His Texas Playboys). But the novel feature of Haley's style, its rhythm, was drawn from black music, although in Haley the rhythm dominated the arrangements much more than it did in Negro records. With Haley, every other beat was heavily accented by the singers and all the instrumentalists at the expense of the relatively flexible rhythms and complex harmonies of dance music records cut for the black audience.

17   "Shake, Rattle and Roll" was in the top ten for twelve weeks from September, 1954; "Rock Around the Clock" was in the list for nineteen weeks, including eight at the top, from May, 1955. By the summer of 1955, roughly two years after Haley's "Crazy Man Crazy", with most of the majors still moving uncertainly, the demand for records with an insistent dance beat was sufficient for three independently manufactured records to reach the top ten in record sales — "Seventeen" by Boyd Bennett (King), "Ain't That a Shame" by Pat Boone (Dot), and "Maybellene" by Chuck Berry (Chess), the last recorded by a black singer.

18   The growth of rock 'n' roll cannot be separated from the emergence, since the Second World War, of a new phenomenon: the adolescent or youth culture. Since the War, adolescents have made a greater show of enjoying themselves than they ever did before. Their impact has been particularly sharp

because there were so few facilities that easily accommodated their new attitudes, interests, and increased wealth. Neither individual communities nor the mass communication industries anticipated the growth of adolescent culture, or responded quickly to it.

19   The initial reaction of society was generally disapproving, which served to reinforce whatever rebellious feelings existed among the adolescents, thereby contributing to an identity and a style which were fostered until, by the early fifties, adolescents really seemed to consider themselves a "new breed" of some kind. Among the creators of popular culture, this self-impression was fostered in particular by Hollywood, whose producers began to adjust their films to the realization that an increasing proportion of their audience were in their teens.

20   Apart from various films dealing with the general social life of adolescents (in family, school, and leisure situations), there were two pictures in the first half of the fifties that focused specifically on the generation conflicts of the time, *The Wild One* (1954) and *Rebel Without a Cause* (1955). With Marlon Brando and James Dean, respectively, these pictures provided figures with whom the new teenagers could identify, figures whose style of dress, speech, movement, facial expressions, and attitudes helped give shape and justification to unrealized feelings in the audience. The plot in both films was clumsy, artificial, and morally compromised, but the undercurrents of frustration and violence in each were sufficient to give the films credibility. The sullen defiance of Brando and the exploited integrity of Dean were simultaneously reflections of and models for large segments of the audience.

21   Cinema was at this time the epitome of "mass culture", drawing situations from the lives of its audience, ordering these situations to fit a dramatic plot, and then returning the packaged product to its source as entertainment. There was little real interchange between the producers and the customers: the customers, having no alternative source of films, could only choose from what was made available to them, and the producers measured their audience's taste almost entirely in terms of the way they spent money. The producers thus tended to put their own money into formulas that had already proved successful. New ideas were notoriously difficult to introduce into this arrangement.

22   Despite these rigidities, the film industry realized and responded to the needs of its audience faster than did the music industry. The film industry, for example, was prepared to accept Negro styles of speech into scripts much faster than ASCAP would allow these styles to infiltrate radio broadcasts: "Dig", "flip", "cat", "jive", "square", and the rest of be-bop talk all made their way on to the screen with apparently no strong opposition — although of course black people themselves weren't very often evident on the screen. So, while in the film the images and the script were telling a new story in new words, as in *The Wild One* and *Rebel Without a Cause,* the music on the sound track remained the big band music that the new young audience had already rejected. Their rejection became explicit in a third film, *Blackboard Jungle* (released in 1955, the same year as *Rebel Without a Cause*), which was a major factor in accelerating the popularity of rock 'n' roll.

23   *Blackboard Jungle,* adapted from the novel by Evan Hunter, was about a teacher's experience in a vocational high school in the Bronx. His students, of various national and racial origins, were near-delinquents whose threatened violence gave the plot most of its dramatic strength.

24   One of the main scenes in the novel, where the students came into open defiance and conflict with a teacher, described an attempt by a teacher to establish rapport with his class by playing records from his collection. He began with Bunny Berigan's "I Can't Get Started". The collective reaction of the class was: "So it's a guy singing. Does he stack up against Como? Where does he shine to Tony Bennett? Guys singing are a dime a dozen. . . . Ain't he got no stuff by The Hilltoppers?" The teacher tried again—Harry James, Will Bradley, Ray McKinley, Ella Mae Morse. The students grew more restless. "What the hell is this, a history lesson? Come on, let's have some music." Their impatience turned to violence, and they broke up the teacher's treasured collection, throwing the records across the classroom. The teacher broke down in tears.

25   The scene accurately expressed the dislocation between the cultures of two generations.

26   Hunter's book was published in 1954, and in the relatively short space of time between the date of publication and the release of the film late in 1955, the musical culture of the young had gone a step beyond the terms of the novel. In the film version (directed by Richard Brooks), it was the relentless rhythm of Bill Haley's "Rock Around the Clock" that emphasized the rejection of the relatively sophisticated "swing" of the jazz records played by the teacher. By late 1955, Tony Bennett and Perry Como were as obsolete as Bunny Berigan and Will Bradley, so far as the self-consciously youthful adolescents were concerned. The film version of *Blackboard Jungle* was a large success and a much discussed movie. What the presence in it of the music of Bill Haley, rather than of Tony Bennett and Perry Como, helped to establish in the minds of both adolescents and adults was the connection between rock 'n' roll and teenage rebellion.

Reading Sources: "The Rise of Rock and Roll"

Read the selection, surveying it to identify key terms and important concepts. Highlight these phrases and ideas, and then answer these questions.

1. What key terms are repeated throughout the essay? How do these terms help readers to follow Gillett's ideas?
2. Whom does Gillett consider the key figures of early rock and roll? Why is each important?
3. What, according to sociologist David Riesman, is the difference between the majority audience and the minority audience?
4. How does Gillett link paragraphs 10 and 11? paragraphs 11 and 12? What techniques does he use to connect the sentences in paragraph 12?

5. How do dates function as a transitional device in paragraphs 12 through 17?
6. Identify the boundaries of the paragraph cluster introduced by the sentence that begins paragraph 20.
7. Why does Gillett isolate the single sentence in paragraph 25? What is the function of this one-sentence paragraph in the essay?

Reacting to Sources

Reread the selection carefully, making marginal notes to aid comprehension and reinforce connections. Then further annotate the selection if you need to do so in order to answer any of these questions. (You may already have addressed some of the questions in your marginal notes.)

1. Using a dictionary if necessary, supply brief marginal definitions of these words as they are used in this selection: *virtuosity* (5), *relativist* (6), *dissident* (6), *proletarianism* (7), *diffuse* (7), *euphemism* (12), *comprised* (15), *fostered* (19), *compromised* (20), *epitome* (21), *rapport* (24), *dislocation* (25).
2. What purpose does Gillett intend Riesman's remarks to serve? Do Riesman's comments help Gillett achieve this purpose? Explain in a marginal note.
3. Outline the paragraph cluster beginning with paragraph 5 and extending through paragraph 8.
4. In a journal entry, explore this statement: ". . . because the minority audience defines itself as being radical within the music audience, its taste is likely to favour, consciously or unconsciously, music with some element of social comment or criticism in it" (9).
5. Formulate three questions in response to the ideas in paragraph 13.
6. In paragraph 20, in reference to the films *The Wild One* and *Rebel Without a Cause,* Gillett says, "The plot in both films was clumsy, artificial, and morally compromised, but the undercurrents of frustration and violence in each were sufficient to give the films credibility." Explore this idea in a journal entry.
7. Give two examples from the essay to support Gillett's statement in paragraph 22 that "the film industry realized and responded to the needs of its audience faster than did the music industry."
8. Find a statement in the essay for which your own knowledge of rock music and its listeners provides contradictory or supporting evidence. Express that support or contradiction in a journal entry.
9. In a journal entry, explore the similarities between members of the "Beat Generation" as John Tytell characterizes them (pp. 216–221) and the "minority audience" identified by David Riesman (5–8).
10. In a marginal note, explain the significance of the use of rock and roll in the film *Blackboard Jungle.*
11. Later in his book Gillett says, "Both large segments of the general public and the music industry establishment looked upon the growing popularity of rock and roll with uneasiness. There were three main grounds for mistrust and complaint: the rock and roll songs had too much sexuality (or, if not that,

vulgarity), that the attitudes in them seemed to defy authority, and that the singers either were Negroes or sounded like Negroes." Discuss your reaction to these concerns in a journal entry.

Working with Sources

1. Referring to the outline you prepared in "Reacting to Sources," question 3, write a one-hundred-word summary of David Riesman's comments (4 – 8).
2. Write a critique of the ideas in paragraph 18.
3. Write a journal entry in which you explore your reactions to these quotations from "The Rise of Rock and Roll":

   "In almost every respect, the sounds of rhythm and blues contradicted those of popular music. . . . The prevailing emotion was excitement" (1).

   "At his first session with Decca, [Bill Haley] recorded 'Rock Around the Clock' and 'Shake, Rattle and Roll,' which between them were to transform throughout the world the conception of what popular music could be" (15).

   "The growth of rock 'n' roll cannot be separated from the emergence, since the Second World War, of a new phenomenon: the adolescent or youth culture" (18).

   Be sure to integrate the quotations smoothly into your writing.
4. Paraphrase the ideas in paragraph 14.
5. Write a one-paragraph synthesis that blends ideas in paragraph 18 of this essay and paragraph 25 of "The Big Barbecue" (pp. 183 – 192).

Writing with Sources: Using a Single Source

Integrating information from "The Rise of Rock and Roll" with your own ideas, write an essay on one of these topics. Be sure to acknowledge ideas that are not your own.

1. Apply Gillett's comments in paragraph 9 to the rock music of today. Be sure to give specific examples to support your ideas.
2. In paragraph 19 Gillett observes that the identification of adolescents as a special group, a "new breed," led Hollywood producers to "adjust their films to the realization that an increasing proportion of their audience were in their teens." Discuss in what sense this trend continues today in films (or in music or television).
3. In his own observations as well as Riesman's, Gillett associates the emergence of rock and roll with adolescent rebelliousness. Is this association valid? Explain your position.

The Beat Generation

John Tytell

Born in Belgium in 1939 and educated at City College of the City University of New York and at New York University, John Tytell is now Associate Professor of English at Queens College. He has published articles in *Partisan Review, The American Scholar, Commonweal, Literature and Psychology,* and *Studies in the Novel;* he has also edited *The American Experience: A Radical Reader* (1970), and *Affinities: A Short Story Anthology* (1970). In addition, Tytell has published poetry in *Partisan Review, Fiddlehead,* and *Galley Sail Review.* "The Beat Generation" is excerpted from the introduction to his book *Naked Angels* (1976), subtitled "The Lives and Literature of the Beat Generation." In this book Tytell focuses on the group of writers—such as Jack Kerouac, Allen Ginsberg, and William Burroughs—who rebelled against the conformity and materialism of the fifties and turned to experimentation and rebellion in their work and in their lives.

Society everywhere is in conspiracy against the manhood of every one of its members.—Ralph Waldo Emerson *"Self-Reliance"*

1   Jack Kerouac, Allen Ginsberg, William Burroughs, and a group of other writers, artists, and mavericks of inspiration like Neal Cassady, formed a "movement" which began near the end of the Second World War, found its voice during the fifties, and became especially influential in the sixties. Though the movement lacked any shared platform such as the Imagist or Surrealist manifestoes, it cohered as a literary group. While the work of one informed the approach and style of another—in the way that Kerouac's prose line and aesthetic of spontaneity affected Ginsberg's poetic—the mutuality among these men developed more as a result of a mythic outlook on their own lives and interactions.

2   In 1952, Jack Kerouac listed the chief members of the movement in a letter to Ginsberg, explaining that the crucial motivation for their union was the ability to honestly confess each other their deepest feelings. Such open revelation of private matters contradicted the spirit of the age, but led to aesthetic and intellectual discoveries. The Beat movement was a crystallization of a sweeping discontent with American "virtues" of progress and power. What began with an exploration of the bowels and entrails of the city—criminality, drugs, mental hospitals—evolved into an expression of the visionary sensibility. The romantic militancy of the Beats found its roots in American transcendentalism. Their spiritual ancestors were men like Thoreau with his aggressive idealism, his essentially conservative distrust of machines and industry, his desire to return to the origins of man's relations to the land; or Melville, with his adventurous tolerance of different tribal codes; or Whitman, optimistically proclaiming with egalitarian gusto the raw newness and velocity of self-renewing change in America while joyously admiring the potential of the common man.

3   Beginning in despair, the Beat vision was elevated through the shocks of experience to a realization of what was most perilous about American life. One

of the images that best captures the motivating energy of this search is the nakedness that was expressed aesthetically in Jack Kerouac's idea of the writer committing himself irrevocably to the original impulses of his imagination, in Ginsberg's relentless self-exposure in a poem like "Kaddish," in Burroughs' refusal in *Naked Lunch* to disguise the demonic aspects of his addiction. But for the Beats nakedness did not exist simply as an aesthetic standard, it was to become a symbolic public and private stance, making art and action inseparable: thus Allen Ginsberg disrobed at poetry readings, and Kerouac once wrote that he wanted to be like the medieval Tibetan scholar-monk Milarepa who lived naked in caves — and as a supreme final statement Neal Cassady was found naked and dead near a railroad track in Mexico. This emphasis on baring the body and exposing the soul was an intuitive reaction to a betrayal the Beats felt because of mass acceptance of demeaning changes in the American idea of self-determination. Nakedness signified rebirth, the recovery of identity.

4   The Beats saw themselves as outcasts, exiles within a hostile culture, freaky progenitors of new attitudes toward sanity and ethics, rejected artists writing anonymously for themselves. Seeking illumination and a transvaluation of values, they deified Rimbaud who had exclaimed in *Une Saison en Enfer:* "Moi! moi qui me suis dit mage ou ange, dispense de toute morale . . ." [I, who called himself magus or angel — purged of all morality]. Messengers of imminent apocalypse, the Beats believed that they were the angels of holocaust — like Kerouac's portrayal of his friend Neal Cassady as a "burning, frightful, shuddering angel, palpitating across the road." The angel image reappears in Kerouac's writing as it does so frequently in the work of all the Beats. In one of Gregory Corso's letters to Allen Ginsberg, there is a drawing of an angelic Virgin cradling William Burroughs in her arms while Ginsberg and Kerouac hover like desolate cherubim — the picture a brooding reminder of the messianic and reformist impulses of a movement that was steeped in sorrow while yearning for beatitude.

5   Foundlings of the fifties, the Beats were like a slowly burning fuse in a silent vacuum. The postwar era was a time of extraordinary insecurity, of profound powerlessness as far as individual effort was concerned, when personal responsibility was being abdicated in favor of corporate largeness, when the catchwords were coordination and adjustment, as if we had defeated Germany only to become "good Germans" ourselves. The nuclear blasts in Japan had created new sources of terror, and the ideology of technology became paramount; science was seen as capable of totally dominating man and his environment. And the prospects of total annihilation through nuclear explosion, of mass conditioning through the media, only increased the awesome respect for scientific powers.

6   Few periods in our history have presented as much of an ordeal for artists and intellectuals. In *The Prisoner of Sex,* Norman Mailer has wondered how he survived those years without losing his mind. What Allen Ginsberg has called the Syndrome of Shutdown began in the late forties: the move toward a closed society where all decisions would be secret; the bureaucratic disease that Hannah Arendt has characterized as rule by Nobody where ultimately, as in

Watergate, there is no final authority or responsibility; the paralysis caused by the use of technological devices that invade privacy; the increasing power of the Pentagon with its military bases designed to contain a new enemy supposedly (and suddenly) more threatening than the Nazis. The hysteria of rabid anticommunism was far more damaging, as Thomas Mann told the House Un-American Activities Committee, than any native communism; the patriotic blood-boiling became a convenient veil assuring a continued blindness to domestic social conditions that desperately needed attention. An internal freeze gripped America, an irrational hatred that created intense fear and repression, and since any repression feeds on oppression as its necessary rationalization, the red witch-hunts, the censorship of artists and filmmakers, the regimentation of the average man, began with unparalleled momentum and design. The contamination caused by this psychic and moral rigidity has been discussed by Allen Ginsberg in his *Paris Review* interview:

> The Cold War is the imposition of a vast mental barrier on everybody, a vast anti-natural psyche. A hardening, a shutting off of the perception of desire and tenderness which everybody *knows* . . . [creating] a self-consciousness which is a substitute for communication with the outside. This consciousness pushed back into the self and thinking of how it will hold its face and eyes and hands in order to make a mask to hide the flow that is going on. Which it's aware of, which everybody is aware of really! So let's say shyness. Fear. Fear of total feeling, really, total being is what it is.

7   With the exception of the Civil War period, never before had the sense of hopefulness usually associated with the American experience been so damaged.

8   In the late forties and early fifties, the axioms of the upright in America were belief in God, family, and the manifestly benevolent international ambitions of the nation. Americans still conceived of themselves as innocent democratic warriors, protectors of a holy chalice that contained a magic elixir of progress in technology, cleanliness, and order. The middle-class American had become Kipling's white man burdened by a tank that he kept confusing with a tractor. Yet the national consciousness and the face of the land had been inevitably altered by the war effort. Fascism, as Susan Sontag has observed, was not a monstrously sudden growth excised by the war, it is the normal condition of the modern industrial state. As Herbert Marcuse demonstrated in *One Dimensional Man,* productive apparatus tends to become totalitarian to the extent that it determines individual needs and aspirations, and results in a "comfortable, smooth, and reasonable democratic unfreedom." The social goal becomes efficiency; the toll, privacy and freedom. As the war machine of industry became insatiable, the inevitable result was the convenient fiction of the Cold War and the cost of perpetual rearmament. Henry Miller realized the ensuing paradox:

> Never has there been a world so avid for security, and never has life been more insecure. To protect ourselves, we invent the most fantastic instruments of destruction, which prove to be boomerangs. No one seems to believe in the

power of love, the only dependable power. No one believes in his neighbor, or in himself, let alone a supreme being. Fear, envy, suspicion are rampant everywhere.

9   The "war on communism" created an atmosphere of coercion and conspiracy. The nation's legacy of individuality had been changed to a more standardized expectation of what constituted "Americanism." Traditional tolerance of ideological difference had been subverted to a passion for organization and political similitude. It was a bitter and ironic distortion of our history: the character of the country had always been as various as its topography, and the lack of homogeneity meant that Americans had to work to develop a national consciousness resilient enough to embrace the aspirations of multitudes. Suddenly, there was an alleged contagion of treasonous spies, a mania for internal security, a repression that fostered anxiety and discouraged dissent. Some vital ingredient of the "American Dream" was warped and out of control.

10   What was the effect on a generation of such a politics of infidelity, such a time of false securities and mistrust? C. Wright Mills saw the emergence of a "mass society" composed of isolated units, formed by media, encouraged only to consume, never to decide. Other social critics noted the development of a mentality that refused to question authority. *Death of a Salesman* dramatized, in the passive victimization of Willy Loman, the immolation of the American soul in the impersonal abstractions of money for its own sake. Even worse, the psychology of the McCarthy era made truth itself suspect; it became something manipulated by "credible" authorities. As Yale chaplain William Sloan Coffin, Jr. observed, students in the fifties agreed their way through life. Education was a means of earning an income, no longer a way of stimulating critical inquiry or deepening sensibility. Novelist Philip Roth has admitted that he belonged to the most patriotic generation of American schoolchildren, the one most willingly and easily propagandized. For those who had reached their majority during the war, the indignity was greater. William Styron claimed that his generation was "not only not intact, it had been cut to pieces." While the end of the war brought with it an enormous sense of relief and a dull weariness, Styron wrote:

> We were traumatized not only by what we had been through and by the almost unimaginable presence of the bomb, but by the realization that the entire mess was not finished after all: there was now the Cold War to face, and its clammy presence oozed into our nights and days.

The cosmos seemed unhinged to Styron's generation as it confronted the "ruthless power and the loony fanaticism of the military mind."

11   The Beats were part of this beseiged generation. At first, political consciousness was dormant: politics, Blake had maintained long before, was an objectification of "mental war." The violence, tyranny, and corruption of world leaders, as the Buddhist notion of karma explained, was only the realization of every individual's carelessness, deliberate ignorance, and uninvolvement. But young men like Kerouac were sensitively aware of the disappearing landmarks of regional diversity, the end of that special adaptability that had for so long

invigorated the American character. The Beats could still nostalgically recall the time when one could bargain for an article purchased in a general store, when one bought land rather than paper shares in huge corporations, when radio and the airplane represented occasions of tremendous excitement. Kerouac's friend, novelist John Clellon Holmes, reflecting on the late thirties and early forties, saw that it was then — both because of the Depression and the anticipations of the war — that a great fissure had occurred in the American psyche, an uprooting of family relationships, of the sense of place and community that was compounded by a fear of imminent devastation. It was a shared premonition that the entire society was going to be changed in a major way, and that young men were to be particularly sacrificed. In a dream that he recorded, Kerouac noted that somewhere during the war he lost his way and took the wrong path. Holmes offered the image of a broken circuit to suggest the lack of connection to the immediate present felt by the members of his generation. It was as dangerous a condition as a hot electrical wire discharging energy randomly into the universe without a proper destination. The philosophical cause was not so much the horrible fact of the war, as it had been for the Lost Generation of the twenties, but the emergence of the new postwar values that accepted man as the victim of circumstances, and no longer granted him the agency of his own destiny: the illusion of free will, the buoyantly igniting spark in the American character, had been suddenly extinguished.

12   Simultaneously in Europe, a similar merger of bitterness and idealism resulted in Existentialism. Like the Beats, the Existentialists began by negation, refusing to accept the social given. While the Beats agreed with the Existentialist argument that man defines himself through his actions, they also shared a Spenglerian expectation of the total breakdown of Western culture. The Beats danced to the music of the absurdity they saw around them. When Ginsberg's friend Carl Solomon sent him an unsigned postcard reading simply: "VANISHED!" it was a token of an irrepressible anarchic gaiety, but also an ominous warning of the totalitarian potentials of the age — a writer could hobo on the road or be kidnapped to the mental wards, the new concentration camps.

13   It is now clear that during the forties and fifties the Beats were operating on a definition of sanity that defied the expectations of their time, but proved potently prophetic. In other words, it was not only their writing that was important, but the way they chose to live. As Longfellow once remarked about the transcendentalist utopians, it was a "divine insanity of noble minds." In a culture that suspected mere difference in appearance as deviant behavior, or regarded homosexuality as criminal perversion, Allen Ginsberg maintained that "my measure at the time was the sense of personal genius and acceptance of all strangeness in people as their nobility." In the face of the asphyxiating apathy of the fifties, the Beats enacted their desires, seeking a restoration of innocence by purging guilt and shame. The model was Blakean, but it was never a path of easy irresponsibility. Gary Snyder, keeping a journal while working as a fire lookout on Sourdough Mountain in 1953, wrote:

> Discipline of self-restraint is an easy one; being clear-cut, negative, and usually based on some accepted cultural values. Discipline of following desires, *always*

doing what you want to do, is hardest. It presupposes self-knowledge of motives, a careful balance of free action and sense of where the cultural taboos lay.

14   In the terms of their time, the Beats were regarded as madmen, and they suffered the consequences of the reformatory, the insane asylum, public ridicule, censorship, even prison. But what would seem defeat in the eye of ordinary experience simply instigated them to further adventures. The Beats were attracted to "madness" as a sustained presence; a lucid, singular, and obsessive way to illuminate the shadows of the day. Was William Blake, for example, acting madly when he read *Paradise Lost* with his wife while both sat naked in their garden? Melville had once perceived that the difference between sanity and insanity was analogous to the points in the rainbow where one color begins and another ends. As the eye could not distinguish any demarcation, a subjective value judgment was necessary. In the nineteenth century, madness became interpreted as unusual behavior, an affront to agreed social codes — so as long as Blake remained naked in the privacy of his garden, he was merely eccentric. But like the European Surrealists, the Beats wanted their Blake to dance naked in the public garden, and this was interpreted as a threat to public dignity. In the fifties, the Beats were still not quite as overtly political as the Surrealists had been, but they certainly paid for whatever self-assertions they managed with great psychic costs. There is no accident in the lament of the first line of "Howl": "I saw the best minds of my generation destroyed by madness." The Christian mystic Thomas Merton understood the spirit of revolt that inspired the Beat redefinition of sanity:

> We equate sanity with a sense of justice, with humaneness, with prudence, with the capacity to love and understand other people. We rely on the sane people of the world to preserve it from barbarism, madness, destruction. And now it begins to dawn on us that it is precisely the *sane* ones who are the most dangerous.

Recognizing that madness was a kind of retreat for those who wanted to stay privately sane, the Beats induced their madness with drugs, with criminal excess, and the pursuits of ecstasy. They used "madness" — which they regarded as naturalness — as a breakthrough to clarity, as a proper perspective from which to see. At times temporarily broken by the world for their disobedience, they developed, as Hemingway put it in *A Farewell To Arms,* a new strength "at the broken places." As Edmund Wilson argues in "The Wound and the Bow," there exists an inextricable relationship between genius and disease in modern artists who have so precisely predicted and reflected the general insanity surrounding them. The acting out of repressed inhibitions and taboos relieves binding public pressures to conform, and the artist as scapegoat/shaman creates an alternative with his very being.

Reading Sources: "The Beat Generation"

Read the selection, surveying it to identify key terms and important concepts. Highlight these phrases and ideas, and then answer these questions.

1. Before beginning his discussion of the Beats, Tytell presents a long overview of the decade in which this movement "found its voice." Why does he do this?
2. What is the significance of the quotation by Emerson that opens the essay? Is this quotation an appropriate introduction to the essay? Explain.
3. To what kind of audience does Tytell address his essay? How can you tell?
4. Carefully reread the opening sentences of each of the essay's fourteen paragraphs. What repeated key words and ideas serve to link the paragraphs smoothly into a unified essay?
5. What is Tytell's purpose in isolating a single sentence in paragraph 7?
6. Identify the topic sentence of paragraph 12.

Reacting to Sources

Reread the selection carefully, making marginal notes to aid comprehension and reinforce connections. Then further annotate the selection if you need to do so in order to answer any of these questions. (You may already have addressed some of the questions in your marginal notes.)

1. Using a dictionary if necessary, supply brief marginal definitions of these words as they are used in this selection: *mavericks* (1), *informed* (1), *aesthetic* (1), *mythic* (1), *visionary* (2), *transcendentalism* (2), *progenitors* (4), *transvaluation* (4), *apocalypse* (4), *palpitating* (4), *cherubim* (4), *messianic* (4), *beatitude* (4), *rabid* (6), *axioms* (8), *manifestly* (8), *insatiable* (8), *coercion* (9), *immolation* (10), *objectification* (11), *karma* (11), *irrepressible* (12), *anarchic* (12), *purging* (13), *analogous* (14), *demarcation* (14), *affront* (14), *scapegoat* (14), *shaman* (14).
2. Use an encyclopedia if necessary to identify the following people: (Arthur) Rimbaud, Norman Mailer, Hannah Arendt, Thomas Mann, Susan Sontag, Herbert Marcuse, C. Wright Mills, William Styron, Longfellow, Gary Snyder, William Blake, Edmund Wilson.
3. In paragraph 5 Tytell calls the Beats "foundlings of the fifties." Explain the significance of this phrase in a journal entry.
4. In paragraph 6 Tytell refers to Thomas Mann's statement that the hysteria of intense anticommunism presented a greater danger to Americans than native communism. Do you agree or disagree with Mann's point? Explain your position in a journal entry.
5. Give several examples from the essay to support this statement: "Few periods in our history have presented as much of an ordeal for artists and intellectuals" (6).
6. Simplify this statement in a marginal note: "As the war machine of industry became insatiable, the inevitable result was the convenient fiction of the Cold War and the cost of perpetual rearmament" (8).
7. Outline paragraph 10.
8. In a marginal note, explain John Clellon Holmes's image of a broken circuit (11) as it applied to the Beat Generation.

9. Formulate three questions whose answers could help you understand the complex allusions and concepts presented in paragraph 12.
10. In a few sentences, rewrite paragraph 13 to simplify its ideas.
11. In a journal entry, explain what Tytell means by this statement: "The acting out of repressed inhibitions and taboos relieves binding public pressures to conform, and the artist as scapegoat/shaman creates an alternative with his very being" (14).
12. In a journal entry, consider the ways in which the Beats as a group were different from the suburbanites described in "The Big Barbecue" (pp. 183 – 192).

Working with Sources

1. Write a fifty-word summary of paragraph 3.
2. Write a critique of the ideas in paragraph 5.
3. Write a journal entry in which you explore your reactions to these quotations from "The Beat Generation":

   "The Beats saw themselves as outcasts, exiles within a hostile culture, freaky progenitors of new attitudes toward sanity and ethics, rejected artists writing anonymously for themselves" (4).

   "Like the Beats, the Existentialists began by negation, refusing to accept the social given" (12).

   "In the terms of their time, the Beats were regarded as madmen, and they suffered the consequences of the reformatory, the insane asylum, public ridicule, censorship, even prison" (14).

   Be sure to integrate the quotations smoothly into your writing.
4. Paraphrase Allen Ginsberg's comments (quoted by Tytell in paragraph 6).
5. Write a one-paragraph synthesis that blends ideas in paragraph 6 of this essay and paragraph 7 of "I Have Here in My Hand . . . " (pp. 202–205).

Writing with Sources: Using a Single Source

Integrating information from "The Beat Generation" with your own ideas, write an essay on one of these topics. Be sure to acknowledge ideas that are not your own.

1. In paragraph 13 Tytell says, "It is now clear that during the forties and fifties the Beats were operating on a definition of sanity that defied the expectations of their time, but proved potently prophetic." In what sense were the Beats prophetic? Identify trends in our culture that are consistent with the Beats' ideas.
2. Read one of the influential literary works of the Beat Generation — Allen Gins-

berg's poem "Howl," for instance, or a section of Jack Kerouac's novel *On The Road.* Explain in what sense the work is a rebellion against the norms of fifties society as Tytell describes it.

3. The Beat Generation has often been compared to the post–World War I "Lost Generation," a group that included famous writers like Ernest Hemingway and F. Scott Fitzgerald. Read an article in an encyclopedia about the Lost Generation; then compare and contrast the two groups.

Beep Beep

William Manchester

In the fall of 1957 the USSR launched *Sputnik,* the first satellite to orbit the earth. In this essay from his history *The Glory and the Dream* William Manchester assesses the impact of this event on Americans in the fifties. (See p. 300 for biographical information on Manchester.)

1   The first word that a Russian sphere the size of a beachball was circling the earth once every 96.2 minutes, traveling at a speed of 18,000 mph and emitting beeping sounds as it did so, had reached Washington, quite by chance, during a cocktail party in the Soviet embassy at 1125 Sixteenth Street. Scientists from twenty-two countries were observing 1957–58 as an International Geophysical Year, or IGY as they called it—a general sharing of data— and Russian diplomats were entertaining fifty IGY luminaries that historic Friday evening when one of the guests, Walter Sullivan of the *New York Times,* was called away for an urgent telephone call. At the phone he learned of the Tass announcement. He hurried back and whispered to an American scientist, Dr. Lloyd Berkner, who rapped on the hors d'oeuvre table until the hubbub quieted. "I wish to make an announcement," he said. "I am informed by the *New York Times* that a satellite is in orbit at an elevation of 900 kilometers.* I wish to congratulate our Soviet colleagues on their achievement."

2   The room burst into applause. Eminent scientists are indifferent to national loyalties, and the Americans there were particularly generous. Dr. Joseph Kaplan, chairman of the U.S. IGY program, called the Russian achievement "tremendous" and added, "If they can launch one that heavy, they can put up much heavier ones." The White House, however, was momentarily speechless. The advent of the first sputnik astounded U.S. intelligence even though the Soviets had made no great secret of their satellite plans. At an IGY planning conference in Barcelona Russian delegates had spoken openly and confidently of their plans to launch a space vehicle. As early as November 1954, Defense Secretary Wilson had been asked whether he was concerned

* Approximately 559 miles.

over the possibility that the USSR might win the satellite race. He had snorted, "I wouldn't care if they did."

3   That continued to be the Republican line now that Sputnik was an accomplished fact. Administration spokesmen seemed to suggest that the press was making molehills out of molehills. Hagerty issued a statement describing the satellite as a matter "of great scientific interest" but adding that "we never thought of our program as one which was in a race with the Soviet's." Wilson, now in retirement, called the Russian feat "a nice technical trick." Rear Admiral Rawson Bennett, chief of the Office of Naval Research, wondered why there was so much fuss over a "hunk of iron almost anybody could launch." White House adviser Clarence Randall described the space vehicle as "a silly bauble"— thereby infuriating the President—and Sherman Adams said disparagingly that the government wasn't interested in "an outer-space basketball game." (In his memoirs Adams regretted this. "I was only trying to reflect the President's desire for calm poise," he wrote, "but I had to admit on reflection that my observation seemed to be an overemphasis of the de-emphasis.")

4   Others in Washington were in no mood to dismiss Sputnik so lightly. Trevor Gardner, who as former Assistant Secretary of the Air Force had tried to mediate interservice quarrels over who should run the American space program, said bitterly, "We have presently at least nine ballistic missile programs, all competing for roughly the same kind of facilities, the same kind of brains, the same kind of engines and the same public attention." Electronics and airframe experts recalled Wilson's casual attitude toward space research. "The basic reason we're behind the Russians," a major defense contractor said, "is that we haven't gone all out." One of the President's closest aides said he felt an urge to "strangle" Budget Director Percival Brundage. Knowland privately warned Ike that the worldwide impact of the Soviet accomplishment had all but nullified the value of America's Mutual Security program, and some publicists were actually suggesting a negotiated peace with the Russians "before it is too late."

5   The Democrats, predictably, were indignant. Senator Henry Jackson of Washington wanted the President to proclaim "a week of shame and danger." Missouri's Symington demanded a special session of Congress. Fulbright of Arkansas said, "The real challenge we face involves the very roots of our society. It involves our educational system, the source of our knowledge and cultural values. And here the Administration's program for a renaissance of learning is disturbingly small-minded." Majority Leader Johnson saw cosmic implications in the Russian success. "The Roman empire controlled the world because it could build roads," he said. "Later—when men moved to the sea—the British Empire was dominant because it had ships. Now the Communists have established a foothold in outer space. It is not very reassuring to be told that next year we will put a 'better' satellite into the air. Perhaps," he concluded sarcastically, "it will even have chrome trim—and automatic windshield wipers."

6   This was more than partisan oratory. Periodically Americans feel a need to agonize over why the country has gone soft. The last time it had happened had

been in the spring of 1940, when France was falling and the older generation thought American youth too engrossed in swing to hear the Nazi jackboots. Now, as then, the press was aroused. "It is downright terrifying with [Sputnik] staring down at us," the Portland *Oregonian* said, and *Time* said that "the U.S. takes deep pride in its technical skills and technological prowess, in its ability to get things done — first. Now, despite all the rational explanations, there was a sudden, sharp national disappointment that Americans had been outshone by the Red moon." John Kenneth Galbraith had been awaiting publication of *The Affluent Society.* Neither he nor his publishers had expected much of a sale. "Then, in the autumn of 1957," he wrote in an introduction to the second edition, "the Soviets sent up the first Sputnik. No action was ever so admirably timed. Had I been younger and less formed in my political views, I would have been carried away by my gratitude and found a final resting place beneath the Kremlin Wall. I knew my book was home."

7   Americans were learning humility — and humiliation. They had become an international laughingstock. At a scientific conference in Barcelona Leonid I. Sedov, Russia's chief space scientist, taunted a U.S. colleague: "You Americans have a better standard of living than we have. But the American loves his car, his refrigerator, his house. He does not, as we Russians do, love his country." Anti-Americans were derisive. RUSSIANS RIP AMERICAN FACE, read a headline in Bangkok's *Sathiraphab,* and a Beirut professor said dryly of his students, "You would have thought they launched it themselves." The editors of London's *Economist* saw the Russians scoring a brilliant psychological triumph in the Afro-Asian world. French journalists saw the catch, the price the Soviet masses had paid. Thierry Maulnier wrote in *Le Figaro,* "The Russian people can . . . see in the sky a brilliant star which carries above the world the light of Soviet power, thanks to millions of pots and shoes lacking," and *Combat* commented: "We ourselves would like it if the Russians would put some of their pride into the evolution of a better world — an end to the world of concentration camps." But in all Europe only the London *Express,* faithful to Britain's old ally, predicted that somehow the United States would muddle through: "The result will be a new drive to catch up and pass the Russians in the sphere of space exploration. Never doubt for a moment that America will be successful."

8   Americans themselves had plenty of doubts, and the more they knew about the implications of the Soviet achievement the more apprehensive they became. In those first days virtually all the details about the man-made star came from Tass and *Pravda;* the Smithsonian Institution was building an astrophysical observatory in Cambridge to track precisely this sort of phenomenon, but it was unfinished and unable even to correlate visual observations being phoned to it by widely scattered moonwatchers. The Russians disclosed that their first sputnik was a polished steel ball twenty-two inches in diameter, weighing 184.3 pounds and equipped with four radio antennas. Its orbit was higher than U.S. scientists had thought possible. Because of that height it would avoid the atmosphere and could keep circling the earth for years. Sputnik's weight was also stunning; the directors of America's Vanguard Project,

still in the theoretical stage, had been hoping to send a 21.5-pound Navy Viking research projectile to a maximum of 300 miles. That would have required 27,000 pounds of rocket thrust. The Russian catapult had used 200,000 pounds — an incredible figure, clearly indicative of a new source of power.

9   As new data came in and were digested by MIT computers, American appreciation of Soviet technical virtuosity soared. The orbit was stunning. It was elliptical, of course, carrying the sputnik from an apogee 583 miles above the earth to a perigee 143 miles down, but since both of these distances were added to the radius of the earth (3,960 miles) the ellipse was almost a circle, showing that the Russians had precise control as well as power. Moreover, the launch had been daring. The simplest way to orbit the satellite would have been to aim it eastward from the equator, taking advantage of the earth's rotation to give the object about 1,000 mph of free speed — in effect, a tailwind. Vanguard's planners had expected to do this; according to their calculations the Viking rocket, rising due east from Florida, would have had a 914 mph boost. But Vanguard rocketeers working under lights those first nights were astounded to learn that the Russian course was 65 degrees the other way. That indicated that they had power to burn. It had another significance. Vanguard's course would have kept it south of Europe and most of Russia. Sputnik's journey took it over most of the inhabited earth, meaning most of the world's peoples could see it, as well as hear it and read about it — a propaganda coup in itself.

10   Americans would be among the last to have a clear view of it, owing, perhaps, to a sly bit of Muscovite humor. The launch had been timed so that during its first weeks the satellite would pass over the United States during the day, when it would be invisible against the glare of the sun, or at night, when the shadow of the earth would hide it. The curious — and there were tens of thousands of them — had to peer up at daybreak and twilight, when the object could be briefly glimpsed against the gray sky. That would change. The orbit was shifting around the earth at four degrees a day, Dr. Joseph A. Hynek of the Smithsonian observatory explained; on about October 20 the sputnik would come into view overhead for those with binoculars or small telescopes. But Americans, impatient as always, wanted to know everything now. They had been huddling over their radios and television sets since that Friday night when an NBC commentator had told them, "Listen now for the sound which forevermore separates the old from the new." Then they had heard it for the first time, alternating between 20 and 40 megacycles — an eerie A-flat beeping from outer space.

11   It was generally assumed in those early days that the object was sending back signals in cipher, and CIA cryptographers worked in shifts to break the code. A man who could enlighten them happened to be right there in Washington; he was General Anatoly Arkadievich Blagonravov, chief of the three-man delegation Moscow had sent to the IGY conference. There was no code, the general said. The designers had put the beeps in to track the sputnik and reassure themselves that the satellite was still out there. There was nothing in the steel ball except the transmitter and the batteries. The power of the signal

was one watt—just about enough for a conversation between hams in Australia and the United States. In about three weeks the batteries would be exhausted, Blagonravov said, and the beeping would stop. A likely story, Americans snorted. Who could trust a Russian general? There was something fishy about those signals. "Many believe that the whole story has not been told," *Time* noted darkly. The CIA had better get to the bottom of it, the man on the street muttered, or the U.S. taxpayer would know the reason why.

12   Sputnik I dealt the coup de grace to Ford's fading Edsel, which had been introduced to the public the month before, and which was now widely regarded as a discredited symbol of the tinny baubles Americans must thrust aside. There were other scapegoats. The administration was one. It was M. Robert Bendiner who suggested that until now the Republican idea of a scientist had been a man who tore and compared cigarettes on television. Public education was another conspicuous target and did, in fact, have much to answer for. American parents were angered to learn that while their children were being taught "life adjustment," Russian education had been acquiring a reputation for being tough and competitive, ruthlessly winnowing out mediocrities beginning in the fourth grade and awarding to outstanding students the laurels which, in the United States, were reserved for athletes and baton-twirling, tail-twitching cheerleaders.

13   Parental wrath would grow with the publication of John Gunther's *Inside Russia Today,* then in galleys. Gunther reported that "In the schools which prepare for college, the Soviet child must absorb in ten years what an American child gets in twelve — perhaps more." Russian pupils, he said, went to school six hours a day, six days a week, attending classes 213 days a year as against 180 in the United States, and in the last two years of schooling four hours of homework were assigned each day. Gunther continued:

> . . . the main emphasis is on science and technology, for both boys and girls, and herein lies the greatest challenge to our system. In addition to ten solid years of mathematics, every child must take four years of chemistry, five of physics, six of biology. By contrast, only about half of American high schools have *any* physics, and only 64 percent have *any* chemistry. An American authority told me that the average Soviet boy or girl graduating from the tenth grade (our twelfth) has a better scientific education — particularly in mathematics — than most American college graduates!

14   Emphasis on science came early in Soviet schools; pupils began studying optics and quantum theory in grade school. By the mid-1950s the USSR was graduating twice as many scientists and engineers as the United States, and in a sixty-four-page report the National Science Foundation estimated that 14 percent of all Soviet scientists were allowed to pursue basic research — that is, inquiries which may or may not have practical significance. Such work often seems pointless at the time, but it is the restless search for answers by the laboratory man with insatiable curiosity which makes possible the technological miracles of the next generation. Thomas Edison could not have developed the

incandescent lamp without Henry Cavendish and Michael Faraday; the atomic bomb became a reality because in 1905 Albert Einstein had published an obscure volume setting forth the proposition, then wholly inapplicable, that energy is encompassed in every bit of matter; and the H-bomb was created by men who had been studying the stars. Charles E. Wilson thought basic research ridiculous. As Secretary of Defense he had once mocked it as finding out "what makes grass green and fried potatoes brown," a remark scientists now remembered and quoted bitterly. The number of Americans in long-range studies was fractional, and the funds allotted to them — about 450 million dollars a year — represented only one-tenth of one percent of the national income.

15   Now scientists were beginning to speak up. Norbert Wiener had something to say about science and society. Wiener blamed the tight lid government had clamped on research, beginning with radar and the Manhattan Project. The consequence, he said, was that the individual scientist was often not only unaware of the vast problem he was dealing with, but even worse, that his scientific inquisitiveness was frequently discouraged. Physicists pointed out that the Soviets had an 8.3-billion electron-volt particle accelerator (atom smasher), better than America's best, the University of California's betatron, and UCLA's Joseph Kaplan, the U.S. IGY chairman, said, "In oceanography, meteorology, and upper-atmosphere physics, the indications are that they are certainly as good as we are."

16   Edward Teller also spoke up. Though still a pariah among most of his fellow physicists, Teller remained a brilliant and prescient scholar. His Pentagon friends pointed out that in last April's issue of *Air Force* magazine, six months before the first beep, he had gloomily written: "Ten years ago there was no question where the best scientists in the world could be found — here in the U.S. . . . Ten years from now the best scientists in the world will be found in Russia." In the Soviet Union, he had pointed out, science was almost a religion; its ablest men were singled out and treated as a privileged class while their underpaid American colleagues lacked status in their society and could offer few incentives to bright protégés. His appeal for respect for the dignity of scientific inquiry was well taken. The number of cartoons about mad scientists dropped sharply. There were also fewer jokes about them. And it was extraordinary how quickly the word egghead dropped out of the language.

17   For some time Walter Lippmann had been urging his countrymen to consecrate themselves to a national purpose. Few had grasped what he had in mind, but now they knew: the national purpose was to rescue education and, with it, America's next generation. Suddenly Rudolf Flesch's *Why Johnny Can't Read — and What You Can Do About It,* which had come out in 1955 without making much of a dent, was on everyone's best-seller list. Hardly anyone had a good word for schools as they were except people like Dr. Ruth Strang of Teachers College, Columbia, and she and TC were in disgrace. Social critics' heaviest guns trained on just such educators, or, as they were derisively christened, "educationists." Chancellor Lawrence A. Klimpton of the University of Chicago explained how the Strangs and the William Heard Kilpatricks had distorted and misrepresented the ideas of John Dewey. Dewey had held that

thinking begins in an interest, or a concern. But this had been twisted into an insistence that teachers must amuse, or entertain, pupils.

18   Herbert Hoover said that the Communists "are turning out twice or possibly three times as many" scientists "as the U.S." He scorned the "too prevalent high-school system of allowing a thirteen- or fourteen-year-old kid to choose most of his studies." That same week another distinguished engineer from whom more would be heard on this score observed in Detroit that one root of the trouble lay in the "misconception of the worth" of the American high school. "We have always overvalued it," said Rear Admiral Hyman G. Rickover, the man responsible for America's atomic submarines. "It comes out," he continued, "that we have many more children in high school and in college than [Europeans] have in secondary schools and universities, and this makes us proud. But all these comparisons are meaningless because the European secondary school graduate has learned more than most of our college graduates. As to the high school diploma," he added heavily, "the less said about it the better."

19   Even resolute Republicans were uneasy. Clare Boothe Luce, in other ways a steadfast defender of the status quo during the Eisenhower years, found complacency on this issue impossible. She called the sputnik's beep an "outer-space raspberry to a decade of American pretensions that the American way of life is a gilt-edge guarantee of our national superiority." Her husband was also troubled by heretical thoughts. "Turning to Washington for reassurance," *Time* said nervously, "the U.S. saw administrative confusion, sensed a crisis in leadership and demanded action." The stock market tobogganed dizzily downward that week, and with Russia's man-made moon flashing across the skies all America seemed depressed. A contagion of black humor cropped up — proposals to change Project Vanguard's name to Project Rearguard and a story about a Washington reporter who called the U.S. Space Agency, asked how the program was going, and was asked by the girl on the phone, "Sir, are you calling *for* information or *with* information?"

20   Sputnik I's beeps died away in the last week of October, as General Blagonravov had predicted. It was still there and could be tracked, but at least you couldn't hear it any more. Then, just as Americans had begun to catch their breath, Sputnik II went up on November 3. In some ways it was a more breathtaking achievement than its predecessor. The new satellite weighed 1,120.29 pounds — making it six times as heavy as Sputnik I — and its orbit carried it 1,056 miles away from the earth. "The unfathomed natural processes going on in the cosmos," Moscow radio proclaimed, "will now become more understandable to man." It was true; American scientists were envious. A space vehicle that large would house a maze of instruments radioing back data on cosmic rays, solar radiation above the atmosphere, atmospheric temperature and composition, the danger of meteors, the earth's gravitation, its magnetic field, its electric charge, and the cloud patterns of its weather. The Russians had another surprise. There was a little dog of the *laika* breed aboard, strapped with contrivances which would provide other information about the ability of fauna to survive in space.

21   It was another luckless day for administration image makers. Ideally news of the event should have found the leaders of the government at their desks furiously striving to catch up. As it happened, Eisenhower was just returning from a West Point class of '15 reunion and homecoming football game, while a Big Ten game had taken Charlie Wilson's successor, the new Secretary of Defense, Neil McElroy, to Columbus.

22   The United States was in an uproar. The presence of the dog in Sputnik II clearly meant that eventually the Russians intended to put a man on the moon. Most people in the U.S. were determined to beat them there, and they were becoming impatient with the composure of their President. *Time* said: "The storm showed promise of being the most serious that Dwight Eisenhower had ever faced." A headline in the *Pittsburgh Press* begged: SHOOT THE MOON, IKE.

Reading Sources: "Beep Beep"

Read the selection, surveying it to identify key terms and important concepts. Highlight these phrases and ideas, and then answer these questions.

1. Why does Manchester call this essay "Beep Beep"? Is this an effective title for his audience? (For more information on the source of the essay, see the introduction to "With All Deliberate Speed," p. 300.) Explain.
2. List some of the reactions to *Sputnik* on the part of American politicians, foreign journalists, and the American scientific community.
3. What is Manchester's purpose in presenting detail about *Sputnik*'s size, weight, and orbit (paragraphs 8 and 9)?
4. How does Manchester connect paragraphs 3 and 4? 14 and 15? 15 and 16? What techniques does Manchester use to help his readers — some of whom would have no memories of the fifties — to develop a sense of what the *Sputnik* era was like?
5. Manchester's essay is visually divided into two sections. Where does the division occur? How is the shift from one section to the next indicated? Why does Manchester break the essay where he does?

Reacting to Sources

Reread the selection carefully, making marginal notes to aid comprehension and reinforce connections. Then further annotate the selection if you need to do so in order to answer any of these questions. (You may already have addressed some of the questions in your marginal notes.)

1. Using a dictionary if necessary, supply brief marginal definitions of these words as they are used in this selection: *hubbub* (1), *bauble* (3), *nullified* (4), *cosmic* (5), *partisan* (6), *derisive* (7), *virtuosity* (9), *apogee* (9), *perigee* (9),

coup de grace (12), *winnowing* (12), *pariah* (16), *prescient* (16), *resolute* (19), *heretical* (19), *tobogganed* (19), *contagion* (19).

2. Identify: Tass (1), Hagerty (3), Sherman Adams (3), Knowland (4), *Pravda* (8), Edsel (12), Walter Lippman (17), Clare Boothe Luce (19). Use an encyclopedia if necessary.
3. In a marginal note, explain Manchester's purpose in quoting Majority Leader (later President) Lyndon Johnson in paragraph 5.
4. In paragraph 6 Manchester says, "Periodically Americans feel a need to agonize over why the country has gone soft." In a journal entry, explain what Manchester means; then, basing your response on your observations about present-day America, explain why you agree or disagree with him.
5. In a marginal note, explain M. Robert Bendiner's comment, quoted in paragraph 12, that "until now the Republican idea of a scientist had been a man who tore and compared cigarettes on television."
6. Give two examples to support Manchester's general statement in paragraph 15 that "scientists were beginning to speak up."
7. In paragraph 16 Manchester observes, "The number of cartoons about mad scientists dropped sharply. There were also fewer jokes about them. And it was extraordinary how quickly the word egghead dropped out of the language." Explain the significance of these developments in a marginal note.
8. Look up Edward Teller in an encyclopedia. Then, in a marginal note, identify him and explain why he was "still a pariah among most of his fellow physicists . . ." (16).
9. In a few sentences, rewrite paragraph 16 to simplify its ideas.
10. In a journal entry, explain the significance of John Gunther's *Inside Russia Today* and Rudolf Flesch's *Why Johnny Can't Read — and What You Can Do About It.*
11. Formulate three questions whose answers could expand your understanding of the ideas presented in paragraph 22.
12. In a journal entry, consider possible connections between this essay and one of the essays in Chapter 11, "The Impact of Technology." Pay special attention to the impact of technology on the lives of the American people.

Working with Sources

1. Write a fifty-word summary of paragraph 10.
2. Write a critique of the ideas in paragraph 14.
3. Write a journal entry in which you explore your reactions to these quotations from "Beep Beep":

> "Americans were learning humility — and humiliation. They had become an international laughingstock" (7).

> "Sputnik's journey took it over most of the inhabited earth, meaning most of the world's peoples could see it, as well as hear it and read about it — a propaganda coup in itself" (9).

"Sputnik I dealt the coup de grace to Ford's fading Edsel, which had been introduced to the public the month before, and which was now widely regarded as a discredited symbol of the tinny baubles Americans must thrust aside" (12).

Be sure to integrate the quotations smoothly into your writing.

4. Paraphrase the ideas in paragraph 8.
5. Write a one-paragraph synthesis that blends ideas in paragraph 1 of this essay and paragraph 17 of "The Summer Before Salk" (pp. 194–199).

Writing with Sources: Using a Single Source

Integrating information from "Beep Beep" with your own ideas, write an essay on one of these topics. Be sure to acknowledge ideas that are not your own.

1. Reread Manchester's material on the American educational system in paragraphs 12–13 and 17–18, and reconsider these paragraphs in light of your own high-school education. Based on your experience, decide in what respects the education available to high school students today is different from the 1957 norm. Then write an essay in which you argue that today's students are (or are not) equipped to compete in an increasingly science-oriented world.
2. In paragraph 8 Manchester says that Americans had doubts about their ability to compete with the Russians on a technological level and that "the more they knew about the implications of the Soviet achievement the more apprehensive they became." Compare and contrast Americans' reactions to the launching of *Sputnik* with our more recent reactions to Soviet advances on technological, political or athletic and cultural fronts. Be sure to consider whether you find this competition healthy and productive or a negative, even dangerous factor in Soviet-American relations.
3. Consider a recent major technological advance that had a dramatic effect on scientists, politicians, and the American public. Explore the effects of this advance on one of these groups and on your own life.

Writing with Sources: Using Multiple Sources

Integrating information from sources in this chapter with your own ideas, write an essay on one of the topics below. Be sure to acknowledge ideas that are not your own.

1. In "The Beat Generation" (pp. 216–221) John Tytell says, "The postwar era was a time of extraordinary insecurity, of profound powerlessness as far as individual effort was concerned, when personal responsibility was being abdicated in favor of corporate largeness, when the catchwords were coordination and adjustment, as if we had defeated Germany only to become 'good Ger-

mans' ourselves'' (5). In short, the fifties rewarded conformity and discouraged nonconformity. Discuss the effects of this tendency as they are presented in "The Big Barbecue," "The Beat Generation," "I Have Here in My Hand . . . ," and "The Rise of Rock and Roll."

2. Interview your parents or other relatives to collect their impressions of the fifties. You may base your questions on the issues presented in this chapter's readings, or you may consider other areas. Use their reminiscences and information from the readings as source material for an essay in which you compare life in the fifties with life in the eighties.

3. The fifties were a time of contrasts — freedom and repression, commitment and irresponsibility, conformity and experimentation, hope and despair. Explore this idea in an essay.

4. What, if anything, did the prominent figures of the fifties — Jonas Salk, Joseph McCarthy, Dwight Eisenhower, Jack Kerouac and Allen Ginsberg, Elvis Presley — have in common? Why did these people capture the attention of fifties Americans? Write an essay in which you explain their appeal.

5. John Tytell quotes Henry Miller as identifying a basic paradox of the fifties: "Never has there been a world so avid for security, and never has life been more insecure" (8). How did this paradox affect the lives and careers of those who came of age in the fifties? Write an essay in which you discuss this issue.

6. Write an essay in which you consider the effects of new technological advances — television, *Sputnik,* the polio vaccine, and so on — on the lives of children growing up in the fifties.

7

The Changing Image of the Hero

Every society creates heroes who function as role models or embody religious or cultural ideals. In our day when rock singers and movie and television stars have supplanted the soldiers, adventurers, presidents, and business tycoons of previous years, the hero is especially difficult to define. To the ancient Greeks, the hero was an individual who had a mystical and religious function and who was often venerated. In the Middle Ages, knights and saints were considered heroes and heroines, and during the Renaissance, explorers and conquistadors set people's imaginations burning. Certainly the twentieth century has had its share of traditional heroes and heroines — Charles Lindbergh, Amelia Earhart, John Glenn, and Coretta Scott King, to name a few. But with the advent of television, where notoriety is instantaneous, contemporary society seems increasingly to use popular culture figures as its heroes and heroines.

In "The Path of the Hero" Joseph Campbell defines the characteristics that heroes in mythology have in common, and in "Hercules" F. Guirand narrates a representative Greek myth. Next, Antonia Fraser in "Heroes and Heroines" classifies her heroes and heroines and discusses what these figures have in common. In "The Emerging American Hero," Marshall W. Fishwick discusses the heroes and myths that have emerged from American culture. Focusing on a single decade, Roderick Nash in "Heroes of the Nineteen Twenties" examines the heroes who embody the hopes and fears of typical Americans. Finally, in "Faster Than an Express Train," Jules Feiffer focuses on a particularly modern hero — Superman.

The Path of the Hero

Joseph Campbell

Joseph Campbell was born in 1904 in Wichita, Kansas, and received a B.A. and M.A. from Dartmouth College. He was a postgraduate fellow at the University of Paris and the University of Munich. Campbell was a member of the literature department at Sarah Lawrence College, and has written widely on mythology and the effect of mythology on culture. His works include *The Hero with a Thousand Faces* (1949); *The Masks of God*, Volume 1: *Primitive Mythology* (1959); *The Masks of God*, Volume II: *Oriental Mythology* (1962); *The Masks of God*, Volume III: *Occidental Mythology* (1964); and *The Masks of God*, Volume IV: *Creative Mythology* (1968). The following essay from *The Hero with a Thousand Faces* presents the standard path that a mythological adventure hero takes. Called the *monomyth*, this journey varies little in its essential elements from one myth to another and from one culture to another.

1   The standard path of the mythological adventure of the hero is a magnification of the formula represented in the rites of passage: *separation — initiation — return:* which might be named the nuclear unit of the monomyth.[1]

2   *A hero ventures forth from the world of common day into a region of supernatural wonder: fabulous forces are there encountered and a decisive victory is won: the hero comes back from this mysterious adventure with the power to bestow boons on his fellow man.*

3   Prometheus ascended to the heavens, stole fire from the gods, and descended, Jason sailed through the Clashing Rocks into a sea of marvels, circumvented the dragon that guarded the Golden Fleece, and returned with the fleece and the power to wrest his rightful throne from a usurper. Aeneas went down into the underworld, crossed the dreadful river of the dead, threw a sop to the three-headed watchdog Cerberus, and conversed, at last, with the shade of his dead father. All things were unfolded to him: the destiny of souls, the destiny of Rome, which he was about to found, "and in what wise he might avoid or endure every burden."[2] He returned through the ivory gate to his work in the world.

4   A majestic representation of the difficulties of the hero-task, and of its sublime import when it is profoundly conceived and solemnly undertaken, is presented in the traditional legend of the Great Struggle of the Buddha. The young prince Gautama Sakyamuni set forth secretly from his father's palace on the princely steed Kanthaka, passed miraculously through the guarded gate, rode through the night attended by the torches of four times sixty thousand divinities, lightly hurdled a majestic river eleven hundred and twenty-eight cubits

---

[1] The word *monomyth* is from James Joyce, *Finnegans Wake* (New York: Viking Press, Inc., 1939), p. 581.
[2] Virgil, *Aeneid*, VI, 892.

wide, and then with a single sword-stroke sheared his own royal locks —
whereupon the remaining hair, two finger-breadths in length, curled to the
right and lay close to his head. Assuming the garments of a monk, he moved as
a beggar through the world, and during these years of apparently aimless
wandering acquired and transcended the eight stages of meditation. He retired
to a hermitage, bent his powers six more years to the great struggle, carried
austerity to the uttermost, and collapsed in seeming death, but presently
recovered. Then he returned to the less rigorous life of the ascetic wanderer.

5   One day he sat beneath a tree, contemplating the eastern quarter of the
world, and the tree was illuminated with his radiance. A young girl named
Sujata came and presented milk-rice to him in a golden bowl, and when he
tossed the empty bowl into a river it floated upstream. This was the signal that
the moment of his triumph was at hand. He arose and proceeded along a road
which the gods had decked and which was eleven hundred and twenty-eight
cubits wide. The snakes and birds and the divinities of the woods and fields
did him homage with flowers and celestial perfumes, heavenly choirs poured
forth music, the ten thousand worlds were filled with perfumes, garlands,
harmonies, and shouts of acclaim; for he was on his way to the great Tree of
Enlightenment, the Bo Tree, under which he was to redeem the universe. He
placed himself, with a firm resolve, beneath the Bo Tree, on the Immovable
Spot, and straightway was approached by Kama-Mara, the god of love and death.

6   The dangerous god appeared mounted on an elephant and carrying
weapons in his thousand hands. He was surrounded by his army, which extended twelve leagues before him, twelve to the right, twelve to the left, and in
the rear as far as to the confines of the world; it was nine leagues high. The
protecting deities of the universe took flight, but the Future Buddha remained
unmoved beneath the Tree. And the god then assailed him, seeking to break
his concentration.

7   Whirlwind, rocks, thunder and flame, smoking weapons with keen edges,
burning coals, hot ashes, boiling mud, blistering sands and fourfold darkness,
the Antagonist hurled against the Savior, but the missiles were all transformed
into celestial flowers and ointments by the power of Gautama's ten perfections.
Mara then deployed his daughters, Desire, Pining, and Lust, surrounded by
voluptuous attendants, but the mind of the Great Being was not distracted. The
god finally challenged his right to be sitting on the Immovable Spot, flung his
razor-sharp discus angrily, and bid the towering host of the army to let fly at
him with mountain crags. But the Future Buddha only moved his hand to touch
the ground with his fingertips, and thus bid the goddess Earth bear witness to
his right to be sitting where he was. She did so with a hundred, a thousand, a
hundred thousand roars, so that the elephant of the Antagonist fell upon its
knees in obeisance to the Future Buddha. The army was immediately dispersed,
and the gods of all the worlds scattered garlands.

8   Having won that preliminary victory before sunset, the Conqueror acquired in the first watch of the night knowledge of his previous existences, in
the second watch the divine eye of omniscient vision, and in the last watch

understanding of the chain of causation. He experienced perfect enlightenment at the break of day.[3]

9   Then for seven days Gautama — now the Buddha, the Enlightened — sat motionless in bliss; for seven days he stood apart and regarded the spot on which he had received enlightenment; for seven days he paced between the place of the sitting and the place of the standing; for seven days he abode in a pavilion furnished by the gods and reviewed the whole doctrine of causality and release; for seven days he sat beneath the tree where the girl Sujata had brought him milk-rice in a golden bowl, and there meditated on the doctrine of the sweetness of Nirvana; he removed to another tree and a great storm raged for seven days, but the King of Serpents emerged from the roots and protected the Buddha with his expanded hood; finally, the Buddha sat for seven days beneath a fourth tree enjoying still the sweetness of liberation. Then he doubted whether his message could be communicated, and he thought to retain the wisdom for himself; but the god Brahma descended from the zenith to implore that he should become the teacher of gods and men. The Buddha was thus persuaded to proclaim the path.[4] And he went back into the cities of men where he moved among the citizens of the world, bestowing the inestimable boon of the knowledge of the Way.[5]

10   The Old Testament records a comparable deed in its legend of Moses, who, in the third month of the departure of Israel out of the land of Egypt, came with his people into the wilderness of Sinai; and there Israel pitched their tents over against the mountain. And Moses went up to God, and the Lord called unto him from the mountain. The Lord gave to him the Tables of the Law and commanded Moses to return with these to Israel, the people of the Lord.[6]

11   Jewish folk legend declares that during the day of the revelation diverse

---

[3] This is the most important single moment in Oriental mythology, a counterpart of the Crucifixion of the West. The Buddha beneath the Tree of Enlightenment (the Bo Tree) and Christ on Holy Rood (the Tree of Redemption) are analogous figures, incorporating an archetypal World Savior, World Tree motif, which is of immemorial antiquity. Many other variants of the theme will be found among the episodes to come. The Immovable Spot and Mount Calvary are images of the World Navel, or World Axis.

The calling of the Earth to witness is represented in traditional Buddhist art by images of the Buddha, sitting in the classic Buddha posture, with the right hand resting on the right knee and its fingers lightly touching the ground.

[4] The point is that Buddhahood, Enlightenment, cannot be communicated, but only the *way* to Enlightenment. This doctrine of the incommunicability of the Truth which is beyond names and forms is basic to the great Oriental, as well as to the Platonic, traditions. Whereas the truths of science are communicable, being demonstrable hypotheses rationally founded on observable facts, ritual, mythology, and metaphysics are but guides to the brink of a transcendent illumination, the final step to which must be taken by each in his own silent experience. Hence one of the Sanskrit terms for sage is *mūni*, "the silent one." *Sākyamūni* (one of the titles of Gautama Buddha) means "the silent one or sage (*mūni*) of the Sakya clan." Though he is the founder of a widely taught world religion, the ultimate core of his doctrine remains concealed, necessarily, in silence.

[5] Greatly abridged from *Jataka*, Introduction, i, 58–75 (translated by Henry Clarke Warren, *Buddhism in Translations* (Harvard Oriental Series, 3) Cambridge, Mass.: Harvard University Press, 1896, pp. 56–87), and the *Lalitavistara* as rendered by Ananda K. Coomaraswamy, *Buddha and the Gospel of Buddhism* (New York: G. P. Putnam's Sons, 1916), pp. 24–38.

[6] Exodus, 19:3–5.

rumblings sounded from Mount Sinai. "Flashes of lightning, accompanied by an ever swelling peal of horns, moved the people with mighty fear and trembling. God bent the heavens, moved the earth, and shook the bounds of the world, so that the depths trembled, and the heavens grew frightened. His splendor passed through the four portals of fire, earthquake, storm, and hail. The kings of the earth trembled in their palaces. The earth herself thought the resurrection of the dead was about to take place, and that she would have to account for the blood of the slain she had absorbed, and for the bodies of the murdered whom she covered. The earth was not calmed until she heard the first words of the Decalogue.

12   "The heavens opened and Mount Sinai, freed from the earth, rose into the air, so that its summit towered into the heavens, while a thick cloud covered the sides of it, and touched the feet of the Divine Throne. Accompanying God on one side, appeared twenty-two thousand angels with crowns for the Levites, the only tribe that remained true to God while the rest worshiped the Golden Calf. On the second side were sixty myriads, three thousand five hundred and fifty angels, each bearing a crown of fire for each individual Israelite. Double this number of angels was on the third side; whereas on the fourth side they were simply innumerable. For God did not appear from one direction, but from all simultaneously, which, however, did not prevent His glory from filling the heaven as well as the earth. In spite of these innumerable hosts there was no crowding on Mount Sinai, no mob, there was room for all."[7]

13   As we soon shall see, whether presented in the vast, almost oceanic images of the Orient, in the vigorous narratives of the Greeks, or in the majestic legends of the Bible, the adventure of the hero normally follows the pattern of the nuclear unit above described: a separation from the world, a penetration to some source of power, and a life-enhancing return. The whole of the Orient has been blessed by the boon brought back by Gautama Buddha—his wonderful teaching of the Good Law—just as the Occident has been by the Decalogue of Moses. The Greeks referred fire, the first support of all human culture, to the world-transcending deed of their Prometheus, and the Romans the founding of their world-supporting city to Aeneas, following his departure from fallen Troy and his visit to the eerie underworld of the dead. Everywhere, no matter what the sphere of interest (whether religious, political, or personal), the really creative acts are represented as those deriving from some sort of dying to the world; and what happens in the interval of the hero's nonentity, so that he comes back as one reborn, made great and filled with creative power, mankind is also unanimous in declaring. We shall have only to follow, therefore, a multitude of heroic figures through the classic stages of the universal adventure in order to see again what has always been revealed. This will help us to understand not only the meaning of those images for contemporary life, but also the singleness of the human spirit in its aspirations, powers, vicissitudes, and wisdom.

[7] Louis Ginzberg, *The Legends of the Jews* (Philadelphia: The Jewish Publication Society of America, 1911), Vol. III, pp. 90–94.

14   The following pages will present in the form of one composite adventure the tales of a number of the world's symbolic carriers of the destiny of Everyman. The first great stage, that of the *separation* or *departure,* will be shown in Part I, Chapter I, in five subsections: (1) "The Call to Adventure," or the signs of the vocation of the hero; (2) "Refusal of the Call," or the folly of the flight from the god; (3) "Supernatural Aid," the unsuspected assistance that comes to one who has undertaken his proper adventure; (4) "The Crossing of the First Threshold"; and (5) "The Belly of the Whale," or the passage into the realm of night. The stage of *the trials and victories of initiation* will appear in Chapter II in six subsections: (1) "The Road of Trials," or the dangerous aspect of the gods; (2) "The Meeting with the Goddess" (*Magna Mater*), or the bliss of infancy regained; (3) "Woman as the Temptress," the realization and agony of Oedipus; (4) "Atonement with the Father"; (5) "Apotheosis"; and (6) "The Ultimate Boon."

15   *The return and reintegration with society,* which is indispensable to the continuous circulation of spiritual energy into the world, and which, from the standpoint of the community, is the justification of the long retreat, the hero himself may find the most difficult requirement of all. For if he has won through, like the Buddha, to the profound repose of complete enlightenment, there is danger that the bliss of this experience may annihilate all recollection of, interest in, or hope for, the sorrows of the world; or else the problem of making known the way of illumination to people wrapped in economic problems may seem too great to solve. And on the other hand, if the hero, instead of submitting to all of the initiatory tests, has, like Prometheus, simply darted to his goal (by violence, quick device, or luck) and plucked the boon for the world that he intended, then the powers that he has unbalanced may react so sharply that he will be blasted from within and without — crucified, like Prometheus, on the rock of his own violated unconscious. Or if the hero, in the third place, makes his safe and willing return, he may meet with such a blank misunderstanding and disregard from those whom he has come to help that his career will collapse. The third of the following chapters will conclude the discussion of these prospects under six subheadings: (1) "Refusal of the Return," or the world denied; (2) "The Magic Flight," or the escape of Prometheus; (3) "Rescue from Without"; (4) "The Crossing of the Return Threshold," or the return to the world of common day; (5) "Master of the Two Worlds"; and (6) "Freedom to Live," the nature and function of the ultimate boon.[8]

16   The composite hero of the monomyth is a personage of exceptional gifts. Frequently he is honored by his society, frequently unrecognized or disdained.

---

[8] This circular adventure of the hero appears in a negative form in stories of the deluge type, where it is not the hero who goes to the power, but the power that rises against the hero, and again subsides. Deluge stories occur in every quarter of the earth. They form an integral portion of the archetypal myth of the history of the world, and so belong properly to Part II of the present discussion: "The Cosmogonic Cycle." The deluge hero is a symbol of the germinal vitality of man surviving even the worst tides of catastrophe and sin.

He and/or the world in which he finds himself suffers from a symbolical deficiency. In fairy tales this may be as slight as the lack of a certain golden ring, whereas in apocalyptic vision the physical and spiritual life of the whole earth can be represented as fallen, or on the point of falling, into ruin.

17   Typically, the hero of the fairy tale achieves a domestic, microcosmic triumph, and the hero of myth a world-historical, macrocosmic triumph. Whereas the former — the youngest or despised child who becomes the master of extraordinary powers — prevails over his personal oppressors, the latter brings back from his adventure the means for the regeneration of his society as a whole. Tribal or local heroes, such as the emperor Huang Ti, Moses, or the Aztec Tezcatlipoca, commit their boons to a single folk; universal heroes — Mohammed, Jesus, Gautama Buddha — bring a message for the entire world.

18   Whether the hero be ridiculous or sublime, Greek or barbarian, gentile or Jew, his journey varies little in essential plan. Popular tales represent the heroic action as physical; the higher religions show the deed to be moral; nevertheless, there will be found astonishingly little variation in the morphology of the adventure, the character roles involved, the victories gained. If one or another of the basic elements of the archetypal pattern is omitted from a given fairy tale, legend, ritual, or myth, it is bound to be somehow or other implied — and the omission itself can speak volumes for the history and pathology of the example, as we shall presently see.

Reading Sources: "The Path of the Hero"

Read the selection, surveying it to identify key terms and important concepts. Highlight these phrases and ideas, and then answer these questions.

1. Where does Campbell state his thesis? Why does he state it here? How effective would another placement have been?
2. Who is Campbell's audience? Is there any indication that Campbell realizes that the concept of the monomyth is difficult for his readers to grasp? Does he attempt to explain the monomyth in terms that his readers will understand? Is he successful?
3. Why does Campbell include the legend of the Great Struggle of the Buddha? In what way does Campbell signal his reason for including the legend?
4. This selection is part of a book entitled *The Hero with a Thousand Faces*. Where does Campbell give an overview of the book? How does the material in this essay relate to the book?
5. What information does Campbell provide in his footnotes? In what ways are these notes useful to readers?
6. Where does Campbell begin his conclusion? What material does he present in his conclusion?

Reacting to Sources

Reread the selection carefully, making marginal notes to aid your comprehension and to reinforce connections. Then further annotate the selection if you need to do so in order to answer any of these questions. (You may already have addressed some of the questions in your marginal notes.)

1. In a few sentences, define *monomyth* so that a general audience would understand its meaning. Why does Campbell use this term to describe the path that a mythological adventure hero takes?
2. Using a dictionary if necessary, supply brief marginal definitions of these words as they are used in the selection: *mythological* (1), *cubit* (4), *resolve* (5), *assailed* (6), *voluptuous* (7), *omniscient* (8), *enlightenment* (8), *zenith* (9), *nonentity* (13), *vicissitudes* (13), *reintegration* (15), *composite* (16), *apocalyptic* (16), *microcosmic* (17), *macrocosmic* (17), *regeneration* (17), *sublime* (18), *morphology* (18), *archetypal* (18), *pathology* (18).
3. Consult an encyclopedia or a collection of Greek myths and look up the figures to whom Campbell refers in paragraph 3 of his essay: Prometheus, Jason, Aeneas, and Cerberus. In a marginal note explain why Campbell refers to these mythic figures.
4. Make a marginal note in which you list three specific examples to illustrate the main point made in paragraph 16.
5. In a journal entry, explore the ideas expressed in paragraph 16.
6. Write three brief marginal questions in response to the ideas in paragraph 17.
7. Identify Campbell's purpose in the paragraph cluster beginning with paragraph 10 and ending with paragraph 12.
8. Read the essay's introduction. Comment on how the author's life and other writings might have influenced his purpose. Comment on how it influences your acceptance of his ideas.
9. In a journal entry, compare and contrast Campbell's definition of a hero with what Roderick Nash says in "Heroes of the Nineteen Twenties" about Charles Lindbergh (pp. 227–228). Does Lindbergh fit Campbell's definition of a hero? How closely does Lindbergh's journey approximate the mythological journey that Campbell describes?
10. Outline the paragraph cluster beginning with paragraph 4 and ending with paragraph 9.

Working with Sources

1. Write a two-sentence summary of paragraph 16.
2. Write a critique of the ideas in paragraph 18.
3. Write a journal entry in which you explore your reactions to these quotations from "The Path of the Hero."

   ". . . the adventure of the hero normally follows the pattern of the nuclear unit above described: a separation from the world, a penetration to some source of power, and a life-enhancing return" (13).

"Whether the hero be ridiculous or sublime, Greek or barbarian, gentile or Jew, his journey varies little in essential plan" (18).

Be sure to integrate the quotations smoothly into your writing.

4. Paraphrase the paragraph cluster beginning with paragraph 1 and ending with paragraph 3.
5. Write a one-paragraph synthesis that blends ideas in paragraph 13 of this essay with the ideas in paragraph 18 of "Heroes and Heroines" (pp. 253–258).

Writing with Sources: Using a Single Source

Integrating information from "The Path of the Hero" with your own ideas, write an essay on one of these topics. Be sure to acknowledge all ideas that are not your own.

1. Compare your definition of a hero to Campbell's. Use three of your own personal heroes to illustrate your points.
2. Show how a movie, television, or literary character fits Campbell's definition of a hero. Be sure to refer to the categories of the heroic journey that Campbell presents in paragraph 2.
3. Using Campbell's essay as your guide, compose your own heroic myth. Make certain that your hero follows the standard path of mythological adventure and, after enduring trials and tribulations, returns victoriously to the world.

Hercules

F. Guirand

"Hercules" is from the *New Larousse Encyclopedia of Mythology*. To the ancient Greeks, Hercules was the embodiment of the heroic ideal. The offspring of Zeus and a mortal woman, he was both man and demigod. His miraculous birth, his superhuman exploits, and his eventual ascension to Olympus, made him the most popular of the Greek heroes. He was worshipped throughout Greece.

Hercules

1 We are not very certain about the etymology of the word Heracles (the Latinised form being Hercules, which is used here throughout). Various hypotheses have been suggested to explain the name. The ancients claimed that Heracles was thus named because he owed his glory to Hera. The name has also been

translated as 'glory of the air'. But no one of the theories advanced is more convincing than the others.

2 **The Functions of Hercules**   Hercules was thought of as the personification of physical strength. In his aspect of athlete-hero the foundation of the Olympic Games was ascribed to him. Pindar says that he arranged all the rules and details. But the chief function of Hercules was to play the part of a protector. When men were in danger Heracles *Alexikakos* was their chief resort. In consequence he even had medical powers: he was invoked in case of epidemics, while certain medicinal springs at Himera and Thermopylae were sacred to him. Finally, sometimes as Heracles Musagetes he played the cithara. To sum up, he presided over all aspects of Hellenic education and, after being the god of physical prowess, he was the god who sang of victory and accompanied himself on the lyre. More than any other he was the friend and counsellor of men.

3 **Representation and Cult**   The glorious hero, the invincible athlete, is depicted as a man of mature strength, endowed with muscular power, whose head is rather small in relation to his body. Generally Hercules stands, leaning on his heavy club. In this statues and busts we observe a rather sad and severe expression, as though Hercules, the eternal conqueror, never knew repose. His appearance suggests that he is waiting for yet another superhuman task to fulfil.

4   Hercules was venerated like other heros and with the same rites, but his cult was much more general. All Greece honoured him. His exploits, indeed, took place all over the Hellenic world. Thebes and Argos were the centres from which his legend spread.

5 **The Birth of Hercules. His Childhood and First Exploits**   Hercules descended from Perseus, whose son Alcaeus (the Strong) was the father of Amphitryon, the supposed father of Hercules. On the other hand, Electryon (the Brilliant), another son of Perseus, was the father of Alcmene (woman of might). Hercules, then, was born under the sign of strength and light; and, into the bargain, his paternity was divine. Zeus, wishing to have a son who should be a powerful protector of both mortals and Immortals, descended one night to the city of Thebes where he assumed the appearance of Amphitryon and lay with Amphitryon's wife, Alcmene. Shortly afterwards Amphitryon himself returned from a victorious expedition and took his wife in his arms. From the two successive unions Alcmene conceived twins: Hercules and Iphicles.

6   Their birth was not without difficulties. On the day Hercules should have been born Zeus swore a solemn and irrevocable oath before the Olympians that the descendent of Perseus who was about to be born should one day rule Greece. At these words Hera, doubly jealous, hurried to Argos where she caused the wife of one Sthenelus — himself a son of Perseus — to be brought prematurely to bed. She gave birth to Eurystheus. Hastening to Thebes, Hera simultaneously retarded the birth of Hercules. Thus Eurystheus came into the title of ruler of Greece and Zeus, bound by his solemn oath, was obliged to

recognise him. And that was why Hercules all his life found the hardest tasks imposed on him by the rival whom Hera had set up against him. Nor was her vengeance yet satisfied. One night while all in the palace of Amphitryon were asleep, two serpents attacked the infant Hercules. While Iphicles screamed pitifully, Hercules firmly grasped the two monsters, one in each hand, and wrung their necks. To encourage such promise Hercules was then handed over to illustrious tutors. Rhadamanthys taught him wisdom and virtue while Linus taught him music. Linus was killed by the young hero in a fit of temper. Amphitryon then confided his divine offspring to some shepherds who lived in the mountains. There Hercules gave himself over to physical exercise and developed his strength. At the age of eighteen he killed a ferocious lion which came to devour Amphitryon's herds. The hero, while waiting for the beast, hid in the house of King Thespius and, legend recounts, he made use of the occasion to lie in a single night with his host's fifty daughters.

7   Hercules shortly afterwards defended his native city against Orchomenus. He met the herald of Orchomenus, who had come to Thebes to collect the tribute, and cut off his nose and ears, thus starting the war. Amphitryon, fighting beside his two sons, was killed. But Hercules aided by Athene, defeated Erginus, King of Orchomenus. Creon became king of that country and gave his daughter Megara to Hercules as a wife. Their marriage was unhappy. Hera sent Lyssa, the Fury of madness, to Hercules. The hero was seized with the deadly malady, mistook his own children for those of Eurystheus, and massacred them and their mother. After this grim crime Hercules had to flee the country. He went to Argolis where he spent twelve years under the orders of Eurystheus who imposed upon him the most arduous labours. For thus the oracle of Delphi had commanded when Hercules, wishing to remove the stain of his crime, consulted her.

The Twelve Labours

8 **The Nemean Lion**   The first monster that Hercules had to exterminate was the Nemean Lion, the skin of which Eurystheus ordered him to bring back. Hercules attempted in vain to pierce the beast with this arrows, then he engaged it hand to hand and finally strangled it in his powerful grip. But he kept the skin and from it made a garment which rendered him invulnerable. He then returned to Tiryns with his trophy.

9 **The Lernaean Hydra**   This hydra, born of Typhon and Echidna, was an enormous serpent with nine heads. Its den was a marsh near Lerna in the Peloponnese. It would issue forth to ravage the herds and crops; its breath moreover was so poisonous that whoever felt it fell dead.

10   Accompanied by Iolaus, son of Iphicles, Hercules arrived at Lerna, found the monster near the spring of Amymone and forced it to emerge from the marshes by means of flaming arrows. Then he tried to overwhelm it by means of his mighty club. But in vain; for every time he struck off one of the hydra's nine heads two grew in its place. Then Iolaus set the neighbouring forest on

fire and with the help of red-hot brands burnt the serpent's heads. Hercules cut off the final head and buried it. Then he soaked his arrows in the hydra's blood which made them poisonous and deadly.

11 **The Wild Boar of Erymanthus**   This savage beast came down from Mount Erymanthus, on the borders of Arcadia and Achaia, and devastated the territory of Psophis. Hercules succeeded in capturing it and carried it to Tiryns. Eurystheus was so terrified at the sight of the monster that he ran away and hid himself in a bronze jar.

12   On his way to Mount Erymanthus Hercules had received the hospitality of the Centaur Pholus, who in his honour broached a barrel of delicious wine which had been a present from Dionysus. The other Centaurs were attracted by the bouquet of the wine and came running to the house of Pholus, armed with stones and uprooted fir trees, to demand their share of the wine. Hercules drove them off with his arrows. The Centaurs were decimated, and took refuge near Cape Malea.

13 **The Stymphalian Birds**   The marshes of Stymphalus in Arcadia were peopled by monstrous birds whose wings, beaks and claws were of iron. They fed on human flesh and were so numerous that when they took wing the light of the sun was blotted out. Hercules frightened them with brazen cymbals and slew them with arrows.

14 **The Ceryneian Hind**   Eurystheus then ordered Hercules to bring him back the hind of Mount Ceryneia alive. Her hooves were of bronze and her horns of gold. Hercules chased her for an entire year before he at last caught her on the banks of the Ladon.

15 **The Stables of Augeias**   Augeias, King of Elis, owned innumerable herds of cattle among which were twelve white bulls sacred to Helios. One of them whose name was Phaethon was privileged to shine like a star. Unhappily these magnificent animals lived in foul stables, heaped high with manure of many years' accumulation. Hercules undertook to clean them out in one day on condition that the king gave him a tenth part of the herd. In order to do this he breached the walls of the building and, altering the course of the rivers Alpheus and Peneius, made them rush through the cowsheds. When the job was done Augeias, under the pretext that Hercules was merely executing the orders of Eurystheus, refused to fulfil his part of the bargain. Later the hero was to punish this dishonesty.

16 **The Cretan Bull**   Poseidon had given Minos a bull, believing that Minos would offer it in sacrifice to him. As the king did nothing of the sort, Poseidon drove the animal mad. The country was terrorised and Minos appealed to Hercules who at the time happened to be in Crete. The hero managed to capture the animal which he carried on his back across the sea to Argolis.

17 The Mares of Diomedes   Diomedes, son of Ares and king of the Bistones, owned mares which he fed on human flesh. Hercules, accompanied by a few volunteers, approached Thrace and captured these terrible mares, having first killed their guardians. The alert was given, the Bistones rushed upon him and the battle began. Hercules at last vanquished his assailants and Diomedes was given to his own mares to eat.

18   The rescue of Alcestis is usually said to have taken place at this same time. Admetus, King of Pherae, had obtained from the Fates, through the intermediary of Apollo, an assurance that he would not die if someone consented to die in his stead. When the fatal moment arrived his wife, Alcestis, took his place. They were about to bury the unhappy woman when Hercules passed by and engaged in dreadful struggle with Thanatos — Death himself. Hercules succeeded in wrenching Alcestis from death's grasp and returned her to her husband.

19 The Girdle of Hippolyte   Hippolyte, whom some call Melanippe, was the Queen of the Amazons in Cappadocia. As a mark of her sovereignty she possessed a magnificent girdle given to her by Ares. Admete, daughter of Eurystheus, greatly coveted this marvellous adornment, and Hercules was therefore given orders to go and fetch it. Accompanied by several celebrated heroes — Theseus, Telamon, Peleus — he embarked. His first port of call was Paros where he fought with the sons of Minos. Next he reached Mariandyne in Mysia where he helped King Lycus to conquer the Bebryces. In gratitude Lycus built the town of Heracles Pontica.

20   When at last he reached the country of the Amazons Hercules at first encountered no obstacle: Hippolyte agreed to give him the girdle. But Hera was enraged and, disguising herself as an Amazon, spread abroad the story that Hercules planned to abduct the queen. The Amazons seized their weapons. Hercules, believing they had betrayed him, slaughtered the Amazons, together with their queen. He took the girdle and then proceeded towards Troy.

21 The Cattle of Geryon   Geryon was a triple-bodied monster who reigned over the western coast of Iberia or, according to others, over the Epirus. He owned a herd of red oxen which were guarded by the herdsman Eurytion and the dog Orthrus. Hercules, on the orders of Eurystheus, took possession of the oxen after killing Eurytion, Orthrus and finally Geryon. On his return journey he had various adventures. He slew the sons of Poseidon who attempted to steal the oxen, and he had to go to Eryx, king of the Elymans, in Sicily, to recapture an ox which had escaped and been put in the stables of Eryx. Eryx refused to return the beast unless Hercules beat him in a series of boxing and wrestling bouts. Hercules finally overthrew and killed him. In the hills of Thrace Hera sent a gadfly which drove the animals mad; they dispersed through the mountains and Hercules had great trouble in herding them together again. When he had done so he brought the cattle to Eurystheus who sacrificed them to Hera.

22   It was in the course of this expedition that Hercules penetrated Gaul where he abolished human sacrifice. He fought the Ligurians with the aid of stones which Zeus caused to rain down from the sky and which covered the plain of the Crau. The river Strymon refused to let him cross and he filled up its bed with stones.

23 **The Golden Apples of the Hesperides**   Eurystheus next commanded Hercules to bring to him the golden apples which the Hesperides, daughters of Atlas and Hesperus, guarded in their fabulous garden at the western extremities of the world. Hercules first travelled towards the north where, on the banks of the Eridanus, the nymphs of the river advised him to consult Nereus about the route. Hercules succeeded in capturing the prophetic god who told him how to reach the garden of the Hesperides. Crossing Libya Hercules measured his strength with Antaeus, a monstrous bandit who forced all travellers to wrestle with him. Antaeus was the son of Gaea, Mother Earth, and had the power of regaining his strength by touching the earth with his feet. Hercules in the end choked him to death by holding him high in the air in his arms. Hercules was next attacked while asleep by the Pygmies. He sewed them up in his lion skin. Then he arrived in Egypt where Busiris, the king, sacrificed a foreigner every year in order to put an end to a terrible famine. Hercules was chosen as victim, put in chains and conducted to the temple. But he threw off his chains suddenly and slew Busiris and his son Amphidamas (Iphidamas). He then resumed his journey. He crossed Ethiopia where he killed Emathion, son of Tithonus, and replaced him by Memnon. He crossed the sea in a golden barque which the Sun had given him. In the Caucasus he slew with his arrows the eagle which gnawed the liver of Prometheus and finally reached the garden of the Hesperides. He killed the dragon Ladon which guarded the entrance, seized the apples and delivered them to Eurystheus. Eurystheus made him a gift of them and Hercules in his turn presented them to Athene who returned them to the Hesperides.

24   It was also related that Hercules was aided by Atlas on this enterprise. He persuaded Atlas to pick the apples while he, Hercules, meanwhile supported the world on his shoulders. When Atlas returned with the apples he was reluctant to reassume his traditional burden and would have refused to do so had not Hercules outwitted him.

25 **Hercules' Journey to the Underworld**   In despair of ever getting the better of Hercules, Eurystheus, as a final labour, commanded him to fetch Cerberus, guardian of the infernal gates. Hercules first had himself initiated into the infernal mysteries at Eleusis and then, guided by Hermes, he took the subterranean passage which descended at Cape Taenarum. Everything fled before him except Meleager and the Gorgon. Farther on Theseus and Peirithous, who had imprudently ventured into the Underworld, implored his assistance. Hercules saved Theseus, but was prevented from rescuing Peirithous by a sudden earthquake. He relieved Ascalaphus of the boulder which was crushing him, overthrew Menoetes, or Menoetius, the herdsman of Hades, wounded Hades himself and finally obtained the permission of Hades to carry off Cerberus, provided that he could conquer the monster without other weapons than his bare hands. Hercules leapt on Cerberus and at last mastered him by strangulation. Then he dragged the brute by the scruff of its neck back to earth, showed him to Eurystheus, and sent him back to Hades again.

26 Other Exploits of Hercules When he was at last freed from servitude Hercules, far from resting on his laurels, set forth on new adventures. When King Eurytus promised the hand of his daughter Iole to him who vanquished him in an archery contest, Hercules arrived and triumphed. The king refused to keep his word. Shortly afterwards the king's son, Iphitus, asked Hercules to help him search for some stolen horses, and Hercules, distraught with fury, killed him. For this crime Hercules went to Delphi to be purified. The Pythia refused to answer him and Hercules made off with her tripod. A bitter quarrel with Apollo ensued in which Zeus himself had to intervene. At last the oracle condemned Hercules to a year's slavery, and obliged him to hand over his year's wages to Eurytus. It was Omphale, Queen of Lydia, who bought the hero when he was offered for sale as a nameless slave, for three talents. In spite of the tradition which showed Hercules during this period softened by pleasures and dressed in a long oriental robe while he spun wool at the feet of his mistress, he did not remain inactive. He captured the Cercopes, evil and malicious demons who were, perhaps, only a horde of brigands camped near Ephesus. He killed the king of Aulis, Syleus, who forced strangers to work in his vineyards and then cut their throats. He rid the banks of the Sagaris of a gigantic serpent which was ravaging the countryside, and finally threw the cruel Lityerses into the Maeander. Lityerses had been in the habit of forcing strangers to help with his harvest and then of cutting off their heads with a scythe. Omphale was overcome with admiration and restored the hero's freedom.

27 Hercules then offered to rescue Hesione, daughter of Laomedon, King of Ilium. This unfortunate princess had been chained to a rock, as an expiatory victim against an epidemic. A dragon had come to devour her. Hercules prevented the tragedy, but Laomedon refused to give him the reward which had been agreed upon. The hero returned to Ilium with six ships, besieged the town, took it by assault, killed Laomedon and his sons, and gave Hesione in marriage to his friend Telamon. On his return journey he was thrown onto the shores of the island of Cos by a storm raised by Hera. The inhabitants received him badly and he avenged himself by sacking the island and slaying its king, Eurypylus. Next, he took part at Phlegra in the battle between the gods and the giants.

28 Hercules had not forgotten the dishonesty of Augeias in the matter of the Augeian Stables. He marched against him and devastated his domain. He had on this occasion to fight the Molionids, sons of Poseidon. It was said that they had been hatched from a silver egg and had but one body with two heads, four arms and four legs.

29 While he was laying siege to Pylus Hercules did battle with Periclymenus who had the power of metamorphosis. When Periclymenus turned himself into an eagle Hercules destroyed him with a blow of his club.

30   Hercules also restored Tyndareus to his throne after he had been deprived of it by Hippocoon and his sons. Passing through Tegea in Arcadia Hercules seduced Auge, daughter of Aleus and a priestess of Athene. She bore him a son Telephus, whom she hid in the temple of the goddess. Athene, angered by this profanation, sent a plague to the country. Aleus discovered his daughter's shame and drove her away. She took refuse with King Teuthras in Mysia and exposed her child on Mount Parthenius. When Telephus grew to manhood he went in search of his mother. He found her in Mysia and, not recognising her, was on the point of marrying her when Hercules intervened and prevented the incest.

31   The last adventure of Hercules took place in Aetolia and in the land of Trachis. He obtained the hand of Deianeira, daughter of Oeneus, king of the Aetolians, after having triumphed over another suitor, the river-god Achelous. But shortly afterwards the accidental murder of young Eunomus, who served at his father-in-law's table, obliged Hercules to fly from the country, together with his wife. When he arrived at the river Evenus Hercules gave Deianeira to the Centaur Nessus to carry across to the opposite bank. But halfway across Nessus attempted to violate Deianeira. Hercules saw this and at once struck him with an arrow. As Nessus died he gave his blood to Deianeira, telling her that it would preserve the love and fidelity of her husband.

32   Unfortunately Hercules then conceived the fateful idea of going back to punish Eurytus. He slew Eurytus, together with his sons, and brought away Iole whom he had never ceased to love. On his return he stopped at Cenaeum in Euboea to offer a sacrifice to Zeus. Before doing so he sent his companion Lichas to Deianeira in Trachis to fetch a white tunic. Deianeira was worried at the thought that Iole was with her husband and, remembering the words of Nessus, soaked the tunic in the Centaur's blood before sending it to Hercules, hoping thus to regain his love. Scarcely had Hercules put on the tunic when he felt himself devoured by inner fire. Maddened with pain, he seized Lichas by the feet and flung him into the sea; then, tearing up pine-trees by their roots he made himself a funeral pyre, mounted it and ordered his companions to set it alight. All refused. Finally Poeas, father of Philoctetes, lighted the pines and Hercules rewarded him by giving him his bow and arrows.

33   The flames crackled and rose around the hero. At the moment they reached his body a cloud descended from the skies and in an apotheosis of thunder and lightning the son of Zeus disappeared from the eyes of men. He was admitted to Olympus where he was reconciled with Hera. He was married to her daughter Hebe and from then on lived the blissful and magnificent life of the Immortals.

Reading Sources: "Hercules"

Read the selection, surveying it to identify key terms and important concepts. Highlight these phrases and ideas, and then answer these questions.

1. Guirand introduces his essay by giving some information about Hercules. What is the nature of this information, and how does it prepare readers for the story?
2. What visual cues are used in this essay?
3. Make an outline of the events of the essay. In what order are events presented in the essay?
4. What words and phrases does Guirand use to link paragraphs? How successful is he in making sure that readers follow the sequence of events?
5. Does this essay have a thesis or a central idea? If so, what is it? If not, why not?

Reacting to Sources

Reread the selection carefully, making marginal notes to aid your comprehension and to reinforce connections. Then further annotate the selection if you need to do so in order to answer any of these questions. (You may already have addressed some of the questions in your marginal notes.)

1. In a few sentences, rewrite paragraph 3 to simplify its ideas.
2. Using a dictionary, supply brief marginal definitions of these words as they are used in the selection: *personification* (2), *cithara* (2), *invincible* (3), *venerated* (4), *paternity* (5), *malady* (7), *arduous* (7), *oracle* (7), *bouquet* (12), *decimated* (12), *brazen* (13), *intermediary* (18), *servitude* (26), *metamorphosis* (29), *profanation* (30).
3. Consult a dictionary of Greek mythology and provide brief marginal identifications of the following figures: Zeus (5), Hera (6), Athene (7), Typhon, Echidna (9), Poseidon (16), Hermes (25), Cerberus (25), Hebe (33).
4. Write three brief marginal questions in response to the ideas in paragraph 7.
5. Find a statement that makes you question Hercules's status as a hero. Write a marginal comment in which you express your misgivings.
6. Find a passage in the essay that shows Hercules acting heroically. Make a marginal comment explaining why his act is heroic.
7. Write a journal entry in which you develop a definition of the term *hero* that would fit Hercules.
8. In paragraph 3 Guirand says that Hercules's "appearance suggests that he is waiting for yet another superhuman task to fulfill." Explore this idea further in a journal entry.
9. In a journal entry consider the possible connections between this essay and "The Path of the Hero" (pp. 236–241).

Working with Sources

1. Write a one-sentence summary of paragraph 15.
2. Write a critique of the ideas in paragraph 6.
3. Write a journal entry in which you explore your reactions to these quotations from "Hercules."

"To sum up, he presided over all aspects of Hellenic education and, after being the god of physical prowess, he was the god who sang of victory and accompanied himself on the lyre. More than any other he was the friend and counselor of men" (2).

"At the age of eighteen he killed a ferocious lion which came to devour Amphitryon's herds. The hero, while waiting for the beast, hid in the house of King Thespius and, legend recounts, he made use of the occasion to lie in a single night with his host's fifty daughters" (6).

Be sure to integrate the quotations smoothly into your writing.

4. Paraphrase the paragraph cluster beginning with paragraph 21 and ending with paragraph 22.
5. Elsewhere F. Guirand makes the following statement:

"But the chief role of the hero was to act as intermediary between men and the gods. While men after death became insubstantial shadows, heroes retained their original qualities and could intercede for mortals. In brief, the heroes, who were originally idealized men, became demi-gods and in the hierarchy occupied a position midway between men and the Olympians."

Write a one-paragraph synthesis that blends the ideas in this statement with the ideas in paragraph 1 of "Heroes of the Nineteen Twenties" (pp. 270–278).

Writing with Sources: Using a Single Source

Integrating information from "Hercules" with your own ideas, write an essay on one of these topics. Be sure to acknowledge all ideas that are not your own.

1. Show how the twelve labors of Hercules corresponds to the monomyth that Joseph Campbell describes in "The Path of the Hero" (pp. 236–241).
2. Describe the Greeks' idea of a hero. Use material from "Hercules" to support your points. (Keep in mind that many of the heroes of ancient Greece were not only famous, but also were venerated and had cults devoted to their worship.)
3. Compare the characteristics of Hercules to the characteristics of someone whom you would consider a hero. How are they alike and how are they different? What conclusions can you draw about these two heroes?

Heroes and Heroines

Antonia Fraser

Antonia Fraser was born in 1932 in London and graduated from Oxford University in 1952. A prolific writer, she achieved immediate critical acclaim with the publication of *Mary, Queen of Scots* (1969). She followed this success with two more histories, *Cromwell* (1973) and *King James VI and I* (1974). Since then, she has written numerous books including *The Weaker Vessel* (1984) and a mystery, *Oxford Blood* (1985). The following essay is the introduction to *Heroes and Heroines* (1980), which Fraser edited. In it, she discusses hero worship and divides heroes and heroines into several categories.

1   'The living rock amid all rushings-down whatsoever; — the one fixed point in modern revolutionary history, otherwise as if bottomless and shoreless' — thus Thomas Carlyle on Hero-Worship. The date was 1840. In the course of his mighty disquisition on the subject, Carlyle lambasted his own age for denying the desirableness of great men ('I am well aware in these days Hero Worship, the thing I call Hero Worship, professes to have gone out, and finally ceased') before going on to charge his imagined foes at full tilt, grandiloquent sword in hand. He claimed, in a famous phrase, that 'Universal History, the history of what man has accomplished in his world, is at bottom the History of the Great Men who have worked here'.

2   Nearly one hundred and fifty years later, the shade of Carlyle must be satisfied by the fact that hero-worship is alive and well — even if many scholars today would deny furiously his proposition concerning the nature of Universal History. Perhaps Carlyle was needlessly concerned. The truth is that hero-worship is an emotion so primitively strong that it is doubtful whether it will ever be eradicated in human nature. For one thing, like many such passions, it often makes its first — and formative — appearance in early childhood. Of course we do not always carry our infant heroes or heroines with us into adult life. Nevertheless the memory remains, and lurks deep.

3   Adulthood does not necessarily mark the passing of hero-worship altogether, but it often brings with it a change of hero-object. Let us divide our heroes and heroines, roughly speaking, into two categories, the Inspirational and the Challenging: those we admire just because we know we could never emulate them, and those we admire and wish to emulate. An Inspirational heroine might be Odette Sansom: while no-one could possibly aim to find themselves in her unfortunate situation, imprisoned and tortured, anyone can be impressed and encouraged by the courage and tenacity she showed in surviving it. A Challenging heroine, on the other hand, is Florence Nightingale, whose example could lead a young girl to take up nursing (or equally to reorganize a corrupt and inefficient government service).

4   In childhood, unaware as we are of our capacities and the lack of them, our heroes tend to be Challenging. 'all I could never be' has not yet proved such a despairingly large category compared with 'all I might be one day with

luck'. With self-knowledge comes the switch to Inspirational heroes; and in certain instances the same type of hero, once Challenging, moves on to become merely Inspirational. I am thinking of the enormous and life-enhancing category of Sporting Heroes: Don Bradman — Challenging to the eager boy — becomes Inspirational to the middle-aged man.

5   As I grow older, my own tendency is to choose Inspirational heroines more relevant to my way of life than the glamorous idols of my youth. The love objects of my childhood were ninety per cent tragic and one hundred per cent romantic: Mary Queen of Scots epitomized them all; her colourful but sad destiny proved a delightful contrast to life in my parents' happy and high-minded (but not romantic) North Oxford home. Latterly St Teresa of Avila has replaced Mary Queen of Scots, not merely for her Inspirational mysticism, but for combining in her own way — as an organizer of convents — the life of the world with the life of the spirit. Mrs. Gaskell, the good mother, good wife, good housekeeper, good friend (and good writer) has replaced poor Charlotte Brontë — a great writer but one whose tragic personal life is irrelevant to my own. I do not however identify myself with either lady: to do so would be both presumptuous and unnecessary. Perhaps there is something essentially childish about such identification. In the clear light of adult reality, this element passes away from our hero-worship. Something humbler but equally able to transform our own ordinary lives remains.

6   I have assumed in all this that our heroes and heroines are leading us towards something higher than ourselves. Must it necessarily be so? Is it implicit in the very nature of a hero that he represent good rather than evil? Sir Thomas Malory in the *Morte d'Arthur* optimistically suggested that those who 'go after the good and leave the evil shall be brought to good fame and renown'; but the more depressing lesson of history is that these two categories of the good and the renowned are not always coincidental.

7   Certainly heroes are not to be equated with saints, although certain individuals can be both — St. Paul is included in this volume. Heroes, like saints, can also be chosen to illustrate particular virtues. Roland dying at Roncesvalles symbolizes the man who stands firm to the last rather than break his oath — 'Every man should be ready to die for his lord'; just as St Catherine, for example, martyred on a wheel after deliberately confessing the Christian faith at a public banquet of the Emperor Maximus, stands for another type of heroic testimony. Both Roland and St Catherine were, in so far as we know about their distant lives, morally irreproachable.

8   But there are tragic heroes whose qualities and destiny have nothing to do with sanctity. Part of the complex Japanese culture includes a special feeling for those heroes who are 'noble failures'. As Ivan Morris points out in a study of the subject, the Japanese not only admire historical figures like Admiral Togo — 'the Nelson of Japan' — who took on and defeated the forces of the West, but other very different types of hero. These are the men whose single-mindedness will not let them compromise, and who are thus inevitably vanquished: in short, the hero as loser, as described by Yeats, 'Bred to a harder thing than Triumph. . . .'

9   Death is often the harbinger of a heroic reputation. The great Spartacus, leader of the slaves who threw off their bondage, knew what he was about when he killed his horse during the final battle so that he could not escape. Our esteem for a certain type of hero — frequently if not essentially a poet or writer — is often bound up with his or her tragic early death. The premature deaths of Keats, Thomas Chatterton and Lermontov, to take but three examples, are inseparable from the romantic aura which surrounds them. To illustrate this point, Maurice Baring described a witty reversal of historical reputations in *The Alternative:* he suggested that if Shelley had survived to old age, he would have turned into a stuffy club bore, a pillar of the establishment, deeply ashamed of the radical poetry of his youth; Wordsworth, on the other hand, dying young on the barricades, would have had statues put up to him as a hero cut off in his prime. Fortunately longevity has not robbed Wordsworth of his serious-minded worshippers, although the dreamers will continue to prefer Keats, and the radicals Shelley.

10   However noble their deaths, it will be evident that many of the heroes in this book were morally ambivalent during their lifetime. Indeed, the importance of Achilles as a character is that he expresses this ambivalence, something which the Greeks held to be inseparable from the nature of war itself. In other cases, the deeds of certain heroes of myths and legends, descendants of the gods as they may be, do not pass muster by today's standards: Theseus's cruel abandonment of Ariadne is a notable example. The merit of Odysseus (the hero I would most like to meet, envying Princess Nausicaa her encounter, however, rather more than Penelope her marriage) is specifically stated to be his native sharpness. 'How like you to be so wary!' exclaims his patron Pallas Athene of some particular piece of cunning; 'And that is why I cannot desert you in your misfortunes: you are so civilized, so intelligent, so self-possessed.'

11   Other clay-footed candidates, those whose private lives would militate against them — rightly or wrongly — today, include Pericles, who would find it more difficult to stand for probity now than he did in his own lifetime. Sometimes the scandalous private life of a hero is actually interwoven with his public virtues, to his own advantage: in the present volume, Gila Falkus refers to Byron, in a felicitous phrase, as having 'heroism spiced with debauchery'.

12   Moral ambivalence, the private weaknesses which in themselves constitute evidence of humanity, are, however, a far cry from evil. It is surely by definition impossible for a hero to be totally evil. It is true that, as Lucifer was the fairest of the archangels before he fell, outshining 'myriads though bright', traces of this attraction remain in evil's face. Thus wicked people may from time to time in history, alas, be hero-worshipped. It is this possibility — regrettable but part of the human condition — that can cause a periodic revulsion against the very notion of a hero in our society: the profound shudder which follows on the regime of any one of history's magnetic tyrants. But in such a case it is the emotion of hero-worship which is responsible, not the concept of a hero.

13   Like all primitive emotions, hero-worship has its reverse side, inevitably according to the calibre of the man or woman admired. There are certain appalling manifestations, such as the public adoption of the Nazi philosophy,

which have to be ascribed to the guidance of one man — Hitler — a monster, but once some form of national hero. Nevertheless, taking this extreme example, I would firmly contend that Hitler was not a hero, and furthermore that there was nothing of the heroic about him. In this sense, it can be argued that those in Germany who made Hitler their hero before the Second World War were deluded, and attributed to him qualities which he did not happen to possess. Despots and dictators can be benevolent or malevolent, both in themselves and in the effects of their regime. But there can be no wicked heroes.

14   What our heroes and heroines do have in common, beyond some form of virtue, however masked, is an ability to capture the imagination. And this romantic assault is carried through by means of a particular kind of heroic quality, an unmistakable attribute in the eyes of the outside world. In certain cases, the subject himself has been aware of it. Nelson wrote in his memoirs: 'I know it is my disposition that difficulties and dangers do but increase my desire of attempting them.' It is an attitude of mind summed up by Alexander the Great when he was urged to attack the enemy by night: 'Alexander does not steal victories.'

15   Heroism in this volume is however by no means confined to the martial, that vision of Richard the Lionheart quoted by John Gillingham:

> O, still, methinks, I see King Richard stand
> In his gilt armour stain'd with Pagan's blood,
> Upon a galley's brow, like war's fierce God . . .

We have also borne in mind the secondary dictionary definition of those exhibiting 'extraordinary bravery, firmness, fortitude, or greatness of soul, in any course of action'. David Livingstone, Gladys Aylward and Martin Luther King find their place as well as Hannibal, Henry V and Montrose. Wolfe, one of our heroes, went on record as saying that he would rather have written Gray's *Elegy in a Country Churchyard* than stormed the heights of Quebec. Nevertheless in their different ways, all these heroes and heroines appeal to the fires which lie damped within us all, and set them ablaze.

16   Carlyle followed through the idea of a special heroic disposition to its limits. He insisted that a given individual would always emerge as a hero, although the form his heroism took might and would vary from age to age. He was concerned to refute the notion that the age threw up the man. I believe that it is possible sensibly to combine both points of view. There is a special quality of heroism in some individuals, denied to others, but which, given certain circumstances, can remain latent throughout their lives. St Thomas More is a case in point. No-one can deny that he has emerged as one of the peaceable (as opposed to martial) heroes of our history. In our own century alone he stands as an Inspirational example to all those who have upheld their own consciences above the demands of the state. Yet St Thomas More did not seek a heroic role or a martyr's death. Had the matrimonial affairs of Henry VIII taken another course, he could well have ended his life trusted and honoured, the King's good servant. It needed the crucible to test his gold.

17   The present book is divided chronologically into five sections. This seemed the most helpful arrangement to the reader, bearing in mind that one

of the primary purposes of this volume is to act as a kind of reference book. It is intended to trace the distinction between myth and reality in the lives of heroes and heroines, casting a little cold water where necessary: Edith Cavell was not a lovely young woman, Saladin was not a Christian Frankish gentleman! On the other hand, Joshua did exist as a war leader in the thirteenth century BC, even if his true story is not identical with that told in the Bible; the facts concerning Joan of Arc are fascinating in themselves, not merely as a corrective to George Bernard Shaw's dominating dramatic picture.

18   As a result of this planning, certain patterns did emerge amongst the heroes and heroines. I use the word emerge deliberately, since these patterns were not imposed from above; we chose our fifty-two heroes and heroines on their individual merits, after agonizing debate (the reader will undoubtedly have his own candidates for both admission and omission). In the first section, Michael Senior writes of the interrelation of common themes in European mythologies. One of these is the long journey and return of the hero, the most poignant version being the visit of the hero to the kingdom of the dead. But the early heroes are also close to the cycle of nature, as society then was: the classic exposition being the legend of Demeter and Persephone. In the second section on Classical and Biblical heroes, James Chambers points to the vital distinction between the two categories. Classical heroes could and frequently did meet a tragic end, from Leonidas to Cleopatra. The Biblical heroes such as David were on the contrary basically triumphant.

19   The Age of Chivalry brings us, as John Gillingham points out, a preponderance of sovereign princes and only one heroine. Both weightings illuminate for us the nature of the times. On the one hand, this was a highly 'established' society, the heyday of the Christian military aristocracy, and to be outside it was to be outside the pale of heroism, as it was then understood. Even Hereward the Wake was a member of an establishment— even if it was one in the process of being destroyed. On the other hand, the status of medieval women was extremely low.

20   The Age of Patriotism brings with it a series of quite different heroes, who, as Gila Falkus expresses it, have to be seen 'in the context of the aspirations of whole nations', now that the feudal ideals have vanished. Even Bonnie Prince Charlie, at first sight the hero as loser, stands for the nostalgic side of patriotism; for he represents a country which felt itself to be rapidly losing its national identity at the expense of its English neighbour. Abraham Lincoln is an obvious example of a high-minded and patriotic hero; but Davy Crockett stands for another aspect of the American nineteenth-century emergent nationalism— that of the settlers in the west.

21   Lastly, in the twentieth century, Alan Palmer points to the significant fact that so many of the modern heroes and heroines spent time in confinement, from Rosa Luxemburg to Douglas Bader. The prisoner has replaced the king as a symbol of the age. As a corrective to this sad commentary, at least women make their appearance on equal terms.

22   The special nature of a heroine (merely a female hero or something different?) was one reflection provoked by the editing of this book. I am inclined to believe that there was a distinction in the past: with the idea of a

heroine came the notion of a particular frailty overcome. We all know what we mean by a Shakespearean heroine and she is not at all the obverse of a Shakespearean hero. Witty, delightful, bold, a Beatrice, Rosalind, Viola — she must yet prove to have a romantic feminine heart beating softly somewhere beneath the gown or doublet at the end. About an operatic heroine there used to be an even greater hint of frailty — lethal illness at times, as Mimi and Violetta cough their way to the final curtain — and also more than a hint of melodrama. And this carries with it an implication of self-indulgence, a lady going mad in white satin to the sound of her own High C, as Sheridan had it in *The Critic*.

23   More genuinely, Brunnhilde is a heroine, not merely because she sacrifices herself unselfishly for love, but because she shows greater nobility and greater strength than the males around her (personally, I have never found anything the slightest bit heroic about Siegfried's conduct but perhaps that is sexual prejudice). Queen Elizabeth I, with the 'heart and stomach of a king' but the glittering costumes of a delicate woman, knew just how to exploit this combination in the minds of her subjects. No mere king could have done so.

24   Will the distinction vanish in the future with the improving status of women? The trouble is that equal opportunities, if granted, still cannot guarantee equal physical strength. Grace Darling will always be rated a heroine, and her male equivalent merely expected to do his duty. We shall have many more heroines, in sheer numbers. But heroism has enough of the physical about it, I suspect, for a heroine to remain in some ways in a special category.

25   Finally, the experience of editing this book was in itself an uplifting one. It was not only a question of encountering the familiar favourite stories of courage from Boadicea to Captain Scott, and thrilling to them again. I was also introduced to new heroes, foremost amongst them two from Celtic myth, Lleu 'the bright one', whose wife was fashioned from the native wild flowers of his country; and CuChulainn, of the Ulster Cycle, who passed some women washing a blood-stained garment in a stream on his way to battle and, recognizing it to be his own, knew that he had seen into the future, and foretold his own death.

26   The real lesson of this book must be the imperishability of heriosm, as a manifestation of the human will. The running vein of evil in every society is often stressed; these stories of the heroism of others remind us that even in the most terrible circumstances some kind of choice may remain. In the words of Matthew Arnold:

The will is free;
Strong is the soul, and wise and beautiful;
The seeds of godlike power are in us still;
Gods we are, bards, saints, heroes if we will.

Reading Sources: "Heroes and Heroines"

Read the selection, surveying it to identify key terms and important concepts. Highlight these phrases and ideas, and then answer these questions.

1. What is the essay's thesis? Where does Fraser state it?
2. Why does Fraser refer to the words of Thomas Carlyle in the first two paragraphs of her essay? What does this reference add to her essay?
3. What techniques does Fraser use to link ideas between paragraphs 9 and 10? between the sentences in paragraph 9?
4. Into what categories does Fraser divide heroes and heroines? How do these categories help Fraser to structure her essay?
5. What technique does Fraser use to indicate that she is beginning her conclusion? What points does she choose to emphasize?

Reacting to Sources

Reread the selection carefully, making marginal notes to aid your comprehension and to reinforce connections. Then further annotate the selection if you need to do so in order to answer any of these questions. (You may already have addressed some of the questions in your marginal notes.)

1. In a few sentences, rewrite paragraph 3 to simplify its ideas.
2. Using a dictionary if necessary, supply brief marginal definitions of these words as they are used in the selection: *disquisition* (1), *lambasted* (1), *grandiloquent* (1), *mysticism* (5), *harbinger* (9), *aura* (9), *ambivalence* (10), *militate* (11), *felicitous* (11), *debauchery* (11), *myriads* (12), *matrimonial* (16), *melodrama* (22), *imperishability* (26).
3. Using an encyclopedia, make marginal notes explaining the significance of Fraser's references to the following figures: Odette Sansom (3), Florence Nightingale (3), Mary Queen of Scots (5), St. Teresa of Avila (5), Admiral Togo (8), Spartacus (9), John Keats (9), Thomas Chatterton (9), Denise Lermontov (9), Achilles (10), Odysseus, Princess Nausicaa (10), Lord Byron (11), St. Thomas More (16), Edith Cavell (17), Saladin (17).
4. Fraser makes the following statement in paragraph 3: "Adulthood does not necessarily mark the passing of hero-worship altogether, but it often brings with it a change of the hero-object." Do you agree or disagree? Write a brief marginal comment in which you explain your position.
5. Write brief marginal questions in response to the main idea in paragraph 5.
6. Identify the writer's purpose in paragraph 14. In a marginal note, discuss how this purpose is related to the purpose of the entire essay.
7. Read the introduction to the selection. In a journal entry, comment on how Fraser's life and other writings might have influenced her purpose. Comment on how it influences your acceptance of her ideas.
8. In paragraph 14 Fraser says, "What our heroes and heroines do have in common, beyond some form of virtue, however masked, is an ability to capture the imagination." Explore this idea further in a journal entry.
9. In a journal entry, consider the possible connections between the heroic figures in this selection and several of your own heroes and heroines.
10. Outline the paragraph cluster beginning with paragraph 10 and ending with paragraph 12.

Working with Sources

1. Write a one-sentence summary of paragraph 3.
2. Write a critique of the ideas in paragraph 14.
3. Write a journal entry in which you explore your reactions to these quotations from "Heroes and Heroines."

   "In childhood, unaware as we are of our capacities and the lack of them, our heroes tend to be challenging" (4).

   "As I grow older, my own tendency is to choose Inspirational heroines more relevant to my way of life than the glamorous idols of my youth" (5).

   Be sure to integrate the quotations smoothly into your writing.
4. Paraphrase the paragraph cluster beginning with paragraph 22 and ending with paragraph 24.
5. Write a one-paragraph synthesis that blends ideas in paragraph 10 of this essay with the ideas in paragraph 6 of "Hercules" (pp. 243–250).

Writing with Sources: Using a Single Source

Integrating information from "Heroes and Heroines" with your own ideas, write an essay on one of these topics. Be sure to acknowledge all ideas that are not your own.

1. Write an essay in which you discuss how the concept of a hero that you had when you were young is not the same now that you are older.
2. In her essay, Fraser says that hero worship is an emotion that is so strong that "it is doubtful that it will ever be eradicated in human nature" (2). Discuss whether hero worship is good or bad for people. Use examples from your own experience to support your points.
3. Write an essay in which you agree or disagree with the statement that, in the twentieth century, "the prisoner has replaced the king as a symbol of the age" (21).

The Emerging American Hero

Marshall W. Fishwick

Marshall W. Fishwick was born in 1923 in Roanoke, Virginia, and received his B.A. from the University of Virginia, his M.A. from the University of Wisconsin, and his Ph.D. from Yale University. He has taught in a number of American and European colleges and universities, and was president of the organization Fellows in American Studies. His works include *American Heroes* (1954), *The Virginia Tradition* (1955), *The South in the Sixties* (1962), and *American Studies in Transition* (1965). He has contributed articles to *American Historical Review, American Heritage, Yale Review, Saturday Review,* and other magazines and journals. The following essay from *American Heroes* discusses the particular characteristics of the American hero in myth, literature, and history.

"The historic memory goes back through long defiles of doom."—Herman Melville

"Every historical change creates its mythology."—Bronislaw Malinowski

1   Being a modern hero is difficult and perplexing. "It is not only that there is no hiding place for the gods from the searching telescope. There is no such society any more as the gods once supported. The social unit is not a carrier of religious content, but an economic-political organization."[1] Corrado Alvaro finds *The Hero in Crisis,* and Ortega y Gasset, a century suffering from the intervention of the mass man into everything. Harrison Smith ascribes the woes of contemporary fiction to the disappearance of the hero, who is really nothing more than a victim. Technology and science are said to have withered up our grass roots, and capitalism our sense of community. "There is no culture where economic relations are not subject to a regulating principle to protect interests involved," Gasset claims.[2] We are told that once America had a culture without a civilization, and now a civilization without a culture.

2   Others bewail the fate of mythology. "Myths are construed simply by the hard Occidental mind—they are lies," writes John Crowe Ransom in *God Without Thunder.* "They are not nearly good enough for the men in our twentieth century generation, brought up in the climatic blessedness of our scientific world." With many words contemporary critics repeat what Nietzsche said in five: "Dead are all the gods."

3   They are wrong. Mythology cannot be superceded or eliminated. It can and does assume every conceivable form, depending on the culture. Like Proteus, as described by Homer in the *Odyssey,* it "takes all manner of shapes of things that creep upon the earth, of water likewise, and of fierce fire burning."

4   American history, in its several periods and on its various levels, confirms this view. We have been as sure as any people in the past that we are the Chosen People; that (to quote Abraham Lincoln's line) "this nation, under God, shall have a new birth of freedom." Under God, and the guidance of the

---

[1] Joseph Campbell, *The Hero with a Thousand Faces* (New York, 1948), p. 387.
[2] Ortega y Gasset, *The Revolt of the Masses* (New York, 1950), p. 52.

heroes whom He sends down to lead us. The military idol still thrills us. In the 1952 presidential election, as in many others, we put one in the White House. We swoon as readily for the television idol as grandmother did for her favorite vaudeville star, or the Greek for the most fashionable tragic actor. In our fiction the hero seems lost in a labyrinth of despair; but he will come back. He always has.

5   Just as certainly we have not lost our faculty for myth, which is innate in the human race. "It seizes with avidity upon any incidents, surprising or mysterious, in the career of those who have at all distinguished themselves from their fellows, and invents episodes to which it then attaches a fanatical belief," Somerset Maugham observed in *The Moon and Sixpence.* "It is the protest of romance against the commonplace of life."

6   Not the scholar, but the doctor, is the current master of the mythological realm. Like the Wise Old Man in the ancient sagas and fairy tales, he is the knower of secret ways and formulas; the one whose potency can kill modern dragons, apply healing balm to the almost fatal wound, and send the heroic conqueror back into the world to do wonderful deeds. Myths supply the power which carries the human spirit forward. The modern psychoanalyst has only reaffirmed the timeless wisdom of the myth-making witch doctors. The goddess of fertility smiles at us from beneath the thick make-up of the latest screen heroine. Ulysses puts out to sea with the United States Marines. The grasping Midas, the ever-searching Parsifal, the new actors in the romance of Beauty and the Beast, stand this very moment on a busy New York street corner, waiting for the traffic light to change.

7   How could it be otherwise? We simply must have heroes. They give us blessed relief from our daily lives, which are frequently one petty thing after another. Hemmed in by our little horizons, we hear the hero's voice, clear and confident. It releases us, telling us where we go and why. He gives meaning to all we do, and we gladly praise him. He helps us to transcend our drab back yards, apartment terraces, and tenements, and to regain a sense of the world's bigness.

8   This is especially true in the United States, which is long on heroes and short on symbols, myths, and rituals. We are so proud of our material achievements that we underestimate and even belittle our psychic ones. "America? I sometimes think she does not have a corner in her own house," commented Walt Whitman.

9   Like most of the world's heroes, ours have usually been physically attractive, strong, and fearless. A note of fatalism has dominated their lives, in which some catalytic experience has set the popular imagination to work, and kept it going. Episodes involved are not always true. We remember Captain John Smith's head on the block, but not his histories. The image of Washington chopping down a cherry tree has stuck more firmly than the names of all his victories. Just as the pier holds up the bridge, so does the hero support society. A moral materialist, he is concerned with both ideas and matter, never with one to the exclusion of the other.

10   Beyond that, all his fellow Americans demand of him is that he be able to look any man in the eye and tell him to go to hell.

11   We love to exaggerate, as the literature of our heroes and their adventures proves. To exaggerate is essentially to simplify. Subtle shades are removed, leaving only the bold ones in the composition. When we go in for rough-housing, we go whole hog, with such results as those described in a poem which appeared in the Galveston *Weekly Journal* some years ago:

> They fit and fit, and gouged and bit
> And struggled in the mud;
> Until the ground for miles around
> Was kivered with their blood,
> And a pile of noses, ears, and eyes
> Large and massive, reached the skies.

12   Funny and even consciously preposterous, our legendary heroes are cockalorum demigods, exhibiting bold and grotesque imaginations, contempt for authority, and limitless optimism. As Josh Billings said, "They love caustick things; they would prefer turpentine to colone-water, if they had tew drink either. So with their relish of humor; they must have it on the half shell with cayenne."

13   Debunkers who say heroes are men with the ability to fool most of the people all of the time, have not been important in America. Nor have lady bone-worshipers, who unite under high-sounding titles to preserve the trappings of greatness. These modern vestal virgins make an easy target for parody and scorn. Real heroes resist both the venomed darts of the debunkers and the sugary epithets of the adulators.

14   Heroes tend to come in bunches. The Revolution and Civil War produced bumper crops. When our writers or movie-makers look back at those dramatic times, they concur with Wordsworth:

> Bliss was it in that dawn to be alive
> But to be young was very heaven.

15   Both decades were military-dominated. The saddle of a white horse remains the best seat for the aspirant. In this respect the democratic hero is like any other. What democracy offers is the opportunity for every man to get on the horse. It attempts to elevate the aristoi, or naturally superior, rather than an aristocracy, or blue bloods.

16   This proposition thrilled Thomas Jefferson, Andrew Jackson, Ralph Waldo Emerson, and Horace Mann. Walt Whitman wanted *Leaves of Grass* to "transpose the reader into the central position," where he could become the living "fountain." From our indigenous traditions and landscape must come our heroes and myths. Henry Thoreau perceived this, and was confident that it would occur. "Who knows what shape the fable of Columbus will assume, to be confounded with that of Jason and the expedition of the Argonauts?" he wrote. "And Franklin — there may be a line for him in the future classical dictionary. 'He aided the Americans to gain their independence, instructed mankind in economy, and drew down lightning from the clouds.'"

17   Our heroes have exonerated our faith in them and in democracy. With a

strong belief in the land, institutions, and society of the new world, they have piloted us skillfully through rough waters. The ship of state has rolled and pitched; sometimes it has taken on water. The short-sighted have shouted, "Abandon ship." But it has sprung no deep leaks, has never gone aground, and has weathered every blow.

18   Behind every hero is a group of skillful and faithful manipulators. We have tried to discover some of them and examine their motives and techniques. Even when their talents and goals were limited, they did well. Often, as with John Burke, Walt Disney or Charles Siringo, they were not intellectuals. Horatio Alger, Harry Bennett, and Ned Buntline demonstrate that they were not always virtuous. John Filson, W. B. Laughead, and Charles Francis Adams engineered the rise of major figures without even being aware that they were doing so. Owen Francis and Jules Billard were duped by the people they set out to fool. The trait which these hero makers all share is faith in their subjects. They believe, and make us believe, that their candidate's purpose is our own. His greatness seems so real that we equate his lengthened shadow with destiny itself.

19   Certain great men emerge as heroic pattern makers. John Smith in colonial times was such a figure; his buoyant optimism and audacity opened the brave new world. The Revolution produced our first demigod in Washington; our national motto, *E Pluribus Unum,* is a tribute to him. Daniel Boone, assisted by James Fenimore Cooper and others, came to personify the trail-blazer and the trek west.

20   The nineteenth century brought bitter sectionalism and civil war. A second demigod, Abraham Lincoln, appeared to reunite us. The South dreamed of the Confederate victory that might have been and of the General who might have made it possible — Robert E. Lee, symbol of the Lost Cause. Out west men were carrying justice around with them on the hip. A young upstart named William Bonney supposedly killed a man for every one of his twenty-one years. Billy the Kid, as he was called, set the desperado prototype, while Buffalo Cody domesticated the Wild West for the tame east. And the Self-Made Man took over as industry boomed. If we knew just how and why Smith, Washington, Boone, Lincoln, Lee, Bonney, Cody and the Self-Made Man became heroes, we would be well on the way to understanding the American hero.

21   We are too close to the twentieth century to say which of its candidates will endure. Because he took the tycoon's path and dramatized modern American know-how, Paul Bunyan has become capitalism's darling. More romantic is the American cowboy, our prime contribution to the world's mythology, whose fame is growing in a world cluttered by fences and macadam roads.

22   Most of them were built to accommodate the cars which Henry Ford taught America to mass-produce. Our chief mechanical hero, he chugged up Olympus in a model T. Motion pictures created new patterns of leisure, and new opportunities for heroes. Douglas Fairbanks the man, and Mickey the mouse, exemplified the activism, ingenuity, and pluck so highly valued in our culture. They pioneered in celluloid. Bunyan, the Cowboy, Ford, Doug,

Mickey Mouse — five quite different figures which illuminate twentieth century America.

23   Our heroes' path, so silvery and apparently so solid, has usually turned out to be quicksand. These men are finally symbols of the transcience of American culture, fighting their way not into an established hagiography, but into a pinwheel. When the pinwheel loses its initial fire, then out with the pinhead and up with the new.

24   Were this not true, this book could not have been written at all; for otherwise we should have been satisfied with what heroes the good Lord gave us at the first settlement of his favor, or at the initial granting of independence. New generations have demanded new faces. "There's nothing as humiliating as being a has-been," observed Doug Fairbanks. Despite his almost impenetrable vanity, even he finally saw that the man of the hour goes down a one-way street. His biographer shows us Doug at the moment he learns a luxurious four months' cruise has cost him $100,000:

25   "Douglas was amazed. 'I spent a fortune on that damned trip and didn't get a nickel's worth of fun out of it.'

26   " 'You paid the piper, all right,' Robert agreed.

27   " 'Apparently that's all I'm good for. And the worst of it is, *I've got to keep on doing it.*' "[3]

. . .

28   Heroes are not born. They are the products of their time, their insight, and the work of their devotees, who create a mythical image and a second life for them. The key to the hero's existence is function; his province is both history and folklore.

29   Heroes do not make history. They are the products of historic times. No combination of factors can fabricate a hero of the wrong man at the right moment, or the right man at the wrong moment. Only when there is a genuine need for a particular type, and when the qualifying candidate thinks and acts in the heroic manner, is there a culmination. Some who have tried hardest have failed. Others, like Washington, succeeded "without seeking any indirect or left-handed attempts to acquire popularity." One must have the inspired ability to do important and dramatic things memorably. Rehearsing is futile, since no one knows when the moment will come — if at all. The man's character, rather than his action, is critical. General Lee's victories jeopardized our Union; he is today a national hero because he was a man of great character. We are not concerned with Washington and Lincoln's frequent defeats. Knowing what these men were, we know that final victory had to be theirs.

30   Potential heroes, living and dead, are always competing. As in a horse race, one can choose his favorites; but the race must be run before anyone knows who will win. To say that the outcome is unpredictable does not mean that the course has no pattern. We can't tell which individual will become a

[3] Ralph Hancock, *Douglas Fairbanks: The Fourth Musketeer* (New York, 1953), p. 256.

hero. Yet in emerging he will follow one of several set formulas. It is like a mathematician figuring out a life-insurance curve. He cannot predict when a certain individual will die. However, he can tell what percentage of the population will die at what ages, over a long period.

31   American history does not lend weight to the great man theory, or demonstrate that heroes dominate events and institutions. It does not substantiate the wave theory, which holds that men get fame effortlessly because of historical chance. "Here is a hero who did nothing but shake the tree when the fruit was ripe," wrote Nietzsche. But he added, "Do you think that was a small thing to do? Well, just look at the tree he shook!"

32   The firmest ground seems to lie in between these two extremes. More important than man's acts or fate's turns is the common will. Reformers follow individual visions, heroes follow communal ones. "So help me God, I can take no other course!" said Martin Luther. "The greater the man, the less is the province of his will," said Napoleon. "My master is pitiless, for that master is the nature of things."

33   The study of heroes takes on to a point where various academic disciplines cross. Creating heroes seems as simple as sunlight; it is as difficult to explain. Twentieth century scholarship and pedagogy tend to splinter human knowledge into fragments. The broad implications of many things, among them the heroic, elude us. Only by studying wholes can we hope to understand the world about and within us. We must explore the twilight area where fact and fancy meet; where myth and reality become so intertwined that no thoughtful man would claim he could separate them.

34   The old gods have gone; but we shall have new ones. Heroes and myths will emerge from our particular culture, just as they have from all others. They may not fit perfectly the old patterns and definitions — but then, why should they? Despite certain universal qualities which they share with heroes of earlier times, ours will eventually acquire a style and manner of their own. Despite differences of mannerisms and techniques, there is a definite heroic relationship between the Homeric hero and the air force "jet jockey" who travels faster than sound to meet individual enemies far up in the heavens. Good or bad luck, mechanical failure, or a sudden change in the weather are so critical that chance takes on all the aspects of a personal intervening power. As with Ulysses or Aeneas, this man's life and reputation are in the hands of the gods.

35   Eventually America will have a developed mythology and Olympus of her own; such things come slowly. We are, after all, very young, and still close to Mother Europe. Stories have to mellow, and legends grow, before enduring myths and heroes result. The time-unit involved is not months or years, but generations. We must have patience. Our technology can modify, but it cannot destroy nor speed up, the heroic process. A writer will appear who can work as successfully on film as Homer did on papyrus or Shakespeare on paper. The hero is not disappearing in America. Like many things in our dynamic culture, he is simply getting a new look. Our literature, our pageants, and especially our movies hint as to what he will be like when he reaches full stature.

36   "I have imagined," wrote Walt Whitman, "a life which should be that of the average man in average circumstances, and still grand, *heroic*." George Washington Harris gave us in *Sut Lovingood Yarns* a detailed picture of the type developed by the American frontier: "The mussils on his arms moved about like rabbits under the skin which was clear red an' white; and his eyes a deep, sparklin', wickid blue, while a smile fluttered like a hummin' bird round his mouth all the while. When the State-fair offers a premium for *men* like they now does fur jackasses, I means to enter Wirt Staples, an' I'll git it, if there's five thousand entries."

37   Another democratic American hero was Bulkington, in *Moby Dick*. "From his fine stature," wrote Herman Melville, "I thought he must be one of those tall mountaineers from the Alleghenian Ridge in Virginia." When we read this line we remember another by Emerson: "America begins west of the Alleghenies." Bulkingtons are the hope of the new world. When the *Pequod* sets sail, he is appropriately at the helm. The reader and the author know the ship must follow the evil White Whale to the bottom of the ocean. Consequently we have Melville's memorable exhortation to the helmsman: "Bear thee grimly, demi-god! Up from the spray of thy ocean-perishing — straight up leaps thy apotheosis!"

38   The American historian who best understood the emerging American hero was Frederick Jackson Turner. In his 1893 essay on "The Significance of the Frontier in American History," he asserted that "the true point of view in the history of this nation is not the Atlantic coast, it is the Great West." The advance of the heroic settler westward explained American development. His special idol was Daniel Boone, who "helped to open the way for civilization," and whose family "epitomizes the backwoodsman's advance across the continent." Turner even felt that the striking characteristics of the American intellect could be traced directly to the frontier: "That coarseness and strength combined with acuteness and inquisitiveness; that practical, inventive turn of mind, quick to find expedients; that masterful grasp of material things, lacking in the artistic but powerful to effect great ends; that restless, nervous energy; that dominant individualism — these are traits of the frontier, or traits called out elsewhere because of the existence of the frontier.[4]

39   Since Turner's day his ideas have been a focal point for historical speculation and controversy. "The frontier hypothesis," Frederick L. Paxson wrote, "presents the most attractive single explanation of the distinctive trends of American history"; and, he might have added, of the American hero.

40   Across the ocean the hero-worshiping Thomas Carlyle also conjured up a vision of the man who could conquer and control the New World. "How beautiful to think of lean tough Yankee settlers, tough as gutta-percha, with most occult unsubduable fire in their belly, steering over the Western Mountains, to annihilate the jungle, and bring bacon for the Posterity of Adam. There is no *myth* of Athene or Herakles equal to this *fact*."

41   Significantly, for Whitman, Harris, Melville, Emerson, Turner, and Carlyle,

---

[4] F. J. Turner, *The Frontier in American History* (New York, 1920), p. 31.

the common points about our emerging hero are his appearance, his attitude, and his westward trek. Masculine, full-sized, and golden, he believes in the future; he is looking for something beyond the next range of mountains.

42   The vision of such a man, and the democratic society which produces him, is a thrilling thing. Those who see it feel no longer that they must apologize for our many acknowledged shortcomings, and defer to older nations. Instead, they can take the offensive, as did Stephen Vincent Benét when he wrote "American Names":

> You may bury my body in Sussex grass,
> You may bury my tongue at Campmedy,
> I shall not be there. I shall rise and pass.
> Bury my heart at Wounded Knee.

Reading Sources: "The Emerging American Hero"

Read the selection, surveying it to identify key terms and important concepts. Highlight these phrases and ideas, and then answer these questions.

1. What information does Fishwick present in his introduction? How does it prepare readers for the rest of the essay?
2. What is Fishwick's thesis? Why does he state it where he does?
3. What visual cues are used in this selection? How do they help readers follow Fishwick's ideas?
4. What techniques does Fishwick use to convince readers that his research is reliable?
5. What techniques does Fishwick use to link ideas among the paragraphs in the paragraph cluster beginning with paragraph 14 and ending with paragraph 16?

Reacting to Sources

Reread the selection carefully, making marginal notes to aid your comprehension and to reinforce connections. Then further annotate the selection if you need to do so in order to answer any of these questions. (You may already have addressed some of the questions in your marginal notes.)

1. In a few sentences, rewrite paragraph 9 to simplify its ideas.
2. Using a dictionary if necessary, supply brief marginal definitions of these words as they are used in the selection: *Occidental* (2), *labyrinth* (4), *innate* (5), *catalytic* (9), *cockalorum* (12), *cayenne* (12), *debunkers* (13), *adulators* (13), *confounded* (16), *exonerated* (17), *duped* (18), *hagiography* (23).
3. Using a dictionary or encyclopedia, make brief marginal notes explaining Fishwick's use of the following: Ortega y Gasset (1), Nietzsche (2), Proteus (3), Midas, Parsifal (6), Douglas Fairbanks (24), Ulysses, Aeneas (34).

4. Write three brief marginal questions in response to the ideas in paragraph 29.
5. Do you agree or disagree with the statement, "Not the scholar, but the doctor, is the current master of the mythological realm" (6). Write a brief marginal note explaining your position.
6. In a marginal note, give two examples to support Fishwick's general statement, "We love to exaggerate, as the literature of our heroes and their adventures proves" (11).
7. In paragraph 29, Fishwick says, "Heroes do not make history. They are the products of historic times." Explore this idea further in a journal entry.
8. In a journal entry, discuss four heroes who correspond to the general description of heroes presented in paragraph 41.
9. In a journal entry compare the central idea of this essay with the central idea of "Heroes of the Nineteen Twenties" (pp. 270–278).
10. Outline the paragraph cluster beginning with paragraph 38 and ending with paragraph 40.
11. What points does Fishwick make in his conclusion? Write a journal entry in which you supply another conclusion that emphasizes different points. Are there any other points that Fishwick should have made?

Working with Sources

1. Write a two-sentence summary of paragraphs 9 and 10.
2. Write a critique of the ideas in paragraph 29.
3. Write a journal entry in which you explore your reactions to these quotations from "The Emerging American Hero."

   "Like most of the world's heroes, ours have usually been physically attractive, strong, and fearless" (9).

   "The hero is not disappearing in America. Like many things in our dynamic culture, he is simply getting a new look" (35).

   Be sure to integrate the quotations smoothly into your writing.
4. Paraphrase the paragraph cluster beginning with paragraph 19 and ending with paragraph 20.
5. Write a one-paragraph synthesis that blends ideas in paragraph 28 of this essay with the ideas in paragraph 1 of "Heroes of the Nineteen Twenties" (pp. 270–278).

Writing with Sources: Using a Single Source

Integrating information from "The Emerging American Hero" with your own ideas, write an essay on one of these topics. Be sure to acknowledge all ideas that are not your own.

1. Explain why you agree or disagree with the assertion that heroes in America are not disappearing but rather getting a new look. Use your own experience and material from your own reading to support your points.
2. Discuss the qualities that a modern hero or heroine must have. Do you agree with Fishwick's statement that in back of every hero is "a group of skillful and faithful manipulators" (18)?
3. In another essay Fishwick says, "Our heroes have become symbols, just as have Old Glory, the log cabin, and the skyscraper. Washington symbolizes the Revolution, Boone the Westward Trek, Lincoln the Restored Union, Lee the Lost Cause." Discuss two of our contemporary heroes and what they symbolize.

Heroes of the Nineteen Twenties

Roderick Nash

Roderick Nash was born in 1939 in New York City and received his B.A. from Harvard University and his M.A. and Ph.D. from the University of Wisconsin. He has taught at Dartmouth College and the University of California, Santa Barbara, where he chaired the Department of Environmental Studies. Nash was a professional fishing guide and has traveled extensively in the wilderness of northern Canada and the western United States. He has published a number of books on the environment and American culture, including *The American Environment* (1968); *The Call of the Wild* (1970); *American Environment: Readings in the History of Conservation* (1976); *The Wilderness and the American Mind* (1982); and *From the Beginnings: A Biological Approach to American History* (1984). The following selection illustrates Nash's interest in American culture. In it he focuses on the 1920s, a time of great economic and intellectual ferment, and discusses why this period produced a particular type of hero.

1   Heroes abounded in the American 1920s. Their names, especially in sports, have been ticked off so frequently they have become clichés. Less often have commentators paused to probe for explanations. Why were the twenties ripe for heroism? And why did the heroics follow a predictable pattern? Such questions lead to an understanding of the mood of the people, because heroism concerns the public as well as the individual. It depends on achievement but even more on recognition. In the final analysis the hopes and fears of everyday Americans create national heroes.

2   The nervousness of the post–World War I generation provided fertile soil for the growth of a particular kind of heroism. Many Americans felt uneasy as they experienced the transforming effects of population growth, urbanization, and economic change. On the one hand, these developments were welcome as steps in the direction of progress. Yet they also raised vague fears about the passing of frontier conditions, the loss of national vigor, and the eclipse of the individual in a mass society. Frederick Jackson Turner and Theodore Roosevelt, among others, had pointed to the liabilities of the transformation at the

turn of the century. World War I underscored the misgivings and doubts. By the 1920s the sense of change had penetrated to the roots of popular thought. Scarcely an American was unaware that the frontier had vanished and that pioneering, in the traditional sense, was a thing of the past. Physical changes in the nation were undeniable. They occurred faster, however, than intellectual adjustment. Although Americans, in general, lived in a densely populated, urban-industrial civilization, a large part of their values remained rooted in the frontier, farm, and village. Exposure of this discrepancy only served to increase the tightness with which insecure people clung to the old certainties. Old-style pioneering was impossible, but Americans proved ingenious in finding equivalents. The upshot in the twenties was the cult of the hero — the man who provided living testimony of the power of courage, strength, and honor and of the efficacy of the self-reliant, rugged individual who seemed on the verge of becoming as irrelevant as the covered wagon.

3   Sports and the star athlete were the immediate beneficiaries of this frame of mind. The American sports fan regarded the playing field as a surrogate frontier; the athletic hero was the twentieth-century equivalent of the pathfinder or pioneer. In athletic competition, as on the frontier, people believed, men confronted tangible obstacles and overcame them with talent and determination. The action in each case was clean and direct; the goals, whether clearing forests or clearing the bases, easily perceived and immensely satisfying. Victory was the result of superior ability. The sports arena like the frontier was pregnant with opportunity for the individual. The start was equal and the best man won. Merit was rewarded. True or not, such a credo was almost instinctive with Americans. They packed the stadiums of the 1920s in a salute to time-honored virtues. With so much else about America changing rapidly, it was comforting to find in sports a ritualistic celebration of the major components of the national faith.

4   Writing in the *North American Review* for October 1929, A. A. Brill, a leading American psychologist of the Freudian school, took a closer look at the meaning of athletics. Why, he wondered, do men play and why do they select the particular kinds of play they do? Brill was also interested in the reasons spectators came to games. His main point was that sports were not idle diversions but intensely serious endeavors rooted in the values and traditions of a civilization. "The ancestry of sport," Brill declared, "is written very plainly in the fact that the first games among all nations were simple imitations of the typical acts of warriors and huntsmen." The primary motivation of play, according to Brill, was the "mastery impulse" — an inherent aggressiveness in man stemming from the Darwinian struggle for existence. Modern man had largely transcended direct physical struggle, but the need for it persisted in the human psyche. Sports were contrived as substitutes for actual fighting, mock struggles that satisfied the urge to conquer. Brill did not suggest a relationship between American sports and the American frontier, but his argument suggested one. So did the fact that the rise of mass spectator sports and the decline of the frontier were simultaneous in the United States.

5   By the 1920s the nation went sports crazy. It seemed to many that a

golden age of sport had arrived in America. Football received a large portion of the limelight. As they had in the declining days of Rome, fans thronged the stadiums to witness contact, violence, bloodshed, man pitted against man, strength against strength. The vicarious element was invariably present. For a brief, glorious moment the nobody in the bleachers *was* the halfback crashing into the end zone with the winning touchdown. For a moment he shared the thrill of individual success and fought off the specter of being swallowed up in mass society.

6   Big-time professional football began on September 17, 1920, when the American Football Association was organized with the great Indian athlete Jim Thorpe as its first president. When the Green Bay Packers joined the Association in 1921, the saga of pro football was solidly launched. Attendance rose dramatically. On November 21, 1925, the presence on the playing field of the fabled Harold "Red" Grange helped draw 36,000 spectators to a game. A week later 68,000 jammed the Polo Grounds in New York to watch Grange in action. The names of the pro teams were suggestive. As on the frontier of old, it was cowboys versus Indians, or giants versus bears — with the names of cities prefixed.

7   The twenties was also the time of the emergence of college football on an unprecedented scale. Heroes appeared in good supply: Red Grange at Illinois, Knute Rockne's "Four Horsemen" at Notre Dame in 1924, Harold "Brick" Muller who began a dynasty at California that extended through fifty consecutive victories in the seasons 1919 through 1925. Hundreds of thousands attended the Saturday games, an estimated twenty million during the season. Millions more followed the action over their radios and made a Sunday morning ritual of devouring the newspaper accounts of the games of the previous day. To accommodate the crowds colleges and universities built huge new stadiums. Yale's and California's seated eighty thousand; Illinois, Ohio State, and Michigan were not far behind. The number of Americans who attended games doubled between 1921 and 1930. A *Harper's* writer caught the spirit of college football in 1928: "it is at present a religion, sometimes it seems to be almost our national religion." So, once, had been westward expansion.

8   Despite its popularity, football tended to obscure the heroic individual. It was, after all, a team sport. Even Red Grange received an occasional block on his long runs. But in sports pitting man against man or against the clock the heroism latent in competition achieved its purest expression. Americans in the 1920s had a glittering array of well-publicized individuals from which to choose their idol. In golf Robert T. "Bobby" Jones, Walter Hagen, and Gene Sarazen were the dominant figures. Tennis had "Big" Bill Tilden and "Little" Bill Johnson whose epic duels on the center court at Forest Hills filled the stands. The competition was even more direct in boxing with its "knock out," the symbol of complete conquest. During the twenties promoters like Tex Rickard built boxing into a big business. Jack Dempsey and Gene Tunney proved so attractive to the sporting public that a ticket sale of a million dollars for a single fight became a reality. By the end of the decade the figure was two million. Fifty bouts in the twenties had gates of more than $100,000. More than 100,000 fans came to Soldier Field in Chicago on September 22, 1927, to see

the second Dempsey-Tunney fight with its controversial "long count" that helped Tunney retain the championship and earn $990,000 for thirty minutes of work. In a nation not oblivious to the approach of middle age, it was comforting to count the heavyweight champion of the world among the citizenry. Here was evidence, many reasoned, that the nation remained strong, young, and fit to survive in a Darwinian universe. Record-breaking served the same purpose, and in Johnny Weismuller, premier swimmer, and Paavo Nurmi, Finnish-born track star, the United States had athletes who set world marks almost every time they competed. Gertrude Ederle chose a longer course when she swam the English Channel in 1926, but she too set a record and was treated to one of New York's legendary ticker-tape parades.

9   And there was the Babe. No sports hero of the twenties and few of any decade had the reputation of George Herman Ruth. Baseball was generally acknowledged to be the national game, and Ruth played with a superb supporting cast of New York Yankees, but when he faced a pitcher Babe Ruth stood as an individual. His home runs (particularly the 59 in 1921 and the 60 in 1927) gave him a heroic stature comparable to that of legendary demigods like Odysseus, Beowulf, or Daniel Boone. Ruth's unsavory background and boorish personal habits were nicely overlooked by talented sportswriters anxious to give the twenties the kind of hero it craved. The payoff was public adulation of the Babe and of baseball.

10   The twenties also saw the public exposure of corruption in baseball and confronted Americans with the necessity of reviewing their entire hero complex. On September 28, 1920, three members of the Chicago White Sox appeared before a grand jury to confess that they and five other players had agreed to throw the 1919 World Series to Cincinnati for a financial consideration. Gradually the unhappy story of the "Black Sox" unfolded. Big-time gamblers had persuaded selected players to make sure that a bet on the underdog Cincinnati team would pay off. Some of the greatest names in the game were involved, preeminently that of "Shoeless" Joe Jackson. An illiterate farm boy from South Carolina, Jackson's natural batting eye helped him compile a .356 average in ten seasons as a major leaguer. In the process he became one of the most idolized players in baseball. It was Jackson's exit from the grand jury chamber on September 28 that allegedly precipitated the agonized plea from a group of boys: "Say it ain't so, Joe!" According to the newspapers, Jackson, shuffling, head down, replied, "Yes, boys, I'm afraid it is."

11   Reaction to the Black Sox testified to the importance baseball had for many Americans. One school of thought condemned the "fix" in the strongest terms and agitated for the restoration of integrity to the game. It was a serious matter. The Philadelphia *Bulletin* compared the eight players with "the soldier or sailor who would sell out his country and its flag in time of war." Suggesting the link between sports and the national character, the *New York Times* declared that bribing a ballplayer was an offense "which strikes at the very heart of this nation." If baseball fell from grace, what could be honest in America? The question haunted journalists and cartoonists. *Outlook* for October 13, 1920, carried a drawing of a crumpled statue of a ballplayer whose torn side

revealed a stuffing of dollar bills. The statue bore the inscription "The National Game." A small boy wept in the foreground; the caption to the cartoon read "His Idol."

12   Baseball officials and club owners were similarly dismayed at the revelation of corruption and determined to clean up the game. Charles A. Comiskey, owner of the Chicago White Sox, led the way with a public statement that no man involved in the fix would ever wear the uniform of his club again. Other owners followed suit until all organized baseball, even the minor leagues, was closed to the Black Sox. On November 12, 1920, Kenesaw Mountain Landis, a former federal judge, was appointed commissioner of baseball with full control over the game and a charge to safeguard its integrity.

13   The everyday fans' response to the fix differed sharply from that of the sportswriters and owners. Many Americans seemed determined to deny the entire affair; more precisely, they didn't *want* to believe anything could be wrong with something as close to the national ideal as baseball. Like the boys of the "say it ain't so" episode, they begged for evidence that the old standards and values still applied. Especially in 1920 in the United States sports heroes were needed as evidence of the virtues of competition, fair play, and the self-reliant individual. Consequently, when confronted with the scandal, the average American simply closed his eyes and pretended nothing was wrong. The heroes remained heroes. When the Black Sox formed an exhibition team, it received enthusiastic support. Petitions were circulated in the major league cities to reinstate the players in organized baseball. But the most remarkable demonstration on the public's feeling came at the conclusion of the Black Sox trial on August 2, 1921. After deliberating two hours and forty-seven minutes, the jury returned a verdict of *not* guilty. According to the *New York Times* reporter at the scene, the packed courtroom rose as one man at the good news, cheering wildly. Hats sailed and papers were thrown about in the delirium. Men shouted "hooray for the clean sox." The bailiffs pounded for order until, as the *Times* reported, they "finally noticed Judge Friend's smiles, and then joined in the whistling and cheering." Finally the jury picked up the acquitted ballplayers and carried them out of the courtroom on their shoulders!

14   Baseball officials and journalists regarded the acquittal of the Black Sox as a technical verdict secured by the lenient interpretation of the Illinois statute involved. The fans in the courtroom, however, and, presumably, many elsewhere were on the side of the players regardless, and viewed the verdict as a vindication. They were not prepared to believe that baseball or its heroes could become tarnished. The game was too important to the national ego. Following baseball gave Americans an opportunity to pay tribute to what many believed was the best part of their heritage. The game was a sacred rite undertaken not merely to determine the winner of league championships but to celebrate the values of a civilization. As one newspaper account of the scandal put it, to learn that "Shoeless" Joe Jackson had sold out the world series was like discovering that "Daniel Boone had been bought by the Indians to lose his fights in Kentucky."

15   In the gallery of popular heroes in the United States the only rival of the frontiersman and his athletic surrogate was the self-made man. In the 1920s the

archetype was Herbert Hoover, a hero-President hewn out of the traditional rags-to-riches mold. Left an orphan in 1884 at the age of ten, Hoover launched an international career in mining that made him rich. During World War I he became famous, heading the American Relief Commission abroad and the Food Administration at home. A genius in matters of largescale efficiency, Hoover neatly executed apparent miracles. After the decline of Woodrow Wilson in the wake of the Versailles Treaty, Hoover was easily the foremost American beneficiary of war-caused popularity. In 1922, while Secretary of Commerce under Warren G. Harding, he set forth his creed in a slender book entitled *American Individualism*. Apparently oblivious of the doubts that beset intellectuals at the time, Hoover professed his "abiding faith in the intelligence, the initiative, the character, the courage, and the divine touch in the individual." But he also believed that individuals differed greatly in energy, ability, and ambition. Some men inevitably rose to the top of the heap, and for Hoover this was entirely right and proper. It was necessary, moreover, if society were to progress. Hoover's philosophy was the old American one of rugged individualism and free enterprise that the Social Darwinists had decorated with scientific tinsel after the Civil War. Intellectually, Hoover was a bedfellow with Benjamin Franklin and William Graham Sumner.

16   Hoover's social, political, and economic ideas followed from these assumptions. He staunchly defended the unregulated profit system. Society and government owed the people only three things: "liberty, justice, and equality of opportunity." Competition took care of the rest, carrying the deserving to their just rewards and the failures to deserved defeat. Any interference, such as philanthropy to the poor or favoritism to the rich, only dulled *"the emery wheel of competition."* To be sure, Hoover paid lip service to restricting the strong in the interest of the society, but the main thrust of his thought awarded the victors their spoils. Critics were disarmed with three worlds — "equality of opportunity." The state should interfere to preserve it; otherwise, hands off! An exponent of the gospel of efficiency in economic affairs, Hoover believed that the road to the good life lay in the direction of more and better production. His mind equated material success with progress.

17   In the concluding chapter of *American Individualism,* Hoover drew the connection between his philosophy and the frontier. "The American pioneer," he declared, "is the epic expression of . . . individualism and the pioneer spirit is the response to the challenge of opportunity, to the challenge of nature, to the challenge of life, to the call of the frontier." Undismayed by the ending of the geographical frontier in the United States, Hoover declared that "there will always be a frontier to conquer or to hold to as long as men think, plan, and dare. . . . The days of the pioneer are not over."

18   When Hoover was elected President in 1928, these ideals were accorded the nation's highest accolade. They dominated popular thought as they had for three centuries of American history. In fact, all the men who occupied the Presidency from 1917 to 1930 were distinctly old-fashioned in their beliefs and in their public image. The traits are so familiar as to require listing only: Wilson the moralist and idealist; Harding the exemplar of small-town, "just

folks'' normalcy; Coolidge the frugal, farm-oriented Puritan; and Hoover the self-made man. If there was any correlation between a people's taste and its Presidents, then the record of this period underscored nostalgia.

19   Rivaling Hoover in the public mind of the early 1920s as an exponent of self-help and individualism was Edward Bok, the Dutch boy who made good and wrote about it in *The Americanization of Edward Bok* (1920). The book described Bok's immigration from Holland in 1870 at the age of six and his rise from a fifty-cents-a-week window cleaner to editor of the magazine with the largest circulation in the nation, the *Ladies Home Journal*. Bok's autobiography reads as a paean to the American ideal of success. Through luck, pluck, and clean living, he became a confidant and friend of Presidents. Thrift and determination made him rich. Bok played the rags to riches theme to the hilt. "Here was a little Dutch boy," he wrote in his preface, "unceremoniously set down in America . . . yet, it must be confessed, he achieved." His book, Bok promised, would describe "how such a boy, with every disadvantage to overcome, was able . . . to 'make good.'"

20   In the final chapters of his autobiography, Bok stepped back to comment on the liabilities and advantages of America. He did not slight the former, yet in "What I Owe America" Bok brushed all debits aside in order to celebrate America's gift of "limitless opportunity: here a man can go as far as his abilities will carry him." For anyone "endowed with honest endeavor, ceaseless industry, and the ability to carry through, . . . the way is wide open to the will to succeed."

21   The public reception of *The Americanization of Edward Bok* suggests how much Americans in the 1920s wanted to confirm old beliefs. Bok was a hero in the Benjamin Franklin – Horatio Alger mold. His success story demonstrated that passing time and changing conditions had not altered hallowed ideals. His pages suggested no troubling doubts, and, after receiving the Pulitzer Prize for biography in 1921, Bok's book became a best-seller. An inexpensive eighth edition issued in July 1921 enabled it to attain third place on the 1922 lists. But the primary reason for Bok's popularity as hero-author was his ability to tell a nervous generation what it wanted to hear.

22   It has long puzzled students of the Great Crash of 1929 why even the most informed observers in education and government as well as business did not recognize and heed the prior economic danger signals that in retrospect seem so apparent. Part of the explanation possibly lies in the depth of the general commitment to the ideals of rugged individualism and free enterprise that Hoover and Bok articulated and symbolized. This commitment, in turn, lay in the nervousness of the American people. So much about the twenties was new and disturbing that Americans tended to cling tightly to familiar economic forms. They just could not bear to admit that the old business premises based on individualism and free enterprise might be fraught with peril. With Herbert Hoover leading the way, they chose to go down with the economic ship rather than question and alter its suicidal course.

23   Respect for the old-time hero was evident in other aspects of postwar thought. The vogue of the Boy Scouts is an example. Although the movement began in 1910, the twenties was the time of its flowering. There were 245,000 Scouts at the beginning of 1917. 942,500 at the end of 1929. In addition, 275,000 adults volunteered their services as leaders. No youth club and few adult organizations matched this record. The Boy Scout *Handbook,* a manual of ideals and instruction, sold millions of copies. Scouting, apparently, tapped fertile soil in its embodiment of the old-time idea of good citizenship and expertise in the outdoors. The Scout, standing straight in his shorts or knickers and doing the daily good deed that his oath required, was the epitome of the traditional American model of heroic young manhood.

24   In the late 1920s the Boy Scout *Handbook* featured an unusual drawing. In the foreground was a clean-cut Scout, eyes fixed on adventure. Behind him, signifying the heritage from which he sprang, were the figures of Daniel Boone, Abraham Lincoln, and Theodore Roosevelt, men who were staples in the annals of American heroism. But there was also a new face, that of Charles A. Lindbergh of Minnesota. At the age of just twenty-five Lindbergh rose to the status of an American demigod by virtue of a single feat. On May 20, 1927, he took off in a tiny single-engine airplane from New York City and thirty-three hours later landed in Paris. The nonstop, solo run across the Atlantic catapulted the average American into a paroxysm of pride and joy. Overnight Lindbergh became the greatest hero of the decade. There was but little exaggeration in the contention of one journalist that Lindbergh received "the greatest ovation in history." Certainly his return from Paris to the United States generated a reception extraordinary even for an age that specialized in ballyhoo. The *New York Times* devoted more space to Lindbergh's return than it had to the Armistice ending World War I. A virtual national religion took shape around Lindbergh's person. A 1928 poll of schoolboys in a typical American town on the question of whom they most wanted to be like produced the following results: Gene Tunney, 13 votes; John Pershing, 14; Alfred E. Smith, 16; Thomas A. Edison, 27; Henry Ford, 66; Calvin Coolidge, 110; Charles A. Lindbergh, 363. If the amount of national adulation is meaningful, adults everywhere would likely have responded in similar proportions.

25   The explanation of Lindbergh's popularity lies less in his feat (pilots had flown across the Atlantic before) and more in the mood of the people at the time it occurred. The typical American in 1927 was nervous. The values by which he ordered his life seemed in jeopardy of being swept away by the force of growth and change and complexity. Lindbergh came as a restorative tonic. He reasserted the image of the confident, quietly courageous, and self-reliant individual. He proved to a generation anxious for proof that Americans were still capable of pioneering. Even in an age of machines the frontier was not dead—a new one had been found in the air.

26   The reaction to Lindbergh's flight in the national press stressed these ideas. "Lindbergh served as a metaphor," wrote one commentator in *Century.* "We felt that in him we, too, had conquered something and regained lost ground." A writer in *Outlook* made the point more explicitly: "Charles Lindbergh is the heir of all that we like to think is best in America. He is the stuff out of which have been made the pioneers that opened up the wilderness first

on the Atlantic coast, and then in our great West." A newspaper cartoon showed a covered wagon leaving for California in 1849 and next to it Lindbergh's plane taking off for Paris in 1927. Colonel Theodore Roosevelt, the son of the President, remarked that Lindbergh "personifies the daring of youth. Daniel Boone, David Crockett, and men of that type played a lone hand and made America. Lindbergh is their lineal descendant." Calvin Coolidge, who personally welcomed Lindbergh home, simply said that he was "a boy representing the best traditions of this country."

27   For one journalist the most significant part of the Lindbergh phenomenon was not the flight but the character of the man: "his courage, his modesty, his self-control, his sanity, his thoughtfulness of others, his fine sense of proportion, his loyalty, his unswerving adherence to the course that seemed right." His unassuming manner fit the traditional hero's mold. Many observers of the postflight celebration noted how the hero refused to capitalize financially on his popularity. It was telling evidence as an essayist put it, that the American people "are *not* rotten at the core, but morally sound and sweet and good!" The generalization from the individual to society was easily acceptable because Americans in 1927 desperately wanted to keep the old creed alive. Lindbergh's flight was popularly interpreted as a flight of faith — in the American experience and in the American people.

28   Looking back over the 1920s F. Scott Fitzgerald remembered in 1931 that "in the spring of 1927, something bright and alien flashed across the sky. A young Minnesotan who seemed to have nothing to do with his generation did a heroic thing, and for a moment people set down their glasses in country clubs and speakeasies and thought of their old best dreams." Also in 1931 Frederick Lewis Allen recalled that Lindbergh had been "a modern Galahad for a generation which had foresworn Galahads." Both Fitzgerald and Allen were right in their assessment of the public reaction to Lindbergh's flight, but wrong about the dreams he engendered being foreign to the 1920s. Fitzgerald notwithstanding, Lindbergh had a great deal to do with his generation. Allen to the contrary, the Lindbergh craze was not a case of Americans returning to ideals they had forsaken; they had never left them.

Reading Sources: "Heroes of the Nineteen Twenties"

Read the selection, surveying it to identify key terms and important concepts. Highlight these phrases and ideas, and then answer these questions.

1. What information appears in the essay's introduction? How does this information prepare readers for the rest of the essay?
2. What is the essay's thesis? Where does it appear?
3. What technique does Nash use to link ideas between paragraphs 2 and 3?
4. Identify the purpose of paragraph 15. How is this purpose related to the purpose of the entire essay?

5. At what point does Nash begin his conclusion? What information does Nash choose to emphasize?

Reacting to Sources

Reread the selection carefully, making marginal notes to aid your comprehension and to reinforce connections. Then further annotate the selection if you need to do so in order to answer any of these questions. (You may already have addressed some of the questions in your marginal notes.)

1. In a few sentences, rewrite paragraph 2 to simplify its ideas.
2. Using a dictionary if necessary, supply brief marginal definitions of these words as they are used in the selection: *urbanization* (2), *efficacy* (2), *surrogate* (3), *tangible* (3), *credo* (3), *ritualistic* (3), *limelight* (5), *Darwinian* (8), *adulation* (9), *bailiffs* (13), *vindication* (14), *ego* (14), *rite* (14), *staunchly* (16), *exponent* (16), *correlation* (18), *nostalgia* (18), *demigod* (24), *paroxysm* (24), *lineal* (26).
3. Using an encyclopedia, make marginal notes explaining the significance of Nash's references to the following figures: Frederick Jackson Turner, Theodore Roosevelt (2), Benjamin Franklin, William Graham Sumner (15), Horatio Alger (21), F. Scott Fitzgerald (28), Frederick Lewis Allen, Galahad (28).
4. After consulting a dictionary or an encyclopedia, make a brief marginal note explaining Nash's use of the term *Social Darwinist* (15).
5. In a marginal note to paragraph 2, list three things about which the post–World War I generation felt uneasy.
6. Make a marginal note in which you explain Nash's statement, "The American sports fan regarded the playing field as a surrogate frontier" (3).
7. Write three brief marginal questions in response to the ideas in paragraph 13.
8. In paragraph 22, Nash says, "With Herbert Hoover leading the way, [Americans] chose to go down with the economic ship rather than question and alter its suicidal course." Explore this idea further in a journal entry.
9. In a journal entry, consider the possible connections between the central idea of this essay and the central idea of "Heroes and Heroines" (pp. 253–258).
10. Outline the paragraph cluster beginning with paragraph 24 and ending with paragraph 27.

Working with Sources

1. Write a one-sentence summary of paragraph 11.
2. Write a critique of the ideas in paragraph 23.
3. Write a journal entry in which you explore your reactions to these quotations from "Heroes of the Nineteen Twenties."

"Scarcely an American was unaware that the frontier had vanished and that pioneering, in the traditional sense, was a thing of the past" (2).

"He [Lindbergh] proved to a generation anxious for proof that Americans were still capable of pioneering. Even in an age of machines the frontier was not dead — a new one had been found in the air" (25).

Be sure to integrate the quotations smoothly into your writing.

4. Paraphrase paragraph 2.
5. Write a one-paragraph synthesis that blends ideas in paragraph 3 of this essay with the ideas in paragraph 4 of "Heroes and Heroines" (pp. 253 – 258).

Writing with Sources: Using a Single Source

Integrating information from "Heroes of the Nineteen Twenties" with your own ideas, write an essay on one of these topics. Be sure to acknowledge all ideas that are not your own.

1. Discuss two classes of heroes that embody the hopes and fears of young Americans in the 1980s.
2. Compare the heroes of the 1920s with those who are popular today. If you can, account for the differences.
3. Like the 1920s, the 1980s have seen public exposure of corruption in sports. Compare the status that sports figures hold today with the status that they held in the 1920s. How have revelations about point shaving, drugs, and player pay-offs affected our perception of sports figures? Do we, like fans of the 1920s, seem "determined to deny the whole affair"?

Faster Than an Express Train: The Advent of the Super-Hero

Jules Feiffer

Jules Feiffer was born in 1929 in New York City and attended the Art Students League and Pratt Institute. From 1946 to 1951 he ghost-scripted "The Spirit," and during the early 1950s held various art jobs. It was during this time that he began publishing cartoons in the *Village Voice*. As his popularity grew, he also published weekly in the *London Observer* and *Playboy* magazine. His cartoons are now distributed to over one hundred newspapers in the United States and abroad. He has published a number of collections of his cartoons and also has written short plays and movie scripts. The following essay from *The Great Comic Book Heroes* (1965) discusses Superman and the advent of the super-hero. In it, Feiffer shows how Superman and the rest of the super-heroes were particularly suited to the era in which they were created.

Leaping over skyscrapers, running faster than an express train, springing great distances and heights, lifting and smashing tremendous weights, possessing an impenetrable skin — these are the amazing attributes which Superman, savior of the helpless and oppressed, avails himself of as he battles the forces of evil and injustice. — Superman, *Action Comics,* August 1939

1   The advent of the super-hero was a bizarre comeuppance for the American dream. Horatio Alger could no longer make it on his own. He needed "Sha-zam!" Here was fantasy with a cynically realistic base: once the odds were appraised honestly it was apparent you had to be super to get on in this world.

2   The particular brilliance of Superman lay not only in the fact that he was the first of the super-heroes, but in the concept of his alter ego. What made Superman different from the legion of imitators to follow was not that when he took off his clothes he could beat up everybody — they all did that. What made Superman extraordinary was his point of origin: Clark Kent.

3   Remember, Kent was not Superman's true identity as Bruce Wayne was the Batman's or (on radio) Lamont Cranston the Shadow's. Just the opposite. Clark Kent was the fiction. Previous heroes — the Shadow, the Green Hornet, The Lone Ranger — were not only more vulnerable; they were fakes. I don't mean to criticize; it's just a statement of fact. The Shadow had to cloud men's minds to be in business. The Green Hornet had to go through the fetishist fol-de-rol of donning costume, floppy hat, black mask, gas gun, menacing auto-mobile, and insect sound effects before he was even ready to go out in the street. The Lone Ranger needed an accoutremental white horse, an Indian, and an establishing cry of Hi-Yo Silver to separate him from all those other masked men running around the West in days of yesteryear.

4   But Superman had only to wake up in the morning to be Superman. In his case, Clark Kent was the put-on. The fellow with the eyeglasses and the acne and the walk girls laughed at wasn't real, didn't exist, was a sacrificial disguise, an act of discreet martyrdom. *Had they but known!*

5   And for what purpose? Did Superman become Clark Kent in order to lead a normal life, have friends, be known as a nice guy, meet girls? Hardly. There's too much of the hair shirt in the role, too much devotion to the imprimatur of impotence — an insight, perhaps, into the fantasy life of the Man of Steel. Superman as a secret masochist? Field for study there. For if it was otherwise, if the point, the only point, was to lead a "normal life," why not a more typical identity? How can one be a cowardly star reporter, subject to fainting spells in time of crisis, and not expect to raise serious questions?

6   The truth may be that Kent existed not for the purposes of the story but for the reader. He is Superman's opinion of the rest of us, a pointed caricature of what we, the noncriminal element, were really like. His fake identity was our real one. That's why we loved him so. For if that wasn't really us, if there were no Clark Kents, only lots of glasses and cheap suits which, when removed, revealed all of us in our true identities — what a hell of an improved world it would have been!

7   In drawing style, both in figure and costume, Superman was a simplified parody of Flash Gordon. But if Alex Raymond was the Dior for Superman, Joe

Shuster set the fashion from then on. Everybody else's super-costumes were copies from his shop. Shuster represented the best of old-style comic book drawing. His work was direct, unprettied—crude and vigorous; as easy to read as a diagram. No creamy lines, no glossy illustrative effects, no touch of that bloodless prefabrication that passes for professionalism these days. Slickness, thank God, was beyond his means. He could not draw well, but he drew single-mindedly—no one could ghost that style. It was the man. When assistants began "improving" the appearance of the strip it promptly went downhill. It looked as though it were being drawn in a bank.

8   But, oh, those early drawings! Superman running up the sides of dams, leaping over anything that stood in his way. (No one drew skyscrapers like Shuster. Impressionistic shafts, Superman poised over them, his leaping leg tucked under him, his landing leg tautly pointed earthward), cleaning and jerking two-ton get-away cars and pounding them into the sides of cliffs—and all this done lightly, unportentiously, still with that early Slam Bradley exuberance. What matter that the stories quickly lost interest; that once you've made a man super you've plotted him out of believable conflicts; that even super-villains, super-mad scientists and, yes, super-orientals were dull and lifeless next to the overwhelming image of that which Clark Kent became when he took off his clothes. So what if the stories were boring, the villains blah? This was the Superman Show—a touring road company backing up a great star. Everything was a stage wait until he came on. Then it was all worth-while.

9   Besides, for the alert reader there were other fields of interest. It seems that among Lois Lane, Clark Kent, and Superman there existed a schizoid and chaste *ménage à trois*. Clark Kent loved but felt abashed with Lois Lane; Superman saved Lois Lane when she was in trouble, found her a pest the rest of the time. Since Superman and Clark Kent were the same person this behavior demands explanation. It can't be that Kent wanted Lois to respect him for himself, since himself was Superman. Then, it appears, he wanted Lois to respect him for his fake self, to love him when he acted the coward, to be there when he pretended he needed her. She never was—so, of course, he loved her. A typical American romance. Superman never needed her, never needed anyone—in any event, Lois chased *him*—so, of course, he didn't love her. He had contempt for her. Another typical American romance.

10   Love is really the pursuit of a desired object, not pursuit by it. Once you've caught the object there is no longer any reason to love it, to have it hanging around. There must be other desirable objects out there, somewhere. So Clark Kent acted as the control for Superman. What Kent wanted was just that which Superman didn't want to be bothered with. Kent wanted Lois, Superman didn't—thus marking the difference between a sissy and a man. A sissy wanted girls who scorned him, a man scorned girls who wanted him. Our cultural opposite of the man who didn't make out with women has never been the man who did—but rather the man who could if he wanted to, but still didn't. The ideal of masculine strength, whether Gary Cooper's, Li'l Abner's, or Superman's, was for one to be so virile and handsome, to be in such a position of strength, that he need never go near girls. Except to help them. And then

get the hell out. Real rapport was not for women. It was for villains. That's why they got hit so hard.

Reading Sources: "Faster Than an Express Train: The Advent of the Super-Hero"

Read the selection, surveying it to identify key terms and important concepts. Highlight these phrases and ideas, and then answer these questions.

1. What terms does Feiffer emphasize by their placement?
2. What techniques does Feiffer use to link ideas between paragraph 4 and paragraph 5?
3. What technique does Feiffer use to classify the heroes in paragraph 3?
4. How would you describe the tone of this essay? Underline three sentences that illustrate your point.
5. What is the thesis of this essay? At what point in the essay is it stated?

Reacting to Sources

Reread the selection carefully, making marginal notes to aid your comprehension and to reinforce connections. Then further annotate the selection if you need to do so in order to answer any of these questions. (You may already have addressed some of the questions in your marginal notes.)

1. In a few sentences, rewrite paragraph 9 to simplify its ideas.
2. Using a dictionary if necessary, supply brief marginal definitions of these words as they are used in the selection: *fetishist* (3), *fol-de-rol* (3), *accoutremental* (3), *imprimatur* (5), *masochist* (5), *tautly* (8), *unportentiously* (8), *schizoid* (9), *chaste* (9), *ménage à trois* (9), *virile* (10).
3. After consulting an encyclopedia, make marginal notes explaining the significance of Feiffer's references to the following figures: Horatio Alger (1), Dior (7), Gary Cooper (10).
4. Write three marginal questions in response to the ideas in paragraph 9.
5. Feiffer makes this statement in paragraph 10: "The ideal of masculine strength, whether Gary Cooper's, L'il Abner's, or Superman's, was for one to be so virile and handsome, to be in such a position of strength, that he need never go near girls. Except to help them" (10). Do you agree or disagree? Write a brief marginal comment in which you explain your position.
6. In a marginal note, identify Feiffer's purpose in paragraph 8. Identify the purpose of the entire essay.
7. Does Feiffer's tone affect your acceptance of his ideas? What other factors affect your response to his ideas? Explain your responses in a journal entry.
8. In paragraph 2 Feiffer says, "The particular brilliance of Superman lay not only

in the fact that he was the first of the super-heroes, but in the concept of his alter ego" (2). Explore this idea further in a journal entry.

9. In a journal entry, explore the significance of this statement: "The truth may be that Kent existed not for the purpose of the story but for the reader" (6).

10. In a journal entry, consider possible connections or relationships between this selection and "The Emerging American Hero" (pp. 261–268).

Working with Sources

1. Write a one-sentence summary of paragraph 6.
2. Write a critique of the ideas in paragraph 10.
3. Write a journal entry in which you explore your reactions to these quotations from "Faster Than an Express Train: The Advent of the Super-Hero."

   "The advent of the super-hero was a bizarre comeuppance for the American dream. Horatio Alger could no longer make it on his own" (1).

   "[Superman's] fake identity was our real one. That's why we loved him so. For if that wasn't really us, if there were no Clark Kents, only lots of glasses and cheap suits, which, when removed, revealed our true identities — what a hell of an improved world it would have been" (6).

   Be sure to integrate the quotations smoothly into your writing.
4. Paraphrase the paragraph cluster beginning with paragraph 7 and ending with paragraph 8.
5. Write a one-paragraph synthesis that blends ideas in paragraph 1 of this essay with the ideas in paragraph 35 of "The Emerging American Hero" (pp. 261–268).

Writing with Sources: Using a Single Source

Integrating information from "Faster Than an Express Train: The Advent of the Super-Hero" with your own ideas, write an essay on one of these topics. Be sure to acknowledge all ideas that are not your own.

1. Explain why you agree or disagree with the "ideal of masculine strength" that Feiffer describes in paragraph 10.
2. Suppose you were commissioned to create your own super-hero comic book. Your editor has asked you to send a letter in which you describe the character that you will present and your analysis of his or her appeal. Use material from this selection to make your case and to convince the editor that your hero or heroine is just what the contemporary reader wants.
3. Super-hero comic books appeal mainly to adolescent males between the ages of ten and fourteen. Discuss why you feel this group finds super-heroes so appealing.

Writing with Sources: Using Multiple Sources

Integrating information from sources in this chapter with your own ideas, write an essay on one of the topics below. Be sure to acknowledge ideas that are not your own.

1. Joseph Campell describes a common theme in mythology: the journey of the hero. As a number of other writers in this section point out, however, different patterns of heroic behavior emerge in different times and different places. Consider three different kinds of heroes. You may use the categories discussed by the various authors that you have read, or you may develop your own classification.

2. In his essay, Fishwick describes the emerging American hero. As Antonia Fraser observes, however, not many heroines were recognized until recently. Describe the characteristics of an American heroine. Does she fit the traditional stereotype and possess ''a romantic feminine heart'' and a ''greater hint of frailty''? Or does she contain a mixture of qualities that makes her more complex than the hero? Give several examples to support your points.

3. Antonia Fraser, Marshall W. Fishwick, and Roderick Nash would agree that ''every historical change creates its own mythology.'' Using the essays of these authors as your guide, discuss the mythology that our own time and one other time have created. If you can, account for the kinds of heroes that have emerged in the eras that you discuss.

4. Literary and movie heroes often conform to the patterns described by the authors in this section. Choose two characters from different movies or books and demonstrate how they correspond to the themes that you read about in this section.

5. According to R. W. B. Lewis in *The American Adam: Innocence, Tragedy, and Tradition in the Nineteenth Century,* the typical American hero is ''self-reliant and self-propelling,'' ready to confront whatever awaits him. On the other hand, he is also an innocent like Huckleberry Finn, who flees toward the frontier, denying women and the social responsibilities that they represent. Discuss how the frontier has figured into the myth of the American hero. In your essay, mention the ideas expressed by Fishwick, Nash, and Feiffer.

8

Issues in Education

A central issue of our time, education has always been the subject of intense debate among teachers and politicians. Questions about the role of education in our society and about its methods, purpose, and potential impact have led to conflicts and further questions. This chapter considers some of the questions that have inspired concern and controversy.

The chapter begins with two classic essays about education. In "The Aims of Education" Alfred North Whitehead sets forth his view that educators must stress the interrelatedness of ideas, not teach academic subjects in isolation from one another. John Holt, in "School Is Bad for Children," argues that children will learn more effectively if they have some control over their own education. The rest of the chapter's selections consider contemporary social issues as well as strictly educational ones. William Manchester's "With All Deliberate Speed" chronicles the integration of the nation's public schools following the Supreme Court's 1954 decision in the case of Brown vs. Board of Education. In the pair of articles that follows, Angelo Gonzalez and Richard Rodriguez, respectively, argue for and against the practice of teaching non-English – speaking children in their native languages. Next, Jonathan Kozol examines "The Price We Pay," in social and emotional as well as economic terms, for the widespread illiteracy in this country. Finally, in "Who Cares About the Renaissance?" Leslie Brown defends the importance of a liberal arts education in an increasingly technological world.

The Aims of Education

Alfred North Whitehead

Alfred North Whitehead (1861–1947) was known world wide as a mathematician, philosopher, and educator. He graduated from Trinity College, Cambridge, in 1884 and taught mathematics there and then at the University of London. With the noted philosopher Bertrand Russell he wrote *Principia Mathematica* (1910–13), which established the field of inquiry known as symbolic logic. In 1924 Whitehead left England to become a professor of philosophy at Harvard University. A prolific writer, his works include *Science and the Modern World* (1925), *Process and Reality* (1929), and *The Aims of Education and Other Essays* (1929). He retired in 1937 and received the British Order of Merit award in 1945. To his students at Harvard, Whitehead was known as a warm human being and a brilliant teacher. He was deeply interested in education and in stimulating and guiding the self-development of the young. In "The Aims of Education" Whitehead sets forth his views on education and stresses the need to recognize the interdependence among various disciplines and to avoid the narrowness of perspective that he felt characterizes much of a university education.

1   Culture is activity of thought, and receptiveness to beauty and humane feeling. Scraps of information have nothing to do with it. A merely well-informed man is the most useless bore on God's earth. What we should aim at producing is men who possess both culture and expert knowledge in some special direction. Their expert knowledge will give them the ground to start from, and their culture will lead them as deep as philosophy and as high as art. We have to remember that the valuable intellectual development is self-development, and that it mostly takes place between the ages of sixteen and thirty. As to training, the most important part is given by mothers before the age of twelve. A saying due to Archbishop Temple illustrates my meaning. Surprise was expressed at the success in after-life of a man, who as a boy at Rugby had been somewhat undistinguished. He answered, "It is not what they are at eighteen, it is what they become afterwards that matters."

2   In training a child to activity of thought, above all things we must beware of what I will call "inert ideas" — that is to say, ideas that are merely received into the mind without being utilised, or tested, or thrown into fresh combinations.

3   In the history of education, the most striking phenomenon is that schools of learning, which at one epoch are alive with a ferment of genius, in a succeeding generation exhibit merely pedantry and routine. The reason is, that they are overladen with inert ideas. Education with inert ideas is not only useless: it is, above all things, harmful — *Corruptio optimi, pessima*. Except at rare intervals of intellectual ferment, education in the past has been radically infected with inert ideas. That is the reason why uneducated clever women, who have seen much of the world, are in middle life so much the most cultured part of the community. They have been saved from this horrible burden of inert ideas. Every intellectual revolution which has ever stirred humanity into greatness has been a passionate protest against inert ideas. Then, alas, with

pathetic ignorance of human psychology, it has proceeded by some educational scheme to bind humanity afresh with inert ideas of its own fashioning.

4   Let us now ask how in our system of education we are to guard against this mental dryrot. We enunciate two educational commandments, "Do not teach too many subjects," and again, "What you teach, teach thoroughly."

5   The result of teaching small parts of a large number of subjects is the passive reception of disconnected ideas, not illumined with any spark of vitality. Let the main ideas which are introduced into a child's education be few and important, and let them be thrown into every combination possible. The child should make them his own, and should understand their application here and now in the circumstances of his actual life. From the very beginning of his education, the child should experience the joy of discovery. The discovery which he has to make, is that general ideas give an understanding of that stream of events which pours through his life, which is his life. By understanding I mean more than a mere logical analysis, though that is included. I mean "understanding" in the sense in which it is used in the French proverb, "To understand all, is to forgive all." Pedants sneer at an education which is useful. But if education is not useful, what is it? Is it a talent, to be hidden away in a napkin? Of course, education should be useful, whatever your aim in life. It was useful to Saint Augustine and it was useful to Napoleon. It is useful, because understanding is useful.

6   I pass lightly over that understanding which should be given by the literary side of education. Nor do I wish to be supposed to pronounce on the relative merits of a classical or a modern curriculum. I would only remark that the understanding which we want is an understanding of an insistent present. The only use of a knowledge of the past is to equip us for the present. No more deadly harm can be done to young minds than by depreciation of the present. The present contains all that there is. It is holy ground; for it is the past, and it is the future. At the same time it must be observed that an age is no less past if it existed two hundred years ago than if it existed two thousand years ago. Do not be deceived by the pedantry of dates. The ages of Shakespeare and of Molière are no less past than are the ages of Sophocles and of Virgil. The communion of saints is a great and inspiring assemblage, but it has only one possible hall of meeting, and that is, the present; and the mere lapse of time through which any particular group of saints must travel to reach that meeting-place, makes very little difference.

7   Passing now to the scientific and logical side of education, we remember that here also ideas which are not utilised are positively harmful. By utilising an idea, I mean relating it to that stream, compounded of sense perceptions, feelings, hopes, desires, and of mental activities adjusting thought to thought, which forms our life. I can imagine a set of beings which might fortify their souls by passively reviewing disconnected ideas. Humanity is not built that way — except perhaps some editors of newspapers.

8   In scientific training, the first thing to do with an idea is to prove it. But allow me for one moment to extend the meaning of "prove"; I mean — to

prove its worth. Now an idea is not worth much unless the propositions in which it is embodied are true. Accordingly an essential part of the proof of an idea is the proof, either by experiment or by logic, of the truth of the propositions. But it is not essential that this proof of the truth should constitute the first introduction to the idea. After all, its assertion by the authority of respectable teachers is sufficient evidence to begin with. In our first contact with a set of propositions, we commence by appreciating their importance. That is what we all do in after-life. We do not attempt, in the strict sense, to prove or to disprove anything, unless its importance makes it worthy of that honour. These two processes of proof, in the narrow sense, and of appreciation, do not require a rigid separation in time. Both can be proceeded with nearly concurrently. But in so far as either process must have the priority, it should be that of appreciation by use.

9   Furthermore, we should not endeavour to use propositions in isolation. Emphatically I do not mean, a neat little set of experiments to illustrate Proposition I and then the proof of Proposition I, a neat little set of experiments to illustrate Proposition II and then the proof of Proposition II, and so on to the end of the book. Nothing could be more boring. Interrelated truths are utilised *en bloc,* and the various propositions are employed in any order, and with any reiteration. Choose some important applications of your theoretical subject; and study them concurrently with the systematic theoretical exposition. Keep the theoretical exposition short and simple, but let it be strict and rigid so far as it goes. It should not be too long for it to be easily known with thoroughness and accuracy. The consequences of a plethora of half-digested theoretical knowledge are deplorable. Also the theory should not be muddled up with the practice. The child should have no doubt when it is proving and when it is utilising. My point is that what is proved should be utilised, and that what is utilised should — so far as is practicable — be proved. I am far from asserting that proof and utilisation are the same thing.

10   At this point of my discourse, I can most directly carry forward my argument in the outward form of a digression. We are only just realising that the art and science of education require a genius and a study of their own; and that this genius and this science are more than a bare knowledge of some branch of science or of literature. This truth was partially perceived in the past generation; and headmasters, somewhat crudely, were apt to supersede learning in their colleagues by requiring left-hand bowling and a taste for football. But culture is more than cricket, and more than football, and more than extent of knowledge.

11   Education is the acquisition of the art of the utilisation of knowledge. This is an art very difficult to impart. Whenever a text-book is written of real educational worth, you may be quite certain that some reviewer will say that it will be difficult to teach from it. Of course it will be difficult to teach from it. If it were easy, the book ought to be burned; for it cannot be educational. In education, as elsewhere, the broad primrose path leads to a nasty place. This evil path is represented by a book or a set of lectures which will practically

enable the student to learn by heart all the questions likely to be asked at the next external examination. And I may say in passing that no educational system is possible unless every question directly asked of a pupil at any examination is either framed or modified by the actual teacher of that pupil in that subject. The external assessor may report on the curriculum or on the performance of the pupils, but never should be allowed to ask the pupil a question which has not been strictly supervised by the actual teacher, or at least inspired by a long conference with him. There are a few exceptions to this rule, but they are exceptions, and could easily be allowed for under the general rule.

12   We now return to my previous point, that theoretical ideas should always find important applications within the pupil's curriculum. This is not an easy doctrine to apply, but a very hard one. It contains within itself the problem of keeping knowledge alive, of preventing it from becoming inert, which is the central problem of all education.

13   The best procedure will depend on several factors, none of which can be neglected, namely, the genius of the teacher, the intellectual type of the pupils, their prospects in life, the opportunities offered by the immediate surroundings of the school, and allied factors of this sort. It is for this reason that the uniform external examination is so deadly. We do not denounce it because we are cranks, and like denouncing established things. We are not so childish. Also, of course, such examinations have their use in testing slackness. Our reason of dislike is very definite and very practical. It kills the best part of culture. When you analyse in the light of experience the central task of education, you find that its successful accomplishment depends on a delicate adjustment of many variable factors. The reason is that we are dealing with human minds, and not with dead matter. The evocation of curiosity, of judgment, of the power of mastering a complicated tangle of circumstances, the use of theory in giving foresight in special cases — all these powers are not to be imparted by a set rule embodied in one schedule of examination subjects.

14   I appeal to you, as practical teachers. With good discipline, it is always possible to pump into the minds of a class a certain quantity of inert knowledge. You take a text-book and make them learn it. So far, so good. The child then knows how to solve a quadratic equation. But what is the point of teaching a child to solve a quadratic equation? There is a traditional answer to this question. It runs thus: The mind is an instrument, you first sharpen it, and then use it; the acquisition of the power of solving a quadratic equation is part of the process of sharpening the mind. Now there is just enough truth in this answer to have made it live through the ages. But for all its half-truth, it embodies a radical error which bids fair to stifle the genius of the modern world. I do not know who was first responsible for this analogy of the mind to a dead instrument. For aught I know, it may have been one of the seven wise men of Greece, or a committee of the whole lot of them. Whoever was the originator, there can be no doubt of the authority which it has acquired by the continuous approval bestowed upon it by eminent persons. But whatever its weight of authority, whatever the high approval which it can quote, I have no hesitation in denouncing it as one of the most fatal, erroneous, and dangerous concep-

tions ever introduced into the theory of education. The mind is never passive; it is a perpetual activity, delicate, receptive, responsive to stimulus. You cannot postpone its life until you have sharpened it. Whatever interest attaches to your subject-matter must be evoked here and now; whatever powers you are strengthening in the pupil, must be exercised here and now; whatever possibilities of mental life your teaching should impart, must be exhibited here and now. That is the golden rule of education, and a very difficult rule to follow.

15   The difficulty is just this: the apprehension of general ideas, intellectual habits of mind, and pleasurable interest in mental achievement can be evoked by no form of words, however accurately adjusted. All practical teachers know that education is a patient process of the mastery of details, minute by minute, hour by hour, day by day. There is no royal road to learning through an airy path of brilliant generalisations. There is a proverb about the difficulty of seeing the wood because of the trees. That difficulty is exactly the point which I am enforcing. The problem of education is to make the pupil see the wood by means of the trees.

16   The solution which I am urging, is to eradicate the fatal disconnection of subjects which kills the vitality of our modern curriculum. There is only one subject-matter for education, and that is Life in all its manifestations. Instead of this single unity, we offer children—Algebra, from which nothing follows; Geometry, from which nothing follows; Science, from which nothing follows; History, from which nothing follows; a Couple of Languages, never mastered; and lastly, most dreary of all, Literature, represented by plays of Shakespeare, with philological notes and short analyses of plot and character to be in substance committed to memory. Can such a list be said to represent Life, as it is known in the midst of the living of it? The best that can be said of it is, that it is a rapid table of contents which a deity might run over in his mind while he was thinking of creating a world, and had not yet determined how to put it together.

Reading Sources: "The Aims of Education"

Read the selection, surveying it to identify key terms and important concepts. Highlight these phrases and ideas, and then answer these questions.

1. What is Whitehead's thesis? Where does he state it?
2. What terms does Whitehead define at the beginning of his essay? Why does he choose to begin in this way?
3. Which does Whitehead think is more apt to convey disconnected ideas to students, the literary or scientific side of education? Explain your answer.
4. At what point in his essay does Whitehead turn his attention to the "art and science of education"? How does he signal this shift to his readers?
5. Where does Whitehead begin his conclusion? How does he let readers know that he is about to sum up his argument? What points does he choose to emphasize in his conclusion? Why do you think he selects these points?

Reacting to Sources

Reread the selection carefully, making marginal notes to aid your comprehension and to reinforce connections. Then, further annotate the selection if you need to do so in order to answer any of these questions. (You may already have addressed some of the questions in your marginal notes.)

1. In a few sentences, rewrite paragraph 5 to simplify its ideas.
2. Using a dictionary if necessary, supply brief marginal definitions of these words and phrases as they are used in the essay: *inert* (2), *ferment* (3), *passive* (5), *pedants* (5), *depreciation* (6), *embodied* (8), *en bloc* (9), *concurrently* (9), *plethora* (9), *primrose path* (11), *philological* (16).
3. "The Aims of Education" was written in 1916, a time when women were viewed differently from the way they are today (in fact, they did not yet have the right to vote). Underline any passages that refer to women. Make marginal notes in which you indicate how the sentiments expressed in these passages are outdated. Rewrite the passages to bring them into line with the position that women now occupy in society.
4. Whitehead makes this statement: "Of course education should be useful, whatever your aim in life" (5). Do you agree or disagree? Write a brief marginal comment in which you explain your position.
5. Write three brief marginal questions in response to the ideas in paragraph 9.
6. Give two examples to support Whitehead's general statement that "theoretical ideas should always find important applications within the pupil's curriculum" (12).
7. Write a marginal note in which you explain what Whitehead means when he says "no educational system is possible unless every question directly asked of a pupil at any examination is either framed or modified by the actual teacher of that pupil in that subject" (11). Write a journal entry in which you agree or disagree with this statement.
8. Identify Whitehead's purpose in paragraph 14. Identify the purpose of the entire selection.
9. Read the introduction to the selection. In a journal entry, comment on how Whitehead's life and other writings might have influenced his purpose. Comment on how they influence your acceptance of his ideas.
10. In paragraph 4 Whitehead presents two educational commandments. Explore these ideas further in a journal entry.
11. In a journal entry compare this essay's central idea with the central idea of "Who Cares About the Renaissance?" (pp. 326–328).
12. Outline the paragraph cluster beginning in paragraph 6 and ending after paragraph 8.

Working with Sources

1. Write a one-sentence summary of paragraph 3.
2. Write a critique of the ideas in paragraph 11.

3. Write a journal entry in which you explore your reactions to these quotations from "The Aims of Education."

> "In training a child to activity of thought, above all things we must be aware of what I will call 'inert ideas' — that is to say, ideas that are merely received into the mind without being utilized, or tested, or thrown into fresh combinations" (2).

> "The solution which I am urging, is to eradicate the fatal disconnection of subjects which kills the vitality of our modern curriculum" (16).

Be sure to integrate the quotations smoothly into your writing.
4. Paraphrase paragraph 1.
5. Write a one-paragraph synthesis that blends the ideas in paragraph 6 of this selection with the ideas expressed in paragraph 8 of "Who Cares About the Renaissance?" (pp. 326–328).

Writing with Sources: Using a Single Source

Integrating information from "The Aims of Education" with your own ideas, write an essay on one of these topics. Be sure to acknowledge all ideas that are not your own.

1. Explain why you agree or disagree with the following statement: "Even though Whitehead wrote 'The Aims of Education' in 1916, his criticisms of the educational system still apply." To support your points, use your own experiences as well as information from the essay.
2. In his essay, Whitehead says, "Of course, education should be useful, whatever your aim in life" (5). He goes on to say, "The only use of a knowledge of the past is to equip us for the present" (6). Discuss how a knowledge of the past equips us for the present. To support your points, draw freely from your own experience and the reading that you have done for your other courses.
3. Describe the best teacher that you ever had. Make sure you discuss how closely this teacher followed Whitehead's ideas about education.

School Is Bad for Children

John Holt

John Holt (1923–1985) was a teacher, writer, and lecturer who greatly influenced the state of teaching in America. During the 1960s and 1970s, his ideas were central in the formation of open classrooms, where children were free to define their own educational goals and to choose the subjects that they would study. His best-known book on education, *How Children Fail* (1964), blames schools for not meeting the needs of students and was hailed by the *New York Times* as ". . . possibly the most penetrating, and probably the most eloquent book on education to be published in recent years." In addition to numerous magazine articles on education, Holt's books include *How Children Learn* (1967), *Freedom and Beyond* (1972), and *Teach Your Own* (1981). Although Holt's ideas are no longer as influential as they once were, they still have a large following among educators. In "School Is Bad for Children," Holt expresses one of his basic assumptions, that children learn best when they control their own learning.

1   Almost every child, on the first day he sets foot in a school building, is smarter, more curious, less afraid of what he doesn't know, better at finding and figuring things out, more confident, resourceful, persistent and independent than he will ever be again in his schooling — or, unless he is very unusual and very lucky, for the rest of his life. Already, by paying close attention to and interacting with the world and people around him, and without any school-type formal instruction, he has done a task far more difficult, complicated and abstract than anything he will be asked to do in school, or than any of his teachers has done for years. He has solved the mystery of language. He has discovered it — babies don't even know that language exists — and he has found out how it works and learned to use it. He has done it by exploring, by experimenting, by developing his own model of the grammar of language, by trying it out and seeing whether it works, by gradually changing it and refining it until it does work. And while he has been doing this, he has been learning other things as well, including many of the "concepts" that the schools think only they can teach him, and many that are more complicated than the ones they do try to teach him.

2   In he comes, this curious, patient, determined, energetic, skillful learner. We sit him down at a desk, and what do we teach him? Many things. First, that learning is separate from living. "You come to school to learn," we tell him, as if the child hadn't been learning before, as if living were out there and learning were in here, and there were no connection between the two. Secondly, that he cannot be trusted to learn and is no good at it. Everything we teach about reading, a task far simpler than many that the child has already mastered, says to him, "If we don't make you read, you won't, and if you don't do it exactly the way we tell you, you can't." In short, he comes to feel that learning is a passive process, something that someone else does *to* you, instead of something you do for yourself.

3   In a great many other ways he learns that he is worthless, untrustworthy, fit only to take other people's orders, a blank sheet for other people to write on. Oh, we make a lot of nice noises in school about respect for the child and individual differences, and the like. But our acts, as opposed to our talk, say to the child, "Your experience, your concerns, your curiosities, your needs, what you know, what you want, what you wonder about, what you hope for, what you fear, what you like and dislike, what you are good at or not so good at — all this is of not the slightest importance, it counts for nothing. What counts here, and the only thing that counts, is what we know, what we think is important, what we want you to do, think and be." The child soon learns not to ask

questions — the teacher isn't there to satisfy his curiosity. Having learned to hide his curiosity, he later learns to be ashamed of it. Given no chance to find out who he is — and to develop that person, whoever it is — he soon comes to accept the adults' evaluation of him.

4   He learns many other things. He learns that to be wrong, uncertain, confused, is a crime. Right Answers are what the school wants, and he learns countless strategies for prying these answers out of the teacher, for conning her into thinking he knows what he doesn't know. He learns to dodge, bluff, fake, cheat. He learns to be lazy. Before he came to school, he would work for hours on end, on his own, with no thought of reward, at the business of making sense of the world and gaining competence in it. In school he learns, like every buck private, how to goldbrick, how not to work when the sergeant isn't looking, how to know when he is looking, how to make him think you are working even when he is looking. He learns that in real life you don't do anything unless you are bribed, bullied or conned into doing it, that nothing is worth doing for its own sake, or that if it is, you can't do it in school. He learns to be bored, to work with a small part of his mind, to escape from the reality around him into daydreams and fantasies — but not like the fantasies of his preschool years, in which he played a very active part.

5   The child comes to school curious about other people, particularly other children, and the school teaches him to be indifferent. The most interesting thing in the classroom — often the only interesting thing in it — is the other children, but he has to act as if these other children, all about him, only a few feet away, are not really there. He cannot interact with them, talk with them, smile at them. In many schools he can't talk to other children in the halls between classes; in more than a few, and some of these in stylish suburbs, he can't even talk to them at lunch. Splendid training for a world in which, when you're not studying the other person to figure out how to do him in, you pay no attention to him.

6   In fact, he learns how to live without paying attention to anything going on around him. You might say that school is a long lesson in how to turn yourself off, which may be one reason why so many young people, seeking the awareness of the world and responsiveness to it they had when they were little, think they can only find it in drugs. Aside from being boring, the school is almost always ugly, cold, inhuman — even the most stylish, glass-windowed, $20-a-square-foot schools.

7   And so, in this dull and ugly place, where nobody ever says anything very truthful, where everybody is playing a kind of role, as in a charade, where the teachers are no more free to respond honestly to the students than the students are free to respond to the teachers or each other, where the air practically vibrates with suspicion and anxiety, the child learns to live in a daze, saving his energies for those small parts of his life that are too trivial for the adults to bother with, and thus remain his. It is a rare child who can come through his schooling with much left of his curiosity, his independence or his sense of his own dignity, competence and worth.

8   So much for criticism. What do we need to do? Many things. Some are

easy—we can do them right away. Some are hard, and may take some time. Take a hard one first. We should abolish compulsory school attendance. At the very least we should modify it, perhaps by giving children every year a large number of authorized absences. Our compulsory school-attendance laws once served a humane and useful purpose. They protected children's right to some schooling, against those adults who would otherwise have denied it to them in order to exploit their labor, in farm, store, mine or factory. Today the laws help nobody, not the schools, not the teachers, not the children. To keep kids in school who would rather not be there costs the schools an enormous amount of time and trouble — to say nothing of what it costs to repair the damage that these angry and resentful prisoners do every time they get a chance. Every teacher knows that any kid in class who, for whatever reason, would rather not be there not only doesn't learn anything himself but makes it a great deal tougher for anyone else. As for protecting the children from exploitation, the chief and indeed only exploiters of children these days *are* the schools. Kids caught in the college rush more often than not work 70 hours or more a week, most of it on paper busywork. For kids who aren't going to college, school is just a useless time waster, preventing them from earning some money or doing some useful work, or even doing some true learning.

9   Objections. "If kids didn't have to go to school, they'd all be out in the streets." No, they wouldn't. In the first place, even if schools stayed just the way they are, children would spend at least some time there because that's where they'd be likely to find friends; it's a natural meeting place for children. In the second place, schools wouldn't stay the way they are, they'd get better, because we would have to start making them what they ought to be right now—places where children would *want* to be. In the third place, those children who did not want to go to school could find, particularly if we stirred up our brains and gave them a little help, other things to do — the things many children now do during their summers and holidays.

10   There's something easier we could do. We need to get kids out of the school buildings, give them a chance to learn about the world at first hand. It is a very recent idea, and a crazy one, that the way to teach our young people about the world they live in is to take them out of it and shut them up in brick boxes. Fortunately, educators are beginning to realize this. In Philadelphia and Portland, Oreg., to pick only two places I happen to have heard about, plans are being drawn up for public schools that won't have any school buildings at all, that will take the students out into the city and help them to use it and its people as a learning resource. In other words, students, perhaps in groups, perhaps independently, will go to libraries, museums, exhibits, courtrooms, legislatures, radio and TV stations, meetings, businesses and laboratories to learn about their world and society at first hand. A small private school in Washington is already doing this. It makes sense. We need more of it.

11   As we help children get out into the world, to do their learning there, we can get more of the world into the schools. Aside from their parents, most children never have any close contact with any adults except people whose sole business is children. No wonder they have no idea what adult life or work

is like. We need to bring a lot more people who are *not* full-time teachers into the schools, and into contact with the children. In New York City, under the Teachers and Writers Collaborative, real writers, working writers — novelists, poets, playwrights — come into the schools, read their work, and talk to the children about the problems of their craft. The children eat it up. In another school I know of, a practicing attorney from a nearby city comes in every month or so and talks to several classes about the law. Not the law as it is in books but as he sees it and encounters it in his cases, his problems, his work. And the children love it. It is real, grown-up, true, not *My Weekly Reader,* not "social studies," not lies and baloney.

12   Something easier yet. Let children work together, help each other, learn from each other and each other's mistakes. We now know, from the experience of many schools, both rich-suburban and poor-city, that children are often the best teachers of other children. What is more important, we know that when a fifth- or sixth-grader who has been having trouble with reading starts helping a first-grader, his own reading sharply improves. A number of schools are beginning to use what some call Paired Learning. This means that you let children form partnerships with other children, do their work, even including their tests, together, and share whatever marks or results this work gets — just like grownups in the real world. It seems to work.

13   Let the children learn to judge their own work. A child learning to talk does not learn by being corrected all the time — if corrected too much, he will stop talking. *He* compares, a thousand times a day, the difference between language as he uses it and as those around him use it. Bit by bit, he makes the necessary changes to make his language like other people's. In the same way, kids learning to do all the other things they learn without adult teachers — to walk, run, climb, whistle, ride a bike, skate, play games, jump rope — compare their own performance with what more skilled people do, and slowly make the needed changes. But in school we never give a child a chance to detect his mistakes, let alone correct them. We do it all for him. We act as if we thought he would never notice a mistake unless it was pointed out to him, or correct it unless he was made to. Soon he becomes dependent on the expert. We should let him do it himself. Let him figure out, with the help of other children if he wants it, what this word says, what is the answer to that problem, whether this is a good way of saying or doing this or that. If right answers are involved, as in some math or science, give him the answer book, let him correct his own papers. Why should we teachers waste time on such donkey work? Our job should be to help the kid when he tells us that he can't find a way to get the right answer. Let's get rid of all this nonsense of grades, exams, marks. We don't know now, and we never will know, how to measure what another person knows or understands. We certainly can't find out by asking him questions. All we find out is what he doesn't know — which is what most tests are for, anyway. Throw it all out, and let the child learn what every educated person must someday learn, how to measure his own understanding, how to know what he knows or does not know.

14   We could also abolish the fixed, required curriculum. People remember

only what is interesting and useful to them, what helps them make sense of the world, or helps them get along in it. All else they quickly forget, if they ever learn it at all. The idea of a "body of knowledge," to be picked up in school and used for the rest of one's life, is nonsense in a world as complicated and rapidly changing as ours. Anyway, the most important questions and problems of our time are not *in* the curriculum, not even in the hotshot universities, let alone the schools.

15   Children want, more than they want anything else, and even after years of miseducation, to make sense of the world, themselves, and other human beings. Let them get at this job, with our help if they ask for it, in the way that makes most sense to them.

Reading Sources: "School Is Bad for Children"

Read the selection, surveying it to identify key terms and important concepts. Highlight these phrases and ideas, and then answer these questions.

1. What is Holt's thesis? Where does he state it?
2. Why does Holt spend the first seven paragraphs of his essay criticizing schools? What does he hope to accomplish with this strategy?
3. What is the function of paragraph 7?
4. What is the topic sentence of paragraph 8? How does it help readers follow the progression of Holt's ideas?
5. What things does Holt suggest could be done to improve schools? At what points does Holt anticipate objections from his audience? How does he refute them?
6. How effective is Holt's conclusion? What points does he choose to emphasize?

Reacting to Sources

Reread the selection carefully, making marginal notes to aid your comprehension and to reinforce connections. Then further annotate the selection if you need to do so in order to answer any of these questions. (You may already have addressed some of the questions in your marginal notes.)

1. In a few sentences, rewrite paragraph 1 to simplify its ideas.
2. Provide brief marginal definitions of these words as they are used in the selection: *resourceful* (1), *competence* (4), *responsiveness* (6), *resource* (10), *miseducation* (15).
3. In the first half of his essay, Holt criticizes the schools. What does he do in the second half? Mark the point at which he signals transition from one section of the essay to the other.
4. Do you agree or disagree with the following statement: "We should abolish compulsory school attendance. At the very least we should modify it, perhaps

by giving children every year a large number of authorized absences" (8). Write a brief marginal comment in which you explain why.

5. Write three brief marginal questions in response to the ideas in paragraph 4.
6. Give two examples to support Holt's general statement, "As we help children get out into the world, to do their learning there, we can get more of the world into the schools" (11).
7. Using examples from your own experience, write a journal entry that supports or contradicts the ideas Holt expresses in paragraph 3.
8. Reread the introduction to the selection. Comment on how the author's life and other writings might have influenced his purpose. Comment on how they influence your acceptance of his ideas.
9. In a journal entry, briefly define what Holt means by *education*.
10. In a journal entry, compare Holt's thesis in this essay with Whitehead's in "The Aims of Education" (pp. 287–291).
11. Outline the ideas in paragraphs 11 through 12.

Working with Sources

1. Write a one-sentence summary of paragraph 7.
2. Write a critique of the ideas in paragraphs 8 and 9.
3. Write a journal entry in which you explore your reactions to these quotations from "School Is Bad for Children."

> "It is a rare child who can come through his schooling with much left of his curiosity, his independence or his sense of his own dignity, competence and worth" (7).

> "Children want, more than they want anything else, and even after years of miseducation, to make sense of the world, themselves, and other human beings" (15).

Be sure to integrate the quotations smoothly into your writing.
4. Paraphrase paragraph 13.
5. Write a synthesis that blends the ideas in paragraph 11 of this essay with the ideas in paragraph 4 of "The Aims of Education" (pp. 287–291).

Writing with Sources: Using a Single Source

Integrating information from "School Is Bad for Children" with your own ideas, write an essay on one of these topics. Be sure to acknowledge all ideas that are not your own.

1. Explain why you agree or disagree with Holt's statement, "You might say that school is a long lesson in how to turn yourself off . . ." (6). Use material from the essay as well as your own experience to support your points.

2. Examine the value of the schools you have attended. As Holt does, define the problems of the schools in the first half of your essay, and present the things that could be done to improve the situation in the second half.
3. Argue against Holt's proposal to abolish compulsory school attendance. Be sure to identify the main points that he makes and to counter them with arguments of your own. Feel free to support your points with material from your experience and reading.

With All Deliberate Speed

William Manchester

Born in 1922 and educated at the University of Massachusetts, Dartmouth College, and the University of Missouri, William Manchester is currently adjunct professor of history at Wesleyan University. He has worked as a newspaper reporter, a foreign correspondent, and a war correspondent and has won numerous awards for his nonfiction writing. His published books include *Disturber of the Peace* (1951), *The City of Anger* (1953), *Shadow of the Monsoon* (1956), *Beard the Lion* (1958), *A Rockefeller Family Portrait* (1959), *The Long Gainer* (1961), *Portrait of a President* (1962), *The Death of a President* (1967), *The Arms of Krupp* (1968), *Controversy and Other Essays in Journalism* (1967), *American Caesar* (1978), *Goodbye, Darkness* (1978), and *One Brief Shining Moment* (1983). The selection that follows is from his 1974 book *The Glory and the Dream,* a political and social history of the United States between 1932 and 1972.

1   By the U.S. Supreme Court clock it was 12:52 P.M., May 17, 1954. A concealed hand parted the red velour draperies at the front of the Court's magnificent chamber, and nine men robed in black, stepping past the gleaming Ionic columns, seated themselves in the leather chairs at the long mahogany bench. Editors all over the world were awaiting what was already being called the greatest moment in the Court's history since the Dred Scott decision of 1857. Associate Justice Robert Jackson, who was convalescing from a heart attack, had left his hospital bed that morning so that the full Court, including its three southerners would be present for the occasion. In a departure from custom, newsmen had not been given advance copies of the decision. They had no inkling of which way it would go. The new Chief Justice had been on the bench only six months. At the time of his appointment lawyers had been appalled by his total lack of judicial experience, and few in Washington had been willing to predict how he would stand in this case of Brown v. Board of Education of Topeka. Earl Warren was no racist, but he had the reputation of being a staunch believer in states' rights.

2   Wire service reporters who cover Court sessions scribble bulletins in longhand at the press table, just below the bench, and send them on their way in pneumatic tubes. At 12:57 the Associated Press A wire came alive:

Chief Justice Warren today began reading the Supreme Court's decision in the public school segregation cases. The Court's ruling could not be determined immediately.

3 Delivery of an opinion by the Chief Justice meant that he sided with the majority. This was Warren's first important ruling, and for a while all that spectators could be sure of was that he was taking an unconscionable amount of time to say what the decision was. Instead of delivering a brisk text he was meandering, stopping to cite such psychologists and sociologists as Kenneth Clark and Gunnar Myrdal on the mental development of Negro children. At 1:12 the exasperated AP correspondent dispatched a second bulletin. Warren was clearly opposed to segregation on principle, he said, but "the Chief Justice had not read far enough in the court's opinion for newsmen to say that segregation was being struck down as unconstitutional."

4 The decision's constitutional pivot was the Fourteenth Amendment: "Nor shall any state deny to any person the equal protection of the laws . . . ," but there was no judicial precedent for this application of it. The Supreme Court had never ruled on the issue of school segregation. In 1896 it had laid down a "separate but equal" doctrine in a case involving segregation of train passengers. Since then it had found against segregated housing and railroad transportation and ordered Negro students admitted to graduate schools of six southern and border state universities. Now at 1:20 P.M. Warren came to the climax of the ruling:

> To separate [Negro children] from others of similar age and qualifications solely because of their race generates a feeling of inferiority as to their status in the community that may affect their hearts and minds in a way never to be undone . . . We conclude that in the field of public education the doctrine of "separate but equal" has no place. Separate educational facilities are inherently unequal.

5 Segregation in schools, then, was unconstitutional: against the law. And the decision was unanimous, a special triumph for the National Association for the Advancement of Colored People and its scholarly counsel, Thurgood Marshall, himself a graduate of Jim Crow schools. Acknowledging that compliance would take time, the Court said it would withhold further instructions until its fall term. Meanwhile all sides were asked to prepare arguments on when segregation should be abolished and who — a special master or the federal district courts — should establish and enforce the terms under which it would end.

6 In the white South there was gloom. No greater blow to its social structure could be imagined. In seventeen states and the District of Columbia public school segregation was required by law, and four other states permitted it. Altogether, schools with a total population of twelve million children were affected. The first reactions of the authorities responsible for them varied according to their geographical location. In Kansas and Oklahoma, border states, officials were calm; they predicted that the change would be made with little commotion, if any. In Austin Governor Allan Shivers said Texas would submit,

though he warned that full compliance might "take years." After studying the full opinion, Virginia's Governor Thomas Stanley told the press: "I shall call together . . . representatives of both state and local governments to consider the matter and work toward a plan which will be acceptable to our citizens and in keeping with the edict of the court."

7   The Deep South was more hostile. South Carolina's Governor James F. Byrnes, now seventy-five, said he was "shocked." He could scarcely claim to be surprised. In the hope of intimidating the Court, South Carolina had amended its constitution to allow for abandonment of the public school system. The question now was whether it would carry out its threat. Georgia had taken the same step, and its leaders were fiercer. Senator Richard Russell argued that racial matters were in the jurisdiction of the legislative, not the judicial, branch of government, and he accused the Warren Court, as some were already calling it, of "a flagrant abuse of judicial power." Governor Herman Talmadge delivered a diatribe: "The United States Supreme Court . . . has blatantly ignored all law and precedent . . . and lowered itself to the level of common politics . . . The people of Georgia believe in, adhere to, and will fight for their right under the U.S. and Georgia constitutions to manage their own affairs." They would, he said, "map a program to insure continued and permanent segregation of the races."

8   By autumn there was a lot of that sort of rhetoric as local candidates in southern elections fell to quarreling over who would be the greater defender of white supremacy. The Court, wary of civil disorder, set no rigid schedule for compliance. At the same time the justices let it be known that having laid down the law, they meant to see that it was enforced. Federal courts and local school districts were directed to evaluate their situations and study administrative problems. Then they were to take steps toward a "prompt and reasonable start" in carrying out the decision with "all deliberate speed" as soon as was "practicable."

9   President Eisenhower was troubled by all this. He knew there was a certain inevitability in it—that the end of European colonialism in Africa and Asia was bound to be matched in the United States by rising protests against discrimination, and that Americans were increasingly aware that the country's position of world leadership was being jeopardized by racism at home. Still, his innate conservatism distrusted sudden change. Privately he called the Warren appointment "the biggest damfool mistake I ever made." While believing in eventual integration, he argued that "if you try to go too far too fast . . . you are making a mistake." Nixon disagreed. He said that he felt strongly that "civil rights is primarily a moral rather than a legal question." But Ike remained reticent on this very delicate issue. To one of his advisers he said emphatically: "I am convinced that the Supreme Court decision set back progress in the South at least fifteen years. . . . It's all very well to talk about school integration—if you remember you may also be talking about social *dis*integration. Feelings are deep on this, especially where children are concerned. . . . We can't demand perfection in these moral questions. All we can

do is keep working toward a goal and keep it high. And the fellow who tries to tell me that you can do these things by force is just plain nuts."

10   Still, as an old soldier he knew that orders must be obeyed. The Court had interpreted the Constitution; the chief executive had to carry out its instructions. At his direction all District of Columbia schools were integrated at once. He ended segregation on all Navy bases where it was still practiced — Truman had abolished it on Army posts — and overnight, literally over one night, the COLORED and WHITE signs over drinking fountains and rest room doors disappeared from naval installations. Lois Lippman, a Boston Negro, became the first black member of the White House secretarial staff; a few months later another Negro, E. Frederic Morrow, was appointed an administrative assistant to the President. Hagerty saw to it that all these facts reached the press; no one would say that Eisenhower wasn't practicing what he expected of others.

11   Over the next several months Oklahoma, Texas, Kentucky, West Virginia, Maryland, Tennessee, Arkansas, and Delaware reported partial integration in 350 school districts. Elsewhere the picture was less encouraging. Legislatures in Virginia and the Deep South passed complex measures designed to lead to long, involved court battles and circumvent the Supreme Court's ruling. Their governors were speaking stubbornly of "state sovereignty," "nullification," and the "interposition" of state authority to balk enforcement of federal laws — antebellum expressions which had not been heard since the death of John C. Calhoun. Encouraged by the warlike stance of their leaders, southerners on the lower rungs of the social ladder were reviving the Ku Klux Klan and organizing White Citizens' Councils to resist integration. Tempers were short throughout the white South.

12   But there could be no turning back now. Blacks had tempers, too. Over a century earlier de Tocqueville had predicted that once Negroes "join the ranks of free men, they will be indignant at being deprived of almost all the rights of citizens; and being unable to become the equals of the whites, they will not be slow to show themselves their enemies." That was the alternative to substantial integration. The Court had stirred hope in Negro hearts, and it is hope, not despair, that is the fuel of social action. J. Edgar Hoover reported to the White House that the sale of small arms had increased all over the South. In some communities it was up by as much as 400 percent. The most volatile rhetoric was coming from whites, but it was also notable that throughout the winter of 1954 – 55 the Black Muslims, with their gospel of inverted racism and retaliatory violence, were expanding rapidly.

13   Americans found, to their consternation, that they were rapidly moving into an era of racial incidents. Given the deeply held convictions at either end of the spectrum, such episodes were unavoidable. Militant whites vowed to defend the racial status quo, which the NAACP and the new Negro organizations springing up around it were bound to challenge. As often as not the officials in the middle simply came apart. With Thurgood Marshall as her adviser a twenty-six-year-old black woman, Autherine Lucy, announced her intention to enroll at

the University of Alabama. The university trustees were distraught. After three days of unruly crowds at Tuscaloosa, during which her car was stoned and pelted with rocks, Miss Lucy reached the registrar's office, only to be handed this telegram from the trustees: FOR YOUR SAFETY AND THE SAFETY OF THE STUDENTS AND FACULTY MEMBERS OF THE UNIVERSITY, YOU ARE HEREBY SUSPENDED FROM CLASSES UNTIL FURTHER NOTICE. Marshall led her to a court, which lifted the suspension. The trustees then met that night, accused Miss Lucy of making "false, defamatory, impertinent, and scandalous charges" against the university authorities — and ordered her permanent expulsion.

14   Frustration ran high on both sides in such episodes. With the power of the federal courts behind her, Autherine Lucy was bound to win in the end, and the trustees knew it. Only a bullet could stop her — a haunting possibility. Not only were guns and gunmen all around; it was possible, and indeed in some cases probable, that such a killer would go free. The same Constitution which required desegregation entitled a defendant to trial before a jury of his peers. His peers, in large areas of the South, were likely to acquit him. This happened. The first such incident occurred in Greenwood, Mississippi, in August 1955. Emmett Till, a fourteen-year-old black youth from Chicago, was visiting relatives there. Rumor spread that he had insulted a white woman, and three white men dragged him from his relatives' home and drowned him. Witnesses identified two of the three killers to federal agents, but an all-white jury acquitted them. The two — they were half-brothers — were then charged with kidnapping by a U.S. attorney, but a grand jury refused to indict them, and the FBI, which had painstakingly assembled irrefutable evidence, reluctantly closed its file.

15   By the first anniversary of the Supreme Court decision, racism lay like an ugly blight across much of the South. Rabble-rousers stirred up mobs which frightened, and sometimes attacked, blacks insisting on their constitutional rights. The cruelest incidents were in the grade schools, where children, most of them too small to understand the savage struggle being waged over them, were subjected to intimidation and outright terror. The return to school each September is a familiar American ritual. Mothers dress youngsters in new clothes, brush their hair, give them pencil cases, and send them off to their new classrooms. It is at precisely this time that boards of education introduce whatever changes in regulations there are to be — such as desegregation. Beginning the year after the Supreme Court decision and extending to the end of the 1950s, American front pages each fall carried accounts of ghastly demonstrations in front of bewildered pupils. Sometimes there was violence.

16   Two representative incidents erupted almost simultaneously in one week of 1956. In Clinton, Tennessee, mob hysteria was whipped up by John Kasper, a racist zealot from Washington, D.C. (He saw no irony in his charge that desegregation was the work of "outside agitators.") Until Kasper arrived, Clinton had been a quiet backwater town of four thousand people, where twelve black students were preparing to enroll in the local high school. Goaded by him, a thousand Clinton citizens disrupted the school, blocked traffic, battered the cars of Negroes who happened to be passing through, and then threw

themselves on the eight-man Clinton police force shouting, "Let's get the nigger lovers! Let's get their guns and kill them!" After a night of fear 100 state troopers, 633 National Guardsmen, and seven M-41 tanks put down what looked like an incipient revolution. That was a lot of law enforcement for one township, but the country was learning how vulnerable to hotheads schools were. Mansfield, Texas, with a population of 1,450, was even smaller than Clinton. There a federal district court had ordered the integration of three blacks with three hundred white high school students. On registration day four hundred men barged into the school waving placards that read DEAD COONS ARE THE BEST COONS and $2 A DOZEN FOR NIGGER EARS. The three Negro students quickly withdrew. A fourteen-year-old white girl told a reporter: "If God wanted us to go to school together He wouldn't have made them black and us white."

17   It was easy for Americans outside the South to be scornful of it, but it wasn't necessarily fair. The fact that racist vigilantes could disrupt the peace did not make them a majority. In the aftermath of the Clinton disorders the town looked like a stronghold of bigotry. Kasper, arrested on charges of instigating a riot, was freed. In a current election campaign the White Citizens' Council there nominated its own candidate for mayor. Bumper stickers urging his election seemed to be everywhere. In the school students wearing Confederate flags sewn on their sweaters stoned black boys, shouted "Nigger bitches" and "Dirty nigger whores" at black girls, and poured ink over the blacks' books. On the morning of election day a white minister attempting to escort the Negro children past a mob outside the school was badly beaten; so were two people who tried to come to his assistance. The principal expelled a thirteen-year-old white boy for assaulting a black girl and then, after he himself had been threatened, announced that the school was being closed "because of lawlessness and disorder." At that point, just as Clinton seemed lost to decency, the tide shifted. On orders from Attorney General Brownell, the FBI arrested sixteen of the mob's ringleaders. Fifty white high school students, led by the seventeen-year-old football captain, asked people to comply "with the federal court order to provide an education for all the citizens of Anderson County who desire it." Then came a surprise, even to those who thought they knew the town well. The polls closed, the votes were counted—and every segregationist candidate for local office was defeated by a margin of nearly three to one.

18   That year a new phrase was on the lips of public speakers: "the winds of change." The expression came out of Morocco, where French troops transferred from Vietnam were fighting another losing battle against anticolonialists, but it also seemed applicable to the United States. The Warren Court in particular appeared to be a storm center for winds of change. In time its reinterpretations of the Constitution would bar prayer from classrooms, expand defendants' rights to counsel (notably in Miranda v. Arizona), extend freedom of speech and freedom of the press to moviemakers, strike the bonds of censorship from pornographers, and lay down guidelines for legislative apportionment in the states.

19   Diehard conservatives dug in. IMPEACH EARL WARREN billboards went up all over the South. The Chief Justice had become the most controversial figure in the government since Franklin Roosevelt; all turmoil and racial tensions were laid at his door. Yet the Supreme Court was but one of many federal institutions which were acting to alter the system. Congress was fashioning the first of what would eventually be five civil rights acts. The Civil Service Commission was speeding up the advancement of black workers, and federal regulatory agencies were taking a sudden interest in charges of discrimination. One of them, the Interstate Commerce Commission, was weighing a proposal to forbid the interstate segregation of travelers on trains, buses, and in waiting rooms when a black seamstress in Montgomery, Alabama, anticipated it.

Reading Sources: *"With All Deliberate Speed"*

Read the selection, surveying it to identify key terms and important concepts. Highlight these phrases and ideas, and then answer these questions.

1. This selection is a section of a chapter in a book that gives an overview of American history between 1932 and 1972. The selection focuses on the 1954 Supreme Court decision that ruled school segregation unconstitutional. Does it have a thesis? If so, where is it? If not, why not?
2. What are the selection's key terms? How are they emphasized?
3. What techniques does Manchester use to link the sentences in paragraph 9? How do these techniques help readers to follow the paragraph's ideas?
4. Manchester opens the selection with a long, dramatic introduction and delays revealing the court's decision until the end of paragraph 4. Is this opening strategy effective in terms of his essay's content and purpose? Explain.
5. What is Manchester's attitude toward the white southerners who resisted integration? How can you tell? Identify words, phrases, and sentences that reveal his bias.

Reacting to Sources

Reread the selection carefully, making marginal notes to aid comprehension and reinforce connections. Then further annotate the selection if you need to do so in order to answer any of these questions. (You may already have addressed some of the questions in your marginal notes.)

1. Using a dictionary if necessary, supply brief marginal definitions of these words as they are used in this selection: *Ionic* (1), *inkling* (1), *staunch* (1), *pneumatic tubes* (2), *unconscionable* (3), *exasperated* (3), *pivot* (4), *precedent* (4), *compliance* (5), *edict* (6), *flagrant* (7), *diatribe* (7), *blatantly* (7), *rhetoric* (8), *wary* (8), *reticent* (9), *circumvent* (11), *nullification* (11), *antebellum* (11), *volatile* (12), *consternation* (13), *defamatory* (13), *irrefut-*

able (14), *zealot* (16), *irony* (16), *goaded* (16), *incipient* (16), *vigilantes* (17).

2. Using an encyclopedia if necessary, identify each of the following in a marginal note: the Dred Scott decision of 1857 (1), states' rights (1), Kenneth Clark (3), Gunnar Myrdal (3), National Association for the Advancement of Colored People (5), Jim Crow (5), white supremacy (8), (James) Hagerty (10), John C. Calhoun (11), White Citizens' Council (11), de Tocqueville (12), J. Edgar Hoover (12), Black Muslims (12).

3. In his conclusion, Manchester mentions a "black seamstress in Montgomery, Alabama." Later in his book he identifies her as Rosa Parks. Use an encyclopedia or another reference book if necessary to learn why this woman was an important figure in the civil rights movement.

4. Do you agree or disagree with Manchester's statement that ". . . it is hope, not despair, that is the fuel of social action" (12)? Explain your position in a journal entry.

5. In a journal entry, explore the wider implications of Manchester's statement about Autherine Lucy in paragraph 14: "Only a bullet could stop her—a haunting possibility."

6. In a marginal note, summarize President Eisenhower's position on the Supreme Court decision (9).

7. Give two examples from the essay to support Manchester's general statement, "It was easy for Americans outside the South to be scornful of it, but it wasn't necessarily fair" (17).

8. Write three questions to clarify your understanding of the ideas in paragraph 17.

9. Write a journal entry in which you explore the ideas in paragraph 15. If you have personal knowledge or experiences that are pertinent to these ideas, consider how they are related.

10. In a journal entry, contrast the content and tone of the Court's language (paragraphs 2, 4, 8) with the language used by politicians in the Deep South (7). What do you conclude about Manchester's purpose in quoting such language?

11. In a marginal note, explain the significance of the Emmett Till incident (14).

12. In a marginal note, explain Manchester's purpose in quoting the young girl in the last sentence of paragraph 16.

Working with Sources

1. Write a brief summary of paragraph 11.
2. Write a critique of the ideas in paragraph 12.
3. Write a journal entry in which you explore your reactions to these quotations from "With All Deliberate Speed."

> "In the white South there was gloom. No greater blow to its social structure could be imagined" (6).

"But there could be no turning back now" (12).

"The Warren Court in particular appeared to be a storm center for winds of change" (18).

Be sure to integrate the quotations smoothly into your writing.
4. Paraphrase the climax of the Supreme Court ruling quoted by Manchester in paragraph 4.
5. Write a one-paragraph synthesis that blends ideas in paragraph 14 of "With All Deliberate Speed" with paragraph 31 of "The Price We Pay" (pp. 316–323).

Writing with Sources: Using a Single Source

Integrating information from "With All Deliberate Speed" with your own ideas, write an essay on one of these topics. Be sure to acknowledge ideas that are not your own.

1. Classify the different responses to the Court's decision—for instance, the responses of Eisenhower, elected officials in border states, politicians in the Deep South, ordinary white citizens—discussed in Manchester's essay. What does this wide range of positions reveal?
2. In paragraph 15 Manchester says that in the years immediately following the Supreme Court decision, "American front pages each fall carried accounts of ghastly demonstrations in front of bewildered pupils." Locate four such accounts as they occurred in one newspaper in September of 1957, 1958, 1959, and 1960. Then, write an essay in which you analyze any changes in the nature of the "ghastly demonstrations" or in the way they were reported.
3. Examine the full text of the fourteenth amendment to the Constitution. Write a persuasive essay in which you argue that the language of this amendment clearly makes segregation unconstitutional. Use examples from Manchester's essay to support your position against "separate but equal" educational systems.

Bilingualism, Pro: The Key to Basic Skills

Angelo Gonzalez

Bilingualism, Con: Outdated and Unrealistic

Richard Rodriguez

Angelo Gonzalez is the educational director of ASPIRA of New York, Inc., a Hispanic advocacy and civic organization. Richard Rodriguez, the son of Mexican immigrants, holds a Ph.D. in English Renaissance literature and is a lecturer, educational consultant, and writer. Rodriguez caused considerable controversy with his autobiography, *Hunger of Memory* (1982), in which he argues against affirmative action and bilingual education. Both essays originally appeared together in the *New York Times* and responded to the question of whether bilingual education programs should be continued in the public schools. The Gonzalez article is first.

Pro:

1 If we accept that a child cannot learn unless taught through the language he speaks and understands; that a child who does not speak or understand English must fall behind when English is the dominant medium of instruction; that one needs to learn English so as to be able to participate in an English-speaking society; that self-esteem and motivation are necessary for effective learning; that rejection of a child's native language and culture is detrimental to the learning process; then any necessary effective educational program for limited or no English-speaking ability must incorporate the following:

2 Language arts and comprehensive reading programs taught in the child's native language.

3 Curriculum content areas taught in the native language to further comprehension and academic achievement.

4 Intensive instruction in English.

5 Use of materials sensitive to and reflecting the culture of children within the program.

Most Important Goal

6 The mastery of basic reading skills is the most important goal in primary education since reading is the basis for much of all subsequent learning. Ordinarily, these skills are learned at home. But where beginning reading is taught in English, only the English-speaking child profits from these early acquired skills that are prerequisites to successful reading development. Reading programs taught in English to children with Spanish as a first language waste their acquired linguistic attributes and also impede learning by forcing them to absorb skills of reading simultaneously with a new language.

7   Both local and national research data provide ample evidence for the efficacy of well-implemented programs. The New York City Board of Education Report on Bilingual Pupil Services for 1982–83 indicated that in all areas of the curriculum—English, Spanish and mathematics—and at all grade levels, students demonstrated statistically significant gains in tests of reading in English and Spanish and in math. In all but two of the programs reviewed, the attendance rates of students in the program, ranging from 86 to 94 percent, were higher than those of the general school population. Similar higher attendance rates were found among students in high school bilingual programs.

8   At Yale University, Kenji Hakuta, a linguist, reported recently on a study of working-class Hispanic students in the New Haven bilingual program. He found that children who were the most bilingual, that is, who developed English without the loss of Spanish, were brighter in both verbal and nonverbal tests. Over time, there was an increasing correlation between English and Spanish—a finding that clearly contradicts the charge that teaching in the home language is detrimental to English. Rather the two languages are interdependent within the bilingual child, reinforcing each other.

Essential Contribution

9 As Jim Cummins of the Ontario Institute for Studies in Education has argued, the use and development of the native language makes an essential contribution to the development of minority children's subject-matter knowledge and academic learning potential. In fact, at least three national data bases — the National Assessment of Educational Progress, National Center for Educational Statistics-High School and Beyond Studies, and the Survey of Income and Education — suggest that there are long-term positive effects among high school students who have participated in bilingual-education programs. These students are achieving higher scores on tests of verbal and mathematics skills.

10   These and similar findings buttress the argument stated persuasively in the recent joint recommendation of the Academy for Educational Development and the Hazen Foundation, namely, that America needs to become a more multilingual nation and children who speak a non-English language are a national resource to be nurtured in school.

11   Unfortunately, the present Administration's educational policies would seem to be leading us in the opposite direction. Under the guise of protecting the common language of public life in the United States, William J. Bennett, the Secretary of Education, unleashed a frontal attack on bilingual education. In a major policy address, he engaged in rhetorical distortions about the nature and effectiveness of bilingual programs, pointing only to unnamed negative research findings to justify the Administration's retrenchment efforts.

12   Arguing for the need to give local school districts greater flexibility in determining appropriate methodologies in serving limited-English-proficient students, Mr. Bennett fails to realize that, in fact, districts serving large numbers of language-minority students, as is the case in New York City, do have that flexibility. Left to their own devices in implementing legal mandates, many

school districts have performed poorly at providing services to all entitled language-minority students.

A Harsh Reality

13 The harsh reality in New York City for language-minority students was documented comprehensively last month by the Educational Priorities Panel. The panel's findings revealed that of the 113,831 students identified as being limited in English proficiency, as many as 44,000 entitled students are not receiving any bilingual services. The issue at hand is, therefore, not one of choice but rather violation of the rights of almost 40 percent of language-minority children to equal educational opportunity. In light of these findings the Reagan Administration's recent statements only serve to exacerbate existing inequities in the American educational system for linguistic-minority children. Rather than adding fuel to a misguided debate, the Administration would serve these children best by insuring the full funding of the 1984 Bilingual Education Reauthorization Act as passed by the Congress.

Con:

1 How shall we teach the dark-eyed child *ingles?* The debate continues much as it did two decades ago.

2 Bilingual education belongs to the 1960's, the years of the black civil rights movement. Bilingual education became the official Hispanic demand; as a symbol, the English-only classroom was intended to be analogous to the segregated lunch counter, the locked school door. Bilingual education was endorsed by judges and, of course, by politicans well before anyone knew the answer to the question: Does bilingual education work?

3 Who knows? *¿Quien sabe?*

4 The official drone over bilingual education is conducted by educationists with numbers and charts. Because bilingual education was never simply a matter of pedagogy, it is too much to expect educators to resolve the matter. Proclamations concerning bilingual education are weighted at bottom with Hispanic political grievances and, too, with middle-class romanticism.

5 No one will say it in public; in private, Hispanics argue with me about bilingual education and every time it comes down to memory. Everyone remembers going to that grammar school where students were slapped for speaking Spanish. Childhood memory is offered as parable; the memory is meant to compress the gringo's long history of offenses against Spanish, Hispanic culture, Hispanics.

6 It is no coincidence that, although all of America's ethnic groups are implicated in the policy of bilingual education, Hispanics, particularly Mexican-Americans, have been its chief advocates. The English words used by Hispanics in support of bilingual education are words such as "dignity," "heritage," "culture." Bilingualism becomes a way of exacting from gringos a

grudging admission of contrition — for the 19th-century theft of the Southwest, the relegation of Spanish to a foreign tongue, the injustice of history. At the extreme, Hispanic bilingual enthusiasts demand that public schools "maintain" a student's sense of separateness.

7   Hispanics may be among the last groups of Americans who still believe in the 1960's. Bilingual-education proposals still serve the romance of that decade, especially of the late 60's, when the heroic black civil rights movement grew paradoxically wedded to its opposite — the ethnic revival movement. Integration and separatism merged into twin, possible goals.

8   With integration, the black movement inspired middle-class Americans to imitations — the Hispanic movement; the Gray Panthers; feminism; gay rights. Then there was withdrawal, with black glamour leading a romantic retreat from the anonymous crowd.

9   Americans came to want it both ways. They wanted in and they wanted out. Hispanics took to celebrating their diversity, joined other Americans in dancing rings around the melting pot.

Mythic Metaphors

10   More intently than most, Hispanics wanted the romance of their dual cultural allegiance backed up by law. Bilingualism became proof that one could have it both ways, could be a full member of public America and yet also separate, a private Hispanic. "Spanish" and "English" became mythic metaphors, like country and city, describing separate islands of private and public life.

11   Ballots, billboards, and, of course, classrooms in Spanish. For nearly two decades now, middle-class Hispanics have had it their way. They have foisted a neat ideological scheme on working-class children. What they want to believe about themselves, they wait for the children to prove: that it is possible to be two, that one can assume the public language (the public life) of America, even while remaining what one was, existentially separate.

12   Adulthood is not so neatly balanced. The tension between public and private life is intrinsic to adulthood — certainly middle-class adulthood. Usually the city wins because the city pays. We are mass people for more of the day than we are with our intimates. No Congressional mandate or Supreme Court decision can diminish the loss.

13   I was talking the other day to a carpenter from Riga, in the Soviet Republic of Latvia. He has been here six years. He told me of his having to force himself to relinquish the "luxury" of reading books in Russian or Latvian so he could begin to read books in English. And the books he was able to read in English were not of a complexity to satisfy him. But he was not going back to Riga.

14   Beyond any question of pedagogy there is the simple fact that a language gets learned as it gets used. It fills one's mouth, one's mind, with the new names for things.

15   The civil rights movement of the 1960's taught Americans to deal with forms of discrimination other than economic — racial, sexual. We forget class. We talk about bilingual education as an ethnic issue; we forget to notice that

the program mainly touches the lives of working-class immigrant children. Foreign-language acquisition is one thing for the upper-class child in a convent school learning to curtsy. Language acquisition can only seem a loss for the ghetto child, for the new language is psychologically awesome, being, as it is, the language of the bus driver and Papa's employer. The child's difficulty will turn out to be psychological more than linguistic because what he gives up are symbols of home.

Pain and Guilt

16 I was that child! I faced the stranger's English with pain and guilt and fear. Baptized to English in school, at first I felt myself drowning — the ugly sounds forced down my throat — until slowly, slowly (held in the tender grip of my teachers), suddenly the conviction took: English was my language to use.

17 What I yearn for is some candor from those who speak about bilingual education. Which of its supporters dares speak of the price a child pays — the price of adulthood — to make the journey from a working-class home into a middle-class schoolroom? The real story, the silent story of the immigrant child's journey is one of embarrassments in public; betrayal of all that is private; silence at home; and at school the hand tentatively raised.

18 Bilingual enthusiasts bespeak an easier world. They seek a linguistic solution to a social dilemma. They seem to want to believe that there is an easy way for the child to balance private and public, in order to believe that there is some easy way for themselves.

19 Ten years ago, I started writing about the ideological implications of bilingual education. Ten years from now some newspaper may well invite me to contribute another Sunday supplement essay on the subject. The debate is going to continue. The bilingual establishment is now inside the door. Jobs are at stake. Politicians can only count heads; growing numbers of Hispanics will insure the compliance of politicians.

20 Publicly, we will continue the fiction. We will solemnly address this issue as an educational question, a matter of pedagogy. But privately, Hispanics will still seek from bilingual education an admission from the gringo that Spanish has value and presence. Hispanics of middle class will continue to seek the romantic assurance of separateness. Experts will argue. Dark-eyed children will sit in the classroom. Mute.

Reading Sources: "Bilingualism, Pro: The Key to Basic Skills"; "Bilingualism, Con: Outdated and Unrealistic"

Read each selection, surveying it to identify key terms and important concepts. Highlight these phrases and ideas, and then answer these questions.

1. At what point does each author state his thesis? Would another placement have been better? Explain.
2. How do the headings and paragraphing of both essays help readers follow the progression of the authors' ideas?
3. How do both authors use questions to emphasize and link ideas in their essays?
4. What kind of evidence does Gonzalez use to support his points? How does Rodriguez support his assertions? Why does each writer choose that particular strategy?
5. Compare the conclusions of both selections. What points does each author choose to emphasize? Which conclusion do you feel is most effective? Explain.

Reacting to Sources

Reread the selections carefully, making marginal notes to aid your comprehension and to reinforce connections. Then further annotate each selection if you need to do so in order to answer any of these questions. (You may already have addressed some of the questions in your marginal notes.)

1. Compare the introductions of each selection. Make marginal notes in which you explain why each author chose the strategy he did.
2. Provide brief marginal definitions of the following words from the Gonzalez selection: *medium* (1), *detrimental* (1), *linguistic* (6), *impede* (6), *buttress* (10), *rhetorical* (11), *exacerbate* (13); and from the Rodriguez essay: *analogous* (2), *drone* (4), *gringo* (5), *contrition* (6), *relegation* (6), *paradoxically* (7), *metaphor* (10), *pedagogy* (14), *ideological* (19).
3. Define the term *mythic metaphor* that Rodriguez uses in paragraph 10 of his essay.
4. Write a journal entry in which you explain whether the authors' arguments are addressed mainly to an audience of Hispanics or non-Hispanics.
5. Write brief marginal notes agreeing or disagreeing with each of the following statements:

   "Reading programs taught in English to children with Spanish as a first language waste their acquired linguistic attributes and also impede learning by forcing them to absorb skills of reading simultaneously with a new language" (Gonzalez, 6).

   "Proclamations concerning bilingual education are weighted at bottom with Hispanic political grievances and, too, with middle-class romanticism" (Rodriguez, 4).

6. Make a journal entry in which you discuss which author makes a more effective argument. Which essay would be easier for you to counter? Explain.
7. In paragraph 12, Gonzalez attempts to refute an argument made against bilingual education. Write a journal entry in which you evaluate the effectiveness of Gonzalez's refutation.

8. Write three brief marginal questions in response to the ideas in paragraph 5 of Rodriguez's essay.
9. What is Rodriguez's purpose in paragraphs 16 – 19? Make a marginal note in which you explain your reactions to this section of his essay.
10. In a journal entry explore the implications of Gonzalez's statement that "a child who does not speak or understand English must fall behind when English is the dominant medium of instruction" (1).
11. Write a journal entry that explains what Rodriguez means when he says, "Hispanics may be among the last group of Americans who still believe in the 1960's" (7).
12. In a journal entry compare and contrast the central idea of either of these essays with the central idea of "The Price We Pay" (pp. 316 – 323).

Working with Sources

1. Write a one-sentence summary of the main arguments of both selections.
2. Write a one-paragraph critique of each selection.
3. Write a journal entry in which you explore your reactions to these quotations from both selections:

   "Both local and national research data provide ample evidence for the efficacy of well-implemented [bilingual education] programs" (Gonzalez, 7).

   "The official drone over bilingual education is conducted by educationists with numbers and charts. Because bilingual education was never simply a matter of pedagogy, it is too much to expect educators to resolve the matter" (Rodriguez, 4).

   Be sure to integrate the quotations smoothly into your writing.
4. Paraphrase paragraph 1 of Gonzalez's selection. Paraphrase paragraph 15 of Rodriguez's selection.
5. Write a one-paragraph synthesis that blends ideas in paragraph 8 of Gonzalez's selection with the ideas in paragraph 15 of Rodriguez's selection.

Writing with Sources: Using a Single Source

Integrating information from both selections with your own ideas, write an essay on one of these topics. Be sure to acknowledge all ideas that are not your own.

1. Argue for or against bilingual education. Use your own experience as well as the material in the selections to support your point.
2. As Rodriguez points out, many groups — the elderly, gay rights activists, feminists, and various minorities — have asked that the schools teach courses that acknowledge their contributions to American culture. Argue for or against the

idea that the public schools should institute courses that are sensitive to and reflect the backgrounds of the various children within the program.

3. Some would point out that other non–English-speaking immigrant children — such as Jews, Italians, and Poles — were educated in classes where English was the primary language and that bilingual Hispanic children should be treated no differently. Explain why you agree or disagree with this statement. Use your own experience as well as the material in the selections to support your points.

The Price We Pay

Jonathan Kozol

Born in 1936, Jonathan Kozol graduated from Harvard in 1958 and spent the following year as a Rhodes scholar at Oxford. Between 1964 and 1965, Kozol was a teacher in the Boston public schools, where he was profoundly disturbed by the quality of life and the lack of educational resources available to the sutdents in his all-black school. Eventually fired by the school board, who considered him a dangerous radical (among other things, he had taught his fourth graders Langston Hughes's "Ballad of the Landlord"), Kozol was moved by his experiences to write a book. The result was *Death at an Early Age* (1967), subtitled "The Destruction of the Hearts and Minds of Negro Children in the Boston Public Schools," which won the National Book Award. Subsequent books include *Free Schools* (1972), *The Night Is Dark and I Am Far From Home* (1975), *Children of the Revolution* (1978), *Prisoners of Silence* (1980), *On Being a Teacher* (1981), and *Alternative Schools* (1983). Kozol has also been the recipient of several literary awards and fellowships and has served as an educational consultant, a newspaper correspondent, and a visiting lecturer at Yale and other universities. Between 1980 and 1983 he served on the board of directors of the National Literacy Coalition, and in 1985 he published *Illiterate America,* from which "The Price We Pay" is excerpted.

In 1975, a herd of prime beef cattle was destroyed by accident in Chicago. A feedlot worker could not read the labels on the bags that he found piled in the warehouse and fed poison to the cattle by mistake. He thought that he was adding a nutrition supplement to their feed basins . . .
— Story reported in the *New York Times*

1   What does illiteracy cost America in dollars?

2   The Senate Select Committee on Equal Educational Opportunity estimated a figure of $237 billion in unrealized lifetime earnings forfeited by men twenty-five to thirty-four years old who have less than high school level skills. That estimate, made in February 1972, requires serious updating.

3   Direct costs to business and taxpayers are approximately $20 billion.

4   Six billion dollars yearly (estimate: mid-1970s) go to child welfare costs and unemployment compensation caused directly by the numbers of illiterate adults unable to perform at standards necessary for available employment.

5    $6.6 billion yearly (estimate of 1983) is the minimal cost of prison maintenance for an estimated 260,000 inmates — out of a total state and federal prison population of about 440,000 — whose imprisonment has been directly linked to functional illiteracy. The prison population represents the single highest concentration of adult illiterates. While criminal conviction of illiterate men and women cannot be identified exclusively with inability to read and write, the fact that 60 percent of prison inmates cannot read above the grade school level surely provides some indication of one major reason for their criminal activity.

6   Swollen court costs, law-enforcement budgets in those urban areas in which two fifths of all adults are unemployable for lack of literacy skills, not even to speak of the high cost of crime to those who are its victims, cannot be guessed but must be many times the price of prison maintenance.

7   Several billion dollars go to workers' compensation, damage to industrial equipment, and industrial insurance costs directly caused by on-site accidents related to the inability of workers to read safety warnings, chemical-content designations, and instructions for the operation of complex machines.

8   While there is no way to prove direct causation in all cases, and while substantial unemployment would exist in any case among some sectors of the population — whether people were illiterate or not — it is reasonable to believe, based only on an update of the isolated items listed here, that we now incur a minimal annual loss of $20 billion in direct industrial and tax expenditures.

9   Health expenditures necessitated by the inability of the illiterate adult to use preventive health care measures are not documented. We cannot guess the vast expense required for obstetric or abortion services to women whose unwanted pregnancies are often linked to lack of information caused by inability to read. So too with the cost of mental health care and of rehabilitation programs for drug users and for alcoholics. Emotional stress and frequently uninterrupted desperation are familiar patterns in the life of an illiterate adult. If there is no way to calculate these costs, we can believe that they run into many billions.

10   Business interests suffer in at least two ways.

11   In a decade of high unemployment, hundreds of thousands of entry-level and even middle-level jobs remain unfilled for lack of applicants with competence equivalent to need. The *Wall Street Journal* documents, across the nation, "localized difficulties in finding clerical workers, bank tellers, nurses, para-legals . . ." One of the nation's largest job-referral agencies reports that it is now impossible to find the personnel to meet employment orders.

12   A New York insurance firm reports that 70 percent of its dictated correspondence must be retyped "at least once" because secretaries working from recorders do not know how to spell and punctuate correctly. Another insurance firm reports that one illiterate employee mailed out a check for $2,200 in settlement of a dental claim. Payment of $22.00 had been authorized.

13   Less easily documented, but possibly a great deal more important than the problems of the work force, is the loss of contact between business and its clientele. An incorrectly comprehended mailing from a polling agency or from

a market research firm is surely more misleading to the agency than one that is not understood at all. Marketing firms spend millions of dollars in the effort to find out what customers exist for planned or present services and products. Millions of people can't be reached. Millions more will offer useless or misleading answers.

14   Billing, banking, public disclosure information, customers' rights (above all, the right to be informed of what those "rights" might be) depend upon communication through the mails. Yet even notices of undelivered letters left in the mailbox by the postal service will be read only with difficulty by a minimum of 35 million people. They will not be read at all by 25 million more.

15   Certified mail, registered letters, items that call for signature (sometimes for payment) on receipt—all depend upon a superstructure of assumptions that can bear no relevance to millions of adult Americans. Most of us already find ourselves perplexed by complicated mailings that purport to tell us why electric service rises in expense each year, stipulate what portion of the bill is due to fuel expense, what portion represents a state or local tax, and advise us that electric power cannot be cut off to those who are "the elderly, infirm, or parents of small children." How many of those who need this information most can read it? What right has any business firm to call for payment from a customer who did not understand the prior basis of agreement? Legalities aside, the loss of any certitude that real communication has transpired represents a cost-deficient nightmare.

16   Virtually any financial item on the reader's desk—a checkbook or bank statement or a summary of salary deductions—will suggest the endless acreage of governmental and commercial chaos that underlies the seemingly efficient surface of American communication. Illiterates too frequently have no idea if the deductions from their paychecks are correct. Too often they are not. We shall see the bitterness and justified suspicion this creates among those many millions who will have no way to know if they were cheated.

17   If business does not know its clientele, neither does government know its population. We have seen already the spectacular miscalculations of the Bureau of the Census. A nation that does not know itself is no less subject to the consequences of occluded vision than the blind protagonist of classic tragedy. Oedipus tearing at his eyes, Lear in his demented eloquence upon the moors, Gloucester weeping from those "empty orbs"—these are the metaphors of cultural self-mutilation in a stumbling colossus. Eyeless at Gaza, Samson struggled to regain the power to pull down the pillars that destroyed him and his enemies together. The U.S. Bureau of the Census meanwhile sends out printed forms to ask illiterate Americans to indicate their reading levels.

18   "Know thyself" is an injunction that applies to the United States today at least as much as to the body politic or to the separate citizens of Periclean Greece. "Who am I?" This is a question that cannot be answered even in the most mechanical and trivializing sense by an illiterate democracy that governs nonetheless by a persistent faith in written words.

19   Whatever was meant by John Locke's social contract or by Rousseau's general will is rendered meaningless within a context of denied participation.

The governor does not know the governed. The census cannot total up its own demography. The candidate cannot fathom — even where he cares to ascertain — the needs or the beliefs of the electorate. The postman rings twice, leaves his little piece of incoherence in the hollow box, and those who patiently attend upon the answer will be waiting many years to understand why there is no response.

20   *"Divestiture!"*

21   I have this notification on my desk. It came in the same envelope that brings the bill each month from the phone company. "To comply with new mandated calling areas, we have asked the Department of Public Utilities (DPU) for permission to modify our optional calling plans. These modifications redefine the service areas . . . Customers affected by this change are being notified by letter of their service options . . . The FCC had ordered local companies to begin to bill you for an access charge to offset the loss of subsidy formerly provided . . . This has changed. The change will amount to $2.00 monthly on your lines . . . WHAT'S NEXT? Starting in late 1984, other elements of long-distance calling will begin to change . . . You'll be notified of all these changes well before they occur . . ."

22   *What's next?*

23   Who will be notified? Who will be affected? How? By what? By whom?

24   Many of us find it hard to navigate this jargon. Most at least can isolate the crucial words — "$2.00 monthly" — and take proper warning. Illiterates have no hope at all of calculating the expense of local service, let alone long-distance calls.

25   There is, of course, one possible alternative: Damn the rules. Tear up the bill. Call anyone you love or hate. Talk for an hour. Call collect. Call someone in Bolivia, Brazil, Vancouver, or Afghanistan. Nobody will collect the bill. Instead, you will receive another letter.

26   Newspapers are folding. Paper costs are high, but loss of literate readers is much higher. Forty-five percent of adult citizens do not read newspapers. Only 10 percent abstain by choice. The rest have been excluded by their inability to read. Even the most undistinguished daily papers are now written at an estimated tenth grade level. Magazines such as *The Nation, The New Republic, Time, Newsweek,* and *The National Review* are written at a minimum of twelfth grade level. Circulation battles represent a competition for the largest piece of a diminished pie. Enlargement of that pie does not yet seem to have occurred to those who enter these increasingly unhappy competitions. The only successful major paper to be launched in the last decade, *USA Today,* relies on a simplistic lexicon, large headlines, color photographs, and fanciful weather maps that seek to duplicate the instant entertainment of TV.

27   One might have thought that editors and writers, more than any other group in the commercial world, would have demonstrated more alacrity in learning why their clientele has been reduced. Those who live by the word, in this case, now are dying by the intellectual asphyxiation of a populace to whom the word has been denied.

28   Booksellers and publishers of books are feeling the results of mass illiteracy too. According to a spokesman for McGraw-Hill, there was a steady decline throughout the 1970s in the sale and publication of hardcover books. While certain reports suggest that book sales have increased in recent years, they also demonstrate that only the more privileged sector of the population buys them. Growth in sales is caused by greater use of books by only one third of the population. Thirty-seven percent of adults under twenty-one do not read books at all. The United States ranks twenty-fourth in the world in terms of books produced per capita.

29   The legal system flounders in its own morass of indefensible defendants, incoherent witnesses, and injudicious jurists. It was first held in 1582 in England, and subsequently respected in the United States in 1930, that "a deed executed by an illiterate person does not bind him" if its terms have not been read to him correctly. This precedent, if strictly honored in 1984, would throw the legal system into chaos.

30   More disturbing questions have to do with those who serve on juries. High levels of literacy are not demanded by the courts as a prerequisite to jury service, but those who read at only marginal levels are reduced to passive roles in the deliberation of the jury. Lawyers frequently make use of print displays to explicate the details of a complicated case. Once sequestered, juries often study written documents and, sometimes, transcripts of the testimony heard some weeks or even months before. In arduous debate, the semiliterate or illiterate juror is too readily won over by the selectivity of a persuasive reader.

31   If the high rate of convictions for illiterate defendants had not been so solidly established, none of this might represent a prejudicial aspect of the jury system. But trial by a jury of one's peers does, at the minimum, require a fair representation of poor persons. The number of illiterates among the poor and the nonwhite forces a choice that few defense attorneys would regard as any choice at all. Either they must look for jurors who are competent to judge and understand all written data but are of a different class and race than the defendant; or they must attempt to find more sympathetic jurors who may not be able to read documents which other members of the jury will interpret for them. Since interpretation is too seldom neutral, and can never be entirely neutral, the jury process cannot represent a genuine judgment by one's peers.

32   Even one of the most common forms of litigation, that which arises from contract law, is undermined by the pervasive lack of literacy skills. Contracts, according to a treatise published first in 1844, were regarded as non-binding if "an intelligent understanding of [their] terms" was not established. If this view still holds in the United States today, the problem for the courts will be enormous. An obvious example was reported recently in Tennessee. Contracts for the residents of housing projects were examined by some reading specialists and lawyers and were found to have been written well above a college level. Knowing the way most housing agencies are run, we cannot believe that anyone has read these contracts to the tenants; yet it is for breach of terms within such documents that people are evicted.

33   The social ideology of the United States and of Great Britain has been

built on contract law. If this form of law cannot survive the test of reading competence within the population, the contract system and the social edifice that it supports will be no better able to sustain themselves than any other aspect of American society described above.

34   The U.S. military pays a high price too. Thirty percent of naval recruits were recently termed "a danger to themselves and to costly naval equipment" because of inability to read and understand instructions.

35   The Navy reports that one recruit caused $250,000 in damage to delicate equipment "because he could not read a repair manual." The young recruit had tried to hide his inability to read by using common sense and following the pictures that accompanied the text. "He tried [but] failed to follow the illustrations . . . ." How many more illiterates are now responsible for lower-level but essential safety checks that are required in the handling of missiles or the operation of a nuclear reactor?

36   Some of the means used by the military to explain mechanical procedures are devastating in their banal degradation. Books resembling comics are one of the common methods of instruction. A five-page picture book is needed to explain the steps required to release and lift the hood of army vehicles. How long are the comics needed to explain the operation of those vehicles, to tell the semiliterate soldier where to drive and whom he is to rescue, kill, or capture when he gets there?

37   Illiteracy poses greater military risks than this. One that is potentially explosive is the disproportionate number of both poor and nonwhite men who are assigned the most subordinate positions and who therefore represent a disproportionate percentage of the frontline soldiers and of battle casualties in time of war. We have seen some instances of shipboard mutiny in recent years; one such instance was explicitly connected to the point established here. We can expect to see more frightening rebellions of this sort during the years ahead.

38   There are other military dangers. Many citizens will view with grave alarm the passive and noncritical status of uneducated soldiers trained at best to a mechanical efficiency in areas too tightly circumscribed to offer any vision of the moral or immoral consequences of their actions. Whether from the point of view of the most jingoistic citizen, therefore, or from that of the most ardent pacifist, the present situation holds intolerable dangers. On this, if nothing else, both left and right can certainly agree.

39   What is the cost to universities and public schools?

40   Affluent people tend to look upon illiteracy with comfortable detachment. Their sole concern is that their childen may be cheated of an opportunity for college preparation by "adulterated" courses and by "lowered" standards, both of which they have associated with the more inclusive policies of public schools and, in particular, with race desegregation. Many imagine they can isolate their children from these problems; a few by application to exclusive prep schools, the rest by tougher discipline and more remorseless tracking systems in the public schools. Sophisticated parents, on the other hand, have started to perceive that isolation of this sort is seldom possible today and that, where it still seems possible, the price that they will later pay for such short-sighted selfishness is greater than the short-term gain.

41   Excellence at the top, in short, is intimately tied to the collapse of literacy levels at the bottom. Even in the richest suburbs there are well-concealed but frequently extensive neighborhoods inhabited by poor people. Children from those neighborhoods attend the same schools as the children of the rich. More to the point, the line that separates the inner cities from the suburbs will increasingly be broken down in years ahead. Present patterns of resegregation may appease the fearful; legal actions, even if they take another decade will not leave these stark inequities unchanged. As school desegregation is more fully implemented, only the most isolated suburbs will remain exempt.

42   Tracking schemes, at present in resurgent fashion, will be recognized for what they are: archaic pedagogy and divisive social policy. Legal actions will be launched to fight the obvious denial of a child's civil rights which is inherent in the self-fulfilling prophecy of rigid track separations.

43   To state it bluntly: There will at length be no more places for all but the very privileged to hide.

44   Even for those who may contrive to isolate their kids during the years preceding college, higher academic life will be affected by the growing presence of the poorly educated and the semiliterate. Ethnic tensions consequent from this are seen already both in public institutions like the City University of New York and in private institutions such as Boston University. Even at graduate schools like Harvard Law we have seen a rapid growth of interethnic acrimony in the past five years. Nonwhite students with marginal entrance scores remain close to the bottom of the class; few are admitted to the prestigious *Law Review*. Recent policies that have facilitated their admission have been met with strong resistance from those students who have seen "their" place assumed by someone who, according to the test scores, is less qualified than they.

45   Virulent graffiti on the redbrick walls and Georgian porticoes of Harvard University remind us that the price of excellence for very few in early years of public school, if it is an excellence achieved by separation from the children of poor people, is an ethical contamination that even the most honored law school in the nation cannot manage to escape.

46   If conscience cannot turn the tide, perhaps it is the panic of self-interest which will finally do the job. Panic may not be a noble motive for redress of social wrongs, but there are sufficient grounds for panic, and perhaps the only reason that there is not more alarm among the population is the fact that most of us have never stopped to recognize the perils that surround us.

47   Imagine a familiar situation: The traveller walks into an airport lobby to obtain the ticket for a flight which has already been reserved. The well-dressed woman at the ticket desk projects a confident smile as she taps the buttons on a modern console, asks our seating preference, and hands over a computer-printed boarding pass. We never get to meet the men and women in their oil-coated overalls or jeans who do the more important work of checking out the plane we are about to board. Some of us might be alarmed if we should ever wander through the wrong door by mistake and watch the semieducated persons who attempt to figure out the charts and other manuals that instruct them in the safety details that the government requires: details most of us will never find the time to think about until it is too late.

48   Without warning, on May 5, 1983, an Eastern Airlines jumbo jet en route to Nassau from Miami, crowded with passengers enjoying their first cocktail and perusing their newspapers, dropped three miles in the sky. Three engines had gone dead. By luck one engine came to life just as the pilot had prepared the passengers to ditch. The cause of engine failure was at length discovered. Nothing was wrong with the mechanical equipment. Two members of a ground crew had neglected to insert three tiny oil seals described as "O" rings into the fuel line during the routine check that took place prior to departure. The lives of several hundred people came within three minutes of extinction. The maintenance men, it was reported, "hadn't read" the manual of instructions that the airline had prepared. Eastern Airlines never reported, and perhaps has never learned, whether the maintenance men had failed to look at the instructions or whether they had been unable to decipher them.

49   Failure to follow maintenance instructions led another man, in March of 1979, to leave unsecured the open valves that were a major reason for the near-catastrophe at Three Mile Island: a catastrophe which, had it taken place, would have spread its radiation far beyond the precincts of a single neighborhood in Pennsylvania and might have endangered lives as far away as in New Jersey and New York.

50   Neither of these two events can be identified with evidence of inability to read. Nonetheless, the presence of so many millions of unrecognized illiterates in the work force guarantees that hundreds of mistakes, with consequences we may never know, must take place daily. Many more will take place in the years ahead.

51   The Secretary of Education is correct. The nation is at risk. He very likely does not understand the nature of the risk that he describes. We are all held hostage to each other in this nation. There are no citizens, no matter how wealthy, no matter how removed they may believe themselves to be, who will not be forced to pay a formidable price. The items I have summarized above may prove to be among the least important of these costs, but these matters in themselves are great enough to mandate a dramatic, urgent, and immediate political response.

Reading Sources: "The Price We Pay"

Read the selection, surveying it to identify key terms and important concepts. Highlight these phrases and ideas, and then answer these questions.

1. What visual cues are used in this essay?
2. What does Kozol gain by introducing his essay with an excerpt from a newspaper story?
3. Statistics are used throughout the essay. What is the effect of their use on the reader?
4. A number of Kozol's paragraphs (for example, paragraphs 3, 10, 39, and 43) consist of just one brief sentence. What does the use of brief paragraphs like these add to the essay? Is the one-sentence introductory paragraph an effective opening? Explain.
5. What key terms does Kozol rely on in his essay? How does he place emphasis on these terms?
6. What is the thesis of Kozol's essay?
7. Identify the principal areas of our society in which Kozol sees illiteracy as a problem.
8. How does Kozol link paragraphs 39 and 40? Paragraphs 40 and 41?
9. What techniques does Kozol use to link the sentences in paragraph 48? Do you think more obvious transitions in this paragraph would make the narrative more interesting or easier to follow? Would the addition of such transitions have interfered with the effect Kozol wanted his example to convey? Explain.
10. Identify the boundaries of the paragraph cluster introduced by the first sentence of paragraph 29; by the first sentence of paragraph 34. In each case, what key words link the paragraphs in the cluster to one another?

Reacting to Sources

Reread the selection carefully, making marginal notes to aid comprehension and reinforce connections. Then further annotate the selection if you need to do so in order to answer any of these questions. (You may already have addressed some of the questions in your marginal notes.)

1. Using a dictionary if necessary, supply brief marginal definitions of these words as they are used in this selection: *unrealized* (2), *incur* (8), *superstructure* (15), *purport* (15), *stipulate* (15), *transpired* (15), *occluded* (17), *protagonist* (17), *colossus* (17), *injunction* (18), *demography* (19), *fathom* (19), *divestiture* (20), *mandated* (21), *subsidy,* (21), *abstain* (26), *undistinguished* (26), *lexicon* (26), *alacrity* (27), *precedent* (29), *sequestered* (30), *arduous* (30), *pervasive* (32), *breach* (32), *banal* (36), *circumscribed* (38), *jingoistic* (38), *ardent* (38), *remorseless* (40), *archaic* (42), *divisive* (42), *contrive* (44), *acrimony* (44), *virulent* (45), *redress* (46).
2. In brief marginal notes, compose topic sentences for paragraphs 30, 40, and 47.
3. Reread the headnote that introduces this essay. In a journal entry, comment on how Kozol's personal and professional life might have influenced his purpose in this essay.

4. In a journal entry, explain the literary allusions in paragraph 17. Then, explain the paragraph's main point in simplified terms.
5. In a few sentences, rewrite paragraph 18 to simplify its ideas.
6. Consulting an encyclopedia if necessary, identify John Locke's "social contract" and Rousseau's "general will" (19). Then write a marginal note explaining the point Kozol makes with these allusions.
7. In paragraph 21 Kozol presents an example of bureaucratic jargon. In a journal entry, translate the jargon into clear, simple English. Then identify the most obvious differences between the original and your translation.
8. Write a marginal note commenting on the tone and purpose of paragraph 25.
9. In paragraph 26 Kozol says, "The only successful major paper to be launched in the last decade, *USA Today,* relies on a simplistic lexicon, large headlines, color photographs, and fanciful weather maps that seek to duplicate the instant entertainment of TV." In a journal entry, use your own experience to comment on the success of *USA Today* and similar publications.
10. Write three marginal questions to clarify your understanding of the ideas in paragraph 33.
11. Reread paragraph 40. In a journal entry, explain whether you agree with those who "imagine they can isolate their children" or with the "sophisticated parents" whose views Kozol summarizes. Justify your position.
12. Kozol makes this statement: "As school desegregation is more fully implemented, only the most isolated suburbs will remain exempt" (41). Do you agree or disagree? Write a brief marginal comment in which you explain why.
13. Does Kozol have an underlying bias? How can you tell? Explain in a journal entry.

Working with Sources

1. Write a fifty-word summary of paragraphs 30 and 31.
2. Write a critique of the ideas in paragraphs 40 through 43.
3. Write a journal entry in which you explore your reactions to these quotations from "The Price We Pay."

   "What does illiteracy cost America in dollars?" (1)

   "What right has any business firm to call for payment from a customer who did not understand the prior basis of agreement?" (15)

   "We are all held hostage to each other in this nation" (51).

   Be sure to integrate the quotations smoothly into your writing.
4. Paraphrase the ideas in paragraph 18.
5. Write a one-paragraph synthesis that blends ideas in paragraphs 40 – 41 of "The Price We Pay" and paragraphs 4 – 5 of "With All Deliberate Speed" (pp. 300 – 306).

Writing with Sources: Using a Single Source

Integrating information from ''The Price We Pay'' with your own ideas, write an essay on one of these topics. Be sure to acknowledge ideas that are not your own.

1. Kozol explicitly focuses on the economic cost of illiteracy to the nation. Explore the social and emotional costs of illiteracy.
2. Consider the role of television in the life of an illiterate adult. Is its influence primarily positive or negative? Explain your view.
3. Should illiterate adults be allowed to serve on juries? Reread paragraph 31 carefully before you write your essay.

Who Cares About the Renaissance?

Leslie S. P. Brown

Leslie S. P. Brown is an Annenberg graduate fellow at the University of Pennsylvania, where she is working for a doctorate in Italian Renaissance art history. In a ''My Turn'' column in the April 11, 1983, issue of *Newsweek,* she defends her career choice and the choices of other ''young scholars of the past'' like herself.

1   Last September, with the aid of an unusually generous fellowship, I enrolled in a doctoral program in Italian Renaissance art history. Although I had selected this particular career path as a college freshman and had never seriously considered any alternatives, I experienced severe doubts as I packed my bags and prepared to re-enter the academic life after a year away. For although my return to school elicited a few wistful wishes for happiness and success, it primarily provoked a chorus of lugubrious warnings about the ''lack of relevance'' of my chosen field and the uncertainty of my professional and financial future.

2   I coped easily with the tired jokes about Ph.D.'s driving cabs from the lawyers, doctors and M.B.A.'s of my acquaintance. But when a professor who had encouraged me to apply for graduate study sat me down and described in lurid detail his 20 years of frustration and comparative poverty as an academic, I began to be disturbed. And it was something of a shock to hear him say, as he leafed through the pages of his latest book, ''I spent 10 years of my life on this thing, and what do I get? A thousand bucks and a pat on the back from a couple of colleagues. Sometimes I think it isn't worth it anymore.''

3   **Escapists:**   Not surprisingly, there aren't many of us left, we young scholars of the past. Out of a total of 25 art-history majors at the college I attended, the vast majority went to law school. In these days of frantic attempts to gain admission to the best professional schools, the decision to pursue an advanced

degree in literature, history, music or art is often viewed as a symptom of rapidly advancing lunacy — or, at least, as a sign of total disregard for the practical concerns of life. Media articles relentlessly describe the abysmal condition of the job market for Ph.D.'s in the humanities and the worry of department chairmen at universities where students are avoiding Chaucer and baroque music in favor of technical courses. Friends and family consider those of us who have chosen this course as aberrations. Some of us have been accused of being escapists, of refusing to face the constant changes of a technological society, of shutting ourselves up in ivory towers out of fear of competing with our pragmatic and computer-literate peers. In short, we hopeful scholars have had to accept the fact that we are considered anachronisms.

4   Why do we do it, then? Why have we, highly educated and raised, for the most part, by ambitious and upwardly mobile parents, turned our backs on the 20th century in order to bury our noses in dusty books and write articles that only our colleagues will read?

5   Well, in part we do it for love. Despite the gibes and jeers of our friends (and I might note that I have never once accused any of my lawyer friends of rampant materialism), we *are* realists. We are forced to be. We live in tiny, inexpensive apartments, take public transportation (or, more often, walk) and eat cheaply between long hours at the library. Many of us will be paying back huge educational loans for years and may never own a house or buy a new car. It is not a soft life, and sometimes we do complain. But usually we glory in it. We admire our contemporaries who are now making salaries that we only dream about, but we are secure in the knowledge that we have chosen to do what we love best. We have not relegated our joy in literature and art to the status of hobbies, and we can only hope that our passions will help us survive the lean years, the frustration and the occasional intellectual exhaustion.

6   Nor are we less competent or socially aware than our friends in more practical professions. Several of my teachers and classmates have verbal and analytical abilities that would make them gifted lawyers or product managers; a small contingent is making fascinating discoveries about medieval architecture by performing astounding arithmetical gymnastics — with the aid of a computer. Many of us love science — several of my most enjoyable hours have been spent with a telescope in a freezing observatory — and we pay close attention to political developments. And many of us are enthusiastic sports fans. In other words, we are not social cripples or intellectual snobs with no interests beyond our own esoteric and rarefied disciplines. We have chosen to endure the raised eyebrows and the despair of our families because we hope that, with hard work and dedication, we will never have to mourn a lost love of Botticelli or Bach while working in jobs that fail to touch our souls or feed our human hunger for beauty.

7   Not long ago, a bright 16-year-old girl — a mathematics prodigy — asked me who Michelangelo was. When I told her that he was one of the greatest artists who had ever lived, she asked me why she had never heard of him. Unfortunately, she is not alone. Universities today are wondering where they will find scholars of the humanities for new generations of students; perhaps it

will be necessary to tell future freshmen that they cannot study literature, art, music or foreign languages because there is nobody to teach them.

8 **Elegance:** So there is yet another — perhaps less selfish — reason that we persist. We are the men and women who prepare the museum exhibitions and keep the classics alive. We hold up the lessons of history before the world and try to ensure that they will not be forgotten, even if they go unlearned. We scramble for the funding and the grants — increasingly difficult to obtain these days — to save the deteriorating art works, to publish new editions and translations of the great books, to give recitals of the loveliest music. In short, we fight to maintain the pockets of warmth and elegance that provide some relief to others who are tired and harried in a sometimes sterile and technological society. I am not a particularly altruistic person, but my studies have made me deeply sensitive to the alienation and coldness of our times. While I occasionally wish that I had a time machine to deposit me in the 16th century, where I would never have to worry about a bank card or a failed transmission, I believe that I can perform a certain service here and now. My work may go largely unappreciated by many, but a few will be grateful. And that is enough.

Reading Sources: "Who Cares About the Renaissance?"

Read the selection, surveying it to identify key terms and important concepts. Highlight these phrases and ideas, and then answer these questions.

1. What visual cues are used in this selection?
2. In paragraph 3 Brown's subject shifts from "I" to "we"; in paragraph 7 she moves back to "I" again, and in the concluding paragraph she begins with "we" and ends with "I." Are these shifts confusing, or are they justified? Explain.
3. What technique does Brown use to link paragraphs 4 and 5? Is this strategy effective? Explain.
4. Which sentence in paragraph 3 is the topic sentence? Explain.
5. What is Brown's thesis?

Reacting to Sources

Reread the selection carefully, making marginal notes to aid comprehension and reinforce connections. Then further annotate the selection if you need to do so in order to answer any of these questions. (You may already have addressed some of the questions in your marginal notes.)

1. Using a dictionary if necessary, supply brief marginal definitions of these words as they are used in this selection: *elicited* (1), *lugubrious* (1), *lurid* (2),

abysmal (3), *aberrations* (3), *pragmatic* (3), *anachronisms* (3), *rampant* (5), *materialism* (5), *contingent* (6), *esoteric* (6), *rarefied* (6), *prodigy* (7), *altruistic* (8), *alienation* (8).

2. In a marginal note, explain Brown's purpose in paragraph 6. Why do you think she feels such a paragraph is necessary?

3. Do you believe that "the decision to pursue an advanced degree in literature, history, music or art" is really "a sign of total disregard for the practical concerns of life" (3)? Explain your position in a journal entry.

4. Give two examples to support this general statement of Brown's: "In short, we fight to maintain the pockets of warmth and elegance that provide some relief to others who are tired and harried in a sometimes sterile and technological society" (8).

5. In paragraph 5 Brown notes parenthetically that she has never accused her "lawyer friends of rampant materialism." Why do you think she feels she has to say this? Explain your reaction in a marginal note.

6. In paragraph 5 Brown says that she and her fellow young scholars do what they do "for love" and that they "glory in" their lives despite the sacrifices they must make. In a journal entry, explore your reaction to the attitude she expresses.

7. Is there an implied criticism in Brown's view of those who make a choice different from hers? Write a journal entry in which you explain your position.

8. Consider these statements from the selection; "we are secure in the knowledge that we have chosen to do what we love best" (5); "we hope that . . . we will never have to mourn a lost love of Botticelli or Bach while working in jobs that fail to touch our souls or feed our human hunger for beauty" (6); "We hold up the lessons of history before the world and try to ensure that they will not be forgotten, even if they go unlearned" (8). In marginal notes, try to characterize Brown's tone in these and other representative statements. Then, write a journal entry in which you analyze the essay's tone.

9. Find a statement in the essay for which your own knowledge or experience provides contradictory evidence. Write a journal entry that presents this contradiction.

10. In her conclusion Brown says that she occasionally wishes that she could live in the sixteenth century, where she would never have to worry about a bank card or a failed transmission. Find an article about the sixteenth century in an encyclopedia or a history text. Then write a journal entry in which you discuss whether Brown's view of the past as a simpler time is accurate or idealized.

Working with Sources

1. Write a fifty-word summary of paragraph 6.
2. Write a critique of the ideas in paragraph 8.
3. Write a journal entry in which you explore your reactions to these quotations from "Who Cares About the Renaissance?"

"And it was something of a shock to hear him say, as he leafed through the pages of his latest book, 'I spent 10 years of my life on this thing, and what do I get? A thousand bucks and a pat on the back from a couple of colleagues. Sometimes I think it isn't worth it anymore'" (2).

"My work may go largely unappreciated by many, but a few will be grateful. And that is enough" (8).

Be sure to integrate the quotations smoothly into your writing.

4. Paraphrase the ideas in paragraph 4.
5. Write a one-paragraph synthesis that blends ideas in paragraph 7 of "Who Cares About the Renaissance?" with paragraph 51 of "The Price We Pay" (pp. 316 – 323).

Writing with Sources: Using a Single Source

Integrating information from "Who Cares About the Renaissance?" with your own ideas, write an essay on one of these topics. Be sure to acknowledge ideas that are not your own.

1. Should we care about the Renaissance? Or should young Americans direct their time and energy to improving contemporary social conditions? Write an essay supporting your position.
2. Argue in support of your own choice of major or career. You may argue, as Brown does, that your choice is worth the economic sacrifice it may entail, or you may defend your choice as pragmatic or necessary.
3. According to Brown, most educated people have a choice between a career that nourishes "our human hunger for beauty" but keeps us in "comparative poverty" and one that keeps us economically secure but starved for beauty. Are these two choices really mutually exclusive, or is it possible to have both? Explain your opinion.

Writing with Sources: Using Multiple Sources

Integrating information from sources in this chapter with your own ideas, write an essay on one of the topics below. Be sure to acknowledge ideas that are not your own.

1. Richard Rodriguez, Jonathan Kozol, and William Manchester have all done advanced work in the humanities. All three, however, have gone on to do writing that focuses on social issues rather than "[preparing] museum exhibitions . . . [keeping] the classics alive . . . [saving] the deteriorating art works, [publishing] new editions and translations of the great books, [or giving] recitals of the loveliest music." Are they nevertheless somehow fighting to "maintain the pockets of warmth and elegance" in our increasingly technologi-

cal world, just as Leslie Brown says she and her fellow "young scholars of the past" are doing? Take a stand on this issue.

2. Reread paragraph 18 of "With All Deliberate Speed" (p. 305) and make sure you have a good understanding of the phrase "the winds of change." Then write an essay that considers how the winds of change have affected education between the time in which Whitehead wrote and today. In your essay, focus on the central issues considered by Whitehead, Holt, Rodriguez, Gonzales, and Kozol. Can you determine in what direction the winds of change are now blowing?

3. Consider the readings in this chapter and your own experiences in the educational system. What do you believe is the single most important issue facing educators today? Explain.

4. Imagine that you are writing a document in which you establish priorities for government funding for education during the next twenty years. What would the order of your priorities be? Set forth your plan.

5. All of the authors in this section have their own ideas concerning what constitutes an education. After discussing the ideas of three of the authors in this section, develop your own definition of *education*. Draw freely on your own experiences and point out how your definition is similar to or different from the authors you cite.

Religion and Society

On one level, religion is an intensely personal issue. However, its potential influence on our social and political institutions has made religion an emotionally charged topic that warrants public discussion and analysis. The essays in this chapter do not weigh the benefits of one religion against another, or consider the theoretical underpinnings of the Judeo-Christian (or any other) tradition, or explore the origins and development of religious thought. Rather, the essays explore the impact of religion on the larger world.

In the opening selection, "Kennedy's Houston Speech," then-candidate John F. Kennedy expresses his intention to keep his political decisions free from the influence of his religious beliefs, arguing that his devotion to Roman Catholicism would in no way undermine his ability to serve as President of the United States. In the next essay, "Opposing Prefab Prayer," conservative columnist George F. Will presents a novel argument against requiring prayer in the nation's public schools. In "The Cult Boom" A. James Rudin and Marcia R. Rudin define religious cults, distinguish between a cult and a religion, and explain the appeal — and the dangers — of cults to young people. In "The 'Threat' of Creationism" Isaac Asimov explores what he views as another danger: the increasing influence of creationist theology and of the religious groups that support it. In contrast, biochemist Duane Gish makes a case in favor of creationism, arguing in an excerpt from his book *Evolution: The Fossils Say No* that the fossil record provides support for the creationists' explanation of how life began. The chapter closes with "Appeal to Reason and Conscience," a 1948 statement by poet Archibald MacLeish and other prominent citizens arguing against censorship by any religious group.

Kennedy's Houston Speech

John F. Kennedy

John Fitzgerald Kennedy (1917–1963) received his undergraduate and law degrees from Harvard University. After serving in the Navy during World War II, he was elected Congressman and then Senator from Massachusetts. In 1960, he was elected President of the United States. As the first Catholic president, Kennedy faced unique problems because many feared he would allow the church to influence his political decisions. In this speech before the Greater Houston Ministerial Association on September 12, 1960, Kennedy, then a candidate for president, attempted to dispel such fears by reaffirming the principle of the separation of church and state while skillfully defending his own right to practice his religion.

1   I am grateful for your generous invitation to state my views. While the so-called religious issue is necessarily and properly the chief topic here tonight, I want to emphasize from the outset that we have far more critical issues to face in the 1960 election: The spread of Communist influence, until it now festers ninety miles off the coast of Florida — the humiliating treatment of our president and vice president by those who no longer respect our power — the hungry children I saw in West Virginia, the old people who cannot pay their doctor bills, the families forced to give up their farms — an America with too many slums, with too few schools, and too late to the moon and outer space.

2   These are the real issues which should decide this campaign. And they are not religious issues — for war and hunger and ignorance and despair know no religious barriers.

3   But because I am a Catholic, and no Catholic has ever been elected president, the real issues in this campaign have been obscured — perhaps deliberately, in some quarters less responsible than this. So it is apparently necessary for me to state once again — not what kind of church I believe in, for that should be important only to me — but what kind of America I believe in.

4   I believe in an America where the separation of church and state is absolute — where no Catholic prelate would tell the president (should he be Catholic) how to act, and no Protestant minister would tell his parishioners for whom to vote — where no church or church school is granted any public funds or political preference — and where no man is denied public office merely because his religion differs from the president who might appoint him or the people who might elect him.

5   I believe in an America that is officially neither Catholic, Protestant nor Jewish — where no public official either requests or accepts instructions on public policy from the pope, the National Council of Churches or any other ecclesiastical source — where no religious body seeks to impose its will directly or indirectly upon the general populace or the public acts of its officials — and where religious liberty is so indivisible that an act against one church is treated as an act against all.

6   For, while this year it may be a Catholic against whom the finger of

suspicion is pointed, in other years it has been, and may someday be again, a Jew — or a Quaker — or a Unitarian — or a Baptist. It was Virginia's harassment of Baptist preachers, for example, that helped lead to Jefferson's statute of religious freedom. Today I may be the victim — but tomorrow it may be you — until the whole fabric of our harmonious society is ripped at a time of great national peril.

7   Finally, I believe in an America where religious intolerance will someday end — where all men and all churches are treated as equals — where every man has the same right to attend or not attend the church of his choice — where there is no Catholic vote, no anti-Catholic vote, no bloc voting of any kind — and where Catholics, Protestants and Jews, at both the lay and pastoral level, will refrain from those attitudes of disdain and division which have so often marred their works in the past, and promote instead the American ideal of brotherhood.

8   That is the kind of America in which I believe, and it represents the kind of presidency in which I believe — a great office that must neither be humbled by making it the instrument of any one religious group, nor tarnished by arbitrarily withholding its occupancy from the members of any one religious group. I believe in a president whose religious views are his own private affair, neither imposed by him upon the nation nor imposed by the nation upon him as a condition to holding that office.

9   I would not look with favor upon a president working to subvert the First Amendment's guarantees of religious liberty. Nor would our system of checks and balances permit him to do so — and neither do I look with favor upon those who would work to subvert Article VI of the Constitution by requiring a religious test — even by indirection — for it. If they disagree with that safe-guard, they should be out openly working to repeal it.

10   I want a chief executive whose public acts are responsible to all groups and obligated to none — who can attend any ceremony, service or dinner his office may appropriately require of him — and whose fulfillment of his presi-dential oath is not limited or conditioned by any religious oath, ritual or obligation.

11   This is the kind of America I believe in — and this is the kind I fought for in the South Pacific and the kind my brother died for in Europe. No one suggested then that we might have a "divided loyalty," that we did "not believe in liberty" or that we belonged to a disloyal group that threatened the "free-doms for which our forefathers died."

12   And in fact this is the kind of America for which our forefathers died — when they fled here to escape religious test oaths that denied office to members of less favored churches — when they fought for the Constitution, the Bill of Rights, and the Virginia Statute of Religious Freedom — and when they fought at the shrine I visited today, the Alamo. For side by side with Bowie and Crockett died McCafferty and Bailey and Carey — but no one knows whether they were Catholics or not. For there was no religious test at the Alamo.

13   I ask you tonight to follow in that tradition — to judge me on the basis of

my record of fourteen years in Congress — on my declared stands against an ambassador to the Vatican, against unconstitutional aid to parochial schools, and against any boycott of the public schools (which I have attended myself) — instead of judging me on the basis of these pamphlets and publications we all have seen that carefully select quotations out of context from the statements of Catholic church leaders, usually in other countries, frequently in other centuries and rarely relevant to any situation here — and always omitting, of course, the statement of the American Bishops in 1948 which strongly endorsed church-state separation, and which more nearly reflects the views of almost every American Catholic. I do not consider these other quotations binding upon my public acts — why should you? But let me say with respect to other countries, that I am wholly opposed to the state being used by any religious group, Catholic or Protestant, to compel, prohibit or persecute the free exercise of any other religion. And I hope that you and I condemn with equal fervor those nations which deny their presidency to Protestants and those which deny it to Catholics. And rather than cite the misdeeds of those who differ, I would cite the record of the Catholic Church in such nations as Ireland and France — and the independence of such statesmen as Adenauer and De Gaulle.

14   But let me stress again that these are my views — for, contrary to common newspaper usage, I am not the Catholic candidate for president. I am the Democratic party's candidate for president, who happens also to be a Catholic. I do not speak for my church on public matters — and the church does not speak for me.

15   Whatever issue may come before me as president — on birth control, divorce, censorship, gambling, or any other subject — I will make my decision in accordance with these views, in accordance with what my conscience tells me to be the national interest, and without regard to outside religious pressures or dictates. And no power or threat of punishment could cause me to decide otherwise.

16   But if the time should ever come — and I do not concede any conflict to be even remotely possible — when my office would require me to either violate my conscience or violate the national interest, then I would resign the office; and I hope any conscientious public servant would do the same.

17   But I do not intend to apologize for these views to my critics of either Catholic or Protestant faith — nor do I intend to disavow either my views or my church in order to win this election. If I should lose on the real issues, I shall return to my seat in the Senate, satisfied that I had tried my best and was fairly judged. But if this election is decided on the basis that forty million Americans lost their chance of being president on the day they were baptized, then it is the whole nation that will be the loser, in the eyes of Catholics and non-Catholics around the world, in the eyes of history, and in the eyes of our own people.

18   But if, on the other hand, I should win the election, then I shall devote every effort of mind and spirit to fulfilling the oath of the presidency — practically identical, I might add, to the oath I have taken for fourteen years in the Congress. For, without reservation, I can "solemnly swear that I will

faithfully execute the office of president of the United States, and will to the best of my ability preserve, protect and defend the Constitution . . . so help me God."

Reading Sources: "Kennedy's Houston Speech"

Read the speech, surveying it to identify key terms and important concepts. Highlight these phrases and ideas, and then answer these questions.

1. What does Kennedy hope to accomplish in the opening sentence of his speech?
2. In paragraph 3 Kennedy announces his intention to tell his audience "what kind of America I believe in." In subsequent paragraphs he uses variations on this sequence of words to unify his speech. Identify examples of similar word groups in paragraphs 4 – 12.
3. Kennedy's audience is the Greater Houston Ministerial Association. Is there any indication that he has a wider audience in mind? Explain.
4. What effect are Kennedy's references to Jefferson (6), the First Amendment of the Constitution (9), the Bill of Rights (12), and the Alamo (12) calculated to have on his audience? Do these references accomplish the desired result?
5. Is there any indication in Kennedy's style that his remarks were written to be delivered orally? Explain.
6. Kennedy uses many parallel series of words, phrases, and clauses in his speech — for example, "where no Catholic prelate . . . where no church . . . and where no man" (4). Identify several of these series, and determine how each strengthens Kennedy's argument.
7. What is Kennedy's thesis?
8. Evaluate Kennedy's concluding strategy: Is concluding with the oath of office effective? Are there advantages — or disadvantages — to ending his speech with the words "so help me God"? Explain.

Reacting to Sources

Reread the speech carefully, making marginal notes to aid comprehension and reinforce connections. Then further annotate the speech if you need to do so in order to answer any of these questions. (You may already have addressed some of the questions in your marginal notes.)

1. Using a dictionary if necessary, supply brief marginal definitions of these words as they are used in this speech: *festers* (1), *prelate* (4), *bloc* (7), *occupancy* (8), *subvert* (9).
2. In paragraph 1 Kennedy enumerates the "real issues" of the campaign; nevertheless, he goes on in his speech to focus on the issue of his religion. What, then, is his purpose in directing his audience to the issues he cites in paragraph 1? Explain in a journal entry.

3. In paragraph 3 Kennedy says, "because I am a Catholic, . . . the real issues in this campaign have been obscured." What kind of criticism is Kennedy countering here? Explain in a journal entry.
4. In paragraph 4 Kennedy says he does not believe any church or church school should be "granted any public funds or political preference." Do you agree or disagree? Explore this idea further in a journal entry.
5. Outline the paragraph cluster extending from paragraph 4 through paragraph 7.
6. Give an example from your own experience to support Kennedy's statement in paragraph 6 that "in other years it has been, and may someday be again, a Jew — or a Quaker — or a Unitarian — or a Baptist" who falls victim to distrust and discrimination.
7. After consulting an American history textbook, make marginal notes to explain paragraph 9's references to "the First Amendment's guarantees of religious liberty," "our system of checks and balances," and "Article VI of the Constitution." Then rewrite the paragraph to simplify its ideas.
8. In paragraph 11 Kennedy reminds his audience that he fought—and that his brother died—in World War II. In a marginal note, explain why he volunteers this information here and whether he achieves the purpose he intended.
9. Formulate three questions whose answers could help expand your understanding of the ideas in paragraph 13.
10. Does your knowledge that the author of this speech became President of the United States increase his credibility in your eyes, or is it irrelevant to your evaluation of the logic of his points? Explain in a marginal note.
11. In a journal entry, consider possible connections in style and content between this speech and "I Have a Dream" (pp. 115–119).

Working with Sources

1. Write a fifty-word summary of paragraph 13.
2. Write a critique of the ideas in paragraphs 1 and 2.
3. Write a journal entry in which you explore your reactions to these quotations from "Kennedy's Houston Speech":

   "Today I may be the victim — but tomorrow it may be you — until the whole fabric of our harmonious society is ripped at a time of great national peril" (6).

   ". . . I am not the Catholic candidate for president. I am the Democratic party's candidate for president, who happens also to be a Catholic" (14).

   ". . . if this election is decided on the basis that forty million Americans lost their chance of being president on the day they were baptized, then it is the whole nation that will be the loser . . ." (17).

   Be sure to integrate the quotations smoothly into your writing.

4. Paraphrase the ideas in paragraph 7.
5. Write a one-sentence synthesis that blends ideas in paragraph 5 of this speech and paragraph 58 of "The 'Threat' of Creationism" (pp. 354–363).

Writing with Sources: Using a Single Source

Integrating information from "Kennedy's Houston Speech" with your own ideas, write an essay on one of these topics. Be sure to acknowledge ideas that are not your own.

1. How strongly do you agree with Kennedy's ideas on separating church and state? For instance, do you agree that no "public funds or political preference" should be granted to churches or church-related schools, even in the form of tax exemption, or of aid for textbooks; transportation to and from school; or special services like speech and reading programs or psychological counseling — all of which are provided now in some states? Set forth your position.
2. Can a politician be a loyal follower of his or her religion and an effective representative of all his or her constituents as well? Explain.
3. Does the use of churches as sanctuaries for victims of political persecution violate the separation of church and state as Kennedy would interpret it? In any case, should our government allow this practice? Support your position.

Opposing Prefab Prayer

George F. Will

Editor and political columnist George Will was born in 1941 and attended Trinity College, Oxford University, and Princeton University. He taught political science at several colleges and has served as a congressional aide. In 1972, he was appointed Washington editor of the conservative journal *National Review*. Since then, he has been a political columnist for the *Washington Post* and *Newsweek*. His books include *The Pursuit of Happiness and Other Sobering Thoughts* (1979), *The Pursuit of Virtue and Other Tory Notions* (1982), and *Statecraft as Soulcraft: What Government Does* (1982). Will was the recipient of the 1977 Pulitzer Prize for commentary. In "Opposing Prefab Prayer," a 1982 *Newsweek* column, Will takes a stand on a highly controversial issue.

1   I stand foursquare with the English ethicist who declared: "I am fully convinced that the highest life can only be lived on a foundation of Christian belief — or some substitute for it." But President Reagan's constitutional amendment concerning prayer in public schools is a mistake.

2   His proposal reads: "Nothing in this Constitution shall be construed to

prohibit individual or group prayer in public schools or other public institutions. No person shall be required by the United States or by any state to participate in prayer.'' This would restore the status quo ante the 1962 Supreme Court ruling that public-school prayers violate the ban on ''establishment'' of religion. The amendment would not settle the argument about prayer; it would relocate the argument. All 50 states, or perhaps all 3,041 county governments, or all 16,214 school districts would have to decide whether to have ''voluntary'' prayers. But the issue is not really voluntary prayers for individuals. The issue is organized prayers for groups of pupils subject to compulsory school-attendance laws. In a 1980 resolution opposing ''government authored or sponsored religious exercises in public schools,'' the Southern Baptist Convention noted that ''the Supreme Court has not held that it is illegal for any individual to pray or read his or her Bible in public schools.''

3   **The Question:**   This nation is even more litigious than religious, and the school-prayer issue has prompted more, and more sophisticated, arguments about constitutional law than about the nature of prayer. But fortunately Sen. Jack Danforth is an ordained Episcopal priest and is the only person ever to receive degrees from the Yale Law School and the Yale Divinity School on the same day. Danforth is too polite to pose the question quite this pointedly, but the question is: is public-school prayer apt to serve authentic religion, or is it apt to be mere attitudinizing, a thin gruel of vague religious vocabulary? Religious exercises should arise from a rich tradition, and reflect that richness. Prayer, properly understood, arises from the context of the praying person's particular faith. So, Danforth argues, ''for those within a religious tradition, it simply is not true that one prayer is as good as any other.''

4   One person's prayer may not be any sort of prayer to another person whose devotion is to a different tradition. To children from certain kinds of Christian families, a ''nondenominational'' prayer that makes no mention of Jesus Christ would be incoherent. The differences between Christian and Jewish expressions of piety are obvious; the differences between Protestants and Roman Catholics regarding, for example, Mary and the saints are less obvious, but they are not trivial to serious religious sensibilities. And as Danforth says, a lowest-common-denominator prayer would offend all devout persons. ''Prayer that is so general and so diluted as not to offend those of most faiths is not prayer at all. True prayer is robust prayer. It is bold prayer. It is almost by definition sectarian prayer.''

5   Liturgical reform in the Roman Catholic and Episcopal churches has occasioned fierce controversies that seem disproportionate, if not unintelligible, to persons who are ignorant of or indifferent about those particular religious traditions. But liturgy is a high art and a serious business because it is designed to help turn minds from worldly distractions, toward transcendent things. Collective prayer should express a shared inner state, one that does not occur easily and spontaneously. A homogenized religious recitation, perfunctorily rendered by children who have just tumbled in from a bus or playground, is not apt to arise from the individuals wills, as real prayer must.

6   Buddhists are among the almost 90 religious organizations in America that have at least 50,000 members. Imagine, Danforth urges, the Vietnamese Buddhist in a fourth-grade class in, say, Mississippi. How does that child deal with a "voluntary" prayer that is satisfactory to the local Baptists? Or imagine a child from America's growing number of Muslims, for whom prayer involves turning toward Mecca and prostrating oneself. Muslim prayer is adoration of Allah; it involves no requests and asks no blessing, as most Christian prayers do. Reagan says: "No one will ever convince me that a moment of voluntary prayer will harm a child . . ." Danforth asks: how is America — or religion — served by the embarrassment of children who must choose between insincere compliance with, or conscientious abstention from, a ritual?

7 **A Suggestion**:   In a nation where millions of adults (biologically speaking) affect the Jordache look or whatever designer's whim is *de rigueur,* peer pressure on children is not a trivial matter. Supporters of Reagan's amendment argue that a 9-year-old is "free" to absent himself or otherwise abstain from a "voluntary" prayer—an activity involving his classmates and led by that formidable authority figure, his teacher. But that argument is akin to one heard a century ago from persons who said child-labor laws infringed the precious freedom of children to contract to work ten-hour days in coal mines.

8   To combat the trivializing of religion and the coercion of children who take their own religious traditions seriously, Danforth suggests enacting the following distinction: "The term 'voluntary prayer' shall not include any prayer composed, prescribed, directed, supervised, or organized by an official or employee of a state or local government agency, including public school principals and teachers." When religion suffers the direct assistance of nervous politicians, the result is apt to confirm the judgment of the child who prayed not to God but for God because "if anything happens to him, we're properly sunk."

9   It is, to say no more, curious that, according to some polls, more Americans favor prayers in schools than regularly pray in church. Supermarkets sell processed cheese and instant mashed potatoes, so many Americans must like bland substitutes for real things. But it is one thing for the nation's palate to tolerate frozen waffles; it is another and more serious thing for the nation's soul to be satisfied with add-water-and-stir instant religiosity. When government acts as liturgist for a pluralistic society, the result is bound to be a purée that is tasteless, in several senses.

Reading Sources: "Opposing Prefab Prayer"

Read the selection, surveying it to identify key terms and important concepts. Highlight these phrases and ideas, and then answer these questions.

1. Evaluate the effectiveness of Will's title. Is it appropriate in light of his essay's content, purpose, and audience? Explain.

2. What visual cues are used in this essay? Would the essay be as easy to follow without them? Explain.
3. What is Will's principal objection to President Reagan's proposed constitutional amendment?
4. What is Will's view of prayer?
5. In paragraph 6, Will notes that nearly 90 different religions currently are practiced by at least 50,000 people each in America. How does this piece of information strengthen his argument?
6. In one sentence, state Will's thesis.

Reacting to Sources

Reread the selection carefully, making marginal notes to aid comprehension and reinforce connections. Then further annotate the selection if you need to do so in order to answer any of these questions. (You may already have addressed some of the questions in your marginal notes.)

1. Using a dictionary if necessary, supply brief marginal definitions of these words as they are used in this selection: *foursquare* (1), *ethicist* (1), *construed* (2), *status quo ante* (2), *litigious* (3), *attitudinizing* (3), *sectarian* (4), *liturgical* (5), *transcendent* (5), *homogenized* (5), *perfunctorily* (5), *rendered* (5), *abstention* (6), *affect* (7), *religiosity* (9), *pluralistic* (9), *purée* (9).
2. In a marginal comment, explain Will's purpose in opening his essay with the quotation he chooses.
3. Will bases many of his arguments on the views of Senator Jack Danforth. How does Will attempt to establish Danforth's credibility? Does this dependence on one person's perspective strengthen or weaken Will's case? Explain in a journal entry.
4. In a journal entry, explain this distinction: "But the issue is not really voluntary prayers for individuals. The issue is organized prayers for groups of pupils subject to compulsory school-attendance laws" (2).
5. Will makes this statement in paragraph 3: "Religious exercises should arise from a rich tradition, and reflect that richness. Prayer, properly understood, arises from the context of the praying person's particular faith." Do you agree or disagree? Write a journal entry in which you react to Will's comments in the context of your own understanding of prayer.
6. Give two examples from your own experience to support Will's statement that "One person's prayer may not be any sort of prayer to another person whose devotion is to a different tradition" (4).
7. Write three questions to clarify your understanding of the ideas in paragraph 5.
8. In a marginal note, explain what Will means in the last sentence of paragraph 9 by "tasteless, in several senses."
9. Reread the introduction to the selection. Comment in a marginal note about whether Will's background and other writings seem consistent or inconsistent with the views he expresses in this essay.

Working with Sources

1. Write a fifty-word summary of paragraph 2.
2. Write a critique of the ideas in paragraph 7.
3. Write a journal entry in which you explore your reactions to Will's use of the following phrases in "Opposing Prefab Prayer":

   "lowest-common-denominator prayer" (4)

   "homogenized religious recitation" (5)

   "add-water-and-stir instant religiosity" (9)

   Be sure to integrate the quotations smoothly into your writing.
4. Paraphrase President Reagan's proposed amendment and Senator Danforth's suggested modification.
5. Write a one-paragraph synthesis that blends ideas in paragraph 6 of this essay and paragraph 9 of "The Cult Boom" (pp. 343–351).

Writing with Sources: Using a Single Source

Integrating information from "Opposing Prefab Prayer" with your own ideas, write an essay on one of these topics. Be sure to acknowledge ideas that are not your own.

1. Using Will's essay and your own experience as a student as source material, answer the question Will poses in paragraph 3: "Is public school prayer apt to serve authentic religion, or is it apt to be mere attitudinizing, a thin gruel of vague religious vocabulary?"
2. Can voluntary prayer be harmful to a child? In paragraph 6, Will presents two opposing points of view, President Reagan's and Senator Danforth's. Explain why you support one of these two positions.
3. Many people feel that a regularly scheduled moment of silence, in which children could pray if they chose to, is a reasonable alternative to organized school prayer. Would Will agree? Do you? Consider the advantages and disadvantages of instituting a moment of silence in public school classrooms.

The Cult Boom

A. James Rudin and Marcia R. Rudin

A. James Rudin, educated at George Washington University and Hebrew Union College–Jewish Institute of Religion, is a reform rabbi. After his ordination in 1960, he served as an Air Force chaplain before becoming rabbi of congregations in Kansas City, Missouri, and Champaign, Illinois. He went on to serve as the American Jewish Committee's assistant national director of interreligious affairs and as a weekly syndicated radio commentator. In 1977 he coedited *Scripture, Theology and History: Perspectives of Evangelicals and Jews.* Marcia Rudin has been an assistant professor of philosophy and religion at William Paterson College in New Jersey. She has been researching, writing, and lecturing on alternative religious groups for more than ten years. "The Cult Boom" is excerpted from the Rudins' 1980 book, *Prison or Paradise? The New Religious Cults.* In this book they present the case against modern religious cults and suggest specific methods that can be used to counter their influence.

1   A brilliant Ivy League college graduate writes his parents a short cryptic note informing them he has found a new life with the Children of God. They never see their child again.

2   On Manhattan's West Side a former opera coach named Oric Bovar proclaims himself Jesus Christ and attracts followers from the entertainment world who contribute large sums of money to support his cult. When one of his young followers dies Bovar prays over the body for its resurrection in an apartment for three months. Finally health officials intervene and bury the body. On April 14, 1977, Oric Bovar jumps to his death from the window of his tenth-floor West End Avenue apartment.

3   Dr. Joseph Jeffers builds a $200,000 pyramid called the Temple of Yahoshua, 100 miles southwest of St. Louis, Missouri. Jeffers, who claims he is the Son of God, is the founder and leader of a religion called Yahwism.

4   In November, 1978, 911 men, women, and children, members of the Reverend Jim Jones's Guyana jungle utopia, Jonestown, die by drinking a Kool-Aid and cyanide mixture or are shot to death by guards.

What Are the New Religious Cults?

5   What are these new religious cults? Are the cults a new phenomenon, or are they similar to religious cults that have always existed? How many new groups are there? How many members have they attracted? Are they a fad that will pass, or are they a permanent part of the worldwide religious scene? Are they dangerous, or are they a welcome addition to religious and to cultural pluralism?

6   Sociologists define cults as deviant groups which exist in a state of tension with society. They do not evolve or break away from other religions, as do religious sects, but, rather, offer something new and different. Although by definition cults conflict with "the establishment," there are degrees of conflict:

the more total the commitment the cults demand from their followers, the more hostility they meet from society.

7   There have always been religious cults, particularly in unstable and troubled times such as ours. For example, the Roman Empire, which allowed great freedom of religion, was deluged with apocalyptic movements that sprang from the meeting of Eastern and Western cultures. Throughout history there have always been people, both young and old, who have sought personal fulfillment, peace, mystical experience, and religious salvation through such fringe groups.

8   Today's religious cults, however, are different from those of the past for several reasons. Most of all, there has never in recorded history been such a proliferation of cults. The signs of this cult "boom" are everywhere. Bulletin boards on hundreds of college campuses advertise a smorgasbord of religious options. Both conventional newspapers and magazines and "alternative life-style" publications carry advertisements. Cult members recruit and solicit contributions in stores, on street corners, and in public parks, in tourist centers and airports. Everywhere one hears stories of children, brothers and sisters, nieces and nephews, older parents, or friends who become members of one of these groups. Ministers, priests, and rabbis hear desperate pleas for help, as do the major Jewish and Christian organizations.

How Many Cults Are There?

9   Although we do not know the precise number of these cults, we do know that it is large and that the numbers are growing. After an extensive study, Drs. Egon Mayer and Laura Kitch, sociologists at Brooklyn College, concluded that since 1965 more than thirteen hundred new religious groups have appeared in America. Other observers estimate that there are between one and three thousand such groups in the United States alone. Not all are large and well-known. Some last only a short time. Many of these cults are simply the personal creations of their founders and do not outlive them, such as that of Oric Bovar, which came to an end with his suicide.

10   Just as it is difficult to know how many cults there are, so, too, it is difficult to estimate the number of people involved in them. Accurate membership records are not available. The membership figures the cults release are usually highly inflated in order to appear larger and to give the impression that their growth is more rapid than may really be the case. Cult critics who over-react in their concern may inadvertently inflate the figures or may underestimate them. Cult members tend to float from one group to another with the consequence that one individual may be counted in membership figures several times. Dr. Marc Galanter, a psychiatrist at Yeshiva University's Albert Einstein Medical School in New York City who, along with Richard Rabkin and Judith Rabkin, studied the Unification Church in late 1978, discovered that 90 percent of its members had had a previous involvement with another cult, confirming that there is a good deal of "shopping around" within these groups. Some experts estimate there are three hundred thousand cult adherents. Flo

Conway and Jim Siegelman, authors of *Snapping,* assert there are perhaps as many as 3 million past and present cult members in America alone. Dr. Margaret Thaler Singer, a psychiatrist on the staff of the Wright Institute at Berkeley, California, and the University of California in San Francisco and a cult expert, who counsels former cult members, agrees that there are 2 to 3 million people in these groups.

11   Never before have religious cults been so geographically widespread. They are in every area of the United States, in every major city and on college campuses throughout the nation. They have spread to Canada and to Western Europe — Great Britain, France, Holland, Denmark, Italy, and West Germany— where governments are alarmed about their rapid growth. There are cult centers also in Asia, Africa, South America, Israel, Australia, and New Zealand.

12   Today's cultists are trained in the latest methods of group dynamics and "Madison Avenue" public relations, advertising, and media-manipulation techniques. They bring great enthusiasm to their work and make certain that all members are highly visible and effective missionizers. This dedication heightens their efficiency well beyond their numbers.

Why Are Today's Cults Different?

13   One of the major factors which set the new religious cults off from those of the past is their use of new, specific, and highly sophisticated techniques which successfully manipulate thought and behavior of new cult members. Hundreds of former cult members testify this is so in court proceedings, public information hearings concerning the cults, magazine and newspaper interviews, and counseling sessions. Psychiatrists and other professionals who counsel former cultists confirm this. These techniques include constant repetition of doctrine, application of intense peer pressure, manipulation of diet so that critical faculties are adversely affected, deprivation of sleep, lack of privacy and time for reflection, complete break with past life, reduction of outside stimulation and influences, the skillful use of ritual to heighten mystical experience, and the invention of new vocabulary and the manipulation of language to narrow down the range of experience and construct a new reality. Psychiatrists and counselors who treat former cult members say their emotional and intellectual responses have been severely curtailed. Dr. John G. Clark, Jr., Associate Clinical Professor of Psychiatry at Massachusetts General Hospital— Harvard Medical School, who has worked with former cult members for the past six and one-half years says:

> They appear to have become rather dull and their style and range of expression limited and stereotyped. They are animated only when discussing their group and its beliefs. They rapidly lose a knowledge of current events. When stressed even a little, they become defensive and inflexible and retreat into numbing cliches. Their written or spoken expression loses metaphor, irony, and the broad use of vocabulary. Their humor is without mirth.

Observers believe some cults use hypnosis and posthypnotic suggestion.

14   These methods can bring about a complete personality transformation. The cult leader can mold the recruit's new beliefs and personality according to his desires so the new adherent will have total commitment to the group. This can happen very quickly, sometimes within a period of weeks.

15   Authors Conway and Siegelman believe that in most cults there is "a single moment of conversion and transformation," which they term "snapping." This moment is "induced in the course of a cult ritual or therapeutic technique that is deftly orchestrated to create the experience of a momentous psychic breakthrough." After this experience the person is highly vulnerable to suggestion. The cults follow up the process by chanting, meditation, speaking in tongues, or other mental exercises which reinforce the effects of the sudden psychic experience and also act as mechanisms to stifle future doubts. The results of this expert thought manipulation can be neutralized only with great difficulty. In some cases these changes are permanent.

The Religious Cults Are Wealthy

16   Today's religious cults are unique also because of their great wealth. They charge high fees for classes or lectures and sometimes actually take over their members' financial assets. They own extensive property, operate lucrative and diversified businesses, and skillfully extract millions of dollars every year from the public by solicitations. Their incomes are tax-exempt. The People's Temple had over $10 million in various bank accounts at the time of the mass suicides and murders in Guyana. Ex–Unification Church official Allen Tate Wood estimates that movement's income is over $200 million per year.

17   Money buys power. Some cults can afford to hire the best legal minds to help them fight their opponents. They sue journalists who write about them and campaign against legislation that aims to curb their activities. The Unification Church hires top journalists and columnists to write for its newspaper, *News World,* which offers a widespread platform for its political viewpoint. Critics accuse the Unification Church of using its great wealth to influence United States Government policy.

18   Money can also purchase respectability. The cults are changing their tactics. They are less flamboyant and no longer hire Madison Square Garden or the Houston Astrodome for rallies. They are taking many adherents off the streets and putting them into "white collar" jobs. Cultists who are visible to the public dress in a better manner than they did in the past so that outsiders will think the group is less eccentric, and therefore less dangerous. Many Hare Krishna members, for example, now wear wigs and conventional clothing when they solicit on the streets rather than their exotic Indian garb. The Unification Church employs renowned theologians to teach at its seminary and to lecture on the group's behalf. It "dialogues" with Evangelical Christians and desires conversations with other religious groups. It seeks the academic world's stamp of approval by inviting over four hundred fifty prominent academicians to annual conferences sponsored by a Unification Church organization, ICUS (International Conference of the Unity of Science), which pays for their

travel expenses and large honoraria. Some academics are flattered by the invitations, while others refuse to attend the controversial meetings because of the Unification Church connection.

19   Because of their vast wealth and the power and respectability money can buy the contemporary cults are not merely a passing fad. They are not simply temporary way stations for those who may "be into" something else next year, as some hope. They are a permanent and rapidly growing part of the world-wide religious and cultural scene.

Guarding Against Complacency

20   Although the cults are a very real presence on the religious and cultural scene this does not mean that we must be complacent about them. They want people to get used to them, to become resigned to their existence, to tire of worrying and stop fighting against them. They want to be perceived as "new religious movements" rather than as "cults," a negative label which implies that they are at odds with society. They liken themselves to other religious movements which were previously considered radical and which are now, after the passage of time, old, established, and accepted groups. Unification Church officials often compare their legal difficulties and negative public image to the past harassment of the Mormon Church, implying that just as the Mormons were once considered outsiders and were eventually accepted by society, so too the Unification Church will eventually be accepted. They cite cases of extremism in the Roman Catholic Church, claiming that the treatment of their members is no worse, and that there are Catholic parents who are unhappy at their children's decision to join the cloistered nuns' or monks' orders just as parents of Unification Church members are unhappy that their children have renounced the world to dedicate themselves to a new life.

Characteristics of the Cults

21   All religions have at some point in their histories been guilty of excesses. Extremism, fanaticism, and irrationality are found in all religions and, one can argue, are perhaps an essential component of all religious or mystical experiences. However, these new religious cults are *not* like the Roman Catholic Church, the Mormon Church, or other past "new religious movements." The contemporary cults exhibit characteristics that set them apart from past religious cults and from established religions. These fundamental differences make them different in kind as well as degree, and make them a unique phenomenon.

22   What are these characteristics? (One must remember that the following characteristics are generalizations and do not apply equally to all of the groups.)

23   1. Members swear total allegiance to an all-powerful leader whom they may believe to be a Messiah. The leader determines the rules for daily life and proclaims doctrines or "Truths," but generally the leader and his or her "inner circle" are exempt from the rules or prohibitions. These rules, doctrines, or

"Truths" cannot be questioned. The leader's word is the absolute and final authority.

24   2. Rational thought is discouraged or forbidden. The groups are anti-intellectual, placing all emphasis on intuition or emotional experience. "Knowledge" is redefined as those ideas and experiences dispensed by the group or its leader. One can only attain knowledge by joining the group and submitting to its doctrine. One cannot question this "knowledge."

25   If the follower shows signs of doubting he is made to feel that the fault lies within himself, not with the ideas, and he feels intensely guilty about this doubt. Says Rabbi Zalman Schacter, Professor of Religion and Jewish Mysticism at Temple University, "Any group which equates doubt with guilt is a cult."

26   3. The cult's recruitment techniques are often deceptive. The potential follower may not be told what he is getting into and what will be required of him. The Unification Church often does not mention its name or that of Reverend Moon for perhaps several weeks. By then the person is well indoctrinated into the movement. Most cult members probably would not join if they knew ahead of time what was involved. Says Jeannie Mills, who with her husband and five children spent six years in the People's Temple, "Your first encounter with a cult group is going to be a very pleasant experience. . . . How many people would join a church if the leader stood up in front of them and said, 'You'll never have sex anymore, you're not going to have enough food to satisfy your needs, you're going to sleep four to six hours a night, and you're going to have to be cut off entirely from all your family ties?'"

27   4. The cult weakens the follower psychologically and makes him believe that his problems can only be solved by the group. The cult undermines all of the follower's past psychological support systems; all help from other therapy methods, psychologists or psychiatrists, religious beliefs, or parents and friends is discredited and may actually be forbidden. Psychological problems as well as intellectual doubts are soothed away by denying the reality of the conflicting feelings, by keeping the adherent so busy and constantly on the move that he has no time to think about them, and by assurances that faithful following of the cult's teaching will in time assuage them. The cult follower may reach a plateau of inner calm and appear to be free from anxiety. But this placidity may be only a mask for unresolved psychological turmoil which still presents a grave danger to the adherent.

28   The cult may make the follower feel helpless and dependent on the group by forcing him into childlike submission. Former Unification Church member Christopher Edwards relates in his book *Crazy for God* how childlike he felt during a confusing game played during his recruitment:

> During the entire game our team chanted loudly, "Bomb with Love," "Blast with Love," as the soft, round balls volleyed back and forth. Again I felt lost and confused, angry, remote and helpless, for the game had started without an explanation of the rules.

He described how he surrendered himself to the comfortable feeling of being a small child again:

> "Give in, Chris," urged a voice within me. "Just be a child and obey. It's fun. It's trusting. Isn't this the innocence, the purity of love you've been searching for?"

The cults offer total, unconditional love but actually extract a constantly higher and higher price for it — total submission to the group. Explains Edwards:

> Suddenly I understood what they wanted from me. Their role was to tease me with their love, dishing it out and withdrawing it as they saw fit. My role was not to question but to be their child, dependent on them for affection. The kiddie games, the raucous singing, the silly laughter, were all part of a scenario geared to help me assume my new identity.

29   5. The new cults expertly manipulate guilt. The devotee believes the group has the power to "dispense existence," to determine, according to psychologist Moshe Halevi Spero, "who has the right to live or die, physically or metaphorically." Members may be forced to "confess" their inadequacies and past "sins" before the group or certain individuals. In their book *All God's Children* journalists Carroll Stoner and Jo Anne Parke report that "counter-cult activists claim that some religious cults keep dossiers on members and their families — the more secrets the better — in order to use the material as emotional blackmail if the members should decide to leave, and tell of cases where this has happened."

30   6. Cult members are isolated from the outside world, cut off from their pasts, from school, job, family, and friends as well as from information from newspapers, radio, and television. They may be prohibited from coming and going freely into the outside world, or are so psychologically weakened that they cannot cope with it. They are told that the outside world is evil, satanic, and doomed, and that salvation can come only by remaining in the group and giving up everything else.

31   7. The cult or its leader makes every career or life decision for the follower. The Hare Krishna group regulates every hour of activity for those members who dwell in the temples. The cults determine every aspect of the adherent's personal life, including sexual activities, diet, use of liquor, drugs and tobacco, perhaps the choice of marriage partners, and whether, when, and how to bear children. Even if one does not live within the group the cult comes to overpower all other aspects of life. Career and schooling may be abandoned and all other interests discouraged so that the cult becomes the follower's total world.

32   8. Some cults promise to improve society, raise money, and work to help the poor, etc., in order to attract idealistic members. However, their energies are channeled into promoting the well-being of the group rather than towards improving society. All energy and financial resources are devoted to the cult, in some cases to the benefit only of the leaders. Cults usually exist solely for the purposes of self-survival and financial growth. While all religious organizations must be concerned with such practical affairs, these considerations are not their sole raison d'être. — reason or purpose for existing (Gut level purpose) for being

33   9. Cult followers often work full time for the group. They work very long hours, for little or no pay, and in demeaning circumstances and conditions. They are made to feel guilty or unworthy if they protest. If they do work outside the group, salaries are usually turned over to the cult. The lower-eche-lon members may live in conditions of self-denial or extreme poverty while cult leaders live comfortably or even luxuriously.

34   10. The cults are antiwoman, antichild, and antifamily. Women perform the most menial tasks of cooking, cleaning, and street solicitations and are rarely elevated to high decision-making positions in the group. Birth control, abortion, and the physical circumstances of childbirth are often regulated by the group's leaders, who are usually men. The Unification Church teaches that Eve's sin of intercourse with Satan is the root of human estrangement from God. There are reports of sexual abuse of women in the Church of Armageddon. A fourteen-year-old was raped in the Children of God when she disobeyed a leader. Women in the Children of God are encouraged to use sex to recruit new members.

35   There are reports of child neglect and beatings. Children are often improperly cared for and inadequately educated. They are at times taken away from their parents and raised by others in the group or even geographically separated from them. Because some members have now been in a cult for many years, the consequences of the cult experience are affecting a second generation.

36   Family bonds must be subordinated to loyalties to the cult, which may speak of itself as a higher family. Children and parents may not form close relationships because this may threaten group loyalties. Families are often de-liberately broken up, members forced to renounce spouses who do not ap-prove of the group or who leave it. Cult leaders may order "marriages" with other partners even though the follower may be legally married to another either inside or outside of the cult.

37   The followers' ties with their families outside of the group are strained if their family disapproves of the cult, and adherents may be forced to sever connections with them. Families are often prevented by the cult from locating their member or from talking with him or her privately. The cult may tell the adherent that his family is satanic and warn him that it will try to trick him into leaving the group or may try to kidnap him.

38   11. Most cult members believe the world is coming to an end and they are elite members of an "elect" survival group. They believe in a Manichean dualistic conflict between Absolute Good and Absolute Evil. By joining the cult they believe they have affiliated themselves with the Good which will eventu-ally triumph over Evil.

39   They shed their old identities and take on new ones in preparation for this "new age." They have a sense of rebirth, or a starting over, and so often adopt new names, new vocabulary, and new clothing in order to purify them-selves for their new lives.

40   12. Many of these groups have the philosophy that the ends justify the means. Since the "ends" are so important—salvation of souls, salvation of the world, triumph of Good over Evil—any means required to carry them out are

permitted and even encouraged by the cult. There may be a double standard of truth, one for cult members and another for the outside world. The cult member may be encouraged to lie to outsiders. The Unification Church practices what it calls "Heavenly Deception" and the "Hare Krishna Transcendental Trickery." The Children of God believe that since the world is so corrupt they are not subject to its laws and teach their members to subvert the legal system. However, within the cult the members must be truthful to each other and to the cult leaders.

41   13. The cults are often shrouded in an aura of secrecy and mystery. They keep new members in the dark, promising more knowledge about the group as they become more involved in it. Some leaders are rarely, if ever, seen by the average member. The cults may hide financial information from the public.

42   14. There is frequently an aura of violence or potential violence. Two Unification Church recruitment centers are guarded. The Divine Light Mission premises and the Krishnas at their farm in West Virginia have their own security forces which they insist are necessary to protect the cult leaders or to protect themselves from hostile neighbors. Many Way International members take a weapons training course. There was a large arsenal of automatic rifles, shotguns, and handguns at Jonestown. People's Temple followers were closely guarded before Congressman Ryan and members of his party were slain and many adherents took poison or were shot by Jones's security forces.

43   Some cult members have been involved in incidents of beatings or shootings. In May, 1979, a Swiss court sentenced the head of a Divine Light Mission at Winterhur to fourteen years in prison on charges ranging from breach of the peace to attempted murder. In August, 1979, two Unification Church area directors were arrested and charged with shooting at the car of two former members. Christopher Edwards' parents had to hire private detectives to guard their home for several months after he was deprogrammed and had left the Unification Church. Since Edwards' book about his experiences with the Unification Church was published, he has received two death threats. Private investigator Galen Kelly was hospitalized with a concussion for a week in 1979 after, he alleges, a Unification Church member hit him on the head with a rock.

Are the New Cults Dangerous?

44   Observers of the religious scene are divided over the issue of what these new groups in our society mean. Some scholars see the new cults as the "cutting edge" of a healthy and growing spiritual awakening in the Western world. They maintain that the cults promote religious pluralism by ensuring freedom of choice and a variety of religious alternatives. But cult critics perceive them as wild and poisonous weeds invading religion's vineyard. They believe the new cults are actually antipluralistic because they claim to possess the one, only, and final truth. They discourage or forbid their members to discuss other ideas and alternatives and vow to triumph over other viewpoints. This attitude, critics maintain, hinders rather than promotes religious pluralism.

Reading Sources: "The Cult Boom"

Read the selection, surveying it to identify key words and important concepts. Highlight these phrases and ideas, and then answer these questions.

1. What visual cues are used in this essay? How do they help readers to follow the essay's ideas?
2. Evaluate the effectiveness of the essay's opening strategy (1–4).
3. What is a cult?
4. What purpose does paragraph 5 serve in the essay?
5. Why, according to the authors, are today's religious cults different from those of the past?
6. Why is it difficult to determine how many people are involved in cults?
7. How do the authors link paragraphs 9 and 10? What techniques do they use to connect the sentences in paragraph 13?
8. What is "snapping"?
9. The authors quote a variety of experts in their essay. Select three quotations and identify the purpose for which each source is quoted.
10. What key terms do the authors use when they refer to cult members? Are all these terms neutral, or do some have unfavorable connotations? Explain.

Reacting to Sources

Reread the selection carefully, making marginal notes to aid comprehension and reinforce connections. Then further annotate the selection if you need to do so in order to answer any of these questions. (You may already have addressed some of the questions in your marginal notes.)

1. Using a dictionary if necessary, supply brief marginal definitions of these words as they are used in this selection: *pluralism* (5), *apocalyptic* (7), *smorgasbord* (8), *missionizers* (12), *adherent* (14), *complacent* (20), *assuage* (27), *placidity* (27), *raison d'être* (32), *deprogrammed* (43).
2. In a few sentences, rewrite paragraph 13 to simplify its ideas.
3. Outline the paragraph cluster that extends from paragraph 16 through paragraph 19. Can you identify any other paragraph clusters?
4. In paragraph 19 the authors call the cults "a permanent and rapidly growing part of the worldwide religious and cultural scene." Explore the implications of this statement in a journal entry.
5. What efforts, if any, do the authors make to present an objective picture of the cult boom? Is any bias evident? In marginal notes, identify examples of impartial and/or slanted statements.
6. In a marginal note, explain Rabbi Schacter's statement, quoted in paragraph 25.
7. Give three examples from the selection to support the authors' general statement in paragraph 27 that a typical cult "weakens the follower psychologically."

8. Find a statement in the essay for which your own knowledge or experience — about religion, about cults, or about young adult behavior — provides supporting or contradictory evidence. Write a marginal note that presents this support or contradiction.
9. Reread the introduction to the selection. Comment on how the authors' backgrounds might have influenced their purpose. How does your knowledge that A. James Rudin is a rabbi affect your reaction to the essay? Explain in a marginal note.

Working with Sources

1. Write a fifty-word summary of paragraph 20.
2. Write a critique of the ideas in paragraphs 16–19.
3. Write a journal entry in which you explore your reactions to these quotations from "The Cult Boom":

   "There have always been religious cults, particularly in unstable and troubled times such as ours" (7).

   "Extremism, fanaticism, and irrationality are found in all religions and, one can argue, are perhaps an essential component of all religious or mystical experiences" (21).

   ". . . cult critics perceive them as wild and poisonous weeds invading religion's vineyard" (44).

   Be sure to integrate the quotations smoothly into your writing.
4. Paraphrase the topic sentences of paragraphs 23, 24, 26, 27, 29, 30, 31, 32, 33, 34, 38, 40, 41, and 42; then combine them into a paragraph that identifies the fourteen characteristics that set today's cults apart from both established religions and older religious cults.
5. Write a one-paragraph synthesis that blends ideas in paragraph 13 of this essay and paragraph 52 of "The 'Threat' of Creationism" (pp. 354–363).

Writing with Sources: Using a Single Source

Integrating information from "The Cult Boom" with your own ideas, write an essay on one of these topics. Be sure to acknowledge ideas that are not your own.

1. Consider the two opposing views about cults presented in paragraph 44. Then, taking into account your own view of religion in America and the facts about cults presented in this essay, consider whether cults "promote religious pluralism by ensuring freedom of choice and a variety of religious alternatives" or whether they represent a danger to our pluralistic society.
2. There has been a tendency lately for some young adults to become more involved with the religions in which they were brought up, sometimes redis-

covering faith or ritual after a long estrangement. Is there a relationship between the causes behind this rediscovery of traditional religion and the impulses that lead others to join cults, or are they due to entirely different factors?
Write an essay in which you answer this question.

3. In recent years, the rise of acts of terrorism — bombings, hijackings, kidnap-
pings, and assassinations — in the name of religious extremism has led the
media and political leaders to speculate about the dangers of fanatical devotion
to a cause. Do you see a possible cause and effect relationship between the
characteristics identified in "The Cult Boom" (23 – 43) and such extremist
acts? Explain your views.

The "Threat" of Creationism

Isaac Asimov

Born in 1920, Isaac Asimov received his B.S., M.A., and Ph.D. degrees in Chemistry
from Columbia University and has been a Professor of Biochemistry at Boston
University School of Medicine since 1979. Beginning with his first professional short
story in 1938, Asimov has had an extremely prolific career as a writer: his 250th
book was published in 1982, and he has continued to write additional volumes. His
books include *I, Robot* (1950), *The Human Body* (1963), *Asimov's Guide to Shakespeare* (1970), *Asimov's Guide to Science* (1972), *Foundation's Edge* (1982), and
The Robots of Dawn (1983). In addition, he has published two volumes of his
autobiography, and his writings also include books about literature, history,
mathematics, and the Bible. In "The 'Threat' of Creationism," Asimov argues that
evolution, not creationism, should be taught in the schools.

1   Scientists thought it was settled.

2   The universe, they had decided, is about 20 billion years old, and Earth
itself is 4.5 billion years old. Simple forms of life came into being more than
three billion years ago, having formed spontaneously from nonliving matter.
They grew more complex through slow evolutionary processes and the first
hominid ancestors of humanity appeared more than four million years ago.
Homo sapiens itself — the present human species, people like you and me —
has walked the earth for at least 50,000 years.

3   But apparently it isn't settled. There are Americans who believe that the
earth is only about 6,000 years old; that human beings and all other species
were brought into existence by a divine Creator as eternally separate varieties
of beings, and that there has been no evolutionary process.

4   They are creationists — they call themselves "scientific" creationists —
and they are a growing power in the land, demanding that schools be forced to
teach their views. State legislatures, mindful of votes, are beginning to succumb to the pressure. In perhaps 15 states, bills have been introduced, putting
forth the creationist point of view, and in others, strong movements are gaining

momentum. In Arkansas, a law requiring that the teaching of creationism receive equal time was passed this spring and is scheduled to go into effect in September 1982, though the American Civil Liberties Union has filed suit on behalf of a group of clergymen, teachers and parents to overturn it. And a California father named Kelly Segraves, the director of the Creation-Science Research Center, sued to have public-school science classes teach that there are other theories of creation besides evolution, and that one of them was the Bibical version. The suit came to trial in March, and the judge ruled that educators must distribute a policy statement to schools and textbook publishers explaining that the theory of evolution should not be seen as "the ultimate cause of origins." Even in New York, the Board of Education has delayed since January in making a final decision, expected this month, on whether schools will be required to include the teaching of creationism in their curriculums.

5   The Rev. Jerry Falwell, the head of the Moral Majority, who supports the creationist view from his television pulpit, claims that he has 17 million to 25 million viewers (though Arbitron places the figure at a much more modest 1.6 million). But there are 66 electronic ministries which have a total audience of about 20 million. And in parts of the country where the Fundamentalists predominate — the so-called Bible Belt — creationists are in the majority.

6   They make up a fervid and dedicated group, convinced beyond argument of both their rightness and righteousness. Faced with an apathetic and falsely secure majority, smaller groups have used intense pressure and forceful campaigning — as the creationists do — and have succeeded in disrupting and taking over whole societies.

7   Yet, though creationists seem to accept the literal truth of the Biblical story of creation, this does not mean that all religious people are creationists. There are millions of Catholics, Protestants and Jews who think of the Bible as a source of spiritual truth and accept much of it as symbolically rather than literally true. They do not consider the Bible to be a textbook of science, even in intent, and have no problem teaching evolution in their secular institutions.

8   To those who are trained in science, creationism seems like a bad dream, a sudden reliving of a nightmare, a renewed march of an army of the night risen to challenge free thought and enlightenment.

9   The scientific evidence for the age of the earth and for the evolutionary development of life seems overwhelming to scientists. How can anyone question it? What are the arguments the creationists use? What is the "science" that makes their views "scientific"? Here are some of them:

• The argument from analogy.

10   A watch implies a watchmaker, say the creationists. If you were to find a beautifully intricate watch in the desert, far from habitation, you would be sure that it had been fashioned by human hands and somehow left there. It would pass the bounds of credibility that it had simply formed, spontaneously, from the sands of the desert.

11   By analogy, then, if you consider humanity, life, earth and the universe, all infinitely more intricate than a watch, you can believe far less easily that it

"just happened." It, too, like the watch, must have been fashioned, but by more-than-human hands — in short by a divine Creator.

12   This argument seems unanswerable, and it has been used (even though not often explicitly expressed) ever since the dawn of consciousness. To have explained to prescientific human beings that the wind and the rain and the sun follow the laws of nature and do so blindly and without a guiding hand would have been utterly unconvincing to them. In fact, it might well have gotten you stoned to death as a blasphemer.

13   There are many aspects of the universe that still cannot be explained satisfactorily by science; but ignorance implies only ignorance that may some-day be conquered. To surrender to ignorance and call it God has always been premature, and it remains premature today.

14   In short, the complexity of the universe — and one's inability to explain it in full — is not in itself an argument for a Creator.

• The argument from general consent.

15   Some creationists point out that belief in a Creator is general among all peoples and all cultures. Surely this unanimous craving hints at a great truth. There would be no unanimous belief in a lie.

16   General belief, however, is not really surprising. Nearly every people on earth that considers the existence of the world assumes it to have been created by a god or gods. And each group invents full details for the story. No two creation tales are alike. The Greeks, the Norsemen, the Japanese, the Hindus, the American Indians and so on and so on all have their own creation myths, and all of these are recognized by Americans of Judeo-Christian heritage as "just myths."

17   The ancient Hebrews also had a creation tale — two of them, in fact. There is a primitive Adam-and-Eve-in-Paradise story, with man created first, then animals, then woman. There is also a poetic tale of God fashioning the universe in six days, with animals preceding man, and man and woman created together.

18   These Hebrew myths are not inherently more credible than any of the others, but they are our myths. General consent, of course, proves nothing: There can be a unanimous belief in something that isn't so. The universal opinion over thousands of years that the earth was flat never flattened its spherical shape by one inch.

• The argument by belittlement.

19   Creationists frequently stress the fact that evolution is "only a theory," giving the impression that a theory is an idle guess. A scientist, one gathers, arising one morning with nothing particular to do, decides that perhaps the moon is made of Roquefort cheese and instantly advances the Roquefort-cheese theory.

20   A theory (as the word is used by scientists) is a detailed description of some facet of the universe's workings that is based on long observation and, where possible, experiment. It is the result of careful reasoning from those

observations and experiments and has survived the critical study of scientists generally.

21   For example, we have the description of the cellular nature of living organisms (the "cell theory"); of objects attracting each other according to a fixed rule (the "theory of gravitation"); of energy behaving in discrete bits (the "quantum theory"); of light traveling through a vacuum at a fixed measurable velocity (the "theory of relativity"), and so on.

22   All are theories; all are firmly founded; all are accepted as valid descriptions of this or that aspect of the universe. They are neither guesses nor speculations. And no theory is better founded, more closely examined, more critically argued and more thoroughly accepted, than the theory of evolution. If it is "only" a theory, that is all it has to be.

23   Creationism, on the other hand, is not a theory. There is no evidence, in the scientific sense, that supports it. Creationism, or at least the particular variety accepted by many Americans, is an expression of early Middle Eastern legend. It is fairly described as "only a myth."

• The argument from imperfection.

24   Creationists, in recent years, have stressed the "scientific" background of their beliefs. They point out that there are scientists who base their creationist beliefs on a careful study of geology, paleontology and biology and produce "textbooks" that embody those beliefs.

25   Virtually the whole scientific corpus of creationism, however, consists of the pointing out of imperfections in the evolutionary view. The creationists insist, for example, that evolutionists cannot show true transition states between species in the fossil evidence; that age determinations through radioactive breakdown are uncertain; that alternate interpretations of this or that piece of evidence are possible, and so on.

26   Because the evolutionary view is not perfect and is not agreed upon in every detail by all scientists, creationists argue that evolution is false and that scientists, in supporting evolution, are basing their views on blind faith and dogmatism.

27   To an extent, the creationist are right here: The details of evolution are not perfectly known. Scientists have been adjusting and modifying Charles Darwin's suggestions since he advanced his theory of the origin of species through natural selection back in 1859. After all, much has been learned about the fossil record and about physiology, microbiology, biochemistry, ethology and various other branches of life science in the last 125 years, and it is to be expected that we can improve on Darwin. In fact, we have improved on him.

28   Nor is the process finished. It can never be, as long as human beings continue to question and to strive for better answers.

29   The details of evolutionary theory are in dispute precisely because scientists are not devotees of blind faith and dogmatism. They do not accept even as great a thinker as Darwin without question, nor do they accept any idea, new or old, without thorough argument. Even after accepting an idea,

they stand ready to overrule it, if appropriate new evidence arrives. If, however, we grant that a theory is imperfect and that details remain in dispute, does that disprove the theory as a whole?

30   Consider. I drive a car, and you drive a car. I do not know exactly how an engine works. Perhaps you do not either. And it may be that our hazy and approximate ideas of the workings of an automobile are in conflict. Must we then conclude from this disagreement that an automobile does not run, or that it does not exist? Or, if our senses force us to conclude that an automobile does exist and run, does that mean it is pulled by an invisible horse, since our engine theory is imperfect?

31   However much scientists argue their differing beliefs in details of evolutionary theory, or in the interpretation of the necessarily imperfect fossil record, they firmly accept the evolutionary process itself.

▪ The argument from distorted science.

32   Creationists have learned enough scientific terminology to use it in their attempts to disprove evolution. They do this in numerous ways, but the most common example, at least in the mail I receive, is the repeated assertion that the second law of thermodynamics demonstrates the evolutionary process to be impossible.

33   In kindergarten terms, the second law of thermodynamics says that all spontaneous change is in the direction of increasing disorder — that is, in a "downhill" direction. There can be no spontaneous buildup of the complex from the simple, therefore, because that would be moving "uphill." According to the creationist argument, since, by the evolutionary process, complex forms of life evolve from simple forms, that process defies the second law, so creationism must be true.

34   Such an argument implies that this clearly visible fallacy is somehow invisible to scientists, who must therefore be flying in the face of the second law through sheer perversity.

35   Scientists, however, do know about the second law and they are not blind. It's just that an argument based on kindergarten terms is suitable only for kindergartens.

36   To lift the argument a notch above the kindergarten level, the second law of thermodynamics applies to a "closed system" — that is, to a system that does not gain energy from without, or lose energy to the outside. The only truly closed system we know of is the universe as a whole.

37   Within a closed system, there are subsystems that can gain complexity spontaneously, provided there is a greater loss of complexity in another interlocking subsystem. The overall change then is a complexity loss in line with the dictates of the second law.

38   Evolution can proceed and build up the complex from the simple, thus moving uphill, without violating the second law, as long as another interlocking part of the system — the sun, which delivers energy to the earth continually — moves downhill (as it does) at a much faster rate than evolution moves uphill.

39   If the sun were to cease shining, evolution would stop and so, eventually, would life.

40   Unfortunately, the second law is a subtle concept which most people are not accustomed to dealing with, and it is not easy to see the fallacy in the creationist distortion.

41   There are many other "scientific" arguments used by creationists, some taking quite clever advantage of present areas of dispute in evolutionary theory, but every one of them is as disingenuous as the second-law argument.

42   The "scientific" arguments are organized into special creationist textbooks, which have all the surface appearance of the real thing, and which school systems are being heavily pressured to accept. They are written by people who have not made any mark as scientists, and, while they discuss geology, paleontology and biology with correct scientific terminology, they are devoted almost entirely to raising doubts over the legitimacy of the evidence and reasoning underlying evolutionary thinking on the assumption that this leaves creationism as the only possible alternative.

43   Evidence actually in favor of creationism is not presented, of course, because none exists other than the word of the Bible, which it is current creationist strategy not to use.

• The argument from irrelevance.

44   Some creationists put all matters of scientific evidence to one side and consider all such things irrelevant. The Creator, they say, brought life and the earth and the entire universe into being 6,000 years ago or so, complete with all the evidence for an eons-long evolutionary development. The fossil record, the decaying radioactivity, the receding galaxies were all created as they are, and the evidence they present is an illusion.

45   Of course, this argument is itself irrelevant, for it can neither be proved nor disproved. It is not an argument, actually, but a statement. I can say that the entire universe was created two minutes ago, complete with all its history books describing a nonexistent past in detail, and with every living person equipped with a full memory: you, for instance, in the process of reading this article in midstream with a memory of what you had read in the beginning — which you had not really read.

46   What kind of a Creator would produce a universe containing so intricate an illusion? It would mean that the Creator formed a universe that contained human beings whom He had endowed with the faculty of curiosity and the ability to reason. He supplied those human beings with an enormous amount of subtle and cleverly consistent evidence designed to mislead them and cause them to be convinced that the universe was created 20 billion years ago and developed by evolutionary processes that included the creation and development of life on Earth.

47   Why?

48   Does the Creator take pleasure in fooling us? Does it amuse Him to watch us go wrong? Is it part of a test to see if human beings will deny their senses and their reason in order to cling to myth? Can it be that the Creator is a cruel and malicious prankster, with a vicious and adolescent sense of humor?

▪ The argument from authority.

49   The Bible says that God created the world in six days, and the Bible is the inspired word of God. To the average creationist this is all that counts. All other arguments are merely a tedious way of countering the propaganda of all those wicked humanists, agnostics and atheists who are not satisfied with the clear word of the Lord.

50   The creationist leaders do not actually use that argument because that would make their argument a religious one, and they would not be able to use it in fighting a secular school system. They have to borrow the clothing of science, no matter how badly it fits and call themselves "scientific" creationists. They also speak only of the "Creator," and never mention that this Creator is the God of the Bible.

51   We cannot, however, take this sheep's clothing seriously. However much the creationist leaders might hammer away at their "scientific" and "philo-sophical" points, they would be helpless and a laughing stock if that were all they had.

52   It is religion that recruits their squadrons. Tens of millions of Americans, who neither know or understand the actual arguments for — or even against — evolution, march in the army of the night with their Bibles held high. And they are a strong and frightening force, impervious to, and immunized against, the feeble lance of mere reason.

53   Even if I am right and the evolutionists' case is very strong, have not creationists, whatever the emptiness of their case, a right to be heard?

54   If their case is empty, isn't it perfectly safe to discuss it since the empti-ness would then be apparent?

55   Why, then, are evolutionists so reluctant to have creationism taught in the public schools on an equal basis with evolutionary theory? Can it be that the evolutionists are not as confident of their case as they pretend? Are they afraid to allow youngsters a clear choice?

56   First, the creationists arc somcwhat lcss than honest in their demand for equal time. It is not their views that are repressed: Schools are by no means the only place in which the dispute between creationism and evolutionary theory is played out.

57   There are the churches, for instance, which are a much more serious influence on most Americans than the schools are. To be sure, many churches are quite liberal, have made their peace with science and find it easy to live with scientific advance — even with evolution. But many of the less modish and citified churches are bastions of creationism.

58   The influence of the church is naturally felt in the home, in the newspa-pers and in all of surrounding society. It makes itself felt in the nation as a whole, even in religiously liberal areas, in thousands of subtle ways: in the na-ture of holiday observance, in expressions of patriotic fervor, even in total

irrelevancies. In 1968, for example, a team of astronauts circling the moon were instructed to read the first few verses of Genesis as though NASA felt it had to placate the public lest they rage against the violation of the firmament. At the present time, even the current President of the United States has expressed his creationist sympathies.

59   It is only in school that American youngsters in general are ever likely to hear any reasoned exposition of the evolutionary viewpoint. They might find such a viewpoint in books, magazines, newspapers or even, on occasion, on television. But church and family can easily censor printed matter or television. Only the school is beyond their control.

60   But only just barely beyond. Even though schools are now allowed to teach evolution, teachers are beginning to be apologetic about it, knowing full well their jobs are at the mercy of school boards upon which creationists are a stronger and stronger influence.

61   Then, too, in schools, students are not required to believe what they learn about evolution — merely to parrot it back on tests. If they fail to do so, their punishment is nothing more than the loss of a few points on a test or two.

62   In the creationist churches, however, the congregation is required to believe. Impressionable youngsters, taught that they will go to hell if they listen to the evolutionary doctrine, are not likely to listen in comfort or to believe if they do.

63   Therefore, creationists, who control the church and the society they live in and who face the public school as the only place where evolution is even briefly mentioned in a possibly favorable way, find they cannot stand even so minuscule a competition and demand "equal time."

64   Do you suppose their devotion to "fairness" is such that they will give equal time to evolution in their churches?

65   Second, the real danger is the manner in which creationists want their "equal time."

66   In the scientific world, there is free and open competition of ideas, and even a scientist whose suggestions are not accepted is nevertheless free to continue to argue his case.

67   In this free and open competition of ideas, creationism has clearly lost. It has been losing in fact, since the time of Copernicus four and a half centuries ago. But creationists, placing myth above reason, refuse to accept the decision and are now calling on the Government to force their views on the schools in lieu of the free expression of ideas. Teachers must be forced to present creationism as though it has equal intellectual respectability with evolutionary doctrine.

68   What a precedent this sets.

69   If the Government can mobilize its policemen and its prisons to make certain that teachers give creationism equal time, they can next use force to make sure that teachers declare creationism the victor so that evolution will be evicted from the classroom altogether.

70   We will have established the full groundwork, in other words, for legally enforced ignorance and for totalitarian thought control.

71   And what if the creationists win? They might, you know, for there are millions who, faced with the choice between science and their interpretation of the Bible, will choose the Bible and reject science, regardless of the evidence.

72   This is not entirely because of a traditional and unthinking reverence for the literal works of the Bible; there is also a pervasive uneasiness — even an actual fear — of science that will drive even those who care little for Fundamentalism into the arms of the creationists. For one thing, science is uncertain. Theories are subject to revision; observations are open to a variety of interpretations, and scientists quarrel among themselves. This is disillusioning for those untrained in the scientific method, who thus turn to the rigid certainty of the Bible instead. There is something comfortable about a view that allows for no deviation and that spares you the painful necessity of having to think.

73   Second, science is complex and chilling. The mathematical language of science is understood by very few. The vistas it presents are scary — an enormous universe ruled by chance and impersonal rules, empty and uncaring, ungraspable and vertiginous. How comfortable to turn instead to a small world, only a few thousand years old, and under God's personal and immediate care; a world in which you are His peculiar concern and where He will not consign you to hell if you are careful to follow every word of the Bible as interpreted for you by your television preacher.

74   Third, science is dangerous. There is no question but that poison gas, genetic engineering and nuclear weapons and power stations are terrifying. It may be that civilization is falling apart and the world we know is coming to an end. In that case, why not turn to religion and look forward to the Day of Judgment, in which you and your fellow believers will be lifted into eternal bliss and have the added joy of watching the scoffers and disbelievers writhe forever in torment.

75   So why might they not win?

76   There are numerous cases of societies in which the armies of the night have ridden triumphantly over minorities in order to establish a powerful orthodoxy which dictates official thought. Invariably, the triumphant ride is toward long-range disaster.

77   Spain dominated Europe and the world in the 16th century, but in Spain orthodoxy came first, and all divergence of opinion was ruthlessly suppressed. The result was that Spain settled back into blankness and did not share in the scientific, technological and commercial ferment that bubbled up in other nations of Western Europe. Spain remained an intellectual backwater for centuries.

78   In the late 17th century, France in the name of orthodoxy revoked the Edict of Nantes and drove out many thousands of Huguenots, who added their intellectual vigor to lands of refuge such as Great Britain, the Netherlands and Prussia, while France was permanently weakened.

79   In more recent times, Germany hounded out the Jewish scientists of Europe. They arrived in the United States and contributed immeasurably to scientific advancement here, while Germany lost so heavily that there is no telling how long it will take it to regain its former scientific eminence. The Soviet Union, in its fascination with Lysenko, destroyed its geneticists, and set

back its biological sciences for decades. China, during the Cultural Revolution, turned against Western science and is still laboring to overcome the devastation that resulted.

80 Are we now, with all these examples before us, to ride backward into the past under the same tattered banner of orthodoxy? With creationism in the saddle, American science will wither. We will raise a generation of ignoramuses ill-equipped to run the industry of tomorrow, much less to generate the new advances of the days after tomorrow.

81 We will inevitably recede into the backwater of civilization and those nations that retain open scientific thought will take over the leadership of the world and the cutting edge of human development.

82 I don't suppose that the creationists really plan the decline of the United States, but their loudly expressed patriotism is as simple-minded as their "science." If they succeed, they will, in their folly, achieve the opposite of what they say they wish.

Reading Sources: "The 'Threat' of Creationism"

Read the selection, surveying it to identify key terms and important concepts. Highlight these phrases and ideas, and then answers these questions.

1. What visual cues are used in this essay? How do they help readers to follow Asimov's arguments?
2. Why does Asimov open his essay with the very brief paragraph, "Scientists thought it was settled"? Evaluate the effectiveness of this strategy.
3. At whom is Asimov aiming his argument — at those who support creationism, those who already agree with him, or those who are undecided? Explain.
4. What are the creationists' arguments as identified by Asimov? How does he refute each argument?
5. What is the purpose of paragraph 7? What is the purpose of the entire essay?
6. Asimov uses the phrase "army [or armies] of the night" in paragraphs 8, 52, and 76. What do you think he means to suggest by this phrase?
7. Asimov is open about his bias against creationism, but his bias against creationists themselves is more subtle. Identify language that reveals this bias.
8. Why does Asimov explicitly state that his explanation of the second law of thermodynamics is presented "in kindergarten terms" (33)? Why does he later "lift the argument a notch above the kindergarten level" (36)?
9. Why, according to Asimov, do the creationists use scientific rather than religious terminology?
10. What is the intended effect of the series of questions Asimov asks in paragraphs 47–48, 53–55, and 64? Is the desired effect achieved in each case? Explain.
11. How does Asimov connect the ideas in paragraphs 72–74? What techniques does he use to link the ideas within each of these three paragraphs?
12. In one sentence, restate Asimov's thesis. Where in the essay does a version of this thesis statement appear?

Reacting to Sources

Reread the selection carefully, making marginal notes to aid comprehension and reinforce connections. Then further annotate the essay if you need to do so in order to answer any of these questions. (You may already have addressed some of the questions in your marginal notes.)

1. Using a dictionary if necessary, supply brief marginal definitions of these words as they are used in this selection: *hominid* (2), *creationism* (4), *Fundamentalists* (5), *fervid* (6), *secular* (7), *blasphemer* (12), *corpus* (25), *dogmatism* (26), *disingenuous* (41), *humanists* (49), *agnostics* (49), *impervious* (52), *modish* (57), *bastions* (57), *placate* (58), *firmament* (58), *exposition* (59), *pervasive* (72), *vertiginous* (73), *orthodoxy* (77).
2. Identify: American Civil Liberties Union (4), Moral Majority (5), Bible Belt (5), origin of species (27), Copernicus (67). If necessary, refer to an encyclopedia.
3. Give two examples from the selection to support Asimov's general statement in paragraph 4 that the creationists are "a growing power in the land."
4. In a few sentences, rewrite paragraphs 25–26 to simplify the ideas Asimov presents there.
5. Write three questions to clarify your understanding of the ideas in paragraphs 33–39.
6. Outline paragraphs 53–70.
7. From your own experience, do you agree or disagree with Asimov's views in paragraphs 59–61? Write a journal entry in which you explain your position.
8. Throughout his essay, Asimov sets up a dichotomy between creationists and scientists. List a few of the contrasts he identifies. What is his purpose in setting the two groups in opposition? Is this fair? Explain in marginal notes.
9. Find a statement in the essay which your own educational experience can support. Write a journal entry presenting this support.
10. Reread the introduction to the selection. Comment in your journal on how your knowledge of the nature and scope of Asimov's other writings influences your attitude toward this essay.
11. In paragraph 70, Asimov equates the creationists' aims with "legally enforced ignorance and . . . totalitarian thought control." In a marginal note, comment on the possible validity of this statement.
12. Throughout the essay, Asimov makes frequent use of highly charged, emotional language. Identify several examples of such language. Is this technique necessary? Does it strengthen or weaken Asimov's credibility? Explain in a journal entry.

Working with Sources

1. Write a one-hundred-word summary of paragraphs 76–82.
2. Write a critique of the ideas in paragraphs 19–23.

3. Write a journal entry in which you explore your reactions to these quotations from "The 'Threat' of Creationism":

> "They make up a fervid and dedicated group, convinced beyond argument of both their rightness and righteousness" (6).

> ". . . they are a strong and frightening force, impervious to, and immunized against, the feeble lance of mere reason" (52).

> "I don't suppose that the creationists really plan the decline of the United States, but their loudly expressed patriotism is as simple minded as their 'science'" (82).

Be sure to integrate the quotations smoothly into your writing.
4. Paraphrase the ideas in paragraph 73.
5. Write a one-paragraph synthesis that blends ideas in paragraphs 55–58 of this essay and paragraph 7 of "Opposing Prefab Prayer" (pp. 343–351).

Writing with Sources: Using a Single Source

Integrating information from "The 'Threat' of Creationism" with your own ideas, write an essay on one of these topics. Be sure to acknowledge ideas that are not your own.

1. In paragraph 7 Asimov says, "though creationists seem to accept the literal truth of the Biblical story of creation, this does not mean that all religious people are creationists. There are millions of Catholics, Protestants and Jews who think of the Bible as a source of spiritual truth and accept much of it as symbolically true." Keeping this statement in mind, read a Biblical account of the creation of the universe, and write an essay in which you consider whether it is possible for religious people to accept the scientific theory of creation.
2. Review the discussion of the creation of the universe in several biology textbooks. Then write an essay in which you compare these accounts, point by point, with the Biblical version of creation, considering which aspects of the opposing account would be objectionable to supporters of each theory.
3. Are the creationists' goals as Asimov defines them really a threat to our nation? Or does Asimov overstate his case in paragraphs 76–82? (Note that recent court cases in Texas, Arkansas, and Louisiana have ruled against requiring the teaching of creationism in public school biology classes. In addition, California recently *rejected* all proposed high school biology texts for not including enough about evolution. Publishers are now rewriting them.) Write an essay in which you explain your position.

From *Evolution — The Fossils Say No*

Duane T. Gish

Duane Gish, who received his Ph.D. in biochemistry from the University of California, Berkeley, spent eighteen years doing biochemical and biomedical research at Cornell University Medical College, the Virus Laboratory of the University of California, Berkeley, and The Upjohn Company. Today, he is Associate Director of the Institute for Creation Research and Professor of Natural Science at Christian Heritage College in San Diego. A prominent lecturer on creationism and evolution, Gish is also the author of many technical articles in his field. This selection is excerpted from a chapter of his 1978 book *Evolution — The Fossils Say No*. Elsewhere in the same chapter, Gish defines the terms *evolution* and *creationism*. He states that while creationists accept the evolutionists' explanation of the origin of variations within basic animal or plant kinds, they deny "the evolutionary origin of basically different types of plants and animals from common ancestors." By *creation*, Gish states, he means "the bringing into being by a supernatural Creator of the basic kinds of plants and animals by the process of sudden, or fiat, creation."

1   Much evidence from the fields of cosmology, chemistry, thermodynamics, mathematics, molecular biology, and genetics could be inferred in an attempt to decide which model offers a more plausible explanation for the origin of living things. In the final analysis, however, what actually *did* happen can only be decided, scientifically, by an examination of the historical record, that is, the fossil record. Thus, W. LeGros Clark, the well-known British evolutionist, has said:

> That evolution actually *did* occur can only be scientifically established by the discovery of the fossilized remains of representative samples of those intermediate types which have been postulated on the basis of the indirect evidence. In other words, the really crucial evidence for evolution must be provided by the paleontologist whose business it is to study the evidence of the fossil record.[1]

This latter statement also applies to creation.

2   The history of life upon the earth may be traced through an examination of the fossilized remains of past forms of life entombed in the rocks. If life arose from an inanimate world through a mechanistic, naturalistic, evolutionary process and then diversified, by a similar process via increasingly complex forms, into the millions of species that have existed and now exist, then the fossils actually found in the rocks should correspond to those predicted on the basis of such a process.

3   On the other hand, if living things came into being by a process of special

---

[1] *Discovery* (January 1955), 7.

creation, then predictions very different from those based on evolution theory should be made concerning the fossil record. It is our contention that the fossil record is much more in accordance with the predictions based on creation, rather than those based on the theory of evolution, and actually strongly contradicts evolution theory.

. . .

4 **Creation Model.**   On the basis of the creation model, we would predict an explosive appearance in the fossil record of highly complex forms of life without evidence of ancestral forms. We would predict that all of the major types of life, that is, the basic plant and animal forms, would appear abruptly in the fossil record without evidence of transitional forms linking one basic kind to another.

5   We would thus expect to find the fossilized remains, for example, of cats, dogs, bears, elephants, cows, horses, bats, dinosaurs, crocodiles, monkeys, apes, and men without evidence of common ancestors. Each major kind at its earliest appearance in the fossil record would possess, fully developed, all the characteristics that are used to define that particular kind.

6 **Evolution Model.**   On the basis of the evolution model, we would predict that the most ancient strata in which fossils are found would contain the most primitive forms of life capable of leaving a fossil record. As successively younger strata were searched, we would expect to see the gradual transition of these relatively simple forms of life into more and more complex forms of life. As living forms diverged into the millions of species which have existed in the past and which exist today, we would expect to find a slow and gradual transition of one form into another.

7   We would predict that new basic types would *not* appear suddenly in the fossil record possessing all of the characteristics that are used to define its kind. The earliest forms in each group would be expected to possess in incipient form some of the characteristics which are used to define that group while retaining characteristics used to define the ancestral group.

8   If fish evolved into amphibia, as evolutionists believe, then we would predict that we would find transitional forms showing the gradual transition of fins into feet and legs. Of course, many other alterations in the anatomy and physiology of fishes would have to occur to change an animal adapted to living its entire life span in water to one which spends most of its life outside of water. The fin-to-feet transition would be an easily traceable transition, however.

9   If reptiles gave rise to birds, then we would expect to find transitional forms in the fossil record showing the gradual transition of the forelimbs of the ancestral reptile into the wings of a bird, and the gradual transition of some structure on the reptile into the feathers of a bird. These again are obvious transitions that could be easily traced in the fossil record. Of course, many other changes would have been taking place at the same time, such as the conversion

of the hindfeet of the reptile into the perching feet of the bird, reptilian skull into birdlike skull, etc.

10   In the pterosaurs, or flying reptiles, the wing membrane was supported by an enormously lengthened fourth finger. If the pterosaurs actually evolved from a nonflying reptile, then we would predict that the fossil record would produce transitional forms showing a gradual increase in length of the fourth finger, along with the origin of other unique structures.

11   The fossil record ought to produce thousands upon thousands of transitional, or in-between forms. It is true that according to evolutionary geology only a tiny fraction of all plants and animals that have ever existed would have been preserved as fossils. It is also true that we have as yet uncovered only a small fraction of the fossils that are entombed in the rocks. We have, nevertheless, recovered a good representative number of the fossils that exist.

12   Sampling of the fossil record has now been so thorough that appeals to the imperfections in the record are no longer valid. George has stated:

> There is no need to apologize any longer for the poverty of the fossil record. In some ways it has become almost unmanageably rich and discovery is outpacing integration.[2]

13   It seems clear, then, that after 150 years of intense searching a large number of obvious transitional forms would have been discovered if the predictions of evolution theory are valid.

14   We have, for example, discovered literally billions of fossils of ancient invertebrates and many fossils of ancient fishes. The transition of invertebrate into vertebrate is believed to have required many millions of years. Populations are supposed to constitute the units of evolution and, of course, only successful populations survive. It seems obvious, then, that if we find fossils of the invertebrates which were supposed to have been ancestral to fishes, and if we find fossils of the fishes, we surely ought to find the fossils of the transitional forms.

15   We find fossils of crossopterygian fishes which are alleged to have given rise to the amphibia. We find fossils of the so-called "primitive" amphibia. Since the transition from fish to amphibia would have required many millions of years, during which many hundreds of millions, even billions, of the transitional forms must have lived and died, many of these transitional forms should have been discovered in the fossil record even though only a minute fraction of these animals have been recovered as fossils. As a matter of fact, the discovery of only five or six of the transitional forms scattered through time would be sufficient to document evolution.

16   So it would be throughout the entire fossil record. There should not be the slightest difficulty in finding transitional forms. Hundreds of transitional forms should fill museum collections. If we find fossils at all, we ought to find transitional forms. As a matter of fact, difficulty in placing a fossil within a distinct category should be the rule rather than the exception.

[2] T. N. George, *Scientific Progress* 48 (1960), 1.

Reading Sources: From Evolution — The Fossils Say *No*

Read the selection, surveying it to identify key terms and important concepts. Highlight these phrases and ideas, and then answer these questions.

1. What visual cues are used in this selection? How do they help clarify Gish's ideas?
2. Why does Gish quote W. LeGros Clark in paragraph 1? How does Clark's statement help to build Gish's argument?
3. Why does Gish dismiss evidence from "cosmology, chemistry, thermodynamics, mathematics, molecular biology, and genetics" (1) for the purposes of his essay?
4. Analyze Gish's target audience: Is he addressing scientists or the general public? Creationists, evolutionists, or neutral readers? How can you tell?
5. How does Gish use repetition and parallelism to link the paragraph cluster beginning with paragraph 4 to the cluster beginning with paragraph 6?
6. In paragraph 11 Gish concedes two points to his opponents. How does he signal these concessions to his readers? How does he signal his dismissal of these points?
7. In paragraph 11 Gish says, "The fossil record ought to produce thousands upon thousands of transitional, or in-between forms." Identify other statements in the essay that make essentially the same point. Does this repetition strengthen or weaken Gish's argument?
8. In one sentence, state Gish's thesis.

Reacting to Sources

Reread the selection carefully, making marginal notes to aid comprehension and reinforce connections. Then further annotate the selection if you need to do so in order to answer any of these questions. (You may already have addressed some of the questions in your marginal notes.)

1. Using a dictionary if necessary, supply brief marginal definitions of these words as they are used in this selection: *entombed* (2), *mechanistic* (2), *contention* (3), *strata* (6), *incipient* (7).
2. In paragraph 6 of "The 'Threat' of Creationism" (pp. 354–363), Asimov characterizes creationists as "a fervid and dedicated group, convinced beyond argument of both their rightness and righteousness." Using examples of Gish's tone and language, write a journal entry in which you consider whether or not Asimov's description applies to Gish.
3. In this selection, Gish bases his argument for creationism solely on one shortcoming he identifies in the evolutionists' view. What is this single shortcoming? Does this narrow focus strengthen or weaken Gish's argument? Explain in a journal entry.

4. In paragraph 12 Gish says, "Sampling of the fossil record has now been so thorough that appeals to the imperfections in the record are no longer valid." Write a journal entry in which you explore this idea.
5. Write three questions in response to the ideas in paragraph 6.
6. What is the purpose of paragraph 13? Explain in a marginal note.
7. In a marginal note, give two examples from the essay to support Gish's general statement in paragraph 13 that "after 150 years of intense searching a large number of obvious transitional forms would have been discovered if the predictions of evolution theory are valid."
8. Identify a statement with which you strongly agree or disagree, and write a marginal comment explaining your position.
9. Reread the introduction to the essay. Then write a journal entry in which you comment on how your knowledge of Gish's educational and professional background influences your acceptance of his ideas.
10. In a journal entry, reconsider Gish's central point in light of this statement: "Virtually the whole scientific corpus of creationism . . . consists of the pointing out of imperfections in the evolutionary view" ("The 'Threat' of Creationism," paragraph 25).

Working with Sources

1. Write a fifty-word summary of paragraphs 4 – 7.
2. Write a critique of the ideas in paragraph 16.
3. In the October 1981 issue of *Science Digest,* Isaac Asimov debated Duane Gish. Write a journal entry in which you explore your reactions to these statements by Asimov in response to Gish's argument that the fossil record supports creationism.

> "There *are* an immense number of transitional forms, and museums *are* overflowing with them."

> "Fossils were formed rarely and haphazardly. We don't expect a complete story."

> "There are even *living* transitional forms between vertebrates and invertebrates. Balanoglossus, a kind of sea worm, and the tunicates, a subphylum of marine animal, show clear signs of ecinoderm (the phylum that includes starfish) ancestry, and yet they are indisputably related to the vertebrates."

Be sure to integrate the quotations smoothly into your writing.
4. Paraphrase the ideas in paragraphs 2 – 3.
5. Write a one-paragraph synthesis that blends ideas in paragraph 2 of this essay and paragraphs 24 – 28 of "The 'Threat' of Creationism" (pp. 354 – 363).

Writing with Sources: Using a Single Source

Integrating information from the excerpt from *Evolution — the Fossils Say No* with your own ideas, write an essay on one of these topics. Be sure to acknowledge ideas that are not your own.

1. Taking into account Asimov's remarks about the existence of transitional forms in both fossils and living animals and his view that many other such forms remain undiscovered (quoted in Working with Sources, question 3), evaluate the validity of Gish's essay. Is his argument convincing? What kinds of evidence could further strengthen it?
2. Find a series of pictures, in an encyclopedia or a biology book, of many different species of animals. Write an essay for elementary school children in which you argue that, based on their obvious physical characteristics, some of the animals *could* in fact be considered "transitional forms."
3. Stephen Jay Gould, a biologist who teaches the history of science at Harvard, has advanced the theory that evolution actually proceeded in a series of leaps rather than in gradual steps. In an essay, consider how Gould's theory could account for the weakness Gish sees in the theory of evolution.

Appeal to Reason and Conscience

Archibald MacLeish and the Ad Hoc Committee of Protest

During 1947 and 1948, a series of articles by Paul Blanshard critical of the policies of the Roman Catholic Church appeared in *The Nation,* a well-respected liberal periodical. In retaliation, *The Nation* was banned from New York City's public school libraries and subsequently from libraries and schools in other communities. In response to these actions, a group of more than one hundred American writers and intellectuals, led by poet Archibald MacLeish, formed an ad hoc committee of protest. In "Appeal to Reason and Conscience," which appeared in the October 16, 1948 issue of *The Nation,* these prominent literary leaders argue that Americans have a right to express their ideas about religion freely and honestly—even if their opinions offend others.

1   On June 8 the Board of Superintendents of New York City's schools closed the schools to *The Nation,* the oldest liberal magazine in the United States. This action was taken without advance notice to *The Nation* or to the people of the city, without a hearing and without announcement of any kind, either to the magazine or to the public. The only opportunity afforded to the magazine to defend itself or to citizens to be heard, was at a meeting of the board from which the press was excluded, and which was called as a result of

public protest some weeks after the decision had accidentally become known. After this proceeding, the board reaffirmed its decision by unanimous vote.

2   Other communities thereupon followed suit by similar unilateral action. In Massachusetts *The Nation* was banned from the State Teacher's Colleges by a public official who admitted he had not, at the time of the banning, himself investigated the reason given by the New York board for its action.

3   That reason was the publication by *The Nation* in 1947 and 1948 of a series of articles by Paul Blanshard, for many years Commissioner of Investigations and Accounts of the City of New York in the LaGuardia administration. Mr. Blanshard's articles described and criticized the official position of the Catholic Church in such matters as education, science, medicine, marriage and divorce, democracy and fascism. The board stated that there were passages in these articles which a Catholic would find objectionable on grounds of faith.

4   It is the opinion of the undersigned that the action of The New York Board of Superintendents raises an issue of the greatest gravity to the people of the city and of the country. It is not an issue between Catholic and non-Catholic. There are Catholics among us, and none of us, whether Catholic or not, have been moved to protest by reason of hostility to the Catholic faith. Neither is the issue raised a mere issue of fact with regard to the articles themselves. We agree with the board that there are sincere Catholics and men of good will who object on grounds of faith to certain statements in Mr. Blanshard's articles. Indeed, some of us who are not Catholics, disagree with certain of Mr. Blanshard's statements.

5   The issue as we see it is the issue of principle which the board's action and the board's statements in defense of its action present. The question before the board was not the question of the suitability of *The Nation* as a textbook in the city's schools. The question was whether *The Nation,* which had long been one of the periodicals available to New York students, should continue to be available to them. In ruling that it should not, and in giving the publication of the Blanshard articles as justification, the board in effect enunciated two propositions, both of which in our opinion are contrary to American ideas of freedom and destructive of American principles.

6   The first is the proposition that any published material which is regarded, or which could be regarded, as objectionable on grounds of faith or creed by any group in the community should be excluded from the community's schools and school libraries.

7   The second is the proposition that the appearance in any publication of material of this kind justifies the suppression in schools and school libraries of the publication as a whole. In the case of a periodical this means that the past publication of such material justifies the suppression of future issues regardless of the general character and record of the periodical.

8   The vice of the second of these two propositions is apparent upon its face. The exclusion from public institutions, by public officials, of future issues of newspapers, magazines, or other periodicals on the basis of particular material published in the past, rather than on the basis of the character of the

publication as a whole, cannot be defended even as censorship. It is extra-judicial punishment pure and simple, and it involves a power of intimidation and possible blackmail in officials of government which no free society can tolerate and which a free press could not long survive. To permit public officials, in their unlimited, extra-judicial discretion, to stigmatize an established and respected magazine or newspaper as unfit for students to read because of the publication of a specific article or series of articles, or of particular paragraphs in a specific article or series, is to confer an arbitrary and dictatorial power which is wholly foreign to the American tradition and to the laws and Constitution in which the American tradition is expressed.

9   The first proposition — that any publication objectionable on grounds of faith to any group in the community should be suppressed in the schools — though more plausible on its face, is equally vicious in fact. It is a repudiation, on one side, of the principle of freedom of education; on the other, of the principle of the separation of church and state. The meaning of that latter tenet, so far as education is concerned, is that no church may use the public schools as instruments of its propaganda. To give the churches of the country, or any of their members who might seek to exercise it, the power to determine by simple veto what shall *not* be available to students in the public schools, or, worse, for public officials to exclude automatically anything any group might be expected to wish excluded, is to do by negative action what the Constitution and the courts forbid by positive action.

10   The argument offered in defense of this revolutionary proposal is apparently that religion cannot be criticized in American education. There is nothing in American law or in the American tradition which says that religion cannot be criticized in education, nor does the principle of the separation of church and state involve any such consequence. On the contrary, the American Republic was founded, and the American continent was settled, by people whose actions were in large part an expression of their criticism of certain established religions. Criticism of religion can certainly take forms which are unsuitable to schools, just as political controversy can take forms which are the opposite of instructive. But the doctrine that the criticism of religion must be outlawed *as such* in American education is a proposition which has no justification in American experience. Ignorance is notoriously the worst foundation for tolerance, and the American people have never felt that education should teach their children to be blind.

Archibald MacLeish, Eleanor Roosevelt, Herbert H. Lehman, Leonard Bernstein, Lillian Smith, Fannie Hurst, Cass Canfield, William Rose Benet, Henry Seidel Canby, G. Bromley Oxnam, Rex Stout, Max Lerner, Alvin Johnson, Bernard DeVoto, Dorothy Canfield Fisher, Oscar Hammerstein II, Sinclair Lewis, Lewis Mumford, Louis Untermeyer, Elmer Rice, Mark Van Doren, Sumner Welles, Stephen S. Wise, Edward R. Murrow, Reinhold Niebuhr, Allan Nevins, Bud Schulberg, Samuel Hopkins Adams, Truman Capote, Langston Hughes, Henry Steele Commager, Henry Emerson Fosdick, Virginia Gildersleeve, Hamilton Holt, Robert Hutchins, Howard Mumford Jones, Frank P. Graham, Perry Miller, Albert Spalding, Marshall Field III

Reading Sources: "Appeal to Reason and Conscience"

Read the selection, surveying it to identify key terms and important concepts. Highlight these phrases and ideas, and then answer these questions.

1. How do the authors link the sentences in the first two paragraphs?
2. What key terms do the authors of this selection stress through repetition? How does the use of the these terms strengthen their argument?
3. What was the church's actual objection to Blanshard's series of articles?
4. In paragraph 4 the authors declare: "It is not an issue between Catholic and non-Catholic. There are Catholics among us, and none of us, whether Catholic or not, have been moved to protest by reason of hostility to the Catholic faith." Why do they find it necessary to state this?
5. What do the authors hope to gain by using language such as "both of which in our opinion are contrary to American ideas of freedom and destructive of American principles" (5) and "wholly foreign to the American tradition and to the laws and Constitution in which the American tradition is expressed" (8)? Are they successful in achieving their ends?
6. How do the authors use language to call attention to their refutation of the two propositions set forth by the Board of Education? Underline the phrases in paragraphs 5–9 that signal the authors' intention to refute the Board's propositions.

Reacting to Sources

Reread the selection carefully, making marginal notes to aid comprehension and reinforce connections. Then further annotate the selection if you need to do so in order to answer any of these questions. (You may already have addressed some of the questions in your marginal notes.)

1. Using a dictionary if necessary, supply brief marginal definitions of these words as they appear in this selection: *unilateral* (2), *gravity* (4), *enunciated* (5), *suppression* (7), *extra-judicial* (8), *stigmatize* (8), *arbitrary* (8), *plausible* (9), *repudiation* (9), *tenet* (9).
2. What is the purpose of paragraph 3? What is the purpose of the entire selection? Explain in marginal notes.
3. In paragraph 8 the authors say that excluding future issues of *The Nation* from libraries "is extra-judicial punishment pure and simple, and it involves a power of intimidation and possible blackmail in officials of government which no free society can tolerate and which a free press could not long survive." Do you agree with their view, or do you believe the authors are overstating their case? Explain in a marginal note.
4. In a few sentences, rewrite paragraph 8 to simplify its ideas.
5. In paragraph 9 the authors assert that the board's first proposition "is a repudiation, on one side, of the principle of freedom of education; on the other side, of the principle of the separation of church and state." Formulate three questions whose answers could enhance your understanding of this statement.

6. Consider the use, in paragraph 9, of strong words like *vicious, repudiation, propaganda,* and *veto.* Is such language justified? What is the effect of substituting less inflammatory terms? Do this in marginal notes, and comment on the effect in a journal entry.
7. Give two examples that could support the authors' general position, in paragraph 9, against giving "the churches of the country, or any of their members who might seek to exercise it, the power to determine by simple veto what shall not be available to students in the public schools."
8. In paragraph 10 the authors point out that "the American Republic was founded, and the American continent was settled, by people whose actions were in large part an expression of their criticism of certain established religions." Explore this idea further in a journal entry.
9. In a journal entry, consider possible connections between this selection and your own experiences with censorship by your church, your school, or your parents.
10. Review the list of signatures at the end of the selection, and identify as many of the names as you can. How might this list have affected the selection's credibility at the time of its publication? What effect do the names have on your own acceptance of the selection's ideas? Explain in a journal entry.

Working with Sources

1. Write a two-sentence summary of paragraphs 1 and 2.
2. Write a critique of the ideas in paragraph 9.
3. Write a journal entry in which you express your reaction to these quotations:

   "The board stated that there were passages in these articles which a Catholic would find objectionable on grounds of faith" (3).

   "There is nothing in American law or in the American tradition that says that religion cannot be criticized in education, nor does the principle of the separation of church and state involve any such consequence" (10).

   "Congress shall make no law respecting an establishment of religion, or prohibiting the free exercise thereof . . ." (Bill of Rights, Article I).

   Be sure to integrate the quotations smoothly into your writing.
4. Paraphrase the ideas in paragraph 8.
5. Write a one-paragraph synthesis that blends ideas in paragraph 10 of this essay and paragraph 4 of "Kennedy's Houston Speech" (pp. 333–336).

Writing with Sources: Using a Single Source

Integrating information from "Appeal to Reason and Conscience" with your own ideas, write an essay on one of these topics. Be sure to acknowledge ideas that are not your own.

1. The authors end the selection with this statement: "Ignorance is notoriously the worst foundation for tolerance, and the American people have never felt that education should teach their children to be blind." Respond to this statement, considering how it applies to other aspects of American education — the teaching of evolution or sex education, for example.
2. Do you believe certain books or periodicals should be excluded from public libraries? If not, why not? If so, on what grounds, and by whose authority?
3. The authors are careful to note in paragraph 5 that the issue they are addressing is not whether or not *The Nation,* with its articles critical of a religious group's practices, would be suitable as a required text, but simply whether it should be banned from school libraries. Consider the case of a required text that includes passages that might offend members of a particular ethnic, religious, or racial group. Is this a different situation? Should such books be used as texts, providing they meet other criteria for adoption? Explain your position on this issue.

Writing with Sources: Using Multiple Sources

Integrating information from sources in this chapter with your own ideas, write and essay on one of the topics below. Be sure to acknowledge ideas that are not your own.

1. Is it fair for a democratic society to make laws that tell people how to worship, or that restrict their beliefs? Consider the potential conflict between individual liberties and conformity to group norms as it applies to the issues of school prayer, the teaching of creationism, and the formation of religious cults.
2. Can religion be a threat to our society? Explain your viewpoint.
3. Should religion and politics be kept completely separate, or are there areas in which the government has a legitimate reason to interfere in the religious lives of Americans — or instances in which religious groups should interfere in American politics? Explain your position.
4. Consider the rights of Americans who do not believe in any religion, or any god, or whose religious convictions and practices are very different from those of mainstream American religions. Does the Constitution guarantee freedom of religion to them, too? Read the Fourteenth Amendment to the Constitution. Explain what protection, if any, it offers to agnostics, atheists, and members of small religious sects.
5. What do you believe is the greatest challenge facing religion today? Write an essay in which you explain this pressing issue and offer suggestions on how to resolve the problems it presents.

10

Working

Psychologists, psychiatrists, and sociologists have testified to the importance of work. An individual's attitude toward work can affect his or her attitude toward family, friends, and even life itself. For this reason, understanding the complex relationship between the individual and the workplace is important. Equally important is understanding the historical origins of the importance of work and the struggle that various groups have undertaken to gain access to work and improve working conditions. In this century technology, unionization, immigration, and the economic climate have all changed the way individuals perceive work. As a result, a great number of workers feel frustrated and alienated from traditional values about work and success. Recently, a number of writers have challenged contemporary assumptions about work and suggested changes that, if implemented, would radically change the workplace.

Irvin G. Wyllie, in an excerpt from *The Self-Made Man in America,* sheds light on current attitudes toward work by examining the nineteenth-century cult of the self-made man. Next, in "The Phenomenon of Burn-Out" Herbert Freudenberger considers what happens when an individual's ideas about work do not conform to the everyday reality of work. In "The Importance of Work" Gloria Steinem discusses how paid work is important to a woman's self-esteem. Daniel T. Rodgers, in "The Working Day," examines organized labor's struggle to achieve an eight-hour day. In a selection from *Brave New Workplace,* Robert Howard takes a critical look at the changes that are occurring in workplaces all across the country. And finally, in an excerpt from *Working* Studs Terkel surveys the fears and hopes of working people and conveys their longing for a better life.

From *The Self-Made Man in America*

Irvin G. Wyllie

Irvin G. Wyllie was born in Pittsburgh in 1920. He received his Ph.D. in history from the University of Wisconsin in 1949 and taught at a number of colleges and universities. The following selection is excerpted from his book *The Self-Made Man in America: The Myth of Rags to Riches* (1954). In his essay, Wyllie traces the beginnings of the rags-to-riches theme in America and shows how this concept helped define the goals of generations of young workers.

I

1   In the nation's capital on June 29, 1869, the graduating class of the Spencerian Business College assembled for final exercises. The speaker for the occasion was a politician, but he did not talk about Reconstruction, or any other current political issue. Instead, James A. Garfield took up a matter of more personal concern to both his audience and himself, the problem of getting ahead in the world. He asserted that in the aristocracies of the Old World, where society was stratified like the rocks of the earth, it was uncommon for a boy to rise from the lowest to the highest social strata, but in America, where society was as fluid as the ocean, poor boys continually rose to displace those riding the crests. This, he declared, was the chief glory of America.[1] Twelve years later James A. Garfield became President of the United States. His own rise from a log cabin to the White House offered proof of his thesis.

2   To the young men of the Spencerian Business College Garfield's message could scarcely qualify as news. They were already familiar with the tradition of log-cabin Presidents, and their choice of business vocations suggested an equal knowledge, and perhaps greater admiration, of the careers of such men as John Jacob Astor, Peter Cooper, and Cornelius Vanderbuilt. The truth was that even before the Civil War there was considerable worship of self-made men of wealth, and a widespread desire to emulate them. In 1853 *Harper's New Monthly Magazine* reported that to the vast majority of Americans success had long since come to mean achievement in business, and in making money. "The idea instilled into the minds of most boys, from early life," the article declared, "is that of 'getting on.' The parents test themselves by their own success in this respect; and they impart the same notion to their children."[2] Parents had no monopoly on this idea, of course, for writers and orators characteristically loved the rags-to-riches theme and helped to spread it widely. At mid-century the young man who went to church, or to the lyceum, or to the reading rooms of a mercantile library association was bound to hear or read something about the self-made man and his glorious conquest of fortune.

3   The popular American conception of this phenomenon was much nar-

[1] James A. Garfield, *Elements of Success* (Washington, 1881), p. 6. For popular accounts of Garfield's rise, see William M. Thayer, *From Log-Cabin to the White House* (Boston, 1881), and Horatio Alger, *From Canal Boy to President* (New York, 1881).
[2] "Success in Life," *Harper's New Monthly Magazine,* VII (1853), 238.

rower, however, than the dictionary definition which described the self-made man as one who had achieved success in any work without benefit of external advantages, one who had risen from obscurity on the strength of personal merit. Although the dictionary allowed the self-made artist, writer, or clergyman as much honor as the titan of trade, it is a matter of record that actually they were not so highly honored, or so widely worshipped. "Analyze the elements of it," an English observer wrote in 1885, "and you will see that success is identified to some extent with fame; still more with power; most of all, with wealth." [3] And it was not to men of the professions but to a group of successful manufacturers that the term "self-made man" was first applied. On February 2, 1832, Henry Clay was defending the protective tariff in the Senate against charges of his Southern opponents that a tariff would spawn an hereditary industrial aristocracy. Not so, Clay replied. A protective tariff would widen opportunities and enable humble men to rise in the industrial sphere. "In Kentucky," he said, "almost every manufactory known to me is in the hands of enterprising self-made men, who have whatever wealth they possess by patient and diligent labor." [4]

II

4   Though it was an American conceit that the self-made man was peculiar to our shores, he had been known in other lands. Since virtually all societies provided some channels for vertical social circulation, men of this type had been common to all. In the older nations of Europe such institutions as the army, the church, the school, and the political party served as agencies for testing, sifting, and distributing individuals within various social strata. Even in associating the self-made man with wealth America enjoyed no special distinction, for in ancient Greece and Rome successful moneymakers often rose into the ruling class, regardless of social origin. And in the Italian city-states and the commercial centers of Western Europe at the close of the Middle Ages money-making was one of the most common and omnipotent means of social promotion.[5]

5   Seventeenth-century England was especially familiar with the economic definition applied to this class of men, for as the English merchant classes rose to power they inspired a substantial literature of justification. Publicists associated with the English business community turned out many pamphlets, sermons, and guidebooks which pointed out the way to wealth. One of these English classics was Richard Johnson's *Nine Worthies of London* (1592), an account of nine apprentices who rose to positions of honor through the exercise of personal virtue. Another of these handbooks, *A Treatise of the Vocations* (1603), written by William Perkins, a learned Cambridge theologian, was held in special regard by Americans. In the seventeenth century success-minded

[3] Frederick W. Farrar, *Success in Life* (Boston, 1885), p. 21.

[4] William A. Craigie and James R. Hulbert, eds., *A Dictionary of American English* (4 vols., Chicago, 1944), IV, 2065; *Register of Debates in Congress* (14 vols., Washington, 1825–37), VIII, Part 1, 277.

[5] For a discussion of social promotion under European conditions, consult Pitirim Sorokin, *Social Mobility* (New York, 1927), pp. 139, 164–183.

immigrants sometimes carried Perkins' book with them to the New World, and read it for guidance and inspiration.[6] Of course the great majority who came to America had no room for books, but they doubtless carried in their heads an ample store of self-help homilies, for such maxims were common coin in England.

6   It is a commonplace of American colonial history that most immigrants came to the New World in the hope of improving their economic status. The agricultural laborer knew that land here was plentiful, and easily acquired, while tradesmen and day laborers built their hopes around the prospect of the high wages which were a natural consequence of the scarcity of labor. On every side American opportunities damaged class patterns inherited from Europe, and altered old orders of caste and custom. In a land where achievement was more important than titles of nobility there was always the possibility that a nobody could become a man of consequence if he worked hard and kept his eye on the main chance. Ralph Barton Perry put it very well when, speaking of colonial artisans and tradesmen, he observed that "They were neither so unfortunate as to be imbued with a sense of helplessness, nor so privileged as to be satisfied with their present status. They possessed just enough to whet their appetites for more and to feel confident of their power to attain it."[7]

7   After the starving time had passed and commercial towns had sprung up along the Atlantic seaboard, urban dwellers could dream not just of competence but of wealth. Cadwallader Colden, reporting on New York City in 1748, asserted that "The only principle of life propagated among the young people is to get money, and men are only esteemed according to what they are worth — that is, the money they are possessed of."[8] This passion for wealth was one which enjoyed the sanction of religion, especially in New England, where Puritan clergymen assured their congregations that God approved business callings, and rewarded virtue with wealth. Cotton Mather, for example, in *Two Brief Discourses, one Directing a Christian in his General Calling; another Directing him in his Personal Calling* (1701) taught that in addition to serving Christ, which was man's general calling, all men were obliged to succeed in some useful secular employment, in order to win salvation in this life as well as in the next. In *Essays To Do Good* (1710) he argued that prosperity was the gift of God, and that men of wealth were God's stewards, charged with the responsibility of doing good to their fellows.[9] Such doctrines as these, inherited from seventeenth-century England, occupied a central place in the American success rationale.

8   It was no accident that the best-known colonial self-made man was Benjamin Franklin, a product of Puritan Boston. At a tender age he read Cotton

---

[6] Louis B. Wright analyzes English success literature in *Middle Class Culture in Elizabethan England* (Chapel Hill, 1935), pp. 165–200.

[7] Ralph Barton Perry, *Puritanism and Democracy* (New York, 1944), p. 298. See also Arthur M. Schlesinger, "What Then Is the American, This New Man?" *American Historical Review*, XLVIII (1943), 227, 237, 239.

[8] Quoted in T. J. Wertenbaker, *The Golden Age of Colonial Culture* (New York, 1942), p. 48.

[9] The best analysis of Cotton Mather's ideas on business success is in Alfred W. Griswold, "Three Puritans on Prosperity," *New England Quarterly*, VII (1934), 475–493.

Mather's *Essays To Do Good,* later crediting them with having had a profound and lifelong influence on his thought and conduct. He also received advice from his father, a humble Puritan candlemaker, who drummed into his head the meaning of the ancient proverb: "Seest thou a man diligent in his business? He shall stand before kings." Fortified by these principles of self-help Franklin migrated to Philadelphia, the Quaker commercial metropolis, to begin his rise in the printing trade. The story of his upward climb has always enjoyed a prominent place in the folklore of success. Through *Poor Richard's Almanack* (1732–1757) he publicized prosperity maxims which have probably exerted as much practical influence on Americans as the combined teachings of all the formal philosophers. Certainly in the nineteenth century the alleged virtues of the American people closely resembled the virtues of Poor Richard.[10]

9   During the American Revolution Franklin's energies were diverted into other channels, and it was the third decade of the nineteenth century before his self-help themes were revived by a new generation of success propagandists. In the troubled years after 1763 publicists were too busy framing assertions of political independence, too busy contriving Federalist and Republican polemics, to be diverted to the writing of maxims of trade. And despite the gains made in industry, commerce, and finance between the Revolution and the period of Jackson's rise to power, few prophets arose to call young men to action in these spheres. By 1830, however, the impacts of the Industrial Revolution could no longer be ignored; in the great cities of the North and East, journalists, clergymen, lawyers and other spokesmen began to lay the foundations for the powerful nineteenth-century cult of the self-made man.

III

10   Appropriately Benjamin Franklin became the first object of adoration in this cult, the convenient symbol which linked the success traditions of the two centuries. In 1826 Simeon Ide, a Vermont printer, dedicated a new edition of Franklin's *The Way to Wealth* and *Advice to Young Tradesmen* to the mechanics and farmers of New England. He urged every workingman to reflect on his own advantages, and to compare them with the disadvantages that Franklin had encountered, observing that "Perhaps he may, from a comparison, draw the conclusion, that he has greater advantages in his favour, and fewer discouragements to encounter, than had the persevering Franklin. If this be really the case, what other impediment can there be in his way . . . but the want of a resolute determination to merit, by a similar conduct, the good fortune which attended him?" [11] Ide urged any youth who aspired to wealth or station to lean on the counsel and example of Franklin where he might hope to find an almost infallible passport to the ultimatum of his wishes.

[10] For Franklin's influence on the nineteenth-century success ideology, see Louis B. Wright, "Franklin's Legacy to the Gilded Age," *Virginia Quarterly Review,* XXII (1946), 268–279.

[11] Simeon Ide, ed., *Benjamin Franklin, The Way to Wealth, Advice to Young Tradesmen, and Sketches of His Life and Character* (Windsor, Vt., 1826), p. 39.

11   At Boston in 1831 a series of Franklin Lectures was begun with the avowed object of inspiring the young men of that city to make the most of their opportunities. Edward Everett inaugurated the series, proclaiming that the story of Franklin's rise could not be told too often. The most successful men in history, he declared, had been men "of humble origin, narrow fortunes, small advantages, and self-taught." [12] Twenty-six years later, when a statue of Franklin was unveiled in Boston, Robert C. Winthrop again used the occasion to arouse the working class from their lethargy:

> Behold him, Mechanics and Mechanics' Apprentices, holding out to you an example of diligence, economy and virtue, and personifying the triumphant success which may await those who follow it! Behold him, ye that are humblest and poorest in present condition or in future prospect—lift up your heads and look at the image of a man who rose from nothing, who owed nothing to parentage or patronage, who enjoyed no advantages of early education which are not open,—a hundred fold open,—to yourselves, who performed the most menial services in the business in which his early life was employed, but who lived to stand before Kings, and died to leave a name which the world will never forget.[13]

12   Probably the number of poor boys who were actually inspired to great deeds by the example of Franklin was never large, but at least one, Thomas Mellon, founder of a great banking fortune, has testified to the influence of Franklin on his life. In the year 1828 young Mellon, then fourteen years old, was living on a farm outside the rising industrial city of Pittsburgh. After he had read a battered copy of Franklin's *Autobiography* which he had picked up at a neighbor's house, he found himself aflame with a new ambition. "I had not before imagined," he said, "any other course of life superior to farming, but the reading of Franklin's life led me to question this view. For so poor and friendless a boy to be able to become a merchant or a professional man had before seemed an impossibility; but here was Franklin, poorer than myself, who by industry, thrift and frugality had become learned and wise, and elevated to wealth and fame. The maxims of 'Poor Richard' exactly suited my sentiments. . . . I regard the reading of Franklin's *Autobiography* as the turning point of my life." [14] Abandoning the family farm at Poverty Point young Mellon migrated to Pittsburgh, where he made his way as a lawyer and money lender. Later when he had founded his own bank it was Franklin's statue that he placed at the front of the building as a symbol of his inspiration, and in the last years of his life he bought a thousand copies of Franklin's *Autobiography,* which he distributed to young men who came seeking advice and money.

13   Important though Franklin was as a symbol and inspiration, the magnificent economic opportunities of nineteenth-century America constituted a far more important inspiration to young men in quest of wealth. The urge to get ahead was especially strong in areas which had been transformed by the

---

[12] Edward Everett, *Orations and Speeches on Various Occasions by Edward Everett* (Boston, 1836), pp. 298–299.

[13] Robert C. Winthrop, *Oration at the Inauguration of the Statue of Benjamin Franklin* (Boston, 1856), p. 25.

[14] Quoted in Harvey O'Connor, *Mellon's Millions* (New York, 1933), p. 4.

Industrial Revolution; it was no accident that three out of every four nineteenth-century millionaires were natives of New England, New York, or Pennsylvania, and that 70 percent won their fortunes in either manufacturing,
banking, trade, or transporation.[15] Such activities were concentrated in the
cities, in old commercial centers like New York, Philadelphia, and Boston, or
in new industrial towns such as Lawrence, Lowell, Rochester, and Pittsburgh,
cities which held the key to fortune for the ambitious poor. On the eve of the
Civil War it was a backward metropolis indeed that could not boast of its
self-made businessmen, and an American who knew nothing of the careers of
Amos and Abbott Lawrence, Samuel Appleton, John Jacob Astor, Peter Cooper,
Cornelius Vanderbuilt, Stephen Girard, or George Peabody was considered
hopelessly uninformed.

14   In and near the great urban centers sensitive observers divined the
tendency of the age and gave it their sanction. "How widely spread is the
passion for acquisition," exulted William Ellery Channing of Boston, "not for
simple means of subsistence, but for wealth! What vast enterprises agitate the
community! What a rush into all the departments of trade." [16] As Channing saw
it, it was this tendency that explained the progressive vigor of America in the
1840s. Ralph Waldo Emerson agreed. This philosopher who preached self-reliance also pronounced benedictions on those single-minded businessmen who
created the wealth that raised man above the subsistence level, blessed him
with leisure, and gave him access to the masterworks of the human race. "The
pulpit and the press have many commonplaces denouncing the thirst for
wealth," said Emerson; "but if men should take these moralists at their word
and leave off aiming to be rich, the moralists would rush to rekindle at all
hazards this love of power in the people, lest civilization should be undone." [17]

15   As a good Boston Brahmin Oliver Wendell Holmes was no special friend
of business upstarts, but even he conceded that America could be justly proud
of those self-made men who had come forward before the Civil War to form a
new aristocracy. He thought this aristocracy was "very splendid, though its
origin may have been tar, tallow, train-oil, or other such unctuous commodities." [18] Moreover, he believed that after ten years of patient and diligent labor
any enterprising young man might rise into this elite. Holmes was not alone in
this estimate, for John Aiken, an observer of industrial conditions at Lowell,
Massachusetts, reported in 1849 that "He who five years ago was working for
wages, will now be found transacting business for himself, and a few years
hence, will be likely to be found a hirer of the labor of others." [19]

[15] Sorokin, "American Millionaires and Multi-Millionaires," *Journal of Social Forces,* III (1925),
634, 639. See also C. Wright Mills, "The American Business Elite: a Collective Portrait," *The Tasks of
Economic History,* Supplement V (1945), 22.
   [16] William Ellery Channing, "The Present Age," in *The Works of William Ellery Channing*
(Boston, 1887), p. 165. Channing delivered this address to the Mercantile Library Company of Philadelphia, May 11, 1841.
   [17] Ralph Waldo Emerson, *The Conduct of Life* (Boston, 1904), p. 95.
   [18] Oliver Wendell Holmes, *The Autocrat of the Breakfast Table* (Boston, 1892), p. 259.
   [19] John Aiken, *Labor and Wages, at Home and Abroad* (Lowell, 1849), p. 16.

16   In New York, no less than in New England, the glories of accumulation and the precepts of self-help were widely trumpeted. In 1842 the editor of the New York *Sun,* Moses Yale Beach, gave Americans their first directory of men distinguished chiefly for their possession of money when he published his famous *Wealth and Pedigree of the Wealthy Citizens of New York City.* He tried to include all local men worth a hundred thousand dollars or more; at the top of his list of fourteen millionaires he placed the name of John Jacob Astor, a self-made German immigrant, with a fortune estimated at ten million.[20] In order to benefit his readers Beach called attention to those "who by honest and laborious industry have raised themselves from the obscure walks of life, to great wealth and consideration," and singled out "some of the brightest examples of prosperity in this *touch-stone* land as beacons for those ambitious of fortune's favors."[21]

17   Beach had strong competition in this field of publicity in the person of Freeman Hunt, a migrant from Massachusetts who, after locating in New York, began to report the triumphs of American merchants. *Hunt's Merchants' Magazine,* founded in 1839, tried to inform the world of the merchant's doings and of his usefulness to mankind. As publisher of this journal Hunt collected thousands of business anecdotes and maxims of trade which he turned to good account in *Worth and Wealth* (1856), a compilation that established him as a worthy successor to Benjamin Franklin. Two years later he published a two-volume *Lives of American Merchants* (1858), which explained the rules of success through the lives of men who had achieved it.

18   Philadelphia too had self-help prophets to match those of New York and Boston in pointing the way to wealth. Philadelphia's counterpart of Freeman Hunt was Edwin Troxell Freedley, a prolific writer who served manufacturers as Hunt served merchants. Freedley's *Practical Treatise on Business* (1852) rivalled Hunt's *Worth and Wealth* in popularity, and his *Leading Pursuits and Leading Men* (1856) was on the market two years before Hunt's *Lives of American Merchants* was offered for sale. Another Philadelphian who popularized themes of business triumph was Timothy Shay Arthur, onetime watchmaker's apprentice, counting room clerk, and bank agent. Though his fame rested primarily on *Ten Nights in a Barroom* (1854), Arthur was also well known for his self-help homilies, and for his demand for a new kind of American biography. "In this country," he asserted, "the most prominent and efficient men are not those who were born to wealth and eminent social positions, but those who have won both by the force of untiring personal energy. It is to them that the country is indebted for unbounded prosperity. Invaluable, therefore, are the lives of such men to the rising generation. . . . Hitherto, American Biography has confined itself too closely to men who have won

[20] Moses Y. Beach, *Wealth and Pedigree of the Wealthy Citizens of New York City* (4th ed., New York, 1842), p. 3. According to a later estimate New York City boasted twenty millionaires in 1855, most of whom had earned their fortunes in commerce and real estate. See Robert G. Albion, *The Rise of New York Port* (New York, 1939), p. 259.

[21] Beach, *Wealth and Pedigree* (4th ed.), p. 2; *Ibid.* (11th ed., New York, 1846), p. 1.

political or literary distinction. . . . Limited to the perusal of such biographies, our youth must, of necessity, receive erroneous impressions of the true construction of our society, and fail to perceive wherein the progressive vigor of the nation lies. . . . We want the histories of our self-made men spread out before us, that we may know the ways by which they came up from the ranks of the people." [22] Within two years Arthur's demand had been met in the form of Charles C. B. Seymour's *Self-Made Men* (1858), an inspiring account of poor boys who had made their mark in the world.

19   On the eve of the Civil War this rags-to-riches theme had already captured the imagination of young men living close to the centers of business enterprise. A New York clergyman observed that "Their plans, their thoughts, their energies, are, day and night, concentrated to this one point, to become opulent, the sooner the better." [23] This was the appealing dream, born of the opportunities of the urban frontier and nourished by a rising army of self-help propagandists. In the days before Sumter the counting room clerk and the bobbin boy dreamed more of private fortune than of military glory. And though the Civil War imposed military values on the nation, it did so only temporarily. Out of the war came rich new opportunities for acquisition, a new generation of self-made men, and a well-ordered gospel of business success.

Reading Sources: from The Self-Made Man in America

Read the selection, surveying it to identify key terms and important concepts. Highlight these phrases and ideas, and then answer these questions.

1. What visual cues are used in this selection?
2. Identify the major sections in this selection. What techniques does Wyllie use to link their ideas?
3. What is Wyllie's purpose in writing this essay?
4. Where does Wyllie state his thesis?
5. What is the function of Section I of this essay? What points does Wyllie establish and how do they prepare readers for the rest of the essay?
6. What are the main points that Wyllie makes in Section II and III of the essay? How do these sections relate to each other?
7. Where does Wyllie state his conclusion? What points does he emphasize there?

Reacting to Sources

Reread the selection carefully, making marginal notes to aid your comprehension and to reinforce connections. Then further annotate the selection if you need to do

---

[22] Quoted in Freeman Hunt, *Worth and Wealth* (New York, 1856), pp. 350–351. Arthur's best known success handbook was *Advice to Young Men on Their Duties and Conduct in Life* (Boston, 1848).

[23] William H. Van Doren, *Mercantile Morals* (New York, 1852), p. 103.

so in order to answer any of these questions. (You may already have addressed some of the questions in your marginal notes.)

1. In a few sentences, rewrite paragraph 3 to simplify its ideas.
2. Using a dictionary if necessary, supply brief marginal definitions of these words as they are used in the selection: *stratified* (1), *vocations* (2), *emulate* (2), *mercantile* (2), *tariff* (3), *diligent* (3), *omnipotent* (4), *homilies* (5), *stewards* (7), *maxims* (9), *infallible* (10), *ultimatum* (10), *inaugurated* (11), *menial* (11), *tallow* (15), *anecdotes* (17), *opulent* (19), *bobbin* (19), *acquisition* (19).
3. Using a dictionary or encyclopedia, make brief marginal notes explaining the significance of the following figures mentioned in paragraph 13: Amos and Abbott Lawrence, Samuel Appleton, John Jacob Astor, Peter Cooper, Cornelius Vanderbilt, Stephen Girard, George Peabody.
4. Write three brief marginal questions in response to the ideas in paragraph 3.
5. In a marginal note, give two examples from the essay to support Wyllie's assertion, "Appropriately Benjamin Franklin became the first object of adoration in [the cult of the self-made man], the convenient symbol which linked the success traditions of the two centuries" (10).
6. Write a marginal note in which you explain why you agree or disagree with Emerson's words quoted in paragraph 14.
7. In paragraph 13 Wyllie says, "Important though Franklin was as a symbol and inspiration, the magnificent economic opportunities of nineteenth-century America constituted a far more important inspiration to young men in quest of wealth." Explore this idea further in a journal entry.
8. In a journal entry, explore why the selection discusses young men and not young women. You may want to consult an encyclopedia in order to determine the status of women in nineteenth-century America.
9. In a journal entry, consider the possible connections between this selection and "The Importance of Work" (pp. 397–401).
10. Outline the paragraph cluster beginning with paragraph 4 and ending with paragraph 5.

Working with Sources

1. Write a two-sentence summary of paragraph 8.
2. Write a critique of the ideas in paragraph 6.
3. Write a journal entry in which you explore your reactions to these quotations from *The Self-Made Man in America:*

> "And it was not to men of the professions but to a group of successful manufacturers that the term 'self-made men' was first applied" (3).

> "Certainly in the nineteenth century the alleged virtues of the American people closely resemble the virtues of Poor Richard" (8).

"Appropriately Benjamin Franklin became the first object of adoration in this cult, the convenient symbol which linked the success traditions of the two centuries" (10).

Be sure to integrate the quotations smoothly into your writing.
4. Paraphrase the paragraph cluster beginning with paragraph 6 and ending with paragraph 7.
5. Write a one-paragraph synthesis that blends ideas in paragraph 19 with the ideas in paragraph 17 of "The Phenomenon of Burn-Out" (pp. 387–395).

Writing with Sources: Using a Single Source

Integrating information from *The Self-Made Man in America* with your own ideas, write an essay on one of these topics. Be sure to acknowledge all ideas that are not your own.

1. Compare your goals to those of the self-made man and his "glorious conquest of fortune."
2. Wyllie's essay considers only the self-made man in nineteenth-century America. Discuss whether his concept of the self-made man currently defines the goals of young men and women in America. Be specific and use examples from your own experience and reading to support your points.
3. Write a critique of the values associated with the self-made man in America. In your discussion, identify those values you see as positive and those which you believe had a negative consequence for the individual and for society.

The Phenomenon of Burn-Out

Herbert J. Freudenberger with Geraldine Richelson

Herbert J. Freudenberger received his Ph.D. in psychology from New York University and is a graduate of the National Psychological Association for Psychoanalysis. In addition, he is a fellow of the American Psychological Association and is past president of the New York Society of Clinical Psychologists. Freudenberger has published numerous professional articles; he also lectures extensively. "The Phenomenon of Burn-Out" is from his book *Burn-Out: The High Cost of High Achievement* (1980). In his essay, Freudenberger defines *burn-out* and demonstrates how it often results from a work situation in which a person feels that his or her goals or ideals are being consistently frustrated.

1   Have you ever awakened in the morning unable to sleep any longer and equally unable to get out of bed? You lie there for a few minutes, trying to

remember why you woke up in the first place, what it was you were supposed to do.

2   "Ah yes," you think, "work. I have to go to work. But wait, maybe I don't have to go today. Maybe I can call in sick."

3   Then, one by one, you count off the urgencies . . . the appointment at ten, the report you promised, the meeting at two. You throw back the covers. The day has begun.

4   You hope, as you jump into the shower, that the splashing water will wash the heaviness away, and your old vital, energetic self will emerge. What leaves the house instead is a grim, unsmiling figure, a little bent, a little tired, lips and shoulders set against the irritations of the day ahead.

5   And for that figure, the day *will* be irritating. There will be too much work, too many interruptions, too many details, too few rewards. The day will be marked by fatigue and tension. And even the ending of it will bring no moment of exhilaration, because it's not just work. Even family, friends, and social situations have become "weary, stale, flat, and unprofitable."

6   If you recognize yourself in that picture, you're probably wondering how you got that way. Where's that old dynamic you who used to start every day with enthusiasm and vigor? Why is the life you embarked on with such high expectations letting you down at every turn? Why does it seem you have gotten what you wanted only to find you don't want it?

7   Take heart. There *are* answers to those questions. And chances are, you don't have to spend years searching back through all the stages of your life to find them. They may be more readily available than you have been led to believe.

8   More than likely, if you've been functioning well in the past and have seen yourself progress from one level of development to the next, you're not suffering from some deep-rooted psychological problem. You may not need to dig for traumas and other significant events of long ago to explain your decreasing ability to function or to care. That nameless malaise with its physical symptoms, its feelings of depression, anger, and weariness may be a developing case of Burn-Out . . . a demon born of the society and times we live in and our ongoing struggle to invest our lives with meaning.

The Times We Live In

9   Historically, the American dream has been to rise above what one's parents were; to work hard, even play hard; to achieve excellence, which would in turn lead to material comfort, community respect, position, prestige, compliments, security, status. This has been the American dream both for its people and for the nation. In short order, the United States formed itself, sprawled, grew, invented, discovered, industrialized, and surpassed every society of history in wealth, material goods, and self-esteem. We enjoyed more prestige and envy than any other nation. The goal of the world was to come to America to find gold in the streets and freedom in the air.

10   Why, then, with all these goals and visible rewards, which we as Americans have accepted so unquestioningly, has the result been a singular lack of

satisfaction? Why are so many of our best and our brightest beginning to feel empty and unfulfilled? Why does it seem there must always be more accomplishment, more achievement, more effort? WHY, AS A NATION, DO WE SEEM, BOTH COLLECTIVELY AND INDIVIDUALLY, TO BE IN THE THROES OF A FAST-SPREADING PHENOMENON — BURN-OUT?

11   Many men and women who come to me in pain report that life seems to have lost its meaning. Their enthusiasm is gone. They feel uninvolved, even in the midst of family and friends. Their jobs, which used to mean so much, have become drudgery with no associated feeling of reward.

12   Usually these people have come most reluctantly to seek professional help. They are accomplishers and doers who have no room in their philosophies for what they consider weakness. All their lives, they have undertaken tough jobs and prided themselves on their ability to master situations. Whether it was a bad marriage, a difficult child, an exhausting job situation, or economic reverses, they would find a way. They had enough determination and will power to lick anything. Now, however, no matter how great their efforts, the only result seems to be frustration. Some vital spark inside these men and women is burning out, leaving a terrible void.

The Impact of Change

13 We are living in times of change so rapid they've left us without moorings. Think of the roller coaster as it plunges headlong to the bottom. You've plunged along with it, but your system hasn't. Your head snaps, your body lurches, you're giddy and breathless, your stomach is still at the top. You tense yourself to keep up with the ride, but you tingle with a sense of weightlessness as if vital parts of you have been flung away. In a way, you've passed yourself by. Exciting . . . and more than a little scary.

14   Not too different from what we've been living through since World War II. These have been remarkable times, moving forward at breakneck speed. We have probably seen greater change in the past few decades than in all the rest of history. Like the roller coaster, it's been exciting. But for many of us, a little too fast.

15   Think about it. Restraints and taboos have been swept away. In sexual mores alone, we have moved a millennium in about a quarter of a century. The mother who was herself raised to preserve her virginity until her wedding night and who had to observe curfews and bring her dates home for inspection now visits her daughter at college and finds a live-in boyfriend. Obviously, this causes all sorts of conflicts in the mother and, perhaps not so obviously, in the daughter, too. No matter how defiantly a young woman may protest her right to live the way she wants to, she cannot completely have shed the attitudes she learned in her mother's home. Somewhere inside of her, though it may be unconscious, a tug-of-war is taking place between the customs of her contemporaries and the teachings of her childhood.

16   A generation is a very short time span for learning to live with such a prodigious change. Whoever coined the term "sexual revolution" was deadly

accurate; our world went to sleep one night and awoke the next morning having undergone a drastic transformation. And not only in our sexual behavior. Within that same time span, communities have broken down. Divorce has become a commonplace. Women are redefining their roles. Technology has bombarded us with new ways of doing things. Affluence has brought us more leisure than we know how to handle. The credit card seduces us into buying by promoting ready cash. Education has placed us on new plateaus that make us discontent with simpler life-styles. At the same time, TV has exposed us to alluring pictures of people leading the "good life." We're finding, as Alice did in *Through the Looking-Glass,* that "it takes all the running you can do to keep in the same place. If you want to get somewhere else, you must run at least twice as fast as that."

17   Yet if Oliver Wendell Holmes was right (and I believe he was) when he said, "a man's education begins a hundred and fifty years before he is born," we can begin to see the dilemma. We are products, not of this culture alone, but of two conflicting cultures. Within us, the past dies hard. No matter how hedonistic the world may be at the moment, it was pretty puritanical not so long ago. Our parents raised us on *Poor Richard's Almanack* and similar dicta that go all the way back to the Old Testament and exhort us to strive, accomplish, and observe the Ten Commandments.

18   When we stray from these guidelines, we feel uncomfortable and guilty, yet when we follow them, they don't seem to pay off. Others, who are breaking all the rules, appear to be flourishing while our own lives are dull. *We* don't cheat on our taxes or buy hot typewriters, yet we know many who do, and they neither get caught nor suffer from guilty consciences. While we're still driving our beat-up, six-year old Chevy on our way home to our family, they're passing us by in a Mercedes, starting out on a swinging evening. All the fun is "over there" somewhere, just outside our grasp. Very disturbing, since according to everything we've been taught, we should have been rewarded. Somehow, there's a great contradiction between reality and the messages we've been receiving, and we end up confused. I believe it is this climate of confusion that has given rise to the phenomenon of Burn-Out.

19   In a society where we have killed our gods, exorcised our ghosts, separated from our parents, and left our neighborhoods behind, we have little left to cling to. Against what restraints do we forge our standards? According to whose values do we plan our lives? The old rewards and punishments have disappeared. We have to rely on ourselves and ourselves alone. Not an easy task. If we want to fulfill the responsibilities we have accepted, we have to close our ears to the siren's call. Without any longer being sure of what is right or wrong, we have to resist temptation on every side.

20   Such an effort requires a constant buildup of defenses. Without even realizing it, we spend a lot of time erecting structures that can protect us. As we pile layer on layer, the weight bows us under. We begin to make excessive demands on ourselves, all the time draining ourselves of energy. To compensate for the weakness, the burning out we feel, we develop a rigidity. Things must be just so; the slightest deviation causes pain. Our accomplishments must

become ever worthier to prove the rightness of the exhausting struggle. To maintain our position, we must constantly excel.

21   Unfortunately, the harder we try, the more we impair our efficiency. About the only thing we succeed in doing is burning ourselves out more. If we do achieve our goals, we find little pleasure in them because we're too tired to enjoy them. So our efforts end in disappointment; our attitudes in cynicism. Our resources exhaust themselves. Our endeavors produce nothing.

Burn-Out: Who's Prone?

22 In everyday language, especially when it's applied to mechanical objects, Burn-Out is a very common term. If we're working in the backyard with a power saw, and it suddenly gives off a burst of sparks and stops running, we realize the motor has burned out. Same thing with a light bulb when it goes "pooft" and leaves us in the dark. We know precisely what has happened.

23   Unfortunately, however, when good old reliable Paul suddenly tells the client to shove it, or June, a successful career woman, starts coming back from lunch a little tipsy, we don't really know what's going on. We are not familiar with the concept of Burn-Out in human beings, so we look elsewhere for answers. If we are personally affected by the erratic behavior, we react with anger or hurt feelings, punishment or withdrawal. We may decide the person is anything from a "goof-off" to a "pain in the ass," an ingrate to an eccentric, or someone who lost what he once had. On the other hand, if *we are* the ones who are erupting, we will quickly assign the blame to something or someone outside ourselves. Our self-perception, our own self-image, does not allow us to contemplate that what is going wrong may be a function of factors within ourselves.

Emily's Story

24 These numerous denial reactions are doomed to make a bad situation worse. Take the case of Emily, a young woman caught in the maelstrom of reconciling the two sets of mores her generation had been exposed to. She and her husband met in college and married soon after graduation. They settled in Chicago, where they both found good jobs, he with a drug manufacturer, she with a public-relations firm. The two salaries allowed them to live well, and in time they settled into a relaxed, sophisticated routine — dinner out when they wanted it, a nicely furnished apartment, good clothes, weekends away. Emily loved her job, which afforded her some travel and contact with glamorous people. She felt independent and accomplished.

25   As she approached the end of her twenties, she found herself thinking about children. Her husband, Richard, wanted a child, and her parents never visited without asking when she was going to make them grandparents. Emily, herself, had mixed feelings about changing her way of life, but she made an agreement with Richard that he would help out and she could go back to work as soon as she liked. That's what they did. When the baby was six weeks old, they hired a house-

keeper, and Emily returned to her job. Her boss was delighted to see her, and she was equally delighted to be back. She fell back into her office routine with a sense of renewed energy and purpose, determined to make up for her time away. Her work had never been better. She seemed like a fountain of fresh ideas and within a few months was promoted to a position of greater responsibility, servicing major clients and traveling more than she had before.

26   Although Emily wasn't noticing, the situation at home wasn't flourishing like the career. In the world of public relations, there's no such thing as a nine-to-five day. Frequently, events have to be held in the evening or in distant cities. Emily was seldom home, and when she was, she was too tired to be much company. Many evenings, she didn't see her husband and daughter at all or she was "too beat to eat" and wanted nothing more than a hot bath and bed. At first, Richard was accommodating, pitching in with the baby and the meals. He knew how much Emily's career meant to her, and besides, he felt honorbound to abide by the agreement they had made before her pregnancy, especially since he had wanted the child more than she had.

27   As time passed, however, he couldn't help feeling neglected. Emily had become more like a mistress than a wife; more like a visiting aunt than a mother. He tried subtle ways of telling her, but they only served to make Emily defensive. "Gee, Richard, I get enough pressure on the job," she would say. "I don't need grief from you. Besides, it won't go on forever. Things will settle down soon."

28   But things didn't settle down, and Emily showed increasing signs of strain. She vacillated between *not* doing and overdoing. When she felt guilty about her absences from home, she'd compensate by leaving the office early and taking over from the housekeeper. On those evenings, she attended to her daughter's supper, bath, and bedtime, and expected Richard to praise her for her efficiency. Because she was to tired all the time, her judgment was impaired, and she honestly couldn't see how difficult she was being.

29   Things finally came to a head one evening when Richard had an important business meeting and Emily had promised to be home by six-thirty. At five o'clock, her boss called an emergency meeting, and the next thing Emily knew, her watch said ten to eight. She flew out of the office and into a cab, prepared to make apologies and have Richard accept them. But not *that* night. As she opened the door, Richard was standing there with a look on his face she never remembered seeing before. "You are, without a doubt, the most inconsiderate woman I have ever known," he let fly. "Night after night, I sit in this house alone, taking over for you, and the one time I tell you it's important, you don't show up." Emily was horrified. Richard went on and on, spewing forth all the grievances he had been collecting. "Do you realize how selfish you've been?" he finally concluded.

30   That, of course, was the last thing Emily was likely to realize, and she rushed into their bedroom in tears, accusing him silently of being petty and jealous of her success and no better than the other "male chauvinist pigs" she had read about. Over the next weeks she refused to discuss the incident, and the distance between them increased. Finally, when Richard insisted on a confrontation, she said she wanted a trial separation. She left him with the

child and moved in with her friend Gretchen. "He thinks he's doing it all without me. Let him find out," she told Gretchen, expecting a sympathetic ear. "He said I could go back to work, and no matter how tired I was, I never complained. Most nights, I did everything for the baby, and I paid the house-keeper out of my salary. For a year now, I haven't done a thing but go to work and run home to be with him and the baby. I haven't shopped or had my hair done or even gone to the dentist. And *he's* feeling neglected. He's behaving like a two-year-old."

31   Gretchen, who had known Emily and Richard for a long time, was aston-ished at Emily's view of things. In Gretchen's mind—and in the minds of most of their friends—Richard had behaved like a saint, indulging Emily, being supportive, and never complaining although she had clearly been taking advantage of him. Gretchen felt she couldn't let that speech pass without saying something. Trying her best to be tactful, she said, "Emily, sit down. Let me fix you a drink. I want you to listen to a couple of things, and I want you to listen with an open mind. I think you're making a big mistake, Em. Richard has been pretty terrific through all this."

32   "Uh-oh," Gretchen thought, as Emily started to get up from the couch. "Not tactful enough." But Gretchen wasn't one to give up easily, and she put her hand on Emily's shoulder to keep her seated. "No, Em, I want you to hear me. You and Richard made an agreement that you could go back to work. I know that. But be fair about it. You didn't just go back to work. You plunged into a twenty-four-hour whirlwind and stopped being a person, let alone a wife and mother. You don't have to tell me you haven't gone shopping or to the hairdresser. I can see that for myself. But what I also see—and apparently you don't—is that you've been tyrannizing Richard with this 'male chauvinist' crap. He's gone all out to consider your position. Do you honestly think you've considered his?"

33   Emily was furious. She was truly convinced she had leaned over backward to consider her husband and child, so much so that she was exhausted from the strain. If Gretchen couldn't see that, she must be blind. Come to think about it, Gretchen always did have a soft spot for Richard! She, Emily, had been a fool to come here. She'd pack that night and go to a hotel.

34   Emily was reacting in the classic way of a Burn-Out, denying her own contribution to a bad situation and exhibiting signs of paranoia. In her eager-ness to be the model "New Woman," she had become rigid in her defense of herself, insisting that her view of the situation was the *only* view. Instead of listening to Richard and Gretchen, who were merely asking her to examine her behavior, she accused them of plotting against her. Then, to justify that accusa-tion, she invented a romance between them, twisting the facts to suit herself and attributing Richard's understanding of her business trips to his desire to be with Gretchen.

35   Emily was so far along in her Burn-Out and was clinging so hard to her image of herself, she was incapable of seeing that she had lost her priorities and her humanity. Consequently, everything she did compounded her problems instead of ameliorating them. Had she not been so defensive, Emily would at

least have considered the questions Gretchen had raised. Why couldn't she get
to the hairdresser? Other working women did. Why did she have to say "yes"
to every assignment that came up? Did her career really depend upon her
being available round the clock? Did she have to be the "Wonder Woman" of
her profession?

36   Emily had set up impossibly high work standards for herself, based partly
on a deeply entrenched family principle ("Whatever we do, we do it well.")
and her misguided notions of what women's liberation was all about. Even
without a husband and child, she couldn't have lived up to her standards, as
she was shortly to find out. Nobody is Wonder Woman. Everyone needs
balance, and Emily had let her life become totally lopsided. Misguidedly, she
had given herself permission to neglect the most important part of her life
when she should have been curtailing her work effort. That, however, would
have been an admission of weakness in her mind, whereas she was able to
reconcile herself to the failure of her marriage by blaming it on Richard. By
leaving him and the child, she thought she was ridding herself of the source of
her conflict, but in reality she was tipping the scales even further. When, less
than a year later, her Burn-Out became critical enough to force her to take a
leave of absence from her job, she was shocked, although no one else was.

Burn-Out: What Is It?

37 A person who is burning out is not, on the surface, a very sympathetic figure.
He or she may be cranky, critical, angry, rigid, resistant to suggestions, and
given to behavior patterns that turn people off. Unless we're able to probe
beneath the surface and see that the person is really suffering, our tendency
will be to turn away. Sometimes, like Richard, we'll bottle up our own hurts and
frustrations just to keep the peace, but that doesn't work, either. The earlier we
approach a Burn-Out, the more hope we have of eliciting some understanding;
the longer we wait, the more defensiveness we're likely to encounter. That's
true even with ourselves. As we saw with Emily, we'll go to any lengths to deny
we're burning out. Just as she transferred her shortcomings to Richard, we'll
look for anything or anybody we can blame. We look away from ourselves in an
effort to cover up.

38   Burn-Out, however, is not a condition that gets better by being ignored.
Nor is it any kind of disgrace. On the contrary, it's a problem born of good
intentions. The people who fall prey to it are, for the most part, decent individuals who have striven hard to reach a goal. Their schedules are busy, and
whatever the project or job, they can be counted on to do more than their
share. They're usually the leaders among us who have never been able to admit
to limitations. They're burning out because they've pushed themselves too
hard for too long. They started out with great expectations and refused to
compromise along the way.

39   I've never met a Burn-Out who didn't start with some ideal in mind.
Perhaps it was a marriage that was going to be like the marriages in the story-
books. Or children who were going to be the "family jewels." The list is

endless. A talent. A cause. A position in the community. Money. Power. A meteoric career. Whatever. A Burn-Out experience usually has its roots in the area of a person's life that seemed to hold the most promise.

40   Often, Burn-Out is the consequence of a work situation in which the person gets the feeling he's batting his head against the wall day after day, year after year. The helping professions are a good example. Many young, idealistic students who want to do something for the world become doctors, nurses, lawyers, social workers, policemen, teachers, counselors, politicians. They hope to have an impact on the lives they deal with. They envision making people well again, improving world conditions, turning wasted lives into productive ones, or sending educated students into the world.

41   Unfortunately, the helping professions get to see a lot of failure and misery. Doctors and nurses see their patients suffer and die. Teachers face overcrowded classrooms and students with a disdain for learning. Social workers battle against the overwhelming odds of poverty and hopelessness. The people they're trying to help are likely to have surrounded themselves with impenetrable walls. The disappointments mount up until eventually the helpers build walls of their own.

42   Since it hurts too much to care, they tend to anesthetize their feelings and go about their daily routines in a more mechanical and cut-off way. They're still conscientious and hard-working, but they're no longer functioning as whole human beings. In a slow, corrosive process, they remove a vital part of themselves. What happens is similar to what happens in a car that's running on only two cylinders — the cylinders that continue to function have to do a lot of compensating. After a while, the strain becomes too great, and something has to give. In the car, that something may be critical parts of the engine. In a person, it is usually other areas of his life.

43   A Burn-Out is "someone in a state of fatigue or frustration brought about by devotion to a cause, way of life, or relationship that failed to produce the expected reward." Stated another way: *Whenever the expectation level is dramatically opposed to reality and the person persists in trying to reach that expectation, trouble is on the way.* Deep inside, friction is building up, the inevitable result of which will be a depletion of the individual's resources, an attrition of his vitality, energy, and ability to function.

Reading Sources: "The Phenomenon of Burn-Out"

Read the selection, surveying it to identify key terms and important concepts. Highlight these phrases and ideas, and then answer these questions.

1. What visual cues are used in this essay?
2. How long is Freudenberger's introduction? What points does he make with his introduction?
3. What is Freudenberger's thesis? Where does he state his thesis?

4. What techniques does Freudenberger use to link ideas between paragraphs 14 and 15? How does he link ideas among the sentences in paragraph 15?
5. At what point does Freudenberger define *burn-out*? What is the relationship between this definition and the rest of the essay?
6. What ideas does Freudenberger emphasize in his conclusion?

Reacting to Sources

Reread the selection carefully, making marginal notes to aid your comprehension and to reinforce connections. Then further annotate the selection if you need to do so in order to answer any of these questions. (You may already have addressed some of the questions in your marginal notes.)

1. In a few sentences, rewrite paragraph 9 to simplify its ideas.
2. Using a dictionary if necessary, supply brief marginal definitions of these words as they are used in the selection: *millennium* (15), *prodigious* (16), *hedonistic* (17), *puritanical* (17), *exhort* (17), *cynicism* (21).
3. Freudenberger makes this statement in paragraph 19: "In a society where we have killed our gods, exorcised our ghosts, separated from our parents, and left our neighborhoods behind, we have little left to cling to." Do you agree or disagree? Write a brief marginal comment in which you explain why.
4. Write three brief marginal questions in response to the ideas in paragraph 40.
5. In a marginal note, give two examples from the essay to support the writer's general statement, "We are living in times of change so rapid they've left us without moorings" (13).
6. Is Freudenberger aiming his discussion at an audience of experts or of general readers? Make a marginal note in which you explain your answer.
7. Find a statement in the essay which your own experience supports or contradicts. Write a brief marginal note in which you explain why.
8. Read the introduction to the selection. Comment on how Freudenberger's work might have influenced his purpose. In a journal entry, comment on how it influences your acceptance of his ideas.
9. In paragraph 17 Freudenberger says, "No matter how hedonistic the world may be at the moment, it was pretty puritanical not so long ago. Our parents raised us on *Poor Richard's Almanack* and similar dicta that go all the way back to the Old Testament and exhort us to strive, accomplish, and observe the Ten Commandments." Explore this idea further in a journal entry.
10. In a journal entry, explore your reactions to the section of the reading entitled "Emily's Story."

Working with Sources

1. Write a two-sentence summary of paragraph 16.
2. Write a critique of the ideas in paragraph 6.

3. Write a journal entry in which you explore your reactions to these quotations from "The Phenomenon of Burn-Out":

> "Their jobs, which used to mean so much, have become drudgery with no associated feeling of reward" (11).

> "Emily had set impossibly high work standards for herself, based partly on a deeply entrenched family principle . . . and her misguided notions of what women's liberation was all about" (36).

> "They're burning out because they've pushed themselves too hard for too long. They started out with great expectations and refused to compromise along the way" (38).

Be sure to integrate the quotations smoothly into your writing.

4. Paraphrase the paragraph cluster beginning with paragraph 40 and ending with paragraph 42.
5. Write a one-paragraph synthesis that blends ideas in paragraph 43 with the ideas in paragraph 11 of "The Importance of Work" (pp. 397–401).

Writing with Sources: Using a Single Source

Integrating information from "The Phenomenon of Burn-Out" with your own ideas, write an essay on one of these topics. Be sure to acknowledge all ideas that are not your own.

1. Write an essay in which you agree or disagree with Freudenberger's statement that our jobs, "which used to mean so much, have become drudgery with no associated feeling of reward" (11).
2. Write about a time when as a student or as a worker you experienced burn-out. As Freudenberger did with the section of his essay called "Emily's Story," follow your narrative with an analysis of the factors that led to your problems.
3. Write a letter to Freudenberger in which you challenge his assertion, "We are living in times of change so rapid they've left us without moorings" (13).

The Importance of Work

Gloria Steinem

Gloria Steinem was born in Toledo, Ohio, in 1934. After graduating from Smith College in 1956, she studied in India on a Chester Bowles Asian Fellowship. She gained prominence as a journalist and in 1968 helped found *New York* magazine. Always an articulate advocate of women's rights, Steinem helped to establish the National Women's Political Caucus and the Women's Action Alliance. She became a founder and editor of *Ms.* in 1972 and in 1977 was awarded a Woodrow Wilson

International Center for Scholars fellowship. Steinem is still actively involved in the feminist movement and is a contributor to a number of magazines. "The Importance of Work" is from Steinem's most recent book, *Outrageous Acts and Everyday Rebellions* (1983). In this essay she considers the importance of work to women and argues that women, like men, work not just because they have to but because work is "one of life's basic pleasures."

1   Toward the end of the 1970s, *The Wall Street Journal* devoted an eight-part, front-page series to "the working woman" — that is, the influx of women into the paid-labor force — as the greatest change in American life since the Industrial Revolution.

2   Many women readers greeted both the news and the definition with cynicism. After all, women have always worked. If all the productive work of human maintenance that women do in the home were valued at its replacement cost, the gross national product of the United States would go up by 26 percent. It's just that we are now more likely than ever before to leave our poorly rewarded, low-security, high-risk job of homemaking (though we're still trying to explain that it's a perfectly good one and that the problem is male society's refusal both to do it and to give it an economic value) for more secure, independent, and better-paid jobs outside the home.

3   Obviously, the real work revolution won't come until all productive work is rewarded — including child rearing and other jobs done in the home — and men are integrated into so-called women's work as well as vice versa. But the radical change being touted by the *Journal* and other media is one part of that long integration process: the unprecedented flood of women into salaried jobs, that is, into the labor force as it has been male-defined and previously occupied by men. We are already more than 41 percent of it — the highest proportion in history. Given the fact that women also make up a whopping 69 percent of the "discouraged labor force" (that is, people who need jobs but don't get counted in the unemployment statistics because they've given up looking), plus an official female unemployment rate that is substantially higher than men's, it's clear that we could expand to become fully half of the national work force by 1990.

4   Faced with this determination of women to find a little independence and to be paid and honored for our work, experts have rushed to ask: "Why?" It's a question rarely directed at male workers. Their basic motivations of survival and personal satisfaction are taken for granted. Indeed, men are regarded as "odd" and therefore subjects for sociological study and journalistic reports only when they *don't* have work, even if they are rich and don't need jobs or are poor and can't find them. Nonetheless, pollsters and sociologists have gone to great expense to prove that women work outside the home because of dire financial need, or if we persist despite the presence of a wage-earning male, out of some desire to buy "little extras" for our families, or even out of good old-fashioned penis envy.

5   Job interviewers and even our own families may still ask salaried women the big "Why?" If we have small children at home or are in some job regarded as "men's work," the incidence of such questions increases. Condescending or

accusatory versions of "What's a nice girl like you doing in a place like this?" have not disappeared from the workplace.

6   How do we answer these assumptions that we are "working" out of some pressing or peculiar need? Do we feel okay about arguing that it's as natural for us to have salaried jobs as for our husbands — whether or not we have young children at home? Can we enjoy strong career ambitions without worrying about being thought "unfeminine"? When we confront men's growing resentment of women competing in the work force (often in the form of such guilt-producing accusations as "You're taking men's jobs away" or "You're damaging your children"), do we simply state that a decent job is a basic human right for everybody?

7   I'm afraid the answer is often no. As individuals and as a movement, we tend to retreat into some version of a tactically questionable defense: "Womenworkbecausewehaveto." The phrase has become one word, one key on the typewriter — an economic form of the socially "feminine" stance of passivity and self-sacrifice. Under attack, we still tend to present ourselves as creatures of economic necessity and familial devotion. "Womenworkbecausewehaveto" has become the easiest thing to say.

8   Like most truisms, this one is easy to prove with statistics. Economic need *is* the most consistent work motive — for women as well as men. In 1976, for instance, 43 percent of all women in the paid-labor force were single, widowed, separated, or divorced, and working to support themselves and their dependents. An additional 21 percent were married to men who had earned less than ten thousand dollars in the previous year, the minimum then required to support a family of four. In fact, if you take men's pensions, stocks, real estate, and various forms of accumulated wealth into account, a good statistical case can be made that there are more women who "have" to work (that is, who have neither the accumulated wealth, nor husbands whose work or wealth can support them for the rest of their lives) than there are men with the same need. If we were going to ask one group "Do you really need this job?" we should ask men.

9   But the first weakness of the whole "have to work" defense is its deceptiveness. Anyone who has ever experienced dehumanized life on welfare or any other confidence-shaking dependency knows that a paid job may be preferable to the dole, even when the handout is coming from a family member. Yet the will and self-confidence to work on one's own can diminish as dependency and fear increase. That may explain why — contrary to the "have to" rationale — wives of men who earn less than three thousand dollars a year are actually *less* likely to be employed than wives whose husbands make ten thousand dollars a year or more.

10   Furthermore, the greatest proportion of employed wives is found among families with a total household income of twenty-five to fifty thousand dollars a year. This is the statistical underpinning used by some sociologists to prove that women's work is mainly important for boosting families into the middle or upper middle class. Thus, women's incomes are largely used for buying "luxuries" and "little extras": a neat double-whammy that renders us secondary within our families, and makes our jobs expendable in hard times. We may

even go along with this interpretation (at least, up to the point of getting fired so a male can have our job). It preserves a husbandly ego-need to be seen as the primary breadwinner, and still allows us a safe "feminine" excuse for working.

11   But there are often rewards that we're not confessing. As noted in *The Two-Career Couple,* by Francine and Douglas Hall: "Women who hold jobs by choice, even blue-collar routine jobs, are more satisfied with their lives than are the full-time housewives."

12   In addition to personal satisfaction, there is also society's need for all its members' talents. Suppose that jobs were given out on only a "have to work" basis to both women and men — one job per household. It would be unthinkable to lose the unique abilities of, for instance, Eleanor Holmes Norton, the distinguished chair of the Equal Employment Opportunity Commission. But would we then be forced to question the important work of her husband, Edward Norton, who is also a distinguished lawyer? Since men earn more than twice as much as women on the average, the wife in most households would be more likely to give up her job. Does that mean the nation could do as well without millions of its nurses, teachers, and secretaries? Or that the rare man who earns less than his wife should give up his job?

13   It was this kind of waste of human talents on a society-wide scale that traumatized millions of unemployed or underemployed Americans during the Depression. Then, a one-job-per-household rule seemed somewhat justified, yet the concept was used to displace women workers only, create intolerable dependencies, and waste female talent that the country needed. That Depression experience, plus the energy and example of women who were finally allowed to work during the manpower shortage created by World War II, led Congress to reinterpret the meaning of the country's full-employment goal in its Economic Act of 1946. Full employment was officially defined as "the employment of those who want to work, without regard to whether their employment is, by some definition, necessary. This goal applies equally to men and to women." Since bad economic times are again creating a resentment of employed women — as well as creating more need for women to be employed — we need such a goal more than ever. Women are again being caught in a tragic double bind: We are required to be strong and then punished for our strength.

14   Clearly, anything less than government and popular commitment to this 1946 definition of full employment will leave the less powerful groups, whoever they may be, in danger. Almost as important as the financial penalty paid by the powerless is the suffering that comes from being shut out of paid and recognized work. Without it, we lose much of our self-respect and our ability to prove that we are alive by making some difference in the world. That's just as true for the suburban woman as it is for the unemployed steel worker.

15   But it won't be easy to give up the passive defense of "weworkbecause-wehaveto."

16   When a woman who is struggling to support her children and grandchildren on welfare sees her neighbor working as a waitress, even though that neighbor's husband has a job, she may feel resentful; and the waitress (of course, not the waitress's husband) may feel guilty. Yet unless we establish the

obligation to provide a job for everyone who is willing and able to work, that welfare woman may herself be penalized by policies that give out only one public-service job per household. She and her daughter will have to make a painful and divisive decision about which of them gets that precious job, and the whole household will have to survive on only one salary.

17   A job as a human right is a principle that applies to men as well as women. But women have more cause to fight for it. The phenomenon of the "working woman" has been held responsible for everything from an increase in male impotence (which turned out, incidentally, to be attributable to medication for high blood pressure) to the rising cost of steak (which was due to high energy costs and beef import restrictions, not women's refusal to prepare the cheaper, slower-cooking cuts). Unless we see a job as part of every citizen's right to autonomy and personal fulfillment, we will continue to be vulnerable to someone else's idea of what "need" is, and whose "need" counts the most.

18   In many ways, women who do not have to work for simple survival, but who choose to do so nonetheless, are on the frontier of asserting this right for all women. Those with well-to-do husbands are dangerously easy for us to resent and put down. It's easier still to resent women from families of inherited wealth, even though men generally control and benefit from that wealth. (There is no Rockefeller Sisters Fund, no J. P. Morgan & Daughters, and sons-in-law may be the ones who really sleep their way to power.) But to prevent a woman whose husband or father is wealthy from earning her own living, and from gaining the self-confidence that comes with that ability, is to keep her needful of that unearned power and less willing to disperse it. Moreover, it is to lose forever her unique talents.

19   Perhaps modern feminists have been guilty of a kind of reverse snobbism that keeps us from reaching out to the wives and daughters of wealthy men; yet it was exactly such women who refused the restrictions of class and financed the first wave of feminist revolution.

20   For most of us, however, "womenworkbecausewehaveto" is just true enough to be seductive as a personal defense.

21   If we use it without also staking out the larger human right to a job, however, we will never achieve that right. And we will always be subject to the false argument that independence for women is a luxury affordable only in good economic times. Alternatives to layoffs will not be explored, acceptable unemployment will always be used to frighten those with jobs into accepting low wages, and we will never remedy the real cost, both to families and to the country, of dependent women and a massive loss of talent.

22   Worst of all, we may never learn to find productive, honored work as a natural part of ourselves and as one of life's basic pleasures.

Reading Sources: "The Importance of Work"

Read the selection, surveying it to identify key terms and important concepts. Highlight these phrases and ideas, and then answer these questions.

1. At what point does Steinem end her introduction and begin the body of her essay? Why does she provide so much background material in her introduction? What points does she make in her introduction that she does not develop in the rest of her essay?
2. What is the essay's thesis? Does Steinem state or imply her thesis? Explain.
3. Does Steinem rely primarily on logic or on appeals to emotion? Explain.
4. What techniques does Steinem use to link ideas between paragraph 9 and paragraph 10? How does she link the sentences in paragraph 10.
5. Where does Steinem begin her conclusion? What points does she emphasize? What does her essay gain or lose from this choice?

Reacting to Sources

Reread the selection carefully, making marginal notes to aid your comprehension and to reinforce connections. Then further annotate the selection if you need to do so in order to answer any of these questions. (You may already have addressed some of the questions in your marginal notes.)

1. In a few sentences, rewrite paragraph 4 to simplify its ideas.
2. Using a dictionary if necessary, supply brief marginal definitions of these words as they are used in the selection: *influx* (1), *ego* (10), *traumatized* (13), *autonomy* (17).
3. Do you agree or disagree with the following statement, "If we were going to ask one group 'Do you really need this job?' we should ask men" (9).
4. Write three brief marginal questions in response to the ideas in paragraph 11.
5. In a marginal note give two examples to support the writer's general statement, "A job as a human right is a principle that applies to men as well as women. But women have more cause to fight for it" (17).
6. Find a statement in the essay for which your own knowledge or experience provides contradictory evidence. Write a brief marginal note that presents this contradiction.
7. Identify Steinem's purpose in paragraph 19. Identify the purpose of the entire essay.
8. In a journal entry, list the reasons why, according to Steinem, women work.
9. Read the introduction to the selection. Comment on how Steinem's life or other writings might have influenced her purpose. Comment on how it influences your acceptance of her ideas.
10. In a journal entry, consider the possible connections between this essay and "The Self-Made Man in America" (pp. 378–385).
11. At whom is Steinem aiming her remarks? a general audience? feminists? homemakers? Explain your answer in a journal entry.
12. Outline the paragraph cluster beginning with paragraph 9 and ending with paragraph 10.

Working with Sources

1. Write a two-sentence summary of paragraph 17.
2. Write a critique of the ideas in paragraph 14.
3. Write a journal entry in which you explore your reactions to these quotations from "The Importance of Work":

   > "Obviously, the real work revolution won't come until all productive work is rewarded — including child rearing and other jobs done in the home — and men are integrated into so-called women's work as well as vice versa" (3).

   > "Clearly, anything less than government and popular commitment to this 1946 definition of full employment will leave the less powerful groups, whoever they may be, in danger" (14).

   > "But to prevent a woman whose husband or father is wealthy from earning her own living, and from gaining the self-confidence that comes with that ability, is to keep her needful of that unearned power and less willing to disperse it" (18).

   Be sure to integrate the quotations smoothly into your writing.
4. Paraphrase the paragraph cluster beginning with paragraph 17 and ending with paragraph 18.
5. Write a one-paragraph synthesis that blends ideas in paragraph 22 with the ideas in paragraph 1 of the excerpt from *Brave New Workplace* (pp. 410 – 417).

Writing with Sources: Using a Single Source

Integrating information from "The Importance of Work" with your own ideas, write an essay on one of these topics. Be sure to acknowledge all ideas that are not your own.

1. Using your own experience, define the primary attitude of society in general toward women in the workplace. Are the attitudes that you discuss consistent with those that Steinem presents?
2. Discuss how you would create a full employment society. Make sure that you consider both the benefits and the liabilities of such a system.
3. Write an editorial for your local paper in which you argue for or against Steinem's position that all productive work — including child rearing and housework — should be given financial compensation.

The Working Day

Daniel T. Rodgers

Daniel T. Rodgers was born in Darby, Pennsylvania in 1942. He received his B.A. from Brown University in 1965 and his Ph.D. in history from Yale University in 1973. A recipient of the Frederick Jackson Turner Award for historical writing, Rodgers teaches at the University of Wisconsin in Madison. "The Working Day" is from his book *The Work Ethic in Industrial America 1850–1920*. In this essay, Rodgers explores labor's struggle for the eight-hour working day. Far from being of isolated historical interest, this event illustrates the conflict that occurred when traditional work values met with the new realities of the Industrial Revolution.

1   How much of a man's life should work consume? No work-related question is more central than this, and none in the nineteenth and early twentieth centuries divided workers and employers more sharply. The early factory masters took over the traditional sun-to-sun workday, stretched it to between twelve and fourteen hours of labor winter and summer alike with the introduction of gas lighting in the 1830s and 1840s, and brought the full weight of generations of moralizing to bear in justification. "Labor is *not* a curse," they insisted; "it is not the hours per day that a person *works* that breaks him down, but the hours spent in dissipation." Give men "plenty to do, and a long while to do it in, and you will find them physically and morally better." [1]

2   But among workingmen, the drive to shorten the hours of labor was a long and fervent struggle. The campaign began early in the nineteenth century with the appearance of the first self-conscious workingmen's organizations. By the 1840s the ten-hour movement had moved into the New England textile mills, producing a massive flood of shorter-hours petitions, the largest, from Lowell in 1846, containing signatures equivalent to almost two-thirds of the city's cotton mill operatives. [2] After 1850 the shorter-hours demand — now typically put in terms of the eight-hour day — was at the forefront of every organized labor effort. The National Labor Union at its first convention in 1866 declared a federal eight-hour law "the first and grand desideratum of the hour," and, though the organization drifted shortly thereafter toward rival programs of cooperatives and currency reform, many of its member unions clung firmly to the original platform. P. J. McGuire of the Carpenters, for example, told a congressional committee in 1883 that the reduction of working hours was the "primary object" of the union he headed. The American Federation of Labor under Samuel Gompers was a still more persistent champion of the shorter workday — "eight hours to-day, fewer to-morrow," as Gompers defined the cause. The shorter workday was "the question of questions," the

---

[1] Massachusetts Bureau of Statistics of Labor (MBLS), *Tenth Annual Report* (Boston, 1879), p. 149; MBLS, *Report* (Boston, 1870), p. 221; Ohio Bureau of Labor Statistics, *Second Annual Report* (Columbus, 1879), p. 281.

[2] Norman Ware, *The Industrial Worker, 1840–1860* (Boston: Houghton Mifflin, 1924), chaps. 8, 10.

only one which "reaches the very root of society," Gompers declared in the 1880s, and over the next twenty years he labored tirelessly to promote strikes over the issue. Nor did the labor left disagree. For Bill Haywood of the IWW, the only fit motto for the working class was "the less work the better."[3]

3   "However much they may differ upon other matters, . . . all men of labor . . . can unite upon this," Samuel Gompers wrote in defense of the eight-hour issue in 1889.[4] If the unions, particularly the nonfactory building trades unions, led the agitation for the shorter workday, there was more than Gompers's testimony to indicate that the shorter-hours dream had a strong hold on the larger number of nonunionized workers as well. For three decades after 1869, until they turned to the neutral and duller task of compiling purely statistical data, many of the new state bureaus of labor statistics took upon themselves the task of canvassing the opinions of the workingmen they took to be their constituents. Who these often nameless workers were and how their opinions found their way into print is not clear, but, taking opinion samples as they come, none more closely approaches the rank and file of labor than these. And when they posed the working-hours question, the surveys repeatedly turned up strong, often overwhelming support for the shorter-hours demand.[5] "We go into the factory too young and work too hard afterwards," a New Jersey glass blower put the recurrent complaint in the mid-1880s. A decade and a half later, Thomas Jones, a nonunion Chicago machinist, interrupted his testimony on the un-American and anti-Christian policies of trade unions to interject that "we nonunion men are not opposed to more pay and shorter hours; not at all."[6]

4   Twice in the nineteenth century, moreover, the shorter-hours demand mushroomed into popular crusades unsurpassed in their intensity by any other of the era's labor issues. The first wave of enthusiasm began quietly in 1865 with the organization of the Grand Eight-Hour League of Massachusetts by a small group of Boston workingmen. Three years later workingmen's Eight-Hour Leagues had proliferated throughout the Northern states and, together with the trade unions, had succeeded in writing the eight-hour day in the statute books of seven states and forcing an eight-hour law for federal employees through Congress. Riddled with loopholes, the legislation proved a hollow victory, and workers angrily turned to more aggressive tactics. In Chicago some 6,000 to

---

[3] Marion C. Cahill, *Shorter Hours: A Study of the Movement since the Civil War* (New York: Columbia University Press, 1932), p. 35; U.S. Senate, Committee on Education and Labor, *Report upon the Relations between Labor and Capital,* 4 vols. (Washington, D.C., 1885), 1:315, 299, 294; *Twentieth Century Illustrated History of Rhode Island and the Rhode Island Central Trades and Labor Union* (Providence: Rhode Island Central Trades and Labor Union, 1901), p. 143; William D. Haywood and Frank Bohn, *Industrial Socialism* (Chicago: Charles H. Kerr, 1911), p. 62.

[4] Gerald N. Grob, *Workers and Utopia: A Study of Ideological Conflict in the American Labor Movement, 1865–1900* (Evanston, Ill.: Northwestern University Press, 1961), p. 149.

[5] MBLS, *Report* (Boston, 1870), pp. 287–98; New Jersey Bureau of Statistics of Labor and Industries (NJBLS), *Seventh Annual Report* (Trenton, 1885), pp. 237–56; Pennsylvania, *Annual Report of the Secretary of Internal Affairs, Part III: Industrial Statistics* (hereafter *Pennsylvania Industrial Statistics*), 15 (Harrisburg, 1888): 16H-28H; Michigan Bureau of Labor and Industrial Statistics (MichBLS), *Fourteenth Annual Report* (Lansing, 1897), pp. 195–96.

[6] NJBLS, *Seventh Annual Report,* p. 239; U.S. Industrial Commission, *Reports,* 19 vols. (Washington, D.C., 1900–1902), 8:196.

10,000 workers walked off their jobs on 1 May 1867 in a massive demonstration to demand enforcement of the new Illinois eight-hour law, and strikes, rioting, and some machine breaking followed in its wake. A year later in the anthracite coalfields of Pennsylvania, similarly angered workers abandoned the coal pits and, marching from mine to mine, shut down virtually all operations in the state's leading coal-producing county in a bitter three-month strike. Only in the building trades did the first eight-hour campaign bear fruit, and many of those gains evaporated in the depression of the 1870s. But the experience suggested something of the emotional reserves behind the shorter-hours issue.[7]

5   The second eight-hour crusade of the mid-1880s was still larger and more spontaneous than the first. When in 1884 the Federation of Organized Trades and Labor Unions issued a call for a general eight-hour demonstration to take place on 1 May 1886, it was a quixotic gesture on the part of a weak and barely solvent organization. But the call fell on unexpectedly fertile ground. Over the next two years, workers flocked into the labor unions filled with hopes for a shorter working day. The Knights of Labor, the chief recipient of the influx, ballooned from 104,066 members in July 1885 to 702,924 members a year later, and the newcomers threatened to overwhelm the organization. Grand Master Workman Terence Powderly waged a vigorous fight to dampen the strike fever of the local Knights assemblies. In place of a general strike, Powderly proposed an educational campaign and a nationwide essay contest on the eight-hour question and, that failing, championed a less than realistic scheme to shorten the working day through a cooperative agreement between the Knights and a yet unformed general association of the nation's manufacturers. A month before the day set for the demonstration, P. M. Arthur of the strongly organized locomotive engineers denounced the whole affair as a demand for "two hours more loafing about the corners and two hours more for drink." Yet notwithstanding such foot-dragging at the top, 190,000 workers struck for the eight-hour day in the first week of May. In Milwaukee, according to the Wisconsin Bureau of Labor and Industrial Statistics, the shorter hours issue was "*the* topic of conversation in the shop, on the street, at the family table, at the bar, [and] in the counting room." Beginning with a monster picnic on 2 May, the crusade turned grim and bloody as police opened fire on workers intent on shutting down the city's iron and steel works. In Chicago, the center of the movement, May opened with police and worker battles, some five hundred individual strikes, and still more imposing demonstrations.[8]

[7] David Montgomery, *Beyond Equality: Labor and the Radical Republicans, 1862–1872* (New York: Alfred A. Knopf, 1967), chaps. 6–8; Robert Ozanne, *A Century of Labor Management Relations at McCormick and International Harvester* (Madison: University of Wisconsin Press, 1967), pp. 6–7; Clifton K. Yearley, *Enterprise and Anthracite: Economics and Democracy in Schuylkill County, 1820–1875* (Baltimore: Johns Hopkins University Press, 1961), p. 182.

[8] John R. Commons and Associates, *History of Labour in the United States,* 4 vols. (New York: Macmillan, 1918–35), 2:375–86; Donald L. Kemmerer and Edward D. Wickersham, "Reasons for the Growth of the Knights of Labor in 1885–1886," *Industrial and Labor Relations Review* 3 (1950): 213–20; Terence V. Powderly, *Thirty Years of Labor, 1859 to 1889* (Columbus, Ohio: Excelsior Publishing House, 1889), pp. 471–525; Henry David, *The History of the Haymarket Affair* (New York: Farrar and Rinehart, 1936), chaps. 7–8; Wisconsin Bureau of Labor and Industrial Statistics, *Second Biennial Report* (Madison, 1886), pp. 314–71.

6   Despite Samuel Gompers's best efforts over the next decade and a half, the general strike of 1886 was never repeated. Most workers who walked off their jobs in the late nineteenth and early twentieth centuries struck over wage-related issues, not working hours; and where the wage question pressed most heavily or where hours reduction meant a cut in pay, hours demands generally made little headway. Yet, larger on the average than wage strikes, shorter-hours walkouts possessed a peculiar intensity.[9] And in the massive garment workers' strikes of 1910–11, the IWW-led silk workers' walkout in Paterson, New Jersey, in 1913, the great steel strike of 1919, and elsewhere, the shorter-hours issue smoldered under the surface of many of the era's most famous labor disputes long after the experience of 1886 had faded from memory.

7   Where rank-and-file workers divided from union leaders was not over the desirability of shorter working hours — whose appeal cut across lines of ideology and unionization — but over rationale. For most union spokesmen the eight-hour day was essentially a link in a complex economic equation whose upshot was wages. A large number of the late nineteenth century's most influential labor leaders — Gompers, George E. McNeill of the Knights, and Adolph Strasser of the Cigarmakers among them — learned the eight-hour creed in the 1860s from a self-educated Boston machinist, Ira Steward. In Steward's argument, wages fell to the minimum standard of living workers would tolerate, and leisure was the one effective means of raising both. Let "the ragged — the unwashed — the ignorant and ill-mannered" have time "to become ashamed of themselves," to raise their expenses and desires, and the demand for higher wages would no longer be resistible. "The *idea* of eight hours isn't eight hours," Steward insisted; "it is *less poverty!*"[10] As late as 1915, Steward's jingle

> Whether you work by the piece
> Or work by the day
> Decreasing the hours
> Increases the pay

could still be found in the pages of the *American Federationist.* And if this was by then a remnant of an increasingly old-fashioned idea, the argument that pushed Steward's aside in labor circles in the 1890s took an equally instrumental attitude toward leisure. Shorter working hours were a means of spreading the work being relentlessly whittled down by machinery, ironing out the boom and bust cycles of the economy, or employing the unemployed.[11]

8   One can find appeal to all of these arguments among the respondents of the state bureaus of labor statistics; but far more often than union leaders, the men whose ideas were preserved there demanded leisure not as a means but as

---

[9] U.S. Commissioner of Labor, *Twenty-first Annual Report, 1906: Strikes and Lockouts* (Washington, D.C., 1907).

[10] Ira Steward, "A Reduction of Hours an Increase of Wages" (1865), in *A Documentary History of American Industrial Society,* ed. John R. Commons et al., 10 vols. (Cleveland: Arthur H. Clark, 1910–11), 9:290; Montgomery, *Beyond Equality,* pp. 252–53.

[11] Sidney Fine, "The Eight-Hour Day Movement in the United States, 1888–1891," *Mississippi Valley Historical Review* 40 (1953): 441–62.

an end in itself. "I do not believe that God ever created man in order to spend his life in work and sleep, without any time to enjoy the pleasures of the world," a New Jersey miner wrote in 1881. A Pennsylvania workingman reiterated the theme; to know "nothing but work, eat and sleep" was to strip a man of his humanity, to make him "little better than a horse." In an argument particularly appealing to the middle-class moralists, some workingmen proposed to turn the time set free from work into labors of self-education, but in the records of the bureaus of labor statistics such men are few. In 1880 the Massachusetts bureau tried to find out what textile mill operatives would do with more leisure. Most proposed to rest, read the newspaper, visit, look around "to see what is going on," and spend time with their families.[12] For all the complex intellectual rationale behind the eight-hour campaigns, the essential appeal of the shorter day was the obvious one: the promise of relief from toil.

9   It is the privilege of moralists, as vigorously exercised in the mid-twentieth century as in the nineteenth, to point to decay. But the chasm between the work ideals of those who stood inside and outside the new work forms and employee relations was present virtually from the very beginning. "Toil, toil, toil, unending," the sweatshop poet Morris Rosenfeld protested in the plaint that echoed deeply through the most vocal segment of those caught in the new half-free, time-pressed labor of the factories. While the middle-class moralists, torn between the allure and the apparent dangers of leisure, wrestled with questions of pleasure and duty, industrial workers crossed far fewer inner compunctions as they struggled to pare down the looming place of labor in their lives. "Eight Hours for Work. Eight Hours for Rest. Eight Hours for What We Will." To Samuel Gompers, the persuasively symmetrical rallying cry of the eight-hour crusade was the workers' "fling-back" at the ethic of all-consuming industry.[13]

Reading Sources: "The Working Day"

Read the selection, surveying it to identify key terms and important concepts. Highlight these phrases and ideas, and then answer these questions.

1. Why does Rodgers open his essay with a question? Is this an effective strategy?
2. How does Rodgers use dates to help structure his essay? How does this technique help readers to follow his ideas?
3. How does Rodgers link the ideas in paragraph 4 with those in paragraph 5? How does he link ideas within paragraph 4?

---

[12] NJBLS, *Fourth Annual Report* (Somerville, 1881), p. 90; *Pennsylvania Industrial Statistics,* 17 (Harrisburg, 1890): 32E; MBLS, *Twelfth Annual Report* (Boston, 1881), pp. 450–53.
   [13] Philip S. Foner, *American Labor Songs of the Nineteenth Century* (Urbana: University of Illinois Press, 1975), p. 288; Samuel Gompers, *Seventy Years of Life and Labor,* 2 vols. (New York: E. P. Dutton, 1925), 1:54.

4. Underline Rodgers's thesis. Why does he state it where he does?
5. Underline the topic sentence of paragraph 7. What information does Rodgers provide to support this sentence?
6. Where does Rodgers begin his conclusion? What points does he choose to emphasize?

Reacting to Sources

Reread the selection carefully, making marginal notes to aid your comprehension and to reinforce connections. Then further annotate the selection if you need to do so in order to answer any of these questions. (You may already have addressed some of the questions in your marginal notes.)

1. In a few sentences, rewrite paragraph 2 to simplify its ideas.
2. Using a dictionary if necessary, supply brief marginal definitions of these words as they are used in the selection: *dissipation* (1), *fervent* (2), *desideratum* (2), *quixotic* (5), *monster* (5), *sweatshop* (9).
3. In a marginal note, identify Rodgers's purpose. Is his tone appropriate for his purpose? Explain in a journal entry.
4. Does Rodgers show any bias for or against his subject? Explain in a marginal note.
5. Write three brief marginal questions in response to the ideas in paragraph 3.
6. In his essay, Rodgers says, "How much of a man's life should work consume? No work-related question is more central than this . . ." (1). Explore this idea further in a journal entry.
7. In a marginal note, give two examples to support Rodgers's general statement, "But among workingmen, the drive to shorten the hours of labor was a long and fervent struggle" (2).
8. How do the information in the introduction to the essay and the notes following it influence your acceptance of Rodgers's ideas? Explain in a journal entry.
9. In a journal entry, consider the possible relationships between this selection and the ideas in the excerpt from *Brave New Workplace* (pp. 410–417).
10. Outline the paragraph cluster beginning with paragraph 4 and ending with paragraph 5.

Working with Sources

1. Write a two- or three-sentence summary of paragraph 3.
2. Write a critique of the ideas in paragraph 1.
3. Write a journal entry in which you explore your reaction to these quotations from "The Working Day":

    "The early factory masters took over the traditional sun-to-sun workday, stretched it to between twelve and fourteen hours of labor . . ." (1).

"Twice in the nineteenth century, moreover, the shorter-hours demand mushroomed into popular crusades unsurpassed in their intensity by any other of the era's labor issues" (4).

"Where rank-and-file workers divided from union leaders was not over the desirability of shorter working hours — whose appeal cut across lines of ideology and unionization — but over rationale" (7).

Be sure to integrate the quotations smoothly into your writing.

4. Paraphrase paragraph 7.
5. Write a one-paragraph synthesis that blends ideas in paragraph 2 with the ideas in paragraph 3 of the excerpt from *Brave New Workplace* (pp. 410 – 417).

Writing with Sources: Using a Single Source

Integrating information from "The Working Day" with your own ideas, write an essay on one of these topics. Be sure to acknowledge all ideas that are not your own.

1. Recently, a four-day work week, flextime, and job splitting have been proposed as alternatives to the standard work week. Go to the library and locate an article that examines one of these innovations, and then write an essay in which you discuss whether or not this alternative is a good substitute for the traditional work schedule.
2. Increasing foreign competition has caused some manufacturers to wonder if the workday should be extended to nine or even ten hours. Write an essay in which you argue for or against this position.
3. As Rodgers illustrates, labor unions historically were instrumental in winning an eight-hour workday and other benefits for workers. Write an essay in which you discuss whether unions currently perform a useful function for labor. Use your own experience and reading to support your points.

From *Brave New Workplace*

Robert Howard

Robert Howard attended Amherst College, Cambridge University, and the Ecole Normale Supérieure. His articles have appeared in *The New Republic, The Nation, Working Papers, Commonweal,* and other magazines. In the following selection, the introduction to Howard's book *Brave New Workplace* (1985), he examines the effect that technology is having on working life and social values. Howard concludes that far from being the harbinger of meaningful work, the new workplace disguises old problems of work and creates new problems of its own.

1   Few areas of our lives evoke more profound ambivalence than the activity that goes by the name of work. On the one hand, work seems synonymous with promise. It is the means by which we nourish a sense of mastery and achievement in the world. It is the major activity through which we shape our ambitions and our talents and, thus, come to know ourselves. Work also takes us beyond the self. It is our link to society, our chief (and, for many, only) collective activity. Through our work, we dedicate ourselves to an end — a product or service, a professional or occupational group, a human community. In its inherently double nature — simultaneously personal and social — work quite simply makes us who we are.

2   And yet, how often do we think of work as little more than a burden and a problem. It is a source of persistent dissatisfaction, a realm hedged in by necessity and constraint, time irretrievably lost to that unavoidable task of "making" a living. In the apt words of one social researcher, work is "society's most heavily obligated sphere of life." And if the idea of work contains a promise, then the obligations of working life, for many, signify a promise rarely kept.

3   During the past decade, our ambivalence about work has been exacerbated by enormous and nearly permanent change. Social and demographic changes have redrawn the visage of the U.S. labor force, introducing new groups into the workplace — women, minorities, and the baby-boom generation of the young. Economic changes continue to spawn previously unheard-of industries and dispatch familiar ones into decline; to transform entire geographic regions, allocating some to boom and others to dislocation and decay; even to challenge the heretofore dominant position of American industry in the world economy. Most recently (and perhaps most visibly), rapid technological change is revolutionizing the very tools with which we do our work, putting into question traditional occupations, skills, and ideas about what work is.

4   All these changes have contributed to a widespread uncertainty about work. Are the high unemployment levels of recent years to become a permanent fixture of American working life? Can the economy provide the same kind of generalized prosperity that it produced in the 1950s and 1960s in the decades to come? Who will be the winners and who the losers in the new economy that appears to be growing up right before our eyes?

5   At the same time as these changes have engendered myriad questions about work, they have also inspired a new set of promises on the part of that social institution which, more than any other, has shaped the contours of our working life during the past century: the modern corporation. Precisely when work has become so unstable and unsure, American business has begun to articulate a remarkably ambitious vision for the social transformation of working life, a scenario for a future in which we can put aside our ambivalence about work once and for all.

6   This is a book about that vision. It is the story of what I call the "brave new workplace." The pages that follow describe the elements of that vision and the meanings they communicate and tell how it is being put into practice at workplaces across the country and throughout the economy. They also suggest

why this emerging corporate blueprint for the future of work constitutes a danger — not only for workers but for American society as a whole.

7   Just what is this vision of the brave new workplace? Its signs are all around us. They can be found in the media, in the speeches of corporate executives, in best-selling books, sometimes even in the very architecture of working life. They all speak to us of a desired future, often using images deeply rooted in our past.

8   Consider, by way of introduction, a recent advertisement appearing in magazines and newspapers across the country. It features a familiar personality from America's past and a product that will be a fixture of America's future — the IBM Personal Computer. A Chaplinesque figure sits before the soft, off-white keyboard and ice-green screen, his face consumed with wonder and delight. Plucked from his imprisoning assembly line, stripped of his overalls and dressed in a pinstripe suit (so suddenly that his work boots remain, old and worn, a fitting contrast to the high-tech polish of the computer), the character made famous by Chaplin in *Modern Times* is plopped down in the middle of the twenty-first century.

9   "How to test drive the IBM Personal Computer," the headline reads, only the first in a long line of references to that twentieth-century archetype of freedom and mobility, the automobile. Liberated from the drudgery of his factory job, his chair tipped back, his hat blown clean away by a passing breeze, our former assembly-line worker is off on a wild, exhilarating ride into the future of work. As if to underline this message, the punchline of the ad informs us that the IBM Personal Computer is "a tool for modern times."

10   Designed to sell computers, this ad sells a promise as well. Charlie Chaplin was the first popular media figure to express the reality of alienating work on the assembly line. For more than a generation, his film *Modern Times* has provided the images governing how we see industrial work. And yet, here, Chaplin's factory worker finds fulfillment (and, from the look of his suit, a considerable raise in pay) through the wonders of new technology. The computer delivers him from the prison of dirty, boring, alienating work. Within the frame of the ad, the former critic of work becomes a persuasive advocate for technology and for the corporation itself. Through technology and the corporation that provides it, Chaplin seems to be telling us, we too can be, like him, test-driving the IBM Personal Computer. And our work can become a realm of freedom — fluid, infinitely mobile, freighted with enormous possibility.

11   This idea that new technology will usher in an era of more satisfying and meaningful work is a key element in the vision of the brave new workplace. What is interesting about this ad and its use of Chaplin is that it speaks to our fears about technology gone out of control, our becoming a mere appendage of the machine (remember Chaplin trapped in the maw of that voracious conveyor belt), and in doing so allays them.

12   A further elaboration on this theme comes from the ongoing celebration of "high technology" in American culture. It's not merely the fact that we are fascinated with the technology of the silicon chip and awed by the rapid

economic growth of the industries that produce and work with it. High technology also seems to offer us something more, an alternative image of the
corporation itself.

13   One after another, journalists have made pilgrimage to California's Silicon
Valley. The reports they have sent back suggest that these corporations of the
future, far from being impersonal technocratic bureaucracies, are in fact the
embodiment of an egalitarian community. "It does not take long," James
Fallows has written in the *Atlantic,* "for a visitor . . . to the area to sense an
atmosphere different from that of the 'mature' manufacturing industries."
Silicon Valley firms are "more flexible," says Fallows, and "less concerned
with the normal trappings of rank." This "egalitarian and flexible structure,"
adds *New York Times* correspondent Steve Lohr, allows high-tech companies to
"avoid the bureaucratic hierarchy characteristic of most firms."

14   The most committed champions of this theme have been the founders of
Silicon Valley's successful high-tech corporations. Sounding less like corporate
executives than social visionaries, they have elevated the idea of the entrepreneur to the status of a new social ethic. "The rest of the country, and even the
rest of the world, doesn't have a very good idea about Silicon Valley," Steve
Jobs, the almost legendary cofounder of Apple Computer, told an audience at
the first Stanford Conference on Entrepreneurship in April 1982. "There is
something going on here on a scale which has never been seen on the face of
the earth." Jobs called it a "critical mass of entrepreneurial risk culture" and he
claimed that it was producing an epochal social change. "A lot of people ask if
Silicon Valley is ever going to be unionized," Jobs continued. "I say everybody's unionized. . . . There's much greater union here than I've seen anywhere. What we're starting to see is the redefinition of the corporation in
America."

15   Thus, the brave new workplace concerns not only technology but community, the transformation of bureaucracy, the redefinition of the corporation.
And once the new technology resolves the age-old problem of alienation and
the corporation becomes an expression of unity and communal bonds, then the
workplace itself will be a temple dedicated to the cultivation of the self.

16   From the moment you step off the elevator that ferries people to the
Tenneco Employee Center built on top of a parking garage in downtown
Houston, you have the feeling of entering a spacious cathedral. Perhaps it is
the light streaming through the three-story-tall windows. Perhaps it is the
silence broken only by the gentle gurgling of fountains, the muted sound of
voices, a distant laugh. Whatever the reason, you are enveloped in a reverential
atmosphere radiating tranquillity and calm.

17   A few steps from the elevator, you enter a lavish indoor tropical garden.
Its bewildering variety of broadleaf plants and green bamboo shoots arch
toward the sun. The employee cafeteria is right off the garden. It has green
marble floors and tables, and chairs of powder-blue crushed velvet and bronze.

18   One floor down from the main entrance is the sanctuary of this modern-
day cathedral: the Tenneco Health and Fitness Center. Employees ranging from
the lowliest clerk to the highest corporate executive exchange their office

clothes and their diverse social roles for standard gray "Tenneco Health and Fitness Center" T-shirts and shorts. There are saunas and whirlpools in the locker room, racquetball courts, a running track, and an exercise room.

19   From the balcony, you look down on the weight room, divided into male and female sections. Three women work out on the Nautilus weight machines. An elderly man furiously pedals an exercise bicycle while two attendants take his blood pressure and run other tests. Other gray-clad Tenneco employees line up at the three computer terminals on the long table at one end of the weight room. They insert their magnetized company ID cards and punch in their workouts for the day. Each month, they receive a computer printout listing their exercises for the month and, according to their weight, the total amount of calories they have burned.

20   "We have almost perfect statistics," says Barbara Roop, one of the nine full-time members of the Health and Fitness Center staff. "We know how many people use the center, who they are, and what they use it for."

21   "We are trying to build a sense of self-responsibility," adds Mark Land-green, the young director of the center. "We want to make people feel that this is their thing. That produces a good feeling about Tenneco — that Tenneco cares."

22   Recently, the center staff has organized an experiment using these computerized statistics to try to demonstrate a direct link between the workers' health and corporate productivity. A computer tracking system will correlate employee use of the center facilities with a cross section of physiological and organizational indicators. What is the relationship between hypertension and, say, absenteeism? Are the most frequent users of the center also Tenneco's best performers as indicated by promotion records and performance evaluations? The hypothesis, says Barbara Roop, is that "keeping morale up, people feeling good about themselves, helps improve productivity." Of course, all personal information is strictly confidential.

23   Two floors up from the Health and Fitness Center is the complex's executive dining room. Set on the third-floor balcony, it looks out over the tropical garden. Here the crushed-velvet chairs aren't powder-blue but mauve. Lenox china and frest-cut flowers adorn every table. But lest one forget the overriding purpose of the Tenneco Employee Center, there are the menus at every place setting. The number of calories in each item is prominently displayed on the right. The fried breaded scallops tartar have 250, the House Salad (Bibb lettuce, spinach, tomatoes, shredded eggs, and bay shrimp) a mere 210. And those items on the menu starred with an asterisk are selections from the Pritikin Diet.

24   But the message of the brave new workplace does not even stop there. This caring corporation is not reserved for those employees lucky enough to work within its benevolent walls; it extends to everyone. For it is being offered as a model for society as a whole and promoted as the central institution of all social life.

25   "As geographic communities cease to have real social significance for many citizens," Robert Reich has written in one expression of this point of

view, "workplaces are becoming the center of social relationships." And "business enterprises are rapidly becoming the central mediating structures in American society." In the particular future Reich envisions, the corporation will take on the dimensions of a miniature society—for example, taking over from government the administration of a wide range of social programs for its employees, including health care, social security, day care, and disability and unemployment benefits. Even more important, the corporation will become the provider of a crucial social identity for its employees and, ultimately, for all members of society. For the brave new workplace promises a world where "all citizens (and their dependents) will become employee members of some business enterprise."

26   New technology as the harbinger of meaningful work; the corporation conceived, not as an impersonal bureaucracy, but as a caring community; the workplace as a realm of self-fulfillment; business enterprise as the fundamental source of identity in modern society—these are heady claims. Indeed, they are so visionary, so tinged with possibility and marked with the stamp of the future, that they merit the term "utopia." They promise a world where traditional dissatisfactions dissolve in an atmosphere of unity and good feeling, where conflict and division are abolished, and where the ambivalences of modern industrial life disappear behind the glittering facade of a utopian business culture.

27   That this corporate utopia of the brave new workplace has emerged just now should really be no surprise. For it is the ironic culmination of a decades-long reflection on the place of work in American society. For some thirty years, sociologists and journalists, novelists and social critics have tried to gauge the distance between the promise of work and its reality. They have seen work as a unique social problem threatening the very conception of American democracy.

28   Daniel Bell's seminal essay "Work and Its Discontents" is an appropriate place to begin, for it sets the tone of much subsequent writing. In 1956, Bell emphasized the fragmentation and dehumanization of work in the modern industrial factory, traced it to the very principles of efficiency at the foundation of industrial society, and predicted the emergence of a rebellion against those principles in American workplaces. According to Bell, the "revolt against work" had already begun. "It appears in the constant evasion of thought about work," he wrote, "the obsessive reveries while on the job and the substitution of the glamor of leisure for the drudgery of work." At times, this revolt even passed into action in "crazy racings against the clock to vary the deadly monotony" of the assembly line, in "slowdowns" which he termed "the silent war against production standards," and, "most spectacularly," in "the violent eruptions of wildcat strikes."

29   Three years later in 1959, the novelist and social critic Harvey Swados echoed Bell's concerns and charged American society with a systematic denial of what he termed the "problem of work." In an article entitled "Work as a Public Issue," in the *Saturday Review,* Swados charged the "growing white collar classes" with refusing to admit "the possibility that millions of American

workers may in truth be horribly discontented with their jobs." To do so "would disturb the comfortable mass-media concept of America as a land of blissful togetherness" and "do violence to their own self-esteem." And yet, Swados had to admit that critics such as he and Bell were still in the minority. He lamented "the terrible breadth of the chasm that separates those who *think* from those who *do*, those who *ponder* problems of power from those who *wield* power."

30   A decade later, the latent workplace rebellion identified by Bell flared up with increasing visibility. Events such as the 1974 wildcat strike at the General Motors assembly plant in Lordstown, Ohio, undermined the media myth of "blissful togetherness," replacing it with images of "blue collar blues" and "white collar woes." And Studs Terkel's best-selling book *Working* documented what he, like Bell, termed the "violence" of working life and the revolt brewing in the American workplace, and gave that rebellion flesh and blood and the discontented worker a voice.

31   In 1974, a special report to Elliot Richardson, then secretary of health, education, and welfare, endorsed the criticisms of work articulated over the years by Bell, Swados, Terkel, and others. The authors of *Work in America* condemned the "anachronistic authoritarianism" reigning in most American workplaces; predicted that, in a rapidly changing society, such heavy-handed methods would prove counterproductive; and called for an "atmosphere of social experimentation" in which the wholesale redesign of the American workplace could be undertaken. It was as if Swados's dream — work considered as a public issue — had come true.

32   Today, the preoccupation with work has returned to center stage once again — only this time with some important differences. Whereas earlier reflections about work took place during a period of relative prosperity, the current debate is occurring in an atmosphere of economic uncertainty and even crisis. The almost desperate search for new paths to economic success — perhaps best symbolized by the recent fascination with "Japanese management" — has made the problem of work less a social issue than a matter of industrial competitiveness and economic survival. And where earlier observers of working life tended to view the corporation as an obstacle to reform, today more and more see it as the primary vehicle for social change.

33   The allure of the brave new workplace is that it promises a wholesale transformation of working life precisely when we seem to need it the most. When the legitimacy and effectiveness of traditional forms of corporate power and practice have been worn thin by the simultaneous impacts of rapid social, economic, and technological change, here is a brand-new model of corporate life promising to reconcile equity with efficiency, meaningful work with high technology, worker satisfaction with corporate profit, and social renewal with economic prosperity.

34   It is precisely these claims that this book is meant to question. The brave new workplace is certainly a response to past criticisms and present uncertainties. But far from resolving the problems of work, it tends to disguise them, suppress them, and in the process create new problems (as yet unrecognized,

let alone understood) even more difficult to address. For this corporate utopia for work denies the essential fact that work in America is a relationship of unequal power, that conflicts of interest are endemic to working life, and that this new model of the corporation, much like the old, is founded on the systematic denial of influence and control to the large majority of working Americans. . . .

35   The story of the brave new workplace is ultimately about politics — although not in the narrow way that term is usually understood. It is the most recent chapter in the long struggle between two conflicting conceptions of work and society.

36   One is the heir to a basic tenet of traditional capitalism — that work is essentially a private affair and that the only institution with the expertise and the legitimacy to shape it is the private corporation. This was the unquestioned premise on which the company towns of early industrial capitalism were built. It was the justification for what one social historian has called the "tyranny of the foreman" in the early mass-production industries. Even after the advent of industrial unionism, it survived in a modified form in the concept of "management prerogatives" still found in most labor contracts today. And it has found its most recent reincarnation in the antiunion, antigovernment, antipublic ideology of contemporary conservatism exemplified by the Reagan administration.

37   The other conception has been the guiding force of workplace conflict and protest throughout the twentieth century — the idea that work is a public activity far too important to the health of American democracy to be left to the corporation alone. The first efforts at work regulation around the turn of the century, the industrial union movement of the 1930s, and the most recent wave of occupational health and safety and environmental legislation in the 1960s and 1970s all emerged from this same principle. They are part of the ongoing effort to create institutions that represent the public interest at work.

38   Its reassertion of the primacy of the corporation over working life and its parallel devaluation of the public dimension of work make the brave new workplace a characteristically capitalist utopia. And, today, that utopia seems to have the imprimatur of the future and the affinity of extraordinary promise. The premise of this book is that this future is bankrupt and its promises false — and that the brave new workplace is sowing the seeds of new social conflicts at work and creating the conditions for alternative visions of working life.

Reading Sources: from **Brave New Workplace**

Read the selection, surveying it to identify key terms and important concepts. Highlight these phrases and ideas, and then answer these questions.

1. What visual cues are used in this essay? How do they help readers follow Howard's ideas?

2. Where does Howard's introduction end and the body of his essay begin? How do the points he emphasizes prepare readers for the rest of the essay?
3. What is Howard's thesis? How does the selection's title foreshadow this thesis? To what does the title allude?
4. Paragraphs 7 through 26 contain several extended examples. Why does Howard include such a long section devoted to examples? Does this decision strengthen or weaken the essay?
5. What effect does Howard's use of quotations in paragraphs 27 to 30 have on his argument?
6. What techniques does Howard use to link paragraphs 33 and 34? What idea does he question in paragraph 34?
7. Where does Howard begin his conclusion? What points does he decide not to emphasize in his conclusion? Does the essay gain or lose from this choice?

Reacting to Sources

Reread the selection carefully, making marginal notes to aid your comprehension and to reinforce connections. Then further annotate the selection if you need to do so in order to answer any of these questions. (You may already have addressed some of the questions in your marginal notes.)

1. In a few sentences, rewrite paragraph 3 to simplify its ideas.
2. Using a dictionary if necessary, supply brief marginal definitions of these words as they are used in the selection: *ambivalence* (1), *collective* (1), *dislocation* (3), *myriad* (5), *maw* (11), *egalitarian* (13), *bureaucratic* (13), *hierarchy* (13), *entrepreneur* (14), *harbinger* (26), *utopia* (26).
3. Write three brief marginal questions in response to the ideas in paragraph 5.
4. Howard makes this statement in paragraph 11: "This idea that technology will usher in an era of more satisfying and meaningful work is a key element in the vision of the brave new workplace." Do you agree or disagree? Write a brief marginal comment in which you explain why.
5. Give two examples to support Howard's general statement, "For some thirty years, sociologists and journalists, novelists and social critics have tried to gauge the distance between the promise of work and its reality" (27).
6. Find a statement in the essay for which your own knowledge or experience provides contradictory evidence. Write a brief marginal note that explains the contradiction.
7. Identify the purpose of paragraph 26. Identify the purpose of the entire essay.
8. In paragraph 33 Howard says, "The allure of the brave new workplace is that it promises a wholesale transformation of working life precisely when we seem to need it most." Explore this idea further in a journal entry.
9. In a journal entry, consider your reactions to Howard's comments in paragraph 34.

10. Outline the paragraph cluster beginning with paragraph 28 and ending with paragraph 30.

Working with Sources

1. Write a two-sentence summary of paragraph 5.
2. Write a critique of the ideas in paragraph 38.
3. Write a journal entry in which you explore your reactions to these quotations from *Brave New Workplace:*

> "New technology as the harbinger of meaningful work; the corporation conceived, not as an impersonal bureaucracy, but as a caring community; the workplace as a realm of self-fulfillment; business enterprise as the fundamental source of identity in modern society — these are heady claims" (26).

> "It is precisely these claims that this book is meant to question. The brave new workplace is certainly a response to past criticisms and present uncertainties" (34).

> "The story of the brave new workplace is ultimately about politics. . . . It is the most recent chapter in the long struggle between two conflicting conceptions of work and society" (35).

Be sure to integrate the quotations smoothly into your writing.
4. Paraphrase the paragraph cluster beginning with paragraph 33 and ending with paragraph 34.
5. Write a one-paragraph synthesis that blends ideas in paragraph 30 with the ideas in paragraph 7 of the excerpt from *Working* (pp. 420 – 426).

Writing with Sources: Using a Single Source

Integrating information from the excerpt from *Brave New Workplace* with your own ideas, write an essay on one of these topics. Be sure to acknowledge all ideas that are not your own.

1. Explain the meaning work has in your life. Is it "little more than a burden and a problem"? Or is it a major activity by which you shape your ambitions and talents and come to know yourself?
2. Describe briefly some of the changes that you would institute to improve workplaces across the country. Be specific, and support your points with references to your own experiences and reading.
3. Explain why you agree or disagree with Howard's thesis concerning the brave new workplace. Do you agree with him that the workplace that corporate executives envision constitutes a danger for American society, or do you think that it creates a "realm of freedom" that is filled with possibilities?

From *Working*

Studs Terkel

Louis "Studs" Terkel, born in 1912, grew up in Chicago and graduated from the University of Chicago in 1932 and Chicago Law School in 1934. Traveling extensively all over the world, he held a great number of unusual and interesting jobs. He acted in radio soap operas and was a disk jockey, a sports announcer, a television announcer, and an interviewer. Perhaps as a result of these jobs or of growing up during the Great Depression, Terkel developed an interest in presenting history through the words of the ordinary people who experienced it. His oral histories include *Division Street: America* (1967); *Hard Times: An Oral History of the Great Depression* (1970); *Working* (1974); *Talking to Myself* (1977) (an autobiography); *American Dreams: Lost and Found* (1980); and *The Good War* (1984). The following excerpt is from the introduction to *Working,* a book in which Terkel examines the working lives of people from all segments of American society. In this essay, he sums up his feelings about the nature of work in America and defines the common factors that link all workers.

1   This book, being about work, is, by its very nature, about violence — to the spirit as well as to the body. It is about ulcers as well as accidents, about shouting matches as well as fistfights, about nervous breakdowns as well as kicking the dog around. It is, above all (or beneath all), about daily humiliations. To survive the day is triumph enough for the walking wounded among the great many of us.

2   The scars, psychic as well as physical, brought home to the supper table and the TV set, may have touched, malignantly, the soul of our society. More or less. ("More or less," that most ambiguous of phrases, pervades many of the conversations that comprise this book, reflecting, perhaps, an ambiguity of attitude toward The Job. Something more than Orwellian acceptance, something less than Luddite sabotage. Often the two impulses are fused in the same person.)

3   It is about a search, too, for daily meaning as well as daily bread, for recognition as well as cash, for astonishment rather than torpor; in short, for a sort of life rather than a Monday through Friday sort of dying. Perhaps immortality, too, is part of the quest. To be remembered was the wish, spoken and unspoken, of the heroes and heroines of this book.

4   There are, of course, the happy few who find a savor in their daily job: the Indiana stonemason, who looks upon his work and sees that it is good; the Chicago piano tuner, who seeks and finds the sound that delights; the book-binder, who saves a piece of history; the Brooklyn fireman, who saves a piece of life . . . But don't these satisfactions, like Jude's hunger for knowledge, tell us more about the person than about his task? Perhaps. Nonetheless, there is a common attribute here: a meaning to their work well over and beyond the reward of the paycheck.

5   For the many, there is a hardly concealed discontent. The blue-collar

blues is no more bitterly sung than the white-collar moan. "I'm a machine," says the spot-welder. "I'm caged," says the bank teller, and echoes the hotel clerk. "I'm a mule," says the steelworker. "A monkey can do what I do," says the receptionist. "I'm less than a farm implement," says the migrant worker. "I'm an object," says the high-fashion model. Blue collar and white call upon the identical phrase: "I'm a robot." *"There is nothing to talk about,"* the young accountant despairingly enunciates. It was some time ago that John Henry sang, "A man ain't nothin' but a man." The hard, unromantic fact is: he died with his hammer in his hand, while the machine pumped on. Nonetheless, he found immortality. He is remembered.

6   As the automated pace of our daily jobs wipes out name and face — and, in many instances, feeling — there is a sacrilegious question being asked these days. To earn one's bread by the sweat of one's brow has always been the lot of mankind. At least, ever since Eden's slothful couple was served with an eviction notice. The scriptural precept was never doubted, not out loud. No matter how demeaning the task, no matter how it dulls the senses and breaks the spirit, one *must* work. Or else.

7   Lately there has been a questioning of this "work ethic," especially by the young. Strangely enough, it has touched off profound grievances in others, hitherto devout, silent, and anonymous. Unexpected precincts are being heard from in a show of discontent. Communiqués from the assembly line are frequent and alarming: absenteeism. On the evening bus, the tense, pinched faces of young file clerks and elderly secretaries tell us more than we care to know. On the expressways, middle management men pose without grace behind their wheels as they flee city and job.

8   There are other means of showing it, too. Inchoately, sullenly, it appears in slovenly work, in the put-down of craftsmanship. A farm equipment worker in Moline complains that the careless worker who turns out more that is bad is better regarded than the careful craftsman who turns out less that is good. The first is an ally of the Gross National Product. The other is a threat to it, a kook — and the sooner he is penalized the better. Why, in these circumstances, should a man work with care? Pride does indeed precede the fall.

9   Others, more articulate — at times, visionary — murmur of a hunger for "beauty," "a meaning," "a sense of pride." A veteran car hiker sings out, "I could drive any car like a baby, like a woman change her baby's diaper. Lots of customers say, 'How you do this?' I'd say, 'Just the way you bake a cake, miss.' When I was younger, I could swing with that car. They called me Lovin' Al the Wizard."

10   Dolores Dante graphically describes the trials of a waitress in a fashionable restaurant. They are compounded by her refusal to be demeaned. Yet pride in her skills helps her make it through the night. "When I put the plate down, you don't hear a sound. When I pick up a glass, I want it to be just right. When someone says, 'How come you're just a waitress?' I say, 'Don't you think you deserve being served by me?'"

11   Peggy Terry has her own sense of grace and beauty. Her jobs have varied with geography, climate, and the ever-felt pinch of circumstance. "What I

hated worst was being a waitress. The way you're treated. One guy said, 'You don't have to smile; I'm gonna give you a tip anyway.' I said, 'Keep it. I wasn't smiling for a tip.' Tipping should be done away with. It's like throwing a dog a bone. It makes you feel small."

12   In all instances, there is felt more than a slight ache. In all instances, there dangles the impertinent question. Ought not there be an increment, earned though not yet received, for one's daily work—an acknowledgement of man's *being?*

13   An American President is fortunate — or, perhaps, unfortunate — that, offering his Labor Day homily, he didn't encounter Maggie Holmes, the domestic, or Phil Stallings, the spot-welder, or Louis Hayward, the washroom attendant. Or, especially, Grace Clements, the felter at the luggage factory, whose daily chore reveals to us in a terrible light that Charles Dickens's London is not so far away nor long ago.

14   Obtuseness in "respectable" quarters is not a new phenomenon. In 1850 Henry Mayhew, digging deep into London's laboring lives and evoking from the invisible people themselves the wretched truth of their lot, astonished and horrified readers of the *Morning Chronicle*. His letters ran six full columns and averaged 10,500 words. It is inconceivable that Thomas Carlyle was unaware of Mayhew's findings. Yet, in his usual acerbic—and, in this instance, unusually mindless—manner, he blimped, "No needlewoman, distressed or other, can be procured in London by any housewife to give, for fair wages, fair help in sewing. Ask any thrifty housemother. No *real* needlewoman, 'distressed' or other, has been found attainable in any of the houses I frequent. Imaginary needlewomen, who demand considerable wages, and have a deepish appetite for beer and viands, I hear of everywhere. . . . " * A familiar ring?

15   Smug respectability, like the poor, we've had with us always. Today, however, and what few decades remain of the twentieth century, such obtuseness is an indulgence we can no longer afford. The computer, nuclear energy for better or worse, and sudden, simultaneous influences flashed upon everybody's TV screen have raised the ante and the risk considerably. Possibilities of another way, discerned by only a few before, are thought of—if only for a brief moment, in the haze of idle conjecture — by many today.

The drones are no longer invisible nor mute. Nor are they exclusively of one class. Markham's Man with the Hoe may be Ma Bell's girl with the headset. (And can it be safely said, she is "dead to rapture and despair"? Is she really "a thing that grieves not and that never hopes"?) They're in the office as well as the warehouse; at the manager's desk as well as the assembly line; at some estranged company's computer as well as some estranged woman's kitchen floor.

17   Bob Cratchit may still be hanging on (though his time is fast running out, as did his feather pen long ago), but Scrooge has been replaced by the conglomerate. Hardly a chance for Christmas spirit here. Who knows Bob's name in this outfit—let alone his lame child's? ("The last place I worked for, I was let go," recalls the bank teller. "One of my friends stopped by and asked

---

* E. P. Thompson and Eileen Yeo, *The Unknown Mayhew* (New York: Pantheon Books, 1971).

where I was at. They said, 'She's no longer with us.' That's all. I vanished.")
It's nothing personal, really. Dickens's people have been replaced by Beckett's.

> Many old working class women have an habitual gesture which illuminates the years of their life behind. D. H. Lawrence remarked it in his mother: my grandmother's was a repeated tapping which accompanied an endless working out of something in her head; she had years of making out for a large number on very little. In others, you see a rhythmic smoothing out of the hand down the chair arm, as though to smooth everything out and make it workable; in others, there is a working of the lips or a steady rocking. None of these could be called neurotic gestures, nor are they symptoms of acute fear, they help the constant calculation.*

In my mother's case, I remember the illuminating gesture associated with work or enterprise. She was a small entrepreneur, a Mother Courage fighting her Thirty Years' War, daily. I remember her constant feeling of the tablecloth, as though assessing its quality, and her squinting of the eye, as though calculating its worth.

18   *Perhaps it was myopia, but I rarely saw such signs among the people I visited during this adventure. True, in that dark hollow in Eastern Kentucky I did see Susie Haynes, the black lung miner's wife, posed in the doorway of the shack, constantly touching the woodwork, "as though to smooth everything out and make it workable." It was a rare gesture, what once had been commonplace. Those who did signify—Ned Williams, the old stock chaser, Hobart Foote, the utility man—did so in the manner of the machines to which they were bound. Among the many, though the words and phrases came, some heatedly, others coolly, the hands were at rest, motionless. Their eyes were something else again. As they talked of their jobs, it was as though it had little to do with their felt lives. It was an alien matter. At times I imagined I was on the estate of Dr. Caligari and the guests poured out fantasies.*

19   To maintain a sense of self, these heroes and heroines play occasional games. The middle-aged switchboard operator, when things are dead at night, cheerily responds to the caller, "Marriott Inn," instead of identifying the motel chain she works for. "Just for a lark," she explains bewilderedly. "I really don't know what made me do it." The young gas meter reader startles the young suburban housewife sunning out on the patio in her bikini, loose-bra'd, and sees more things than he would otherwise see. "Just to make the day go faster." The auto worker from the Deep South will "tease one guy 'cause he's real short and his old lady left him." Why? "Oh, just to break the monotony. You want quittin' time so bad."

20   The waitress, who moves by the tables with the grace of a ballerina, pretends she's forever on stage. "I feel like Carmen. It's like a gypsy holding out a tambourine and they throw the coin." It helps her fight humiliation as well as arthritis. The interstate truckdriver, bearing down the expressway with a load of seventy-three thousand pounds, battling pollution, noise, an ulcer, and

* Richard Hoggart, *The Uses of Literacy* (New York: Oxford University Press, 1957).

kidneys that act up, "fantasizes something tremendous." They all, in some manner, perform astonishingly to survive the day. These are not yet automata.

21   The time study men of the General Motors Assembly Division made this discomforting discovery in Lordstown. Gary Bryner, the young union leader, explains it. "Occasionally one of the guys will let a car go by. At that point, he's made a decision: 'Aw, . . . it's only a car.' It's more important to just stand there and rap. With us, it becomes a human thing. It's the most enjoyable part of my job, that moment. I love it!" John Henry hardly envisioned that way of fighting the machine — which may explain why he died in his prime.

22   There are cases where the job possess the man even after quitting time. Aside from occupational ticks of hourly workers and the fitful sleep of salaried ones, there are instances of a man's singular preoccupation with work. It may affect his attitude toward all of life. And art.

23   Geraldine Page, the actress, recalls the critique of a backstage visitor during her run in *Sweet Bird of Youth.* He was a dentist. "I was sitting in the front row and looking up. Most of the time I was studying the fillings in your mouth. I'm curious to know who's been doing your dental work." It was not that he loved theater less, but that he loved dentistry more.

24   At the public unveiling of a celebrated statue in Chicago, a lawyer after deep study, mused, "I accept Mr. Picasso in good faith. But if you look at the height of the slope on top and the propensity of children who will play on it, I have a feeling that some child may fall and be hurt and the county may be sued. . . ."

25   In my own case, while putting together this book, I found myself possessed by the mystique of work. During a time out, I saw the film *Last Tango in Paris.* Though Freud said *lieben und arbeiten* are the two moving impulses of man, it was the latter that, at the moment, consumed me. Thus, I saw on the screen a study not of redemption nor of self-discovery nor whatever perceptive critics may have seen. During that preoccupied moment I saw a study of an actor *at work.* He was performing brilliantly in a darkened theater (apartment), as his audience (the young actress) responded with enthusiasm. I interpreted her moans, cries, and whimpers as bravos, huzzahs, and olés. In short, I saw the film as a source of a possible profile for this book. Such is the impact of work on some people.

26   A further personal note. I find some delight in my job as a radio broadcaster. I'm able to set my own pace, my own standards, and determine for myself the substance of each program. Some days are more sunny than others, some hours less astonishing than I'd hoped for; my occasional slovenliness infuriates me . . . but it is, for better or worse, in my hands. I'd like to believe I'm the old-time cobbler, making the whole shoe. Though my weekends go by soon enough, I look toward Monday without a sigh.

27   The danger of complacency is somewhat tempered by my awareness of what might have been. Chance encounters with old schoolmates are sobering experiences. Memories are dredged up of three traumatic years at law school. They were vaguely, though profoundly, unhappy times for me. I felt more than a slight ache. Were it not for a fortuitous set of circumstances, I might have

become a lawyer—a determinedly failed one, I suspect. (I flunked my first bar examination. Ninety percent passed, I was told.)

28   During the Depression I was a sometime member of the Federal Writers' Project, as well as a sometime actor in radio soap operas. I was usually cast as a gangster and just as usually came to a violent and well-deserved end. It was always sudden. My tenure was as uncertain as that of a radical college professor. It was during these moments — though I was unaware of it at the time — that the surreal nature of my work made itself felt. With script in hand, I read lines of stunning banality. The more such scripts an actor read, the more he was considered a success. Thus the phrase "Show Business" took on an added significance. It was, indeed, a business, a busy-ness. But what was its meaning?

29   If Freud is right — "his work at least gives him a secure place in a portion of reality, in the human community" * — was what I did in those studios really work? It certainly wasn't play. The sales charts of Procter & Gamble and General Mills made that quite clear. It was considered *work*. All my colleagues were serious about it, deadly so. Perhaps my experiences in making life difficult for Ma Perkins and Mary Marlin may have provided me with a metaphor for the experiences of the great many, who fail to find in their work their "portion of reality." Let alone, a secure place "in the human community."

30   Is it any wonder that in such surreal circumstances, status rather than the work itself becomes important? Thus the prevalence of euphemisms in work as well as in war. The janitor is a building engineer; the garbage man, a sanitary engineer; the man at the rendering plant, a factory mechanic; the gravedigger, a caretaker. They are not themselves ashamed of their work, but society, they feel, looks upon them as a lesser species. So they call upon a promiscuously used language to match the "respectability" of others, whose jobs may have less social worth than their own.

(The airline stewardess understands this hierarchy of values. "When you first start flying . . . the men you meet are airport employees: ramp rats, cleaning airplanes and things like that, mechanics. . . . After a year we get tired of that, so we move into the city to get involved with men that are usually young executives. . . . They wear their hats and their suits and in the winter their black gloves.")

Not that these young men in white shirts and black gloves are so secure, either. The salesman at the advertising agency is an account executive. "I feel a little downgraded if people think I'm a salesman. Accounting executive — that describes my job. It has more prestige than just saying, 'I'm a salesman.'" A title, like clothes, may not make the man or woman, but it helps in the world of peers — and certainly impresses strangers. "We're all vice presidents," laughs the copy chief. "Clients like to deal with vice presidents. Also, it's a cheap thing to give somebody. Vice presidents get fired with great energy and alacrity."

* Sigmund Freud, *Civilization and Its Discontents* (New York: W. W. Norton and Co., 1962).

31   At hospitals, the charming bill collector is called the patients' representative! It's a wonderland that Alice never envisioned. Consider the company spy. With understandable modesty, he refers to himself as an industrial investigator. This last — under the generic name, Security — is among the most promising occupations in our society today. No matter how tight the job market, here is a burgeoning field for young men and women. Watergate, its magic spell is everywhere.

32   In a further bizarre turn of events (the science of medicine has increased our life expectancy; the science of business frowns upon the elderly), the matter of age is felt in almost all quarters. "Thirty and out" is the escape hatch for the elderly auto worker to the woods of retirement, some hunting, some fishing. . . . But thirty has an altogether different connotation at the ad agency, at the bank, at the auditing house, at the gas company. Unless he/she is "with it" by then, it's out to the woods of the city, some hunting, some fishing of another sort. As the work force becomes increasingly younger, so does Willy Loman.

Dr. John R. Coleman, president of Haverford College, took an unusual sabbatical during the early months of 1973. He worked at menial jobs. In one instance, he was fired as a porter-dishwasher. "I'd never been fired and I'd never been unemployed. For three days I walked the streets. Though I had a bank account, though my children's tuition was paid, though I had a salary and a job waiting for me back in Haverford, I was demoralized. I had an inkling of how professionals my age feel when they lose their job and their confidence begins to sink."* Dr. Coleman is 51.

33   Perhaps it is this specter that most haunts working men and women: the planned obsolescence of people that is of a piece with the planned obsolescence of the things they make. Or sell. It is perhaps this fear of no longer being needed in a world of needless things that most clearly spells out the unnaturalness, the surreality of much that is called work today.

Reading Sources: from Working

Read the selection, surveying it to identify key terms and important concepts. Highlight these phrases and ideas, and then answer these questions.

1. What points does Terkel include in his opening paragraph? Relate these points to the rest of the selection.
2. What visual cues are used in this selection?
3. What knowledge does Terkel assume his audience has? At what points in the

---

* *New York Times,* June 10, 1973.

selection does he allude to people or things with which he expects his audience to be familiar?

4. What is the main idea of Terkel's essay? Does he state his thesis? Explain.
5. What use does Terkel make of quotations? Do they add to his essay, or do they distract the reader? Explain.
6. Terkel uses the pronoun "I" in his discussion. What is the effect of this strategy? What conclusions can you draw from this about Terkel and his relationship to his audience?

Reacting to Sources

Reread the selection carefully, making marginal notes to aid your comprehension and to reinforce connections. Then further annotate the selection if you need to do so in order to answer any of these questions. (You may already have addressed some of the questions in your marginal notes.)

1. In a few sentences, rewrite paragraph 5 to simplify its ideas.
2. Using a dictionary if necessary, supply brief marginal definitions of these words as they are used in the selection: *Orwellian* (2), *Luddite* (2), *torpor* (3), *sacrilegious* (6), *precincts* (7), *increment* (12), *obtuseness* (14), *ante* (15), *estranged* (16), *banality* (28), *euphemisms* (30), *generic* (31), *connotation* (32), and *obsolescence* (33).
3. In a marginal note, explain the point that Terkel is making in paragraphs 16 and 17 with his references to Edwin Markham, Charles Dickens, and Thomas Beckett. Use an encyclopedia if necessary.
4. Terkel makes this statement in paragraph 7: "Lately there has been a questioning of this 'work ethic,' especially by the young." Do you agree or disagree? Write a brief marginal comment in which you explain why.
5. Write three marginal questions in response to the ideas in paragraph 19.
6. In a marginal note give three original examples to support Terkel's general statement, "Thus the prevalence of euphemisms in work as well as war" (30).
7. In a journal entry consider whether Terkel's conclusions are objective or biased.
8. At several points in his essay Terkel mentions John Henry, the mythical figure who died trying to beat a steam-driven pile driver. Find the various references to John Henry, and in a journal entry, explain the use that Terkel is making of this figure.
9. Find a statement in the essay for which your own knowledge or experience provides contradictory evidence. Write a journal entry that presents this contradiction.
10. In a journal entry, explore the possible connections between this selection and "The Self-Made Man in America" (pp. 378–385).
11. Outline the paragraph cluster beginning with paragraph 30 and ending with paragraph 31.

Working with Sources

1. Write a one-sentence summary of paragraph 19.
2. Write a critique of the ideas in paragraph 7.
3. Write a journal entry in which you explore your reactions to these quotations from *Working:*

    "This book, being about work, is, by its very nature, about violence — to the spirit as well as to the body" (1).

    "To maintain a sense of self, these heroes and heroines play occasional games" (19).

    "Perhaps it is this specter that most haunts working men and women: the planned obsolescence of people that is of a piece with the planned obsolescence of the things they make" (33).

    Be sure to integrate the quotations smoothly into your writing.
4. Paraphrase the paragraph cluster beginning with paragraph 14 and ending with paragraph 15.
5. Write a one-paragraph synthesis that blends ideas in paragraph 3 with the ideas in paragraph 17 of "The Importance of Work" (pp. 397–401).

Writing with Sources: Using a Single Source

Integrating information from the excerpt from *Working* with your own ideas, write an essay on one of these topics. Be sure to acknowledge all ideas that are not your own.

1. Explain why you support or contradict Terkel's assessment of work.
2. Read the following statement by Donna Murray, a bookbinder, one of "the happy few" to whom Terkel refers in paragraph 4 of his essay. After doing so, write an essay in which you support Terkel's contention that those who enjoy their work find meaning "well over and beyond the reward of the paycheck."

    "Oh, I think it's important. Books are things that keep us going. Books — I haven't got much feeling for other things. I adore the work. Except sometimes it becomes very lonesome. It's nice to sit beside somebody, whether it's somebody who works with you or whether it's your husband or your friend. It's just lovely, just like a whisper, always. . . . If you were really brainy, you wouldn't waste your time pasting and binding. But if you bind good books, you make something good, really truly good. Yes, I would like to make a good book hold good and I would like to be involved in a pact that will not be broken, that holds good, which would really be as solid as the book.

    "Keeping a four-hundred-year-old book together keeps the spirit alive. It's an alluring kind of thing, lovely, because you know that belongs to us.

Because a book is life, like one man is a life. Yes, yes this work is good for me, therapeutic for old age . . . *just keep going* with the hands.''

3. Interview five people about their jobs. Then write an essay in which you compare and contrast the attitudes of these individuals toward work.

Writing with Sources: Using Multiple Sources

Integrating information from sources in this chapter with your own ideas, write an essay on one of the topics below. Be sure to acknowledge ideas that are not your own.

1. Assess your own attitude toward work. Support your points with examples of jobs that you have had and with references to the ideas of the authors in this section.
2. In ''The Phenomenon of Burn-Out'' Herbert J. Freudenberger says, ''Historically, the American dream has been to rise above what one's parents were; to work hard . . . to achieve excellence . . .'' (9). Write an essay in which you consider whether the work ethic still flourishes in America. Use material from as many of the essays in this section as you can to support your contentions.
3. Write an essay in which you consider what Gloria Steinem has to say about the importance of work to women in light of what Studs Terkel and Herbert J. Freudenberger have to say about the physical and emotional costs of working.
4. Daniel Rodgers begins ''The Working Day'' with the question, ''How much of a man's life should work consume?'' Write an essay in which you discuss how any three of the authors in this section would answer this question.
5. Of all the selections in this chapter, only one, ''Brave New Workplace,'' directly deals with the effect of new technology on attitudes toward work. In an essay, consider how technological advances such as computers and industrial robots might affect the work ethic and the position that work occupies in people's lives. Use the ideas of several authors in this chapter to support your points.

11

The Impact of Technology

As the pace of technology increases, problems develop. Even as we are excited by new discoveries, and by the seemingly unlimited promise of discoveries to come, we may be perplexed by the technology, concerned about its effects on our lives, and perhaps even overwhelmed by the changes we must make to accommodate it. The essays in this chapter deal with the impact of various scientific and technological developments on society and with society's responses to those developments.

In "The Advent of Printing" James Burke examines the social and economic climate that encouraged the invention of movable type and considers the immediate effects of that invention. The next three essays consider the effects of technology on work. Douglas Liversidge's "The Luddites: Machine Breakers of the Early Nineteenth Century" focuses on a group of English workers who saw technology as a threat to their livelihood; Paul Starr's "Medical Practice and the Local Transportation Revolution" explains how advances like paved roads, the telephone, and particularly the automobile changed the nature of doctors' practices in nineteenth- and early twentieth-century America; and Susan Strasser's "At the Flick of a Switch" considers the impact of the development of gas and electricity on the work of women during the same period. In the next essay, "Why Smaller Refrigerators Can Preserve the Human Race," Appletree Rodden explains how the move toward larger refrigerators has had a negative effect on our society. Finally, in "The Soul of a New Machine," Tracy Kidder discusses the effects on our lives of that quintessential symbol of twentieth-century technology, the computer.

The Advent of Printing

James Burke

Writer and television producer James Burke was born in 1936 and received his Bachelor's and Master's degrees from Oxford University. After serving as the BBC's chief reporter on the Apollo missions to the moon, he began his own weekly television series, "The Burke Special," in 1972. In 1979 "Connections," a series of programs he produced for the BBC, was broadcast on public television in the United States. The series and its companion volume (from which "The Advent of Printing" is excerpted) examined the "ideas, inventions, and coincidences" that led to today's most important technological advances. One of these inventions was movable type.

Beginning in 1347, the Black Death—bubonic plague—claimed millions of victims all over Europe. When the plague ended, most people were better off than they had been before. Fewer people competed for jobs, and production rose. As the demand for luxuries increased, dress became more and more extravagant: The upper classes bought silk, and the peasants bought linen. As Burke says, "the widespread and increasing use of linen in the late fourteenth century represents one of those crucial moments in the history of the process of change when the sequence of events suddenly changes direction and context." As worn-out linen clothing was discarded, linen rag became available for high-quality, durable paper. This, along with movable type, laid the groundwork for printing and the widespread distribution of inexpensive books.

1   At the end of the fourteenth century paper-making was a growth industry, functioning as it did in times of rising economic strength and consequent administrative paperwork. The paper-making techniques had originally come to Europe with the Arabs, who had picked them up when they overran Samarkand in A.D. 751 just after the Chinese had sent a team of paper-makers there to set up a factory. By 1050 the Byzantine Empire was importing Arab paper, and in Europe paper was first made in Muslim Spain at Xativa, south of Valencia. The first evidence of a paper mill working on water power is at Fabriano, in the Italian Marches, in 1280. The paper mills used the same basic technology as the fulling mills which preceded them. Rotten linen rags were pounded in water by trip hammers, together with gums, until a white pulp was produced. The pulp was laid in thin layers on wire mesh to drain, and then pressed in a screw press (similar to those used for pressing olives) until most of the moisture had been squeezed out of it, when it was hung to dry. The wire mesh itself is another example of the accidental way in which change comes about, because at the same time as the paper boom the sartorial excesses that followed the Black Death were giving employment to drawers of precious metal wire used in cloth-of-gold and -silver, so the wire mesh techniques were available for the paper industry to use, almost as if planned. Most of the early paper mills were set up in the foothills of mountains, to profit from abundant supplies of water power.

2   The demand for paper was high because it was comparatively cheap in

relation to its competitor on the market, parchment. Between two and three hundred sheepskins or calfskins were needed to produce enough material for a large Bible, and the preparation of the skins was time-consuming and therefore costly. As the supply of the new linen rag paper increased, its price fell. By 1300 in Bologna, northern Italy, paper was only one-sixth of the price of parchment, and its price continued to fall. As Europe recovered from the plague and trade revived, the demand for manuscript went up to meet the increasing paperwork as the notaries produced the documentation that went with burgeoning business. The universities already had their own manuscript-copying departments, and in time private citizens went into the business. In the middle of the fifteenth century, for example, a certain Vespasiano da Bisticci ran a copying shop in Florence employing more than fifty scribes. Since the Black Death had killed off many of the literate members of the community, those who were left commanded astronomically high prices. The situation was clearly unacceptable: on the one hand scribes who cost too much, on the other, paper so cheap you could cover the walls with it. Craftsmen all over Europe must have been working on the solution to the problem, since in essence it was obvious: there had to be some form of automated writing.

3   It had been tried before. The Chinese had been using porcelain block-printing techniques to put characters on paper for more than a thousand years. In Korea, from about 1370 onwards, some form of interchangeable copper blocks had been used to do the same thing. In Europe the blocks were made of wood and used to print playing cards, calendars, prayers and occasionally capital letters in manuscripts. There were also a few books with entire pages printed by one block, but these were expensive and besides, the wooden blocks eventually wore down.

4   The credit for the great leap of imagination that followed is usually given to a goldsmith from Mainz in Germany called Johann Gansfleisch, better known to the world by his mother's family name which he adopted — Gutenberg. He first appears enrolled in the Strasbourg militia as a goldsmith member, just before his family returned to Mainz, which they had left during a rising against the members of the city's ruling class. Gutenberg's father had been an official in the bishop's mint in Mainz, and from him Johann had learned the tricks of handling soft metals which were to prove vital when it came to printing. Apparently he had made an arrangement with three fellow-townsmen to make hand mirrors to sell to pilgrims leaving the city on a pilgrimage to Aix-la-Chapelle. Unfortunately somebody in the partnership had got the date of the pilgrimage wrong. After they had signed the agreement they discovered that the pilgrims would not be leaving until 1440, a year later than they had expected. Naturally there was some consternation, since presumably money had already been spent. At this point, Gutenberg promised to teach his partners 'a thing' he had been thinking about for some time. No more is heard of what this was, but later on, after another partnership with two other men called Fust and Shoeffer, the wrangling and lawsuits give the impression that Gutenberg's 'thing' had been a technique for printing. The main problem in developing automated printing was the creation of movable type, and in this

Gutenberg had two great advantages. He knew how to work soft metals, and the language he used had only twenty-three letters in it (no j, v, or w). This may have been the reason the Chinese had never taken the matter of movable type further, since with a language made up of thousands of characters the problem was too immense to handle.

5   Gutenberg's aim was to make movable type that would not wear down easily, that would be uniform in size, and that would lie side by side accurately and uniformly enough to produce an even line of print. Each letter would have to be cast in an identical mould, and this was where knowledge of metal-working came in. The mould would have to be made of metal that would melt only at a much higher temperature than that from which the letter was to be made. Initially the mould was made in copper or brass, with the letter punched into it with a steel punch of the type used for placing hallmarks on precious metal. Early experiments may have been tried using a small box with the letter punched into the closed end, into which was poured the molten tin-lead alloy. The problem was that the box would have to be split apart to take out the cooled letter. Any doubts that have ever been expressed about Gutenberg as the inventor of printing are based on the fact that he appears to have solved the casting problem at a stroke, with a system that was working perfectly the first time we hear of it. Arguments run that he must have heard of other tests and designs, notably by men such as the Dutchman Laurens Coster, who were trying to do the same thing. Whoever designed the final mould, it is a work of genius. In order to save breaking the mould every time a letter was cast, a mould was made in three sections that slid together and were held in place by a large curved iron spring; after casting these parts slid apart, to be used again. The product was called mitred type. The greatest advantage was that the mould made all letters of the same dimensions. The space taken by a cross-section of each letter was identical, as were the space types, so that the printing was regular. The form — the stalk behind the letter face itself — was the same height, so that each letter would press on the paper with equal firmness. The problem of uniform pressure was minimized by the fact that the paper used was thick and soft, and was wetted slightly before printing, and it was further helped by the use of a linen or grape screw-press to push the letters in their bed-shaped box down on to the paper with equal pressure all the way across. But it was the interchangeability of the letters that lay at the heart of the new invention.

6   The earliest dated example of the new technology in action is the Mainz Psalter, printed at the order of the Archbishop in 1457. (There are other pieces of early printed material, but they are undated.) The introduction displays the pride felt by the printers at their achievement. It reads: 'This volume of the Psalms, adorned with a magnificence of capital letters and clearly divided by rubrics, has been fashioned by a mechanical process of printing and producing characters, without use of a pen, and it was laboriously completed, for God's Holiness, by Joachim Fust, citizen of Mainz, and Peter Schoeffer of Gersheim, on Assumption Eve in the year of Our Lord, 1457.' If you look closely at the original text, you will see that there are many more than the basic twenty-three letters. There are lines above some letters. Others are joined together, and

others abbreviated in forms that are no longer recognizable. This is because the first printers had to produce the nearest thing to a manuscript they could, or the work would not be accepted by readers used to the script techniques of the scribes, which included abbreviations and even a form of shorthand. To have printed the texts in full would have insulted the reader's intelligence, as a printer would today if he printed 'To-day Ma-ry is go-ing to vi-sit her un-cle.'

7   The advent of printing, whether due to a German or a Dutchman — or even, as has been suggested, to an Englishman — was one of the most critical events in the history of mankind. Printing first and foremost made it easy to transmit information without personal contact, and in this sense it revolutionized the spread of knowledge, and craft technique in particular. 'How to do it' books were among the first off the press, written about almost every field of human activity from metallurgy, to botany, to linguistics, to good manners. Printing also made texts consistent, by ending the copying errors with which manuscripts were rife. In doing so it placed on the author the responsibility for accuracy and definitive statement, since many more people were now likely to read his material who might know at least as much about it as he did himself. This in turn encouraged agreement on the material, and because of this, spurred academic investigation of subjects and the development of agreed disciplines. Just as learning became standardized, so did spelling. Authorship became an object of recognition, and this led to the concept of 'mastership' in a subject, which in turn led to the fragmentation of knowledge into specialized areas, emphasizing the separation of the 'expert' from the rest of the community. The earliest books would have been read by men who could doubtless as easily have turned their hand to the lyre or the sword or the pen or the architect's drawing, and it may be said that with the coming of the book they were the last generation to be able to do so. The new texts also conferred prestige on the inventor, who could now publicly claim association with his invention and expect to be identified with it. And as the books began to circulate, carrying ideas to readers who no longer had to have access to a manuscript copyist producing rare and expensive editions, the speed of change born of the interaction of ideas accelerated.

Reading Sources: "The Advent of Printing"

Read the selection, surveying it to identify key terms and important concepts. Highlight these phrases and ideas, and then answer these questions.

1. This selection, like the entire book from which it is excerpted, focuses on the ways in which one event made possible — or even caused — another. Identify the transitional words and phrases that are used throughout the selection to make causal connections explicit.

2. How does Burke signal the flashback in papagraph 3? Where else does he depart from his chronological narrative to go back in time? How does he signal such time shifts to his readers?

3. What is the "great leap of imagination" Burke mentions in paragraph 4?
4. What were the advantages of paper over parchment? What were the advantages of Gutenberg's movable type over previous methods of printing?
5. This selection is directed at a wide popular audience. How can you tell that it is not aimed at historians or at technicians?
6. This selection has long paragraphs unbroken by visual cues. What kind of visual cues might help readers follow Burke's ideas more easily? Explain.
7. In paragraph 7 Burke enumerates the effects of printing on our history. Highlight the paragraph to identify the major effects he considers.

Reacting to Sources

Reread the selection carefully, making marginal notes to aid comprehension and reinforce connections. Then further annotate the selection if you need to do so in order to answer any of these questions. (You may already have addressed some of the questions in your marginal notes.)

1. Using a dictionary if necessary, supply brief marginal definitions of these words as they are used in this selection: *fulling* (1), *sartorial* (1), *burgeoning* (2), *scribes* (2), *consternation* (4), *hallmarks* (5), *rubrics* (6), *conferred* (7).
2. In your journal, draw a diagram to illustrate the major cause and effect relationships Burke uncovers.
3. What, if anything, does Burke's description in paragraph 1 of the paper-making process add to the reader's understanding of the selection? Explain in a journal entry.
4. In marginal notes, clarify the connection between the increasing administrative paperwork Burke mentions briefly in paragraphs 1 and 2 and the rise of printing.
5. In paragraph 2 Burke says, "The situation was clearly unacceptable: on the one hand scribes who cost too much, on the other, paper so cheap you could cover the walls with it." In a marginal note, explain how this unacceptable situation came about.
6. Write one or two questions in response to the ideas presented in each of the selection's seven paragraphs.
7. What is Burke's purpose in paragraph 4 in telling his audience of Gutenberg's foiled plan to sell mirrors to pilgrims on their way to Aix-la-Chapelle? In a journal entry, analyze Burke's possible motive. Would the selection be more effective without this material?
8. Prepare a topic outline of paragraph 5.
9. In paragraph 5 Burke says, "it was the interchangeability of the letters that lay at the heart of the new invention." Explain this idea in a marginal note.
10. In a marginal note, give two examples in addition to those Burke supplies to support his general statement in paragraph 7 that the advent of printing "was one of the most critical events in the history of mankind."
11. In a journal entry, consider possible connections between the advent of printing and the advent of word processing.

Working with Sources

1. Write a fifty-word summary of paragraph 2.
2. Write a critique of the ideas in paragraph 7.
3. Write a journal entry in which you explore your reactions to these quotations from "The Advent of Printing":

    "there had to be some form of automated writing" (2).

    "Whoever designed the final mould, it was a work of genius" (5).

    "as the books began to circulate, . . . the speed of change born of the interaction of ideas accelerated" (7).

    Be sure to integrate the quotations smoothly into your writing.
4. Paraphrase the ideas in paragraph 3.
5. Write a one-paragraph synthesis that blends ideas in paragraph 7 of this selection and paragraph 11 of the excerpt from "The Soul of a New Machine" (pp. 474 – 477).

Writing with Sources: Using a Single Source

Integrating information from "The Advent of Printing" with your own ideas, write an essay on one of these topics. Be sure to acknowledge ideas that are not your own.

1. Assess the impact of printing on your own life. If you like, you may consider how this impact has changed—increased or diminished—as you have grown older.
2. Choose any historical period from 1600 to the present with which you are familiar, and describe how the key events of that era would have been affected by the absence of printing facilities. If you like, you may focus on one particular historical event.
3. Compare the immediate effects of the advent of printing (listed in paragraph 7) with the effects of computer technology on modern American society.

From *The Luddites: Machine Breakers of the Early Nineteenth Century*

Douglas Liversidge

Born in 1913 in Yorkshire, England, Douglas Liversidge is a journalist and freelance writer. His books include popular biographies, for children and adults, of Saint Francis of Assisi, Saint Ignatius of Loyola, Stalin, Lenin, and Elizabeth II, as well as several popular books about Arctic exploration. (During 1949–50, as a correspondent for Reuters news service, Liversidge was the first British journalist to visit both polar regions.) *The Luddites: Machine Breakers of the Early Nineteenth Century* was published in 1972. In this book, Liversidge explains that in 1806, Napoleon's blockade of the British Isles weakened Britain's foreign trade; five years later, hostilities with the United States cost England the United States market. British industry was seriously threatened, and the result was massive unemployment and extreme poverty, particularly in industrial areas. At the same time, machines had begun to replace craftsmen, and workers were growing increasingly frightened and uneasy. In response to their frustration with widespread unemployment and poverty, groups of men began sneaking into factories at night and smashing the machines that threatened their livelihoods. This violent response to industrialization began near Nottingham on March 11, 1811. The attacks, perpetrated by men who began to call themselves Luddites, eventually spread to Lancashire, Cheshire, and Yorkshire. Today, the term *Luddite* has come to be applied to anyone who opposes technological change. In the selection that follows, Douglas Liversidge examines the fear and discontent that nurtured the Luddite movement and describes its earliest acts of revenge.

Smouldering Discontent

1 The setting was Regency England—a period of disruptive change and industrial strife; the date was March 11 in the year 1811. The hosiery town of Nottingham was thronged more than usual that day and, as the citizens went about their business, they eyed with curiosity the arrival of groups of men. Bystanders guessed rightly that the newcomers were framework-knitters from the countryside and from their mutterings and angry words it was clear that something was amiss. Some hundreds in all, they made for a prearranged rendezvous—the market place.

2   They had come into Nottingham to air trade grievances and, as the more articulate of them harangued the mob, it was as if a sullen smouldering discontent had burst into flame. The crowd roared approval as speakers passionately denounced low wages and other abuses—the festering sores in the trade. Some knitters were without work and their vehement cry was for more work as well as better wages.

3   Trouble had been brewing for some weeks, for, ill-fed and working in their humble homes that were mostly unheated, the workers' nerves had grown taut under the added strain of a cold and cheerless winter.

4   At first the knitters (also known as stockingers) had tried to redress their

wrongs in discussions with the hosiers who employed them. But, tantalisingly, although some manufacturers were willing to ease the knitters' plight, there was a hard core who, spurred on by a mixture of commercial depression and greed, not only kept wages low, but threatened to reduce them even further.

5   Faced with these keenly competitive pressures, and with fraudulent practices which undercut prices, the more scrupulous hosiers could do nothing beyond sympathise with the men.

6   In these inflammatory circumstances, reason ebbed away, leaving in its place a mounting rage which finally exploded into violence. In Arnold, a small township close to Nottingham, knitters had smashed their way into workshops of their hated masters and confiscated the jack-wires from the knitting frames. The machines were thus left dismembered and useless.

7   It was the workers' warning to the uncompromising attitude of the offending hosiers, and a warning which grew swiftly in magnitude, for stockingers in other parts were quick to emulate their Arnold brethren.

8   These outbreaks had persisted throughout February and into March, the enraged knitters carrying off their jack-wire prizes and secreting them in local churches. These rough tactics were intended to force the hosiers into submission but, stubbornly, they refused to yield to the knitters' demands. This defiance was to breed some of the worst rioting and disturbances in British history.

9   By March 11, negotiations had come to an end and the men in the market-place at Nottingham clamoured impatiently for militant action.

10   So threatening was the crowd that the authorities, fearing mob rule in the streets, called out the special constables. But this was not enough. As night approached, a tense excitement ran through Nottingham. A troop of Dragoons paraded the streets, and the stockingers, still shouting insults, were urged to return peaceably to their homes.

11   There was a feeling of relief when, about nine o'clock, the mob broke up and began to leave the town. It seemed as if the crisis had been averted. But, in fact, the main drama was about to begin. Someone must have suggested going to Arnold, for that is where some stockingers decided to march.

12   This time it was not just a matter of removing the jack-wires. The knitters now ran wild, brusquely forcing their way into homes housing machines rented from the hosiers who had antagonised them. By the time daylight returned, at least sixty stocking frames were in complete ruin.

13   All through this noisy night, however, the machine-breaking went on with public approval, for the people generally sympathised with the framework-knitters and even goaded them on. Onlookers cheered as heavy hammers and axes smashed into wood. Moreover, when the Dragoons arrived, the rioters had all dispersed and the public denied all knowledge of the culprits. Frustrated, all that the Dragoons could do was clear the streets.

14   It was as if an explosion had reverberated from one hill to another. The violence at Arnold was echoed in the neighbouring villages on other nights. And, always, it was only the frames belonging to hostile hosiers that were wrecked.

15   In the next few weeks, these nocturnal forays, undertaken by relentless gangs of stockingers terrorised the whole of the north-western area of the

county. The strident sound of breaking wood grew all too familiar, raids sometimes occurring in different villages on the same night. And as the rioters grew more confident, workshops were entered even in daylight.

16   For the time being at least, the stockingers had the advantage; relying on surprise raids, they could attack with relative ease. The authorities were baffled and ill-prepared, and lacked the manpower to counter the frame-breakers. Help from the public was out of the question. It was obvious that people witnessed the destruction, but no one could be found who would inform against those concerned. Even the victims whose frames were broken preferred to stay silent. Some did so out of fear, but others — overcharged in rent— detested the hosiers as much as the frame-breakers.

17   At first the authorities set up a nightly watch, enrolling special constables; then they sought what military aid that was readily available. But this was scarce, for Britain was at war with France, and Napoleon still threatened.

18   Despite these measures, the disturbances went on. In desperation, attractive rewards were now offered to anyone exposing the machine-breakers, and experienced officials from Bow Street Court in London conducted inquiries in the affected areas. But little was exposed. Then, early in April, the raids — so far confined to the north-western area of Nottinghamshire — subsided as quickly as they had begun.

19   The summer that followed was one of smouldering discontent. Trade worsened and the farmers reported a bad harvest. Yet although the distress of the hungry people deteriorated, there were no more cases of violence.

General Ludd

20 Not until the night of November 4 were the attacks renewed. Without warning, six frames were wrecked in Bulwell, a village of some two thousand souls. The spirit of riot was again ignited. More outbreaks erupted on the following nights.

21   Machine-wrecking now took an even more dramatic turn. Framework-knitters from Arnold, augmented by others, assembled secretly in Bulwell forest. In military style, they responded to the commands of a man who went under the name of "General Ludd". Numbering about seventy, they set off for Bulwell, for the workshop of Edward Hollingsworth, a hosier loathed by the knitters.

22   Hollingsworth, anticipating trouble, had barricaded his windows and doors and planned an armed defence. He had also removed some of his frames to safety in Nottingham. But the nature and ferocity of the attack, carried out with the precision of a military sortie, caught him unawares. The attackers, calling themselves Luddites, were armed as well. Soon shots shattered the night and an Arnold man, John Westley, fell dead. Yet his death merely made the Luddites more tenacious. They compelled the defenders to submit, smashed a number of frames, then quickly dispersed.

23   From then on such attacks were more frequent, and "Luddism" became a household word. Whenever it was mentioned, it brought to mind bands of rioters organised to destroy machinery.

24   The origin of the name itself is unusual. One version claims that in 1779 there lived in a Leicestershire village a boy called Ned Ludd. He was of weak intellect and became, unfortunately, the butt of other boys. Once, he chased one of his tormentors into a house, but failed to catch him. The frustrated Ned vented his wrath on two frames which happened to be there. Henceforth, whenever any machines were broken, the breakages were attributed to Ludd.

25   A variant of this tale, published by the *Nottingham Review,* claims that Ned Ludd, a boy apprenticed to learn framework knitting at Anstey, near Leicester, was thrashed for laziness and retaliated by hammering to pieces his hated frame.

26   The Luddites signed their proclamations "Ned Ludd", and at times gave Sherwood Forest as their address. One such declaration to the Home Office contended that a Charter granted by Charles II to the stocking trade permitted the framework-knitters to wreck all machines which made goods in a deceitful manner. Moreover, they could break the frames of hosiers who failed to pay the regular prices agreed to by hosiers and men. Indeed, "all Frames of whatsoever description the workmen of whom are not paid in the current coin of the realm will invariably be destroyed."

27   But, at the same time, the Luddites denounced any robbery which went on in the course of frame-breaking attacks.

Regency England

28   To get some idea why men resorted to this form of violence, one must first picture the England of those times. Early in the nineteenth century, agriculture still dominated the English scene. More than half the nation lived a rural life and over one-third was actively engaged in farming.

29   By present-day standards, towns were small and more nearly allied to the villages and the countryside. Indeed, of the densely populated cities and towns of today, not many had populations of 20,000 in the early nineteenth century. These centres relied greatly on the neighbouring villages, for industry — including the most recent, such as cotton manufacture — was mostly in rural areas. And what industrial machines prevailed were worked mostly by hand, usually in homes or workshops. When other power was required, it was mainly water power and not steam.

30   Even in the cotton industry, which was to figure so prominently in the Industrial Revolution later in the century, the machine or factory system was still limited. In the spinning process, for instance, water power predominated, but there was still employment for manual workers. Steam-driven factories were few. In cotton weaving, steam looms were also not very prevalent and the hand-worker was still supreme.

31   The woollen and worsted industries were even more dependent on the hand-workers who also operated in cottage or country workshops.

32   The locomotive was still in its infancy. Few railways existed and canals were the major arteries of trade for bulk cargo. By and large, roads were in a poor state. The movement of goods was, therefore, necessarily slow.

33   No matter what the drawbacks in communications were, the chief industries were expanding, and imports and exports — in spite of the economic strain of a gruelling war with France — had grown. However, in these troublesome times trade was poised precariously. The major industries, such as coal-mining, textiles, hosiery and lace, relied more and more on foreign trade. To begin with, many of the raw materials (for instance, cotton and wool) were brought from other countries. And to pay for them, Britain had to sell roughly one-sixth to one-third of her commodities overseas.

34   Trade was also important for the necessities of life. British farmers could not grow enough food for the rapidly increasing population, so it was essential to import food supplies.

35   Why the population grew so rapidly it is hard to assess. What is factual is that the population growth coincided with the growth of farming and industry. But whether improved farming and industry bred a bigger population or whether the needs of a larger population caused the development of agriculture and industry, is not easy to say. Actually the birth rate rose throughout the eighteenth century, increasing more rapidly in the early nineteenth century. In terms of figures, it is believed that an estimate made by Gregory King in 1695, when he reckoned the population of England and Wales to be 5.5 million, is reasonably correct. In 1801 — the first time that a population census was taken in Britain — the population totalled almost 11 million. This had soared to 16.5 million by 1831.

36   So, for all her food and industrial essentials Britain depended increasingly on foreign rade. Consequently, any serious disruption to the incoming flow of commodities would clearly have a harsh effect on the people.

37   In this early-nineteenth century scene, although London business houses were strengthening their commercial power, the hard core of the nation's industries was in the provinces. Firms were owned by partners rather than companies, and manufacturers and businessmen generally maintained a close association with their workers.

38   Of all forms of employment, agriculture was paramount. But it was now being subjected to the greatest change. The medieval system of open-field farming was rapidly giving way to enclosure; so much so that well over 3,000,000 acres were enclosed during the first twenty years of the nineteenth century.

39   Hedgerows and ditches now criss-crossed the countryside, and new stone farmhouses ousted the humble dwellings of mud and thatch. This process put an end to many of the old-time lease-holders who had worked a few strips of common land. Now they had to face a future either working as farm labourers or trying to find employment in industry.

40   But even in industry a transformation had already begun. Textile manufacturers were installing machines which replaced the country craftsmen, who, when they were not cultivating the land, had devoted time to spinning wool or knitting lace and stockings. Gradually the old system was being stifled and of this the people involved were only too well aware. In desperation many felt compelled to riot.

Reading Sources: from The Luddites: Machine Breakers of the Early Nineteenth Century

Read the selection, surveying it to identify key terms and important concepts. Highlight these phrases and ideas, and then answer these questions.

1. What visual cues are used in this selection? How do they emphasize Liversidge's key ideas?
2. Liversidge occasionally interrupts his narrative with flashbacks, so historical events are not necessarily presented in chronological order. Why does Liversidge present some events out of sequence?
3. What techniques does Liversidge use to link the section introduced by paragraph 28 to the rest of the essay?
4. Because Liversidge is British, he uses some spellings and phrasing not used by American writers. Identify examples of British variants, making sure you know the American equivalents of each.
5. In paragraph 6 Liversidge states, "In these inflammatory circumstances, reason ebbed away, leaving in its place a mounting rage which finally exploded into violence." What were the "inflammatory circumstances"?
6. In paragraph 1 Liversidge describes England in 1811 as in "a period of disruptive change and industrial strife." Where does he elaborate on this statement? What changes in agriculture and industry so upset workers that they turned to violence?
7. What is the probable origin of the name Luddites?
8. Does Liversidge seem to expect his readers to be familiar with the historical events he describes? Explain.
9. Is Liversidge's account an objective one, or does he reveal his sympathy for (or disapproval of) the Luddites' actions? Explain.

Reacting to Sources

Reread the selection carefully, making marginal notes to aid comprehension and reinforce connections. Then further annotate the selection if you need to do so in order to answer any of these questions. (You may already have addressed some of the questions in your marginal notes.)

1. Using a dictionary if necessary, supply brief marginal definitions of these words as they are used in this selection: *Regency* (1), *harangued* (2), *vehement* (2), *taut* (3), *redress* (4), *Dragoons* (10), *brusquely* (12), *nocturnal* (15), *forays* (15), *strident* (15), *augmented* (21), *loathed* (21), *sortie* (22), *tenacious* (22), *vented* (24), *paramount* (38), *hedgerows* (39).
2. Outline the major events recounted in the essay, making sure you present them in the order in which they actually occurred.
3. What purpose does paragraph 9 serve in this essay? Explain in a marginal note. Then, identify any other paragraphs in the selection that serve a similar function.

4. In paragraph 13 Liversidge notes that "the people generally sympathised with the framework-knitters and even goaded them on." Explore this idea further in a journal entry.
5. In one sentence, rewrite paragraph 35 to simplify its ideas.
6. What is Liversidge's purpose in explaining Britain's dependence on foreign trade (33–36)? In a marginal note, explain the connection between the information in this paragraph cluster and the forces motivating the Luddites.
7. Formulate three questions whose answers could help you understand the ideas in paragraphs 38–39.
8. In a journal entry, consider possible links between this essay and your own attitude toward the acceptance of new inventions.
9. Read the document reprinted below—the Luddites' declaration of their grievances—and write a journal entry explaining how it enhances your understanding of the events Liversidge describes.

Whereas by the charter granted by our late sovereign Lord Charles II by the Grace of God King of Great Britain France and Ireland, the framework knitters are empowered to break and destroy all frames and engines that fabricate articles in a fraudulent and deceitful manner and to destroy all framework knitters' goods whatsoever that are so made and whereas a number of deceitful unprincipled and intriguing persons did attain an Act to be passed in the 28th year of our present sovereign Lord George III whereby it was enacted that persons entering by force into any house shop or place to break or destroy frames should be adjudged guilty of felony and as we are fully convinced that such Act was obtained in the most fraudulent interested and electioneering manner and that the honourable the Parliament of Great Britain was deceived as to the motives and intentions of the persons who obtained such Act we therefore the framework knitters do hereby declare the aforesaid Act to be null and void to all intents and purposes whatsoever as by the passing of this Act villainous and imposing persons are enabled to make fraudulent and deceitful manufactures to the discredit and utter ruin of our trade. And whereas we declare that the aforementioned Charter is as much in force as though no such Act had been passed. . . . And we do hereby declare to all hosiers lace manufacturers and proprietors of frames that we will break and destroy all manner of frames whatsoever that make the following spurious articles and all frames whatsoever that do not pay the regular prices heretofore agreed to [by] the masters and workmen—All print net frames making single press and frames not working by the rack and rent and not paying the price regulated in 1810: warp frames working single yarn or two coarse hole—not working by the rack, not paying the rent and prices regulated in 1809—whereas all plain silk frames not making work according to the gage—frames not marking the work according to quality, whereas all frames of whatsoever description the workmen of whom are not paid in the current coin of the realm will invariably be destroyed. . . .

Given under my hand this first day of January 1812.
God protect the Trade.

Ned Lud's Office
Sherwood Forest.

Working with Sources

1. Write a fifty-word summary of paragraphs 29–32.
2. Write a critique of the ideas in paragraph 16.

3. Write a journal entry in which you explore your reactions to these quotations from *The Luddites: Machine Breakers of the Early Nineteenth Century:*

"it was as if a sullen smouldering discontent had burst into flame" (2).

"The spirit of riot was again ignited" (20).

"In desperation many felt compelled to riot" (40).

Be sure to integrate the quotations smoothly into your writing.
4. Paraphrase the ideas in paragraphs 24–25.
5. Write a one-paragraph synthesis that blends ideas in paragraph 6 of this selection and paragraph 14 of the excerpt from *The Soul of a New Machine* (pp. 474–477).

Writing with Sources: Using a Single Source

Integrating information from the selection from *The Luddites: Machine Breakers of the Early Nineteenth Century* with your own ideas, write an essay on one of these topics. Be sure to acknowledge ideas that are not your own.

1. Many people today feel threatened — psychologically as well as economically — by the increasing domination of machines, particularly computers. Whether or not workers actually fear being replaced by machines, they may still feel that their failure to master them could result in a loss of employment. Explore the causes and effects of these feelings and suggest possible solutions to the problems they cause.
2. Are "smouldering discontent" and "inflammatory circumstances" like the ones Liversidge describes an excuse for violence? What alternative measures, if any, could the Luddites have taken? Consider the possibility of achieving change through nonviolent action, both for the Luddites and for discontented groups in twentieth-century America.
3. This selection does not consider the outcome of the Luddites' protests, which is treated elsewhere in Liversidge's book. What became of the movement's supporters? How did the protests affect the knitting industry in the years to follow? Consult a good encyclopedia to find the answers to these and any other questions you may have, and write an essay in which you evaluate the effects of the Luddite uprisings.

Medical Practice and the Local Transportation Revolution

Paul Starr

Paul Starr, who received his B.A. from Columbia University and his Ph.D. from Harvard, is now Associate Professor of Sociology at Harvard. He previously coauthored *The Discarded Army: Veterans After Vietnam.* The following essay is excerpted from his 1982 book *The Social Transformation of American Medicine,* which won the 1984 Pulitzer Prize in general nonfiction, the 1984 Bancroft Prize in American history, and the 1983 C. Wright Mills Award in sociology. In this well-received work of scholarship, Starr traces two movements in American medicine: first, "the rise of professional sovereignty"; and second, "the transformation of medicine into an industry and the growing, though still unsettled, role of corporations and the state."

The Changing Ecology of Medical Practice

The Local Transportation Revolution

1   Low use of professional services was the fundamental constraint on medicine in early American society. Many physicians found it extremely difficult to support themselves solely from medical practice. A second occupation, usually farming, often proved necessary. "The resources of a farm," Benjamin Rush observed in his advice to medical students, "will prevent your cherishing, even for a moment, an impious wish for the prevalence of sickness in your neighborhood."[1] Later, many doctors, especially in small town and frontier areas, ran drug stores; and druggists, if they were not previously doctors, often took up medical practice as part of their work. (One historian records a doctor who, "not satisfied with his practice, robbed stagecoaches on the side" before he was captured in 1855 and sent to prison.[2] But he may have been looking for excitement.) Starting out in practice frequently meant protracted underemployment and hardship. "The fact is," stated the *Boston Medical and Surgical Journal* in 1836, "there are dozens of doctors in all great towns, who scarcely see a patient from christmas-time to christmas-coming."[3]

2   This pattern, Ivan Waddington has shown, is typical of medical practice in preindustrial societies. In eighteenth- and early nineteenth-century France and England, as in the United States, the demand for professional advice was limited by the inability of the great mass of the population to afford services and the persistence of traditional and domestic forms of treatment. Doctors had difficulty setting themselves up in practice and many abandoned the

---

[1] Benjamin Rush, "Observations on the Duties of a Physician, and the Methods of Improving Medicine; Accommodated to the Present State of Society and Manners in the United States," in *Medical Inquiries and Observations* (Philadelphia: J. Conrad, 1805), 390.

[2] Richard Dunlop, *Doctors of the American Frontier* (Garden City, N.Y.: Doubleday, 1962), 129–30.

[3] *Boston Medical and Surgical Journal* 15 (November 30, 1836), 273.

occupation entirely.[4] The structural problem everywhere was the same: Given the limited extent of the market, physicians could not lucratively monopolize the medical work available in the society. In Europe, a small elite of physicians confined itself to practice among the rich and separated itself from other practitioners. This "status professionalism" had broken down in America. The more numerous American physicians, scattered among small communities or overcrowded in the towns, struggled on under modest circumstances.

3   The inadequacy of local markets stemmed partly from Americans' ingrained self-reliance, their disbelief in the value of professional medicine, and the ease with which competitors entered the field. Some may wish to argue that all these factors were ultimately reducible to the ineffectiveness of contemporary therapeutics. It is not clear, however, that doctors' economic problems would have been resolved if they had the scientific knowledge of 1920 under the economic and cultural conditions of 1850 or even 1880. I leave aside, for the moment, the question of whether such knowledge would have been as widely recognized as authoritative. The basic problem would have remained the same: Most families could not have afforded to rely on physicians' services.

4   The heart of the economic problem was not that the physicians' fees were so high, but that the real price of medical care was so much higher than their fees. The price of medical services consists not only of the direct price (the physician's fee, the charge for a hospital room) but also of the indirect price — the cost of transportation (if the patient travels to the doctor or sends another person to summon one) and the foregone value of the time taken to obtain medical care. In most discussions, only the direct price is taken into account, but this bias is unwarranted.[5]

5   In the early and mid-nineteenth century, the indirect price of medical services probably outweighed the direct price. Dispersed in a heavily rural society, lacking modern transportation, the great majority of the population was effectively cut off from ordinary recourse to physicians because of the prohibitive opportunity cost of travel. For a farmer, a trip of ten miles into town could mean an entire day's lost work. Contemporary observers and historians have continually drawn attention to the isolation of rural life and most small communities before the twentieth century. This was as much an economic as a psychological fact.

6   The self-sufficiency of the household in early American society was never complete, but it was quite extensive, particularly in the frontier, back-country, and rural communities where most Americans lived. Families produced not only food for their own consumption, but also clothes, furniture, household utensils, farm implements, building materials, and many other necessities.

---

[4] Ivan Waddington, "The Development of Medicine as a Modern Profession," in *A Social History of the Bio-medical Sciences,* ed. Massimo Piattelli-Palmarini (Milan: Franco Maria Ricci, forthcoming).

[5] For a general discussion of indirect prices, see Gary Becker, "A Theory of the Allocation of Time," *The Economic Journal* 75 (September 1965), 493–517.

After 1815 household manufacturers rapidly declined in New England; according to Rolla Tryon, the transition to shop and factory-made goods there was nearly accomplished by 1830. Elsewhere it took longer; the presence of a large frontier population through mid-century meant that the transition was "always taking place but never quite completed" in the country as a whole. "As soon as manufactured goods could be supplied from the sale or barter of the products of the farm, the home gave up its system of manufacturing, which had been largely carried on more through necessity than desire. Generally speaking, by 1860 the factory, through the aid of improved means of transportation, was able to supply the needs of the people for manufactured commodities." [6]

7   A similar, but slower transition from the household to the market economy took place in the production of personal services. For rural families, the time it took to procure specialized services outside the household greatly increased their cost. The growth of cities, the advent of modern means of transportation, and the building of hard roads radically altered the structure of prices. By reducing the opportunity and transportation costs for services, urbanization and improved transportation generally promoted the substitution of paid, specialized labor for the unpaid, unspecialized labor of the household or local community. Getting a haircut, visiting a prostitute, and consulting a doctor all became, on the average, less expensive because of reduced costs of time.

8   Data contained in nineteenth-century fee tables provide a basis for estimating the relation between direct and indirect prices. The fee bills published by medical societies may be poor indicators of average charges, but they are probably reliable as indicators of the relative value of different services. In addition to a basic fee for a physician visit, almost all nineteenth-century fee schedules list a charge per mile if the doctor needed to travel out of town. The charge for mileage represents an estimate of the foregone value to the doctor of the time spent in traveling, plus the expense of his personal transportation (a horse, or horse and buggy). We may assume that time had about the same value for patients as for their physicians. (This assumption probably holds for the nineteenth century, though it would be untenable today because of the high median income of physicians relative to the population at large.) Thus the monetary value doctors assigned to travel may give us an estimate of the indirect prices faced by patients when they called on the doctor.

9   Nineteenth-century fee bills vary from one region to another, especially between urban and rural areas, but the importance of indirect prices is evident everywhere. A few examples will suffice to make the point. In 1843 in Addison County, Vermont, the fee for each visit by a doctor was 50 cents at less than half a mile; $1.00 between a half mile and two miles; $1.50 between two and four miles; $2.50 between four and six miles and so on. In Mississippi the same year, according to a report in a Boston journal, a visit cost $1, while the

---

[6] Rolla M. Tryon, *Household Manufactures in the United States, 1640–1860* (Chicago: University of Chicago Press, 1917), 243, 11. See also Stuart Bruchey, *The Roots of American Economic Growth, 1607–1861* (New York: Harper & Row, 1965), 26–31.

charge for travel was $1 per mile during the day ($2 at night).[7] These ratios between charges for service and mileage are typical. Even at relatively short distances, the share of the total price due to traveling and opportunity costs exceeded the physician's ordinary fee; at a distance of five or ten miles, the mileage charges typically amounted to four or five times the basic fee for a visit.[8]

10   For major services, the indirect price became less significant; the fee for serious operations could overshadow the charge for mileage. So indirect prices especially limited use of physicians' services in routine illness. In rural areas, many families would not think of calling in a doctor except under the most grave conditions.

11   When patients were treated at home, before the advent of the telephone, the doctor had to be summoned in person. So the costs of travel were often doubled, as two people, the physician and an emissary, had to make the trip back and forth. Furthermore, since the doctor was often out on calls, there was no guarantee that he would be found when someone went in search of him. A doctor from the District of Columbia, observing that no physician in Washington during the 1840s or 1850s kept regular office hours, later recalled, "Patients and other persons wishing to consult [a doctor] waited at irregular times for indefinite periods, or went away and came back, or followed in pursuit in the direction last seen, and sometimes waited at houses to which it was known the doctor would come. . . . The only certain time at which one could be found was when [one was] in bed and had not instructed the servant to deny the fact."[9]

12   Before the construction of hard roads, according to one Illinois practitioner, "the doctor did not often go more than ten miles from his home."[10] Within that radius were a limited number of patients. The size of the market might be enough to keep village practitioners hard at work, but not enough to enable them to set the terms of business and limit their practice to an office. The doctor of the early and mid-nineteenth century passed much of his day (and many of his nights) traveling along back country roads. Autobiographies of nineteenth-century doctors dwell on these long periods of solitude and the weariness that often came over them on their rides. As one doctor put it, he spent "half of his life in the mud and the other half in the dust."[11] In several nineteenth-century fee schedules, a fee for an entire day's attendance by a doctor is given as $5 or $10. (The average daily income for doctors, depending on locality, probably fell within or below this range.) These same fee schedules list the charge for an office visit at $1.00 or $1.50.[12] It seems likely,

[7] These data have been culled from Rosen, *Fees and Fee Bills,* 15–16, which contains numerous other fee tables that would make the point equally well.

[8] Direct estimates of transportation and opportunity costs indicate that the cost of travel exceeded the basic consultation fee at about two miles. See my calculations in "Medicine, Economy and Society in Nineteenth-Century America," *Journal of Social History* 10 (Summer 1977), 604–05.

[9] Samuel C. Busey, *Personal Reminiscenses and Recollections* . . . (Washington, D.C., 1895), 157–58.

[10] Thomas N. Bonner, *Medicine in Chicago, 1850–1950* (Madison, Wis.: American Historical Research Center, 1957), 200.

[11] Ibid.

[12] Rosen, *Fees and Fee Bills,* 30, 41.

therefore, that doctors in the early and mid-1800s were seeing no more than an average of five to seven patients a day (in urban areas perhaps more, in rural areas less).

13   The high costs of travel contributed to the individualism and isolation of medical practice. The country practitioner had to rely on his own devices; consultations were not readily available. Practitioners might be long out of touch with new developments; or if apprised of them, completely on their own in carrying them out. "The first appendectomy many a doctor saw was the first he himself performed after this operation came into use in the late 1880s and the 1890s," remarks a historian of medicine in Oregon.[13]

14   As more Americans and more physicians began to live in larger towns and cities, they came in closer contact with both their patients and their colleagues. The proportion of Americans living in towns of 2,500 or more increased from just 6 percent in 1800 to 15 percent by 1850; it then jumped to 37 percent in 1890 and 46 percent in 1910.[14] In the late nineteenth century, doctors moved to cities even more rapidly than the population as a whole. Between 1870 and 1910, the number of physicians per 100,000 people grew from 177 to 241 in the large cities, while it fell from 160 to 152 in the rest of the country—this during a time when the overall ratio of doctors to population was still increasing.[15]

15   The rise of cities was brought about partly by the building of canals and the development of steamboats and railroads. This "transportation revolution" widened the markets of cities and enabled the larger and stronger producers to penetrate what were previously fragmented local markets. On a more modest scale, the railroads and the telegraph helped widen doctors' markets by expanding the territory they could cover. This proved a boon especially to consultants; one mentions logging ten thousand miles of railroad travel in a half year.[16] If the railroad did not take physicians all the way to their destination, a carriage might be waiting for them when they alighted. Doctors were such frequent users of railroads that some treated injuries to railroad workers in exchange for a travel pass. The railroads also brought in patients from a distance and naturally doctors wanted to be in towns along the routes to enjoy the benefits. In cities, they had a similar incentive to locate along the routes followed by streetcars.[17]

16   The transportation revolution of the nineteenth century has generally been considered from the standpoint of regional and long-distance flows of commodities, information, and even disease. But there was also a revolution in local travel. One historian remarks, "The automobile and the telephone did

[13] O. Larsell, *The Doctor in Oregon: A Medical History* (Portland, Ore.: Binsford & Mort, 1947), 160.

[14] U.S. Bureau of the Census, *Historical Statistics,* 11–12. See also Adna F. Weber, *The Growth of Cities in the Nineteenth Century* (New York: Macmillan, 1899).

[15] American Medical Association, Committee on Social Insurance, *Statistics Regarding the Medical Profession* (Chicago: American Medical Association, 1916), 38–39.

[16] Victor C. Vaughan, *A Doctor's Memories* (Indianapolis: Bobbs-Merrill, 1926), 269.

[17] On the role of railroads in bringing in patients from a distance, see Helen Clapesattle, *The Doctors Mayo* (Minneapolis: University of Minnesota Pess, 1941), 348–53. For further discussion of doctors' relation to railroads, see Chapter 6.

not greatly lower the cost of transportation as had been the case with the railroad in the 19th century."[18] Though this may be true of inter-city transportation between two points along main routes, it does not apply to local travel.

17   The telephone made it less costly to reach a physician by greatly reducing the time formerly spent tracking down the peripatetic practitioner on foot. Phones first became available in the late 1870s. Curiously, the first rudimentary telephone exchange on record, built in 1877, connected the Capital Avenue Drugstore in Hartford, Connecticut, with twenty-one local doctors.[19] (Drugstores had often served as message centers for physicians.) The first telephone line in Rochester, Minnesota, set up in December 1879, connected the farmhouse of Dr. William Worrall Mayo with Geisinger and Newton's drugstore downtown.[20] As telephones became more widespread, families could, of course, keep continually in touch with the doctor without a visit. In an apt analogy, one manual for medical practice in 1923 commented that the telephone had become as necessary to the physician as the stethoscope.[21]

18   As automobiles, first produced in the 1890s, became more reliable after the turn of the century, they further reduced time lost in travel. Doctors were among the earliest to buy cars. Physicians who wrote to the *Journal of the American Medical Association,* which published several supplements on automobiles between 1906 and 1912, reported that an auto cut the time required for house calls in half. "It is the same as if the day had forty-eight hours instead of twenty-four," a doctor from Iowa rejoiced.[22] Besides making calls in one-half the time," wrote a physician from Oklahoma, "there is something about the auto that is infatuating, and the more you ride the more you want to ride."[23] In a 1910 survey of readers that drew 324 replies concerning automobiles, three out of five doctors said they had increased their income; answering a slightly different question, four out of five agreed that it "pays to own a car." The survey asked physicians using either automobiles or horses to give their annual mileage and costs, including maintenance and depreciation. The 96 physicians still using horses reported costs that work out to 13 cents a mile; for the 116 who owned low-priced cars (under $1,000), the cost per mile was 5.6 cents. It came to 9 cents for 208 doctors who owned cars priced over $1,000. However, the initial investment in purchasing a car was greater than in buying a horse.[24] "To assert that it costs no more to run a car than to keep up a team is absurd," insisted one physician. "But if one considers the time saved on the road, and

[18] Samuel Hays, "Introduction" to *Building the Organizational Society,* ed. Jerry Israel (New York: Free Press, 1972), 9–10. On the subject of changing transportation costs, see George Rogers Taylor, *The Transportation Revolution* (New York: Rinehart, 1951) and especially Allen Pred, *Urban Growth and the Circulation of Information* (Cambridge: Harvard University Press, 1973).

[19] John Brooks, *Telephone: The First Hundred Years* (New York: Harper & Row, 1976), 65; Marion May Dilts, *The Telephone in a Changing World* (New York: Longmans Green, 1941), 9.

[20] Clapesattle, *The Doctors Mayo,* 135–36.

[21] Verlin C. Thomas, *The Successful Physician* (Philadelphia: Saunders, 1923), 146.

[22] George Kessel, "Would Not Practice Without an Auto," *Journal of the American Medical Association* [hereafter referred to as *JAMA*] 50 (March 7, 1908), 814.

[23] J. A. Bowling, "Testimony from the Southwest," *JAMA* 46 (April 21, 1906), 1179.

[24] "A Compilation of Automobile Statistics," *JAMA* 54 (April 9, 1910), 1273–74.

the consequent additional business made possible, to say nothing of the lessened discomfort, a busy practitioner will find a large balance on the side of the motor car."[25]

19   Besides saving time, the automobile, like the railroad, widened the doctors' market geographically. In 1912, a Chicago physician noted that the residential mobility of patients required doctors to drive a car. "Chicago today is a city of flats [apartments], and people move so, that a patient living within a block today may be living five miles away next month. It is impossible to hold one's business unless one can answer calls quickly, and this is impossible without a motor car. I have not only held my own, but have increased my business by making distant calls promptly . . . [averaging] about 75 miles a day . . . "[26]

20   Just as telephones, automobiles, and hard roads enabled physicians to cut down on traveling costs, so they enabled patients to do the same in visiting doctors' offices. Reduced traveling time in both directions cut the cost of medical care and raised the supply of physicians' services, by increasing the proportion of doctors' time available for contact with patients.

21   The reduction of indirect prices from the local transportation revolution and the rise of cities put medical care within the income range of more people; in this way, it had the same effect as cost reductions from new technology in manufacturing. Underlying the shift from household to market in manufactured goods were radical changes in productivity that drastically altered relative prices. In the production of textiles, for example, family manufacture was virtually eliminated in a remarkably short period. In 1815 the power loom was introduced in Massachusetts; by 1830 the price of ordinary brown shirting had fallen from 42 to 7.5 cents a yard. A woman at home could weave 4 yards of the cloth in a day; one worker in a factory, tending several power looms, could turn out 90 to 160 yards daily. There was no way women at home could compete.[27]

22   In medicine, no radical or sudden change in technology drastically cut the cost of producing physicians' services; there was only the gradual erosion of indirect prices that came from more rapid transportation and more concentrated urban life. Though difficult to measure, the "productivity" of physicians (measured simply as services to patients per day) significantly increased. I mentioned before that physicians probably averaged no more than five to seven patients a day in the mid-nineteenth century. In contrast, by the early 1940s, the average load of general practitioners, rural and urban, was about eighteen to twenty-two patients daily.[28] Such figures suggest a gain in produc-

---

[25] H. A. Stalker, "The Automobile as a Physician's Vehicle," *JAMA* 52 (March 7, 1908), 812.

[26] C. A. Hibbert, "Transient Flat Life Requires Physician to Cover Wide Territory," *JAMA* 58 (April 6, 1912), 1080. For more on the subject, see Lewis Mayers and Leonard V. Harrison, *The Distribution of Physicians in the United States* (New York: General Education Board, 1924), and Michael L. Berger, "The Influence of the Automobile on Rural Health Care, 1900–1929," *Journal of the History of Medicine and the Allied Sciences* 28 (October 1973), 319–35.

[27] Tryon, *Household Manufacturers,* 275–76, 291–93.

[28] Antonio Ciocco and Isidore Altman, "The Patient Load of Physicians in Private Practice, A Comparative Statistical Study of Three Areas," *Public Health Reports* 58 (September 3, 1943), 1329–51.

tivity for practicing doctors on the order of 300 percent. For surgeons, the gains have been much larger, considering the infrequency of surgery before antisepsis.

23   The local transportation evolution also improved the efficacy of treatment by reducing the isolation of medical practice. It made possible more rapid intervention in emergencies, and the ambulance was meant to accelerate that process. Reduced distances may also have had a psychological effect: Increasingly, one came to expect the doctor's intervention. Improved access ultimately brought greater dependency.

Reading Sources: "Medical Practice and the Local Transportation Revolution"

Read the selection, surveying it to identify key terms and important concepts. Highlight these phrases and ideas, and then answer these questions.

1. Why, according to Starr, did most nineteenth-century American physicians find it difficult to support themselves from their practices alone?
2. What does Starr mean by the "indirect price of medical services"? How does this concept help him make his point?
3. In the first half of this essay, Starr summarizes the obstacles faced by early nineteenth-century physicians because of the lack of modern transportation; in the second half, he discusses the effects on medical practice of improved transportation. Where does he begin the second part of his essay? How does he signal to his readers the shift in focus from problem to solution?
4. What key terms are repeated in this essay? How do they help readers to follow Starr's ideas?
5. How do the opening sentences in Starr's paragraphs provide continuity in his essay? Consider each sentence's function carefully.
6. Starr occasionally inserts first-person comments into his discussion — for example, "I leave aside, for the moment, . . . " (3) and "I mentioned before . . . " (22). Do these comments interrupt the flow of the essay? What purpose do they serve? Do they violate the scholarly tone of the essay? On balance, are they useful or intrusive?
7. To whom is this essay directed — physicians, historians, or the general public? How can you tell?
8. Locate any paragraph clusters in Starr's essay, and identify the focus of each.
9. What is Starr's thesis?

Reacting to Sources

Reread the selection carefully, making marginal notes to aid comprehension and reinforce connections. Then further annotate the selection if you need to do so in order to answer any of these questions. (You may already have addressed some of the questions in your marginal notes.)

1. Using a dictionary if necessary, supply brief marginal definitions of these words as they are used in this selection: *protracted* (1), *lucratively* (2), *ingrained* (3), *foregone* (4), *recourse* (5), *barter* (6), *procure* (7), *untenable* (8), *suffice* (9), *emissary* (11), *apprised* (13), *boon* (15), *peripatetic* (17).
2. In a few sentences, rewrite paragraph 1 to simplify its ideas.
3. Formulate three questions whose answers could clarify your understanding of the ideas in paragraph 2.
4. In a marginal note, explain what Starr means in paragraph 5 by "opportunity cost."
5. In marginal notes, give two examples from the essay to support Starr's statement that "the self-sufficiency of the household in early American society was . . . quite extensive . . . " (6). When—and why—did this situation change? Explain in a marginal note.
6. In paragraph 10 Starr says, "In rural areas, many families would not think of calling in a doctor except under the most grave conditions." In a marginal note, explain why this was so.
7. What function does paragraph 16 serve in the essay? What function does paragraph 20 serve? Explain in marginal notes that pinpoint each paragraph's central idea.
8. In a journal entry, list the ways in which the railroad, the telephone, and the automobile changed the nature of medical practice.
9. Outline the paragraph cluster consisting of paragraphs 21 and 22, making sure your outline highlights the comparison Starr is making.
10. In a journal entry, explain what Starr means by "transportation revolution."
11. In the last line of the essay Starr says, "Improved access ultimately brought greater dependency." Explore this idea further in a journal entry.
12. Reread the selection's headnote and the bibliographic and explanatory notes that accompany the selection. How does this information affect your acceptance of Starr's ideas? Explain in a marginal note.
13. In a journal entry, explore possible connections or relationships between this essay and the excerpt from "Rich Doctors, Poor Nurses" in Chapter 1 (p. 9).

Working with Sources

1. Write a two-sentence summary of paragraph 12.
2. Write a critique of the ideas in paragraph 13.
3. Write a journal entry in which you explore your reactions to these quotations from "Medical Practice and the Local Transportation Revolution":

> "The heart of the economic problem was not that the physicians' fees were so high, but that the real price of medical care was so much higher than their fees" (4).

> "Doctors were among the earliest to buy cars" (18).

"In medicine, no radical or sudden change in technology drastically cut the cost of producing physicians' services; there was only the gradual erosion of indirect prices that came from more rapid transportation and more concentrated urban life" (22).

Be sure to integrate the quotations smoothly into your writing.
4. Paraphrase the ideas in paragraph 3.
5. Write a one-paragraph synthesis that blends ideas in paragraphs 18 – 19 of this selection and paragraph 11 of "Why Smaller Refrigerators Can Preserve the Human Race" (pp. 469 – 472).

Writing with Sources: Using a Single Source

Integrating information from "Medical Practice and the Local Transportation Revolution" with your own ideas, write an essay on one of these topics. Be sure to acknowledge ideas that are not your own.

1. In paragraph 8, discussing the nineteenth century, Starr says, "We may assume that time had about the same value for patients as for their physicians." He notes, however, that this notion "would be untenable today because of the high median income of physicians relative to the population at large." Explain how the nineteenth-century transportation revolution contributed to this change.
2. In paragraphs 13 and 23 Starr offers a contrast between the early physicians' isolation and their lack of isolation today, arguing in paragraph 23 that medical treatment has become more efficient as a result. Consider other results of this change: advantages and disadvantages of either the increased availability of medical care for patients or the increased availability of support services for physicians.
3. Has improved access to medical care actually made us more dependent on physicians? Using examples from your own experience and observations, explain your position.
4. Analyze the relationship between improved transportation facilities and the development of a profession or service other than medicine.

At the Flick of a Switch

Susan Strasser

Born in 1948, Susan Strasser received her Bachelor's degree from Reed College and her Master's and Doctoral degrees in history from the State University of New York at Stony Brook. Since 1975 she has taught American history and labor studies at the Evergreen State College in Olympia, Washington. "At the Flick of a Switch" is a chapter in her 1982 book, *Never Done: A History of American Housework*. This book vividly describes the domestic burdens on the wife and mother in the typical nineteenth-century household, chronicling the drudgeries of cooking, cleaning, and doing laundry. Strasser goes on to explain how post–Civil War industrialization changed the nature of these tasks and, in turn, the nature of women's daily lives.

1   Gas and electricity, the new fuels for home heating and lighting, altered family relations not only by changing Americans' sense of household space but by totally revamping their conception of time. Gas and electric heat dulled the distinctions between summer and winter, removing the winter work from household routine — no more wood chopping, fuel hauling, hopper tending, or fire building. Gas and electric cooking made summer meals almost as comfortable to prepare as winter meals were; gas and electric light made winter evenings as bright as summer. Seasonal differences, fading at the same time because of food preservation and transportation, and because of the simple fact that an increasingly urban population had less reason to spend time outdoors, held less sway over daily human routines. Artificial light merged night and day; central heat and the new fuels introduced warm winter mornings without work; gas and electric cookstoves with individual burners offered an afternoon cup of tea or warm milk at two in the morning even in the summer. The seasonal differences held no great attraction for people who spent so much time and labor attempting to brighten winter nights and stay warm; the new fuels appealed precisely because they saved all that work. No one complained about moving from private production of energy to consumption of heat and light publicly produced for profit, although few could afford to purchase energy until after the turn of the century.

2   Painter Rembrandt Peale, who initially installed gas lighting as a brilliant curiosity to illuminate the paintings and stuffed animals in his eclectic Baltimore museum, established America's first gas company in that city in 1816. Along with four other investors, he gained a charter from the city and a contract to lay pipes along the streets and erect street lights; the company built a manufacturing plant that inaugurated American commercial gas lighting in 1817. Propaganda from the whale oil and tallow interests impeded the Baltimore company's progress; twenty years later, only two miles of gas main had been laid. Nonetheless, other cities began to consider gas as a fuel for public use.

3   In New York, a municipal committee investigated the possibilities for a municipally owned gasworks and build a rudimentary experimental system, eventually concluding that the high costs should be borne, not by the city, but by private investors operating under a city charter. In 1823, the city chartered the New York Gas Light Company and contracted with it to lay pipes and manufacture enough gas to light Broadway from the Battery to Grand Street within two years, and to light other areas at the city's request after five years. Samuel Leggett, the gas company's first president and also president of the Franklin Bank, gathered a board of directors composed of substantial citizens, which offered four thousand shares to the public at fifty dollars each; owing to the board's reputation and the success of gas stocks in London, the issue sold out immediately. By 1830, the company had expanded substantially — its capital, labor force, manufacturing and storage capacity, area of operation, and

number of subscribers all boomed — and other groups of investors began to establish competitive firms to challenge its monopoly.

4   Municipal gas systems were expensive to start; they required all the manufacturing capacity of any industrial concern, plus the distribution systems, the pipes and fittings. The only Americans with that kind of money had made it in commerce and finance; most farmers still operated outside the money economy, the growing class of wage laborers had nothing to spare, and even the few who operated the new manufacturing concerns had only enough to reinvest in their own plants, still dependent themselves on the commercial interests. From the start, bankers and merchants controlled the gas companies everywhere, establishing systems in most major cities during the 1820s and 1830s, and in smaller towns during the next two decades. By the beginning of the Civil War, state legislatures had chartered over three hundred companies to operate in towns of all sizes.

5   Although the New York company at first manufactured gas from oil and rosin, a method used by some companies until the middle of the century, most gas manufacture until the 1870s used soft or bituminous coal, heated in an airtight furnace to produce "coal gas" (cooled and collected in a series of pipes) and its major by-product, coke (which is to coal as charcoal is to wood). Manufactured separately as a fuel for ironmaking, coke went to waste as a gas by-product, while the gas went to waste in coke ovens; nineteenth-century ironmakers considered the retort ovens that would save both expensive, the market for gas limited, and retort-oven coke inferior. Coal gas provided unsteady, smelly light at about fifteen to seventeen candlepower.

6   As improved lamp designs and the new kerosene fuel began to brighten both American lighting and oil's competitive prospects, coal gas became less attractive. Soon after kerosene hit the market, two inventors, Frenchman Tessie du Motay and American T. S. C. Lowe, independently developed "water gas." This new illuminant, produced by reacting steam with superheated coke or hard anthracite coal, provided twenty-two to thirty-five candlepower when mixed with oil vapors or other gases. First introduced in Pennsylvania in 1873, it rapidly supplanted coal gas after 1880; by 1890, America's 742 city gasworks produced more water gas than coal gas.

7   Natural gas competed with manufactured gas only in limited geographical areas. Thomas Jefferson mentioned a "burning spring" in West Virginia in his *Notes on Virginia,* later dedicated as a park by George Washington; salt-well drilling produced natural gas in 1815 in Charleston and in 1820 in Pittsburgh, but nobody wanted or used the gas. The first intentional gas well, dug in Fredonia, New York, in 1821, provided enough gas for thirty burners, each of two candlepower. Improved by storage systems and lead pipes, the Fredonia well attracted international attention. General Lafayette, touring the United States and greeted at a Fredonia hotel blazing with light at two o'clock in the morning, remarked that he had better leave a place "evidently too near to Hades"; the German explorer Alexander von Humboldt called Fredonia gas the eighth wonder of the world. But even the Fredonians failed to recognize the commercial potential of their gas, not organizing a company to make improve-

ments until 1858; more important, most of the early producers of petroleum failed to exploit the natural gas that accompanied the oil. A few manufacturers used natural gas during the 1870s, and many more during the 1880s in places near gas fields, particularly the Pittsburgh area. In 1891, the Indiana Natural Gas and Oil Company built the first high-pressure long-distance pipeline, running 120 miles between the northern Indiana gas fields and Chicago. However, natural gas did not outstrip manufactured gas until the 1930s, and even then remained more popular for industrial purposes than for domestic use.

8   Domestic use provided only a small market for manufactured gas as well, until the end of the century; although gas companies abounded, their product primarily lighted city streets and public places. The simplest fixtures — T-shaped iron pipes (usually with two burners, one at each end of the T) or plain elbows with one burner at the end — provided light for factories, prisons, hospitals, schools, and plebeian saloons. More fashionable bars and stores often used gas pillars, ornamental standards on pedestals or mounted on the bar or counter, with branches at the top capped by burners and shades. One firm, Cornelius and Baker, supplied a wide variety of fixtures for government buildings; by 1859, they had lit nearly all of the state capitols and many rooms in the White House, and had commissions for the United States Capitol and the Treasury Building. These chandeliers and brackets incorporated statuettes representing Produce, Commerce, Liberty, and the like, along with American eagles, buffaloes, corn, Indians, state heroes, and American presidents. The company's apparatus for lighting the Senate and House chambers in the Capitol spaced gas jets so closely that they could all be ignited by a single pilot light — 2,500 burners "lighted instantaneously" on the Senate side.

9   Fixtures in some private homes displayed similar ostentation. A. T. Stewart, owner of the largest dry-goods firm in the world, lit his marble mansion at Fifth Avenue and Thirty-Fourth Street in New York with twelve-light bronze chandeliers, ornamented with procelain, etched glass shades, and Egyptian Revival heads. Stewart's house, completed in 1869 and generally acclaimed as the finest in the city, predated most other millionaires' mansions, but even the Vanderbilts' "bourgeois brownstone," which they ultimately abandoned for palaces on Fifth Avenue and in Newport, included in 1873 a splendid glass chandelier.

10   Not everyone who used gas had as much money as Stewart or the Vanderbilts, but only relatively wealthy people could afford the installation cost or the fuel itself before the end of the century. Those who bought it used it almost exclusively for lighting; at the end of the century, gas was still very much a "fuel of the future" for domestic cooking and heating. Despite the many gas companies and gas mains, the fuel might have disappeared quickly when faced with its first serious competition, electricity, during the 1880s, had it not been for the Welsbach burner, or gas mantle, invented in 1885 and first manufactured in the United States in 1887. Thanks to this treated cotton mesh cylinder that created an incandescent light, gas lighting maintained "an increasingly futile rearguard action" until about 1910.

11   The Welsbach mantle kept the gas companies alive while they estab-

lished themelves firmly in some localities; at least two early-twentieth-century studies of working people's houses in New York, for example, showed a majority with gas lighting. Meanwhile, the companies devoted themselves to promoting other domestic uses for their fuel, especially cooking. Despite the new mantle, gaslights flickered more than electric ones, required ventilated fixtures, and produced soot; unlike both kerosene and electric lamps, which could be moved around a room, gas fixtures had to be installed permanently. Faced with this obvious competition, the gas lighting companies allied themselves with the gas appliance manufacturers in the National Commercial Gas Association in 1905; this organization applied itself to merchandising the fuel, developing new appliances, training sales personnel, and producing showroom displays and demonstrations. A national advertising campaign, jointly sponsored by gas companies and appliance manufacturers in 1912–1913, promoted many uses for gas; by 1918, its future was assured, despite the serious competition.

12   This competition displayed itself at the World's Columbian Exposition in Chicago, which opened in May 1893. The exposition, commemorating the four-hundredth anniversary of Columbus's discovery of America, surpassed all the other nineteenth-century world's fairs — London's 1851 Crystal Palace, the 1889 Paris exposition for which the Eiffel Tower was built, and the 1876 Philadelphia Centennial. Within 3 of the 150 buildings of the White City, designed by the most famous architects of the day, model kitchens offered women fair visitors a glimpse of the future. The Women's Building kitchen, primarily used by home economists for twice-daily cooking lectures, contained seats for the audience and a platform with a gas stove and a table. The Electrical Building featured a complete model house, with electric stoves, hot plates ("Dishes are kept hot on the table by dainty, polished electric warming furnaces connected by wires under the table"), washing and ironing machines, fans, dishwashers, and carpet sweepers. Its gas counterpart, located in the Horticultural Building, promised to "delight all housekeepers" with its gas stoves, hot-water heater, refrigerators and coolers, and automatic dishwasher. Most of the delighted housekeepers went home to wood and coal stoves and houses without plumbing; these were the only dishwashers they would see in a lifetime. To them, electric cooking was no more fantastic than gas.

13   Electric lighting had started in competition with gas. Others had long experimented with arc lights and dynamos; Thomas Edison's major achievement was not the light bulb but a total system "for generating, controlling, measuring, distributing, and utilizing power." Edison, who made his first fortune manufacturing stock tickers for Western Union, had already established the nation's first research-and-development firm at Menlo Park, New Jersey, a well-equipped laboratory and a permanent staff dedicated to full-time invention in an organized fashion, aimed at making "a minor invention every ten days, and a big one every six months or so." When he decided to tackle the problem of incandescent lighting, a decision based on the greater potential financial rewards that lighting held over such possible areas of invention as the telephone and phonograph, he limited the research by fixing the price at the price of gaslight. He could profit only by lowering costs as much as possible, and

designed the rest of the system (generators, light sockets, junction boxes, safety fuses, underground conductors, and much more) to do that. The system as a whole, first demonstrated in 1879 and first established commercially at the Edison Electric Illuminating Company's Pearl Street power station in New York in 1882, proved competitive with gas, exactly as intended in its design.

14   Setting up the system required financing far beyond the research-and-development stage; Edison needed help, and turned to big businessmen for support in forming the Edison Electric Light Company, a forerunner of General Electric. With other bankers and the president of Western Union, J. P. Morgan provided major financial backing for the several Edison companies; his partner served as director and treasurer of Edison Electric Light until 1883; and his New York mansion served as an early demonstration of the Edison system. Morgan himself helped to form General Electric in 1892, and served on its board until his death in 1913. Henry Villard, the president and financier of the Northern Pacific Railroad, financed some of Edison's early work and created the merger that became General Electric. That merger, combining two of the three large electrical equipment manufacturers (Edison General Electric and Thompson-Houston, leaving Westinghouse independent), represented as well a merger of New York and Boston financial interests. These financiers were important to the merger "because the electrical manufacturers were the first American industrialists not intimately connected with railroads who found it necessary to go to the capital markets for funds in order to build their initial enterprise."

15   Dominated by these outside financial interests, the board of General Electric continued to exert powerful control over the operations of the salaried managers. The top management, in turn, held tight rein over the middle management, building large central staffs and carefully defining their responsibilities, creating "the basic organizational form used by modern American industrial enterprises." The sales department, with its own vice-president and a manager for each major product, responsible for coordinating its production and marketing, met monthly with the manager for foreign sales and the advertising director to consider "pricing, competitors' activities, market conditions, customers' needs and concerns, and the processing of major orders." Coordination between sales and production departments, central to all modern corporations, was particularly important at General Electric because its salesmen, knowing more about the technical aspects of the equipment than their customers, had frequent contact with them, serving as installers and repairmen; many GE salesmen, like those in other technologically advanced industries, had engineering degrees.

16   Most of this sales and service force handling GE's early industrial products served the large manufacturers that demanded power-generating equipment. Eventually, however, households joined the electrical industry's consumer market; their ignorance established a similar dependence on servicemen. The new terminology that came along with electrical equipment — watts and amps and volts — could be confusing. Some local lighting companies supplied alternating current, others direct, well into the 1930s; equipment came de-

signed for use with either or both, and voltage varied likewise in different localities and for different appliances. Women's magazines and household manuals explained the terms, suggesting that ignorance in these matters led to misunderstandings about why the toaster burned the toast or why the waffle iron didn't work like Cousin Mary's. In the end, though, the whole thing was a matter for experts. "It is unwise to attempt repairs yourself," advised one article after explaining watts and meter reading. You might treat a slight cold or a small cut, suggested a manual called *The Electric Home,* "but for a real sickness you would call a physician." Likewise, you might wish to fix a cord or socket or change a fuse yourself, "but beyond this consult your electrical contractor or lighting company. They are your electrical doctors." Wires embedded in the walls of the house, like gas lines and plumbing pipes but quite unlike anything common in households before 1900, contributed to this dependence on servicemen.

17   Ignorance, combined with the genuine dangers of fire and electrocution, engendered fear. Mrs. Cornelius Vanderbilt, who in 1881 went to a costume ball dressed as an electric light, demanded that her Fifth Avenue house's entire new electrical system be removed a short time later because it caused a small fire. Electrical companies that hoped to attract a broader clientele than the Vanderbilts and the Morgans had to counteract such fears in order to establish the new fuel as the competitor Edison had designed it to be. They never did so by explaining the mysteries of the ampere or by addressing fears about fire and electrocution directly; instead, in the budding tradition of the advertising industry that was emerging at the same time, they diverted attention to the product's advantages.

18   For the first thirty years or so, the only households that could afford electricity could also afford domestic servants. Electricity, its proponents claimed, promised freedom from the ages-old servant problem: electrical appliances could not talk back. A Columbian Exposition guidebook described gracious living in the electric future at the model house in the Electrical Building. A servant answered an electric bell, ushered the visitor into the reception room, and turned on a phonograph, which kept the guest occupied with a selection from *Faust* until the hostess appeared. She kept contact with the servants "by electric calls daintily fashioned." Electricity could, then, serve even those with servants. But it also could dispense with them: "About the time the dinner is over the servant gets angry at something and picks up her 'duds' and goes off in a huff." The fortunate mistress of the home of the future sends her guests to the parlor, "excuses herself for a moment," sends the dishes upstairs on the electric dumbwaiter, does them in the electric dishwasher "in five minutes," and dries them in the electric dish dryer. If the servant is not replaced by the time washday comes, the mistress "need have no fear of breaking her aristocratic back leaning over tubs or ruining her pretty hands by constant soaking in hot suds," but can wash them in an automatic washer that drains and fills for washing, rinsing, and bluing, hang them to dry in front of electric radiators in the garret, run them through the electric ironer, and be "none too tired to go to the opera in the evening."

19   By 1917, the disappearing servant was commonplace; many of the women who had formed the servant population were taking other jobs instead, the popular press moaned about the servant problem, and a variety of reformers proposed solutions. General Electric joined in. Advertising light bulbs to the middle-class readers of *McClure's,* they suggested that electricity had other uses besides light. "Housework is hard work—and the problem of help in the home is growing more and more acute." Both the work and the problem could be simplified with "electrical servants," dependable for the "muscle part of the washing, ironing, cleaning and sewing." They could cool or heat the house, percolate the coffee, or "do all your cooking—without matches, without soot, without coal, without argument—in a cool kitchen. Don't go to the Employment Bureau. Go to your Lighting Company or leading Electric Shop to solve your servant problem." The first step, buying Edison Mazda light bulbs to save "enough current to operate several electrical appliances without increasing your electric bill," would "light the way to lighter housework." In an ad directed at women short of servants who used electricity only for lighting, the company sold light bulbs but promoted the entire industry.

20   After World War I, pictures of servants vitually disappeared from advertising for women; most ads depicted housewives doing their own housework. Many new ads treated household tasks as expressions of emotion: a new bride showed her love by "washing tell-tale gray out of her husband's shirts"; a mother cleaning the bathroom sink protected her family from disease. A Muncie, Indiana electric company advertisement of the 1920s suggested that electricity promoted good motherhood. "This is the test of a successful mother —she puts first things first. She does not give to sweeping the time that belongs to her children." Men, ran the ad, were "judged successful according to their power to delegate work. Similarly the wise woman delegates to electricity all that electricity can do. She cannot delegate the one task most important. Human lives are in her keeping; their future is molded by her hands and heart." As live-in servants disappeared from households and electricity entered them, the electric companies suggested that housewives could use the new fuel to save time for more important tasks.

21   Some of the appliances offered as "electric servants" did save time. The electric iron, first patented in 1882 and first sold in 1893, relieved women of the hot work involved in continually heating heavy flatirons, although carefree ironing had to wait until about 1927 for the adjustable automatic thermostat. Before that, electric irons were either on or off. Immensely helpful and relatively inexpensive, irons became the most popular electric appliances during the 1920s. Fifty-nine percent of the households in Zanesville, Ohio, where interviewers for a market research firm knocked on every door in 1926, had them; 82 percent of that firm's sample of somewhat wealthier families in thirty-six other cities ironed with electricity.

22   Almost as many had vacuum cleaners: 53 percent in Zanesville and 60 percent in the other towns. Nonelectric carpet sweepers—always dominated by the Bissell company—had literally swept the nation beginning in the 1880s; David Kenney patented the first electric suction cleaner in 1907. The

two most popular vacuum cleaner types had both appeared by the time of the Zanesville study: the Hoover, which beat the rug with a power-driven brush, was patented in 1908 and had created a national market by 1919; the Electrolux, the first tank or cylinder type cleaner, imported from Sweden in 1924, sold well enough immediately that by 1931 the company had decided to manufacture cleaners in the United States. Many companies, large and small, sold vacuum cleaners house-to-house; by 1926, an edition of Marion Harland's famous 1871 cookbook, *Common Sense in the Household,* "Revised for Gas and Electricity," maintained that "almost every woman who lives in or near a town of any size" had seen a vacuum cleaner demonstration, "and even the dweller in remote country districts has probably had the automobile of the demonstrator stop at her door."

23   Harland's daughter, who wrote the revision, loved these machines. Their superiority to brooms and carpet sweepers, she wrote, "is at once apparent." The "swiftness and ease" of the work "seem miraculous." "It is like play to see ravelings, lint, feathers and hair and other scraps drawn into the maw of the cleaner and vanish from sight." The numerous attachments made short work of cleaning hangings, tufted furniture, cornices, picture frames, "and remote corners under bureaus and bookcases." Best of all, she wrote, the vacuum cleaner "has in a measure done away with housecleaning. The old fashion of having a semi-annual upheaval," that old household earthquake, when carpets were removed, hangings taken down, pictures and books displaced, "and general misery produced through the household, is no longer essential to cleanliness." Delivered from this "bondage," housekeepers could look forward to the next step: "Not yet has a machine been devised which will mechanically mop up a floor or take china from the shelf and wash it, but it is probably on the way and when it comes it will undoubtedly be run by electricity!"

24   None of the other small electric appliances sold as well as vacuum cleaners and irons. Hot plates, heating pads, grills, percolators, room heaters, and fans appeared in some households by 1926, but only about a fifth of Zanesville households owned toasters, which far outstripped all these others. The first electric toasters, appearing around 1910, adapted the wire-frame designs long used on top of the stove; GE's 1912 Radiant Toaster, a frame holding one slice of bread, produced a slice a minute, "Crisp, Delicious, Golden-Brown Toast on the Breakfast Table." Automatic toasters, first widely marketed by Toastmaster after 1926, timed the process so that the cook could leave the table. "How many times *each week* do you have to throw out burned slices of toast?" the company asked in a 1927 *Saturday Evening Post* ad. "This amazing new invention" ended that waste and annoyance in "three fascinating operations": drop in a slice of bread, then press two levers (one set the current, the other operated the timer), and "Pop! up comes the toast automatically when it's done, and the current is automatically turned off. The toast is made in a jiffy because both sides are toasted *at the same time.* There is no guesswork."

25   Other specialized cooking devices, designed for one function alone, appeared on the market in the 1920s and early 1930s; although few families bought them, electric waffle irons, chafing dishes, and coffee makers promised

further freedom from the stove and the kitchen. A woman could prepare her family's entire meal at the table, or cook it in the kitchen and keep it warm in the dining room; she could serve her guests and enjoy their company at the same time. By 1934, she could buy even the most highly specialized appliances — egg cookers (with "no moving parts to wear out or cause trouble"), corn poppers ("useful not only for making pop-corn at Hallowe'en parties and gatherings, but also for roasting chestnuts and freshening nuts"), doughnut bakers (which made four greaseless doughnuts at a time "right on the dining room table"), wiener cookers ("furnished in different sizes and colors to suit one's fancy"), and baby-bottle warmers ("which you can place on your bedside table at night" for two o'clock feedings).

26   Most of the early ads for electric appliances celebrated their economy: the 1912 GE Radiant Toaster made toast for one-tenth of a cent per slice, the 1909 Hoover suction Sweeper would "Sweep With Electricity For 3¢ a Week," the 1913 GE Even Heat electric iron promised "Real Economy" over its competitors, even at fifteen cents per "average family ironing," because it ironed faster, "thereby requiring less electricity." Most GE ads promoted the current-saving Edison Mazda light bulbs: "Replace the old-style lamps and you can enjoy using these electrical appliances without any increase in the monthly bills for current." By the 1920s, economy no longer dominated the ads, which now celebrated electricity's ability to relieve women of burdensome chores. "What Every Woman Wants," one utility-sponsored ad stated, was an all-electric kitchen, "A Kitchen Where Work Is Easy!" The 1927 Toastmaster ad used the words "automatic" and "automatically" seven times and noted the "gleaming nickel" finish that made it "an attractive piece for the dining table," but never mentioned economy at all.

27   As electric service spread to more households, the price of current dropped; in 1912, when about 16 percent of American dwelling units had electric service, a kilowatt hour cost about nine cents, while the 35 percent who had it in 1920 paid seven and a half cents and the 68 percent in 1930 paid six cents. Customers spent more money on electricity, however; as time went on, they installed more lights, bought more appliances, and used more current. The average annual use per customer doubled between 1912 and 1930. Still, most of them limited themselves to lights, irons, vacuum cleaners, and the curling irons that created the fashionable hairstyles of the 1920s. American consumption of electricity in 1930, although greatly increased over the past and still on the rise, suggests that while every woman might well have wanted an all-electric kitchen, it was scarcely more a reality then than it had been at the Columbian Exposition in 1893: the average customer used only 547 kilowatt hours. Customers in 1970 bought thirteen times that much electricity.

28   Electric service, available in most cities by the turn of the century, spread rapidly in urban areas after World War I. By 1920, almost half of the nonfarm dwelling units in America had electric service; a massive Bureau of Labor Statistics study conducted in forty-two states in 1918–1919 reported that some members of all economic groups had electricity, although poorer households used less current. At the beginning of the Depression, 85 percent of nonfarm

dwellings had electric service. Farm homes lagged far behind — only about 10 percent had electricity in 1930 — until after 1935, when Franklin D. Roosevelt created the Rural Electrification Administration. The REA made long-term loans to farmers' cooperatives, state and local governments, and nonprofit organizations, enabling farmers (not individually eligible for the loans) to electrify at minimum cost. By 1941, 35 percent of farm homes had electricity. The REA liberalized the loan policy in 1944; more than half of farm homes were electrified by 1946.

29   Few dared or bothered to comment on the broad social effects of so fundamental a transition. Once produced by household members who chopped wood, hauled coal, and tended kerosene lamps, energy now became a commodity, something people bought from corporations whose motive was profit. Once burdened by hard work, women could now buy "electric servants" that did the work for them. Once framed by nature, daily life now stood independent of the seasons and the daily movements of the sun. What could it all mean? Were women now at leisure, free to pursue lives in the world outside the household, or to change their roles within it?

30   One group that did ask those questions, a graduate seminar at Bryn Mawr College in 1925–1926, produced a comprehensive bibliography of books and articles about electricity in the household. The students "established the fact that practically no work has been done on this subject, and that we have no actual knowledge as to the social and economic effects of the introduction of electricity in the home." They found almost no written conjecture on what they understood to be fundamental questions about daily life, except for discussions of electricity and the servant question, a relationship without clarity about cause and effect. They guessed that most of the change lay in the future, for electricity had not yet touched the lives of the unskilled laboring classes; they speculated that electricity might even return production to the home, decentralizing manufacturing by bringing back some of the work that industrialization had removed — a possible revival of home sewing, for example. Without predicting exactly what might happen, the Bryn Mawr researchers knew something would, because of two "relatively recent factors": "first the rapidly declining cost of electric current — and second, the fact that electricity in the near future will be practically everywhere available and in unlimited quantity."

31   Those assumptions, upon which all discussion of electricity rested until they were shattered during the 1970s, allowed Americans to take electric power and its social effects for granted for about half a century. The Bryn Mawr students correctly predicted that electricity would help free American women from much of the "monotony and drudgery" that they called "so largely the portion of womankind the world over"; their prediction that production would return to the home proved considerably less accurate. In fact, electricity contributed to its further removal, and the industry that produced electric power and electric appliances followed the patterns of expansion, centralization, and corporate domination by large investors that characterized the process of industrialization in other industries. Electric power's predecessor and competitor, gas, under the control of local bankers and financiers, had set the

majority of American households apart from affluent homes and many public places during the first half of the nineteenth century. Even wealthier investors dominated the electrical industry, initially created and designed to return maximum profits to the financiers, not to free housewives from monotony and drudgery; from the start, the industry promoted dependence on manufactured products and on the experts who understood them well enough to keep them in repair.

32   Women welcomed electricity and gas in the early part of the century because they no longer had to haul fuel, build fires, and clean lamps; they knew that electric vacuum cleaners and washing machines would relieve them of backbreaking labor. Now, with energy conservation a serious issue for both the nation and their own pocketbooks, American women must evaluate their dependence on extravagant energy consumption and on an industry devoted to wasteful production of unnecessary goods planned for obsolescence. Hooked on power, devoted to the electric can opener along with the electric light, to electric knives and toothbrushes along with vacuum cleaners, and continuing to buy that power and those appliances from the same corporations — now even fewer, larger, and more centralized — American households become ever more prey to the effects of corporate decision making on daily life.

PAGE 455   Baltimore gas company: Louis Stotz and Alexander Jamison, *History of the Gas Industry* (New York: Press of Stettiner Bros., 1938), pp. 13–16.
New York City gas company: Stotz and Jamison, *History of the Gas Industry,* pp. 20–40.

PAGE 456   Three hundred gas companies: see chronological list in Denys Peter Myers, *Gaslighting in America: A Guide for Historic Preservation* (Washington, D.C.: U.S. Department of the Interior, Heritage Conservation and Recreation Service, 1978), pp. 249–52. See also Edgar W. Martin, *The Standard of Living in 1860: American Consumption Levels on the Eve of the Civil War* (Chicago: University of Chicago Press, 1942), pp. 96–97.

PAGE 456   Coke and gas manufacturing: Victor S. Clark, *History of Manufactures in the United States,* vol. 2, *1860–1893* (New York: McGraw-Hill Book Co. for Carnegie Institution of Washington, 1929), pp. 515–16.
Coal gas and water gas methods of manufacture: Clark, *History of Manufactures,* vol. 2, p. 516; Stotz and Jamison, *History of the Gas Industry,* pp. 4–5; Elizabeth Mickle Bacon, "The Growth of Household Conveniences in the United States from 1865 to 1900" (unpublished Ph.D. dissertation, Radcliffe, 1942); "Gas, an Ideal Fuel," (New York: Dominick and Dominick, 1930), pp. 6–7.
Natural gas: "Gas, an Ideal Fuel," p. 5; Stotz and Jamison, *History of the Gas Industry,* pp. 67–91; Clark, *History of Manufactures,* vol. 2, p. 517; Alfred M. Leeston, John A. Crichton, and John C. Jacobs, *The Dynamic Natural Gas Industry* (Norman: University of Oklahoma Press, 1963), pp. 4–9.

PAGE 457   Public-building fixtures: Myers, *Gaslighting in America,* pp. 3, 35, 43, 115–27.
Stewart and Vanderbilt fixtures: Myers, *Gaslighting in America,* pp. 141–43, 147.
"An increasingly futile rearguard action": Myers, *Gaslighting in America,* p. 207.
Living Among Workingmen's Families in New York City (New York: Russell Sage Foundation, Charities Publication Committee, 1909), p. 117; New York City Bureau of Standards, *Report on the Cost of Living for an Unskilled Laborer's Family in New York City* (n.p., n.d. — 1915 stamped in Library of Congress copy), p. 36.

PAGE 458   Columbian Exposition: William E. Cameron, *The World's Fair, Being a Pictorial History of the Columbian Exposition* (Chicago: Chicago Publication & Lithograph Co., 1893), pp. 327, 467, 718.

PAGE 458   A total system "for generating," etc.: Reyner Banham, *The Architecture of the Well-Tempered Environment* (Chicago: University of Chicago Press, 1969), pp. 60–61.
"A minor invention every ten days": Edison, quoted in David F. Noble, *America by Design: Science, Technology, and the Rise of Corporate Capitalism* (New York: Oxford University Press, 1977), p. 8.
Edison's financial backing: Noble, *America by Design*, pp. 8–9; Alfred D. Chandler, Jr., *The Visible Hand: The Managerial Revolution in American Business* (Cambridge, Mass.: Harvard University Press, 1977), pp. 426–28.

PAGE 459   Financiers and electrical manufacturers: Chandler, *Visible Hand*, p. 426.
"The basic organizational form": Chandler, *Visible Hand*, p. 417.
"Pricing, competitors' activities": Chandler, *Visible Hand*, p. 430.
Electrical salesmen: Chandler, *Visible Hand*, pp. 309–10.
Toaster and Cousin Mary's waffle iron: "When You Buy Electrical Equipment," *American Cookery* 29 (February 1925): 606.
"It is unwise to attempt repairs": R. C. Tarr, "Electrical Measurements in the Household," *American Cookery* 29 (March 1925): 606.

PAGE 460   Mrs. Cornelius Vanderbilt: David P. Handlin, *The American Home: Architecture and Society, 1815–1915* (Boston: Little, Brown & Co., 1979), p. 474.
Columbian Exposition model house: Cameron, *The World's Fair*. p. 327.
GE ad in *McClure's*: "The Lamp That Lights the Way to Lighter Housework," *McClure's*, September 1917, p. 55.

PAGE 461   Ads after World War I, and "tell-tale gray" quotation: Ruth Schwartz Cowan, "Two Washes in the Morning and a Bridge Party at Night: The American Housewife Between the Wars," *Women's Studies* 3 (1976): pp. 149–51.
Muncie electric company ad: quoted in Robert S. Lynd and Helen Merrell Lynd, *Middletown: A Study in Modern American Culture* (New York: Harcourt, Brace & World, 1929), p. 173.
Electric irons: Earl Lifshey, *The Housewares Story: A History of the American Housewares Industry* (Chicago: National Housewares Manufacturers Association, 1973), pp. 229–31.
Zanesville and thirty-six other cities: R. O. Eastman, Inc., *Zanesville and Thirty-Six Other American Communities: A Study of Markets and of the Telephone as a Market Index* (New York: Literary Digest, 1927), pp. 68–69.
Carpet sweepers and vacuum cleaners: Lifshey, *Housewares Story*, pp. 290–300.

PAGE 462   "Almost every woman": Marion Harland, *The New Common Sense in the Household" by Marion Harland Revised for Gas and Electricity by her Daughter Christine Terhune Herrick* (New York: Frederick A. Stokes Co., 1926), p. 323.
The New Common Sense on vacuum cleaners: Harland, *New Common Sense*, pp. 322–25.

PAGE 462   Toasters: Lifshey, *Housewares Story*, pp. 254–57; in Zanesville: Eastman, Inc., *Zanesville*, p. 71.
Toastmaster ad: *Saturday Evening Post*, March 5, 1927, reproduced in Lifshey, *Housewares Story*, p. 256.
Highly specialized appliances: E. S. Lincoln, *The Electric Home, a Standard Ready Reference Book* (New York: Electric Home Publishing Co., 1934), pp. 344–47.

PAGE 463   Economy in ads: reproduced in Lifshey, *Housewares Story:* GE toaster, p. 255; Hoover sweeper, p. 297; GE iron, p. 233.
"Replace the old-style lamps": 1912 GE ad reproduced in Lifshey, *Housewares Story*, p. 226.
"What Every Woman Wants": reproduced in Lifshey, *Housewares Story*, p. 226.

Electricity statistics: U.S. Department of Commerce, Bureau of the Census, *Historical Statistics of the United States, Colonial Times to 1970* (Washington, D.C.: Government Printing Office, 1975), p. 827.

Bureau of Labor Statistics study: U.S. Department of Labor, Bureau of Labor Statistics, *Cost of Living in the United States,* Bulletin no. 357 (Washington, D.C.: Government Printing Office, 1924), p. 391.

PAGE 464   Bryn Mawr graduate seminar: Quoted in Belle Boone Beard, *Electricity in the Home* (New York: Workers Education Bureau Press, 1927), p. 11.

"Relatively recent factors": Beard, *Electricity in the Home,* p. 9.

Reading Sources: *"At the Flick of a Switch"*

Read the selection, surveying it to identify key terms and important concepts. Highlight these phrases and ideas, and then answer these questions.

1. This selection discusses the development of both gas and electricity. Where does Strasser move from her discussion of gas to her treatment of electricity? How does she signal her change of subject to her readers?
2. Why, according to Strasser, was control of the gas companies in the hands of bankers and merchants?
3. What device does Strasser use to link paragraphs 8 and 9? 24 and 25?
4. What was the role of the 1893 Columbian Exposition in the development of advances in technology?
5. What was the significance of Edison's decision to link the price of electricity to the price of gaslight?
6. Highlight several points Strasser supplies to support this statement in paragraph 16: "In the end . . . the whole thing was a matter for experts."
7. In what respects were the predictions of the Bryn Mawr College study (1925– 26) about the future of electricity accurate? Which of their predictions proved inaccurate?
8. What is Strasser's thesis? How does her detailed factual information support this thesis?

Reacting to Sources

Reread the selection carefully, making marginal notes to aid comprehension and reinforce connections. Then further annotate the selection if you need to do so in order to answer any of these questions. (You may already have addressed some of the questions in your marginal notes.)

1. Using a dictionary if necessary, supply brief marginal definitions of these words as they are used in this selection: *hopper* (1), *tallow* (2), *impeded* (2), *rudimentary* (3), *rosin* (5), *plebian* (8), *incandescent* (10), *engendered* (17), *bluing* (18), *garret* (18), *ravelings* (23).
2. Prepare a complete outline of the successive developments in the improve-

ments in gas and electrical technology as presented by Strasser. Be sure to include dates in your outline whenever possible.

3. Consider the wide geographical range from which Strasser draws her sources, her inclusion of accounts drawn from the writings and experiences of many different observers, and the range in the level of print and nonprint sources she cites. How does the nature and variety of these sources strengthen the essay? Explain in a journal entry.

4. In paragraph 11 Strasser says, "The Welsbach mantle kept the gas companies alive. . . ." Explain why in a marginal note.

5. In paragraph 12 Strasser says, "Most of the delighted housekeepers went home [from the Columbian Exposition] to wood and coal stoves and houses without plumbing; these were the only dishwashers they would see in a lifetime. To them, electric cooking was no more fantastic than gas." Write a journal entry in which you explore this comment further.

6. In a journal entry, consider Strasser's tone in this essay. Where does her matter-of-fact tone give way to irony? How is such irony consistent with her essay's purpose?

7. In marginal notes, identify the roles of each of these people in the development of gas and electricity: Samuel Leggett (3), Tessie du Motay and T. S. C. Lowe (6), Thomas Edison (13), J. P. Morgan (14), David Kenney (22).

8. In a journal entry, explore the connections between the rise of electricity and the "disappearing servant."

9. Write a journal entry in which you respond to the questions Strasser poses in paragraph 29.

10. In the essay's conclusion Strasser says, "American women must evaluate their dependence on extravagant energy consumption and on an industry devoted to wasteful production of unnecessary goods planned for obsolescence." Do you agree or disagree? Explain your position in a journal entry.

Working with Sources

1. Write a fifty-word summary of paragraphs 27–28.
2. Write a critique of the ideas in paragraph 17.
3. Write a journal entry in which you explore your reactions to these quotations from "At the Flick of a Switch":

"at the end of the [nineteenth] century, gas was still very much a 'fuel of the future' for domestic cooking and heating" (10).

"Electric service, available in most cities by the turn of the century, spread rapidly in urban areas after World War I" (28).

"Hooked on power . . . American households become ever more prey to the effects of corporate decision making on daily life" (32).

Be sure to integrate the quotations smoothly into your writing.

4. Paraphrase the ideas in paragraph 1.
5. Write a one-paragraph synthesis that blends ideas in paragraph 32 of this selection and paragraph 23 of "Medical Practice and the Local Transportation Revolution" (pp. 445 – 452).

Writing with Sources: Using a Single Source

Integrating information from "At the Flick of a Switch" with your own ideas, write an essay on one of these topics. Be sure to acknowledge ideas that are not your own.

1. Strasser's essay traces the development of gas and electricity, but its central purpose is not to contrast them. Assess the relative merits of the two fuels at each of several key stages in their development.
2. Strasser devotes paragraphs 19 and 20 and sections of paragraphs 24 – 26 to analyzing the methods through which advertisers in the late nineteenth and early twentieth centuries promoted the benefits of electricity. Consider the ways in which today's print and television advertising promote electricity and the labor-saving devices it makes possible. What features do today's advertisements share with earlier ones? In what ways are they different? How do you account for the similarities and the differences you observe?
3. Paragraph 25 identifies a number of "highly specialized appliances" available in the 1930s. Today, these and many other such specialized electrical gadgets still exist. Identify and evaluate a number of these appliances in order to reach a conclusion about the value of the contribution they make to our lives.

Why Smaller Refrigerators Can Preserve the Human Race

Appletree Rodden

Appletree Rodden, a former biochemical researcher at Stanford University, later became a member of the Staatstheater Ballet Company. He now lives in Kassel, West Germany. In this essay, published in *Harper's* in 1975, Rodden suggests that we stop and think about whether or not bigger and more complex technology will necessarily change the quality of our lives for the better.

1   Once, long ago, people had special little boxes called refrigerators in which milk, meat, and eggs could be kept cool. The grandchildren of these simple devices are large enough to store whole cows, and they reach temperatures comparable to those at the South Pole. Their operating costs increase

each year, and they are so complicated that few home handymen attempt to repair them on their own.

2   Why has this change in size and complexity occurred in America? It has not taken place in many areas of the technologically advanced world (the average West German refrigerator is about a yard high and less than a yard wide, yet refrigeration technology in Germany is quite advanced). Do we really need (or even want) all that space and cold?

3   The benefits of a large refrigerator are apparent: a saving of time (one grocery-shopping trip a week instead of several), a saving of money (the ability to buy expensive, perishable items in larger, cheaper quantities), a feeling of security (if the car breaks down or if famine strikes, the refrigerator is well stocked). The costs are there, too, but they are not so obvious.

4   Cost number one is psychological. Ever since the refrigerator began to grow, food has increasingly become something we buy to store rather than to eat. Few families go to market daily for their daily bread. The manna in the wilderness could be gathered for only one day at a time. The ancient distaste for making food a storage item is echoed by many modern psychiatrists who suggest that such psychosomatic disorders as obesity are often due to the patient's inability to come to terms with the basic transitoriness of life. Research into a relationship between excessive corpulence and the size of one's refriger- ator has not been extensive, but we might suspect one to be there.

5   Another cost is aesthetic. In most of Europe, where grocery marketing is still a part of the daily rhythm, one can buy tomatoes, lettuce, and the like picked on the day of purchase. Many European families have modest refrigera- tors for storing small items (eggs, milk, butter) for a couple of days, but the concept of buying large quantities of food to store in the refrigerator is not widely accepted. Since fresh produce is easily available in Europe, most people buy it daily.

6   Which brings to mind another price the large refrigerator has cost us: the friendly neighborhood market. In America, time is money. A large refrigerator means fewer time-consuming trips to the grocery store. One member of a deep-freeze-owning family can do the grocery shopping once or twice a month rather than daily. Since shopping trips are infrequent, most people have been willing to forego the amenities of the little store around the corner in favor of the lower prices found in the supermarket.

7   If refrigerators weren't so large — that is, if grocery marketing were a daily affair — the "entertainment surcharge" of buying farm-fresh food in a smaller, more intimate setting might carry some weight. But as it is, there is not really that much difference between eggs bought from Farmer Brown's wife and eggs bought from the supermarket which in turn bought them from Eggs Incorporated, a firm operated out of Los Angeles that produces 200,000 eggs a day from chickens that are kept in gigantic warehouses lighted artificially on an eighteen-hour light-and-dark cycle and produce one-and-a-half times as many eggs — a special breed of chickens who die young and insane. Not much difference if you don't mind eating eggs from crazy chickens.

8   Chalk up Farmer and Mrs. Brown as cost number four of the big refrigera- tor. The small farmer can't make it in a society dominated by supermarkets and

big refrigerators; make way for superfarmers, super yields, and pesticides (cost number five).

9   Cost number six of the big refrigerator has been the diminution of regional food differences. Of course the homogenization of American fare cannot be blamed solely on the availability of frozen food. Nonetheless, were it not for the trend toward turning regional specialties into frozen dinners, it might still be possible to experience novelty closer to home.

10   So much for the disadvantages of the big refrigerator. What about the advantages of the small one? First of all, it would help us to "think small," which is what we must learn anyway if the scary predictions of the Club of Rome *(The Limits of Growth)* are true. The advent of smaller refrigerators would set the stage for reversing the "big-thinking" trends brought on with the big refrigerator, and would eventually change our lives.

11   Ivan Illich makes the point in *Tools for Conviviality* that any tool we use (the automobile, standardized public education, public-health care, the refrigerator) influences the individual, his society, and the relationship between the two. A person's automobile is a part of his identity. The average Volkswagen owner has a variety of characteristics (income, age, occupation) significantly different from those of the average Cadillac owner. American society, with more parking lots than parks, and with gridded streets rather than winding lanes, would be vastly different without the private automobile. Similar conclusions can be drawn about any of the tools we use. They change us. They change our society. Therefore, it behooves us to think well before we decide which tool to use to accomplish a given task. Do we want tools that usurp power unto themselves, the ones called "non-convivial" by Illich?

12   The telephone, a "convivial tool," has remained under control; it has not impinged itself on society or on the individual. Each year it has become more efficient, and it has not prevented other forms of communication (letter writing, visits). The world might be poorer without the telephone, but it would not be grossly different. Telephones do not pollute, are not status symbols, and interact only slightly (if at all) with one's self-image.

13   So what about the refrigerator? Or back to the more basic problem to which the refrigerator was a partial answer: what about our supply of food? When did we decide to convert the emotion-laden threat of starvation from a shared community problem (of societal structure: farm-market-home) to a personal one (of storage)? How did we decide to accept a thawed block taken from a supermarket's freezer as a substitute for the voluptuous shapes, smells, and textures of fresh fruits and vegetables obtained from complex individual sources?

14   The decision for larger refrigerators has been consistent with a change in food-supply routes from highly diversified "trails" (from small farms to neighborhood markets) to uniform, standardized highways (from large farms to centrally located supermarkets). Desirable meals are quick and easy rather than rich and leisurely. Culinary artistry has given way to efficiency, the efficiency of the big refrigerator.

15   People have a natural propensity for running good things into the ground. Mass production has been a boon to mankind, but its reliance on homogeneity

precludes its being a paradigm for all areas of human life. Our forebears and contemporaries have made it possible to mass-produce almost anything. An equally challenging task now lies with us: to choose which things of this world should be mass-produced, and how the standards of mass production should influence other standards we hold dear.

16   Should houses be mass-produced? Should education? Should food? Which brings us back to refrigerators. How does one decide how large a refrigerator to buy, considering one's life, one's society, and the world, and not simply the question of food storage?

17   As similar questions are asked about more and more of the things we mass-produce, mass production will become less of a problem and more of a blessing. As cost begins to be measured not only in dollars spent and minutes saved, but in total richness acquired, perhaps smaller refrigerators will again make good sense. A small step backward along some of the roads of "techno-logical progress" might be a large step forward for mankind, and one our age is uniquely qualified to make.

Reading Sources: "Why Smaller Refrigerators Can Preserve the Human Race"

Read the selection, surveying it to identify key terms and important concepts. Highlight these phrases and ideas, and then answer these questions.

1. Evaluate Rodden's opening strategy. What are the advantages and disadvan-tages of his first paragraph's tone and style?
2. Why does Rodden present the benefits of large refrigerators before moving on to discuss their costs?
3. How does Rodden use repetition and parallelism to focus his readers' attention on the costs of a large refrigerator? Highlight each of the costs he enumerates.
4. How does Rodden signal to his readers that he is moving from a discussion of the disadvantages of large refrigerators to the advantages of small ones? Could another transitional strategy have been more effective? Explain.
5. Rodden uses an informal style marked by contractions, colloquialisms like "chalk up" (8), and incomplete sentences. Identify as many examples as possi-ble of this essay's informal style. How can you account for such style in a sophisticated periodical aimed at well-educated readers?
6. Evaluate the effectiveness of Rodden's use of rhetorical questions (those which the reader is not expected to answer).
7. In one sentence, state Rodden's thesis.

Reacting to Sources

Reread the selection carefully, making marginal notes to aid comprehension and reinforce connections. Then further annotate the selection if you need to do so in order to answer any of these questions. (You may already have addressed some of the questions in your marginal notes.)

1. Using a dictionary if necessary, supply brief marginal definitions of these words as they are used in this selection: *manna* (4), *psychosomatic* (4), *transitoriness* (4), *corpulence* (4), *aesthetic* (5), *amenities* (6), *diminution* (9), *homogenization* (9), *behooves* (11), *convivial* (12), *impinged* (12), *voluptuous* (13), *propensity* (15), *precludes* (15), *paradigm* (15), *forebears* (15).
2. Does Rodden really believe smaller refrigerators can preserve the human race? In a journal entry, explain the essay's title.
3. Outline the paragraph cluster beginning with paragraph 4 and extending through paragraph 9.
4. Formulate three questions whose answers could help broaden your understanding of the ideas in paragraph 5.
5. In a marginal note, explain what Rodden means in paragraph 7 by the expression "entertainment surcharge."
6. In paragraph 11 Rodden says, "Similar conclusions can be drawn about any of the tools we use. They change us. They change our society." Explore this idea further in a journal entry.
7. In a marginal note, give two examples of your own to support this statement of Rodden's: "People have a natural propensity for running good things into the ground" (15).
8. Are there passages in this essay that make you suspect Rodden is not being completely serious? If so, write a journal entry in which you identify any such passages and explain why you feel they were not intended to be taken seriously. If not, explain why you feel Rodden is serious throughout.
9. In a marginal note, explain what Rodden means by this statement: "Mass production has been a boon to mankind, but its reliance on homogeneity precludes its being a paradigm for all areas of human life" (15).
10. Do you agree or disagree with Rodden's concluding sentence? Explain your feelings in a journal entry, giving examples to support your position.
11. In a journal entry, apply Rodden's criticism of large refrigerators to the personal computer. Are his arguments valid in this case?
12. Is Rodden fair? Does he display a bias? Explain in a journal entry.
13. In a journal entry, explore the implications of the ideas Rodden presents in paragraph 16.

Working with Sources

1. Write a one-paragraph summary of paragraphs 4–9.
2. Write a critique of the ideas in paragraph 12.
3. Write a journal entry in which you explore your reactions to these quotations from "Why Smaller Refrigerators Can Preserve the Human Race":

    "In America, time is money" (6).

"Desirable meals are quick and easy rather than rich and leisurely" (14).

"Should houses be mass-produced? Should education? Should food?" (16).

Be sure to integrate the quotations smoothly into your writing.

4. Paraphrase the ideas in paragraph 4.
5. Write a one-paragraph synthesis that blends ideas in paragraph 12 of this selection and paragraph 17 of "Medical Practice and the Local Transportation Revolution" (pp. 445 – 452).

Writing with Sources: Using a Single Source

Integrating information from "Why Smaller Refrigerators Can Save the Human Race" with your own ideas, write an essay on one of these topics. Be sure to acknowledge ideas that are not your own.

1. Consider the flaws in Rodden's argument, and write an essay arguing the continuing need for large —and perhaps even larger— refrigerators.
2. Write an essay with this thesis: "A small step backward along some of the roads of 'technological progress' might be a large step forward for mankind, and one our age is uniquely qualified to make" (17). Support your thesis with examples.
3. Answer the question Rodden poses in paragraph 2: "Why has this change in size and complexity occurred in America?" You might want to consider parallel developments such as the growth of suburbia, the growth of supermarkets, the increasing number of automobiles, and the rising number of women entering the work force.

From *The Soul of a New Machine*

Tracy Kidder

Tracy Kidder was born in 1945. He received his B.A. from Harvard and a Master's degree in fine arts from the University of Iowa. After serving in Army intelligence in Vietnam, he became a writer. Today he is a contributing editor for the *Atlantic Monthly* and a contributor to newspapers and magazines like *The New York Times Book Review, Science '83,* and *Country Journal.* His first book was *The Road to Yuba City: A Journey into the Juan Corona Murders* (1974); most recently, he has published *House* (1985). Kidder is best known, however, for his 1982 book, *The Soul of a New Machine,* winner of both the Pulitzer Prize and the American Book Award. The book follows a group of Data General Corporation engineers as they try, over a period of a year and a half, to create a super-minicomputer. In the following excerpt from the book, Kidder takes a break from the National Computer Conference, a yearly fair held by the computer industry, to reflect on the impact of computers on our society.

1   Norbert Wiener coined the term *cybernetics* in order to describe the study of "control and communication in the animal and the machine." In 1947 he wrote that because of the development of the "ultra-rapid computing machine, . . . the average human being of mediocre attainments or less" might end up having "nothing to sell that is worth anyone's money to buy." Although Wiener clearly intended this as a plea for humane control over the development and application of computers, many people who have written about these machines' effects on society have quoted Wiener's statement as though it were a claim of fact; and some, particularly the computer's boosters, have held the remark up to ridicule — "See, it hasn't happened."

2   Since Wiener, practically every kind of commentator on modern society, from cartoonists to academic sociologists, has taken a crack at the sociology of computers. A general feeling has held throughout: that these machines constitute something special, set apart from all the others that have come before. Maybe it has been a kind of chronocentrism, a conviction that the new machines of your own age must rank as the most stupendous or the scariest ever; but whatever the source, computers have acquired great mystique. Almost every commentator has assured the public that the computer is bringing on a revolution. By the 1970s it should have been clear that *revolution* was the wrong word. And it should not have been surprising to anyone that in many cases the technology had served as a prop to the status quo. The enchantment seemed enduring, nevertheless. So did many of the old arguments.

3   "Artificial intelligence" had always made for the liveliest of debates. Maybe the name itself was preposterous and its pursuit, in any case, something that people shouldn't undertake. Maybe in promoting the metaphorical relationship between people and machines, cybernetics tended to cheapen and corrupt human perceptions of human intelligence. Or perhaps this science promised to advance the intelligence of people as well as of machines and to imbue the species with a new, exciting power.

4   "Silicon-based life would have a lot of advantages over carbon-based life," a young engineer told me once. He said he believed in a time when the machines would "take over." He snapped his fingers and said, "Just like that." He seemed immensely pleased with that thought. To me, though, the prospects for truly intelligent computers looked comfortably dim.

5   To some the crucial issue was privacy. In theory, computers should be able to manage, more efficiently than people, huge amounts of a society's information. In the sixties there was proposed a "National Data Bank," which would, theoretically, improve the government's efficiency by allowing agencies to share information. The fact that such a system could be abused did not mean it would be, proponents said; it could be constructed in such a way as to guarantee benign use. Nonsense, said opponents, who managed to block the proposal; no matter what the intent or the safeguards, the existence of such a system would inevitably lead toward the creation of a police state.

6   Claims and counterclaims about the likely effects of computers on work in America had also abounded since Wiener. Would the machines put enormous numbers of people out of work? Or would they actually increase levels of employment? By the late seventies, it appeared, they had done neither. Well, then, maybe computers would eventually take over hateful and dangerous jobs and in general free people from drudgery, as boosters like to say. Some anecdotal evidence suggested, though, that they might be used extensively to increase the reach of top managers crazed for efficiency and thus would serve as tools to destroy the last vestiges of pleasant, interesting work.

7   Dozens of other points of argument existed. Were computers making nuclear war more or less likely? Had the society's vulnerability to accident and sabotage increased or decreased, now that computers had been woven inextricably into the management of virtually every enterprise in America? . . .

8   . . . Observing the familiar chaos of a New York City street, I was struck by how unnoticeable the computer revolution was. You leave a bazaar like the NCC [National Computer Conference] expecting to find that your perceptions of the world outside will have been altered, but there was nothing commensurate in sight — no cyborgs, half machine, half protoplasm, tripping down the street; no armies of unemployed, carrying placards denouncing the computer; no TV cameras watching. . . . Computers were everywhere, of course — in the café's beeping cash registers and the microwave oven and the jukebox, in the traffic lights, under the hoods of the honking cars snarled out there on the street (despite those traffic lights), in the airplanes overhead — but the visible differences somehow seemed insignificant.

9   Computers had become less noticeable as they had become smaller, more reliable, more efficient, and more numerous. Surely this happened by design. Obviously, to sell the devices far and wide, manufacturers had to strive to make them easy to use and, wherever possible, invisible. Were computers a profound, unseen hand?

10   In *The Coming of Post-Industrial Society*, Daniel Bell asserted that new machines introduced in the nineteenth century, such as the railroad train, made larger changes in "the lives of individuals" than computers have. Tom West liked to say: "Let's talk about bulldozers. Bulldozers have had a hell of a lot bigger effect on people's lives." The latter half of the twentieth century, some say, has witnessed an increase in social scale — in the size of organizations, for instance. Computers probably did not create the growth of conglomerates and multinational corporations, but they certainly have abetted it. They make fine tools for the centralization of power, if that's what those who buy them want to do with them. They are handy greed-extenders. Computers performing tasks as prosaic as the calculating of payrolls greatly extend the reach of managers in high positions; managers on top can be in command of such aspects of their businesses to a degree they simply could not be before computers.

11   Obviously, computers have made differences. They have fostered the development of spaceships — as well as a great increase in junk mail. The computer boom has brought the marvelous but expensive diagnostic device known

as the CAT scanner, as well as a host of other medical equipment; it has given rise to machines that play good but rather boring chess, and also, on a larger game board, to a proliferation of remote-controlled weapons in the arsenals of nations. Computers have changed ideas about waging war and about pursuing science, too. It is hard to see how contemporary geophysics or meteorology or plasma physics can advance very far without them now. Computers have changed the nature of research in mathematics, though not every mathematician would say it is for the better. And computers have become a part of the ordinary conduct of businesses of all sorts. They really help, in some cases.

12   Not always, though. One student of the field has estimated that about forty percent of commercial applications of computers have proved uneconomical, in the sense that the job the computer was bought to perform winds up costing more to do after the computer's arrival than it did before. Most computer companies have boasted that they aren't just selling machines, they're selling *productivity*. ("We're not in competition with each other," said a PR man. "We're in competition with labor.") But that clearly isn't always true. Sometimes they're selling paper-producers that require new legions of workers to push that paper around.

13   Coming from the fair, it seemed to me that computers have been used in ways that are salutary, in ways that are dangerous, banal and cruel, and in ways that seem harmless if a little silly. But what fun making them can be!

14   A reporter who had covered the computer industry for years tried to sum up for me the bad feelings he had acquired on his beat. "Everything is quantified," he said. "Whether it's the technology or the way people use it, it has an insidious ability to reduce things to less than human dimensions." Which is it, though: the technology or the way people use it? Who controls this technology? Can it be controlled?

15   Jacques Ellul, throwing up his hands, wrote that technology operates by its own terrible laws, alterable by no human action except complete abandonment of technique. More sensible, I think, Norbert Wiener, prophesied that the computer would offer "unbounded possibilities for good and for evil," and he advanced, faintly, the hope that the contributors to this new science would nudge it in a humane direction. But he also invoked the fear that its development would fall "into the hands of the most irresponsible and venal of our engineers." One of the best surveys of the studies of the effects of computers ends with an appeal to the "computer professionals" that they exercise virtue and restraint. . . .

Reading Sources: from **The Soul of a New Machine**

Read the selection, surveying it to identify key terms and important concepts. Highlight these phrases and ideas, and then answer these questions.

1. List the positive and negative effects of the advent of computers as identified by Kidder.

2. How does Kidder link paragraphs 1 and 2? 6 and 7? 11 and 12? What techniques does he use to connect the ideas in paragraph 6?
3. Throughout the selection, Kidder gives his readers a sampling of the ideas of others, from Norbert Wiener and Daniel Bell to his fellow workers. Why does Kidder present this variety of opinions?
4. Paragraph 11 summarizes some of the computer's effects on society. Highlight the verbs in the paragraph that indicate this causal connection.
5. In one sentence, state Kidder's thesis.

Reacting to Sources

Reread the selection carefully, making marginal notes to aid comprehension and reinforce connections. Then further annotate the selection if you need to do so in order to answer any of these questions. (You may already have addressed some of the questions in your marginal notes.)

1. Using a dictionary if necessary, supply brief marginal definitions of these words as they are used in this selection: *chronocentrism* (2), *mystique* (2), *metaphorical* (3), *imbue* (3), *inextricably* (7), *commensurate* (8), *abetted* (10), *prosaic* (10), *fostered* (11), *proliferation* (11), *salutary* (13), *banal* (13), *quantified* (14), *insidious* (14), *venal* (15).
2. Kidder mentions Norbert Wiener and Daniel Bell in this selection, and he quotes information from their books. In a reference work, locate information to help you identify these two men and evaluate their books. Then write a journal entry in which you assess the wisdom of Kidder's decision to refer to them.
3. What is "artificial intelligence"? Explain in a marginal note.
4. In paragraph 2 Kidder notes that commentators on modern society tend to agree that computers are "something special, set apart from all the [machines] that have come before." Do you agree or disagree? Explain your position in a journal entry.
5. In paragraph 5 Kidder briefly summarizes arguments for and against a National Data Bank. Would you support or oppose such a system? Explain in a journal entry.
6. Does Kidder seem to be concluding that computers have been a positive or a negative force in our society? Or does his position lie somewhere between the two extremes? Explain in a journal entry.
7. What purpose does paragraph 8 serve in this selection? Explain in a marginal note.
8. Write three questions whose answers could enhance your understanding of the ideas in paragraph 10.
9. Give three examples to support Kidder's general statement in paragraph 11 that "computers have become a part of the ordinary conduct of business of all sorts."
10. In a marginal note, identify Jacques Ellul (15). Use a reference work to help you if necessary.

11. In a journal entry, consider possible connections between this essay and your own experiences with computers.

Working with Sources

1. Write a two-sentence summary of paragraph 6.
2. Write a critique of the ideas in paragraph 9.
3. Write a journal entry in which you explore your reactions to these quotations from *The Soul of a New Machine:*

   "Almost every commentator has assured the public that the computer is bringing on a revolution" (2).

   "Obviously, computers have made differences" (11).

   "Who controls this technology? Can it be controlled"? (14)

   Be sure to integrate the quotations smoothly into your writing.
4. Paraphrase the ideas in paragraph 3.
5. Write a one-paragraph synthesis that blends the ideas of Daniel Bell and Tom West, quoted in paragraph 10 of this selection, and paragraph 1 of "At the Flick of a Switch" (pp. 454 – 467).

Writing with Sources: Using a Single Source

Integrating information from the selection from *The Soul of a New Machine* with your own ideas, write an essay on one of these topics. Be sure to acknowledge ideas that are not your own.

1. Is the computer "bringing on a revolution," or is it rather "a prop to the status quo" (2)? Write an essay supporting your position.
2. In paragraph 8 Kidder observes that computers are an all-pervasive — although often unnoticeable — force in our society. Compare the unseen presence — and power — of the computer with the subtle but significant influence of another machine.
3. In paragraph 11 Kidder summarizes some of the differences computers have made in our lives. Consider the narrower question of the effects of the computer on your life as a student.

Writing with Sources: Using Multiple Sources

Integrating information from sources in this chapter with your own ideas, write an essay on one of the topics that follow. Be sure to acknowledge ideas that are not your own.

1. As technology has brought change, it has also brought problems. Give a series of examples to support this thesis. Whenever possible, suggest solutions to the problems you identify.
2. Consider the causal relationships among several different technological advances — those described in this chapter's selections , or others with which you are familiar. How does one advance pave the way for another? How does one predict problems with another? How does one make another necessary? possible? problematic? Respond to some or all of these questions.
3. Consider the effects — both positive and negative — on your own day-to-day life of several different technological improvements.
4. Choose one machine or appliance that was not in regular use fifty years ago. Briefly summarize its uses today, and then consider how your life would be different without it.
5. Does our dependence on machines have the power to dehumanize our society? To what extent, if any, does a machine-dominated society risk sacrificing its respect for the individual? Discuss these ideas.

PART III

Essays for Further Reading

The section that follows includes three chapters: "Coming of Age," "The Nature of Violence," and "Life in America." Unlike previous chapters, whose questions were designed to guide you through the process of reading and reacting to sources and extracting information from them, these chapters assume that you no longer need such close guidance. By now, you should be able to question and comment on material on your own, selecting useful ideas and integrating them logically into your writing. Therefore, the question sets "Reading Sources," "Reacting to Sources," and "Working with Sources" are not included. In this section, you are encouraged to work on your own to develop papers on the topics suggested in "Writing with Sources: Using a Single Source" at the end of each essay and "Writing with Sources: Using Multiple Sources" at the end of each chapter.

12

Coming of Age

Growing-up rituals and experiences differ from person to person and society to society, depending on factors like sex, ethnicity, geographic location, and economic and social class. Despite such differences, however, certain similarities are also apparent: growing up is a time of questioning and learning, a time to develop a sense of oneself and a sense of how that self can connect with others. The authors of the six essays in this chapter represent a variety of backgrounds and a variety of perspectives on the growing-up experience.

For Joyce Howe, a Chinese-American woman born in 1958, the most vivid memories of her childhood center on the laundry her parents operated, and she recalls those memories in "Indelible Marks: Growing Up in a Chinese Laundry." Alfred Kazin's essay "At School in Brownsville" calls up memories of elementary school in the 1920s in a Brooklyn, New York, neighborhood of Eastern European immigrants. The focus of "Beauty: When the Other Dancer Is the Self," by Alice Walker, a black woman who grew up in Georgia, is on the author's changing self-image and how it was influenced by how others saw her. Ron Kovic, a Vietnam veteran from Long Island, New York, examines his patriotism and how it affected his later life in *Born on the Fourth of July*. Susan Allen Toth, in "Bookworm," considers the role of the Ames, Iowa, public library in her life. Finally, Russell Baker, a southerner, tells of his early decision to become a newspaper reporter in "Starting Out in Journalism."

Indelible Marks: Growing Up in a Chinese Laundry

Joyce Howe

Joyce Howe was born in 1958 and grew up in New York City, where her father owned a laundry. In this essay, published in the *Village Voice*, Howe tells the story of her life as a child of a laundryman, focusing on her memories of her father's work and her own changing attitudes toward that work.

1   It is a Sunday afternoon, and I am in a friend's East Village apartment, watching him sort laundry. He and his roommate throw a month's worth of dirty wash into large white drawstring bags and stretched-out pillowcases for the short trek down Second Avenue to a laundry where for four dollars the owner will wash 15 pounds.

2   The sheets, underwear, socks, towels, polos, and T's are bundled up into their bags, but the long-sleeved cotton shirts — the young professional uniforms —are set aside. The next day, these will be brought around the corner to the Chinese laundry, to the featureless man behind the counter, Mr. Lee or Mr. Chan, whose English is bad, who irons out the creases, and promises they will be ready next Wednesday.

3   "Oh, you're going to the Chinks!" laughs a visitor from the Upper West Side, whom I have just met. My face reddens. "In Riverdale, that's how we said we were going to the Chinese laundry," he says. I laugh. As the daughter of a former Chinese laundryman, I figure I have learned how.

4   My older sisters and I grew up in the back of laundries. In 1964, when I was six years old, we moved from my father's first laundry on Amsterdam Avenue to his last, in Jackson Heights. All of us lived in the rear rooms of the business just as the nearly 8000 mostly lone laundrymen in New York did at the turn of the century. A single long curtain divided the workplace from home.

5   I grew up with the sight of my stocky father wringing the milky, hand-mixed starch solution, that turned even the limpest collar stiff, from a clean shirt into a pail. Or my father was bent low over the "hong-chong," an ironing bed, built waist-high along the laundry wall from planks and boards and covered with a felt pad and muslin hammered in with tacks. (The "hong-chong" was traditionally used for storage too; a sheet of cloth hung down from it, hiding boxes of tickets, starch, and other tools.) In his right hand, the old heavy wood-handled electric iron glided across the front of a customer's button-down shirt or smoothed the corner of a cotton handkerchief.

6   My father preferred the dull smooth-bottomed irons with their own metal plates to the modern chrome steam irons, and he wet the wrinkled cloth with spray from two triggered hoses hanging overhead. As children, my sisters and I had terrific water-gun fights with those hoses.

7   My father, now 66, ran a laundry for almost 30 years. Born in Albany in 1916, he learned the business from his father, a former farmer from Canton who, with his wife, had sailed to America that same year. His father (my Goong, or paternal grandfather) had come to Albany with the same hopes of a

prosperous life that all immigrants bring. Still, I know very little about him, and very little about my father's youth. What I, the youngest of four daughters, know comes only from an old gilt-framed photograph sitting on my parents' dresser and from those occasions, perhaps fewer than 10, when I have asked questions and my father has answered.

8   The black-and-white photograph is a formal portrait of my grandparents and their three children — my father and his two younger sisters — taken sometime in the late 1920s. Goong sits tall; his thin body is hidden in a dark, American suit, a bow tie tight at this throat. There is a gentle look about his mouth, the barest smile on a long face which I like to think was kind. My father does not look like him at all. In the photo, he stands as an adolescent, in short pants and suit jacket, to the right of my seated grandmother; her bound feet are not noticeable. It is she whom my father resembles — the same broad forehead and nose, the full lips and heavy brows, the face set tight, betraying nothing.

9   What *do* I know? I know that my father, who raised his children as agnostics, was once an altar boy in an Albany Catholic church, and that after finishing the eighth grade he left school to work full time in his ailing father's store. I know that neighborhood children ran in and out of that store, calling Goong and my father names, like "Chink" or "Chinaman." Even now, when I bring up discrimination, he remembers the name-calling. He is insistent that such things no longer happen, certain that things are now better. He has told me that at age 18, Goong sent him off to China with a family friend, a laundryman from nearby Mechanicsville, for Chinese education. While there, according to his father's wishes, he met and married the friend's youngest daughter, my mother. Goong died during the year or so my father was away. A short time later, my grandmother died.

10   My father sailed back to the U.S. alone. He sold his father's laundry. After service in the army, he apprenticed with an uncle in Manhattan. This bachelor uncle, who'd arrived in New York years before, was debilitated by an old opium habit begun long ago to relieve the tedium of his work day.

11   My mother, because of strict immigration laws forbidding the entry of Chinese females into the country, was still in Canton. The pretty young wife, whom he hardly knew, wrote letters to my father, describing how she and my oldest sister who was born after he left, fled their rural village to escape the invading Japanese — how for days, they stayed with whoever would take them in. In each letter she asked for money, and my father always sent it. His literacy in Chinese was limited, so his uncle read my mother's letters aloud, translating my father's prompt responses into delicate Chinese script.

12   After his uncle's death (my father blames it on the opium), the laundry at 966 Amsterdam Avenue, on whose plate-glass window was painted the name "Jim Lee Laundry" in red for luck, was left to him. In 1949 my mother and oldest sister, then 12 years old, arrived in New York. My sister later married a young Chinese immigrant and for $4500, they soon bought their own laundry, 20 blocks south of my father's. They are still there, and the laundry is one of the few remaining in the area.

13   In Queens, on the block where we moved, my father was known as the man who ran the Chinese laundry, like Ernie who ran the deli, Benny the upholsterer, and the butcher a few doors down. To all of his customers he was Joe. And they — middle-aged housewives, young bachelors and students, mainly white — were known to him by a first name or by the unique indelible "mark" on their collars and hems. (This "mark," consisting of one or more characters, was written on each item for the duration of a customer's patronage; if he switched laundries, the new establishment usually did not bother changing it.) With all of them, as tickets, laundry bills, and change passed from hand to hand over the wide counter, my father exchanged comments: "Too much of this rain, huh?", "Yeah, the Mets looked lousy last night," or "How's the wife and the kids?"

14   Saturday was his busiest day. It was not only the day more customers came in and out, but it was also one of the three days on which the long and tedious job of laundry-sorting was done. The entire floor of the store became a dumping ground for soiled clothes. My father divided the laundry into piles: 10 to 15 sheets and pillowcases were bundled up into one sheet and the ticket stubs of the customers whose laundry made up the bundle were then stapled together and put aside for later identification. "Wet items," such as towels, underwear, and socks were separated into two categories — light and dark; shirts were separated into four categories — colored, white, starch, and no starch. Each pile of "wet items" and shirts was then placed in a laundry bag with its respective tag.

15   The bags and bundles were picked up Sunday morning by the truck drivers, who had names like Rocky and Louie, from the wholesale laundry or "wet wash" contracted by my father. ("Hand laundry" has been a misnomer since the late 1930s and '40s, when a whole new industry of Chinese-operated wholesale laundries and pressing concerns sprang up and contracted to do the actual washing and pressing for laundrymen.) Every Sunday, we were awakened from our sleep by the sound of the drivers' keys turning in the front door's locks.

16   When the "wet wash" drivers returned Monday with the previous day's load, the sheets and pillowcases, or "flat pieces," were wrapped in a heavy brown paper which my mother later would use for tablecloths. The shirts returned in the same bags they went out in. My father pulled out the bag of shirts to be starched and hand-ironed, leaving the rest for the shirt-press truck to pick up that night. On Tuesday night, they returned — clean, pressed, folded — in large square cardboard boxes, each shirt ringed in its own pale blue paper band.

17   For a short time, we had our own automatic dryer to take care of the damp "wet items" when they returned. After it broke down, irreparably, the dryer retired, and was left to hold stacks of comic books and board games. My sisters and I took turns making pilgrimages to the local laundromat, our metal shopping cart bent from the weight of the load. We wheeled those three blocks three times a week. On my turn, I always hoped that no one I knew would see me as I struggled with two hands to keep laundry and cart intact when maneu-

vering the high curbs. Even then, the irony of going from the laundry to the laundromat was not lost.

18   Of course, there were days when the system was off, when the shirt press might return its load late, or when my father didn't feel well enough to wrap every package. On those days, we were all expected to help. We made sure that the promise my father had made to customers on Saturday that their shirts would be ready by Wednesday was kept. Behind the tan curtain drawn across our plate-glass window every evening at seven and the door's pulled venetian blind, we settled into a tableau. My family formed a late-night assembly line, each member taking his place amid the shelves, boxes, white cones of string, rolls of wrapping paper, and the familiar fragrance of newly laundered cloth.

19   There were those customers who took an interest in my father's life and in his children, who gave my sisters and me candy, and asked how we were doing in school. Without offering any of his own, my father heard their problems, while making sure it was only a little starch they wanted or that their shirts should be hung rather than folded.

20   I was always glad when these customers came in. In my child's eyes, their interest somehow legitimized us. My sisters and I, who often wished our father ran a candy store instead, were not just seen as three faceless Chinese daughters with braids, dutifully making change, delivering laundry or cleaning up. We became individuals, known by our first names, with other concerns.

21   Hearing my father converse with the customers reassured me that not everyone saw his life revolving entirely around his livelihood. His identity was not solely that of the role of Chinese laundryman. He had interests in the outside world. He read the *Daily News* and the *Post*. He bet on the harness races with Benny the upholsterer, who drove him to the track. During the baseball season, he sat in the back, on the orange vinyl couch discarded from a friend's take-out restaurant, and watched the day games on TV, getting up at the sound of the front door's chimes as someone came in.

22   I needed the reassurance of others. It seemed as if it would be easier, on those endless forms handed out in school, to fill in "candy store owner" in the space for "father's occupation." Instead of "Chinese laundryman," my sisters taught me to write "Chinese laundry proprietor," as if the latter were somehow more respectable. No one else we knew at school lived behind a store.

23   Shouldn't our American-born father — who drank beer with his rice at dinner, who took us to James Bond movies and amusement parks, to LaGuardia airport to watch the planes take off — be something more than another laundryman? He wasn't an immigrant like his father, another Chinaman who came to find gold but found the washing industry instead.

24   My father retired when he was 60. I was a sophomore away at college; my family had bought a three-family brick house three years before. His average weekly income of $400 (considered "good business" for a hand laundry) had gradually plummeted to a low of $175 as the racial and economic face of our Jackson Heights neighborhood changed from middle-class whites to lower-income Hispanics. When his rent ($200 when he moved in 14 years earlier) threatened to double, my father let the laundry go.

25   There would have been no one to pass it on to. No only son to try and make a go of it. His younger children—who had spent hours after school and during weekends learning to sort laundry, count change quickly, and securely tie string—were all too grown, all too educated.

26   According to the New York Chinatown History Project, which has put together a traveling exhibit on the history of Chinese laundry workers in the United States, only an estimated 1000 hand laundries remain in the New York metropolitan area. The city's Department of Consumer Affairs, which licenses all "establishments which take in laundry" (except for dry cleaners) every two years, reports that as of September 13, there were only 305 licensed hand laundries in New York.

27   When my father retired, he referred his remaining customers to another laundry, owned by friends, two blocks away. His laundry and former home have since become in turn, a dry cleaner, a dress shop, a bodega, and another dress shop named "Fuego." On the few times I've driven by, I've looked carefully for its latest occupant, catching a quick glimpse of an iron gate instead.

28   I have a favorite photo of my father. It is in color. Taken two or three years ago in the garden which he and my mother tend behind the family house, my shirt-sleeved father is kneeling among the leafy green cabbage, tomato plants, and other vegetables growing in straight rows. His fine white hair is combed back from the broad forehead, black-rimmed spectacles frame his eyes. Looking straight at the camera, he is smiling.

29   I showed it once to my friend, laughing proudly, "Doesn't he look like a Russian dissident intellectual here?" But of course, he is not. The man in the photograph is my father. He used to run a Chinese laundry.

Writing with Sources: Using a Single Source

Integrating information from "Indelible Marks: Growing Up in a Chinese Laundry" with your own ideas, write an essay on one of these topics. Be sure to acknowledge ideas that are not your own.

1. Interview one of your parents, and then write a narrative essay tracing his or her professional life. Include background about your parent's childhood and education, and summarize each stage in his or her professional development.
2. Give an example of an incident or situation in which you felt ashamed of one of your parents. Looking back, do you feel your attitude was justified? Would your reaction be different today?
3. What indelible marks were made on you as a child by the work your parents did? Respond to this question in an essay.

At School in Brownsville

Alfred Kazin

Alfred Kazin was born in 1915 in Brooklyn, New York, and received his B.S. from City College of the City University of New York (1935) and his M.A. from Columbia University. He has been a literary editor for *The New Republic* and a contributing editor for *Fortune* magazine. He also has taught literature at a number of colleges and universities including Harvard University, Smith College, Amherst College, New York University, Princeton University, the University of California at Berkeley, and Hunter College. An outstanding literary critic, Kazin has received the George Polk Memorial Award for Criticism (1966), the Brandeis University Creative Arts Award (1973), and the Hubbell medal from the Modern Language Association (1982). Kazin has published a number of outstanding books, including *On Native Grounds* (1942), *A Walker in the City* (1951), *The Inmost Leaf* (1955), *Contemporaries* (1962), *Starting Out in the Thirties* (1965), *Bright Book of Life* (1973), *New York Jew* (1978), and *An American Procession* (1984). The following essay, from *A Walker in the City*, focuses on Kazin's experiences in elementary school during the 1920s in Brownsville, a Brooklyn neighborhood then inhabited by Jewish immigrants from eastern Europe.

1   All my early life lies open to my eye within five city blocks. When I passed the school, I went sick with all my old fear of it. With its standard New York public-school brown brick courtyard shut in on three sides of the square and the pretentious battlements overlooking that cockpit in which I can still smell the fiery sheen of the rubber ball, it looks like a factory over which has been imposed the façade of a castle. It gave me the shivers to stand up in that courtyard again; I felt as if I had been mustered back into the service of those Friday morning "tests" that were the terror of my childhood.

2   It was never learning I associated with that school: only the necessity to succeed, to get ahead of the others in the daily struggle to "make a good impression" on our teachers, who grimly, wearily, and often with ill-concealed distaste watched against our relapsing into the natural savagery they expected of Brownsville boys. The white, cool, thinly ruled record book sat over us from their desks all day long, and had remorselessly entered into it each day—in blue ink if we had passed, in red ink if we had not—our attendance, our conduct, our "effort," our merits and demerits; and to the last possible decimal point in calculation, our standing in an unending series of "tests"—surprise tests, daily tests, weekly tests, formal midterm tests, final tests. They never stopped trying to dig out of us whatever small morsel of fact we had managed to get down the night before. We had to prove that we were really alert, ready for anything, always in the race. That white thinly ruled record book figured in my mind as the judgment seat; the very thinness and remote blue lightness of its lines instantly showed its cold authority over me; so much space had been left on each page, columns and columns in which to note down everything about us, implacably and forever. As it lay there on a teacher's desk, I stared at it all day long with such fear and anxious propriety that I had no trouble believing that God, too, did nothing but keep such record books, and that on

the final day He would face me with an account in Hebrew letters whose phonetic dots and dashes looked strangely like decimal points counting up my every sinful thought on earth.

3   All teachers were to be respected like gods, and God Himself was the greatest of all school superintendents. Long after I had ceased to believe that our teachers could see with the back of their heads, it was still understood, by me, that they knew everything. They were the delegates of all visible and invisible power on earth — of the mothers who waited on the stoops every day after three for us to bring home tales of our daily triumphs; of the glacially remote Anglo-Saxon principal, whose very name was King; of the incalculably important Superintendent of Schools who would someday rubberstamp his name to the bottom of our diplomas in grim acknowledgment that we had, at last, given satisfaction to him, to the Board of Superintendents, and to our benefactor the City of New York — and so up and up, to the government of the United States and to the great Lord Jehovah Himself. My belief in teachers' unlimited wisdom and power rested not so much on what I saw in them — how impatient most of them looked, how wary — but on our abysmal humility, at least in those of us who were "good" boys, who proved by our ready compliance and "manners" that we wanted to get on. The road to a professional future would be shown us only as we pleased *them. Make a good impression the first day of the term, and they'll help you out. Make a bad impression, and you might as well cut your throat.* This was the first article of school folklore, whispered around the classroom the opening day of each term. You made the "good impression" by sitting firmly at your wooden desk, hands clasped; by silence for the greatest part of the live-long day; by standing up obsequiously when it was so expected of you; by sitting down noiselessly when you had answered a question; by "speaking nicely," which meant reproducing their painfully exact enunciation; by "showing manners," or an ecstatic submissiveness in all things; by outrageous flattery; by bringing little gifts at Christmas, on their birthdays, and at the end of the term — the well-known significance of these gifts being that they came not from us, but from our parents, whose eagerness in this matter showed a high level of social consideration, and thus raised our standing in turn.

4   It was not just our quickness and memory that were always being tested. Above all, in that word I could never hear without automatically seeing it raised before me in gold-plated letters, it was our *character.* I always felt anxious when I heard the word pronounced. Satisfactory as my "character" was, on the whole, except when I stayed too long in the playground reading; outrageously satisfactory, as I can see now, the very sound of the word as our teachers coldly gave it out from the end of their teeth, with a solemn weight on each dark syllable, immediately struck my heart cold with fear — they could not believe I really had it. Character was never something you had; it had to be trained in you, like a technique. I was never very clear about it. On our side *character* meant demonstrative obedience; but teachers already had it — how else could they have become teachers? They had it; the aloof Anglo-Saxon principal whom we remotely saw only on ceremonial occasions in the assembly

was positively encased in it; it glittered off his bald head in spokes of triumphant light; the President of the United States had the greatest conceivable amount of it. Character belonged to great adults. Yet we were constantly being driven onto it; it was the great threshold we had to cross. *Alfred Kazin, having shown proficiency in his course of studies and having displayed satisfactory marks of character . . .* Thus someday the hallowed diploma, passport to my further advancement in high school. But there — I could already feel it in my bones — they would put me through even more doubting tests of character; and after that, if I should be good enough and bright enough, there would be still more. *Character* was a bitter thing, racked with my endless striving to please. The school — from every last stone in the courtyard to the battlements frowning down at me from the walls — was only the stage for a trial. I felt that the very atmosphere of learning that surrounded us was fake — that every lesson, every book, every approving smile was only a pretext for the constant probing and watching of me, that there was not a secret in me that would not be decimally measured into that white record book. All week long I lived for the blessed sound of the dismissal gong at three o'clock on Friday afternoon.

5   I was awed by this system, I believed in it, I respected its force. The alternative was "going bad." The school was notoriously the toughest in our tough neighborhood, and the dangers of "going bad" were constantly impressed upon me at home and in school in dark whispers of the "reform school" and in examples of boys who had been picked up for petty thievery, rape, or flinging a heavy inkwell straight into a teacher's face. Behind any failure in school yawned the great abyss of a criminal career. Every refractory attitude doomed you with the sound "Sing Sing." Anything less than absolute perfection in school always suggested to my mind that I might fall out of the daily race, be kept back in the working class forever, or — dared I think of it? — fall into the criminal class itself.

6   I worked on a hairline between triumph and catastrophe. Why the odds should always have felt so narrow I understood only when I realized how little my parents thought of their own lives. It was not for myself alone that I was expected to shine, but for them — to redeem the constant anxiety of their existence. I was the first American child, their offering to the strange new God; I was to be the monument of their liberation from the shame of being — what they were. And that there was shame in this was a fact that everyone seemed to believe as a matter of course. It was in the gleeful discounting of themselves — what do we know? — with which our parents greeted every fresh victory in our savage competition for "high averages," for prizes, for a few condescending words of official praise from the principal at assembly. It was in the sickening invocation of "Americanism" — the word itself accusing us of everything we apparently were not. Our families and teachers seemed tacitly agreed that we were somehow to be a little ashamed of what we were. Yet it was always hard to say why this should be so. It was certainly not — in Brownsville! — because we were Jews, or simply because we spoke another language at home, or were absent on our holy days. It was rather that a "refined," "correct," "nice"

English was required of us at school that we did not naturally speak, and that
our teachers could never be quite sure we would keep. This English was
peculiarly the ladder of advancement. Every future young lawyer was known by
it. Even the Communists and Socialists on Pitkin Avenue spoke it. It was bright
and clean and polished. We were expected to show it off like a new pair of
shoes. When the teacher sharply called a question out, then your name, you
were expected to leap up, face the class, and eject those new words fluently off
the tongue.

7   There was my secret ordeal: I could never say anything except in the most
roundabout way; I was a stammerer. Although I knew all those new words from
my private reading — I read walking in the street, to and from the Children's
Library on Stone Avenue; on the fire escape and the roof; at every meal when
they would let me; read even when I dressed in the morning, propping my
book up against the drawers of the bureau as I pulled on my long black stockings — I could never seem to get the easiest words out with the right dispatch,
and would often miserably signal from my desk that I did not know the answer
rather than get up to stumble and fall and crash on every word. If, angry at
always being put down as lazy or stupid, I did get up to speak, the black
wooden floor would roll away under my feet, the teacher would frown at me in
amazement, and in unbearable loneliness I would hear behind me the groans
and laughter: *tuh-tuh-tuh-tuh.*

8   The word was my agony. The word that for others was so effortless and so
neutral, so unburdened, so simple, so exact, I had first to meditate in advance,
to see if I could make it, like a plumber fitting together odd lengths and shapes
of pipe. I was always preparing words I could speak, storing them away,
choosing between them. And often, when the word did come from my mouth
in its great and terrible birth, quailing and bleeding as if forced through a
thornbush, I would not be able to look the others in the face, and would walk
out in the silence, the infinitely echoing silence behind my back, to say it all
cleanly back to myself as I walked in the streets. Only when I was alone in the
open air, pacing the roof with pebbles in my mouth, as I had read Demosthe-
nes had done to cure himself of stammering; or in the street, where all words
seemed to flow from the length of my stride and the color of the houses as I
remembered the perfect tranquillity of a phrase in Beethoven's *Romance in F* I
could sing back to myself as I walked — only then was it possible for me to
speak without the infinite premeditations and strangled silences I toiled
through whenever I got up at school to respond with the expected, the exact
answer.

9   It troubled me that I could speak in the fullness of my own voice only
when I was alone on the streets, walking about. There was something unnatural
about it; unbearably isolated. I was not like the others! I was not like the
others! At midday, every freshly shocking Monday noon, they sent me away to a
speech clinic in a school in East New York, where I sat in a circle of lispers
and cleft palates and foreign accents holding a mirror before my lips and
rolling difficult sounds over and over. To be sent there in the full light of the
opening week, when everyone else was at school or going about his business,

made me feel as if I had been expelled from the great normal body of human-ity. I would gobble down my lunch on my way to the speech clinic and rush back to the school in time to make up for the classes I had lost. One day, one unforgettable dread day, I stopped to catch my breath on the corner of Sutter Avenue, near the wholesale fruit markets, where an old drugstore rose up over a great flight of steps. In the window were dusty urns of colored water floating off iron chains; cardboard placards advertising hairnets, Ex-Lax; a great illus-trated medical chart headed THE HUMAN FACTORY, which showed the exact course a mouthful of food follows as it falls from chamber to chamber of the body. I hadn't meant to stop there at all, only to catch my breath; but I so hated the speech clinic that I thought I would delay my arrival for a few minutes by eating my lunch on the steps. When I took the sandwich out of my bag, two bitterly hard pieces of hard salami slipped out of my hand and fell through a grate onto a hill of dust below the steps. I remember how sickeningly vivid an odd thread of hair looked on the salami, as if my lunch were turning stiff with death. The factory whistles called their short, sharp blasts stark through the middle of noon, beating at me where I sat outside the city's magnetic circle. I had never known, I knew instantly I would never in my heart again submit to, such wild passive despair as I felt at that moment, sitting on the steps before THE HUMAN FACTORY, where little robots gathered and shoveled the food from chamber to chamber of the body. They had put me out into the streets, I thought to myself; with their mirrors and their everlasting pulling at me to imitate their effortless bright speech and their stupefaction that a boy could stammer and stumble on every other English word he carried in his head, they had put me out into the streets, had left me high and dry on the steps of that drugstore staring at the remains of my lunch turning black and grimy in the dust.

Writing with Sources: Using a Single Source

Integrating information from "At School in Brownsville" with your own ideas, write an essay on one of these topics. Be sure to acknowledge all ideas that are not your own.

1. Think about your elementary school experiences and write an essay describing your memories.
2. In paragraph 2 of this selection Kazin says, "It was never learning that I asso-ciated with that school: only the necessity to succeed. . . ." Explain what Kazin means by this statement and explain why you agree or disagree with him.
3. Describe an experience that made you feel, as Kazin did, as if you "had been expelled from the normal body of humanity."

Beauty: When the Other Dancer Is the Self

Alice Walker

Alice Walker was born in 1944 and received her B.A. from Sarah Lawrence College in 1966. She is the author of numerous books of fiction, poetry, and essays. Her books include *Once* (1968), *The Third Life of George Copeland* (1970), *In Love and Trouble* (1973), *Langston Hughes, American Poet* (1973), *Revolutionary Petunias* (1974), *Meridian* (1976), *I Love Myself When I Am Laughing* (1979), *Good Night, Willie Lee, I'll See You in the Morning* (1979), *You Can't Keep a Good Woman Down* (1981), *The Color Purple* (1982), and *In Search of Our Mothers' Gardens* (1983), from which "Beauty: When the Other Dancer Is the Self" is excerpted. Walker has been the recipient of a number of prestigious awards for her writing, including the American Book Award and the Pulitzer Prize. In the selection that follows, Walker presents a series of vividly remembered scenes to recreate key incidents from her childhood and young adulthood.

1   It is a bright summer day in 1947. My father, a fat, funny man with beautiful eyes and a subversive wit, is trying to decide which of his eight children he will take with him to the county fair. My mother, of course, will not go. She is knocked out from getting most of us ready: I hold my neck stiff against the pressure of her knuckles as she hastily completes the braiding and then beribboning of my hair.

2   My father is the driver for the rich old white lady up the road. Her name is Miss Mey. She owns all the land for miles around, as well as the house in which we live. All I remember about her is that she once offered to pay my mother thirty-five cents for cleaning her house, raking up piles of her magnolia leaves, and washing her family's clothes, and that my mother — she of no money, eight children, and a chronic earache — refused it. But I do not think of this in 1947. I am two and a half years old. I want to go everywhere my daddy goes. I am excited at the prospect of riding in a car. Someone has told me fairs are fun. That there is room in the car for only three of us doesn't faze me at all. Whirling happily in my starchy frock, showing off my biscuit-polished patent-leather shoes and lavender socks, tossing my head in a way that makes my ribbons bounce, I stand, hands on hips, before my father. "Take me, Daddy," I say with assurance; "I'm the prettiest!"

3   Later, it does not surprise me to find myself in Miss Mey's shiny black car, sharing the back seat with the other lucky ones. Does not surprise me that I thoroughly enjoy the fair. At home that night I tell the unlucky ones all I can remember about the merry-go-round, the man who eats live chickens, and the teddy bears, until they say: that's enough, baby Alice. Shut up now, and go to sleep.

4   It is Easter Sunday, 1950. I am dressed in a green, flocked, scalloped-hem dress (handmade by my adoring sister, Ruth) that has its own smooth satin petticoat and tiny hot-pink roses tucked into each scallop. My shoes, new T-strap patent leather, again highly biscuit-polished. I am six years old and have learned one of the longest Easter speeches to be heard that day, totally

unlike the speech I said when I was two: "Easter lilies / pure and white / blossom in / the morning light." When I rise to give my speech I do so on a great wave of love and pride and expectation. People in the church stop rustling their new crinolines. They seem to hold their breath. I can tell they admire my dress, but it is my spirit, bordering on sassiness (womanishness), they secretly applaud.

5   "That girl's a little *mess*," they whisper to each other, pleased.

6   Naturally I say my speech without stammer or pause, unlike those who stutter, stammer, or, worst of all, forget. This is before the word "beautiful" exists in people's vocabulary, but "Oh, isn't she the *cutest* thing!" frequently floats my way. "And got so much sense!" they gratefully add . . . for which thoughtful addition I thank them to this day.

7 *It was great fun being cute. But then, one day, it ended.*

8 I am eight years old and a tomboy. I have a cowboy hat, cowboy boots, checkered shirt and pants, all red. My playmates are my brothers, two and four years older than I. Their colors are black and green, the only difference in the way we are dressed. On Saturday nights we all go to the picture show, even my mother; Westerns are her favorite kind of movie. Back home, "on the ranch," we pretend we are Tom Mix, Hopalong Cassidy, Lash LaRue (we've even named one of our dogs Lash LaRue); we chase each other for hours rustling cattle, being outlaws, delivering damsels from distress. Then my parents decide to buy my brothers guns. These are not "real" guns. They shoot "BBs," copper pellets my brothers say will kill birds. Because I am a girl, I do not get a gun. Instantly I am relegated to the position of Indian. Now there appears a great distance between us. They shoot and shoot at everything with their new guns. I try to keep up with my bow and arrows.

9   One day while I am standing on top of our makeshift "garage"—pieces of tin nailed across some poles—holding my bow and arrow and looking out toward the fields, I feel an incredible blow in my right eye. I look down just in time to see my brother lower his gun.

10   Both brothers rush to my side. My eye stings, and I cover it with my hand. "If you tell," they say, "we will get a whipping. You don't want that to happen, do you?" I do not. "Here is a piece of wire," says the older brother, picking it up from the roof; "say you stepped on one end of it and the other flew up and hit you." The pain is beginning to start. "Yes," I say. "Yes, I will say that is what happened." If I do not say this is what happened, I know my brothers will find ways to make me wish I had. But now I will say anything that gets me to my mother.

11   Confronted by our parents we stick to the lie agreed upon. They place me on a bench on the porch and I close my left eye while they examine the right. There is a tree growing from underneath the porch that climbs past the railing to the roof. It is the last thing my right eye sees. I watch as its trunk, its branches, and then its leaves are blotted out by the rising blood.

12   I am in shock. First there is intense fever, which my father tries to break

using lily leaves bound around my head. Then there are chills: my mother tries to get me to eat soup. Eventually, I do not know how, my parents learn what has happened. A week after the "accident" they take me to see a doctor. "Why did you wait so long to come?" he asks, looking into my eye and shaking his head. "Eyes are sympathetic," he says. "If one is blind, the other will likely become blind too."

13   This comment of the doctor's terrifies me. But it is really how I look that bothers me most. Where the BB pellet struck there is a glob of whitish scar tissue, a hideous cataract, on my eye. Now when I stare at people—a favorite pastime, up to now—they will stare back. Not at the "cute" little girl, but at her scar. For six years I do not stare at anyone, because I do not raise my head.

14 Years later, in the throes of a mid-life crisis, I ask my mother and sister whether I changed after the "accident." "No," they say, puzzled. "What do you mean?"

15   *What do I mean?*

16   I am eight, and, for the first time, doing poorly in school, where I have been something of a whiz since I was four. We have just moved to the place where the "accident" occurred. We do not know any of the people around us because this is a different county. The only time I see the friends I knew is when we go back to our old church. The new school is the former state penitentiary. It is a large stone building, cold and drafty, crammed to overflowing with boisterous, ill-disciplined children. On the third floor there is a huge circular imprint of some partition that has been torn out.

17   "What used to be here?" I ask a sullen girl next to me on our way past it to lunch.

18   "The electric chair," says she.

19   At night I have nightmares about the electric chair, and about all the people reputedly "fried" in it. I am afraid of the school, where all the students seem to be budding criminals.

20   "What's the matter with your eye?" they ask, critically.

21   When I don't answer (I cannot decide whether it was an "accident" or not), they shove me, insist on a fight.

22   My brother, the one who created the story about the wire, comes to my rescue. But then brags so much about "protecting" me, I become sick.

23   After months of torture at the school, my parents decide to send me back to our old community, to my old school. I live with my grandparents and the teacher they board. But there is no room for Phoebe, my cat. By the time my grandparents decide there *is* room, and I ask for my cat, she cannot be found. Miss Yarborough, the boarding teacher, takes me under her wing, and begins to teach me to play the piano. But soon she marries an African—a "prince," she says—and is whisked away to his continent.

24   At my old school there is at least one teacher who loves me. She is the teacher who "knew me before I was born" and bought my first baby clothes. It is she who makes life bearable. It is her presence that finally helps me turn on the one child at the school who continually calls me "one-eyed bitch." One day I simply grab him by his coat and beat him until I am satisfied. It is my teacher who tells me my mother is ill.

25 My mother is lying in bed in the middle of the day, something I have never seen. She is in too much pain to speak. She has an abscess in her ear. I stand looking down on her, knowing that if she dies, I cannot live. She is being treated with warm oils and hot bricks held against her cheek. Finally a doctor comes. But I must go back to my grandparents' house. The weeks pass but I am hardly aware of it. All I know is that my mother might die, my father is not so jolly, my brothers still have their guns, and I am the one sent away from home.

26   "You did not change," they say.

27   *Did I imagine the anguish of never looking up?*

28 I am twelve. When relatives come to visit I hide in my room. My cousin Brenda, just my age, whose father works in the post office and whose mother is a nurse, comes to find me. "Hello," she says. And then she asks, looking at my recent school picture, which I did not want taken, and on which the "glob," as I think of it, is clearly visible, "You still can't see out of that eye?"

29   "No," I say, and flop back on the bed over my book.

30   That night, as I do almost every night, I abuse my eye. I rant and rave at it, in front of the mirror. I plead with it to clear up before morning. I tell it I hate and despise it. I do not pray for sight. I pray for beauty.

31   "You did not change," they say.

32 I am fourteen and baby-sitting for my brother Bill, who lives in Boston. He is my favorite brother and there is a strong bond between us. Understanding my feelings of shame and ugliness he and his wife take me to a local hospital, where the "glob" is removed by a doctor named O. Henry. There is still a small bluish crater where the scar tissue was, but the ugly white stuff is gone. Almost immediately I become a different person from the girl who does not raise her head. Or so I think. Now that I've raised my head I win the boyfriend of my dreams. Now that I've raised my head I have plenty of friends. Now that I've raised my head classwork comes from my lips as faultlessly as Easter speeches did, and I leave high school as valedictorian, most popular student, and *queen,* hardly believing my luck. Ironically, the girl who was voted most beautiful in our class (and was) was later shot twice through the chest by a male companion, using a "real" gun, while she was pregnant. But that's another story in itself. Or is it?

33   "You did not change," they say.

34 It is now thirty years since the "accident." A beautiful journalist comes to visit and to interview me. She is going to write a cover story for her magazine that focuses on my latest book. "Decide how you want to look on the cover," she says. "Glamorous, or whatever."

35   Never mind "glamorous," it is the "whatever" that I hear. Suddenly all I can think of is whether I will get enough sleep the night before the photography session: if I don't, my eye will be tired and wander, as blind eyes will.

36   At night in bed with my lover I think up reasons why I should not appear on the cover of a magazine. "My meanest critics will say I've sold out," I say. "My family will now realize I write scandalous books."

37   "But what's the real reason you don't want to do this?" he asks.

38   "Because in all probability," I say in a rush, "my eye won't be straight."

39   "It will be straight enough," he says. Then, "Besides, I thought you'd made your peace with that."

40   And I suddenly remember that I have.

41   *I remember:*

42   I am talking to my brother Jimmy, asking if he remembers anything unusual about the day I was shot. He does not know I consider that day the last time my father, with his sweet home remedy of cool lily leaves, chose me, and that I suffered and raged inside because of this. "Well," he says, "all I re-member is standing by the side of the highway with Daddy, trying to flag down a car. A white man stopped, but when Daddy said he needed somebody to take his little girl to the doctor, he drove off."

43   *I remember:*

44   I am in the desert for the first time. I fall totally in love with it. I am so overwhelmed by its beauty, I confront for the first time, consciously, the meaning of the doctor's words years ago: "Eyes are sympathetic. If one is blind, the other will likely become blind too." I realize I have dashed about the world madly, looking at this, looking at that, storing up images against the fading of the light. *But I might have missed seeing the desert!* The shock of that possibility — and gratitude for over twenty-five years of sight — sends me literally to my knees. Poem after poem comes — which is perhaps how poets pray.

ON SIGHT

I am so thankful I have seen
The Desert
And the creatures in the desert
And the desert Itself.

The desert has its own moon
Which I have seen
With my own eye.

There is no flag on it.

Trees of the desert have arms
All of which are always up
That is because the moon is up
The sun is up
Also the sky
The stars
Clouds
None with flags.

If there *were* flags, I doubt
the trees would point.
Would you?

45   *But mostly, I remember this:*

46   I am twenty-seven, and my baby daughter is almost three. Since her birth

I have worried about her discovery that her mother's eyes are different from other people's. Will she be embarrassed? I think. What will she say? Every day she watches a television program called "Big Blue Marble." It begins with a picture of the earth as it appears from the moon. It is bluish, a little battered-looking, but full of light, with whitish clouds swirling around it. Every time I see it I weep with love, as if it is a picture of Grandma's house. One day when I am putting Rebecca down for her nap, she suddenly focuses on my eye. Something inside me cringes, gets ready to try to protect myself. All children are cruel about physical differences, I know from experience, and that they don't always mean to be is another matter. I assume Rebecca will be the same.

47   But no-o-o-o. She studies my face intently as we stand, her inside and me outside her crib. She even holds my face maternally between her dimpled little hands. Then, looking every bit as serious and lawyerlike as her father, she says, as if it may just possibly have slipped my attention: "Mommy, there's a *world* in your eye." (As in, "Don't be alarmed, or do anything crazy.") And then, gently, but with great interest: "Mommy, where did you *get* that world in your eye?"

48   For the most part, the pain left then. (So what, if my brothers grew up to buy even more powerful pellet guns for their sons and to carry real guns themselves. So what, if a young "Morehouse man" once nearly fell off the steps of Trevor Arnett Library because he thought my eyes were blue.) Crying and laughing I ran to the bathroom, while Rebecca mumbled and sang herself off to sleep. Yes indeed, I realized, looking into the mirror. There *was* a world in my eye. And I saw that it was possible to love it: that in fact, for all it had taught me of shame and anger and inner vision, I *did* love it. Even to see it drifting out of orbit in boredom, or rolling up out of fatigue, not to mention floating back at attention in excitement (bearing witness, a friend has called it), deeply suitable to my personality, and even characteristic of me.

49   That night I dream I am dancing to Stevie Wonder's song "Always" (the name of the song is really "As," but I hear it as "Always"). As I dance, whirling and joyous, happier than I've ever been in my life, another bright-faced dancer joins me. We dance and kiss each other and hold each other through the night. The other dancer has obviously come through all right, as I have done. She is beautiful, whole and free. And she is also me.

Writing with Sources: Using a Single Source

Integrating information from "Beauty: When the Other Dancer Is the Self" with your own ideas, write an essay on one of these topics. Be sure to acknowledge ideas that are not your own.

1. Walker develops her essay through a series of scenes instead of a continuous narrative. Write an essay about your own childhood in which you use this technique to highlight key incidents that are connected by a common theme.
2. How has your own physical appearance affected your life? Write an essay dis-

cussing this idea, considering how your appearance, your perception of your appearance, and the perceptions of others affected you, and how each changed as you grew older.

3. Write an essay in which you explore the connection between self-acceptance —coming to terms with who you are and learning to accept the things that cannot be changed—and growing up.

From *Born on the Fourth of July*

Ron Kovic

Born on the Fourth of July, 1946, in Massapequa, New York, Ron Kovic had a typical 1950s American boyhood. He played Little League, marched in Boy Scout parades, felt chills when he heard "The Star-Spangled Banner," and imagined himself leading troops into battle. After graduation from high school, he joined the marines and served two tours of duty in Vietnam. On his second tour, Kovic was seriously wounded and paralyzed from the chest down. After returning home, he became active in Vietnam Veterans Against the War and wrote the book *Born on the Fourth of July* (1976), in which he outlines the events that led to his disillusionment with the military. The following selection, excerpted from *Born on the Fourth of July*, gives an account of Kovic's early years.

1   For me it began in 1946 when I was born on the Fourth of July. The whole sky lit up in a tremendous fireworks display and my mother told me the doctor said I was a real firecracker. Every birthday after that was something the whole country celebrated. It was a proud day to be born on.

2   I hit a home run my first time at bat in the Massapequa Little League, and I can still remember my Mom and Dad and all the rest of the kids going crazy as I rounded the bases on seven errors and slid into home a hero. We lost the game to the Midgets that night, 22 to 7, and I cried all the way home. It was a long time ago, but sometimes I can still hear them shouting out in front of Pete's house on Hamilton Avenue. There was Bobby Zimmer, the tall kid from down the street, Kenny and Pete, little Tommy Law, and my best friend Richie Castiglia, who lived across from us on Lee Place.

. . .

3   When we weren't down at the field or watching the Yankees on TV, we were playing whiffle ball and climbing trees checking out birds' nests, going down to Fly Beach in Mrs. Zimmer's old car that honked the horn every time it turned the corner, diving underwater with our masks, kicking with our rubber frog's feet, then running in and out of our sprinklers when we got home, waiting for our turn in the shower. And during the summer nights we were all over the neighborhood, from Bobby's house to Kenny's, throwing gliders,

doing handstands and backflips off fences, riding to the woods at the end of the block on our bikes, making rafts, building tree forts, jumping across the streams with tree branches, walking and balancing along the back fence like Houdini, hopping along the slate path all around the back yard seeing how far we could go on one foot.

4   And I ran wherever I went. Down to the school, to the candy store, to the deli, buying baseball cards and Bazooka bubblegum that had the little fortunes at the bottom of the cartoons.

5   When the Fourth of July came, there were fireworks going off all over the neighborhood. It was the most exciting time of year for me next to Christmas. Being born on the exact same day as my country I thought was really great. I was so proud. And every Fourth of July, I had a birthday party and all my friends would come over with birthday presents and we'd put on silly hats and blow these horns my Dad brought home from the A&P. We'd eats lots of ice cream and watermelon and I'd open up all the presents and blow out the candles on the big red, white, and blue birthday cake and then we'd all sing "Happy Birthday" and "I'm a Yankee Doodle Dandy." At night everyone would pile into Bobby's mother's old car and we'd go down to the drive-in, where we'd watch the fireworks display. Before the movie started, we'd all get out and sit up on the roof of the car with our blankets wrapped around us watching the rockets and Roman candles going up and exploding into fountains of rainbow colors, and later after Mrs. Zimmer dropped me off, I'd lie on my bed feeling a little sad that it all had to end so soon. As I closed my eyes I could still hear strings of firecrackers and cherry bombs going off all over the neighborhood.

6   Every Saturday afternoon we'd all go down to the movies in the shopping center and watch gigantic prehistoric birds breathe fire, and war movies with John Wayne and Audie Murphy. Bobbie's mother always packed us a bagful of candy. I'll never forget Audie Murphy in *To Hell and Back*. At the end he jumps on top of a flaming tank that's just about to explode and grabs the machine gun blasting it into the German lines. He was so brave I had chills running up and down my back, wishing it were me up there. There were gasoline flames roaring around his legs, but he just kept firing that machine gun. It was the greatest movie I ever saw in my life.

7   Castiglia and I saw *The Sands of Iwo Jima* together. The Marine Corps hymn was playing in the background as we sat glued to our seats, humming the hymn together and watching Sergeant Stryker, played by John Wayne, charge up the hill and get killed just before he reached the top. And then they showed the men raising the flag on Iwo Jima with the marines' hymn still playing, and Castiglia and I cried in our seats. I loved the song so much, and every time I heard it I would think of John Wayne and the brave men who raised the flag on Iwo Jima that day. I would think of them and cry. Like Mickey Mantle and the fabulous New York Yankees, John Wayne in *The Sands of Iwo Jima* became one of my heroes.

8   We'd go home and make up movies like the ones we'd just seen or the ones that were on TV night after night. We'd use our Christmas toys — the Matty Mattell machine guns and grenades, the little green plastic soldiers with

guns and flamethrowers in their hands. My favorites were the green plastic men with bazookas. They blasted holes through the enemy. They wiped them out at thirty feet just above the coffee table. They dug in on the front lawn and survived countless artillery attacks. They burned with high-propane lighter fluid and a quarter-gallon of gasoline or were thrown into the raging fires of autumn leaves blasting into a million pieces.

9   On Saturdays after the movies all the guys would go down to Sally's Woods — Pete and Kenny and Bobbie and me, with plastic battery-operated machine guns, cap pistols, and sticks. We turned the woods into a battlefield. We set ambushes, then led gallant attacks, storming over the top, bayonetting and shooting anyone who got in our way. Then we'd walk out of the woods like the heroes we knew we would become when we were men.

10   The army had a show on Channel 2 called ''The Big Picture,'' and after it was over Castiglia and I crawled all over the back yard playing guns and army, making commando raids all summer into Ackerman's housing project blasting away at the imaginary enemy we had created right before our eyes, throwing dirt bombs and rocks into the windows, making loud explosions like hand grenades with our voices then charging in with our Matty Mattel machine guns blazing. I bandaged up the German who was still alive and had Castiglia question him as I threw a couple more grenades, killing even more Germans. We went on countless missions and patrols together around my back yard, attacking Ackerman's housing project with everything from bazookas to flame-throwers and baseball bats. We studied the Marine Corps Guidebook and Richie brought over some beautiful pamphlets with very sharp-looking marines on the covers. We read them in my basement for hours and just as we dreamed of playing for the Yankees someday, we dreamed of becoming United States Marines and fighting our first war and we made a solemn promise that year that the day we turned seventeen we were both going down to the marine recruiter at the shopping center in Levittown and sign up for the United States Marine Corps.

11   We joined the cub scouts and marched in parades on Memorial Day. We made contingency plans for the cold war and built fallout shelters out of milk cartons. We wore spacesuits and space helmets. We made rocket ships out of cardboard boxes. And one Saturday afternoon in the basement Castiglia and I went to Mars on the couch we had turned into a rocket ship. We read books about the moon and Wernher von Braun. And the whole block watched a thing called the space race begin. On a cold October night Dad and I watched the first satellite, called *Sputnik,* moving across the sky above our house like a tiny bright star. I still remember standing out there with Dad looking up in amaze-ment at that thing moving in the sky above Massapequa. It was hard to believe that this thing, this *Sputnik,* was so high up and moving so fast around the world, again and again. Dad put his hand on my shoulder that night and without saying anything I quietly walked back inside and went to my room thinking that the Russians had beaten America into space and wondering why we couldn't even get a rocket off the pad.

· · ·

12   That spring before I graduated, my father took me down to the shopping

center in Levittown and made me get my first job. It was in a supermarket not far from the marine recruiting station. I worked stacking shelves and numbing my fingers and hands unloading cases of frozen food from the trucks. Working with Kenny each day after school, all I could think of, day after day, was joining the marines. My legs and my back ached, but I knew that soon I would be signing the papers and leaving home.

13   I didn't want to be like my Dad, coming home from the A&P every night. He was a strong man, a good man, but it made him so tired, it took all the energy out of him. I didn't want to be like that, working in that stinking A&P, six days a week, twelve hours a day. I wanted to be somebody. I wanted to make something out of my life.

14   I was getting older now, I was seventeen, and I looked at myself in the mirror that hung from the back of the door in my room and saw how tall and strong I had suddenly become. I took a deep breath, flexing my muscles, and stared straight into the mirror, turning to the side and looking at myself for a long time.

15   In the last month of school, the marine recruiters came and spoke to my senior class. They marched, both in perfect step, into the auditorium with their dress blue uniforms and their magnificently shined shoes. It was like all the movies and all the books and all the dreams of becoming a hero come true. I watched them and listened as they stood in front of all the young boys, looking almost like statues and not like real men at all. They spoke in loud voices and one of them was tall and the other was short and very strong looking.

16   "Good afternoon men," the tall marine said. "We have come today because they told us that some of you want to become marines." He told us that the marines took nothing but the best, that if any of us did not think we were good enough, we should not even think of joining. The tall marine spoke in a very beautiful way about the exciting history of the marines and how they had never lost and America had never been defeated.

17   "The marines have been the first in everything, first to fight and first to uphold the honor of our country. We have served on distant shores and at home, and we have always come when our country has called. There is nothing finer, nothing prouder, than a United States marine."

18   When they were finished, they efficiently picked up their papers and marched together down the steps of the stage to where a small crowd of boys began to gather. I couldn't wait to run down after them, meet with them and shake their hands. And as I shook their hands and stared up into their eyes, I couldn't help but feel I was shaking hands with John Wayne and Audie Murphy. They told us that day that the Marine Corps built men — body, mind, and spirit. And that we could serve our country like the young president had asked us to do.

19   We were all going in different directions and we had our whole lives ahead of us, and a million different dreams. I can still remember the last stickball game. I stood at home plate with the sun in my face and looked out at Richie, Pete, and the rest. It was our last summer together and the last stickball game we ever played on Hamilton Avenue.

20   One day that summer I quit my job at the food store and went to the little red, white, and blue shack in Levittown. My father and I went down together. It was September by the time all the paperwork was completed, September 1964. I was going to leave on a train one morning and become a marine.

21   I stayed up most of the night before I left, watching the late movie. Then "The Star-Spangled Banner" played. I remember standing up and feeling very patriotic, chills running up and down my spine. I put my hand over my heart and stood rigid at attention until the screen went blank.

Writing with Sources: Using a Single Source

Integrating information from the excerpt from *Born on the Fourth of July* with your own ideas, write an essay on one of these topics. Be sure to acknowledge all ideas that are not your own.

1. Discuss the significance of Kovic's statement, "For me it began in 1946 when I was born on the Fourth of July."
2. Kovic illustrates how movies did a lot to form his attitudes toward war and patriotism. Explain how movies and television have influenced your attitudes about this or any other subject.
3. Kovic concludes his essay by saying that he and his friends were all going in different directions. Write an essay in which you illustrate how you and two or three of your high school friends have gone in different directions.

Bookworm

Susan Allen Toth

Susan Allen Toth was born in 1940 in Ames, Iowa, and attended Smith College (B.A.), the University of California at Berkeley (M.A.), and the University of Minnesota (Ph.D.). She taught at San Francisco State College before assuming her present position teaching English at Macalester College in St. Paul, Minnesota. In her mid-thirties, Toth began to write fiction and autobiographical memoirs, contributing articles to magazines like *Harper's, Redbook,* and *Ms.* She has published two autobiographical books, *Blooming: A Small Town Girlhood* (1981), from which "Bookworm" is excerpted, and *Ivy Days: Making My Way Out East* (1984), a chronicle of her years at Smith College. In "Bookworm," Toth recalls with affection the Ames Public Library and some of the books and people she encountered there.

1   Whenever I hear the words *inner sanctum* I think of the Ames Public Library. It was a massive stone temple, with imposing front steps that spread on either side into two flat ledges, overhung by evergreens. Waiting for my

mother to pick me up, I could sit almost hidden on the cool stone blocks, surveying passing cars with a removed superiority. Safely perched on my pedestal, surrounded by my stacks of new books, I always felt unusually serene, bolstered by the security of the library behind me and the anticipation of the books beside me. Even to the moment of leaving it, my visits to the library were high occasions.

2   Entering the Ames Public Library I could feel its compelling power immediately. Inside the front doors a split staircase climbed elaborately to the main entrance on the second floor, and trudging up the marble steps I was enveloped by the cavernous space. A chilly breeze always seemed to be blowing up my back. Few buildings in Ames had such grandeur; the only one that reminded me of the library was the college's Memorial Union, which had an entrance hall dedicated to the dead of World War I and inlaid with tablets of granite you weren't supposed to walk on. The library, and the Union Hall, seemed to be places where things lay precariously at rest, just below the surface, waiting to be summoned up again.

3   I always worried when I went to the library that I might have to go to the bathroom. That meant getting a key from the front desk and descending the staircase again, but turning this time down one more flight of steps into darkness. The locked toilets were in the basement, a storage area known to no one but the janitor and Miss Jepson, the head librarian. Shadows lurked every-where down there, steps echoed noisily, the light switch was impossible to find. Once I felt the door and fumbled with the key, it didn't always turn right in the lock, and I often had to go back upstairs, embarrassed, to ask an an-noyed librarian to come down and try. When the heavy door of the ladies' toilet finally swung shut after I got inside, I was afraid that it might lock itself again. As the day wound on, no one would hear my cries for help behind that wooden block, and night would find me alone and helpless in the dark bowels of the library. I tried to avoid all this by not going to the bathroom. Sometimes I had to cross my legs and pinch myself in the car in order to make it home safely.

4   But if I didn't have to go down to the basement, I was seldom as happy anywhere as I was at the library. It was a place in which you always knew exactly where you belonged. At the entrance stood a circular wooden enclo-sure, only entered by librarians, who flipped up a small wooden shelf. There all books were checked in and out. When you came in the door, the librarian on duty glanced up and mentally checked you in as well. Directly behind the librarians' sentry post was adult fiction, both on the main floor and on a dark mezzanine above. For a long time I wasn't allowed up there. To the left was the map, newspaper and periodical room, where I seldom ventured either. Grown-ups who worked downtown sometimes came and ate their lunches at the big tables there, surrounded by spread-out newspapers whose rustlings blended with the quiet sounds of munched lettuce. My world lay to the right.

5   The west wing of the library was divided into sections for Children and Juniors. At first I nested happily in the Children's Room, with its small round tables and equally small chairs. I liked knowing that adults looked ridiculous trying to squat on those chairs, though of course that was also why a few years

later I was ready to escape to the Junior Room, which had adult-sized chairs that didn't make you feel as though you were a baby. Besides its coziness and small scale, the Children's Room held two of the most important places in the whole library. One was the curtained door to Miss Jepson's office, which you never entered unless you were going to have a Serious Talk with her. The other was a window, a three-sided display case at child's-eye level that held a changing miniature diorama. I always rushed to see it before I went anywhere else in the library. All children did. Usually it was a scene from a familiar book, like *Goldilocks* or *Rumpelstiltskin,* though sometimes I had to guess. Nobody I knew had miniatures like the library's, tiny kettles, braided rugs, hand-knit doll aprons, and I could stand for fifteen minutes admiring the elaborate sets. It was like a small theatre with the actors all frozen into a single moment. Like a theatre, it had a small velvet curtain that was kept drawn when the scene was being changed. Its inner doors, or backstage, were entered from inside Miss Jepson's office, although she personally never had anything to do with the actual changing of displays. That, like most menial tasks, was left to Mrs. Erhard and her assistants.

6   The Children's collection was not a large one, and before long I roamed through it confidently. I gorged myself on books, lugging home piles as high as I could carry, sometimes begging for Mrs. Erhard's permission because she was so sure I couldn't read them all in a week. But I could. At home I read before school, after school, with a book on my lap at dinner, and at night before I went to bed. I read with equal avidity about Horton hatching an egg and about East of the sun and West of the moon. I moved without pausing from Rabbit Hill to the tower of the Little Lame Prince. It was like having a box of assorted chocolates, all tempting, with unknown centers. I wanted to bite into each one right away to see what it was like.

7   About this time I first heard myself called a bookworm. One of the boys in my class saw me struggling off the city bus on a day when my mother hadn't been able to pick me up at the library. "Whaddya think ya are, a bookworm or something?" he said with a sneer. I had my chin on the top of my stack of books to keep them steady, so I couldn't open my mouth very far to respond. "I am NOT," I said defiantly, as the stack quivered. But I felt caught, labeled with something dirty and unpleasant. I didn't like worms. After that I looked around carefully when I was carrying a load of books, and if a friend was with me I made her carry part of mine. But not even the fear of being known as a bookworm could stop my reading.

8   As I looked ahead to the Junior Room, I could see that it held at least four times as many books as did Children's. I worried about how I was going to tackle such a task; I felt the order and serenity that emanated from the library dictated that I approach my reading in a suitably controlled way. So in third grade I decided to compile a miniature card catalogue, like the library's, for each book I read. My mother bought me a pile of index cards and a small metal file box. Now I felt official, part of the library itself, as I sat down at a polished maple table and importantly spread out my stack of cards. On each card I noted author, title, and one or two sentences of plot summary so I could remember

what I'd read. Then I created an elaborate series of abbreviations, which today I can barely decipher, like "N.G." for "No Good," or "Exc." for "Excellent," as well as a series of numbers which must have been an attempt to compare each book with the others. I can no longer remember why *Caddie Woodlawn* might have been a "2," let alone "G," as opposed to *The Five Little Peppers,* which was "3" and "V.G." Soon I was spending more time making notes and inventing annotations than I was reading, a fact which Mrs. Erhard pointed out to me one day. She looked at a few of my cards and laughed. My feelings were hurt. I had thought of myself as preparing for a job like hers. Not long afterward I put the card catalogue away.

9   When I moved to the Junior Room, probably at the age of ten or eleven, I decided, like many omnivorous readers, to begin with the A's and read through to the Z's. I thought this was obviously the best way of making sure I didn't miss anything. Though three walls of this large room were lined with books, I didn't think it would be impossible to cover it all. The Ames Public Library did have a human scale to it. I might have done so, too, except I found somewhat to my surprise that I was developing tastes. I didn't really like books about horses. I wasn't very interested in boy detectives. I didn't want to read anything if the author was trying too hard to be educational. I was happy through the B's, where I found *Sue Barton, Rural Nurse; Sue Barton, Public Nurse;* and *Sue Barton, Superintendent of Nurses;* but after that I bogged down quickly. I skipped ahead to the L's, where I had discovered Maude Hart Lovelace's sequential adventures of Betsy, Tacy, and Tib, and promised myself I would someday return to the C's. But I never did.

10   When I abandoned my plan of methodically reading everything in the library, I was stimulated by new freedom of choice. I began to explore the nonfiction sections, which had never interested me before, and gradually I realized that within the walls of the Ames Public Library could probably be found the answers to any questions I would ever have. All my problems could be solved if I could only find the right book. At twelve, when *The Teen-Agers' Complete Guide To Beauty* fell into my hands, I thought I had found just such an authority. It was written, its cover assured me, by a successful New York teen-age model named Barbie Betts, whose unfamiliar face and name didn't deter me from believing every word she had to say. I checked out her book and renewed it twice, until Mrs. Erhard said I would have to ask Miss Jepson to change the rules if I wanted to renew it again. Then I reluctantly released it back to the shelves.

11   My mother hated *The Teen-Agers' Complete Guide To Beauty.* It upset our home for weeks. I fervently believed that if I followed all its instructions, I would be transformed into the girl of my dreams, thin, graceful, well dressed and well groomed. Barbie Betts felt especially strongly about the importance of good grooming, a phrase I had previously connected only with horses. She suggested that I make my evening bath a beauty routine, buy a pumice stone for the rough skin on my elbows, soak my cuticles in olive oil, powder carefully between my toes. Although my mother muttered loudly that she couldn't see anything wrong with the way I looked, I disappeared each night for an hour

into the bathroom with a tray of beauty aids and soaked, scrubbed, powdered. I got wrinkles from staying so long in the water and the places I scrubbed turned very pink, but I didn't look different at all. Nobody ever stopped to admire my cuticles or tell me how nice my elbows felt. I eventually gave up and only continued halfheartedly to brush my hair one hundred strokes a night.

12   Then I turned my full attention to the problem of being well dressed. Barbie Betts said that the key to a successful wardrobe was not money but organization. I tried to follow her directions about sorting my clothes, coordinating them into interchangeable outfits, and then color-coding each outfit with markers in the closet. This took days of heaped clothes on the floor, disastrous experiments with colored paper glued to hangers, and hours of frustrated weeping when I discovered I lacked several crucial essentials of the master plan, like a wide black leather belt and a white wool skirt, which my mother said we couldn't afford. Near despair, I thought perhaps I could transform my environment even if I myself remained a lump of raw material. I studied intently Barbie Betts's pictures of model bedrooms, which were frilly and feminine, and asked my mother if we could at least buy a headboard and make a canopy. She sighed. I wept again. I gradually realized that I could never carry out Barbie Betts's full-scale plans, and I was convinced halfway measures wouldn't work. I was doomed to a life of unmatched sweaters and tufted chenille bedspreads.

13   But when my dream of beauty failed, I retreated, as always, to other dreams. The Ames Public Library had an unending supply of them. I was too old by now for *The Blue Fairy Book* and *The Green Fairy Book,* but for solace I soon found Elizabeth Goudge. For at least a year I wandered blissfully through English cathedral towns and country inns, where I met benevolent grandfathers with spiritual secrets and freckled fun-loving boys who grew up into gentle sweethearts. If only I had lived a hundred years ago in England, I thought, how satisfying life would have been.

14   As I moved toward high school, I began to consider what I was going to be when I grew up, a question I felt it was time I took seriously. Despite my attraction to Sue Barton, I doubted whether I would make a good nurse. The only one I knew in real life was at school, a cross-faced tough-jawed woman who didn't believe you were sick unless you threw up copiously in the hall. Then she grumbled, took your temperature, and sent you home. I would have to be pretty lucky to escape that kind of life and find one like Sue Barton's, who married her Doctor Bill in the end. For a long while I thought I could be a foreign correspondent, since I liked to write and loved the idea of travel, but the career guides I began to read assiduously all seemed discouraging about a woman's chances as a reporter. My inevitable choice was the career I had been nurturing in my bones since my first trip up those marble steps. I decided to become a librarian.

15   Although librarians didn't make much money, my career guides warned me, they had something else that appealed to me as much as constant proximity to all those books. They had power. Not many women in Ames visibly wielded that, but Miss Jepson did. Even her deputy, Mrs. Erhard, had a derived air of

stern authority. Miss Jepson, whose white hair and wrinkled pink skin made her seem agelessly preserved, was a definite-minded woman whose tongue had an almost audible snap. Whenever she submitted a budget request to the Ames City Council, she was able to get almost everything she wanted. No one dared to argue long with Miss Jepson. She personally selected each book the library ordered and gave the impression that she had read them all first. No detail of the library's operation escaped her inspection; she knew it so well I thought for a long time she must live there, in a secret suite connecting to her office.

16   The most impressive symbol of Miss Jepson's power was her locked glass case. This was a small cabinet in her office where she kept books whose literary or scholarly worth was unquestioned but whose text or illustrations she deemed obscene. Only Miss Jepson had the key. If you wanted to read one of Those Books, you had to knock at Miss Jepson's curtained door, enter when you heard her gruff voice, and then sit down facing her to explain why you felt it necessary to check out that particular book. If your reasons were unsatisfactory, it stayed in the locked case.

17   If I ever wanted a book in that case, I don't remember what it was. But I did have several uncomfortable conversations in Miss Jepson's office. One was the culmination of my struggles with her deputy, Mrs. Erhard, who had to enforce Miss Jepson's edicts. The rule that got me into trouble was the strict age limitation placed upon moving from the Junior to the Adult collection. Although sometimes Mrs. Erhard might stretch a year or two to let a child take something from Juniors', she was not going to yield so much as a month when it came to Adults'. I think the dividing line for Adults' was entrance into the downtown high school; whatever it was, it came too late for me. I was impatient to be exploring the stacks of novels on the mezzanine long before Mrs. Erhard thought I should. We would stand at the checkout desk and argue over my confiscated books, as I pointed out that my mother let me read everything in her library at home. Mrs. Erhard said what my mother did at home was her business, but in the Ames Public Library I was not yet an adult and could not check out adult books. Besides, she asked slyly, had I read every single book in the Junior section? I admitted I hadn't. With a triumphant smile, Mrs. Erhard lifted her wooden drawbridge and left. A few minutes later she was back, holding a small pile of Junior books. Had I read any of these? She could recommend them all highly.

18   I agreed ungraciously to try them. But I had no intention of giving in. Back home, I complained vehemently to my mother, until she agreed to call Miss Jepson for a little chat. Whatever my mother said must have worked. The next week Mrs. Erhard glared at me and told me to report to Miss Jepson's office. There Miss Jepson looked me up and down, asked me a few questions about books, impressed upon me the rarity of exceptions to the library's rules, and told me from now on I could check out three adult books a week.

19   After that I wandered freely among the adults, though I tried to choose checkout times when a student assistant was replacing Mrs. Erhard. I was afraid she might veto some of my choices. I remember trembling when I carried *The Empress of Byzantium* from its shelf to the desk, hoping Mrs. Erhard hadn't

read it. I had already seen enough to know she wouldn't approve. *The Empress of Byzantium,* whose author I had never heard of, should have been in Miss Jepson's locked case. I discovered it by accident, as I often uncovered marvels in the library, pulling down books because of their elegant gold lettering or well-worn bindings or unusual color. Adult fiction was particularly suited for this kind of browsing, since the mezzanine had narrow aisles just wide enough to brace your back against one shelf while you sat on the rubber-tiled floor and ruffled through the books opposite. Whatever first attracted me to *The Empress of Byzantium* soon fled my mind when I saw what the book held inside: sex, sadism, and a graphic style that left little to my active imagination. I remember nothing about the plot, but I do recall one particular scene that galvanized me. The heroine, who had recently given birth, was in bed with her husband. He resented the child, I think, and they had some kind of argument followed by what I could dimly recognize as lovemaking. He grabbed her, began to nibble on her nipples until little drops of milk leaked out, and sucked until she managed to push him away. She was shocked; so was I. I couldn't remember seeing anyone breastfeed a baby, but I thought husbands were probably repelled by it. I read greedily through as much of the book as I could manage that afternoon, brought it home and hid it in my closet, and then carried it furtively back to the library the next week. I looked at Mrs. Erhard with a new respect. If she had read all the books in the adult section, she probably knew all about sex too.

20   Not only did librarians have access to all important knowledge, but in the Ames Public Library they had social power as well. It was not that either Miss Jepson or Mrs. Erhard attended coffee parties, played bridge, or belonged to the Country Club, but rather that they carefully used their ability to select student assistants. Miss Jepson's hand-picked band, chosen from high-school applicants after a long screening process culminating in an intensive interview behind her curtained door, were dedicated to becoming future librarians. They had to be serious, devoted, and of high moral character. The training they received from Miss Jepson and Mrs. Erhard was supposed to be the equivalent of a library degree; in return the student assistants had to agree to work a steady number of hours after school and weekends all through high school. Like dedicating yourself to a convent, you knew that to withdraw from this agreement after acceptance, and worse, after months of training, was to fail disgracefully.

21   When I was just beginning junior high school, I desperately admired Miss Jepson's student librarians. One of them was Shelley McNulty, the oldest daughter of one of the most respected families in town. Her dignified father served communion at our church, and her mother played golf regularly with the wife of the head of the Leichner Clinic. Shelley herself was gravely beautiful, with warm dark eyes and softly curling short hair. She was quiet, graceful, assured, all the things I had given up hope of being after abandoning Barbie Betts's optimistic teen-age program. Only the best boys were permitted to take her out, and she never went steady with any of them, not because they didn't ask her, but because her parents didn't approve. Everyone in high school knew

how special she was; Shelley had already been Homecoming Queen and was an obvious shoo-in for Senior Sweetheart in her last year. If Shelley McNulty was going to be a librarian, I could hardly have aspired to any career more socially sanctioned.

22   As I grew older, however, and Shelley eventually moved on to college and away from the library, I found to my dismay that my dedication to her model began to waver. My future had seemed quite set. By the time I was in eighth grade, I had already had one serious talk with Miss Jepson about becoming an assistant when I was a sophomore. But as the time approached, although I still loved the library, I was no longer quite so sure that I could give up all my after-school hours and weekends. In ninth grade, I tried being a student helper in our school library, and I was disappointed. Although I enjoyed shelving books, finding the infinitesimally exact Dewey decimal numbers between which to sandwich each volume, noting with pride the tidiness of the arrangement when I had finished, I found that within a day all the books were messed up again. Other people kept taking them out. I had always thought of the library as a personal possession, and I wasn't altogether comfortable about sharing it. Since nobody asked me questions about where things were, I didn't get a chance to show off my superior knowledge either. Mainly I sat on a high stool behind the one-drawer card catalogue and guarded the checkout slips. It was against the rules to read while you were being a student helper. Not many kids wandered back to the library to talk, and none of them were boys. My volunteer hours became duller, and shorter.

23   When Miss Jepson called me into her office as a new sophomore, to check her list of promised disciples, I had to tell her that I was too busy. I said I wanted to work on the high-school newspaper, act in some plays, and attend all the out-of-town football games. As I faintly concluded this feeble list, Miss Jepson's eyes seemed to crackle and give off small sparks of light. "All I can say is that I'm disappointed in you, Susan," she said, her firm mouth tightening even more. "I hope you have made the right choice. You know your decision will close the door here to you permanently. I'm sorry because I think you would have been a fine librarian." I had no reply. I backed out of her office and left the library that day without even checking out any books.

24   Although I tended to avoid Miss Jepson for a while after that, I certainly didn't give up the library. I continued my regular visits there during high school, and while in college I managed to squeeze trips to the library into my brief vacations home. I sought it out increasingly as a place of quiet more than as a source of knowledge. Although I was now aware that other libraries had more books and more impressive buildings, the Ames Public Library was my own private refuge. If I had a difficult paper to write, I knew I could spread it out on the shiny maple tables in the Junior Room. I would make notes, sort piles of paper, look out the tall windows at the elm trees, and take little breaks to wander past the familiar shelves, plucking out old friends that seemed like once-loved dolls carefully packed away for someone else. Few people came into the library when I spent my afternoons there, and I would be lulled by the soft padding of the librarians' feet, the gentle thud of the heavy front door, the

rare whispers from the Children's Room next door. Sometimes during college vacations I would just go there to write letters. Miss Jepson nodded at me then and asked me how I liked Smith; I smiled at her as one adult to another. Eventually I no longer even wondered about the books in her little glass case. Perhaps now I had read them all.

25   But although the Ames Public Library eventually became simply a pleasant place to visit, I still think of it at odd times. When something troubles me, I feel an urge to go to the library to get a book on it, though now that I can afford to buy books occasionally, I sometimes go to the bookstore instead. My crowded shelves hold all the books I thought would help: advice and guidance on needlepoint, cats, England, loneliness, parenting, and antique jewelry. Last spring, when I decided it was time for me to get my body in shape, I went downtown in a self-satisfied glow to outfit myself for exercise. I had planned to buy some properly cushioned shoes. But I passed by a bookstore first, stopped to browse, and spent my money instead on *The Complete Book of Running*. I thought I had better read about running first to see whether I would like it.

Writing with Sources: Using a Single Source

Integrating information from "Bookworm" with your own ideas, write an essay on one of these topics. Be sure to acknowledge ideas that are not your own.

1. To Toth, the Ames Public Library was a special place that in many ways seems to symbolize the world of her childhood. Describe a similarly memorable place from your own childhood and explain its impact on you then and now.
2. How did reading help to shape your life? Choose four or five memorable books you read as a child, and explain how each affected you. Try to convey to your readers exactly why each book had such an impact on you.
3. Susan Allen Toth grew up in the 1940s and 50s in a small college town in Iowa. What competing influences did you and your peers have that kept books from having the same place in your lives as they had in hers? In your essay give examples of such competing pursuits and explain the relative appeal of each.

Starting Out in Journalism

Russell Baker

Russell Baker was born in 1925 in Loudoun County, Virginia, and received a B.A. from Johns Hopkins University in 1947. Baker began his newspaper career working for the *Baltimore Sun* and eventually became its London bureau chief, writing a spirited weekly series for that paper. In 1954 he joined the staff of the *New York Times,* where he covered the White House, the State Department, and Congress before accepting the opportunity in 1962 to write the "Observer" column for the

Times. In this column he quickly established himself as a keen political satirist. In 1979, he won the George Polk Award for commentary and the Pulitzer Prize for distinguished commentary. He has written a number of books, most recently *So This is Depravity* (1980), a collection of his columns, *Growing Up* (1982), for which he won the Pulitzer Prize for biography, and *The Rescue of Miss Yaskell and Other Pipe Dreams* (1983), a collection of his newspaper articles. The following selection, from *Growing Up,* presents Baker's story of how he first got started in journalism.

1   I began working in journalism when I was eight years old. It was my mother's idea. She wanted me to "make something" of myself and, after a levelheaded appraisal of my strengths, decided I had better start young if I was to have any chance of keeping up with the competition.

2   The flaw in my character which she had already spotted was lack of "gumption." My idea of a perfect afternoon was lying in front of the radio rereading my favorite Big Little Book, *Dick Tracy Meets Stooge Viller.* My mother despised inactivity. Seeing me having a good time in repose, she was powerless to hide her disgust. "You've got no more gumption than a bump on a log," she said. "Get out in the kitchen and help Doris do those dirty dishes."

3   My sister Doris, though two years younger than I, had enough gumption for a dozen people. She positively enjoyed washing dishes, making beds, and cleaning the house. When she was only seven she could carry a piece of short-weighted cheese back to the A&P, threaten the manager with legal action, and come back triumphantly with the full quarter-pound we'd paid for and a few ounces extra thrown in for forgiveness. Doris could have made something of herself if she hadn't been a girl. Because of this defect, however, the best she could hope for was a career as a nurse or schoolteacher, the only work that capable females were considered up to in those days.

4   This must have saddened my mother, this twist of fate that had allocated all the gumption to the daughter and left her with a son who was content with Dick Tracy and Stooge Viller. If disappointed, though, she wasted no energy on self-pity. She would make me make something of myself whether I wanted to or not. "The Lord helps those who help themselves," she said. That was the way her mind worked.

5   She was realistic about the difficulty. Having sized up the material the Lord had given her to mold, she didn't overestimate what she could do with it. She didn't insist that I grow up to be President of the United States.

6   Fifty years ago parents still asked boys if they wanted to grow up to be President, and asked it not jokingly but seriously. Many parents who were hardly more than paupers still believed their sons could do it. Abraham Lincoln had done it. We were only sixty-five years from Lincoln. Many a grandfather who walked among us could remember Lincoln's time. Men of grandfatherly age were the worst for asking if you wanted to grow up to be President. A surprising number of little boys said yes and meant it.

7   I was asked many times myself. No, I would say, I didn't want to grow up to be President. My mother was present during one of these interrogations. An elderly uncle, having posed the usual question and exposed my lack of interest in the Presidency, asked, "Well, what *do* you want to be when you grow up?"

I loved to pick through trash piles and collect empty bottles, tin cans with pretty labels, and discarded magazines. The most desirable job on earth sprang instantly to mind. "I want to be a garbage man," I said.

8   My uncle smiled, but my mother had seen the first distressing evidence of a bump budding on a log. "Have a little gumption, Russell," she said. Her calling me Russell was a signal of unhappiness. When she approved of me I was always "Buddy."

9   When I turned eight years old she decided that the job of starting me on the road toward making something of myself could no longer be safely delayed. "Buddy," she said one day. "I want you to come home right after school this afternoon. Somebody's coming and I want you to meet him."

10   When I burst in that afternoon she was in conference in the parlor with an executive of the Curtis Publishing Company. She introduced me. He bent low from the waist and shook my hand. Was it true as my mother had told him, he asked, that I longed for the opportunity to conquer the world of business?

11   My mother replied that I was blessed with a rare determination to make something of myself.

12   "That's right," I whispered.

13   "But have you got the grit, the character, the never-say-quit spirit it takes to succeed in business?"

14   My mother said I certainly did.

15   "That's right," I said.

16   He eyed me silently for a long pause, as though weighing whether I could be trusted to keep his confidence, then spoke man-to-man. Before taking a crucial step, he said, he wanted to advise me that working for the Curtis Publishing Company placed enormous responsibility on a young man. It was one of the great companies of America. Perhaps the greatest publishing house in the world. I had heard, no doubt, of the *Saturday Evening Post*?

17   Heard of it? My mother said that everyone in our house had heard of the *Saturday Post* and that I, in fact, read it with religious devotion.

18   Then doubtless, he said, we were also familiar with those two monthly pillars of the magazine world, the *Ladies Home Journal* and the *Country Gentleman*.

19   Indeed we were familiar with them, said my mother.

20   Representing the *Saturday Evening Post* was one of the weightiest honors that could be bestowed in the world of business, he said. He was personally proud of being a part of that great corporation.

21   My mother said he had every right to be.

22   Again he studied me as though debating whether I was worthy of a knighthood. Finally: "Are you trustworthy?"

23   My mother said I was the soul of honesty.

24   "That's right," I said.

25   The caller smiled for the first time. He told me I was a lucky young man. He admired my spunk. Too many young men thought life was all play. Those young men would not go far in this world. Only a young man willing to work and save and keep his face washed and his hair neatly combed could hope to

come out on top in a world such as ours. Did I truly and sincerely believe that I was such a young man?

26   "He certainly does," said my mother.

27   "That's right," I said.

28   He said he had been so impressed by what he had seen of me that he was going to make me a representative of the Curtis Publishing Company. On the following Tuesday, he said, thirty freshly printed copies of the *Saturday Evening Post* would be delivered at our door. I would place these magazines, still damp with the ink of the presses, in a handsome canvas bag, sling it over my shoulder, and set forth through the streets to bring the best in journalism, fiction, and cartoons to the American public.

29   He had brought the canvas bag with him. He presented it with reverence fit for a chasuble. He showed me how to drape the sling over my left shoulder and across the chest so that the pouch lay easily accessible to my right hand, allowing the best in journalism, fiction, and cartoons to be swiftly extracted and sold to a citizenry whose happiness and security depended upon us soldiers of the free press.

30   The following Tuesday I raced home from school, put the canvas bag over my shoulder, dumped the magazines in, and, tilting to the left to balance their weight on my right hip, embarked on the highway of journalism.

31   We lived in Belleville, New Jersey, a commuter town at the northern fringe of Newark. It was 1932, the bleakest year of the Depression. My father had died two years before, leaving us with a few pieces of Sears, Roebuck furniture and not much else, and my mother had taken Doris and me to live with one of her younger brothers. This was my Uncle Allen. Uncle Allen had made something of himself by 1932. As salesman for a soft-drink bottler in Newark, he had an income of $30 a week; wore pearl-gray spats, detachable collars, and a three-piece suit; was happily married; and took in threadbare relatives.

32   With my load of magazines I headed toward Belleville Avenue. That's where the people were. There were two filling stations at the intersection with Union Avenue, as well as an A&P, a fruit stand, a bakery, a barber shop, Zuccarelli's drugstore, and a diner shaped like a railroad car. For several hours I made myself highly visible, shifting position now and then from corner to corner, from shop window to shop window, to make sure everyone could see the heavy black lettering on the canvas bag that said THE SATURDAY EVENING POST. When the angle of the light indicated it was suppertime, I walked back to the house.

33   "How many did you sell, Buddy?" my mother asked.

34   "None."

35   "Where did you go?"

36   "The corner of Belleville and Union Avenues."

37   "What did you do?"

38   "Stood on the corner waiting for somebody to buy a *Saturday Evening Post*."

39   "You just stood there?"

40   "Didn't sell a single one."

41   "For God's sake, Russell!"

42   Uncle Allen intervened. "I've been thinking about it for some time," he said, "and I've about decided to take the *Post* regularly. Put me down as a regular customer." I handed him a magazine and he paid me a nickel. It was the first nickel I earned.

43   Afterwards my mother instructed me in salesmanship. I would have to ring doorbells, address adults with charming self-confidence, and break down resistance with a sales talk pointing out that no one, no matter how poor, could afford to be without the *Saturday Evening Post* in the home.

44   I told my mother I'd changed my mind about wanting to succeed in the magazine business.

45   "If you think I'm going to raise a good-for-nothing," she replied, "you've got another think coming." She told me to hit the streets with the canvas bag and start ringing doorbells the instant school was out next day. When I objected that I didn't feel any aptitude for salesmanship, she asked how I'd like to lend her my leather belt so she could whack some sense into me. I bowed to superior will and entered journalism with a heavy heart.

46   My mother and I had fought this battle almost as long as I could remember. It probably started even before memory began, when I was a country child in northern Virginia and my mother, dissatisfied with my father's plain workman's life, determined that I would not grow up like him and his people, with calluses on their hands, overalls on their backs, and fourth-grade educations in their heads. She had fancier ideas of life's possibilities. Introducing me to the *Saturday Evening Post,* she was trying to wean me as early as possible from my father's world where men left with their lunch pails at sunup, worked with their hands until the grime ate into the pores, and died with a few sticks of mail-order furniture as their legacy. In my mother's vision of the better life there were desks and white collars, well-pressed suits, evenings of reading and lively talk, and perhaps — if a man were very, very lucky and hit the jackpot, really made something important of himself — perhaps there might be a fantastic salary of $5,000 a year to support a big house and a Buick with a rumble seat and a vacation in Atlantic City.

47   And so I set forth with my sack of magazines. I was afraid of the dogs that snarled behind the doors of potential buyers. I was timid about ringing the doorbells of strangers, relieved when no one came to the door, and scared when someone did. Despite my mother's instructions, I could not deliver an engaging sales pitch. When a door opened I simply asked, "Want to buy a *Saturday Evening Post?*" In Belleville few persons did. It was a town of 30,000 people, and most weeks I rang a fair majority of its doorbells. But I rarely sold my thirty copies. Some weeks I canvassed the entire town for six days and still had four or five unsold magazines on Monday evening; then I dreaded the coming of Tuesday morning, when a batch of thirty fresh *Saturday Evening Posts* was due at the front door.

48   "Better get out there and sell the rest of those magazines tonight," my mother would say.

49   I usually posted myself then at a busy intersection where a traffic light

controlled commuter flow from Newark. When the light turned red I stood on
the curb and shouted my sales pitch at the motorists.

50 "Want to buy a *Saturday Evening Post?*"

51 One rainy night when car windows were sealed against me I came back
soaked and with not a single sale to report. My mother beckoned to Doris.

52 "Go back down there with Buddy and show him how to sell these magazines," she said.

53 Brimming with zest, Doris, who was then seven years old, returned with
me to the corner. She took a magazine from the bag, and when the light turned
red she strode to the nearest car and banged her small fist against the closed
window. The driver, probably startled at what he took to be a midget assaulting
his car, lowered the window to stare, and Doris thrust a *Saturday Evening Post*
at him.

54 "You need this magazine," she piped, "and it only costs a nickel."

55 Her salesmanship was irresistible. Before the light changed half a dozen
times she disposed of the entire batch. I didn't feel humiliated. To the contrary.
I was so happy I decided to give her a treat. Leading her to the vegetable store
on Belleville Avenue, I bought three apples, which cost a nickel, and gave her one.

56 "You shouldn't waste money," she said.

57 "Eat your apple." I bit into mine.

58 "You shouldn't eat before supper," she said. "It'll spoil your appetite."

59 Back at the house that evening, she dutifully reported me for wasting a
nickel. Instead of a scolding, I was rewarded with a pat on the back for having
the good sense to buy fruit instead of candy. My mother reached into her
bottomless supply of maxims and told Doris, "An apple a day keeps the doctor
away."

60 By the time I was ten I had learned all my mother's maxims by heart.
Asking to stay up past normal bedtime, I knew that a refusal would be explained
with, "Early to bed and early to rise, makes a man healthy, wealthy, and wise."
If I whimpered about having to get up early in the morning, I could depend on
her to say, "The early bird gets the worm."

61 The one I most despised was, "If at first you don't succeed, try, try
again." This was the battle cry with which she constantly sent me back into the
hopeless struggle whenever I moaned that I had rung every doorbell in town
and knew there wasn't a single potential buyer left in Belleville that week.
After listening to my explanation, she handed me the canvas bag and said, "If
at first you don't succeed . . ."

62 Three years in that job, which I would gladly have quit after the first day
except for her insistence, produced at least one valuable result. My mother
finally concluded that I would never make something of myself by pursuing a
life in business and started considering careers that demanded less competitive
zeal.

63 One evening when I was eleven I brought home a short "composition"
on my summer vacation which the teacher had graded with an A. Reading it
with her own schoolteacher's eye, my mother agreed that it was top-drawer
seventh grade prose and complimented me. Nothing more was said about it

immediately, but a new idea had taken life in her mind. Halfway through supper she suddenly interrupted the conversation.

64   "Buddy," she said, "maybe you could be a writer."

65   I clasped the idea to my heart. I had never met a writer, had shown no previous urge to write, and hadn't a notion how to become a writer, but I loved stories and thought that making up stories must surely be almost as much fun as reading them. Best of all, though, and what really gladdened my heart, was the ease of the writer's life. Writers did not have to trudge through the town peddling from canvas bags, defending themselves against angry dogs, being rejected by surly strangers. Writers did not have to ring doorbells. So far as I could make out, what writers did couldn't even be classified as work.

66   I was enchanted. Writers didn't have to have any gumption at all. I did not dare tell anybody for fear of being laughed at in the schoolyard but secretly I decided that what I'd like to be when I grew up was a writer.

Writing with Sources: Using a Single Source

Integrating information from "Starting Out in Journalism" with your own ideas, write an essay on one of these topics. Be sure to acknowledge all ideas that are not your own.

1. As Baker does, recall some of your earliest memories of your parents.
2. Describe your first job and how your parents reacted to it.
3. In paragraph 6 Baker says, "Fifty years ago parents still asked boys if they wanted to grow up and be President, and asked it not jokingly but seriously." Discuss why the situation is different today.

Writing with Sources: Using Multiple Sources

Integrating information from sources in this chapter with your own ideas, write an essay on one of the topics below. Be sure to acknowledge ideas that are not your own.

1. How did your childhood environment, experiences, and friends help to shape your adult life, particularly your choice of a college, major, and potential career? Explore these ideas.
2. Identify several milestones in your life — incidents that helped you to grow up. In what sense was each experience a significant force in your maturity?
3. A number of authors in this section focus on a disillusioning experience that they had as children or young adults. Compare the disillusioning experiences that two of the authors in this section had, and discuss how these experiences helped the individuals adjust their view of the world.

4. Assess the roles played by the parents of any three authors in this section. Would you consider them nurturing? How significant were they in the development of their children?
5. In spite of their different backgrounds, all the individuals in this section grew up to be writers. Analyze the experiences that several of the authors in this section had in common. What experiences did they have — even at a young age — that link them together?

13

The Nature of Violence

Pick up any paper today and you are sure to see ample evidence that we live in violent times. The causes of this violence are complex and extend back — so some people think — to our origins as human beings. Other observers believe that we do not have to look quite so far to find the roots of violence. They point to sports such as boxing, hockey, and football and to movies and television as the primary culprits. Still others blame the culture as a whole and say that violence has indeed shaped our consciousness. As examples these critics point to our folk heroes, our love of guns, and especially our history and reach the conclusion that violence has always been a part of our national character.

In "Violence as an American Tradition" Arthur Schlesinger reveals the violent underside of American history. Next, in "Group Violence," John Langone examines the dynamics of group violence and suggests causes for group behavior. In "Values and Violence in Sports Today" Brenda Jo Bredemeier and David L. Schields examine what happens when the values of sports spill over into the real world. Maria W. Piers, in "Crucifix and Clockwork Orange," argues that violence in the arts and on television does not in itself cause violent behavior in children. Phillip Knightly, in "The First Televised War," takes the position that journalists, by toning down the violence of the Vietnam War for prime-time audiences, deceived the American public. Finally, in "A Mirror to Man," Robert Claiborne considers whether violence in our species is innate or is a response to our environment.

Violence as an American Tradition

Arthur M. Schlesinger, Jr.

Arthur Schlesinger, born in 1917 in Columbus, Ohio, received his B.A. from Harvard University in 1938. A distinguished teacher and historian, he served on Adlai Stevenson's presidential campaign staff in 1952 and 1956. He was a special assistant to President John F. Kennedy from 1961 to 1963 and to President Lyndon Johnson from 1963 to 1964. Schlesinger is a trustee for the Robert F. Kennedy Center of the Performing Arts and the Robert F. Kennedy Memorial. He is the director of the Harry S. Truman Library Institute, the John Fitzgerald Kennedy Library, and the Ralph Bunche Institute. His awards include the Pulitzer Prize for history for *The Age of Jackson* (1946) and for biography for *A Thousand Days* (1966); the Francis Parkman Prize (1957); the Bancroft Prize (1958); the National Book Award in 1966 for *A Thousand Days* and in 1979 for *Robert Kennedy and His Times;* the National Institute for Arts and Letters Gold Medal for History (1967); the Ohio Governor's Award for History (1973); the Sidney Hillman Foundation Award (1973); and the Fregeme Prize for Literature (1983). The following selection, from Schlesinger's book *The Crisis of Confidence: Ideas, Power, and Violence in America* (1969), discusses how violence permeates our history and appears to have become a part of the American character.

1   Self-knowledge is the indispensable prelude to self-control; and self-knowledge, for a nation as well as for an individual, begins with history. We like to think of ourselves as a peaceful, tolerant, benign people who have always lived under a government of laws and not of men. And, indeed, respect for persons and for law has been one characteristic strain in the American tradition. Most Americans offer this respect most of their lives. Yet this is by no means the only strain in our tradition. For we also have been a violent people. When we refuse to acknowledge the existence of this other strain, we refuse to see our nation as it is.

2   We must recognize that an impulse to destroy coexists with our impulse to create — that the destructive impulse is in us and that it springs from some dark intolerable tension in our history and our institutions. We began, after all, as a people who killed red men and enslaved black men. No doubt we often did this with a Bible and a prayerbook. But no nation, however righteous its professions, could act as we did without doing something fearful to itself — without burying deep in itself, in its customs, its institutions, its conditioned reflexes and its psyche, a propensity toward violence. However much we pretended that Indians and Negroes were subhuman, we really knew that they were God's children too. It is almost as if this initial experience fixed a primal curse on our nation — a curse which still shadows our life.

3   It was a curse we have always flinched to acknowledge. In this respect our written history is revealing; for history, after all, is the record of a nation's consciousness. "To our reproach," Jefferson wrote in 1782, "it must be said that though for a century and a half we have had under our eyes the races of black and of red men, they have never yet been viewed by us as subjects of

natural history." This reproach, initially directed at scientists, applied in the next century and a half just as much as historians. White historians wrote of Indian wars, of slavery and so on; but they held racial events at a distance, treated them as isolated phenomena of a remote time and rarely connected them in any organic way with the development of the American character. They were engaged in the process Freud called "repression"—"the function of rejecting and keeping something out of consciousness." Repression, Freud added, "is, at bottom, an attempt at flight."

4   The evidence that such repression took place in the writing of American history is abundantly provided by American literature. For, if history is the record of a nation's consciousness, novels, short stories and poems are the mirror of a nation's unconscious. And, where our history has segregated race from the main course of American development, our literature has involuntarily perceived race as very near the heart of American life; it has been pervaded, indeed haunted, by images of racial unrest, aggression and guilt. What white America declined to confront in its explicit portrayal of the past, it could not escape in the dreams and fantasies that underlie artistic creation. "The Negro," said Richard Wright, "is America's metaphor." The colored American has been the symbol of white America's capacity for sin, the permanent but forgotten weight on the American conscience.

5   Our great writers have felt this, even if they did not precisely know what they were feeling. How else to account for the fact that the relationship between white man and colored man has been one of the grand themes of American fiction—a more basic theme, as Leslie Fiedler has insisted, than the relationship between man and woman? Leatherstocking and Chingachgook, Ishmael and Queequeg, Huck and Jim—these have signified the artists' compulsion to come to terms with the tragedy the historians have suppressed. There has always been in American literature what Melville called "the blackness of darkness beyond." But literature could only register this terrible wound; it could not heal it; it left the guilt hidden and malignant in the national unconscious, finding outlet in spasms of violence.

6   Perhaps nothing shaped our national unconscious more than the institutionalization of violence in the slavery system. "The whole commerce between master and slave," wrote Jefferson, "is a perpetual exercise of the most boisterous passions, the most unremitting despotism on the one part, and degrading submissions on the other. . . . The parent storms, the child looks on, catches the lineaments of wrath, puts on the same airs in the circle of smaller slaves, gives a loose to the worst of passions, and thus nursed, educated, and daily exercised in tyranny, cannot but be stamped by it with odious peculiarities. The man must be a prodigy who can retain his manners and moral undepraved by such circumstances." And Jefferson foresaw that slavery would demand retribution. "I tremble for my country when I reflect that God is just; that his justice cannot sleep forever; that considering numbers, nature and natural means only, a revolution of the wheel of fortune, an exchange of situation is among possible events. . . . The Almighty has no attribute which can take side with us in such a contest." Yet Jefferson himself retained his slaves; and, like him, his

countrymen, denying what they were doing, armed themselves with oblivious-
ness.

7   Mark Twain's meditation on the French Revolution illuminates with grim
exactitude the attitude of white America toward black America, from Nat
Turner to the latest ghetto riot:

> There were two "Reigns of Terror" if we would but remember it and consider it;
> the one wrought murder in hot passion, the other in heartless cold blood; the one
> lasted mere months, the other had lasted a thousand years; the one inflicted death
> upon ten thousand persons, the other upon a hundred millions; but our shudders
> are all for the "horrors" of the minor Terror, the momentary Terror, so to speak;
> whereas, what is the horror of swift death by the ax compared wih lifelong death
> from hunger, cold, insult, cruelty, and heartbreak? What is swift death by lightning
> compared with death by slow fire at the stake? A city cemetery could contain the
> coffins filled by the brief Terror which we have all been so diligently taught to
> shiver at and mourn over; but all France could hardly contain the coffins filled by
> the older and real Terror—that unspeakably bitter and awful Terror which none
> of us has been taught to see in its vastness or pity as it deserves.

8   Nor did we confine violence to red men and black men. Habits were
contagious. The first century after independence were years of indiscriminate
violence—wars, slave insurrections, Indian fighting, urban riots, murders,
duels, beatings. Members of Congress went armed to the Senate and House. In
his first notable speech, in January 1838, before the Young Men's Lyceum of
Springfield, Illinois, Abraham Lincoln named internal violence as the supreme
threat to American political institutions. He spoke of "the increasing disregard
for law which pervades the country; the growing disposition to substitute the
wild and furious passions, in lieu of the sober judgment of Courts; and the
worse than savage mobs, for the executive ministers of justice." The danger to
the American republic, he said, was not from foreign invasion. "At what point
then is the approach of danger to be expected? I answer, if it ever reach us, it
must spring up amongst us. It cannot come from abroad. If destruction be our
lot, we must ourselves be its author and finisher. As a nation of free men, we
must live through all time, or die by suicide."

9   So the young Lincoln named the American peril—a peril he did not fear
to locate within the American breast. Indeed, the sadness of America has been
that our worst qualities have so often been the other face of our best. Our
commitment to morality and our faith in experiment have been sources of
America's greatness. But they have also led Americans into temptation. For our
moralists have sometimes condoned murder if the cause was deemed good; so
Emerson and Thoreau applauded John Brown of Osawatomie. And our pragma-
tists have sometimes ignored the means if they approved the result; so Jefferson could write, "To lose our country by a scrupulous adherence to written
law, would be to lose the law itself, with life, liberty, property . . . thus
absurdly sacrificing the end to the means." Moralism and pragmatism have
hardly provided infallible restraints on the destructive instinct.

10   No one understood the American ambiguity better than Lincoln. No one
saw more poignantly the desperate need to control and transcend a national

propensity toward violence. This was the preoccupation of his life. "When . . . you have succeeded in dehumanizing the Negro," he said twenty years after his Springfield speech; "when you have put him down to be but as the beasts of the field; when you have extinguished his soul in this world and placed him where the ray of hope is blown out as in the darkness of the damned, are you quite sure that the demon you have roused will not turn and rend you?" It was both ironic and fortunate that a man who so profoundly perceived the curse of violence in American society should have been President during the greatest explosion of internal violence in our history.

11   Throughout the Civil War Lincoln tried unremittingly to discipline the destructive impulse; this effort produced his most majestic prose. "We are not enemies, but friends," he said of the rebels in his First Inaugural. "Though passion may have strained, it must not break our bonds of affection." And in his Second Inaugural: "With malice toward none; with charity for all; with firmness in the right, as God gives us to see the right, let us strive on to finish the work we are in; to bind up the nation's wounds." In the end our greatest enemy of violence and hate became our greatest victim of violence and hate.

12   The impulses of violence and civility continued after Lincoln to war within the American breast. The insensate bloodshed of the Civil War exhausted the national capacity for violence and left the nation emotionally and psychologically spent. For half a century America remained substantially at peace (the Spanish-American War lasted only a few weeks). For nearly a century after Appomattox we appeared on the surface the tranquil and friendly people we still like to imagine ourselves to be. The amiability of that society no doubt exerted a restraining influence. There were still crazy individuals, filled with grievance, bitterness and a potential for violence. But most of these people expended their sickness in fantasy; the Guiteaus and the Czolgoszes were the exception. These years of stability, a stability fitfully recaptured after the First World War, created the older generation's image of a "normal" America.

13   Yet even in the kindly years we did not wholly eradicate the propensity toward violence which history had hidden in the national unconscious. Walt Whitman noted "the battle, advancing, retreating, between democracy's convictions, aspirations, and the people's crudeness, vice, caprices," and William James commented, "Angelic impulses and predatory lusts divide our heart exactly as they divide the hearts of other countries." Mark Twain wrote of "The United States of Lyncherdom" and attributed "To the Person Sitting in Darkness" (i.e., those living in underdeveloped countries) this proposition about the United States: "There must be two Americas: one that sets the captive free, and one that takes a once-captive's new freedom away from him, and picks a quarrel with him with nothing to found it on; then kills him to get his land." Nor was Jack London's *The Iron Heel* a novel about czarist Russia. In certain moods, indeed, we prided ourselves on our violence; we almost considered it evidence of our virility. "Above all," cried Theodore Roosevelt, "let us shrink from no strife, moral or physical, within or without the nation, provided we are certain that the strife is justified." The fatal susceptibility always lurked under

the surface, breaking out in Indian wars and vigilantism in the west, in lynchings in the south, in labor riots and race riots and gang wars in the cities.

14   It is important to distinguish collective from individual violence — the work of mobs from the work of murderers; for the motive and the effect can be very different. There can, of course, be murder by a mob. This was such a national problem at the turn of the century that Theodore Roosevelt, who as it turned out was not all that gratified by the beauties of strife, reminded white America in a passionate State of the Union message

> that every lynching represents by just so much a loosening of the bands of civilization; that the spirit of lynching inevitably throws into prominence in the community all the foul and evil creatures who dwell therein. No man can take part in the torture of a human being without having his own moral nature permanently lowered. Every lynching means just so much moral deterioration in all the children who have any knowledge of it, and therefore just so much additional trouble to the next generation of Americans.

But not all mobs aim at murder. Collective violence — rioting against what were considered illegal British taxes in Boston in 1773, or dangerous Papist influence sixty years later, or inequitable draft laws in New York in 1863, or unfair labor practices in Chicago in 1937 — is more characteristically directed at property and process than at people. In many cases (though by no means all), the aim has been to protest rather than protect the status quo; and the historian is obliged to concede that collective violence has often forced those in power to recognize long-denied rights. Extra-legal group action, for better or worse, has been part of the process of American democracy. Violence, for better or worse, *does* settle some questions, and for the better. Violence secured American independence, freed the slaves and stopped Hitler.

15   But this has ordinarily been the violence of a mass. The individual who commits violence is less likely to be concerned with reforming conditions than with punishing persons. On occasion his purpose is to protect the status quo by destroying men who symbolize or threaten social change (a tactic which the anarchists employed in reverse). A difference exists in psychic color and content between spontaneous mass convulsions and the premeditated killing of individuals. The first signifies an unstable society, the second a murderous society. America has exhibited both forms of violence. The second is more ominous. "Of the last seven elected Presidents," Theodore Roosevelt said in 1901 after the assassination of William McKinley, "he is the third who has been murdered, and the bare recital of this fact is sufficient to justify great alarm among all loyal American citizens." Of the ten Presidents who followed McKinley, four at one time or another in their lives were targets of assassination attempts. The United States has compiled a record in this field not often exceeded by those banana republics on whose politics North Americans look with such disdain.

16   Along with a devotion to law, a covert relish in violence has been an abiding strain in American history. Dr. Karl Menninger's observation about

contemporary American applies equally to the American past: "The crime and punishment ritual is part of our lives. . . . We need criminals to identify ourselves with, to envy secretly, and to punish stoutly. They do for us the forbidden, illegal things we *wish* to do and, like scapegoats of old, they bear the burdens of our displaced guilt and punishment." Our popular heroes have been precisely those who joined the themes of violence and law — the quiet, strong, lonely men, from frontier marshals to private eyes, who drew their guns in order to establish order. But can personal violence and public law be truly joined? The effort to do so made America, in the words of Martin Luther King, "a schizophrenic personality, tragically divided against herself."

Writing with Sources: Using a Single Source

Integrating information from "Violence as an American Tradition" with your own ideas, write an essay on one of these topics. Be sure to acknowledge all ideas that are not your own.

1. Consulting an encyclopedia or a history book, write an essay that either supports or contradicts Schlesinger's statement that "we have . . . been a violent people" (1). Support your thesis with a series of examples.

2. According to Henry David Thoreau in his essay "Civil Disobedience," "Unjust laws exist: shall we be content to obey them, or shall we endeavor to ammend them, and obey them until we have succeeded, or shall we transgress them at once?" Like Thoreau, many Americans have traditionally felt civil disobedience is a just response to unjust laws. Discuss the attitude toward civil disobedience Schlesinger expresses when he says, "Indeed, the sadness of America has been that our worst qualities have so often been the other face of our best. Our commitment to morality and our faith in experiment have been sources of America's greatness" (9).

3. In paragraph 16 Schlesinger quotes Dr. Karl Menninger, who says, "We need criminals to identify ourselves, to envy secretly, and to punish stoutly. . . ." Schlesinger continues, "Our popular heroes — from marshals to police — join the themes of violence and law and draw their guns to establish order." Go through the weekly television guide in your Sunday paper and count the number of prime-time network programs that fit this description. Then use your findings to support the thesis, "More than just entertainment, prime-time television is a reflection of inner tensions that are central to the American character."

Group Violence

John Langone

John Langone, born in 1929 in Cambridge, Massachusetts, received a B.S. from Boston University and was a special student at the School of Medicine at Harvard University. He was a Kennedy Fellow in medical ethics at Harvard University, a fellow at the Center for Advanced Sciences at Stanford, and a Fulbright Fellow in Japan. Langone traveled with the National Science Foundation to Antarctica and to the South Pole in 1972, and to Israel in 1973, to report on developments in science and medicine. Currently, Langone is a teacher, an editor, and a staff writer for *Discover* magazine. He has written a number of nonfiction books including *Vital Signs: The Way We Die in America* (1974); *Human Engineering: Marvel or Menace?* (1978); *Long Life: What We Know and Are Learning About the Aging Process* (1978); *Women Who Drink* (1980); *Thorny Issues: How Ethics and Morality Affect the Way We Live* (1981); and *Violence: Our Fastest Growing Public Health Problem* (1984). The following selection, from *Violence: Our Fastest Growing Public Health Problem*, examines the factors that lie at the root of mob violence.

There is no grievance that is a fit object of redress by mob law. —Abraham Lincoln

1   Violence can be done by individuals with their own private motives, and by individuals working for the motives of a special group. Many times, when one person assaults another it is for highly personal reasons: a drug dealer murders an undercover agent to escape arrest, a woman kills a lover who has been cheating on her to punish him and the other woman, an irate employee murders the manager who fired him, a young man provokes a brawl to prove he is tough, a woman is raped because her attacker was once spurned by a high school girlfriend and now hates all women.

2   But quite often, individuals commit violent acts not only to satisfy themselves but also to gain some benefit for a group of people. They may belong to a lynch mob that takes the law into its own hands and executes a suspect before he or she has had a fair trial; they may be members of a secret society of misguided zealots that uses violence to intimidate; they may be participants in a family feud, a private war waged for generations to avenge the death of one of its members long ago; they may be political terrorists who use violence to force change, or to call attention to their cause, or to avenge some real or imagined or long-past insult or wrong. Some people may not even be members of the group for whom they commit violence: a hired assassin, for instance, might not be at all concerned with the philosophy or actions of the world leader he has been paid to eliminate, nor have any personal grudge against him. But whether such hired killers formally belong to an organization is not all that important; their reasons for maiming and killing are usually to further the aims of that group.

3   Let us begin our discussion of group violence by looking at what psychologists call crowd behavior, popularly known as mob psychology. Certainly, there are no formal membership requirements, no dues to be paid, to join a

lynch mob or a student riot. Unlike some of the other forms of group violence to be discussed later, mob violence is often unplanned and unorganized; a mob's members lose their ability to think rationally, so intent are they on acting as one; its leadership generally depends on who can shout the loudest, or who is strong enough to get to the front of the crowd fastest. Moreover, a mob generally breaks up rather quickly once its purpose has been achieved. Says one sociology textbook, "In crowd behavior, irrational as it always is, the impulse to follow a suggested course of action is obeyed at once; whereas, in any form of rational behavior, there is always delay enough to permit comparisons and evaluations."[1]

4   Experts in mob psychology say the anatomy of a riot begins with a precipitating event, a trigger. This may be the arrest of someone the crowd believes to be innocent or a scapegoat; an assault on a white by a black, or vice versa; a simple official act, like the dedication of a statue of a controversial figure; the parking of a foreign car near an automobile factory that suffered high unemployment because of foreign-car imports; or merely the announcement that a state has approved the construction of a nuclear power plant.

5   As word of the triggering event spreads, the crowd becomes angrier; finally, violence erupts, escalating from shouting and occasional rock throwing to open street war as the rioters clash with police, others in authority, or those who oppose their views. Such a situation has been compared to the outbreak of a disease epidemic. Dr. John P. Spiegel, who headed the Lemberg Center for the Study of Violence at Brandeis University, once said of mass violence, "You just can't ignore it, isolate it, or hope that it will cure itself."[2]

6   Often, the common hostility of a crowd has been festering for some time, and is not just a sudden eruption. If, for instance, a hostile mob has gathered at a civil rights parade, the concerted action taken when some incident or person ignites the violence is the result of a long-standing racial conflict simmering in each member of the crowd. Matters are obviously made much worse, and the mob becomes more inflamed, if whatever it is that provokes the riot has not been dealt with fairly, or at all, by authorities.

7   A mob generally behaves in ways that its individual members would shun if alone: few members of a riotous crowd would, for example, stand alone in front of a policeman and shout obscenities at him; nor would many people break a store window in broad daylight and help themselves to a television set or a wristwatch; and it is highly unlikely that mob members would, acting alone, attempt to crash a gate at a navy base to protest the docking of a nuclear submarine. It is the *gathering* of individuals, with their strong, shared feeling, that gives the individuals within the group their sense of courage and power, and allows each to release impulses usually kept under control. Wartime and periods of insurrection contain proof of that. For example, on Easter Monday in

---

[1] R. L. Sutherland and Julian L. Woodward, *Introductory Sociology,* 2nd edition (Philadelphia: J. B. Lippincott, 1940), p. 317.

[2] "Is Mass Violence an Epidemic Disease?," *Medical World News,* September 1, 1967, p. 48.

1282, on the island of Sicily, a riot broke out after a French soldier insulted a Sicilian woman in front of a church at the hour of evening worship, or vespers; in what came to be known as the Sicilian Vespers, the riot swelled to a political revolt against the Angevin French who ruled the island, and virtually the entire French population was murdered. In Nanking, China, during World War II, drunken Japanese soldiers and sailors slaughtered 150,000 Chinese and raped some 5,000 women in an outbreak of mob brutality that seems almost inconceivable.

8   Mob action, like the violence it spawns, is not new. Dissent has a long history, and mobs have gathered since at least the early Roman days — when loud protests were lodged even then against the high cost of living — to air economic, political, and social grievances, or to vent their anger against other groups. In China in 1900, for example, a branch of a sect known as the White Lotus — also called Boxers — rose up against foreigners. Missionaries were murdered, a German official was assassinated, and later some two hundred foreigners were driven to seek refuge in the British legation. They were besieged by the Boxers for two months, and were finally rescued by an expedition of soldiers from America, Great Britain, France, Germany, Russia, and Japan. A few years later, on January 22, 1905, Russian peasant workers marched on Saint Petersburg to present a petition to the czar. They were attacked by the czar's troops and hundreds of unarmed workers were killed.

9   In the United States, mobs turned against immigrants, especially Orientals and Irish Catholics, in the 1800s. Native-born Americans, fearful that the immigrants would gain political power, and angry that they were taking jobs for cheaper pay, regularly attacked the immigrants in the streets. During the same period, bloody labor riots erupted in cities across the United States, and many lives were lost. In 1886, for instance, there was the celebrated Haymarket riot in Chicago. It occurred when police tried to break up a labor protest meeting organized by anarchists — people who believe that all forms of government are unnecessary and undesirable. Someone threw a bomb, killing seven policemen and wounding seventy other people. A few years later, during the so-called Homestead strike at the Carnegie Steel Company plant in Pennsylvania, an armed clash took place between workers and detectives hired by the company; a number of men were killed, and soon after, the state militia had to be sent in to restore order.

10   Even today, workers are sometimes set upon. In 1983, when a group of independent truckers went on strike, thousands of trucks that defied the strike and kept on rolling were damaged by rocks thrown from bridges, by nails spread on the highways, and by gunfire. Many drivers were injured and one was killed.

11   Race has also been a factor in mob violence. During World War I (1914 – 1918), many blacks took jobs in defense factories. The whites were afraid that the blacks would take their jobs and move into white neighborhoods. Several violent incidents occurred — the worst in East Saint Louis in 1917 when some forty blacks and ten whites were killed during a riot. Similar racial violence

broke out after World War II (1939–1945) and has continued through the years. Among the worst in recent years were the riots in the Watts section of Los Angeles in 1965, and in Newark and Detroit in 1967.

12   In the sixties and seventies, mob violence was common during the student protests against the war in Vietnam (1957–1975). In one of the largest such demonstrations, thousands of young people gathered in Chicago during the 1968 Democratic National Convention and battled with police in the streets. Around the same time, militant black students regularly resorted to violence to back up demands for more Afro-American history and culture courses in their colleges.

13   But of all this mob violence, the two incidents that stand out in recent years, perhaps for the emotional impact they had on Americans, were the tragic student deaths at Kent State University in Ohio in 1970, and the riot at Attica state prison in New York the following year. The two events were unrelated — the Kent State incident came during demonstrations against President Nixon's decision to send U.S. forces into Cambodia, and the Attica uprising stemmed from charges that inmates, most of them black, had been mistreated by white guards. But both places have become unofficial national monuments to the tragic consequences of confrontation.

14   The Kent State incident began with students throwing rocks, bricks, and bottles at National Guardsmen, and guardsmen firing tear gas. Then, some of the guardsmen knelt and pointed rifles at demonstrators, who shouted, "Shoot, shoot, shoot!" The kneeling guardsmen did not fire. But moments later, it happened. "I heard the first shot," one account quoted a guardsman as saying. "I had my rifle at my shoulder, not sighting, just at my shoulder. I had my finger on the trigger and fired when the others did. I just didn't think about it. It just happened. How can you think at a time like that? Right after the first shot, it sounded like everyone squeezed off one round, like at the range, drawn out. I fired once. I just closed my eyes and shot. I didn't aim at anyone in particular. I just shot at shoulder level toward the crowd." An estimated sixty shots were fired, and thirteen seconds later, when it was over, four of the student demonstrators had been killed, nine wounded. Two reporters who were there that day wrote, "Most of the victims were dressed in bell-bottoms and flowered Apache shirts, and most had Rolling Stone haircuts. Some carried books. The guardsmen wore battle helmets, gas masks, fatigues, and combat boots. The two sides looked, to each other, like the inhabitants of different worlds. . . . Blood shimmered on the grass. Bullet holes marked the trees. A generation of college students said they had lost all hope for the System and the future."[3]

15   The Attica incident was just as chaotic. The revolt involved some one thousand prisoners, who held thirty-eight guards and civilian workers hostage for four days. Faced with the possibility that the convicts would carry out threats to kill the hostages, New York Governor Nelson Rockefeller ordered

---

[3] Joe Eszterhas and Michael D. Roberts, *Thirteen Seconds: Confrontation at Kent State* (New York: Dodd, Mead & Co., 1970), pp. 163, 8.

state troopers to storm the facility. In the assault, which included use of a tear-gas-spraying helicopter, thirty-two prisoners and nine guards and employees were killed. Rockefeller, who had turned down a request that he personally visit the prison during the revolt, defended the action, saying, "There was no alternative but to go in." Adding to the depth of the tragedy were reports that many of the hostages had died of bullet wounds, rather than by knife attacks from convicts — an indication that, as commonly happens in scenes of mob violence, some people were killed unintentionally. Shortly after the riot was quelled, Rockefeller acknowledged that it was possible state troopers had killed some of the hostages. "If you recreate the circumstances of that situation — where the troopers had instructions to shoot the executioners who had been assigned to each of the prisoners [a reference to convicts menacing hostages] and who were standing there with a knife at his throat — then you add to that the helicopter coming in with the gas, and the effect of the gas — which first creates a cloud and then has an effect on the individual — you have a scene of chaos that is one in which accidents can very well happen."[4]

16   Both the Kent State tragedy and the awful ending to the Attica revolt raise questions about how much force should be used to put down a disturbance. Often, as has been seen, the mob itself loots and burns and kills; other times, however, it is the authorities who lose control and riot. The Boston Massacre of March 5, 1770, is a familiar example of such a situation, and one that is sometimes used when the events at Kent State are being discussed. The stationing of British soldiers in Boston in 1768 had provoked a good deal of anger among the citizens. Matters came to a head when more troops were sent to the city to protect customs commissioners. A mob of men and boys, led by a black named Crispus Attucks, began throwing missiles at the soldiers, who responded by firing into the crowd, killing five. Some witnesses regarded the unfortunate incident as a lawless affair that discredited both soldiers and the crowd; others have seen it as a historically significant event, an important preliminary to the American Revolution. Whatever it was, it lends substance to the old expression that a policeman's lot is not a happy one. "Police often vacillate between brutal suppression and inaction," said Dr. Spiegel. "If they use excessive force, they encourage the use of counterforce. If they do nothing, they encourage rioters and looters."[5]

17   The Kent State and Attica incidents may also make it somewhat easier to justify the violent explosion of a mob. Many people become angered after being maltreated, as at Attica, or provoked, as were the guardsmen at Kent State, and it is quite natural, although perhaps wrong, to lash out occasionally at the people believed responsible. When nobody listens to a complaint that appears to be legitimate, when nobody tries to rectify a bad situation, a violent act is perhaps the only way left to focus attention on the wrong, and help get something done about it.

[4] *New York Times,* September 16, 1971, p. 1.
[5] "Is Mass Violence an Epidemic Disease?," *Medical World News,* September 1, 1967, p. 48.

Writing with Sources: Using a Single Source

Integrating information from "Group Violence" with your own ideas, write an essay on one of these topics. Be sure to acknowledge all ideas that are not your own.

1. Describe a time when you did something as a member of a group that you would not have done if you had been alone. In your essay, relate your experience to the "mob psychology" that Langone discusses in paragraph 3.
2. Consult a history book or a newspaper and find an example of mob violence. Then, in an essay, determine whether or not the mob action follows the "anatomy of a riot" that Langone discusses in paragraph 4.
3. Explain why you agree or disagree with Langone's statement, "When nobody listens to a complaint that appears to be legitimate, when nobody tries to rectify a bad situation, a violent act is perhaps the only way left to focus attention on the wrong, and to help get something done about it" (17). Support your thesis with examples.

Values and Violence in Sports Today

Brenda Jo Bredemeier and David L. Shields

Brenda Jo Bredemeier is an assistant professor of sport psychology in the department of physical education at the University of California at Berkeley. David L. Shields is a visiting research fellow with the department of physical education at the University of California at Berkeley and is the author of *Prejudice to Pluralism* (1986). In the following article, Bredemeier and Shields discuss the attitudes toward violence that athletes reveal in their games and in their lives.

1   To be good in sports, you have to be bad. Or so many athletes, coaches and sports fans believe. Heavyweight champion Larry Holmes, for example, revealed a key to his success during a *60 Minutes* interview with Morley Safer: Before he enters the ring, he said, "I have to change, I have to leave the goodness out and bring all the bad in, like Dr. Jekyll and Mr. Hyde."

2   Even sports fan Ronald Reagan suggested that normally inappropriate ways of thinking and acting are acceptable in sports. When he was governor of California, he reportedly told a college team during a pep talk that in football, "you can feel a clean hatred for your opponent. It is a clean hatred since it's only symbolic in a jersey."

3   Does success today really depend on how well an athlete or team has mastered the art of aggression? The question is usually answered more by ideology than by evidence. But there is a more fundamental question that needs to be asked: Is it really OK to be bad in sports? In particular, is aggression an acceptable tactic on the playing field? If it is morally unacceptable, the debate about its utility misses the mark.

4   It seems odd to ask whether being bad is all right. But in contact sports particularly, acts of aggression are seldom condemned, usually condoned and often praised. Sport is a "world within a world" with its own unique conventions and moral understandings.

5   Lyle and Glenn Blackwood of the Miami Dolphins are nicknamed "the bruise brothers." Their motto—"We don't want to hurt you, just make you hurt"—aptly expresses the ambiguity many people feel about sport aggression. To reduce such ambiguity, many athletes appeal to game rules, informal agreements or personal convictions to decide the legitimacy of aggressive acts. As one collegiate basketball player told us in an interview: "It's OK to try to hurt somebody if it is legal and during the game. If the guy doesn't expect it, it's a cheap shot. That's no good. You can be aggressive and do minor damage without really hurting him and still accomplish your goal."

6   As social scientists, we are interested in the moral meaning athletes and fans attach to aggression. Do sport participants think about aggression in moral terms? Does the maturity of athletes' moral reasoning influence their aggressive behavior? What are the unique characteristics of sport morality and how does this "game reasoning" influence the perceived legitimacy of aggression?

7   Most recommendations for reducing sport aggression have focused on rules and penalties against fighting, beanballs, slugging and other forms of violence. We believe, however, that reducing athletic aggression requires the transformation of both external sports structures such as rules and penalties and internal reasoning structures. To reduce aggression, we must first understand the meaning athletes attach to it.

8   By aggression, we mean acts that are intended to inflict pain or injury. Robust, physically forceful play not meant to harm another player is better termed assertion. Unfortunately, this distinction is often blurred on the mat, the ice and the Astroturf.

9   We believe that aggression is more than a convention; it is a moral issue and can be investigated as such. If this is true, there should be an inverse relationship between the maturity of athletes' moral reasoning and their acceptance of aggression. Our research suggests that this relationship exists. The higher their level of moral reasoning, the less aggression athletes practice and condone.

10   Establishing a link between moral reasoning and sport aggression is only the first step in understanding it. It is still not clear why many people find everyday aggression objectionable but have few moral qualms when they or others hurl a beanball at a batter. We can develop a more complete portrait of athletic aggression by exploring the unique patterns of moral reasoning that sport encourages.

11   Some social scientists have noted a curious fact that athletes and fans take for granted. Sport is set apart both cognitively and emotionally from the everyday world. Anthropologist Don Handelman, for example, has observed that play "requires a radical transformation in cognition and perception." Sociologist Ervin Goffman has described play activities as enclosed within a unique "social membrane" or conceptual "frame."

12   In a 1983 interview, Ron Rivera, then a linebacker with the University of California at Berkeley and now with the Chicago Bears, described the personality transformation he undergoes on the field. The off-field Ron, he said, is soft-spoken, considerate and friendly. When asked to describe the on-field Ron, he replied, "He's totally opposite from me. . . . He's a madman. . . . No matter what happens, he hits people. He's a guy with no regard for the human body." Elaborating further, Rivera revealed, "I'm mean and nasty then. . . . I'm so rotten. I have a total disrespect for the guy I'm going to hit."

13   Does this personality transformation include a fundamental change in moral reasoning? To explore this possibility, we designed a study to see whether the same people would use similar levels of moral reasoning in response to hypothetical dilemmas set in sport-specific and daily life contexts. One "sport dilemma," for example, centered on Tom, a football player who is told by his coach to injure an opponent to help Tom's team win. One of the "daily life" dilemmas hinged on whether a person should keep his promise to deliver some money to a rich man or use it to help his hungry kin.

14   We presented four dilemmas to 120 high school and college athletes and nonathletes and asked them to reason about the best way to resolve each dilemma. Most of the students clearly perceived a difference between morality in sport and in everyday life. One comment by a high school female basketball player exemplified this perspective: "In sports, it's hard to tell right from wrong sometimes; you have to use game sense." Both athletes and nonathletes used lower-level egocentric moral reasoning when thinking about dilemmas in sport than when addressing moral issues in other contexts.

15   These and other findings suggest that moral norms which prescribe equal consideration of all people are often suspended during competition in favor of a more egocentric moral perspective. One male college basketball player explained the difference this way: "In sports you can do what you want. In life it's more restricted. It's harder to make decisions in life because there are so many people to think about, different people to worry about. In sports you're free to think about yourself."

16   This theme was echoed by many others who referred to sport as a field where each person or team seeks personal triumph and where opponents need not be given equal consideration.

17   There are several reasons sports may elicit an egocentric style of game reasoning. The very nature of competition requires that self-interest be temporarily adopted while the athlete strives to win. In everyday life, such preoccupation with self almost inevitably leads to moral failings. But in sport, participants are freed to concentrate on self-interest by a carefully balanced rule structure that equalizes opportunity. Players are guarded against the moral defaults of others by protective rules and by officials who impose sanctions for violations. Moral responsibility is thus transferred from the shoulders of players to those of officials, the enforcers of the rules, and to coaches, whom the players learn to see as responsible for all decisions.

18   If the nature of competition encourages egocentricity, the "set aside" character of sport helps to justify it. Sport consists of artificial goals that are

achieved through arbitrarily defined skills and procedures. Although running across a line or shooting a ball through a hoop is all-important in the immediate game context, neither has significant consequences outside sports. This lack of any "real world" meaning to sport actions helps make egocentric reasoning seem legitimate.

19   Not all sport goals, of course, lack real-world implications. In boxing, for example, where the goal involves damage to another person, serious injury or even death is possible. Another exception is professional sports, and even some collegiate and high school sports, where winners may receive prizes, bigger paychecks, more perks or expanded educational and professional opportunities. The moral implications of harm as a sport goal (boxing) and extrinsic rewards contingent on sport performance (in professional and quasi-professional sports) still need to be investigated.

20   The dynamic of competition, the structural protection provided by officials and rules and the relatively inconsequential implications of sport intentions combine to release sport participants from the usual demands of morality. But game-specific moral understandings do not completely replace everyday morality. Just as sport exists in a unique space and time within the everyday world, so game reasoning is a form of "bracketed morality." The transformed morality that occurs in sport does not take the place of everyday morality; rather, it is embedded in the broader, more encompassing morality of daily life.

21   Because of this, most athletes limit the degree of sport aggression they accept as legitimate in line with their general understanding of the rights of others. Coordinating these two sets of standards is not easy. Consider, for example, how one athlete reasoned about the football dilemma in which Tom is told to injure his opponent:

22   "If Tom looks at it as a game, it's OK to hurt the guy — to try to take him out of the game. But if he looks at the halfback as a person, and tries to hurt him, it's not OK." Asked, "How do you decide which to go by?" the athlete explained, "When you're on the field, then the game is football. Before and after, you deal with people morally."

23   This man recognized that aggression can be viewed from two contrasting viewpoints but eliminated his ambivalence by subordinating everyday morality to game reasoning. For him, an opponent is a player, not a person. This objectification of opponents reduces an athlete's sense of personal responsibility for competitors.

24   Among some of the other athletes we interviewed, accountability was alleviated by simply "not thinking about it." As one athlete stated succinctly, "In sports you don't think about those things [hurting others]; mostly you don't think about other people, you just think about winning."

25   Most athletes, however, tried to coordinate game and everyday morality by distinguishing between legitimate and illegitimate aggression. As one man explained: "Some [aggressive acts] are not acceptable. The game is a game. You go out to win, but there's a line — limitations — there are rules. . . . You try to dominate the other player, but you don't want to make him leave the game."

26   Another athlete put it this way: "Tom shouldn't try to hurt him. He should just hit him real hard, stun him, make him lose his wind, make sure he's too scared to run the ball again."

27   Players use a complex moral logic in attempts to coordinate the goal of winning with the need to respect limits to egocentricity. Some athletes identify the rules as the final arbiter of legitimacy, but most appeal to less formal criteria. Themes such as intimidation, domination, fairness and retribution are continuously woven into participants' fabric of thought, providing a changing picture of what constitutes legitimate action.

28   Shifting expectations, created by the fast-paced and emotionally charged action, can readily lead to perceived violations or "cheap shots." Cheap shots, of course, are in the eye, or ribs, of the beholder. As a college basketball player explained, physical contact may be interpreted by athletes as either assertive or aggressive, depending on their perception of intent: "I've played with guys who try to hurt you. They use all kinds of cheap shots, especially elbows in the face and neck. But that's different than trying to maintain postion or letting a guy know you're there. An elbow can be for intimidation or it can be for hurting. I just use elbows in the regular course of the game."

29   Given the complex and variable conditions of sport, it is not surprising that among the athletes we interviewed there was not a clear consensus about the line between legitimate and illegitimate aggression. Generally, we found that the more mature the athletes' moral reasoning, the less aggression they accepted as legitimate — both for the fictitious character Tom in the hypothetical football dilemma and for themselves as they reasoned about personal aggression.

30   Yet even the more morally mature athletes often accepted minor forms of aggression as legitimate game strategy. In fact, such minor aggression was sometimes viewed as a positive, enhancing aspect of the game. As a high school player explained: "Football is a rough game and if it weren't for rules people would get hurt real bad — even killed. Some people just want to hurt other people real bad." Asked, "Should the present rules be changed to reduce football injuries?" he replied, "No. Nobody will want to play if the rules get so uptight that you can't hit hard."

31   Moral research inevitably leads beyond descriptions about what people do to questions about what people ought to do. Perhaps most athletes accept some aggression as "part of the game," but should they? Should any degree of aggression be considered legitimate?

32   Based on what we have learned about game reasoning, we believe two criteria can be employed to distinguish morally mature athletes' judgments of aggression which they may perceive as legitimate from aggression which certainly is not. First, any act intended to inflict an injury that is likely to have negative consequences for the recipient once the game has ended is illegitimate. The legitimacy of game reasoning depends partly on the irrelevance of sport action to everyday life. Consequently, inflicting such "game-transcending" injuries as a broken leg or a concussion cannot be morally justified.

33   Second, game reasoning is also legitimated because it occurs within a

situation that is defined by a set of rules that limit the relevant procedures and skills which can be used during the game. Therefore, any act is illegitimate if it occurs apart from the strategic employment of game-relevant skills, even if such an act is intended to cause only minor injury or mild discomfort. Such behavior impinges upon the protective structure that releases participants from their normal moral obligations.

34   The implications of our research on athletes' game reasoning may extend to other spheres of life. If game reasoning is distinct from the morality of general life, are there other context-specific moralities, such as business reasoning or political reasoning? Perhaps the list could be extended indefinitely. While every context raises unique moral issues, however, we agree with most moral-development theorists that the fundamental structure of moral reasoning remains relatively stable in nearly all situations.

35   Sport is employed frequently as a metaphor for other endeavors, and game language is often utilized in discussions of such diverse topics as business, politics and war. A recent book by Thomas Whisler of the University of Chicago, *Rules of the Game,* has little to do with sport and everything to do with corporate boardrooms.

36   The borrowing of sport images and language may reflect a tendency to transplant game morality from its native soil to foreign gardens. If this is the case, game reasoning has social implications that extend far beyond the limited world of sport. Game morality is legitimated by protections within the sport structure, but most other contexts lack such safeguards. If game reasoning leads to manipulation to gain job advancement, for example, are adequate laws available and enforced to guarantee equal opportunity? Can the dirty tricks of politics be legitimated as if they were just a game? Does game reasoning encourage a view that nuclear war is winnable, propelling us toward the "game to end all games"? And if it does, who consents to play these games?

Writing with Sources: Using a Single Source

Integrating information from "Values and Violence in Sports Today" with your own ideas, write an essay on one of these topics. Be sure to acknowledge all ideas that are not your own.

1. Describe your behavior and the behavior of your teammates while participating in a sport. Do you perceive the "world within a world" that the authors mention in paragraph 4? Explain.
2. Psychologist Jeffery H. Goldstein of Temple University explains fan violence by saying, "The people watching an aggressive sport are likely to become more aggressive themselves; thus, the sequence of events tends to perpetuate itself — the fans themselves feel aggressive, they sense or see aggression and then they act aggressively." Drawing on material from "Values and Violence in Sports Today" and Goldstein's remarks, as well as your own experience as a spectator, consider the truth of this statement.

3. Describe the dangers of employing sport as a metaphor for endeavors such as business, politics, and war. Before writing this essay, look through several newspapers and news magazines to gather examples of this phenomenon.

Crucifix and Clockwork Orange

Maria W. Piers

Maria W. Piers was born in 1911 in Vienna. She received her Ph.D. from the University of Vienna in 1939 and did additional work at Northwestern University and the Chicago Institute of Psychoanalysis. She has taught at the University of Chicago and is Distinguished Professor of Child Development at the Erikson Institute for Early Education, affiliated with Loyola University of Chicago. Piers is also on the board of advisors for the Advisory Committee for Family Viewing and the American Parents Committee. Among the many books that she has written on the subject of child development are *Growing Up With Children* (1966), *The Wages of Neglect* (1969), *Play and Development* (1972), *Infanticide* (1978), and *The Gift of Play* (1980). The following essay, from *Infanticide,* examines the effects on children of violent themes in the arts.

1   Tourists vacationing in my native Austria are likely to eat three meals a day in a *Gaststube* with cozy benches, checkered tablecloths, and all of the attributes of homeyness. In a corner of the *Gaststube,* however, they find, almost invariably, the realistic effigy of a corpse: Christ on the cross. Such an effigy can be seen in virtually every farmhouse, nailed over many a stable door, and often by the roadside. Occasionally, in place of a crucifix one finds a pietà or the statue of some martyred saint. Tourists come and go; but the native children stay, and they are the ones who grow up in the constant presence of representations of bloodshed.

2   Has it changed the national character? Has the perennial sight of the crucifix made the Austrians more violent? The accusation hurled at the media implies, obviously, that representation of violence turns impressionable young people into brutes.

3   What about the Austrians? They have no doubt produced their share of street crime, gang violence, and murder. They also committed a sizable number of large-scale bloody deeds, not the least of which was their participation in the Holocaust. But can one rightly say that the proneness of Austrians to bloodshed exceeds that of people who grew up under the portraits of the neatly uniformed Kaiser Wilhelm, or Hitler, or Stalin, or the paternally benevolent Mao? And what about those who grow up under the likenesses of the ladylike Queen or the meditating Buddha, that epitome of peace? Which patriotic or religious symbols have a more pernicious influence on the young? In terms of the amount of bloodshed, it is clearly a toss-up.

4   On the other hand, violent themes have been a mainstay of all the arts in

general, with some exceptions such as love lyrics. But nowhere is violence as prevalent as it is in the drama. For thousands of years — and to this very day — the drama by definition has dealt with the most awesome human passions, and perhaps most frequently among these, violence. What does this do to the audience? People who attend *Macbeth* or *Oedipus Rex,* or view the film *Clockwork Orange,* do not show a significantly higher incidence of brutality than those who do not.

5   The origin of the drama is religious. Although in our modern civilization it is no longer experienced as such (since theater attendance is connected with "scalpers'" fees, traffic jams, parking problems, and other sobering impediments), it is, even now, a festive occasion. As soon as the curtain rises, members of the audience are emotionally transported onto the stage and share with tears and laughter and angry indignation in the fate of the protagonists. The drama gives us an opportunity to experience vicariously a kind of gratification of our most secret and most unacceptable wishes, without inviting the least bit of trouble, either with the law or with ourselves. And as we emerge from the performance, we usually feel relieved, uplifted or thoughtful. But we are not disposed to plan, let alone commit, a violent deed. If anything, attending a play decreases the probability of violence.

6   It seems that the vast majority of theater-goers or TV watchers experience vicarious suffering more strongly than people do when looking at a crucifix. Without dwelling on the many obvious differences between a static representation and a play or movie, we might rather contemplate what the two kinds of representation have in common. They are both public portrayals of fearsome, painful sets of facts made bearable by certain formal elements. It is the lack of attention to such formal elements that makes many a television drama trashy. Not, however, their content.

7   The prevalence of violence in drama, the crucifix symbol, and many other gruesome themes of two thousand years of Christian iconography all bear witness that the portrayal of the almost unbearable has been deemed not merely worthy, but indeed necessary, by artists and frequently also by those who commission artists' work. Artistic depiction of gruesome events is a form of mastery of a sense of horror. Portrayal of the horrible, the ugly, or the unbearable in a variety of static or dramatic, visual or auditory art forms can be regarded as a set of adaptive mechanisms and therefore a biological must. This is why art is ubiquitous. There is no civilization without some form of art, and the theme of violence is an essential part of it.

8   In view of the universality of symbolically expressed violence, it is strange indeed that in recent years the public and the press have been campaigning with increased vehemence against television violence — not against the trashy way in which it is often shown, but against the content and only the content. Thus, Joseph Morgenstern argued in *Newsweek* (1972)

> For the better part of two decades, evidence has been accumulating that violence in the mass media can breed aggressive behavior in the mass audience, especially among children. Supporting documents from last month's report to the Surgeon General on "Television Violence" give us the strongest suggestions to date that

violent TV programs can have harmful effects on large groups of normal kids. It's unlikely, though, that millions of outraged parents will lower the boom on the broadcasters. Much of the adult audience is on a violence trip of its own at the movies.

What the report actually said was somewhat different.

9   In 1972, public indignation had reached such heights that, upon the request of Senator Pastore of Rhode Island to Secretary of Health, Education and Welfare Finch, the Surgeon General had commissioned a group of experts to investigate the impact of television violence on children. The conscientious research of highly competent experts from a variety of fields connected with child development led to the conclusion that "first, there is evidence that any sequence by which viewing television violence causes aggressive behavior is most likely applicable only to some children who are predisposed in that direction. . . . Second, . . . that the way children respond to violent film material is affected by the context in which it is presented. Such elements as parental explanations, the favorable or unfavorable outcome of the violence, and whether it is seen as fantasy or reality [!] make a difference. Generalization about all violent content are misleading." (U.S. Public Health Service 1972.)

10   It is, incidentally, remarkable that the Surgeon General's report stresses parental explanation, but does not consider the possibility that the overt *behavior* of parents may influence the child's responses to the screen or, in-deed, the parents' unconscious thoughts or wishes. What is also remarkable about this extensive and voluminous report is the tentative, cautious wording. It is studded with laudable "ifs" and "maybes." Yet, not only *Newsweek* but lay people and even professional educators and sectors of the scientific commu-nity reacted as if the report had proved conclusively that TV violence engenders real violence in the young.

11   This distorted view persisted. On October 29, 1973, one year after the Surgeon General's report, the *U.S. News and World Report* stated:

> Murder and mayhem, bigger and bolder than ever, again is erupting on U.S. television screens — to the rising anger of Congressmen, press, clergy and other citizens across America.
>   The point made by critics: All this comes only 18 months after the nation's television industry was urged by Congressmen to review its policies on violence — and indicated that it would do so.
>   A sampling of current programs shows that already this season networks have aired such films as *Bonnie and Clyde, The Wild Bunch* and *In Cold Blood* that graphically depict scores of bloody shootings. Such shows would have been held off the screen a few years ago.

The article ends on this note:

> Explicit portrayals of violence on the screen — make-believe or real — are being weighted increasingly against public concern over the rising scale of violence in real-life America.

12   Among the scientific authorities most frequently quoted in the magazines and educational journals is Albert Bandura, a psychologist. Bandura designed a series of experiments to investigate the degree to which children are apt to

imitate aggressive behavior shown by adult models in real life, on film, and as cartoon characters on film. "The result," states Bandura (1963), "leaves little doubt that exposure to violence heightens aggressive tendencies in children." In view of such weighty conclusions, it behooves us to be explicit about Bandura's definition of violence and his design for "adult-modeling."

13   To find out if and to what extent children would imitate violent adults in real life or fictional situations, Bandura had a group of children sit in a corner with some toys and an adult in another with some Tinker Toys, a large inflated Bobo doll and a mallet. Suddenly the adult began attacking the Bobo doll in ways that children rarely would, e.g., he sat on the doll, punched it repeatedly in the nose, pummeled its head with the mallet, tossed it up in the air aggressively and kicked it around the room. The attack was accompanied by verbal invectives: "Sock him in the nose!" "Knock him down!" "Throw him in the air!" "Kick him!"

14   A second group of children saw a film of the same scene, while a third watched a movie of the scene on a TV console; in this last case the adult was costumed as a cartoon cat. A fourth group serving as a control group saw none of these aggressive models.

15   Not unexpectedly, the children exposed to adult sham violence followed the adult lead and viciously attacked the Bobo doll. The children were apparently not asked what they thought they were doing or what they thought the adult was doing. (One cannot help wondering whether the children thought the adult had lost his marbles.) In real life, of course, we rarely deal with Bobo dolls. The point is that normal, well-cared-for children — even young ones — know that a Bobo doll can be attacked with impunity and without guilt feelings whereas people of flesh and blood cannot.

16   Other studies, carefully designed, come to conclusions vastly different from those reached by Bandura. Let us look at the one done by Feshbach and Singer (1971). The two researchers exposed a group of boys, selected at random, to TV programs with aggressive content and another group, serving as a control, to programs of a non-aggressive nature. They also examined the boys for aggressive tendencies. Their conclusion was:

> . . . exposure to aggressive content produces a decrement in aggression, relative to exposure to non-aggressive t.v. in boys who have strong aggressive tendencies coupled with weak inhibitory and ego controls. The one exception to this pattern is fantasy aggression. . . . boys below the median in fantasy aggression being most strongly affected by exposure to the aggressive or the control diet.

In other words, boys with well-functioning egos, including a well-developed ability to sublimate, do not become violent, even if they watch violence on television. By contrast, boys who are already prone to acting out instead of merely fantasizing, do get upset when they watch some TV programs. These same boys seem to get "turned on" whether the program is violent or not. Almost any visual stimulus apparently ignites their excitement.

17   Another study, done by Milgram and Shotland (1970), raised even more doubts about the claimed cause-and-effect relationship between fictionalized violence and antisocial behavior. To test the idea that antisocial action seen on

TV causes imitation, the researchers "created a program in which the act—breaking into a charity bank—is shown repeatedly, and with considerable impact." They then created a series of "assessment situations in which antisocial acts and imitation could easily occur."

18   The first experiment took place at a theater where a group of children saw one of four "stimulus programs." The children were "then tested at a gift distribution center." The researchers found that one of the four programs did provoke imitation but that the trend did not have statistical significance. The test results, suggestive as they were, had not accounted for all the variables. In particular, the possibility existed that "the high level of frustration experienced by the subjects obscured the effects of the stimulus program." A second experiment was devised to eliminate this frustration. "Result: no evidence of imitation." A third was designed to find out if another variable, namely "a model or booster placed in the assessment situation might interact with the stimulus program and produce an effect." The result was the same. A final experiment aimed at reducing "the time delay between seeing the television act and the occasion for imitating it by embedding both in the same situation." Again the result was the same: "no evidence of imitation."

19   In sum, it stands to reason that those whose research projects were a simplistic examination of the cause-and-effect relationship between seeing and doing violence were bound to come up with very different results from those researchers whose work took into account the complexities of motivation and the many variables affecting behavior. Yet, what is most amazing is that the careful research showing no connection between television and violence is completely disregarded, whereas studies allegedly proving such a connection are unquestioningly, almost gratefully, accepted.

20   It is as if people can understand and acknowledge only that which supports their most cherished prejudices; as if they were anxious to blame TV, to make of it a scapegoat, despite the well-known fact that violence has its roots in complex social conditions and in a person's intrapsychic make-up. Children do not become brutal just because they happen to watch TV programs that feature brutal acts. And adults do not commit violence crimes merely because they have seen the film *Clockwork Orange* seventeen times. At this juncture I want to make it very clear that I am neither defending the often inferior network programs, nor suggesting that everybody should be obligated to partake of a daily horror show after dinner—for his evening catharsis, as it were. If I seem to be exculpating the media, it is rather for three reasons:

1. Reliable research shows that blood-dripping murder mysteries activate only these youngsters who are already endangered and ready to act out.
2. We have no reason to object to the representation of the human passions as such. These passions have been the raw material for the world's greatest literature. Any attack on this content is censorship and might lead to a serious depletion of culture. We might, however, insist that violence be depicted in a far more artistic form than is presently the case.
3. What makes us so sure that the roots of violence are to be found on TV? Could it be that, by pointing a finger at the media, we deliver ourselves from

any further obligation to change the conditions of children's lives? — conditions that have been proven to stunt their moral (and intellectual and affective) development: the insufficient care, protection, and health measures, and the massive exposure to crime found in slums.

21   If we manage to project it all onto an institution, then our own sins of omission don't bother us anymore. It seems we are dealing here with a modern version of the defense system: the media now takes the place of the Jew, the Witch, and the Infanticidal Mother.

Writing with Sources: Using a Single Source

Integrating information from "Crucifix and Clockwork Orange" with your own ideas, write an essay on one of these topics. Be sure to acknowledge all ideas that are not your own.

1. Explain why you agree or disagree with Piers's assertion in paragraph 19 that the roots of violence are not to be found on television.
2. The following remarks are contained in an article by David Pearl, chief of the Behavioral Sciences Research Branch of the National Institute of Mental Health, on the effects of televised violence on viewers:

   The more time viewers spend watching television, the more they will conceive the world to be similar to television portrayals. Thus people who view a great deal of television — and who consequently see a great deal of violence — are more likely to view the world as a mean and scary place. These heavy viewers also exhibit more fear, mistrust, and apprehension than do light viewers. Because there are more victims than there are aggressors, this finding may ultimately be of more significance than the direct relationship between televised violence and aggression.

   Discuss if these conclusions contradict or support Piers's thesis.
3. Present some of the possible benefits of experiencing violence vicariously in drama, art, or religious symbols.

The First Televised War

Phillip Knightly

Phillip Knightly was born in 1929 in Australia. After working as a reporter, he eventually became a special correspondent for the *Sunday Times* of London. Along with other members of the *Times*'s Insight Team, he is author of *The Philby Conspiracy, The Secret Lives of Lawrence of Arabia,* and *The Pearl of Days* (a history of the *Times*). The following selection is from Knightly's book *The First Casualty: The War Correspondent as Hero, Propagandist, and Myth Maker* (1975). The title of the book comes from a statement made by Senator Hiram Johnson in 1917: "The first casualty when war comes is truth." In this selection, Knightly discusses the way television coverage misrepresented the nature of the war in Vietnam and, as a result, did little to change public opinion about the war.

1   The most intrusive medium in Vietnam was television, and, as the war went on, the hunger of editors for combat footage increased. "Before they were satisfied with a corpse," Richard Lindley, a British television reporter, said. "Then they had to have people dying in action." [1] Michael Herr described a truck carrying a dying ARVN soldier that stopped near a group of correspondents. The soldier, who was only nineteen or twenty, had been shot in the chest. A television cameraman leaned over the Vietnamese and began filming. The other correspondents watched. "He opened his eyes briefly a few times and looked back at us. The first time he tried to smile . . . then it left him. I'm sure he didn't even see us the last time he looked, but we all knew what it was that he had seen just before that." [2] The Vietnamese had seen the zoom lens of a sixteen-millimetre converted Auricon sound camera capturing his last moments of life on film that, if the flight connections worked and the editors back at the network liked it, would be shown in America living rooms within forty-eight hours.

2   This little item would not be exceptional. During the Tet offensive, a Vietnamese in a checked shirt appeared on television being walked—that is, dragged—between two soldiers. The soldiers took him over to a man holding a pistol, who held it to the head of the man in the checked shirt and blew his brains out. All of it was seen in full colour on television (and later in a memorable series of photographs taken by Eddie Adams of the AP).

3   Any viewer in the United States who watched regularly the television reporting from Vietnam—and it was from television that 60 percent of Americans got most of their war news—would agree that he saw scenes of real-life violence, death, and horror on his screen that would have been unthinkable before Vietnam. The risk and intrusion that such filming involved could, perhaps, be justified if it could be shown that television had been particularly effective in revealing the true nature of the war and thus had been able to change people's attitudes to it. Is there any evidence to this effect? . . .

4   . . . The director of CBS News in Washington, William Small, wrote: "When television covered its 'first war' in Vietnam it showed a terrible truth of war in a manner new to mass audiences. A case can be made, and certainly should be examined, that this was cardinal to the disillusionment of Americans with this war, the cynicism of many young people towards America, and the destruction of Lyndon Johnson's tenure of office." [3] A *Washington Post* reporter, Don Oberdorfer, amply documents, in his book *Tet,* the number of commentators and editors (including those of Time Inc.) who had to re-examine their

[1] *London Sunday Times,* November 26, 1967.
[2] *Christian Science Monitor,* May 29–June 30, 1970.
[3] *Sunday Times,* October 19 and October 10, 1971; *The Times,* July 12, 1971.

attitudes after extensive television—and press—coverage brought home to them the bewildering contradictions of a seemingly unending war.

5   Television's power seems to have impressed British observers even more than American. The director-general of the Royal United Service Institution, Air Vice-Marshal S. W. B. Menaul, believes that television had "a lot to answer for [in] the collapse of American morale in relation to the Vietnam war." The then editor of the *Economist,* Alistair Burnet, wrote that the television reporting of Vietnam had made it very difficult for two American administrations to continue that war, "which was going on in American homes," irrespective of the merits or demerits of why the United States was actually involved in Vietnam. Robin Day, the BBC commentator, told a seminar of the Royal United Service Institution that the war on colour-television screens in American living rooms had made Americans far more anti-militarist and anti-war than anything else: "One wonders if in future a democracy which has uninhibited television coverage in every home will ever be able to fight a war, however just. . . . The full brutality of the combat will be there in close up and colour, and blood looks very red on the colour television screen." And the Director of Defence Operations, Plans and Supplies at the Ministry of Defence, Brigadier F. G. Caldwell, said that the American experience in Vietnam meant that if Britain were to go to war again, "we would have to start saying to ourselves, are we going to let the television cameras loose on the battlefield?" [4]

6   All this seems very persuasive, and it would be difficult to believe that the sight, day after day, of American soldiers and Vietnamese civilians dying in a war that seemed to make no progress could not have had *some* effect on the viewer. Yet a survey conducted for *Newsweek* in 1967 suggested a remarkably different conclusion: that television had encouraged a majority of viewers to *support* the war. When faced with deciding whether television coverage had made them feel more like "backing up the boys in Vietnam" or like opposing the war, 64 percent of viewers replied that they were moved to support the soldiers and only 26 percent to oppose the war. A prominent American psychiatrist, Fredric Wertham, said, in the same year, that television had the effect of conditioning its audience to accept war, and a further *Newsweek* enquiry, in 1972, suggested that the public was developing a tolerance of horror in the newscasts from Vietnam—"The only way we can possibly tolerate it is by turning off a part of ourselves instead of the television set."

7   Edward Jay Epstein's survey of television producers and news editors, for his book *News from Nowhere,* showed that more than two-thirds of those he interviewed felt that television had had little effect in changing public opinion on Vietnam. An opinion commonly expressed was that people saw exactly what they wanted to in a news report and that television only served to reinforce existing views. *The New Yorker*'s television critic, Michael J. Arlen, reported, on several occasions, that viewers had a vague, unhappy feeling that they were not getting "the true picture" of Vietnam from the medium. [5] So if it was true

---

[4] J. Lucas, *Dateline Vietnam* (New York: Award Books, 1967), p. 15.
[5] F. Harvey, *Air War Vietnam* (New York: Bantam, 1967), p. 115.

that television did not radically change public opinion about the war, could it have been because of the quality of the coverage?

8   Television is a comparatively new medium. There were 10,000 sets in the United States in 1941; at the time of Korea there were 10 million, and at the peak of the Vietnam War 100 million. There was some television reporting in Korea, a lot of it daring—an American general had to order the BBC camera-man Cyril Page to get down off the front of a tank to which he had tied himself so as to get a grandstand view of the battle as the tank went into action. But, until Vietnam, no one knew what problems the prolonged day-by-day coverage of a war by television would produce. The first was surprising—a lack of reality. It had been believed that when battle scenes were brought into the lving room the reality of war would at last be brought home to a civilian audience. But Arlen was quick to point out, in *The New Yorker,* that by the same process battle scenes are made less real, "diminished in part by the physical size of the television screen, which, for all the industry's advances, still shows one a picture of men three inches tall shooting at other men three inches tall." [6] Sandy Gall of ITN found shooting combat footage difficult and dangerous, and the end result very disappointing. "I think you lose one dimension on television's small screen and things look smaller than life; the sound of battle, for example, never coming across. I am always let down when I eventually see my footage and think, Is that all? The sense of danger never comes across on television and you, the correspondent, always look as though you had an easy time of it" [7]

9   For many Americans in Vietnam, there emerged a strange side to the war that became directly related to television—the fact that the war seemed so unreal that sometimes it became almost possible to believe that everything was taking place on some giant Hollywood set and all the participants were extras playing a remake of *Back to Bataan.* GIs—and even correspondents— brought up on Second World War movies shown on television, used to seeing Errol Flynn sweeping to victory through the jungles of Burma or Brian Donlevy giving the Japanese hell in the Coral Sea, tended to relate their experiences in Vietnam to the Hollywood version of America at war.* Michael Herr, making a dash, with David Greenway of *Time,* from one position at Hué to another, caught himself saying to a Marine a line from a hundred Hollywood war films: "We're going to cut out now. Will you cover us?" One should not be surprised, therefore, to find that GIs sometimes behaved, in the presence of television cameras, as if they were making *Dispatch from Da Nang.* Herr describes soldiers running about during a fight because they knew there was a television crew nearby. "They were actually making war movies in their heads, doing little guts and glory Leatherneck tap dances under fire, getting their pimples shot off for the networks." [8]

10   So it is not difficult to understand how, when seen on a small screen, in

[6] Harvey, p. 184.
[7] *Washington Post,* February 23, 1966.
* The arrival in 1965 of Flynn's son, Sean, as a correspondent tended to confirm this feeling.
[8] Interview with John Shaw.

the enveloping and cosy atmosphere of the household, sometime between the afternoon soap-box drama and the late-night war movie, the television version of the war in Vietnam could appear as just another drama, in which the hero is the correspondent and everything will come out all right at the end. Jack Laurence of CBS, an experienced war correspondent, who spent a lot of time in Vietnam, had this possibility brought home to him in Israel during the 1973 conflict. He was in a hotel lobby, and a couple who had just arrived from the United States recognised him and said, "We saw you on television and we knew everything was going to be all right because you were there." [9] There is not much a television correspondent can do about such a situation as that; it seems inherent in the nature of the medium. However, correspondents, or, more fairly, their editors, do have something to answer for in their selection of news in Vietnam.

11   Years of television news of the war have left viewers with a blur of images consisting mainly of helicopters landing in jungle clearings, soldiers charging into undergrowth, wounded being loaded onto helicopters, artillery and mortar fire, air strikes on distant targets, napalm canisters turning slowly in the sky, and a breathless correspondent poking a stick microphone under an army officer's nose and asking, "What's happening up there, Colonel?" (The only honest answer came, in 1972, from a captain on Highway 13. "I wish the hell I knew," he said.) The networks claimed that combat footage was what the public wanted; that concentrating on combat prevented the film's being out of date if it was delayed in transmission; that it was difficult to shoot anything other than combat film when only three or four minutes were available in the average news program for events in Vietnam; and that the illusion of American progress created by combat footage shot from only one side was balanced by what the correspondent had to say.

12   This is simply not true. To begin with, combat footage fails to convey all aspects of combat. "A cameraman feels so inadequate, being able to record only a minute part of the misery, a minute part of the fighting," said Kurt Volkert, a CBS cameraman. "You have to decide what the most important action is. Is it the woman holding her crying baby? Is it the young girl cringing near her house because of the exploding grenades? Or is it the defiant looking Vietcong with blood on his face just after capture?" [10] When the cameraman's thirty minutes of combat footage are edited down to three minutes — not an unusual editing ratio — the result is a segment of action that bears about as much relation to the reality in Vietnam as a battle scene shot in Hollywood does. In fact, the Hollywood version would probably appear more realistic.

13   The American viewer who hoped to learn something serious about Vietnam was subjected, instead, to a television course in the techniques of war, and he was not sufficiently exposed either to what the war meant to the people over whose land it was being fought, or to the political complexities of the situation, or even to the considered personal views of reporters who had spent

[9] Harvey, p. 104.
[10] P. Jones Griffiths. *Vietnam, Inc.* (New York: Macmillan, 1971), p. 60.

years covering the situation. Yet, even by the networks' own standards, the limited aspects of the war that the viewer was permitted to see could produce excellent television. One of the most dramatic pieces of film on the war was shot by a CBS team on Highway 13 late in April 1972. A South Vietnamese mine, intended to stop advancing enemy tanks, had caught a truck loaded with refugees. The film showed dead children, distressed babies, and a woman weeping over the body of her son. The reporter, Bob Simon, described what had happened and then, with perhaps the best sign-off line from Vietnam, said simply, "There's nothing left to say about this war, nothing at all." "Morley Safer's Vietnam," an hour-long report by the CBS correspondent in Saigon, was Safer's own explicit view, and was hailed by *The New Yorker*'s critic, Michael J. Arlen, as "one of the best pieces of journalism to come out of the Vietnam war in any medium." But film like this was rare.

14   Competition for combat footage was so intense that it not only forced American television teams to follow each other into what the BBC's correspondent Michael Clayton called "appallingly dangerous situations," but it also made editors reluctant to risk allowing a team the time and the freedom to make its own film of the war. Where were the television equivalents of Martha Gellhorn's series on Vietnamese orphanages and hospitals, or Philip Jones Griffiths' searing book on the nature of the war, *Vietnam Inc.*? True, television was handicapped by its mechanics — a three-man, or even a two-man, team loaded with camera, sound equipment, and film is less mobile and more dependent on military transport, and in a dangerous situation more vulnerable, than a journalist or a photographer. In its presentation, too, television is sometimes handicapped by its commercial associations. The Vietnamese cameraman Vo Suu filmed the brutal shooting of a Vietcong suspect by General Nguyen Ngoc Loan during the Tet offensive. NBC blacked out the screen for three seconds after the dead man hit the ground, so as to provide a buffer before the commercial that followed. (What television *really* wanted was action in which the men died cleanly and not too bloodily. "When they get a film which shows what a mortar does to a man, really shows the flesh torn and the blood flowing, they get squeamish," says Richard Lindley. "They want it to be just so. They want television to be cinema.")[11]

15   American television executives showed too little courage in their approach to Vietnam. They followed each other into paths the army had chosen for them. They saw the war as "an American war in Asia — and that's the only story the American audience is interested in," and they let other, equally important, aspects of Vietnam go uncovered.

Writing with Sources: Using a Single Source

Integrating information from "The First Televised War" with your own ideas, write an essay on one of these topics. Be sure to acknowledge all ideas that are not your own.

[11] Jones Griffiths, p. 62.

1. In paragraph 9 Knightly observes, "the war seemed so unreal that sometimes it became almost possible to believe that everything was taking place on some giant Hollywood set. . . ." Discuss the images of war that Hollywood has created. You may consider either old movies or new movies, or if you wish, you may compare an old movie to a new movie.
2. Discuss a current event or a historical occurrence that you feel was distorted by television.
3. In paragraph 14, Knightly says that television was squeamish about showing the violence of the Vietnam war. Some critics would argue that today television goes out of its way to show graphic violence and death. Consider which position accurately defines the current state of television.

A Mirror to Man

Robert Claiborne

Robert Claiborne was born in 1919 in England and received his B.A. from New York University in 1942. After working as a lathe operator, factory worker, union official, music teacher, and folksinger, he became associate editor of *Scientific American* in 1957. He has been managing editor of *Medical World News,* an editor of the *Life Science Library,* and a lecturer on ecology for the New School for Social Research. At present, he is a senior editor of *Hospital Practice,* a magazine for physicians. Among the many books Claiborne has written are *Time* (1966); *Climate, Man, and History* (1970); *On Every Side the Sea* (1971); *The First Americans* (1973); *God or Beast: Evolution and Human Nature* (1974); *Cell Membranes: Biochemistry, Cell Biology and Pathology* (1975); and *Our Marvelous Native Tongue: The Life and Times of the English Language* (1983). He has also contributed articles to *Harper's, The Nation, Science Digest, Smithsonian,* and other periodicals. In the following selection from *God or Beast: Evolution and Human Nature,* Claiborne discusses the anthropological and environmental reasons for violence in human beings.

1   There is nothing about the environmental view as I, along with most environmentalists, would define it that excludes a biological, evolutionary component in human violence. As I have several times noted, evolution has indeed given man the potential for violence, chiefly because during his five-million-year residence in open country he was often confronted with predators — animal and sometimes human — whose threat to himself, his females, and his young could only be met by violence. But to recognize this potential is merely to say that man is sometimes violent, which we knew anyway. What we also know, however, is that he is clearly much *more* violent in some cultures, in some environments, and at some times. A thousand years ago, homicide was almost a weekly occurrence among the Viking settlers of Iceland; today, among the biological descendants of those same settlers, it is a rarity. The Pueblo tribes of the American Southwest were basically pacific, their Navaho and Apache neighbors were anything but; white Americans kill one another considerably oftener than white Englishmen, despite the two nations' shared heritage

of language, law, and literature. And one could continue to list such contrasts almost indefinitely.

2   If, then, we — meaning my friends and I, among many others — are concerned about the increasing violence in our world and want to do something about it, our only rational approach is to take man's evolutionary nature, violent potential and all, as given, and go on from there. Human nature, millions of years in the making, is not going to change in our lifetime, or our grandchildren's. What we must inquire is why that nature expresses itself in violent actions so much more often at some times and places than at others. As always, wisdom begins with asking the right questions. If we ask "How can we eliminate violence from human affairs?" the answer is very probably "No way!"; man's evolutionary nature, if nothing else, will take care of that. But if we ask rather, "How can we *minimize* violence?" the chances are that we can find an answer, since a number of cultures have, by accident or design, done so.

3   We have already seen how aggression and violence in baboons can vary enormously in different environments. Ardrey describes the baboon as "a born bully, a born criminal, a born candidate for the hangman's noose [!]. . . . He is ugly. He has the yellow-to-amber eyes that one associates with the riverboat gambler [!!]." And while we need not take this anthropomorphic fantasy very seriously, there is no doubt that the animal's potential for violence is roughly equivalent to our own. We have seen, indeed, how DeVore's male grassland baboons typically ganged up to confront danger, and also typically threatened (and occasionally attacked) one another as part of their struggle for dominance. Rowell's savanna baboons, on the other hand, could and did escape danger by retreating to nearby trees, with the result that the males showed no taste for violent confrontation with predators   in fact, they usually, thanks to their size, outran the females. And, very significantly, they also showed little interest in playing the dominance game among themselves. Well, if Ardrey's "born criminal" can turn pacifist where the environment recommends this course, perhaps there is hope for man!

4   Among our primate relatives (and surely among our own ancestors) aggression and violence are (and were) heavily influenced by the amount of stress and tension in the group. A prime source of such stress, as with the baboons, is the presence of enemies in the neighborhood plus the absence of ways to escape them. A second source, it appears, is crowding, whose effects in engendering violence have been observed in both wild and captive primates. Kenji Yoshiba, observing langurs in the Dharwar Forest of southwest India, found aggressive threats between troops far more common than among the langurs described by Phyllis Jay and others. There was virtually no dominance conflict among males of a given troop because most of the troops had only a single adult male, but the area was infested by all-male gangs which on occasion would attack one of the male-female troops, in particular its male leader, sometimes managing to drive him away permanently. There would then ensue a series of fights between the "conquering" males, to the point where all but one of them was driven off. Sometimes, though not always, the new leader would then proceed to kill the troop's infants — those born before his accession to power — which by primate standards is very odd behavior indeed.

5   The reason for the radical differences between Yoshiba's and Jay's langurs is not altogether clear. Danger from predators is certainly not the answer, since the former were if anything less endangered than the latter. The only significant environmental difference was population density. Yoshiba reports that at Dharwar it was more than thirteen times that reported by Jay. He himself suspects that sexual tension among "unaffiliated" males may also have played a part, but he does not try to guess why so many males were unaffiliated — that is, why most of the mixed troops included only one adult male.

6   Whatever the precise role of crowding in generating stress and conflict among the Dharwar langurs — and it is hard to believe that it did not play a considerable role — there is no doubt that it can produce serious and sometimes fatal conflicts among captive primates. Again the reasons are not wholly clear, but a very important one is evidently the impossibility of avoiding conflict. In the wild, so long as the population is not too dense, a threatened animal can, and often does, simply remove itself from the situation until the threatener has had a chance to cool off; in captivity, the only "solution" may be to fight it out.

7   Other factors inducing stress and other abnormal behavior of various types among captive primates are lack of stimulation (in human terms, boredom), sudden changes in environment (in human terms, culture shock), and, possibly, overstimulation of certain kinds. S. D. Singh, comparing urban and rural populations of rhesus monkeys in India, found the former much more aggressive than the latter, both toward one another and toward humans. And a virtually universal source of stress, anger, and often violence among primates — and most or all other mammals — is what is loosely called frustration, in which an animal's normal response to a situation is blocked by some other aspect of the situation. Thus a male chimp attacked by another male may respond by fighting back, but if that response is blocked by fear will often "take out" its anger on a female or smaller male, or may engage in shaking branches and other angry displays until it cools down. Very probably akin to this sort of frustration was the production of "neurosis" in dogs in the famous experiments by Pavlov: the animals, having first been trained to expect food at the sound of a bell, were then given instead an electric shock. Pushed in two contradictory directions by their responses, they rapidly became tense, fearful, and sometimes vicious.

8   Let us now consider to what extent these stress-and-violence factors may be relevant to violence in man. Specifically, let us examine the environmental, "ecological" situation of the groups in our society that are generally conceded to be a prime focus of violence: the urban, slum poor. These people have committed more than their "share" of violent acts probably for as long as there have been urban slums: in the fifteenth-century Paris of François Villon, in the eighteenth-century London limned by Hogarth, and in twentieth-century New York, Chicago, and Detroit. Neither race nor religion seems to make much difference; in my own city, New York, the "Hell's Kitchen" area of a century ago, populated largely by poor, slum Irish, was quite as dangerous as today's black Harlem or Puerto Rican "El Barrio."

9   The first thing we can say about these ghetto ecosystems is that their

inhabitants feel endangered. The "outside world" — which for them means primarily the (white) landlord and various (usually white) government officials, especially the police — is seen as hostile, and not without reason.* It is seldom possible for the ghetto inhabitant to cope effectively with these threats, since he lacks the power, nor can he escape from them; even could he afford to move to another neighborhood (and he often can't) he is likely to find all sorts of obstacles in the way, from real estate agents who won't sell or rent to him, to neighbors who don't want his kids in school with theirs.

10   The second thing about the ghetto ecosystem is that it is crowded. Poverty, high rents, and the obstacles to moving out make for the highest population densities in urban American, and some of the highest in the world. Continuing down the list, we find that the ghetto dweller, having been transplanted from the Caribbean or the rural American South, frequently suffers from culture shock and also, since he is often unemployed or underemployed, from boredom. And of course he is frequently frustrated, like the chimp whose urge to fight back is blocked by fear. Nor does frustration stop there: he is also continuously urged, by the press and, especially, television, to buy the beautiful and enticing products of American industry, yet the normal response to this urging — to earn money through a job, or a better job — is blocked by discrimination, by his own lack of skills, or by the simple unavailability of jobs of any kind. *In short, if an expert in primate psychology had set about constructing in his laboratory an environment calculated to produce the maximum stress, tension, and violence among his animals, he would have produced something very like our urban ghettos — dangerous, crowded, frustrating, and boring.* The result is as predictable as any of Skinner's rat and pigeon experiments: violence. And of course the violence feeds on itself. To the extent it is directed at other ghetto dwellers (as most ghetto violence is) it makes the environment even more dangerous and stressful, to the extent it is directed toward outsiders, such as the police, the ultimate result is the same. For the cops, of course, are primates too, and the more endangered *they* feel, the more aggressive and trigger-happy they become.

11   Thus far we have considered the ghetto dweller simply as a primate; let us now consider him as a human primate. As we saw in the preceding chapter, man is the most curious and manipulative of the primates, and the only creative one. Evolution has designed him, as it were, to make patterns, and enjoy doing so, from the pattern of a flint hand axe to that of a computer. He is an animal that needs to keep busy, and if he is prevented from doing so in socially approved ways, on the job, he is quite likely to devise less attractive ways of his own. In this sense, Ardrey is perfectly correct in saying that "we" enjoy destruction; we do — so long as we can find no constructive activity to occupy us. The old principle that Satan finds work for idle hands is something that all of us have from time to time seen at work in our own children; it is no less true of other people's children, or of adults.

---

* Many police, of course, perceive the ghetto dwellers as hostile and dangerous, also not without reason.

12   Man is also the primate most prone to imitate, the most adept at observation learning. And if we look at the flickering images which children, in and out of the ghetto, daily observe, we find them saturated with violence, from John Wayne to Superfly. The man who purveys sexual images to teenagers goes to jail; he who purveys violent ones goes to the bank. What effect these violent images have on the normal, middle-class kid is arguable; their probable effect on the ghetto teenager, predisposed to violence by the tensions and stresses — and, by now, also the traditions — of his environment, is not. In this sense, too, Ardrey is right: violence *is* applauded in our culture, but not much of the applause comes from "us." Rather, it comes from a relatively small group of men who have become rich and powerful by portraying violence as romantic, admirable, and manly.* I am all in favor of ending this applause — and reinforcement — for violence. If we can legitimately prevent kids from observing copulation on the screen or tube — and I know of no one who disputes this — then I see no reason why we cannot equally restrict their exposure to mayhem and murder. While we are about it, we might also devote some thought to the curious situation whereby military pilots who engaged in wholesale violence are feted at the White House while men who refused to take the violent way are pilloried "without pity" from the same quarter.

13   But muting our culture's applause for violence, though it may ameliorate the problem, will not solve it. Such positive reinforcement is, in Skinnerian terms, merely the contingency that makes violence more likely to occur; it does not itself generate violence. Much the same can be said of such "negative reinforcements" as tougher courts and cops and longer jail sentences for the violent; they may, just possibly, somewhat diminish violence but they will leave untouched the forces that generate it. To tackle *that* problem means to set about changing the environment which subjects millions of our fellow citizens to the daily fears, tensions, stresses, and frustrations which beget violence in primates as predictably as clouds beget rain.†

14   I do not propose to specify just how we should set about this; space, and a certain modesty, forbid it. Were I asked for a good place to start, however, I would suggest a governmental guarantee of a job at decent wages for every man and woman able to work. This would, quite rapidly, abolish both the poverty and the idleness that are among the important roots of violence — and would incidentally end the hypocrisy of sermonizing about the work ethic to people for whom no work is available. Economists and sociologists, to be sure,

* The plot of a recent John Wayne horse opus can be summed up as follows: little boys become men by learning to kill. Also worth noting is that a good deal of Wild West movie and TV violence has only the most tenuous connection with the historical realities of life on the American frontier. Psychiatrist Kent E. Robinson has pointed out, for example, that Wyatt Earp, an archetype of the rough, tough, shoot-'em-up western sheriff, in fact killed just one man during his three years as marshall. He established law and order not by his readiness for shoot-outs but because he established the first U.S. gun-control law: a system of fines for anyone wearing or discharging firearms in the town. Modern law-and-order advocates, please note.

† Ironically, Ardrey, who dislikes Skinner's theories as much as I do, has in this area unwittingly joined the behaviorists, since his proposals for dealing with violence amount to no more than changing the reinforcements which it entrains.

will at this point exclaim, "But most of these people have no marketable skills — how can they be given jobs?" I have no patience with this argument. If people don't have the skills, train 'em. I don't mean poverty-program training in the "skills" of *how to get* a job, which in the absence of jobs to be gotten is merely an expensive con game.* Nor do I mean the abstract skills involved in "learning a trade" into which the trainee may then find his way blocked by limited opportunity or trade-union exclusiveness. Rather I mean the concrete skills of a veritable job into which the trainee will literally move immediately on graduation — or, better, before it, working while he is learning.

15   And if the trainee should prove, because of limited literacy or for other reasons, to be untrainable? Then let us for God's sake find, or invent, some job he can do without training; if a man can only dig sewer ditches, there are surely plenty of sewers that need digging if our rivers and lakes are to be cleaned up. For something like a quarter of a century the federal government has been subsidizing numbers of technologically backward and/or managerially incompetent industries, two prime examples being railroading and shipbuilding; is it too much to suggest that it also subsidize technologically backward individuals?

16   In proposing that we attack idleness and the other environmental factors that breed violence, I will surely be accused by some biopoliticians of bleeding-heartism, do-goodism, and similar sins: in Ardrey's words, of offering alibis for violence, "presenting greater sympathy for the violator than the violated." As it happens, I have only modest sympathy for the violator — and none at all if he threatens to violate me — but my sympathy is irrelevant to the argument. To cope with the problem of violence, I submit, we do not need sympathy — which, as somebody once observed, is good for a handout at the Salvation Army and not much else — but simple common sense: a willingness to accept the law of cause and effect as it applies to our own species. One does not need sympathy to recognize the fact that if you kick a dog he may bite you, and that if you kick a man he'll kick you back if he can. The study of human evolution, as I have noted earlier, tells us that man, in the specifics of what he does, can be the most unpredictable of animals, but it also tells us that under certain circumstances his nature makes him predictably likely to do certain *kinds* of things. And since we are evidently not going to change his nature, we are foolish indeed if we do not get on with changing the circumstances.

17   Cholera, once a terrifying plague in Europe and America, is an "environmental" disease, in the sense that if the food or drinking water in your environment is contaminated with Vibrio cholerae it is very likely to make you very sick. Nowadays, cholera can be treated quite effectively with antibiotics and quantities of intravenous fluids; at the same time, of course, the sufferer is segregated so that his body wastes cannot infect others. Yet cholera continues to flare up periodically where conditions permit, which is to say in most places where pure water supplies and adequate sewage systems are lacking, sickening

---

* And is seen as such by the trainees, who are by no means as dumb as some psychologists and educationists would like to believe.

tens of thousands and killing at least hundreds. It is the same with violence. We can, and should, segregate the violent; we can and should learn to treat them so that they are no longer violent. But unless we clean up the environmental conditions that stimulate, aggravate, and liberate the potential for violence that evolution has bred into us, it will continue to flare up from time to time — and kill some of us.

Writing with Sources: Using a Single Source

Integrating information from "A Mirror to Man" with your own ideas, write an essay on one of these topics. Be sure to acknowledge all ideas that are not your own.

1. Describe ways that our culture could end the reinforcement of violence.
2. Explain why you agree or disagree with Claiborne's assertion in paragraph 8 that the "urban, slum poor" are "a prime focus of violence."
3. In his essay, Claiborne says that stress often leads to anger and sometimes to violence. Describe an event in your life that followed this pattern.

Writing with Sources: Using Multiple Sources

Integrating information from sources in this chapter with your own ideas, write an essay on one of the topics below. Be sure to acknowledge ideas that are not your own.

1. Use three of the selections in this section to account for the prevalence of violence in American culture.
2. At a summer sports camp, Brenda Jo Bredemeier, coauthor of "Values and Violence in Sports Today," measured the aggressive tendencies in elementary school children to determine their level of moral reasoning. The children who demonstrated higher moral reasoning described themselves as being less verbally and physically aggressive in both sports and daily life, while those with less mature reasoning described themselves as being more aggressive. Using the selections in this chapter, discuss how sports, television, and family environment could affect the moral reasoning of children.
3. In "A Mirror to Man," Claiborne says that we should "attack the idleness and the other environmental factors that breed violence." Using the ideas of the authors in this chapter, write an essay that supports the thesis, "By focusing on 'daily fears, tensions, stresses, and frustrations,' Claiborne oversimplifies the causes of violence in our society."
4. The following remarks concerning the 1985 Brussels soccer riots — in which many sports fans lost their lives — appeared in the *New Statesman,* a British magazine.

Leaving the shores of England merely exacerbates the already dominant narrow chauvinism of the fans, widens the gap between them and the team they are supporting. Foreign territory frees the fan of all restrictions but his mass solidarity with other English lads. He strips off his shirt within minutes of arrival at Ostend. The group code demands that he jeers at every aspect of life in the host country. He uses any aggressive patriotic catchphrase . . . both in casual conversation and shrieked at the Italians.

And then there is the need to drink, not to get tipsy, but to get paralytic. A duty-free liter of Drambuie disappeared easily enough amongst a small group during my half-hour flight. The amount of drink served up by nervous but delighted publicans in Brussels was staggering. Once drunk, there is a standard practice of getting onto the tables and stamping. And the drunker one gets, the more intense all other modes of behavior become, until what is left is a lunatic hatred and blind aggression toward anything that does not conform.

And one fatal and final rule: English fans think they must have an end of the ground to themselves. A far-off corner of the . . . foreign field must be forever England. The fans must have 'Lebensraum' in the stadium. And this is the clause in the British fans' sick book of rules of which the flag-waving Italians in Z Block were fatally unaware. They committed the provocation of being Italian. So the charges of the Liverpool fans were required under the code of conduct for two reasons: One — just to get at the 'spics.' Two — to purify Z Block and establish English rule at that end of the ground. This meant forcing a terrified crowd against barriers and concrete walls; forcing and forcing them until victory. It could only have led to murder.

Use the ideas of John Langone and Brenda Jo Bredemeier and David L. Shields to explain these occurrences.

5. When asked by critics to explain the excessive violence in his film *A Clockwork Orange,* the film director Stanley Kubrick said, "Man isn't a noble savage, he's an ignoble savage. . . . I'm interested in the brutal and violent nature of man because it's a true picture of him." Using material from any three selections in this chapter, explain why you agree or disagree with Kubrick's assessment of human nature.

14

Life in America

What makes the American people uniquely American is more than just our common history or political system. Our identity is also rooted in our fads and our pastimes, in our games and our eating habits, and in the settings in which we feel most at home.

The essays in this chapter consider six developments in U.S. life that are uniquely American. In "The Jeaning of America — and the World" Carin C. Quinn traces the rise of blue jeans from utilitarian work clothes to their present position as a symbol of the United States. Marvin Kaye's essay "Over the Rainbow without Passing Go" examines the development and the continuing appeal of the board game Monopoly, and Susan Strasser's "You Deserve a Break" treats the rising popularity of fast food. Americans' almost fanatical devotion to exercise is challenged in Robert Lipsyte's "What Price Fitness?" and the phenomenal impact of shopping malls on our lives is analyzed by William Ecenbarger in "Why Americans Love Their Malls." Finally, in "Night as Frontier" sociologist Murray Melbin explains how the nighttime has taken the place of the American West as new territory which we are now beginning to explore.

The Jeaning of America — and the World

Carin C. Quinn

Carin C. Quinn received her Master's degree in American Studies from California State University at Los Angeles in 1976. In this essay, first published in *American Heritage* magazine, she traces the history of that peculiarly American symbol, blue jeans, detailing their versatility and explaining their continuing popularity.

1   This is the story of a sturdy American symbol which has now spread throughout most of the world. The symbol is not the dollar. It is not even Coca-Cola. It is a simple pair of pants called blue jeans, and what the pants symbolize is what Alexis de Tocqueville called "a manly and legitimate passion for equality. . . ." Blue jeans are favored equally by bureaucrats and cowboys; bankers and deadbeats; fashion designers and beer drinkers. They draw no distinctions and recognize no classes; they are merely American. Yet they are sought after almost everywhere in the world — including Russia, where authorities recently broke up a teen-aged gang that was selling them on the black market for two hundred dollars a pair. They have been around for a long time, and it seems likely that they will outlive even the necktie.

2   This ubiquitous American symbol was the invention of a Bavarian-born Jew. His name was Levi Strauss.

3   He was born in Bad Ocheim, Germany, in 1829, and during the European political turmoil of 1848 decided to take his chances in New York, to which his two brothers already had emigrated. Upon arrival, Levi soon found that his two brothers had exaggerated their tales of an easy life in the land of the main chance. They were landowners, they had told him; instead, he found them pushing needles, thread, pots, pans, ribbons, yarn, scissors, and buttons to housewives. For two years he was a lowly peddler, hauling some 180 pounds of sundries door-to-door to eke out a marginal living. When a married sister in San Francisco offered to pay his way West in 1850, he jumped at the opportunity, taking with him bolts of canvas he hoped to sell for tenting.

4   It was the wrong kind of canvas for that purpose, but while talking with a miner down from the mother lode, he learned that pants — sturdy pants that would stand up to the rigors of the digging — were almost impossible to find. Opportunity beckoned. On the spot, Strauss measured the man's girth and inseam with a piece of string and, for six dollars in gold dust, had [the canvas] tailored into a pair of stiff but rugged pants. The miner was delighted with the result, word got around about "those pants of Levi's," and Strauss was in business. The company has been in business ever since.

5   When Strauss ran out of canvas, he wrote his two brothers to send more. He received instead a tough, brown cotton cloth made in Nîmes, France — called *serge de Nîmes* and swiftly shortened to "denim" (the word "jeans" de-

rives from Gênes, the French word for Genoa, where a similar cloth was produced). Almost from the first, Strauss had his cloth dyed the distinctive indigo that gave blue jeans their name, but it was not until the 1870s that he added the copper rivets which have long since become a company trademark. The rivets were the idea of a Virginia City, Nevada, tailor, Jacob W. Davis, who added them to pacify a mean-tempered miner called Alkali Ike. Alkali, the story goes, complained that the pockets of his jeans always tore when he stuffed them with ore samples and demanded that Davis do something about it. As a kind of joke, Davis took the pants to a blacksmith and had the pockets riveted; once again, the idea worked so well that word got around; in 1873 Strauss appropriated and patented the gimmick—and hired Davis as a regional manager.

6   By this time, Strauss had taken both his brothers and two brothers-in-law into the company and was ready for his third San Francisco store. Over the ensuing years the company prospered locally, and by the time of his death in 1902, Strauss had become a man of prominence in California. For three decades thereafter the business remained profitable though small, with sales largely confined to the working people of the West — cowboys, lumberjacks, railroad workers, and the like. Levi's jeans were first introduced to the East, apparently, during the dude-ranch craze of the 1930s, when vacationing Easterners returned and spread the word about the wonderful pants with rivets. Another boost came in World War II, when blue jeans were declared an essential commodity and were sold only to people engaged in defense work. From a company with fifteen salespeople, two plants, and almost no business east of the Mississippi in 1946, the organization grew in thirty years to include a sales force of more than twenty-two thousand, with fifty plants and offices in thirty-five countries. Each year, more than 250,000,000 items of Levi's clothing are sold — including more than 83,000,000 pairs of riveted blue jeans. They have become, through marketing, word of mouth, and demonstrable reliability, the common pants of America. They can be purchased pre-washed, pre-faded, and pre-shrunk for the suitably proletarian look. They adapt themselves to any sort of idiosyncratic use; women slit them at the inseams and convert them into long skirts, men chop them off above the knees and turn them into something to be worn while challenging the surf. Decorations and ornamentations abound.

7   The pants have become a tradition, and along the way have acquired a history of their own — so much so that the company has opened a museum in San Francisco. There was, for example, the turn-of-the-century trainman who replaced a faulty coupling with a pair of jeans; the Wyoming man who used his jeans as a towrope to haul his car out of a ditch; the Californian who found several pairs in an abandoned mine, wore them, then discovered they were sixty-three years old and still as good as new and turned them over to the Smithsonian as a tribute to their toughness. And then there is the particularly terrifying story of the careless construction worker who dangled fifty-two stories above the street until rescued, his sole support the Levi's belt loop through which his rope was hooked.

Writing with Sources: Using a Single Source

Integrating information from "The Jeaning of America—and the World" with your own ideas, write an essay on one of these topics. Be sure to acknowledge ideas that are not your own.

1. What items, in addition to jeans, might be considered symbols of American culture? Give examples of articles of clothing, accessories, games and toys, foods, or recreational pursuits that you see as typically American in some way, and then decide what these items have in common.
2. Describe some of the clothing fads that developed during your high school years. Whenever possible, try to account for each fad's emergence, continued popularity, and eventual decline.
3. Try to predict the increasing popularity of another clothing item — one now in existence or one yet to be developed — that could share the universal and continuing appeal of jeans. Be sure to describe the article of clothing in detail and explain its appeal carefully.

Over the Rainbow without Passing Go

Marvin Kaye

Born in 1938, Marvin Kaye received his B.A. from Pennsylvania State University and his M.A. from the University of Denver. He worked as a newspaper reporter and as a senior editor for a publishing company before turning to freelance writing. His published books include *The Histrionic Holmes* (1971), *A Lively Game of Death* (1972), *The Grand Ole Opry Murders* (1974), and *The Story of Monopoly, Silly Putty, Bingo, Twister, Frisbee, Scrabble, Et Cetera* (1973; originally published as *A Toy is Born*), from which "Over the Rainbow without Passing Go" is excerpted. In addition to writing short stories and mystery novels and editing anthologies of stories, Kaye also has training in the theatre as an actor, director, and playwright. He has worked as senior editor of a prominent toy trade magazine and as a professional magician. In the essay that follows, he traces the development of the popular board game Monopoly.

1   It brought riches to an impoverished Philadelphia salesman.

2   It saved a New England manufacturing firm from bankruptcy.

3   It convinced countless thousands of housewives, farmers, laborers, businessmen, and teachers that all they had to do to get rich quick was to invent a new game.

4   It was Monopoly.

5   Not only did Parker Brothers' familiar real estate trading game with the Atlantic City street names on the board enable its originator to retire a million-

aire at forty-six, but Monopoly went on to become the all-time best seller of all copyrighted board games.

6   And it wouldn't stand a chance if it were invented today.

7   "We didn't even think it was any good back in the Depression, when it was first brought to us," said a Parker Brothers executive. "Monopoly breaks just about every rule of what a good game is supposed to be!"

8   The fact that the game requires a four-page instruction book to explain it would be the first strike against Monopoly if it were introduced in the nineteen-seventies. Even though many contemporary "educational" and/or "adult" games require books — literally — to explain rules of play, a mass-distribution family game is usually expected to avoid complexities.

9   What's more, the average Monopoly game can take several hours to play. (In the nineteen-forties, punsters used to call it Monotony.) And originally, the only way to buy an unowned property was to land on it — auctioning off appears to have been an afterthought designed to speed things up. Parker Brothers officials maintain that a game of Monopoly need not take forever, but some gamesters actually like to stretch it out with their own rules. "To many players," said one executive, "Monopoly is almost a mystical, ritualistic thing."

10   The creation of Monopoly is generally attributed to Charles B. Darrow, but game historians point to the Landlord's Game, patented in 1904 by Lizzie J. Magie and featuring purchasable properties, including utilities; a "public park" corner corresponding to Monopoly's "Free Parking," and a "Go to Jail" space. Darrow evidently added several new elements to the pattern of the Magie game.

11   After the 1929 crash, forty-year-old Darrow's business as a sales rep for engineering firms plummeted to nearly nothing. To keep a little money coming in, he produced jigsaw puzzles in his workshop for his neighbors and did any odd jobs he could find. He also devised a contract bridge score pad that gave players the proper hand valuations, bids, and responses in concise form for easy reference. Then, in 1930, Darrow began to turn an idea around in his mind for a game that would involve "plenty of money for the player to invest or speculate with." Real estate interested him, so he chose that as the theme. On the other hand, borrowing and credit were excluded, because Darrow personally didn't believe in them. "I buy everything with cash," he once told a reporter. "If everybody did, I guess the country would go broke, but that's the way *I* buy."

12   The first version of Darrow's game was rather primitive. The board was hand-drawn on a round piece of linoleum and colored with any paint samples Darrow could find at a local paint store. He typed the title cards on cardboard and fashioned the houses and hotels from remnants picked up at a nearby lumber yard. There were no dice or tokens at first, and the game didn't even have a box.

13   Just before the crash, Darrow had taken his wife, Esther, on a vacation to Atlantic City. It seemed so pleasant in his memory — in contrast to the times that followed — that the seashore resort took on a special significance in his mind and he decided to name the properties in his game after Atlantic City streets. When designing the game board, he tried to keep the streets in the consecutive sequence from the Inlet to Park Place at the Boardwalk. But he ran short of interesting names, so he had to go out of sequence and borrow one from nearby Margate (Marven Gardens, which he altered to Marvin Gardens). A second naming problem involved railroads. He needed four, one for each side of the board, but could only find three that serviced the resort: the Pennsylvania, the B & O, and the Reading. So Darrow added the Short Line, actually a freight bus company running between Philadelphia, New York, and Atlantic City.

14   At first, Darrow had no plans to sell or make "the game," as he called it. He and his wife began playing it just for fun, sometimes inviting friends to participate. Soon their acquaintances began requesting copies to take home. "It was a funny thing," the inventor once remarked, "but almost invariably the winner wanted a copy, while the loser was convinced that he could win the next game — so he'd frequently want a game, too. Well, I hadn't anything better to do, so I began to make the games. I charged people four dollars a copy."

15   It took him a whole day to make up one game. The materials cost about $2.25, so he was realizing about $1.75 profit on each — not bad money in the early nineteen-thirties. As more and more people, friends of friends, began asking for Darrow to make up copies of "the game," he found his time increasingly taken up with typing title cards and painting linoleum pieces. Finally, Darrow made an arrangement with a printer friend to take over the production of the game. Darrow was somewhat afraid that he might be unable to pay for the service, but his friend assured him that the printing firm would wait until Darrow's customers paid him.

16   By this time, orders were coming in from more and more distant places, and some department store buyers were also starting to stock up on Darrow's real estate game. Darrow never spent a penny on advertising. The fame of Monopoly spread entirely by word of mouth — even from as far away as California, orders trickled in.

17   In a very short time, the former salesman was amazed to see that the pastime he'd drawn on his kitchen table had sold seventeen thousand pieces. In order to meet the number of orders still arriving in the mail, he realized he'd either have to borrow money and go into game manufacturing himself or else sell out to an established supplier. He chose the latter course. "Taking the precepts of Monopoly to heart," he said, "I did not care to speculate."

18   Parker Brothers was the first supplier Darrow approached, and the response was not enthusiastic. In the firm's opinion, a good game took only a few minutes to learn, and the rules had to be easy enough for a nine-year-old to absorb quickly; furthermore, the longest time any family game should take was about an hour.

19   The company founder, George Parker, had been intrigued by the idea of a financial game as far back as the eighteen-nineties, when the first important governmental investigations of trusts and monopolies were in progress. A genius in the areas of game invention and marketing, George Parker had turned

what fellow New Englanders considered a frivolous pastime into a highly successful business in just five years. According to a booklet published by the firm, the idea of a game named Monopoly occurred to him at the time of the investigations, but he merely filed the name away in his mind for the future.

20   Parker Brothers did not recognize Darrow's game at first, but Darrow persisted. He gave personal demonstrations of his game in department stores in Philadelphia, and it became extremely popular there. Then New York's prestigious F.A.O. Schwarz sold two hundred sets out of a printing of five thousand. On this sales evidence from two key East Coast cities, Parker Brothers — very reluctantly — agreed to take the remainder of the printing on consignment.

21   By Christmas of that year (1934), Parker Brothers had sold every single piece. Darrow was delighted, but the company executives merely sat back and breathed a sigh of relief.

22   This period of relaxation for Parker lasted exactly ten days. Before 1935 was more than a few days old, a veritable tidal wave of orders began pouring in from all parts of the country for more Monopoly sets. Demand quickly reached colossal proportions, and the firm's Salem, Massachusetts, headquarters was almost buried under sacks of mail. Laundry baskets were hauled to the plant to contain the mountains of paper. A Boston office-machinery company was called in to handle Parker's increased bookkeeping. The account executive took one look at the laundry baskets crammed with orders and positively refused to take on the job, no matter what the price.

23   Naturally the company reconsidered its earlier opinion of Darrow's game, and in a very short time Monopoly's creator signed a contract turning over his interest in the game to Parker Brothers on a continuing royalty basis. His very first check was for seven thousand dollars, and soon Darrow could retire for life.

24   As for Parker Brothers, twenty thousand Monopoly sets a week were leaving the factory by mid-February of 1935. Three years earlier, the company had been on the verge of bankruptcy; when Monopoly began to climb in 1935, sales reached as much as eight hundred thousand dollars a week. By the next year, sales topped $1 million and the firm was solidly back on its feet.

25   The craze has shown little sign of abating since then. For a time, the game began to level off into a steady yearly seller. But as soon as the economy gets the least bit rocky, Monopoly takes a sharp upward swing. Most games tend to sell better during times of economic setback, since games give the consumer more hours of enjoyment than, say, movies or other one-time-only forms of entertainment.

26   However, the record year for Monopoly sales was not in the thirties, the period usually associated with the "Monopoly craze," but in 1971. And that year capped a steady fourteen-year growth pattern.

27   Foreign-language and other overseas editions of Monopoly account for part of this growth. In England, the game is called Trafalgar Square, while in Germany, it's Wienerstrasse. Other versions are sold in fourteen other languages, including Flemish, Chinese, Japanese, Greek, and Hebrew.

28   Monopoly appeals to all age groups and is often played in flabbergasting

collegiate marathons. World records have been set for the longest games played in an elevator, in a tree, and on a gigantic replica board. At De Anza College in Cupertino, California, students played Monopoly for twelve hours while submerged in a swimming pool, using special diving equipment hooked up to a respirator and weighted game pieces supplied by Parker Brothers so the play components would not float up to the surface.

29   The longest single Monopoly game yet documented was played from noon on Wednesday, July 21, 1971, to 4 P.M. of Tuesday, August 24 — a total of 820 hours — by twenty players in Danville, California. Another impressive Monopoly event is the annual Detroit tournament held in formal evening clothes. Sponsored by the USMA — United States Monopoly Association — the event invites competition for "the Davis Cup of the board-game playing world," the Stein-Fishbub Trophy.

30   Possibly the wackiest "happening" in Monopoly history occurred in Pittsburgh when some college boys played an endurance game that lasted for days. At last it became obvious to the participants that the bank was about to be "broken." They sent a wire to Parker Brothers explaining that $1 million was desperately needed to ward off another Depression. Parker, which prints about $2.4 billion of legally counterfeit bills daily for its games, took speedy action, packing up a million dollars of Monopoly money and sending it by plane to Pittsburgh. Meantime, a wire had been sent from Salem to the Pittsburgh branch of Brink's. When the airplane landed, an armored car received the money and rushed it to the fraternity house under escort.

31   There is only one major country in the world where Monopoly is not a popular game. Predictably, the game is banned in the Soviet Union as "too capitalistic." Yet even behind the Iron Curtain, it is possible that a few game-sters may enjoy bargaining for Boardwalk and Park Place. During the 1959 American National Exhibition in Moscow, scene of the Nixon-Khrushchev "kitchen debate," six Monopoly sets were placed on display. By the time the exhibit was ended, all of the sets had been stolen.

32   The true mystery of Monopoly lies in its continued popularity. Why should a game that defies the major criteria for a good family game maintain its position as "number one"?

33   Initially, of course, the timing for introducing Monopoly was perfect. People out of work loved playing tycoon, and men who were homeless needed to build dream castles.

34   But the game has far outlived its period, and it shows no signs of dwindling in appeal. Perhaps the reason for Monopoly's long-term success is simply that the game is just great fun. It provides opportunities for fantasized speculation, acceptable miserliness, and interpersonal conflict. Furthermore, Monopoly maintains an unusual balance between luck and freedom of judgment.

35   Could a hit like Monopoly ever happen again? That is the question that impels would-be millionaires in American towns, cities, and rural districts to keep trying, year after year, to come up with the game that will make them secure for life.

36   The odds are pretty small. Darrow himself tried to repeat his success a few years later with Bulls and Bears, a stockmarket game. It went nowhere.

37   With the competition of company inventors and professional freelancers to consider, a conservative estimate of the odds confronting today's amateurs might be about five thousand to one. Yet the pot of gold at rainbow's end is too alluring to ignore.

38   Besides, it stands to reason that somebody has to come up with another Monopoly someday — and Parker Brothers is patiently waiting for it to happen. The company welcomes the thousands of ideas submitted each year; each suggested game is reviewed and many are played before the company reaches a decision.

39   For one of these days, Parker hopes to need those laundry baskets again.

Writing with Sources: Using a Single Source

Integrating information from "Over the Rainbow without Passing Go" with your own ideas, write an essay on one of these topics. Be sure to acknowledge ideas that are not your own.

1. In paragraph 6 Kaye asserts that despite its phenomenal success, Monopoly "wouldn't stand a chance if it were invented today." Argue for or against this assertion, using your knowledge of and experience with contemporary games to support your position.
2. Consider the role of games — one particular one or several — in your life. You may discuss street games, board games, fantasy or role-playing games, or computer games.
3. Assess the relative merits of Monopoly and another board game — or compare the appeal of Monopoly to that of a more elaborate electronic game.

You Deserve a Break

Susan Strasser

The development of the fast-food industry in response to changes in the lifestyle of American families has in turn had a dramatic impact on the way we live today. In this essay, Susan Strasser traces the rise of fast-food restaurants in the 1960s and 1970s, explores the impact of this phenomenon on our eating habits both in restaurants and in the home, and considers the social and psychological implications of the increasingly dominant role of the fast food industry. [For further information about Susan Strasser, see the introduction to "At the Flick of a Switch," pp. 454–455].

1   When Charlotte Perkins Gilman described the food of her ideal future, she envisioned kitchenless houses; individuals and families would patronize establishments that served hot cooked food ready to eat, produced according to the industrial principles of the division of labor and economies of scale. Eighty years later, her dream has come true at McDonald's, Kentucky Fried Chicken, Taco Bell, Arby's, Pizza Hut, and the innumerable smaller restaurant chains that compete with these industry leaders; as Gilman hoped, many men and women stop by these establishments to pick up dinner on the way home from work, or bring their families to eat there. Her accurate prophecy stopped there: she expected that the system that ended women's kitchen fatigue would serve better food than the private home, in better surroundings, thus contributing to general human progress and liberation. Instead, industrial food preparation has controlled and distorted the central ritual of daily life by subordinating all of its values to profit, and decisions about intimate matters get made in the central offices of large corporations.

2   Restaurant eating predated the twentieth century: travelers patronized inns and taverns in colonial America, and Lorenzo Delmonico established the first modern restaurant in New York around 1834, but at the turn of the century, most people ate nothing but meals prepared at home. Only the very wealthy went out for dinner. Workers and schoolchildren brought lunches from home: in Homestead, Pennsylvania, steelworkers' wives took pains to make good cold lunches after the mill owners refused to let them bring hot ones to the plant, while in Manchester, New Hampshire, boardinghouses hired young boys to bring hot lunches to the textile factories. Progressive reformers organized lunches as a major feature of their charitable work, establishing school lunch programs for children from impoverished immigrant households and opening cafeterias to provide cheap lunches for workers, especially single women who boarded in other people's houses and could not bring lunch from home. For the first half of the century, commercial establishments serving prepared lunches proliferated: drug and variety store lunch counters gave downtown shoppers a place to rest and pick up a bite to eat; company and school cafeterias became daily gathering places, their food the butt of many jokes; soda fountains and drive-ins served hungry teen-agers their between-meal snacks. By the end of the 1950s, Americans ate out frequently, although dinner at a restaurant still usually marked a special occasion.

3   All that accelerated during the 1960s and 1970s, as married women with children joined the labor force in unprecedented numbers and as chain restaurants, especially fast-food chains, restructured the restaurant industry. The number of fast-food restaurants nearly tripled during the sixties, while the number of other restaurants declined 9 percent; burger and fried chicken and taco and pizza places crowded the "strips" in every developed suburb, moving into large cities during the seventies, as traditional "Mom and Pop" restaurants closed their doors forever. Rich people consumed more restaurant meals than poor ones, employed people ate out more often than the unemployed, young people more than older ones, men more than women, but by the end of the 1970s everybody ate out somtimes, about a third of the population on any

given day spending about a third of the nation's food dollars on restaurant meals. By 1978, dinner made up about 40 percent of those meals; although most people preferred medium-priced table-service restaurants for their evening meal, they increasingly patronized both takeout and sit-down fast-food restaurants for dinner. . . .

4   The typical restaurant eating experience changed during the sixties and seventies as the Mom and Pop restaurants died out and the chains took over, dominated by the fast-food burger, and chicken operations. Mom's daily special, which she served on thick china plates to customers sitting at tables or on stools, gave way to paper-wrapped sandwiches garnished with precise amounts of ketchup, served by a teen-ager over the counter. The Bureau of Labor Statistics reported that between 1958 and 1972, the number of chain restaurants and drinking establishments almost doubled, while owner-operated restaurants and bars without paid help declined by one-third. The top hundred chains accounted for 25 percent of commercial food-service sales in 1970, 40 percent in 1978, and would go to 50 percent by 1982, according to a food market research firm; one-third of the $23 billion those hundred firms took in during 1977 went to only five companies: McDonald's, Kentucky Fried Chicken, Pillsbury (which owned Burger King and Steak and Ale), International Dairy Queen, and Big Boy. Real growth in commercial food-service sales during the seventies, reported the publisher of a restaurant trade magazine, "can be entirely attributed to the top 100 chain restaurant companies. . . ."

5   As fast-food companies tightened their control over operations and sold out to food conglomerates that could provide them with expansion money, fast food assumed the structure of other American industries, dominated by a few large corporations. As fast foods grew, those few large corporations increasingly dominated not only their industry and their franchisees but Americans' daily lives: McDonald's and Burger Chef and the innumerable smaller chains revamped American eating habits. The average person consumed almost five times as many frozen potatoes in 1976 as in 1960; the fast-food industry used three-quarters of the frozen french fries. Soft-drink consumption more than doubled during the same period. Americans averaged 1.2 pounds of ice milk apiece in 1950, 7.4 pounds in 1976. The consumption of salad and cooking oils tripled between 1947–1949 and 1976. Canned tomatoes, tomato products, and pickles all showed similar increases, testifying to the carloads of ketchup and piles of pickles that garnished all the hamburgers sold with all those fries and shakes.

6   Nor, if the women's magazine writers had their way, would the new foods keep to their place on the street corner. "Everyone's busy these days," declared the *Ladies' Home Journal* in a 1977 article entitled "Fast Food at Home." "But even in the busiest of families, there's no need to go out: food at home can be just as fast, with the added personal touch of grace and style." The *Journal* recommended stocking up on processed foods in cans, jars, and packages and depending on them for the main course. "For instance, frozen fish fillets get topped with a cheese slice, slipped in a bun and served with a side of deli-coleslaw and chips. Round out with a tall glass of tomato juice and

melon balls for dessert. It's the closest thing to non-cooking — without stepping a foot off the premises." Dependent on the food processors for advertising revenue, the *Journal* turned their products into the true competition for fast foods, supplementing the processors' own advertising efforts: Mrs. Paul assured people that they didn't "have to eat out" if they bought her frozen fish sticks. Swanson marketed "take-out style" chicken, Banquet tried their "Outs eat out" campaign, and Contadina and Carnation offered a four-dollar refund on their products to demonstrate that "Eating At Home Pays Off."

7   *Seventeen* and *Mademoiselle,* more allied to the makeup industry than to the food processors and appealing to different audiences, encouraged the new eating habits even more directly. *Seventeen,* apparently suspecting that its readers suffered fast-food withdrawal during the winter, told them in January 1978 that they need not "give up [their] favorite fast foods when it's cold outside" and provided recipes for frozen yogurt, fishburgers, fried pies, frosted shakes, pizza, fried chicken, and coleslaw. While some of these dishes, such as the chicken and the pizza, depended heavily on convenience foods, others such as the fried pies and the frozen yogurt took work and time — "fast foods" only in the sense that they imitated the fare of fast-food restaurants. *Mademoiselle* appealed not to hungry teens but to younger career girls seeking to "whip up company dinner in minutes, from stuff you pick up on the way home. . . . Hide that carton, can or bucket, ritz up the goods, add some candles and wine and they'll never guess the help you had with dinner. (And if they do, they've got to admire your wit . . . and nerve.) Presentation is all — and a twist on the traditional helps. Like melting cheese on the takeout chicken's mashed potatoes. Or toning up Chinese with a tea pot." No recipes followed; readers needed none, since the article recommended simply taking food out of cartons, putting it onto elegant plates, and serving it with tasteful utensils. The Shop section, listing stores where readers could purchase goods pictured throughout the magazine, itemized the plates and utensils; nobody had to be told where to buy fried chicken and mashed potatoes in red-striped cartons.

8   Fast foods have changed eating habits far beyond the food itself; they have invaded the mealtime ritual even at home. The chief executive officer of Kraft, Inc., maintained that eating out accustomed people to "portion control" and therefore to accepting a processor's statement that a package of macaroni and cheese serves four. "Generally speaking," one writer claimed in *Advertising Age,* "the homemaker no longer sets the table with dishes of food from which the family fills their plates — the individual plates are filled and placed before the family, no second helpings." Eating out even accustoms diners at the same table to eating different foods, putting home meals of different prepared foods within the realm of possibility and altering the nature of parental discipline; freed from the "shut up — you'll eat what we're eating" rule, children experience the pleasures and also the isolation of individual free choice at earlier ages. The common bowl that all diners shared until all the food was eaten both represented and fostered important attitudes toward families, toward sharing, and toward food.

9   Children learned those attitudes at the daily family dinner, once the

central ritual of the day and now a dying institution, following the lead of the family lunch (which largely disappeared long before the beginning of the century) and the family breakfast (now defunct in three-quarters of American households). A survey taken during the summer and fall of 1977 showed that families got together for only half their meals on the weekends, when they presumably had the most time to do so; many who had not entirely abandoned family dinners no longer ate together daily. Individual family members eat whenever, wherever, and with whomever they like; one drug company advertised bottled vitamins to mothers in 1980 on the claim that they could not be sure teen-agers were eating properly. "In one generation," according to *Advertising Age*, "we have gone from a traditional food producing society to a food grazing society — one where we eat wherever we happen to be."

10   When Americans graze their way to the fast-food outlets, they encounter and participate in a series of new rituals. As a University of Michigan anthropologist points out, writing specifically about McDonald's, behavior there shares important features with other rituals in all cultures: stylized, repetitive, stereotyped events occur in special places, include costumes and set sequences of words and actions, "translate enduring messages, values, and sentiments into observable action," and "signal" people's "acceptance of an order that transcends their status as individuals." People arrive at McDonald's — and to a lesser extent at the other chains — knowing what they will eat, what they will pay, what to say to the counter person and how she or he will respond, what the restaurant will look like — in short, knowing exactly what to expect and how to behave; children learn these expectations and behaviors early in life. For some, the ritual constitutes an attraction of these restaurants; they neither wish to cook nor to chat with a waitress as she intones and delivers the daily specials. The fast-food ritual requires no responsibility other than ordering (with as few words as possible) and paying; nobody has to set or clear the table, wash the dishes, or compliment the cook on her cuisine, the traditional responsibilities of husbands and children at the family dinner.

11   If, like other rituals, fast-food restaurant behavior signals acceptance of an order that transcends people's status as individuals, there can be no mistaking the order: corporate intrusion into daily life, the ultimate domination of the public sphere over the formerly private. Advertising, as Leon J. Shapiro and Dwight Bohmbach told Madison Avenue in *Advertising Age*, "has replaced 'pinching the tomatoes' and hand selecting in our choice of foods. A wood-cut illustration of an old-fashioned kitchen on a meat analog package; 'grandfather' smacking his lips over a synthetic lemonade . . . these symbols now tell us what to expect from food someone else picked, prepared and packaged for us." The corporations attempt to compensate for stripping food of its emotional content by using symbols like these and the healthy nuclear families in the McDonald's ads. They try to convince consumers that they can regain what they have lost if they substitute one set of products for another: "Eating at home always pays off . . . in good eating, homey surroundings, and economy," Contadina and Carnation claim, offering a refund to consumers who buy their products instead of Pizza Hut's. Or they develop new "product concepts," like

the takeout and frozen ethnic foods that Shapiro and Bohmbach maintain "help
to satisfy the desire for really traditional dishes" and the "new" kinds of
fast-food restaurants that have inside tables. The advertisers do not care whether
anybody actually believes that Taco Bell sells "really traditional" Mexican food
or whether families achieve intimacy sitting around a table at Kentucky Fried
Chicken. They intend merely to "help to satisfy" a desire sufficiently to sell a
product especially attractive to working mothers, whose children prefer fast
foods — and the safe ritual, individual choice, and freedom from responsibility
that go with them — to anything mothers might cook when they get home from
work.

12   The big companies and their advertising wizards have met resistance from
the consumer groups that have lobbied successfully for regulation over advertising, product names, and packaging information, from the health-foods
movement, and from leisure-time gourmet cooking, but none of these challenge the fundamental problem. The consumer movement generally takes
corporate control as given and attempts to limit its powers: although some regulation is better than none, nutritional packaging information helps concerned
consumers make intelligent choices between two processed foods, without
challenging the corporations' power to determine what appears in the stores
on the sole basis of profit. The health-foods movement has brought nutritional
awareness beyond packaging, but the large corporations easily co-opted
consumers' nutritional concerns by producing "health foods" like the granola-
type breakfast cereals, many of them loaded with sugar and salt, and most more
expensive than other products. Gourmet cooking will always be the province
of people with money; past the initial investment in cookbooks and equipment,
this hobby requires continual spending on expensive ingredients, including
the unprocessed foods that may some day be available only to the wealthy, and
to those with backyards and green thumbs, because they produce lower profits
than highly processed foods.

13   None of this resistance attacks either the most profound causes or the
most profound effects of an increasing dilemma; nutritional labeling and
gourmet cookbooks cannot save American culture, insofar as it is reflected in
and formed by daily eating habits and rituals, from the control of the corporate
boardroom. Under that control, most people will increasingly lose their power
to decide about their food, their choices limited to the products of one corporation or another, all uniform, geared to the average palate and produced on
the basis of decisions made, not about flavor or quality or freshness, but about
profit. They will eat even more of their meals in surroundings that distort
fundamental rituals, where corporate managers have decided everything — the
color of the floor, the clothing of the teen-ager at the counter, the words
employees use, and the amount of ketchup on a hamburger — on the basis of
market research, or they will buy food from those restaurants and from factories
by way of supermarkets and bring it home, where the public ritual has over-
taken the private. Their food at home will be processed; like cotton and wool,
now luxury fabrics, fresh broccoli and raw chicken will be supplanted by more
profitable synthetics.

14   Although the corporate executive and the advertising copywriter will

remain able longer to afford unprocessed foods and expensive restaurants, they too graze for food, grabbing a bite in transit, and they too have lost the family dinner. Undoubtedly many of them recognize the long-run and society-wide implications of their work; a few may even quit their jobs when the emotional costs run high, to be replaced by others who do the same work. But those who form American eating habits do so in their roles as corporate executives and advertising copywriters, not as individual human beings. A few making decisions for the many, chosen without any semblance of democracy, they make those decisions according to corporate balance sheets, which never reflect emotional costs.

Notes

PAGE 566   Homestead lunches: Margaret Byington, *Homestead: The Households of a Mill Town* (New York: Russell Sage Foundation, 1910), p. 64.
Manchester lunches: Tamara K. Hareven and Randolph Langenbach, *Amoskeag: Life and Work in an American Factory-City* (New York: Pantheon Books, 1978), p. 223.
Number of fast-food restaurants nearly tripled: Richard B. Carnes and Horst Brand, "Productivity and New Technology in Eating and Drinking Places," *Monthly Labor Review,* September 1977, p. 12.

PAGES 566–567   Who eats out and where: See Gallup surveys in the following: "45,728,000 Adults Go Out to Eat Daily," *Food Service Marketing,* April 1978, p. 8; "Where Are Americans Eating Out?" *Food Service Marketing,* April 1978, pp. 71–73; "Working Women Are Boon to Food Service," *Food Service Marketing,* June 1978, p. 12.

PAGE 567   General growth of fast foods: John C. Maxwell, Jr., "Fast-feeders Draw a Bead on Continued Growth," *Advertising Age,* September 11, 1978, pp. 117–18.
Bureau of Labor Statistics: Carnes and Brand, "Productivity and New Technology," p. 11.
Top hundred chains: Phillip L. Rane, "Are 'Mom and Pops' Dead?" *Food Service Marketing,* November 1978, p. 12.
Frozen-potato consumption: Kiechel, "Food Giants Struggle," p. 52; Louise Page and Berta Friend, "The Changing United States Diet," *Bioscience,* March 1978, p. 194.
Soft drinks and ice milk: Leo J. Shapiro and Dwight Bohmbach, "Eating Habits Force Changes in Marketing," *Advertising Age,* October 30, 1978, p. 65.
Salad and cooking oils: Page and Friend, "Changing United States Diet," p. 193.
"Everyone's busy these days": "Fast Food at Home," *Ladies' Home Journal,* October 1977, p. 138.

PAGE 568   "Eating At Home Pays Off!": Carnation and Contadina ad, *Parade,* February 11, 1979.

PAGE 568   *Seventeen* article: "Homemade Takeouts," *Seventeen,* January 1978, pp. 76–77.
Mademoiselle article: "Four Fast-Food Makeovers," *Mademoiselle,* February 1979, pp. 160–61.
Kraft executive and "Generally speaking, the homemaker no longer sets the table": Larry Edwards, "Soft Sales Challenge Food Marketers," *Advertising Age,* October 30, 1978, p. 27.
Breakfast defunct: Shapiro and Bohmbach, "Eating Habits Force Changes," p. 65.

PAGE 569   One drug company: Roche ad, *Ladies' Home Journal,* August 1980, p. 6.
"In one generation": Shapiro and Bohmbach, "Eating Habits Force Changes," p. 27.
"Translate enduring messages": Conrad P. Kottak, "Rituals at McDonald's," *Natural History,* January 1978, p. 74.
Advertising "has replaced 'pinching the tomatoes'": Shapiro and Bohmbach, "Eating Habits Force Changes," p. 66.

Writing with Sources: Using a Single Source

Integrating information from "You Deserve a Break" with your own ideas, write an essay on one of these topics. Be sure to acknowledge ideas that are not your own.

1. Evaluate the role of fast food — convenience foods as well as meals in chain restaurants — on your own life and the lives of your friends and family. If possible, consider how your eating habits have changed as a result of the increasing availability of fast food.
2. In what other respects have our eating habits changed over the past generation? Interview an older friend or relative about the kinds of meals he or she ate twenty or thirty years ago, and compare the two time periods with respect to the kinds of foods consumed and the settings in which meals were eaten.
3. For a society on the move, fast food is not the only convenience item required. Examine ways in which other aspects of our lives are speeding up, and assess the usefulness of a number of products and services designed to help us keep up our increasingly hectic pace.
4. Write a defense of fast food, arguing against Strasser's key points.

What Price Fitness?

Robert Lipsyte

Robert Lipsyte was born in 1938. He received a B.A. and an M.A. from Columbia University. Between 1957 and 1971 he was a sports writer for *The New York Times,* and during that time he won a number of awards for journalism. More recently he has written books for children and adults, many focusing on sports themes, and several screenplays. Lipsyte is currently a correspondent for CBS television. In "What Price Fitness?" he surveys the history of the fitness craze in America. He discusses what he views as our nation's growing obsession with working out, arguing that it has, for some, gone beyond the limits of healthy exercise.

1   One recent Sunday morning I went to my local community center for a "personal physical fitness review." A matched pair of trim, perky, helpful young people took my vital signs and administered simple tests for muscular strength, flexibility and cardiorespiratory endurance. Except for my flexibility, which was below average, everything was normal or fair or average or O.K. No red flags and no gold stars. I was told, in a friendly and positive way, that there was a lot of room for improvement and that more walking, running and swimming, plus aerobic exercises, stretching and racquetball would make me more fit, help me carve off 10 pounds of fat and probably contribute to my overall health. The young people counseled against lifting weights; it would add nothing to my fitness or health. They suggested moderate activity, especially at

first, and a medical checkup. They were sensible, supportive and, according to everything I've been reading and hearing, absolutely right.

2   So, now what?

3   This current fitness craze, the biggest in a series that predates the Revolution, has produced more confusing information than can be lifted or leaped over by a well-conditioned young athlete. I am 48 years old and my own sports confessional is a typically sorry story. I make an effort to run or swim at least three times a week, but I travel too often and too irregularly to maintain a pattern. Even when I manage to get into a regular rhythm of exercise, I am not passionate about it. I'm not sure why, since I enjoy the process and always feel better for having done it. I covet the better bodies in the locker-room no more than I covet the better cars in the parking lot; I'd like one, sure, but not enough really to extend myself.

4   I haven't smoked in almost 20 years. I don't drink nearly enough, if recent studies are to be believed that suggest two drinks a day may be protective against heart attacks. But I always wear a seat belt and no one in my family died early from heart disease. On the other hand, I keep being turned down by all those mail-order life insurance solicitations after they learn that six years ago I completed a course of chemotherapy for cancer, my only serious illness.

5   In the early 1960's, still firm from Army basic training, I began swimming in a Manhattan YMCA and running in Riverside Park, along the Hudson River. This was fairly aberrant behavior at the time; such people were called "health nuts." I explained to friends that a sportwriter needed to get out and jiggle around a little so as to better understand the people he was writing about. Actually, I did it because I liked it. In the park I was usually alone except for an occasional boxer, who ran in combat boots and a watch cap, and stopped to snort and throw a flurry of punches. I'd feel tough just running behind him.

6   Swimming was a pleasure of the flesh. I felt thin and long and hard, the water sliding along my body like a tongue. Dried off, I felt physically satisfied and mentally sharp. It wasn't until the late 1960's that I also felt morally righteous. Career soldiers had always worked out, to be fit to kill, but it took the consumer movement to give political blessing to a personal act; so-called natural foods and jogging were a progressive response to an establishment that wanted us passive, blissed out in front of televised sports, too impacted by beer and junk food to prevent the robbery of our health and our country.

7   Tennis was the most visible participatory sport of the late 1960's and early 70's, replaced in the middle of the decade by jogging, which became the symbol of the fitness movement. A river of runners was fed by streams from the human potential movement, the women's movement, the so-called sexual revolution, the men's fashion movement. Jogging is the cheapest and most accessible of personal sports; with a companion it is the most sociable. I think the whole world should jog instead of eating lunch. If the whole world did it — very slowly, on soft ground — I would, too.

8   The current symbol is aerobic exercise, particularly as seen on those frenetic, hard-rock cable-television classes led by dancers I think of as the Stepford Other Women. They are perfect people, and they never stop moving or

talking, "Come on, you can do it," and "Bring that bum up." There is a Miami
Vice look to their clothing and to the sets — harsh, bright, unnatural colors.
The more I look at those aerobics teachers, the more I think, No, I can't do it,
better get Sonny and Tubbs.

9   The next symbol may well be weight-training machines; more than a
billion dollars was spent on exercise devices last year, most of it on equipment
for the home. It will be possible to sculpt a single muscle at a time, to create
an objet d'art of flesh, your own. I'll never have the patience for that.

10   Nevertheless, I am a window shopper at what I have come to think of as
the Fitness Fair, that multibillion-dollar market for designer headbands and
honest advice, grunt-along cassettes that can leave you for dead on the living-
room rug, and comfortable shoes that might possibly liberate your heart and
mind after they delight your feet. There is salvation in getting my body in gear,
but there are just too many guides who claim to know the Only Way. The
Fitness Fair calls to me because some of its booths have what I want, if only I
can find them.

11   The American fitness boom is a cyclical phenomenon, predominantly
middle-class, layered by money, sex, religion, charismatic entrepreneurs and
fear of an early death. What else is new?
The names and the bodies are new. Benjamin Franklin called for swimming
and running in the new "leisure" of 1743. In 1772, Dr. Benjamin Rush, an
early model of the progressive, socially committed American physician, delivered his "Sermon on Exercise," and after Independence he published empirical
observations to back it up; wounded British soldiers who hurried after their
retreating units recovered more quickly than those who stayed behind. This was
not revolutionary. Hippocrates and Galen noted the value of exercise. By the
Renaissance, nutrition and exercise were recognized as ways human beings
could wrest control of their destiny from "God's will."

12   The Age of Jackson produced my own favorite health guru, Sylvester
Graham, unfortunately best remembered now for the Graham cracker, an irony.
As a nutritional reformer who waved the banner of bran, he would probably
not have touched the sweet contemporary version. Graham became nationally
prominent in the 1830's; the country was turning from "heroic" medicine
toward natural healing, it was disturbed by the anonymous and often unhealth-
ful practices in the new mass production of food, and it was terrified by an
impending cholera epidemic. Graham espoused exercise, vegetarianism and
gentle, perfunctory sex between long-term partners. He believed that mastur-
bation and the sexual chase stimulated the imagination to a level that debilitated the body.

13   The Graham boarding houses, where people came to regain their health,
were the Pritikin Longevity Centers of their day, and, like Nathan Pritikin,
Graham believed that physical activity was essential. "Go to the gymnasium,"
counseled Graham, "swing upon and climb the poles and ropes and ladders
and vault upon the wooden horse . . . walk and run and jump or labor on the
farm."

14   As Stephen Nissenbaum, a history professor at the University of Massachu-

setts, notes in his 1980 book, "Sex, Diet, and Debility in Jacksonian America," scholars of the period disagree over the political foundations of Graham's theories of minimal consumption. Was he trying to neutralize the growing power of capitalism (Thoreau practiced something like the Graham system during his two years at Walden Pond) or was Graham preparing the rising bourgeoisie for capitalism by teaching them self-restraint? Feminism owed much to the teachings of Graham and his disciples, on health reform, temperance and woman's role as "the final umpire" in the bedroom.

15   According to Harvey Green in his forthcoming "Fit for America," the pre – Civil War fitness craze that Graham dominated grew out of "the millennial spirit of religious enthusiasm and a concern for the fate of the Republic after the death of the great leaders of the 18th century." After the Civil War, however, it was concern for the body more than the spirit that produced a second great fitness craze, writes Green, who teaches history at the University of Rochester.

16   German immigrants, many doctors among them, brought to this country their calisthenic systems and their water cures. Public schools and community recreation centers became laboratories for the new physical educators. The explosion of team sports — baseball for the masses, football for the collegians — was part of an "athletic revival," particularly among the well-to-do "brain" workers of the Northeast. They ate "Granula" cereals, bought rowing machines and flocked to indoor gyms.

17   The third major fitness craze, which began as America entered the 20th century, added to religion and health another strand — regeneration in a time of national midlife crisis. More than a century old at the time, America had not fulfilled all its promise. There was ethnic and racial tension, crime in the cities. Family farms were disappearing. Social dissension was becoming institutionalized: labor unions were on the rise, as was opposition to established political parties; women were demanding the vote. Yet there was a surge of physical activity because the new urban dweller needed to be made fit for the assembly line, child-bearing and trench warfare.

18   If our current fitness craze seems to combine elements of all crazes past, perhaps it is because they are not discrete events but the continuation of a single movement that is interrupted only by economic depression and war. For most of the 1930's, middle-class America was too hard-pressed to touch its toes, although thousands of ball fields, tennis courts, golf courses, swimming pools and ski trails were built by the Works Progress Administration. There was Charles Atlas, of course, but the national role model was a President, Franklin D. Roosevelt, who could not stand unaided.

19   But after World War II came three Presidents with personal commitments to physical activity. Harry S. Truman's "constitutional" was a brisk daily walk that left the press corps breathless. Dwight D. Eisenhower's golf game legitimatized personal sport, and his recovery from a heart attack opened public discussion of coronary disease. It also introduced Eisenhower's personal physician, the bicycle-riding Paul Dudley White, who advocated exercise for everybody, including the aged and the ill.

20   In 1956, Eisenhower founded the President's Council on Youth Fitness to

bring American youngsters up to the strength and stamina levels of European children. The Council grew in status under the Kennedy Administration. There were vigorous new school physical-education programs and politicians campaigning on jogging trails. Indoor tennis courts in upscale suburbs opened sport to millions of women who hadn't been given a real chance to play at anything after kindergarten.

21   The Fitness Fair became crowded again. Sneaker and ski companies paid under-the-table millions to amateur stars to wear their products on television. Cigarette and liquor companies moved into tournament sponsorship. The subspecialty of sports medicine became popular among doctors who wanted to treat the separated shoulders of rich, otherwise healthy celebrities who could get them close to the action. In 1968, Dr. Kenneth H. Cooper published "Aerobics," establishing the statistical measurements of fitness.

22   But by that year, when President Lyndon B. Johnson amended the council's name to Physical Fitness and Sports, the glorious promise of the exercise movement—which promised an early start toward a lifetime of fitness—had been subverted. Children's fitness test scores, measured every 10 years by the council, declined in the 1970's. Gym class was again something to be excused from. There was no national program of exercise and no nutritional information for pre-schoolers and pregnant mothers and senior citizens. There were a few highly publicized private charities that sponsored events for the retarded and the handicapped, but almost all the money and attention was directed instead toward elite athletes, professional and Olympic, and to the customers of relatively expensive, established consumer sports, particularly bowling, golf and tennis.

23   Two apostate tennis players, George A. Sheehan and James F. Fixx, would become the spiritual and practical advisers to the next hopeful development, the running fancy.

24   Sheehan, a New Jersey cardiologist, was 44 years old when he broke his hand against a wall in a fit of pique at being called out in the middle of the night. To stay in shape while his hand healed, he began running. Sheehan discovered on the road more agon and epiphany than anyone since St. Paul. His columns, lectures and books ("This Running Life," "Running and Being," et al.) are erudite and good-natured guides; he elevates the act of exercise. He inveighs against the pride and arrogance of fitness prigs, and he warns that fitness schedules must be "respected, not worshipped."

25   Sheehan's writings informed Fixx, a magazine editor who was 35 when he pulled a muscle playing tennis. He started running to strengthen his legs. Eventually, he quit his two-pack-a-day cigarette habit, lost 60 pounds and became rich and famous with the 1977 publication of "The Complete Book of Running," that rarity in the fitness field, a nonauthoritarian, reader-friendly manual; it became a No. 1 best seller.

26   By then the streets were alive with the sound of sneakers slapping, Pulse rate was a better conversational gambit than astrological sign as the Lite Generation jogged from singles bar to salad bar, from gouty sauces to righteous nutrition.

27   Fixx observed an "unabashedly narcissistic strain" in the lunge for

"self-betterment," but he was basically nonjudgemental. Flabby commentators saw the end of altruism and political involvement, even a hint of fascism in the unforgiving demands of the calisthenic commandos. Some older men felt truly threatened by young professional women wearing jogging shoes from home to office. (What happened to femininity, to elegance, to catch 'em and keep 'em?)

28   Women may have gotten more from the Fitness Fair than men, simply because they started with so much less. Denied most athletic outlets, tranquilized, kept weaker and slower, women exploded into the empowering new world. They were spending a large percentage of the fitness dollar by 1984, the year the Olympic Games staged its first marathon for women. That same year, the New York City Marathon offered identical prizes to the first male and female finisher—$25,000 and a Mercedes-Benz. No wonder that the most famous contemporary fitness entrepreneur is a woman, Jane Fonda, and that she is just about the only barker at the Fair with a social consciousness.

29   But the craze is more talk than action, more style than sweat. Two and half billion dollars was spent on athletic shoes last year, but school and community physical-education programs are local and isolated and the first to go in a cutback. People in their 30's, who benefited from Eisenhower's Youth Fitness, are probably the hard core of the current boom. There is no similarly trained generation to fill their sneakers.

30   In fact, the United States Department of Health and Human Services recently reported that today's children—raised in an era of suburban car pools, television and video games—are softer and weaker than ever. The department also reported that only about 20 percent of American adults are exercising for aerobic fitness. Alas, there may be more compelling reasons to exercise.

31   A man says to me in the health-club locker room in Chicago's Ritz-Carlton Hotel: "At least I did one good thing today." It is 7:30 A.M.

32   What else can he do? Work harder? The company doesn't love him. If the way the railroad mistreated his father didn't teach him that, the last 20 years of reorganizations and closings and layoffs and mergers have. What else can he do? Buy another machine? How many BMW's, VCR's and PC's does one person need? Get into his family? His wife's out jogging, too, clearing her mind for briefs, and the kids are available only for quality time.

33   So he "works out." He wraps himself into himself, and no matter how much pain and/or injury he self-inflicts, even if he recapitulates the Type A overdrive, the paranoia, the reflexive competition of his professional life, he believes he is doing himself good; chasing the dreads, frying off fat, getting stronger, looking younger, becoming better!

34   Meanwhile, the very best bodies of America are in prison, pumping iron in the belly of the beast. Murderers, rapists, armed robbers, predominantly poor boys who never got good coaching on the outside, finally into a routine where the first level of survival—food, shelter, clothing—is included with the price of powerlessness. Watch them take charge of their last possession, their bodies, sculpting them into something to be proud of, something that will carry them from day to day, like a soap opera or a merger deal or an absorbing

war, a reason to get up in the morning, something to think about. How are those lats coming along? What fearful symmetry in the pecs. Did you see how they looked at me today? I can't button the top of my shirt. My neck's gonna be as wide as my head. Here comes The Terminator. The Terminator.

35   A new sign recently appeared alongside the indoor track on which I lumber, 16 laps to the mile. It read, "Don't Give These Signals a Second Thought. Act Immediately." The sign went on to list the symptoms of heart attack. I had seen an identical sign before, on the refrigerator door of a sedentary writer. That was troubling, but appropriate. But not here. Would you hang a sign on the Fountain of Youth, "Don't Drink the Water"?

36   A few weeks earlier, a doctor had died soon after jogging on the track. It was the local angle of a national story. Vigorous exercise kills people. Every time this happens, fitness advocates maintain that anyone who dies running could as easily have died tying his shoelaces — and probably would have died much sooner if he had never run. Fitness skeptics, who are not in vogue these days, might wonder if it wasn't the sudden intensity of exercise that overtaxed the runner's flawed system. If he had never run, if he had missed that particular crisis, perhaps he would have lived longer. As yet, there is no overwhelming scientific evidence for either point of view.

37   Fitness and health are not synonymous. In 1984, when Fixx dropped dead at 52 while running, he proved that it is possible to run fast, frequently, and be on one's last legs. Fixx's autopsy revealed advanced atherosclerosis, that progressive circulatory disease in which plaque attached to the inside of arteries eventually closes the blood vessels. A moment comes when the body needs a rush of oxygen-bearing blood that cannot be delivered. Fixx was fit when he died, but he was not healthy.

38   The simplest measurement of fitness is the time it takes for your pulse to return to its normal or "resting" beat after vigorous exercise raises it to a "target rate" for a few minutes. That target is generally figured by this formula: 70 percent of 220 minus your age. The sooner it recovers, the more fit your are. The more you exercise, the quicker your pulse returns to normal. No responsible sports-medicine doctor will claim that a faster recovery means you are healthier, but some will say it shows that your heart is stronger.

39   How much imagination do you need to extrapolate a stronger heart into the promise of a longer life? These are the magic words that bring us into the Fitness Fair. Even if we also hope to be firm, to be hip, to be spiritual, to be stronger longer, it is the prospect of prolonging life that justifies the money, time and hard work that must be spent at the Fair.

40   The scientific studies that support this dream that the race will continue as long as you can run it are controversial. One of the most famous was a study of London transport workers, published in 1953. Sedentary bus drivers had more coronary disease than conductors. The conclusion was that physical activity offers protection from heart attacks, or at least reduces their severity. Within a few years, even the people who had conducted the study were picking it apart. Men who chose to be drivers, or were hired as drivers, tended to be fatter than conductors, who also had less stress in their jobs and more social in-

teraction. Nevertheless, that study has informed the Fair for more than 25 years. It is what fitness advocates wanted to believe, and it seemed logical.

41   If some physical activity is better than none, reason some, perhaps a great deal of physical activity is best of all. In 1975, Dr. Thomas J. Bassler, a California pathologist and long-distance runner, offered what has been called the "Marathon Hypothesis," which flatly stated that anyone who could run the marathon would never die of a heart attack. He has since fine-tuned his hypothesis to credit the life style of the marathon runner rather than the running itself, but his disciples have taken off in a number of directions short only of suggesting you might live forever if you could run far enough. Does it seem unduly skeptical to wonder if those who choose the marathon, invariably small, wiry, health-conscious folk who don't smoke and eschew animal fats, wouldn't live as long if they ran only 13 miles? Sixteen laps?

42   In "The Complete Book of Running," Fixx wrote that scientific evidence, although "inconclusive . . . clearly suggests that running is more likely to increase than decrease longevity." In his 1980 "Second Book of Running," he introduces Stanford epidemiologist Ralph S. Paffenbarger Jr., whose studies of longshoremen led him to believe that exercise reduces the incidence of heart attacks.

43   Dr. Paffenbarger's study has been attacked as "flawed" by Dr. Henry A. Solomon, a New York cardiologist who calls exercise "a public health hazard." In his 1984 "The Exercise Myth," Dr. Solomon worried over "all those who have bought the mistaken idea that strenuous effort promotes health and longevity."

44   The best of the fitness advocates, like Dr. Sheehan, never suggest that one's life will last longer because of exercise. But they say this: However long you do live, if you exercise, you will have more energy, more clear thoughts, more good time.

45   I drag myself to the track, wince at the warning sign, imagine the iron flower blooming in my chest. But once I am warm with movement, I feel fine, solve problems, have random thoughts. I am alone with myself in personal selfish quality time. For the rest of the day, I am better at whatever I do for having exercised.

46   It's a bargain and I wish I could leave it at that. If I'm willing to accept that fitness does not necessarily prolong life, why do I feel a twinge of guilt if I don't work out? I hear them chanting from the booths, If you don't exercise you will become depressed. Cholesterol will choke your blood vessels. Your fat cells will breed cancer. Quit your whining about the manipulated stresses of modern life, the carcinogens in the air, in the water, in the food. If you get sick it's your own fault.

47   I can't figure out if this is another chapter in the old battle between "heroic" medicine and the natural healers or the cry of the Fitness Fair barkers: They'll say anything to get us to swallow their iron supplements and pump their iron weights. Or is it a conspiracy to divide us, to subvert collective action and create an orthodoxy of isolated individualism, millions straining to be perfect, and thus even more unfit in an increasingly imperfect world?

48   But you have to keep moving. Keep your eyes open, but stuff your ears. Whatever you do has to be better than nothing, even if some barker calls it "garbage yardage," not fast enough for aerobic value. You will burn about the same number of calories per mile no matter how fast you are going, so something is happening. There is no machine that is necessarily better than sit-ups and push-ups and pull-ups. And if you are in pain, your body is not happy. So find something comfortable and pleasurable and do it regularly. It may become an obsession and you will bore everybody about it. Or you may just putter along feeling better. Like me.

49   I am not going to take the results of my "physical fitness review" to heart. I'll try to bring my flexibility up to average and I'll continue to try to do something at least three times a week. But I am not going to force myself into the leap from average to good and beyond, because I know that will mean, for me, an end to the joy of jiggling around. It will mean another list of other people's rules and deadlines to live by, a new set of charts and protocols, the Only Ways of wishful science. I want to be fit for life, not for the Fitness Fair.

50   And so I'm looking for a place to park my car two or three miles from the office so I can walk back and forth at Harry Truman's "constitutional" pace. I'll take a Harry every day, a heart-thumping Harry. You take a Harry. If you see me, wave. But don't stop moving.

Writing with Sources: Using a Single Source

Integrating information from "What Price Fitness?" with your own ideas, write an essay on one of these topics. Be sure to acknowledge ideas that are not your own.

1. Is America's preoccupation with exercise really a potentially dangerous obsession? Or is it just a harmless — or even beneficial — fad? Draw on your own experience to support or challenge Lipsyte's thesis.
2. Can Lipsyte's observations be applied to team sports as well as to exercise? Compare the forces that motivate players on amateur or professional sports teams with the forces that drive personal fitness adherents.
3. Explore possible relationships between the typically American drive for success in business and the pursuit of fitness described by Lipsyte.

Why Americans Love Their Malls

William Ecenbarger

In this magazine article William Ecenbarger, a freelance writer, examines one of the most typically American of modern settings: the shopping mall. Focusing on the King of Prussia mall near Philadelphia, the country's largest shopping complex, Ecenbarger discusses the interchangeability of malls throughout the country and the role of the shopping mall as a social institution, characterizing the mall as "Main Street in the America of the ninth decade of the 20th century."

1   Every day, except Christmas, New Year's and Easter, they come by the tens of thousands to the King of Prussia shopping mall. They come in Mercedes-Benzes — Main Line, high-fashion women, with the aura of money that makes head waiters and bell captains jump the world over, fluttering like exotic birds preening their plumage; they come in Ford station wagons — middle-class couples from mortgaged suburban homes on the outskirts of their income, their wallets thick with credit cards and their children teetering on the edge of their patience; they come tightly packed in rusty Volkswagen Beetles — adolescents wearing jeans and sweatshirts with the names of Ivy League colleges arched across the front; they come on SEPTA buses — old people sitting and watching, deja-viewing, remembering the days when penny postcards cost only a nickel.

2   For the 500,000 people who live within 20 minutes' driving time, the King of Prussia mall is Main Street in the America of the ninth decade of the 20th century. Instead of sidewalks, there are promenades lined with flowers and well-mannered trees. The blare of traffic is replaced by soft music and the tinkle of fountains.

3   But this Main Street is carefully planned so the environment is stable and timeless, like a casino. There are no clocks, other than those for sale. Unlike the old Main Streets, there are no doors on the stores, making entering and leaving easier. No door is even nicer than an open door. Signs on windows are not allowed, for they draw shoppers' eyes away from the displays. The colors of the mall itself are off-white, quiet and restrained, giving the stores and their merchandise the opportunity to shine. The entries and passageways are tiled; store interiors are carpeted. Mall managers know that people tend to walk faster on hard surfaces, slower on soft ones.

4   The King of Prussia mall — actually there are two connected malls, the Plaza at King of Prussia and the Court at King of Prussia — is in many respects similar to the other 23,000 American shopping malls. But in one respect it's unique — it's the largest shopping complex in the United States. How big is the King of Prussia mall? From a distance, it looks big enough to apply for statehood — a shimmering, glassy mountain of 350 stores circled like a wagon train on an asphalt prairie. It has more stores than most cities' downtowns, including Philadelphia's. There are 37 shoe stores and 70 places to eat. The management hands out maps for shoppers. The mall is part of most tour packages created by the nearby Valley Forge Country Convention and Visitors Bureau. So large is its

parking lot that professional car thieves come here with orders — make, year and color.

> ". . . available at Bertha's Kitty Boutique, located in the 'Dales — Roy 'n' Dale, Clydesdale, Airedale, Teasdale, Chippendale, Mondale and other fine shopping centers everywhere."
> — Spoof by Garrison Keillor on *A Prairie Home Companion*.

5   They are the new America, all these Dales and Plazas and Centres and Galleries and Pavilions. Charles Kuralt, CBS's peripatetic reporter, has noted that "what used to be farms or woods or country crossroads have become malls, and if you want to find America today, this is where you have to look." Shopping malls are now the third most-frequented place by the average American, topped only by home and the work place. A Rutgers University study found that adolescents tend to describe their homes not in terms of towns but rather in terms of malls — as, "three miles from the King of Prussia mall."

6   There's a mall on the site of the Long Island airstrip where Lindbergh left for Paris in 1927. There's a mall in Shillington, Pa., where the Berks County poorhouse used to be that was the locale for John Updike's novel *The Poorhouse Fair*. There's a mall on the site of the old Willow Grove Amusement Park, where John Philip Sousa played more than 60 years ago. There's even a mall in Dublin on the site of Barney Kiernan's pub, which was the location for a scene in James Joyce's *Ulysses*. The Rev. Jerry Falwell broadcasts his *Oldtime Gospel Hour* from a mall he owns, and George Wallace was shot and seriously wounded in a mall while campaigning for the presidency in 1972.

7   New Jerseyans now can get their driver's licenses issued or renewed at shopping malls, no-frills medical care is available at thousands of mall clinics, and Sears stores offer insurance, securities and real estate. At the Plymouth Meeting Mall in Montgomery County, a 225-member Presbyterian Church has been operating since 1966, next to Sal's Pizza. It boasts the largest baptismal font in the world — 24,000 gallons.

8   For all its modernity, today's shopping mall assumes an ancient role — that of the Athenian agora, the Roman forum and the medieval cathedral square — as well as the role of the American downtown. The mall is a place where people gather to exchange goods and money, greetings and gossip. But whereas our predecessors coped with the problem of scarcity, mall-goers cope with the problem of multiple choice, and the mall is an arena for America's new national pastime — shopping. Baseball? On a given Saturday, more people go to the King of Prussia mall to shop than go to Veterans Stadium to watch the Phillies.

> "So thees ees Amereeka!"
> — Russian visitor, seeing Bloomingdale's, in the film *Moscow on the Hudson*

9   They come to Bloomingdale's on Sundays after church — exchanging trendier-than-thou looks, glittering like ocean liners in the night. A mother and daughter, linked arm-in-arm like the O's in the store logo, pass beneath the golden portal. A blond woman, gusting perfume, emerges with a brimming

shopping bag, dusts a bench with her eyes, sits down and lights a cigarette in a holder.

10   Bloomingdale's, the store "like no other," the epitome of high fashion and high prices. Its King of Prussia store was designed by Gyo Obata, the architect of the Dallas – Fort Worth Airport, the Smithsonian Institution's National Air and Space Museum, and the Winter Olympic Center at Lake Placid. Bloomingdale's puts its highest fashion on the second floor, and so by design, other high-fashion tenants — Peck & Peck, Cache, T. Edwards, and others — are arrayed on the Court's second level, across from the fabled store. A video game room here would be as out of place as a pair of brown shoes with a tuxedo. Before "Bloomie's" opened in 1981, the people who shop here shopped only in Main Line boutiques, or in Center City, or in New York.

11   The basic strategy of a mall is simple: You space out the department stores so that to get from one to the other, shoppers have to walk past the store-fronts of the smaller tenants. Although Bloomingdale's bats cleanup at King of Prussia, there are six other heavy hitters, and together they form a kind of National Retailing Hall of Fame, of which Lyman Gustave Bloomingdale is but one member.

12   There is Adam Gimble, an immigrant peddler from Bavaria, who opened his first store in 1842 at Vincennes, Ind. And Richard Warren Sears, who, it was said, could sell a breath of air, started a firm with Alvah Curtis Roebuck in 1893 that would become the world's largest retailer. There's John Wanamaker, who went into business in Philadelphia with his famous "money-back" guarantee in 1861. James Cash Penney opened a dry-goods store in Kemmerer, Wyo., in 1902, and soon small-town Americans were circulating petitions entreating him to locate a store in their community. Louis Bamberger and Abraham Abraham and Isidor Straus also are enshrined at King of Prussia.

13   So is Frank W. Woolworth, who started his chain of variety stores in Utica, N.Y., in 1879. And Henry Sands Brooks, who opened a men's store in New York when the city's population was 125,000. Under his two sons, it grew into Brooks Brothers, the nation's oldest men's store. Theodore Roosevelt, Ulysses S. Grant and Woodrow Wilson took their oaths of office in Brooks suits; Franklin Roosevelt wore a Brooks cape at the Yalta Conference, and when Lincoln was assassinated he was wearing a coat, waistcoat and trousers from Brooks. Lena Bryant, a Lithuanian immigrant, created a special dress for pregnant women, and thus the maternity-wear business was born. So flustered was she by her initial success that when she opened her first bank account, she errone-ously gave her name as Lane Bryant, and she was too timid to admit her mistake.

> "You see the main thing today is — shopping. Years ago, a person, if he was unhappy, didn't know what to do with himself — he'd go to church, start a revolution, something. Today, you're unhappy? Can't figure it out? What is the salvation? Go shopping."
> —Arthur Miller's 1968 play, *The Price*

14   Although the National Register of Historic Places credits Market Square in Lake Forest, Ill., built in 1916, with being the nation's first planned shop-

ping district, the modern mall really is a product of four post–World War II developments — the baby boom, which provided the shoppers; the movement to suburbia, which got shoppers away from the downtowns in clusters; the superhighway, which got them to the malls quickly; and television, which tempted them to go there.

15   Much of the mall is evolutionary, beginning when Sears and Montgomery Ward placed their stores outside of downtown shopping areas and offered convenient parking. Smaller stores soon clustered around the retail giants. In 1930, Strawbridge & Clothier opened a department store in Ardmore at Suburban Square — the first shopping center to have a major department store as its leading tenant. Southdale Shopping Center, near Minneapolis, opened in 1956 and was the first large, enclosed mall. The bigger regional malls, like that at King of Prussia, came along when it was discovered that adding a second major department store to a center would increase the sales of the first.

16   Over the next quarter-century, malls were built at the rate of 1,000 a year, fueled by the demands of Americans under the influence of affluence. Today, Americans purchase one billion pairs of shoes a year, about five pairs for every resident. Of course, not everybody gets five new pairs of shoes a year. Shopping is largely a preoccupation of the middle and upper classes. It has never been much fun for the poor.

17   Psychologists say shopping is an expression of power, a therapy for depression and guilt, and a cure for boredom, depression and loneliness. Shoppers are bombarded with opportunities to make themselves more lovable, comfortable, attractive, successful, powerful, healthy, intelligent and just plain happy. There are freelance "shopping consultants" for people who have everything to spend but time. For a fee, advisers will come into your home, remove unacceptable items from your wardrobe and then take you by the hand to the shopping mall for replacements.

18   Not surprisingly, the shopping binge has yielded some dangerous side effects (Malladies? Mallaise? Mal de Mall?). There are compulsive shoppers who buy everything in sight, and a psychological specialty is developing to purge the urge to splurge. Groups called $penderMender$ have formed on the West Coast, and Dr. Richard Hogan, a clinical psychologist in Cerritos, Calif., says that if all the nation's shopping addicts were to clasp hands, "they'd stretch from mall to mall." Shopping malls are high on the list of things dreaded by victims of agoraphobia — literally, "fear of the market place" but more recently fear of any specific place that causes "panic attacks" — sweaty palms, dry mouths, dizziness and heart palpitation. There are several Shoplifters Anonymous groups in the Philadelphia area to aid compulsive thieves. One effective treatment is to have clients go into stores without shopping bags, with their pockets sewn shut, and make purchases quickly, without browsing.

> "Standin' On the Corner Watchin' All the Girls Go By"
> — Song from Broadway's *Most Happy Fella*

19   They come to the mall and for 75 hours each week, they can navigate the waters of prosperity. They stroll past hardware, software, ready-to-wear, wash-

and-wear; past displays of kitchen utensils where the pot calls the kettle turquoise; past drugstores selling cigarettes and relief for emphysematics; past bookstores offering advice on losing weight and making fudge; past delicatessens where ceramic hams and plastic cheeses hang from the ceiling. A man prods his wife to leave a shoe display; she shoots him a look that belongs in a scabbard. An adolescent couple strolls by holding hands; shopping today is something you do on a date. Kids toss pennies into a fountain; they will be collected later and given to local charities, who receive about $100 a month this way.

20   The idea of the mall as Main Street, and as the logical extension of Olde Tyme America, is one that is diligently promoted in the mall. There's Ye Olde Tobacco Barrell, and over here is Hickory Farms. And there's Frontier Fruit & Nut, the Dress Barn, the Lamplighter, County Seat, Gold Rush, Village Silver. . . . The very idea of smallness, so difficult to conjure in a vast enclosed mall, is continually suggested.

21   There is nothing haphazard about the stores in the mall, and when sales seem to be running below expectations, mall managers adjust the "tenant mix" in much the same way a mechanic adjusts the air-fuel mixture on the carburetor of a balky automobile. Take out a shoe store, replace it with a record store, bring in more kids.

22   Main Street never had background music, and the music of the mall is more than a compendium of easy listening. It has been carefully engineered, by Muzak at King of Prussia, to direct behavior by encouraging shopping and improving employee performance.

23   No one ever owned Main Street, but somebody owns the King of Prussia mall — a fact that has raised a long, unresolved dispute over free speech in the mall. Almost anyone could get on a soapbox or pass out leaflets along Main Street. Not so in the mall.

24   In 1972, the U.S. Supreme Court held that the First Amendment does not protect political activities inside privately owned shopping malls, but in 1980 the court handed down a decision that invited individual states to consider the issue under the free-speech guarantees of their own constitutions. Since then several states, including Pennsylvania and New Jersey, have come down in favor of free speech over property rights at the mall.

25   But the issue remains complex and clouded. Last Christmas, Salvation Army bell ringers, who provide food, clothing and toys to about five million poor people during the holiday season, were banned from dozens of shopping malls across the nation because merchants and mall managers felt the clanging disrupted business. (The Salvation Army has clanged away unimpeded for more than two decades at King of Prussia.)

26   The American Civil Liberties Union has been fighting legal battles against malls. "It's a truism of modern life in America that large shopping centers have replaced urban downtowns as places where people gather," says Steven Shapiro of the New York ACLU. "To deny all free speech in them is to cut off a significant avenue of communication." Thus far, the free speech issue has not been raised at the King of Prussia mall.

"In the 1950s the franchise companies began their explosive growth by introduc-ing corporate methods of finance and marketing to traditional small businesses. While once restaurants and barber shops were individual operations financed by the savings of one family, the chain builders discovered that they could raise huge sums by licensing outlets to owner-operators. Pooling funds from hundreds of small investors and borrowing from large institutions, franchise entrepreneurs could build big, eye-catching outlets. They could display standardized products in attractive surroundings. Compared to the gleaming chain stores, local businesses would seem shoddy and outdated."
—*Roadside Empires* by Stan Luxenberg, 1985

27   If you blindfolded the average American, put him on a plane and depos-ited him in an undisclosed shopping mall, it might take a while for him to figure out where he was — even what state he was in. The shopping mall has achieved a kind of placelessness, partly because it is weatherproof, but mainly because most mall stores are parts of large national franchises, and no two are different.

28   At King of Prussia, three of every four stores are national franchises or parts of chains, and many of the others are linked to smaller, regional chains. The Video Concepts music store is a link in a 203-outlet chain whose head-quarters is in Englewood, Colo. There are 108 other Anderson Little apparel stores, all owned by F.W. Woolworth. Merle Norman Cosmetics has about 2,600 "studios" whose affairs are directed from Los Angeles.

29   Most of the 37 shoe stores at King of Prussia are chains, and three of them — Burt's, Chandler's and Wild Pair — are owned by a single firm, Edison Bros. Shoes Inc., of St. Louis, which also owns two King of Prussia apparel stores — Joan Bari and Jeans West. One of the newer franchises is the cookie stores, and King of Prussia already has two — The Original Great American Chocolate Chip Co. (245 stores nationwide, Atlanta, Ga.) and the Famous Chocolate Chip Cookie Co. (75 stores, Fairfield, N.J.).

30   On the old Main Street, responsibility wore a face. In a sense, this is still true at the mall — but it takes some long-range vision to see it. Anyone buying women's clothing at mall shops is likely to be dealing with one of two men — Milton Petrie, president of Petrie Stores (1,400 outlets nationwide) or Leslie H. Wexner, chairman of The Limited, Inc. (2,200 stores nationwide). Petrie owns seven King of Prussia stores (G & G, Stuart's, Marianne, Brooks Fashions, Casual Corner and two Gaps) and lives in Manhattan, Southampton and Nassau. Wexner owns three King of Prussia stores (Lane Bryant and the two Limiteds) and lives in Manhattan, Vail and Palm Beach.

31   In most cases, mall owners prefer franchised operations over local stores for the same reason shoppers seem to like them — predictability. They have brand-name drawing power, making them more likely to produce traffic, and they have large financial bases, making them less likely to miss the rent. Mall owners like to keep the menus of their food outlets complementary rather than competitive, and they often find it difficult to control the menus of local entrepreneurs.

32   The trend toward franchised retailing is likely to continue, and Luxenberg worries in his book about the effect this will have on the next generation of

consumers. "As children become acquainted with fast food, they also learn about the muffler chains, hair salons, and motels they will one day patronize. More important, they come to believe that nationally advertised products sold in shiny outlets are superior to local goods.

> Where the useless stretch of trees
> an orange sphere lke a golf ball
> announces the Shopping Mall, open
> for Thursday evening shopping.
> There, tonight, droves of teenagers hunt
> one another, alert on a memorized pavement.
> —Joyce Carol Oates

33   They come to the mall on weekends and after school, all those Jasons and Kimberleys and Scotts and Buffys — carefree and voluble, the ends of their sentences crashing into the beginnings of the next. Mallingering. Wishful winking. Life in the fast aisle.

34   At Space Port, a hundred boys with twitching fingers stand in a darkened room, hypnotized by screens as orange lasers zap purple spaceships. One boy plays Kung Fu Master while a companion mocks his inexpertise and eats a doughnut, with laughter and crumbs spilling from his mouth. Just outside where the boys are is where the girls are, smuggling giggles to each other, smiling, smirking, sipping. At Frederick's of Hollywood, a girl with hair the color of paprika twitchy-smiles at a display of diaphanous musical panties that play wedding bells, and her friend munches a hot dog topped with something resembling one of the less publicized ingredients of scrapple.

35   In the movie *Fast Times at Ridgemont High,* the adolescent characters migrate with impunity between school and the shopping mall. They go home only occasionally. The mall has become a giant baby sitter that, so long as you have money or a credit card, gives you all the candy you want. Bloomingdale's has christened them the "Saturday Generation." The more obnoxious among them are called "mall rats" by retailers — though there seems to be no equivalent term of opprobrium for obnoxious adults.

> "The old man disliked bars and bodegas. A clean, well-lighted cafe was a very different thing. Now, without thinking further, he would go home to his room. He would lie in the bed and finally, with daylight, he would go to sleep. After all, he said to himself, it is probably only insomnia. Many must have it."
> —Ernest Hemingway, *A Clean, Well-Lighted Place*

36   They come to the mall early, before the stores open, all those Georges and Marthas and Herberts and Claras. Under doctors' orders, they form walking clubs and stroll measured distances between Sears and Wanamaker's, Gimbels and Bloomingdale's. Doctors recommend malls for exercise because they are safe and weatherproof.

37   Later in the day, they sit in benches at the bird fountain in front of Gimbels, watching preschool children on a circular train ride, yawning, smoking, agreeing, polishing their idleness, wagging their tales. In the aisle between Rosela's Jewelry from the Sea and the Lazy Llama, the American Association of

Retired Persons is setting up a senior citizens' tax-assistance booth while across the way at Ye Olde Tobacco Barrell a gray-haired man dressed in a dark-blue suit is buying cigars while one is clasped between his teeth, a sagging ash hanging from its parent leaf.

38   For the elderly, the mall is warm and relaxing, like going to Florida. And it is Hemingway's clean, well-lighted place — an antidote for loneliness.

39   Though the young and the old visit the mall most often and are most visible, the best customers are between the ages of 30 and 44. One in every five of these shoppers comes from 30 or more miles away. The average King of Prussia shopper spends $64 at the Plaza, $80 at the Court. The national average for malls is $35.

40   About 38 percent of all the money spent at King of Prussia is spent during the six-week Christmas holiday period, which begins on the day after Thanksgiving and is called "Black Friday" by Upper Merion police, who operate the traffic lights by computer from their headquarters. Still, the left turn into the parking lot can take a half hour.

41   Kravco spent $125,000 last year promoting Christmas at King of Prussia. The Plaza and the Court each had their own Santa. They were local talent, but many of the nation's malls get their Santas from Western Temporary Services in Los Angeles, which has a Santa Division offering malls "a Santa a child can believe in."

> ". . . 30 percent of the people who come in here will never steal anything, 40 percent will steal if they have the opportunity, and the remaining 30 percent will steal anything."
> —William Bragg, security chief for Bamberger's

42   They come to the King of Prussia mall and are watched. At Bamberger's, they are watched on a closed-circuit television network whose cameras appear as silver globes hanging from the ceiling; they are watched from "perches"— tiny rooms with one-way mirrors behind displays of merchandise; they are watched by clerks, who are trained to recognize suspicious shoppers; they are watched by floor detectives who dress and behave like other shoppers.

43   In a third-floor room behind a door marked "Restricted Area," an investigator flicks his eyes across eight black-and-white television screens that just now are labeled Pacesetter, Clubhouse, Coats & Better Dresses, Children's, Jr. Sportswear, Young Men's, and Waterford.

44   His eyes alight on Young Men's, where three young men at a rack of jeans seem to be more interested in who's around than what's hanging on the rack. From a perch, a concealed detective radios that he, too, is watching the trio and that one of them has gone into a fitting room. The investigator zooms the camera to the fitting room door and waits. After five minutes, the young man emerges and walks out of camera range. The perched detective calls in, "You can pull off. They've left the area."

45   In this manner, Bamberger's fights the mounting losses from shoplifting that afflict all retailers. Like the one above, most incidents end before they

begin. But Bamberger's investigates about 300 cases of suspected shoplifting a month, and about 40 of these end up with prosecution. The store's policy is to prosecute every case it can, but many cases are tough to prove, and a false shoplifting arrest can lead to million-dollar damage suits against the retailer.

46 Bamberger's does not make public the amount of money it loses each year to shoplifting, but the FBI estimates that American retailers are losing between $15 billion and $25 billion — making shoplifting the nation's costliest crime. As a result, prices are 5 to 8 percent higher than they would be in an ideal world where there were no violations of the Eighth Commandment. Retailers have been taking an increasingly tough stance, and last year, shoplifting arrests passed the one million mark nationwide.

47 Mall-adroit professional shoplifters often work for extensive stolen-goods operations that actually have layaway plans for their regular customers and accept credit cards. Some women professionals are called "crotch workers" because they are adept at placing merchandise, including items the size of videocassette recorders, between their thighs and then walking normally.

48 Bamberger's Bragg, whose official title is "training and special-projects coordinator," says the professionals represent a small part of the shoplifting problem. Far more serious are amateurs, who steal only for their personal use, and store employees, who account for at least half of all thefts and are the reason that one of the Bamberger's cameras is focused on the loading dock.

49 "There are three conditions that must be met for shoplifting," says Bragg. "Need, temptation and opportunity. We can't control need, and we even increase temptation by advertising and store displays. But we can control opportunity, and that's the name of our game."

50 Not surprisingly, it is the amateurs who are most often caught, and fame is no deterrent to prosecution. Frank Wills, the night security guard who discovered the Watergate break-in in 1972 and summoned police, was convicted of shoplifting a $12 pair of sneakers last year in Augusta, Ga. Unlike the Watergate conspirators, Wills got the maximum penalty — a year in jail.

"We're safe! It's a shopping center!"
— Lily Tomlin in *The Incredible Shrinking Woman*

51 They come to the King of Prussia Mall with shopping lists — professional car thieves with orders from superiors for "1981 Volvo, dark blue" and "1974 Ford Mustang, light green." With 12,422 mostly filled parking spaces, the mall is a shoppers' wonderland for car thieves, professional and amateur, and the vast mazes of stores, filled with people of property and abundance, offer ideal working conditions for other types of criminals. It is not surprising that as the shopping mall evolved into a downtown, it should succumb to the woes of the downtown, including crime. Asked why he robbed banks, Willie Sutton said because that's where the money is. Now the banks are in the malls. So are the women and the children.

52 Christopher Wilder, a psychopath who was shot and killed in a battle with police in April 1984, lured at least six women from shopping centers and murdered them in a bloody coast-to-coast rampage. Adam Walsh, the child whose abduction and murder was dramatized in a television movie, was taken from a Hollywood, Fla., shopping mall in 1981.

53   Most of the serious crime at King of Prussia has been against property. Gimbels' fur department was stripped by burglars in 1969 and again in 1970; a holdup man made off with about $100,000 in cash and checks from Korvette's in 1970; a well-dressed woman showed clerks a handgun at Bailey, Banks & Biddle in 1972 and filled her handbag with diamond rings valued at $10,000, and in 1978 an armored car guard was relieved of $39,000 by two gunmen as he walked from Gimbels.

54   Though malls may not be as safe as most people think, they are still relatively safe. Lt. Frank Ferlick of the Upper Merion police says about 20 percent of all the department's calls originate at the King of Prussia complex, but most of them involve property crimes. "We get a lot of retail theft, theft from vehicle, vehicle theft, bad checks and purse snatchings. We occasionally have indecent exposures, assaults and drug-related offenses."

55   Mall operators have become increasingly concerned about crime in the mall in recent years, and one reason is that victims of violent crimes are beginning to sue malls on grounds they failed to provide adequate security. A woman who was shot in the parking lot of an Ohio mall that had been the scene of 43 other serious crimes recently won a $2 million settlement from the management.

> "The shopping center is no longer merely a physical place where retail sales occur. It has become an integral part of the social structure of most communities and will continue to expand that role in the future."
> —Urban Land Institute, *Shopping Development Handbook,* 1985

56   Developers are almost unanimous in concluding that the boom in mall building is over. The saturation point has been reached in most areas, and today 49 percent of all retail sales occur in shopping malls. Malls now occupy 60,000 acres of America, and there's one within seven driving miles of every resident of the eight-county Philadelphia area.

57   A leading trend in the industry today is to go back to the older malls for renovation and expansion. The 21-year-old Cedarbrook Mall in Cheltenham Township was nearly vacant three years ago, but today it has a new owner who has rejuvenated it and is signing up new tenants.

58   In addition, the mall has become suburbia's gift to the downtown. Gallery I and Gallery II now offer mall-style shopping in Center City. New York has Trump Tower, Chicago has Water Tower Place, Pittsburgh has One Oxford Center, and Baltimore has Harborplace. Mail-order shopping has more than doubled since 1976, and electronic shopping by computer seems a future alternative to the mall. But neither of these will replace the social aspect of the mall.

59   The best things about American shopping malls is that they are clean, they are relatively safe, and they bring people together in an age of social isolation. Someday, the King of Prussia mall and others like it will go the way

of the agora and the forum, but for now and the foreseeable future, they will be the place Americans go to buy an ever-increasing range of goods as well as to see and be seen along Main Street. And when they finally pass from the American scene, elbowed out by some new marvel, people will miss them and be nostalgic about them.

60   They come to the Garden Food Court for mall-nutrition. Shoppers stop here to rest their martyred feet and oil the squeaky day. Clerks take their lunch breaks and lean over toward each other in animated shoptalk. Small children tongue-lash huge lollipops while their parents munch on the delicacies from All American Hero, Gold 'n Nuggets, Mexican Village and 1 Potato 2. Twelve of the 70 places to eat at King of Prussia are clustered here around a common seating area. A random survey here discloses that very few shoppers know how King of Prussia got its name. Most just shake their heads. One thinks it was named after a czar. And a few think the town was named after the mall.

61   But it really doesn't seem to matter. Outside, they come and go in cars, vans and buses. Traffic is nearly always backed up at the lights that reduce chaos to mere confusion along Route 202, where an island separates the busy northbound and southbound lanes. On the island, stranded in Crusoe-like isolation, is an old inn that was built before the Revolution. For nearly two centuries, the inn was in the center of downtown King of Prussia. It was open for business until 1952, and in its later years, it was famous for its mint juleps.

62   In 1951, the inn was condemned by the state so Route 202 could be widened, but local history buffs have managed to keep away the wrecker's ball for 34 years. The inn is still owned by the Pennsylvania Department of Transportation, but the history buffs still insist on preserving it. Vibrations from the relentless flow of traffic toward the mall threaten its stability daily, and its benefactors have been shoring up the foundation and strengthening beams for years. It was called the King of Prussia Inn to honor Frederick von Steuben, who was the king of Prussia and who lent military support to George Washington during the Valley Forge encampment a few miles away. The town was named after the inn, and the mall was named after the town.

63   The King of Prussia Inn is surrounded by a chain-link fence that is sagging and doesn't do its job. It has become a favorite target for vandals, and inside, the walls are lined with graffiti. One message says, "Willard Ain't Here Tonight."

64   He's probably across the street, at the King of Prussia mall.

Writing with Sources: Using a Single Source

Integrating information from "Why Americans Love Their Malls" with your own ideas, write an essay on one of these topics. Be sure to acknowledge ideas that are not your own.

1. Ecenbarger sees the shopping mall as a quintessentially American gathering place. What other places play a similar role in our society? What common

characteristics do such places share? How do you account for the influence of
these places on our lives?

2. What different roles has your local shopping mall played in your life? Write an
   autobiographical essay that traces the influence of this place on you over the
   years.

3. American teenagers now spend more time in shopping malls than anywhere
   else except at home or at school. Interview an older friend, relative, or teacher
   about his or her childhood and adolescence. What gathering places or social
   institutions dominated their lives as the shopping mall dominates the lives of so
   many young people today? How are the places and institutions that they identify
   similar to or different from the shopping malls of today? What do these similarities and differences reveal about modern American society?

Night as Frontier

Murray Melbin

Murray Melbin was born in 1927 and educated at New York University (B.A.),
Cornell University (M.S.), and the University of Michigan (Ph.D.). He is currently
Professor of Sociology at Boston University, where he has taught since 1969. The
author of *Alone and With Others: A Grammar of Interpersonal Behavior* (1972),
Melbin has been the recipient of a number of fellowships and research grants in his
field. "Night as Frontier" was originally published in the *American Sociological
Review* in 1978 and conforms to that journal's documentation style. This scholarly
essay won the annual prize in social psychology from the American Association for
the Advancement of Science. Melbin advances a provocative hypothesis, characterizing the night as America's last frontier—a frontier of time rather than of space—
and drawing a detailed comparison between the mid-nineteenth-century development of the American West and the development of nighttime America today. The
lawlessness of the night and the independence of the nighttime "pioneers" are just
two of the traits Melbin compares to their counterparts in the early American West.
Melbin goes on to consider the implications of the nighttime society and its possible
impact on life in America.

*While the settlement of some of the world's land areas was coming to an end,
there began an increase in wakeful activity over more of the 24-hour day.
This trend of expansion in time is continuing, especially in urban areas. The
hypothesis that night has become the new frontier is supported by the premise
that time, like space, can be occupied and is treated so by humans. A set of
evidence, including results of several field experiments, shows that nighttime
social life in urban areas resembles social life on former land frontiers. The
research data refers mainly to contemporary Boston and to the U.S. West a
century ago.*

1   Humans are showing a trend toward more and more wakeful activity at all
hours of day and night. The activities are extremely varied. Large numbers of

people are involved. And the trend is worldwide. A unifying hypothesis to account for it is that night is a frontier, that expansion into the dark hours is a continuation of the geographic migration across the face of the earth. To support this view, I will document the trend and then offer a premise about the nature of time and its relation to space. Third, I will show that social life in the nighttime has many important characteristics that resemble social life on land frontiers.

The Course of Expansion

2 We were once a diurnal species bounded by dawn and dusk in our wakeful activity. Upon mastering fire, early humans used it for cooking and also for sociable assemblies that lasted for a few hours after darkness fell. Some bustle throughout the 24-hour cycle occurred too. Over the centuries there have been fires tended in military encampments, prayer vigils in temples, midnight betrothal ceremonies, sentinels on guard duty at city gates, officer watches on ships, the curing ceremonies of Venezuelan Indians that begin at sundown and end at sunrise, innkeepers serving travelers at all hours. In the first century A.D., Rome was obliged to relieve its congestion by restricting chariot traffic to the night hours (Mumford, 1961:217).

3   Yet around-the-clock activity used to be a small part of the whole until the nineteenth century. Then the pace and scope of wakefulness at all hours increased smartly. William Murdock developed a feasible method of coal-gas illumination and, in 1803, arranged for the interior of the Soho works in Birmingham, England to be lighted that way. Other mills nearby began to use gas lighting. Methods of distributing coal-gas to all buildings and street lamps in a town were introduced soon after. In 1820 Pall Mall in London became the first street to be lit by coal-gas. Artificial lighting gave great stimulus to the nighttime entertainment industry (Schlesinger, 1933:105). It also permitted multiple-shift factory operations on a broad scale. Indeed by 1867 Karl Marx (1867:chap. 10, sec. 4) was to declare that night work was a new mode of exploiting human labor.

4   In the closing decades of the nineteenth century two developments marked the changeover from space to time as the realm of human migration in the United States. In 1890 the Bureau of the Census announced that the land frontier in America had come to an end, for it was no longer possible to draw a continuous line across the map of the West to define the edge of farthest advance settlement. Meanwhile, the search for an optimum material for lantern lights, capable of being repeatedly brought to a white heat, culminated in 1885 in the invention of the Welsbach mantle — a chemically impregnated cotton mesh. The use of the dark hours increased thereafter, and grew further with the introduction of electric lighting.

5   The most systematic evidence of steadily increasing 24-hour activity in the U.S. is the growth of radio and television broadcasting. Broadcasters authorize surveys to learn about the market that can be reached in order to plan programs and to set advertising rates. The number of stations active at given hours and

the spread of those hours around the clock reflect these research estimates of the size of the wakeful population—the potential listeners. Although not shown in the table, television hours in Boston ended at 11:30 p.m. in 1949, and then widened to include the Late Show and then the Late Late Show in the intervening years until 1974. Each medium has moved increasingly to 24-hour programming and mirrors the growth in nighttime activity.

6   In the present decade, for the first time, the U.S. Bureau of Labor Statistics (1976) asked about the times of day that people worked. In 1976, of 75 million in the work force, 12 million reported they were on the job mainly after dark and 2.5 million of those persons worked a full shift beginning about midnight. Since these figures do not include *the clientele* that used such establishments as restaurants, hospital emergency wards, gambling rooms, and public transportation, these numbers are conservative estimates of how many people are up and about at night.

7   Today more people than ever are active outside their homes at all hours engaged in all sorts of activities. There are all-night supermarkets, bowling alleys, department stores, restaurants, cinemas, auto repair shops, taxi services, bus and airline terminals, radio and television broadcasting, rent-a-car agencies, gasoline stations. There are continuous-process refining plants, and three-shift factories, post offices, newspaper offices, hotels, and hospitals. There is unremitting provision of some utilities — electric supply, staffed turnpike toll booths, police patrolling, and telephone service. There are many emergency and repair services on-call: fire fighters, auto towing, locksmiths, suppliers of clean diapers, ambulances, bail bondsmen, insect exterminators, television repairers, plate glass installers, and funeral homes.

Space and Time Frontiers and Settlements

8 Time, like space, is part of the ecological niche occupied by a species. Although every type exists throughout the 24-hour cycle, to reflect the way a species uses its niche we label it by *the timing of its wakeful life.* The terms diurnal and nocturnal refer to the periods the creatures are active. We improve our grasp of the ecology of a region by recognizing the nighttime activity of raccoons, owls and rats, as well as by knowing the spatial dispersion of these and other animals. The same area of a forest or meadow or coral reef is used incessantly, with diurnal and nocturnal creatures taking their active turns. We make geographic references to humans in a similar way. We refer to an island people or a desert people, or the people of arctic lands as a means of pointing out salient features of their habitats.

9   This similar treatment of time and space rests on the assumption that both of them are containers for living. Consider the dictionary definition of the word *occupy*: "2. To fill up (take time or space): *a lecture that occupied three hours*" (*American Heritage Dictionary,* 1970:908). Geographers study activities rather than physical structures to decide whether and how people occupy space (Buttimer, 1976:286). The mere presence of buildings and related physical structures in places like Machu-Pichu, Petra, and Zimbabwe do not make us believe they are habitations now. The once-boisterous mining centers

in the American West that have become ghost towns are settlements no longer. Conversely, we say a farming region in which people are active is inhabited even though buildings are few. The presence of human-built structures is not the criterion for occupying a region, it is people and their activities.

10   Like rural settlements, the occupation of time need not be dense. For example, London Transport lists 21 all-night bus routes. On many of these routes "all-night" service means no more than once an hour. Yet, even though the bus does not pass during the intervening 59 minutes, the schedule is said to be continuous. If an active moment interacts with quiet moments around it, the entire period is taken as occupied.

11   Of course, no time has ever been used without also using it in some place. No space has ever been used without also using it some hours of the day. Space and time together form the container of life activity. We forget this in the case of former frontiers because expansion then occurred so dramatically across the land. Less notice was paid to the 16 hours of wakefulness because the daily use of time was rather constant as the surge of geographic expansion kept on over the face of the earth. As time use remained unchanged, it was disregarded in human ecological theory. In different eras, however, expansion may proceed more rapidly in either space or time. Recently expansion is taking place in time. Since people may exploit a niche by distributing themselves and their activities over more hours of the day just as they do by dispersing in space, a frontier could occur in the time dimension too.

12   A *settlement* is a stable occupation of space and time by people and their activities. A *frontier* is a pattern of sparse settlement in space or time, located between a more densely settled and a practically empty region. Below a certain density of active people, a given space-time region is a wilderness. Above that point and continuing to a higher level of density, the presence of people in activities will make that area a frontier. Above that second cutoff point the further denseness of active people turns the area into a fully inhabited region. In a given historical period the frontier's boundaries may be stable or expanding. When expanding the frontier takes on the aspect of venturing into the unknown and is often accompanied by novelty and change.

Similarities Between Land Frontiers and Time Frontiers

13   Two kinds of evidence would support the hypothesis of night as frontier. One is that the forces for expansion into the dark hours are the same as those resulting in expansion across the land. That is, a single causal explanation should account for the spread of people and their activities, whether in space or in time. I offered such an outline in another essay; it includes enabling factors, demand push, supply pull, and stabilizing feedback (Melbin, 1977). The other line of evidence is that the same important features of social life should be found both in time and in space frontiers. The rapid expansion in after-dark activity has been taking place mostly in urban areas. Therefore the culture of the contemporary urban nighttime should reveal the same patterns and moods found in former land frontiers.

14   I have chosen to review life in the U.S. West in the middle of the nine-

teenth century along with the present-day nighttime. Of course there were other land frontiers and the hypothesis should apply to all of them. However there are good reasons to begin by demonstrating it for the U.S. West. One is that the archives holding information about this westward flow are thorough, well organized, and readily available. Another reason is that the U.S. West has continuity with expansion into the night. The movement westward reached the California coast. California's main cities have since become areas of great activity in the dark hours, as if the flow across the continent swerved into the nighttime rather than spilling into the sea.

15   Specifically, the land frontier to be discussed is the area west of the Mississippi River during the middle decades of the nineteenth century, about 1830–1880. The urban nighttime will be any major urban area during the stretch from about midnight to 7:30 a.m. during the decades of the 1960s and 1970s. Most of my examples will be findings from a recent study of Boston. There are many aspects in which social life at night is like the social life of other frontiers.

1. Advance Is in Stages

16   There is a succession of steps in colonizing any new region. People ventured into the western outskirts "in a series of waves . . . the hunter and the fur trader who pushed into the Indian country were followed by the cattle raiser and he by the pioneer farmer" (Turner, 1965:59; 1893:12, 19–20). Life styles were distinctive in each stage as well. The hunters and trappers did not dwell like the miners who followed, and they in turn lived differently from the pioneer farmers who came later (Billington, 1949:4–5). Although living conditions were generally crude then, there was a decided increase in comfort for the farmers settled in one place compared with the earlier-day trappers who were usually on the move.

17   There is also a succession of phases in settling the nighttime. Each stage fills the night more densely than before and uses those hours in a different way. First came isolated wanderers on the streets; then groups involved in production activities, the graveyard-shift workers. Still later those involved in consumption activities arrived, the patrons of all-night restaurants and bars, and the gamblers who now cluster regularly by midnight at the gaming table in resorts.

18   The rates of advance are unequal in both cases. Population gains and development are not unbroken. In the West economic growth was erratic. Similarly, during the oil embargo of 1973–1974 there was some retreat from nighttime activity, as restaurants and auto service stations and other businesses cut back hours of serving the public.

2. Population Is Sparse and Also More Homogenous

19   At first only a few people venture into the new region. The frontier line in the U.S. West was drawn by the Census Bureau through an area of density of two to six inhabitants per square mile. The other side of the line was tabbed the "wilderness." The demographic composition of the western frontier was mostly

vigorous young males with proportionately fewer females and aged persons than found in the populations of the eastern states (Riegel, 1947:624; Godkin, 1896:13; Dick, 1937:7, 232). This demographic picture fits the night as well. There are fewer people up and about and most of them are young males.

3. There Is Welcome Solitude, Fewer Social Constraints, and Less Persecution

20 The land frontier offered tranquility, a place for relief from feelings of being hemmed in. It was appealing to escape into the wilderness, to leave deceit and disturbance, and vexing duties and impositions of the government behind (Robbins, 1960:148). The outer fringes offered escape from persecution too. Mormons and Hutterites both made their ways westward to avoid harassment from others.

21 In a parallel way, many have enjoyed the experience of walking at night along a street that is ordinarily jammed during the day. Individuals who are up and about then report a feeling of relief from the crush and anonymity of daytime city life. The calm of those hours is especially appealing to young people, who come to feel that they possess the streets. (A test of this proposition must of course control for the fear of criminal assault in the dark; I will discuss this further in items 7 and 8 below.) Also, a portion of the people out at night are those avoiding social constraints and perhaps persecution. Street people and homosexuals, for example, find more peace in the dark because surveillance declines. Some night owls are urban hermits. Some individuals who are troubled or stigmatized — such as the very ugly or obese — retreat from the daytime to avoid humiliation and challenge. In this way the night affords an outlet. Like the West it serves an insulating function that averts possible tensions from unwanted encounters.

4. Settlements Are Isolated

22 Initially migration beyond the society's active perimeter is scattered. The land frontier settlements were small and apart from one another. There was little communication across districts and much went on in each in a self-sufficient way. People in the East did not think of the relevance of borderland activities for their own existence and the pioneers were indifferent to outside society (Billington, 1949:96, 746).

23 As the city moves through phases of the day it switches from coordinated actions to unconnected ones. Pockets of wakeful activity are separated from one another, are small scale compared to daytime events, and there is less communication between the pockets. The people of the daytime give little thought to those active in the dark and do not view them as part of the main community.

5. Government Is Initially Decentralized

24 Whatever high-level group may decide the laws and policies for a nation or a community, outside the purview of superiors there are subordinates who make decisions that would otherwise be the domain of the higher-ups or subject to their approval. As the land frontier moved farther from the national center of policy making, the interpretation of the law and judicial decisions were carried out by individuals who were rarely checked on and who rarely consulted with their superiors.

25   Today, although many organizations and cities are continually active, their primary administrators — directors, heads of departments, mayors — are generally on duty only during the daytime. At night they go to sleep and a similar decentralization of power follows. To some extent this is an explicit delegation of authority. But discretion is stretched for other reasons too. Night nurses decide not to wake up the doctor on duty because he gets annoyed at being disturbed for minor problems (Kozak, 1974:59). The style and content of the way the organization or the city is run at night changes accordingly. For example, for the same types of cases, decisions by police officers at night will be based less on professional role criteria and more on personal styles. This results in more extreme instances of being strict and lenient, arbitrary and humane.

6. New Behavioral Styles Emerge

26 Both land and time frontiers show more individualism because they are remote, the environment is unusual (compared with the centers of society), and others subjected to the same conditions are tolerant. Those who traveled to the western borders broke from ordinary society. The casual observance by others, the constituted authority, and the familiar settings and the norms they implied were gone. This left room for unconventional behavior.

27   Deviance was also *created* out west. Many pioneer wives lived on the plains for extended periods without ordinary social contacts, especially when their husbands left on journeys for days or weeks. These women often became withdrawn and untalkative, so shy and uneasy with strangers that they would run away when one approached (Humphrey, 1931:128). From the evidence at hand, these were normal, happy women in the cities when they were growing up, but they were affected by the frontier environment. On the western boundary people were used to this behavior on the part of lonely, isolated women and accepted it. In the eastern cities the same conduct would have been taken as odd.

28   There is also a popular image of the night as the haunt of weirdos and strange characters, as revealed in comments like "I don't know where they hide during the day but they sure come out after dark." Moreover, at night one can find people who, having lived normal lives, are exposed to unusual circumstances that draw them into unconventional behavior. The milieu harbors a deviant subculture that is tolerated and even expected.

7. There Is More Lawlessness and Violence

29 Both land frontier and the nighttime have reputations as regions of danger and outlawry. Interestingly, both do not live up to the myths about them, for the patterns of aggression are selective and localized.

30   On the one hand there is clear evidence of lawlessness and violence. Walter P. Webb observed that the West was lawless "because the law that was applied there was not made for the conditions that existed. . . . It did not fit the needs of the country, and could not be obeyed" (cited by Frantz and Choate, 1955:83). There was also a lack of policemen and law enforcement agencies were few (Riegel, 1947:627; Billington, 1949:480). There was violence in the gold fields (Hollon, 1974:211). In the cow towns, mining camps and boom towns in the early days, practically everyone carried guns. Fighting words, the ring of revolvers, and groans of pain were common sounds out there. Some western settlements were renowned for concentrations of gamblers and gougers and bandits, dance-hall girls and honky-tonks and bawdy houses. Horse thieving was widespread. The stage coach was held up many times. There was habitual fear of attack from either Indians or renegades. In the face of this, the people practiced constant watchfulness and banded together for self-protection (Billington, 1954:8; Doddridge, 1912:103). Towns had vigilante groups. The covered wagons that crossed the plains were accompanied by armed convoys.

31   Yet the violence was concentrated in certain places; otherwise killings and mob law were remarkably infrequent. Such infamous towns as Tombstone and Deadwood, and the states of Texas and California had more than their share of gunfights (Frantz and Choate, 1955:83; Billington, 1949:63; Hollon, 1973:96). But the tumult in the cow towns was seasonal, and took place when the cowboys finally reached Abilene, Ellsworth, and Dodge City after the long drive. And the mayhem was selective. Flint (1826:401) wrote, "Instances of murder, numerous and horrible in their circumstances, have occurred in my vicinity . . . in which the drunkenness, brutality, and violence were mutual. . . . [Yet] quiet and sober men would be in no danger of being involved." Concerning violence, Hollon (1973:97 – 8) concludes that there was

> a natural tendency to exaggerate the truth and emphasize the exception . . .
> not a single shoot-out took place on main street at Dodge City or any of the
> other Kansas cow towns in the manner of the face-to-face encounter presented
> thousands of times on television.

Why, then, did the land frontier have the reputation of a "Wild West?" One reason may be that outlaw killers were drifters, so the same person may have contributed exploits over large areas. Another reason was boredom. The stories of violence persisted and spread because there was little to do or to read about in pioneer homes. The tedium of daily life was countered by exciting stories told and retold around the stove in the general store.

32   It is plausible that western desperados and nighttime muggers would have similar outlooks. Both believe there is less exposure, which improves their chances for succeeding at the risks they take. One relied on dry-gulching; the other uses the dark to set an ambush. Escape is easy because both could move from the scene of the crime into unpopulated areas and elude pursuers.

33   The nighttime has been noted also as a place of evil. It is thought of as crime-ridden and outside of ordinary social control. Medieval and Renaissance cities had no public illumination. Assaults by ruffians and thieves were so common after dark that wayfarers took to paying others to precede them through the streets carrying lighted torches. In the seventeenth century this escort-for-hire was called a "link boy" in London, and a "falot" (lantern companion) in Paris. Deliveries of black market goods to stores, such as fuel oil to gasoline stations during the oil embargo of 1973–1974, was accomplished under cover of darkness. Lawlessness is possible then because police coverage is sparse (Boston *Globe,* 1977:1). In addition, the officers on duty make themselves unavailable by sleeping in their cars, an old custom in New York City where the practice is called "cooping" (*New York Times,* 1968).

34   In Boston today, carrying arms is more common at night. For fear of mugging or rape, escort services are provided on many college campuses for women returning to their dorms at night, or for women on the evening shift going from their places of work to the parking lot or subway station. An escort is provided for nurses at Boston City Hospital because of an increase in robberies in that area. And some apartment houses, with their sentries at the door, become vertical stockades to which people in the city retreat at night.

35   However, like the former West, lawlessness and violence at night are concentrated in certain hours in certain places and are otherwise uncommon. Fights reach their peak about midnight, as shown in Figure 3, but are least frequent from 2:30 to 11:00 a.m. The area of Boston in which many brawls and muggings take place, where prostitution is rampant and bars and lounges feature nude go-go dancers, is called the "combat zone." A large transient population of relatively young males come into the area to patronize the moviehouses featuring X-rated films and become drunk and aggressive in bars and on the streets. Although this description may approximate what was once reported of mining towns in the West, these combat zones do not function so after 2:30 a.m. or during the daytime. In the daytime the areas are parts of business districts. Many people shop at department stores nearby, or otherwise pass through and patronize eating places and businesses there. So the combat zone designation refers to these places only at certain hours and is not true for all the city all night.

8. There Is More Helpfulness and Friendliness

36 Hollon (1974:211–2) remarks that "For every act of violence during the frontier period, there were thousands of examples of kindness, generosity, and sacrifice. . . ."

37   Reports of life on the land frontier are replete with accounts of warmth toward strangers, of community house building and barn raisings, and of help for those in need (Darby, 1818:400; Frantz and Choate, 1955:64; Billington, 1949:96, 167; Riegel, 1947:81). Travelers returning from the outskirts said they were treated more kindly than they had been in the cities (Flint, 1826:402–03; Hollon, 1974:212).

38   At first these stories of openhanded western hospitality may seem inconsistent in the face of the high risks of thievery and violence. But the circum-

stances are actually related to one another. Dick (1937:510) observed that "As the isolated settlers battled against savage men, . . . and loneliness, they were drawn together in a fellowship." Billington (1972:166) added,

> Cooperation is normal within every in-group, but accentuates when the in-group is in conflict with an out-group and group solidarity is strengthened. This was the situation in frontier communities where conflicts with Indians, with raw nature, and with dominating Easterners heightened the spirit of interdependence.

39   Because the night is a time of more violence and people feel more vulnerable then, those up and about have a similar outlook and behave toward others as pioneers did in the West. At night people are more alert to strangers when they pass on the street. Each tries to judge whether the other is potentially dangerous. Upon deciding that the other is to be trusted, one's mood shifts from vigilance to expansiveness. If not foe, then friend. Aware that they are out together in a dangerous environment, people identify with each other and become more outgoing. The sense of safety that spreads over those together at night in a diner or in a coffee shop promotes camaraderie there.

40   Also, on both frontiers people may be more hospitable because they have time to devote to strangers. Pioneers had plenty to do; yet often they had nothing to do. They were not closely synchronized in daily tasks as people were in the eastern cities, and the norm of punctuality was not emphasized. In the city during the day, the mood of pressured schedules takes hold of folk and makes their encounters specific and short. The tempo slows markedly after midnight. The few who are out then hurry less because there are fewer places to rush to. Whereas lack of time inhibits sociability and helpfulness, available time clears the way for them.

9. Exploitation of the Basic Resource Finally Becomes National Policy

41 Westward expansion began long before anyone officially recognized the land frontier's possibilities for our society. It took years to realize even that the U.S. West was habitable. At one time the land west of the Missouri River was labeled on maps as the Great American Desert. Almost no one thought that some day many people would want to migrate and settle there (Hicks, 1948:508). Nor was the catch phrase "Manifest Destiny" applied to colonizing the West until 1845, centuries after the effort had been under way. In 1837 Horace Greeley introduced the slogan "Go West, Young Man, go forth into the Country." He looked upon such migration as a means of relief from the poverty and unemployment caused by the Panic of 1837. In 1862, with the passage of the Homestead Act, it became a deliberate policy of the U.S. government to use the western territory to help relieve the conditions of tenant farmers and hard-pressed city laborers. The policymakers finally saw the exploitation of western space as a means of solving social problems.

42   Similarly, in the first 150 years after Murdock's coal-gas illumination was introduced, there was no national consciousness in England or the United States about colonizing the nighttime. People went ahead, expanding their activities into the dark hours without declaring that a 24-hour community was being forged. Now in the 1970s policy makers have begun talking about cheap time at night the way they once spoke of cheap western land. V. D. Patrushev (1972:429) of the Soviet Union writes that "Time . . . is a particular form of national wealth. Therefore it is imperative to plan the most efficient use of it for all members of a society." Daniel Schydlowsky (1976:5), an economist who specializes in development in Latin America and who recently ended a three-year study there, has concluded that multiple-shift work would produce remarkable gains in reducing unemployment and improve the economies of overpopulated developing cities. His claim for the use of time echoes the attitudes of nineteenth century proponents of the use of western lands as a solution for those who were out of work.

43   The advocates of westward expansion also saw it as a way to draw off great numbers of people from the cities and forestall crowding there (Smith, 1950:8, 238). Today Dantzig and Saaty (1973:190–3) recommend dispersing activities around the clock as a means of reducing congestion. And Meier (1976:965) writes, "Scarce land and expensive human time can also be conserved by encouraging round-the-clock operation. . . . By such means people can live densely without stepping on each other's toes."

10. Interest Groups Emerge

44 As the U.S. frontier matured, the population became more aware of its own circumstances and organized to promote its own concerns. Turner (1893:207; 1965:54) remarked that the West felt a keen sense of difference from the East.

45   Sections are geographically-based interest groups. One hundred years ago the West gave rise to such pressure groups and farm bloc organizations as the Greenback Party, the National Grange, and the Populists. The Granger movement, for example, grew with the westerners' problems with transportation in their region. There were no significant river or canal systems out west and so the settlers were at the mercy of railroads. But the rates in the newer regions of the West were far higher than those in the East, and it was protest against this disparity that aided the movement in the 1870s (Robbins, 1960:271).

46   The night also isolates a group from the main society. Antagonism may develop as daytimers deprecate the nighttimers and the latter resent the neglect shown by the others. People active after dark find their life style differing from that of daytime society, become aware of having a separate identity, and evolve into interest groups. New alignments in the tradition of sectionalism begin to emerge. This has already happened for two groups usually linked with the nighttime: homosexuals and prostitutes. The Gay Liberation Front is one nationwide organization devoted to the rights of homosexuals. Prostitutes also have a union. Appropriately they adopted the name of a creature renowned in the U.S. West for howling at night — the coyote. COYOTES (Call Off Your Old Tired Ethics) seek legislation to decriminalize their activities and protest courtroom discrimination against women who earn their living by prostitution (Boston *Globe*, 1976a).

47   An actual day vs. night contest has already been fought in Boston. The city's airport is flanked by residential neighborhoods and its afterdark activity became a nuisance to people wanting an undisturbed night's sleep. In 1976 dwellers in those neighborhoods, as private citizens and through two organized groups — Fair Share, and the Massachusetts Air Pollution and Noise Abatement Committee — made a concerted effort to stop airplane flights between 11 p.m. and 7 a.m. It led to counterarguments by the business community stressing the economic benefit of continuing the flights. The pro-nighttime group was a coalition among commercial interests, airline companies, unions, and airport employees holding jobs at night (some of whom lived in those very neighborhoods). This group argued that the curfew would result in the loss of thousands of jobs, millions of dollars in sales, and further would discourage business investment in the New England area. Joined by the governor, the mayor and many legislators, the coalition successfully won a decision from the Massachusetts Port Authority that the nighttime flights should be kept going. (Some proposals for noise reduction during the night accompanied the decision.) A month later, Eastern Airlines announced it was adding an airbus and expanding its staff at the airport "as a direct result of the recent decision . . . not to impose a night curfew at Logan [airport]." As one businessman put it, "The curfew decision was regarded as the shootout at the OK Corral" (Boston *Globe,* 1976b; 1976c).

Conclusion

48 What is the gain in thinking of night as a frontier? A single theoretical idea gives coherence to a wide range of events: the kind of people up and about at those hours, why they differ from daytimers in their behavior, the beginnings of political efforts by night people, the slow realization among leaders that public policy might be applied to the time resource. Even the variety of endeavors becomes understandable — from metal smelting plants to miniature golf courses, to mayor's complaint offices, to eating places, to computerized banking terminals that dispense cash. The niche is being expanded. Bit by bit, all of society migrates there. To treat this as a sequel to the geographic spread of past centuries is to summarize the move within familiar ecological concepts of migration, settlement, and frontier.

49 Though I have reviewed materials for one period in U.S. history, these conditions are features of all frontiers. They should apply to the Russians crossing the Urals, to the Chinese entering Manchuria during the Ch'ing dynasty, to the Boers settling South Africa, to Australians venturing into the Outback, to present-day Brazilians colonizing the Amazon interior, as well as to Americans migrating into the night. The patterns are confirmed by essays in Wyman and Kroeber's anthology on frontiers.

50 We should also consider the uniqueness of this new frontier. Each settlement beyond established boundaries has its own qualities. Here are some differences between the West and the night: (1) On the land frontier settlers lived rudely with few services at hand. At night a large portion of the total range of activities is services. (2) Utilities cost more on the western fringes; at night the fees for telephone calls, electricity, and airplane travel are lower. (3) While western settlements were in remote contact with the East, day and night are joined so that either can be affected quickly by events in the other. Twenty-four hour society is more constantly adjusting, more unstable. (4) Looking westward, pioneers saw no end to the possibilities for growth, but we know that expansion into the night can only go as far as the dawn. (5) The land frontier held promise of unlimited opportunity for individuals who ventured there. Miners and pioneers endured hardships because they lived for the future. They hoped to make their fortunes, or at least a better life. At night there are large numbers of unskilled, menial, and dirty tasks; but charwoman and watchman and hospital aide and porter are dead-end jobs. Many people so employed are immigrants or members of minority groups and this expanding margin of society is a *time ghetto.* The ghetto encloses more than minorities and immigrants, for ultimate control in 24-hour organizations remains with top management in the daytime. Policy making, important decisions, employee hiring, and planning are curtailed during off-hours. Since evening and night staffs are prevented from taking many actions that would lead to the recognition of executive ability, and since their performance is not readily observable by the bosses, all have poorer chances for advancement. (6) The western frontier's natural resources were so extensive that we became wasteful and squandered them. At night there is nothing new to exploit but time itself, so we maximize the use of fixed assets and become more frugal. (7) Migrating westward called for rather significant capital investment—outlays for a covered wagon, mining equipment, cattle, the railroad. There is little extra capital required for a move to the night. Instead, the incessant organization's need for more personnel reflects a swing toward more labor intensive operations. So the night frontier may appeal to developing countries with meager treasuries and teeming populations of unemployed.

51   This expansion is also unusual because it happens in time rather than in space. We change from a diurnal into an incessant species. We move beyond the environmental cycle —alternating day and night— in which our biological and social life evolved, and thus force novelty on these areas. (8) In the past a single set of minds shut down an enterprise one day and started it up the next. It permitted easy continuity and orderly administration. For coverage around the clock, we introduce shifts of personnel. Several times a day another set of minds takes over the same activity and facilities. (9) A physiological upset is imposed on people who work at night and maintain ordinary recreation and social life on their days off. Each time they switch their active hours they undergo phase shifts in body rhythms such as heartbeat, temperature, and hormonal production. The several days' malaise that results was known to such workers long before air travel across time zones popularized the phrase "jet fatigue."

52   We may believe we understand the forces, the conditions under which humans enlarge their niche, but what is the probable line of development? Forecasting is called for despite the difficulties of social prediction. We should consider the possibilities of an era in which unremitting activity is even more

commonplace. What is the carrying capacity of the 24-hour day? What will happen when saturation occurs? Time will have extraordinary leverage as it gets used up, for time is a resource without direct substitute. It is unstretchable; we cannot do with it as we did with land by building up toward the sky and digging into the ground. Time is unstorable; we cannot save the unused hours every night for future need.

53   In his essay "The Frontier in American History," Frederick Jackson Turner (1893:38) reviewed the impact of the advance into western lands upon our society and remarked, "And now, four centuries from the discovery of America, at the end of a hundred years of life under the constitution, the frontier has gone." But it has not gone. During the era that the settlement of our land frontier was being completed, there began — into the night — a large-scale migration of wakeful activity that continues to spread over the world.

References

American Heritage Dictionary of the English Language
  1970   Boston: Houghton Mifflin.
Becker, Howard
  1963   Outsiders: Studies in the Sociology of Deviance. New York: Free Press.
Billington, Ray Allen
  1949   Westward Expansion. New York: Macmillan.
  1954   The American Frontiersman. London: Oxford University Press.
  1972   "Frontier democracy: social aspects." Pp. 160–84 in G. R. Taylor (ed.), The Turner Thesis Concerning the Role of the Frontier in American History, 3rd ed. Lexington, Ma.: Heath.
Boston Globe
  1976a   "Prostitutes speak of pride, but they are still victims." June 25:1, 10.
  1976b   "Dukakis decides to go against Logan curfew." August 12:1, 20.
  1976c   "Logan anti-noise plan offered." August 13:35.
  1977   "Boston police today." April 4:1, 3.
Brandeis, Louis D. and Josephine Goldmark
  1918   The Case Against Night Work for Women. Rev. ed. New York: National Consumers League.
Bryan, James H, and Mary Ann Test
  1967   "Models and helping: naturalistic studies in aiding behavior." Journal of Personality and Social Psychology 6:400–7.
Buttimer, Anne
  1976   "Grasping the dynamism of lifeworld." Annals of the Association of American Geographers 66:277–92.
Dantzig, George B, and Thomas L. Saaty
  1973   Compact city. San Francisco: Freeman.
Darby, William
  [1818]
  1969   "Primitivism in the lower Mississippi valley." Pp. 399–401 in M. Ridge and R. A. Billington (eds.), America's Frontier Story. New York: Holt.
Darley, John and C. Daniel Batson
  1973   " 'From Jerusalem to Jericho': a study of situational and dispositional variables in helping behavior." Journal of Personality and Social Psychology 27:100–8.
Dick, Everett
  [1937]
  1954   The Sod-House Frontier, 1854–1890. New York: Appleton-Century.

Doddridge, Joseph
  [1912]
  1969 "Life in the old west." Pp. 101–6 in M. Ridge and R. A. Billington (eds.), America's Frontier Story. New York: Holt.
Feldman, Roy E.
  1968 "Response to compatriot and foreigner who seek assistance." Journal of Personality and Social Psychology 10:202–14.
Flint, Timothy
  [1826]
  1969 "Frontier society in the Mississippi valley." Pp. 401–3 in M. Ridge and R. A. Billington (eds.), America's Frontier Story. New York: Holt.
Forbes, Gordon B., R. D. TeVault, and H. F. Gromoll
  1972 "Regional differences in willingness to help strangers: a field experiment with a new unobtrusive measure." Social Science Research 1:415–9.
Frantz, J. B. and J. E. Choate
  1955 The American Cowboy: The Myth and Reality. Norman: University of Oklahoma Press.
Godkin, Edwin L.
  [1896]
  1969 "The frontier and the national character." Pp. 13–6 in M. Ridge and R. A. Billington (eds.), America's Frontier Story. New York: Holt.
Hicks, John D.
  1948 The Federal Union. Boston: Houghton Mifflin.
Hollon, W. Eugene
  1973 "Frontier violence: another look." Pp. 86–100 in R. A. Billington (ed.), People of the Plains and Mountains. Westport, Ct.: Greenwood Press.
  1974 Frontier Violence. New York: Oxford University Press.
Humphrey, Seth K.
  1931 Following the Prairie Frontier. Minneapolis: University of Minnesota Press.
Ibsen, Henrik
  [1890]
  1950 Hedda Gabler. Tr. E. Gosse and W. Archer. Pp. 42–74 in J. Gassner (ed.), A Treasury of the Theatre. New York: Simon and Schuster.
Jackson, W. Turrentine
  1973 "Pioneer life on the plains and in the mines." Pp. 63–85 in R. A. Billington (ed.), People of the Plains and Mountains. Westport, Ct.: Greenwood Press.
Kozak, Lola Jean
  1974 "Night people: a study of the social experiences of night workers." Michigan State University, Summation 4:40–61.
Latané, Bibb and John Darley
  1970 The Unresponsive Bystander. New York: Appleton-Century.
Marx, Karl
  [1867]
  1906 Capital. New York: Modern Library.
Meier, Richard L.
  1976 "A stable urban ecosystem." Science 192:962–8.
Melbin, Murray
  1977 "The colonization of time." In T. Carlstein, D. Parkes, and N. Thrift (eds.), Timing Space and Spacing Time in Social Organization. London: Arnold.
Milgram, Stanley
  1970 "The experience of living in cities." Science 167:1461–8.
Mumford, Lewis
  1961 The City in History. New York: Harcourt Brace.
National Industrial Conference Board
  1927 Night Work in Industry. New York: National Industrial Conference Board.

New York Times
  1968 " 'Cooping': an old custom under fire." December 15: Sec. 4, 6E.
Patrushev, V. D.
  1972 "Aggregate time-balances and their meaning for socio-economic planning." Pp. 429–40 in A. Szalai (ed.), The Use of Time. The Hague: Mouton.
Riegel, Robert E.
  1947 America Moves West. New York: Holt.
Robbins, Roy M.
  1942 Our Landed Heritage. Princeton: Princeton University Press.
Schachter, Stanley
  1959 The Psychology of Affiliation. Stanford: Stanford University Press.
Schlesinger, Arthur
  1933 The Rise of the City: 1878–1895. New York: Macmillan.
Schydlowsky, Daniel
  1976 "Multiple shifts would produce 'revolutionary results' for Latin American economy." Boston University, Spectrum 4 (September 9):5.
Smith, Henry Nash
  [1950]
  1957 Virgin Land. New York: Vintage.
Sumner, William Graham
  [1906]
  1960 Folkways. New York: New American Library.
Szalai, Alexander (ed.)
  1972 The Use of Time. The Hague: Mouton.
Turner, Frederick Jackson
  [1893]
  1920 The Frontier in American History. New York: Holt.
  1932 The Significance of Sections in American History. New York: Holt.
  [1965]
  1969 America's Great Frontiers and Sections. Unpublished essays edited by W. R. Jacobs. Lincoln: Nebraska University Press. U.S. Bureau of the Census
  1975 Historical Statistics of the United States, Vol. 1: ser. A195–209. Washington, D.C.: U.S. Government Printing Office.
U.S. Bureau of Labor Statistics
  1976 Current Population Survey. Unpublished paper. May 12: Table 1. Washington, D.C.
U.S. Office of Management and Budget
  1974 Social Indicators, 1973. Washington, D.C.: U.S. Government Printing Office.
Wispé, Lauren G. and Harold B. Freshley
  1971 "Race, sex, and sympathetic helping behavior: the broken bag caper." Journal of Personality and Social Psychology 17:59–64.
Wyman, Walker D. and Clifton B. Kroeber (eds.)
  1957 The Frontier in Perspective. Madison: University of Wisconsin Press.
Young, Michael and Peter Willmott
  [1973]
  1975 The Symmetrical Family. Harmondsworth, England: Penguin.

Writing with Sources: Using a Single Source

Integrating information from "Night as Frontier" with your own ideas, write an essay on one of these topics. Be sure to acknowledge ideas that are not your own.

1. Observe the night life of your own community, your college or university

campus, or your dormitory over a period of one week. In what ways does the activity you observe conform to Melbin's observations? Where do your observations differ from his? How can you account for these differences?

2. What additional activities are likely to move into the nighttime hours during your lifetime? How will this movement change the way you live? Speculate about this subject in an essay.

3. What will the next American frontier be? Try to predict the direction of the next wave of expansion, explaining why you made the choice you did.

Writing with Sources: Using Multiple Sources

Integrating information from sources in this chapter with your own ideas, write an essay on one of the topics below. Be sure to acknowledge ideas that are not your own.

1. What common elements are shared by the development of Monopoly and the development of blue jeans? Compare the stories of these two phenomena. How are these developments typical of some aspect of life in America?

2. After having read the selections in this chapter and considered some of the directions in which our society seems to be moving, you should be prepared to make some predictions about the trends of the future. Set forth some of your predictions for the next twenty years.

3. During the same time Americans have been preoccupied with physical fitness, they have also become increasingly dependent on fast food. Explore this apparent contradiction and attempt to explain why these two parallel trends might have developed concurrently.

4. Are Americans becoming increasingly alike, losing their individuality as they pursue the same social and recreational goals? Consider this possibility.

5. Behind the development of the fads discussed in this chapter — shopping malls, fast food, toys and games, clothing items, exercise equipment — lies the spirit of American entrepreneurship and big business. After surveying advertisements in a number of popular magazines, discuss the relationship between business interests and the introduction of new fads into our lives.

Appendix A

Plagiarism

Presenting someone else's words or ideas as if they were your own is *plagiarism*. There are two kinds of plagiarism, intentional and unintentional.

Intentional plagiarism occurs when a student buys a research paper or asks a friend to write the concluding section of his lab report or copies a critique from a professional journal, hoping the professor will not be aware of the original source. Intentional plagiarism also occurs when an author claims credit for an article written by somebody else. This kind of plagiarism has serious consequences: It can lead to failing courses, having degrees withheld, being sued, or even being fired. Both because of these deterrents and because of their self-respect, most writers do not intentionally present other people's ideas and words as if they were their own.

However, *unintentional plagiarism* — forgetting to document a source or to include quotation marks around the words of others — sometimes appears in the writing of perfectly honest people, and it can incur the same serious consequences as intentional plagiarism. To avoid unintentional plagiarism, you must keep track of your sources so that you can distinguish between ideas and thoughts that need not be documented and ideas and thoughts that must be documented.

Information Not Requiring Documentation

Personal information — any observations you make, any statistics you compile from surveys you conduct, or any conclusions you reach from original experiments you have run — need not be acknowledged. For instance, if you observe the behavior of people arriving at airports after flights of more than six hours and then write a paper presenting your observations and conclusions, you need not provide any special citation. You would certainly want to explain the facts on which you base your findings, but you would need no other documentation.

Another category of information that does not require documentation is facts, ideas, or expressions that are considered *common knowledge*. You can consider as common knowledge any fact that is readily available in any reference book. For example, if you were writing an essay on nuclear warfare, you would not have to document the fact that the first atomic bomb was dropped on Hiroshima on August 6, 1945. That date is widely available in newspapers, magazines, textbooks, professional journals, and encyclopedias. Even if you had to look up the date — perhaps because you could not remember the exact year or day — you would still not need to document information that can be found in so many sources.

Finally, you do not have to document a passing reference to a famous work or idea that you expect the reader to recognize. Such a reference is called an *allusion*. You also do not have to document well-known quotations. Consider the following examples.

> The landlord was a Dickensian misanthrope.

> "To be or not to be?" That seems to remain the question.

Your readers could be expected to recognize that the first sentence refers to Charles Dickens's splendidly wicked villains and that the second quotes a well-known soliloquy spoken by Shakespeare's Hamlet.

Information Requiring Documentation

You must acknowledge any words, facts, ideas, or statistics that are not either your own or general knowledge. Common sense and ethics should be your guides. So, although you do not need to document well-known quotations ("Something is rotten in the state of Denmark"), you must document material that your readers might think was your own. Your source might be a book or a professional journal, but it could just as easily be an interview, a computer program, or a television series. You might use an entire paragraph or chart from your source, or you might use only a few words. You might cite your source once or twice or many times. You may quote your source exactly or you may summarize or paraphrase important information. No matter how you use your source; or how frequently you quote it; or how much of it you quote, paraphrase, or summarize, you must provide proper documentation. (See Appendix B for examples of documentation format.)

Guides for Avoiding Plagiarism

The examples that follow illustrate acceptable and unacceptable use of sources and thus demonstrate the difference between plagiarism and the legitimate integration of other people's ideas and words into your own writing.

Using Quotation

Whenever you quote a source, even if you use only a phrase, you must provide proper documentation.

Original Source Albert Einstein, ''Atomic War or Peace,'' 1945, 170.

The *release of atomic energy* has not created a new problem. It has merely made more urgent the necessity of solving an existing one. One could say *that it has affected us quantitatively, not qualitatively. As long as there are sovereign nations possessing great power, war is inevitable.*

Plagiarism: Albert Einstein believed that the discovery of nuclear power did not really initiate new problems. He thought that *the release of atomic energy affected us quantitatively, not qualitatively* (170).

[Although Einstein's name is mentioned, and the page reference appears after the sentence, the phrases ''release of atomic energy'' and ''affected us quantitatively, not qualitatively'' are not enclosed in quotation marks as they should be. Even though the phrases are embedded in an original sentence, they still must be identified as direct quotations.]

Acceptable: Albert Einstein believed that the discovery of nuclear power did not really initiate new problems. He thought that ''the release of atomic energy . . . affected us quantitatively, not qualitatively'' (170).

[The quotation has been properly documented; ellipses indicate that words have been deleted from the original.]

Acceptable: Albert Einstein believed that the discovery of nuclear power did not really initiate new problems. Einstein recognized that gaining the ability to use atomic energy made the difficulties that we already faced greater, but it did not add any new difficulties (170).

[The quotation has been recast as a legitimate paraphrase and has been properly documented.]

Plagiarism: We should face the fact that *''as long as there are sovereign nations possessing great power, war is inevitable.''*

[Although the directly quoted words are correctly enclosed in quotation marks, the source is not cited.]

Acceptable: We should face the fact that ''as long as there are sovereign nations possessing great power, war is inevitable'' (Einstein 170).

[The quotation has been properly documented. The author's name and the page number follow the quotation.]

or

Acceptable: Einstein urged his readers to face the fact that ''as long as there are sovereign nations possessing great power, war is inevitable'' (170).

[The quotation has been properly documented. The author's name is mentioned in the phrase that introduces the quotation, so only the page number must follow the directly quoted words.]

NOTE: Consult Chapter 2, pages 29–31, for a detailed explanation and examples of integrating quotations into your writing.

Using Paraphrase

When you *paraphrase* another writer's work, you restate in your own words the main points of a passage. In addition, you follow the author's original order and maintain the original emphasis. To avoid plagiarism when you paraphrase, make certain that you do not use any exact, or nearly exact, phrases or sentences from your source. In addition, a paraphrase must be accurately documented.

Original Source   Gloria Steinem, "The Importance of Work," 1983, 401.

In many ways, women who do not have to work for simple survival, but who choose to do so nonetheless, are on the frontier of asserting this right for all women.

Plagiarism: In a number of ways, women who do not have to earn a living simply to survive, but who elect to do so nevertheless, are on the frontier of establishing this prerogative for all women (Steinem 401).

[Even though the original author and page number are cited, this sentence is not a legitimate paraphrase. It copies Steinem's sentence pattern exactly and merely substitutes synonyms for her key words.]

Plagiarism: On the frontier of asserting the right for all women to work are the women who choose to work even though they do not have to do so in order to survive (Steinem 401).

[The writer of this sentence has changed the sentence pattern but still uses the original words. Citing the author's name and the original page number does not exempt such an imitative sentence from the charge of plagiarism.]

Acceptable Paraphrase: Steinem maintains that every woman's right to work will be established by those women who are financially secure, yet who opt, nevertheless, to work outside the home (401).

[This sentence accurately conveys Steinem's idea yet uses neither the structure nor the phrasing of the original quotation.]

NOTE: Consult Chapter 2, pages 32–36, for an explanation and examples of writing paraphrases.

Using Summary

Whenever you summarize someone else's ideas, even though you use your own words, you must provide proper documentation.

Read the following original source and the summary that follows it.

Original Source   Ronald B. Adler and Neil Towne, *Looking Out/Looking In,* 3rd edition, pp. 13–14.

Nonverbal Communication Serves Many Functions   Just because this chapter deals with nonverbal communication, don't get the idea that our words and our actions are unrelated. Quite the opposite is true: Verbal and nonverbal communication are interconnected elements in every act of communication. Nonverbal behaviors can operate in several relationships to verbal messages.

First, nonverbal behaviors can *repeat* what is said verbally. If someone asked you for directions to the nearest drugstore, you could say, "North of here about two blocks," and then repeat your instructions nonverbally by pointing north.

Nonverbal messages may also *substitute* for verbal ones. When you see a familiar friend wearing a certain facial expression, you don't need to ask, "How's it going?" In the same way, experience has probably shown you that other kinds of looks, gestures, and other clues say, "I'm angry at you" or "I feel great" far better than words.

A third way in which verbal and nonverbal messages can relate is called *complementing.* If you saw a student talking to a teacher, and his head was bowed slightly, his voice was low and hesitating, and he shuffled slowly from foot to foot, you might conclude that he felt inferior to the teacher, possibly embarrassed about something he did. The nonverbal behaviors you observed provided the context for the verbal behaviors—they conveyed the relationship between the teacher and student. Complementing nonverbal behaviors signal the attitudes the interactants have for one another.

Nonverbal behaviors can also *accent* verbal messages. Just as we can use *italics* in print to underline an idea, we can emphasize some part of a face-to-face message in various ways. Pointing an accusing finger adds emphasis to criticism (as well as probably creating defensiveness in the receiver). Shrugging shoulders accent confusion, and hugs can highlight excitement or affection. As you'll see later in this chapter, the voice plays a big role in accenting verbal messages.

Nonverbal behavior also serves to *regulate* verbal behavior. By lowering your voice at the end of a sentence, "trailing off," you indicate that the other person may speak. You can also convey this information through the use of eye contact and by the way you position your body.

Finally—and often most significantly—nonverbal behavior can often *contradict* the spoken word. People often simultaneously express different and even contradictory messages in their verbal and nonverbal behaviors. A common example of this sort of "double message" is the experience we've all had of hearing someone with a red face and bulging veins yelling, "Angry? No, *I'm not angry!*"

Plagiarism: Nonverbal communication can operate in at least six ways in relation to verbal communication. First, nonverbal messages can reiterate verbal messages. Second, nonverbal behaviors may take the place of what is said verbally. Third, verbal and nonverbal messages can complement each other. In addition, verbal communications can be emphasized by nonverbal behaviors. And, of course, nonverbal messages can work to control verbal communication. The last, and most important, function of nonverbal behaviors is their ability to convey the opposite of what has been said.

[The writer has summarized conclusions originally made by Adler and Towne. Even though the writer has, for the most part, substituted new phrasing and has not included Adler and Towne's analysis of each kind of nonverbal message, the summary still presents the original authors' ideas, and therefore the authors must be acknowledged. In addition, the writer should not follow so closely Adler and Towne's sentence structure.]

> *Acceptable summary:*   According to Adler and Towne, "nonverbal behaviors can operate in several relationships to verbal messages." The authors suggest six connections between verbal and nonverbal communications. Nonverbal behaviors can repeat, replace, complement, emphasize, control, or contradict verbal communications (13–14).

[This summary includes all of Adler and Towne's main points and in addition correctly places in quotation marks the one phrase that is directly borrowed from the original passage. The summary is properly documented since the author's names are given in the introductory phrase, and the page references are provided.]

Identifying Facts, Statistics, and References That May Be Considered Common Knowledge

As we explained above, you need not document any sources that provide information that is familiar to most of your readers, available in many sources, or clearly used as an allusion. Consider the following statements based on "The U.S. Was Wrong" by Gar Alperovitz (p. 165).

> *Common knowledge:*   The United States intelligence system was instrumental in bringing World War II to an end.

[This information can be found in many sources and is accepted as accurate by most experts in the field. No citation is necessary. Note, of course, that the writer has not lifted any phrases or copied the sentence structure of the original source.]

> *Original:*   Mr. Truman's private diaries also record his understanding of the significance of this option. On July 17, 1945, when Stalin confirmed that the Red Army would march, Mr. Truman privately noted: "Fini Japs when that comes about."

> *Plagiarism:*   In his private journal, Truman commented on Stalin's confirmation that the Red Army would make its move on July 17, 1945.

[The connection between Truman's journal and Stalin's announcement is the original idea of Gar Alperovitz and must be acknowledged.]

> *Acceptable:*   Truman commented in his private journal on Stalin's confirmation that the Red Army would make its move on July 17, 1945 (Alperovitz 166).

The following examples, drawn from *Great Expectations: America and the Baby Boom Generation* by Landon Y. Jones (pp. 22–24), also clarify the difference between facts that must be documented and facts that can be considered common knowledge.

Common knowledge: Most people who were born after 1945 have had thousands of hours of exposure to television by the time they reach adulthood.

[This idea, including the date of the beginning of the "baby boom," is available in many places.]

Original: According to a 1976 study by Cleveland State University, the number of hours devoted to media by the 18–24 age group rose from 13.9 in 1965, when only a few baby boomers were in that category, to 18.5 in 1975, when it was composed entirely of that generation.

Plagiarism: In 1965 people ages 18–24 devoted 13.9 hours per week to various media. In 1975, the number of hours for the same age group rose to 18.5.

[These statistics are available only from a specific study cited by Landon Y. Jones, so these numbers and dates must be properly documented.]

Acceptable: Landon Y. Jones cites a Cleveland State University Study made in 1976. This study shows that in 1965 people ages 18–24 devoted 13.9 hours per week to various media. In 1975, the number of hours for the same age group rose to 18.5 (23).

[Both the original source (the Cleveland State University study) and the source used by the writer (Landon Y. Jones's article) have been acknowledged.]

Common knowledge: Most baby boomers grew up in families that owned television sets.

[Widely known and acknowledged as true. Requires no documentation.]

Original: The glowing blue light also plunged the boom children into an environment that was as alien to their parents' experience as if they'd moved to never-never land. It was an alternate reality that was absorbing but strangely discombobulating.

Plagiarism: Television was one factor that alienated baby boomers from their parents.

[Although Landon Y. Jones implies that television was a factor in alienating baby boomers from their parents, this idea must be noted as his opinion. One authority's viewpoint must not be stated as if it were common knowledge.]

Acceptable: Landon Y. Jones believes that television introduced baby boomers into an environment that was radically different from that of their parents (23).

[Here Jones's idea is credited to him and is not stated as though it were accepted fact.]

Finally, consider the following statements based on the Declaration of Independence (p. 86).

Common knowledge: Certainly all of us hold those same "truths to be self-evident." We believe that all people are "created equal" and that all people have the right to "life, liberty and the pursuit of happiness."

Original: We hold these truths to be self-evident, that all men are created equal, that they are endowed by their Creator with certain unalienable rights, that among these are life, liberty and the pursuit of happiness. . . . But when a long train of abuses and usurpations, pursuing invariably the same object evinces a design to reduce them under absolute despotism, it is their right, it is their duty, to throw off such government, and to provide new guards for their future security.

[The quotations from the Declaration of Independence are familiar to most readers, and therefore they do not require a citation. Readers can be reasonably expected to recognize these phrases as allusions to the Declaration.]

Plagiarism: When a long train of abuses and usurpations forces people to live under absolute despotism, it is their right to throw off such government and to fight to establish their independence.

[The phrases from the Declaration of Independence that are incorporated are not immediately identifiable as coming from that source; thus they must be enclosed in quotation marks and documented.]

Acceptable: "When a long train of abuses and usurpations" forces people to live "under absolute despotism, it is their right . . . to throw off such a government" and to fight to establish their independence (Jefferson 86).

[These sentences are now correctly punctuated with quotation marks, and ellipses indicate omitted words. In addition, the source is accurately documented.]

Taking Accurate Notes to Prevent Unintentional Plagiarism

When you are taking notes, make sure to differentiate clearly between your own words and ideas and the words and ideas of your sources. The first two of the following note cards (p. 617) illustrate two potentially confusing notes that could lead the notetaker to plagiarize inadvertently. The third note card (p. 618) demonstrates accurate notetaking and labeling that will prevent accidental plagiarism.

Original Source   John M. Darley and Bibb Latané, "Why People Don't Help in a Crisis," 17.

Even if a person defines an event as an emergency, the presence of other bystanders may still make him less likely to intervene. He feels that his responsibility is diffused and diluted. Thus, if your car breaks down on a busy highway, hundreds of drivers whiz by without anyone's stopping to help — but if you are stuck on a nearly deserted country road, whoever passes you first is likely to stop.

Inaccurate
Note Card

Crisis Reactions   Darley and Latané
                                    p. 26

          Even if
a person defines an event as
an emergency, the presence of
other bystanders may still make
him less likely to intervene.
Darley and Latané ran tests
to prove their theory.

[In the note card above, the student has written her own original thoughts immediately after the direct quotation taken from the source. Because she has not differentiated between the quotation and her own observations, she risks presenting the authors' ideas as her own.]

Inaccurate
Note Card

Crisis Reactions   Darley and Latané,
                                    p. 26

    Although people may be
aware of an emergency, the
presence of bystanders often
makes them less apt to
help. People in a crowd
believe that their accountability
is diffused and diluted.

[Here the student has paraphrased the original source, but has not enclosed in quotation marks the phrase taken directly from Darley and Latané. If he uses the paraphrase as it appears here, he will be plagiarizing even if he cites the original authors and page number.]

Accurate
Note Card

> Crisis Reactions   Darley and Latané,
>   p. 26
>
> A person in an emergency
> may be less apt to help if
> there are other people with
> him. "He feels that his
> responsibility is diffused
> and diluted."
>
> [Darley and Latané ran tests
> to prove their theory.]

[On this note card the student has clearly indicated which words and thoughts are original and which are directly quoted from the source. The direct quotation is placed within quotation marks, and the student's own observation is placed within brackets. It will be easy to use this material correctly and to document it properly because the note was recorded accurately.]

Exercise 1

I. *Directions:* Read the following examples and decide which of them demonstrate the legitimate use and accurate documentation of the original source. When you find examples of plagiarism or errors in documentation, make the necessary corrections.

---

    1. Original Source   From "Why People Don't Help in a Crisis," John M. Darley and Bibb Latané, page 18:

        Thus, the stereotype of the unconcerned, depersonalized *homo urbanus,* blandly watching the misfortunes of others, proves inaccurate.

A. *Using the Source*
The stereotype of the uncaring, impersonal urban dweller, unconcernedly viewing the miseries of others, turns out to be untrue.

B. *Using the Source*
Most of us are appalled at the thought of the unconcerned, depersonalized urban dweller, blandly watching the misfortunes of others (Darley and Latané 28).

C. *Using the Source*
"The stereotype of the unconcerned, depersonalized *homo urbanus*" has been challenged by some experts.

2. ***Original Source*** From "Rich Doctors, Poor Nurses," David Osborne, page 9:

Most American doctors have put in eight hard years of higher education, followed by three to five years of residency. In recent years most have racked up $20,000, $30,000, or even $50,000 in debts, depending on family finances and tuition levels.

A. *Using the Source*
Most doctors who get their training in the United States must serve a residency that can last up to five years.

B. *Using the Source*
It is not unusual for doctors to owe from $20,000 to $50,000 when they finally finish their schooling and residency.

C. *Using the Source*
After putting in "eight hard years of higher education" and serving a residency of up to five years, many American doctors find themselves deeply in debt (Osborne 12).

3. ***Original Source*** From "The Importance of Work," Gloria Steinem, page 398:

If all the productive work of human maintenance that women do in the home were valued at its replacement cost, the gross national product of the United States would go up by 26 percent.

A. *Using the Source*
The gross national product in this country would rise by 26 percent if all the productive work of human maintenance women do at home were valued at what it would cost to replace it (Steinem 398).

B. *Using the Source*
We need to recognize the enormous value of the work done by women in their homes as they nurture their families. It is amazing to realize that our gross national product would rise 26 percent if women's maintenance work were to be done by paid replacement workers (Steinem 398).

C. Using the Source
The work done by women in the home as they nurture their families would
cost a great deal if it were done by paid replacement workers.

4. *Original Source* From "Modern Man Is Obsolete," Norman Cousins,
page 176.

Julian Huxley, the English biologist, draws a sharp distinction between human
nature and the *expression* of human nature.

A. Using the Source
There is a sharp distinction between human nature and the *expression* of
human nature (Cousins 176).

B. Using the Source
The English biologist Julian Huxley sees a clear difference "between human
nature and the *expression* of human nature" (176).

C. Using the Source
Norman Cousins claims that there is a "sharp distinction between human
nature and the *expression* of human nature (176)."

5. *Original Source* From "That Day at Hiroshima," Alexander H.
Leighton, page 144.

Like the children of Hamelin to the piper, they came rushing, at the sound of our
approach, from doorways and alleyways and from behind houses, to line up by the
road and cheer.

A. Using the Source
The children at Hiroshima might be compared to the children of Hamelin.
They came hurrying and cheering at the sound of approaching visitors.

B. Using the Source
"Like the children of Hamelin to the piper," the children of Hiroshima came
rushing at the sound of the approaching visitors. The children peered out from
doorways and alleyways and from behind houses. They stood beside the road
and cheered (144).

C. Using the Source
We might describe modern advocates of nuclear power as being like the
children who followed the Pied Piper.

Exercise 2

Use the passage on page 621 as the source for this exercise.

Patterns of Marital Residence

In societies in which newly married couples customarily live with or close to their kin, there are several residence patterns that may be established. Since children in all societies are required to marry outside the nuclear family (because of the incest taboo), and since couples in almost all societies live together after they are married (with a few exceptions),[2] it is not possible for an entire society to practice a system in which all married offspring reside with their own parents. Some children, then, have to leave home when they marry. But which children remain at home and which reside elsewhere? Societies vary in the way they typically deal with the problem of which married children stay near their kin and which leave. Actually, there are only four societal patterns which occur with any sizable frequency. They are:

1. *Patrilocal residence:* the son stays and the daughter leaves, so that the married couple lives with or near the husband's parents (67 percent of all societies).[3]
2. *Matrilocal residence:* the daughter stays and the son leaves, so that the married couple lives with or near the wife's parents (15 percent of all societies).
3. *Bilocal residence:* either the son or the daughter leaves, so that the married couple lives with or near either the husband's parents or the wife's parents (7 percent of all societies).
4. *Avunculocal residence:* both son and daughter normally leave, but the son and his wife settle with or near his mother's brother (4 percent of all societies).

A fifth pattern of residence, of course, is neolocal, in which the newly married couple does not live with or near kin.

5. *Neolocal residence:* both son and daughter leave; married couples live apart from the relatives of either spouse (5 percent).

Carol R. Ember and Melvin Ember, *Anthropology,* 2d edition.

Write the following:

1. A legitimate paraphrase of the first two sentences, properly documented.
2. A summary of the entire passage, properly documented.
3. A sentence using your own words to lead into a direct quotation from some part of the passage, properly documented.
4. Two or three original sentences that use phrases taken directly from the passage, properly documented.
5. A sentence using a statistic from the passage that requires documentation, properly documented.
6. A sentence using an idea mentioned in the passage that would be considered common knowledge and would therefore require no documentation.

Appendix B

Documentation

What to Document

Documentation enables your readers to identify your sources and to evaluate the quality of your work. It also enables them to locate the books and articles you cite. Therefore, you should carefully document the following kinds of information:

1. All direct quotations
2. All summaries or paraphrases of portions of your source
3. All opinions, judgments, and insights of others
4. All tables, graphs, and charts that you get from your sources

Be careful, however, not to overdocument. Inexperienced writers often feel that the more notes, the better the paper. Too many notes and references distract a reader. If, in a single paragraph, you cite information from two consecutive pages of a book, document it with one note, not two, at the end of the paragraph. Keep in mind, however, that you must document each *quotation* separately.

When to document is largely a matter of judgment. As a beginning researcher you should document any material about which you have questions. By doing so you avoid any hint of plagiarism. For a complete discussion of what information should and should not be documented, see Appendix A.

Different fields have different documentation formats. When you are writing a paper that requires documentation, always find out from your instructor which format you should use.

The most commonly used documentation formats are explained and illustrated in the pages that follow.*

---

*The documentation described in the next two sections follows the guidelines set in the MLA *Handbook for Writers of Research Papers,* 2nd ed. (New York: MLA, 1984).

Parenthetical Documentation

MLA parenthetical documentation, used by most disciplines in the humanities, consists of the author's last name and a page number inserted within the text and keyed to a list of works cited at the end of the paper.

> More and more women writers in our century, primarily in the last two
>
> decades, are assuming as their right fullness of work <u>and</u> family life
>
> (Olson 32).

If you use more than one source by the same author, include a short title.

> Prior to the modern age, which began with the expropriation of the
>
> poor and then proceeded to emancipate the new propertyless classes, all
>
> civilizations have rested upon the sacredness of private property
>
> (Arendt, <u>Human Condition</u> 61).

If the title or author's name is included in the text, omit it in the parenthetical reference.

> Three classic revolutions of modern times — the American, the French,
>
> and the Russian — are discussed by Hannah Arendt in her work <u>On</u>
>
> <u>Revolution</u> (342).

Place each parenthetical reference as close as possible to the material it documents. Keep in mind that you punctuate differently for *indirect references; direct quotations that are not set off from the text;* and *double-spaced quotations set off from the text.*

Parenthetical documentation for *indirect references* should appear *before* all punctuation marks.

> Contrary to the opinion of many scholars, Arendt believes that Lenin
>
> did not want to give all power to the <u>Soviets</u> (269).

Parenthetical documentation for *direct quotations that are not set off from the text* should appear *before* the final punctuation but after the ending quotation marks.

> As Arendt states, "Tocqueville read something into American society
>
> which he knew from the French Revolution" (109).

Long quotations of more than four typed lines must be set off from your text. Indent ten spaces from the left-hand margin, double-space, and do not add quotation marks.

Parenthetical documentation for *quotations that are set off from the text* should appear two spaces *after* the final punctuation.

> . . . this danger of confusing public happiness and private welfare was
>
> present even then, although one may assume that the delegates to the
>
> Assembly still held fast to the general belief of colonial publicists. (125)

Sample References   Parenthetical references provide a straightforward and easy method of documentation. Even so, the following situations call for special attention:

Citing a work by more than one author

> Such publications either reinforced the old trivializing categories or
>
> concocted new ones equally trivializing (Humez and Stavely 13).

Citing a volume and page number

> In the 1880s about 5.2 million foreigners arrived in the United States,
>
> and the figure rose to more than 8 million between 1900 and 1910
>
> (Graebner II: 259).

Citing a work without a listed author

> More than any other writer, Borges lived in and through literature
>
> ("The Talk of the Town" 21).

> As many as 60 commercial satellites will need a boost into orbit between
>
> now and 1990 ("Fumbling in Space: The Ariane Fiasco").

Note: Omit a page reference if you are citing a one-page article.

Citing an indirect source

> As Rosa Luxemburg pointed out, these revolutionary programs needed
>
> most of all "to be carried out energetically in practice" (qtd. in Arendt
>
> 267).

Using Explanatory Notes with Parenthetical References   Explanatory notes
— providing bibliographic information or offering remarks that are necessary but
that might distract your readers — may be used along with parenthetical documentation. These notes are indicated by a raised number in the text and are listed on a
numbered page, entitled "Notes," following the last page of your text.

Use explanatory notes to cite more than one source in a single reference.
Multiple references in a single pair of parentheses within the text distract readers.

> Both scholars agree that a clear definition of evil must be reached
>
> before the human community can act to eradicate its results.[1]

> Notes
>
> [1] Ernest Becker, The Structure of Evil (New York: Macmillan, 1968) 9;
>
> William Irwin Thompson, Evil and World Order (New York: Harper,
>
> 1977) 34.

Use notes to provide comments or explanations that are needed to clarify a
point in the text.

> Many scholars have questioned the validity of creationism and have
>
> challenged the claims of its supporters.[2]

> Notes
>
> [2] For a detailed discussion of the claims of creationists and for examples
>
> of the ways scientists have refuted their hypotheses, see Philip Kitcher,
>
> Abusing Science: The Case Against Creationism, Cambridge: MIT P, 1982.

Listing the Works Cited

The list of sources that you used in your paper is called the "Works Cited" section.
If your instructor tells you to list all the sources you read, whether you actually cite
them or not, use the title "Works Consulted."

Begin the list of works cited on a new page, after your explanatory notes, or
after the last page of your paper, if you have no explanatory notes. Number the list
of works cited as the last page of the text. (If the paper ends on page 8, the works
cited page is page 9.) List items in alphabetical order according to the authors' *last*
names. If one of your sources is unsigned, as is the case with some magazine and

newspaper articles, use the first main word of your title as your guide. The first line of each entry should begin at the left-hand margin, and subsequent lines should be indented five spaces from the left-hand margin. The list of works cited is double-spaced throughout, within, and between items.

Sample Entries: Books

A book by one author

Olsen, Tillie. <u>Silences.</u> New York: Dell, 1980.

Note: To conserve space you should not include "incorporated," "publishers," or "company" after the name of the publisher. Thus Dell Publishing Co., Inc., is shortened to "Dell."

A book by two or more authors

Humez, Alexander, and Keith Fitzgerald Stavely.   <u>Family Man: What</u>

<u>Men Feel About Their Wives, Their Children, Their Parents, and</u>

<u>Themselves.</u> Chicago: Contemporary, 1978.

Note: list only the first author's name in reverse order. List subsequent authors' names in normal order.

Linde, Hans A., et al.   <u>Legislative and Administrative Processes.</u>

Mineola, New York: Foundation, 1981.

Note: If there are three or more authors, list only the first author followed by the abbreviation *et al.* ("and others").

Two or more books by the same author

Arendt, Hannah, <u>The Human Condition.</u>   Chicago: U of Chicago P, 1958.

- - -. <u>On Revolution.</u>   New York: Viking, 1965.

Note: Give the author's name in the first entry. For subsequent entries use three spaced hyphens in place of the name.

An edited book

Eliot, George. <u>Adam Bede.</u> Ed. Stephen Gill. Middlesex, England:

Penguin, 1980.

Note: Include the country for cities outside the United States or for cities whose names may be ambiguous or unfamiliar to readers.

An essay appearing in a book

Miller, Susan. "Classical Practice and Contemporary Basics." The

Rhetorical Tradition and Modern Writing. Ed. James J. Murphy.

New York: MLA, 1982. 46–57.

An anthology or compilation

Murphy, James J., ed.   The Rhetorical Tradition and Modern Writing.

New York: MLA, 1982.

A multivolume work

Graebner, Norman A., et al.   A History of the United States.   2

vols. New York: McGraw, 1970. Vol. 2

Note: If you use only one volume of a multivolume work, include the volume number in your citation.

The foreword, preface, or afterword of a book

Rich, Adrienne. Foreword. Working It Out. Eds. Sara Ruddick and

Pamela Daniels. New York: Pantheon, 1977.

An encyclopedia article

"Panama Canal." New Encyclopaedia Britannica: Macropaedia. 1974 ed.

Note: Entries appear in alphabetical order, so a volume number is not needed. If an article is signed, then begin your reference with the author's name. Unfamiliar works should include full publication information.

A reprint

Lewis, Janet.   The Wife of Martin Guerre.   1941. Chicago: Swallow,

1967.

A pamphlet or bulletin

"Existing–Light photography."   Rochester: Kodak, 1985.

A government publication

United States. Farmers Home Administration. <u>Farm Labor Housing</u>

<u>Loans and Grants.</u> Washington: GPO, 1966.

Note: Include the name of the government first, followed by the name of the agency.

Sample Entries: Articles

An article in a scholarly journal with continuous
pagination throughout an annual volume

Cooper, Marilyn M. "The Ecology of Writing." <u>College English</u> 48

(1986): 364–375.

Note: Citations for articles give the pages on which the full article appears. The abbreviations "p." and "pp." are not included in the page reference.

An article in a scholarly journal that has separate pagination in each issue

Greenwald, Elissa. "The Ruins of Empire: Reading the Monuments in

Hawthorne and James." <u>The CEA Critic</u> 46.3 (1984): 48–59.

Note: For a journal that has separate pagination in each issue, add a period and the issue number after the volume (e.g. 46.3 for volume 46, issue number 3).

An article in a weekly magazine

Castro, Janice. "Bounty from Uncle Sam." <u>Time</u> 18 Aug. 1986: 38.

Note: The date is put in parentheses only when a volume number is mentioned.

An unsigned article in a weekly magazine

"Fumbling in Space: The Ariane Fiasco." <u>Newsweek</u> 9 June 1986: 36.

An article in a monthly magazine

Lemann, Nicholas. "The Origins of the Underclass." <u>The Atlantic</u> July

1986: 54–68.

Card, Emily. "New Twists in Banking: What You Can Expect in a

Changing Market." <u>Ms.</u> Sept. 1986: 71+.

Note: When the pagination of an article is not continuous — for example, it begins on page 71, is interrupted on pp. 72–73 by an advertising supplement, and continues on p. 74 — include only the first page number followed by a (+) sign.

An article in a daily newspaper

Cos, Meg. "Goodness Gracious Snakes Alive! Do People Really Call

Thisss Art?" The Wall Street Journal 21 Nov. 1985, eastern

ed.: 33.

An editorial

"Who's Minding the Archives?" Editorial. The Boston Globe 22 Aug.

1984, evening ed.: 22.

Sample Entries: Nonprint Sources

Computer software

Resident Speller. Computer software. S and K Technology, 1984.

Material from a computer service

Marshall, James, and Michael Peters. "New Perspectives on Piaget's

Philosophy." Educational Theory Sept. 1986: 125–36. ERIC EJ

332 420.

Note: Enter material from a computer service — such as BRS, DIALOG, or ERIC — just as you would other printed material, but identify the information service and the identifying number at the end of the entry.

A lecture

Odell, Lee. Crisis and Renewal: A Maturing Discipline." Conference on

College Composition and Communication, New Orleans, 13 March

1986.

A letter

McNeece, Anne T. Letter to the author. 6 Aug. 1986.

An interview

Wyeth, Andrew. Personal interview. 15 April 1985.

A film

Spielberg, Steven, dir. <u>The Color Purple</u>. With Whoopi Goldberg, Danny

Glover, Margaret Avery, and Rae Dawn Chong. Warner Brothers,

1986.

Note: The citation should include the title (underlined), distributor, and date. Other information, such as the director, writer, and performers, can also be given.

A television or radio program

"Among the Wild Chimpanzees." <u>National Geographic</u>. Narr. Jane

Goodall. PBS. WQED, Pittsburgh. 10 Aug. 1986.

Note: Because "Among the Wild Chimpanzees" is one part of the series *National Geographic,* it is placed in quotation marks.

<u>Traveling Muse</u>. Narr. Clarence Washington. WBUR-FM, Boston. 22

Aug. 1984.

Endnotes and Footnotes

Some instructors prefer that you use endnotes or footnotes rather than parenthetical documentation. There are three parts to endnote and footnote documentation: (1) the number in the text that refers to your note; (2) the note itself; and (3) the bibliography at the end of the paper. The note number directly follows the material you are documenting and is typed slightly above the line. Notes are numbered consecutively throughout the paper and placed *after* all punctuation.

". . . the Hegelian dialectic."[3]

The number is not followed by a period, asterisk, or other symbol.

First References: Books   If your endnote is a first reference to a book, it will contain the following information.

1. A number that matches the number in the text
2. Author (name as it appears on the title page) — first name, middle name or initial, and last name
3. Book title (underlined)
4. City of publication
5. Publisher } enclosed in parentheses
6. Year of publication
7. Page reference

Indent the first line of each note five spaces, and begin it with a number (typed slightly above the line) corresponding to the note number in the text. After the first line, type all the lines that follow flush with the left margin. Endnotes are double-spaced within notes as well as between notes. (Footnotes are single-spaced within the note and double-spaced between notes.) Unless you are told otherwise, use endnotes rather than footnotes in your papers.

Sample endnote

⁴ William Irwin Thompson, <u>Evil and World Order</u> (New York:

Harper, 1977) 34.

Sample footnote

⁵ Ernest Becker, <u>The Structure of Evil</u> (New York: Macmillan,

1968) 9.

With endnotes and footnotes, insert punctuation exactly as it appears in these sample references.

A book by one author

¹ Tillie Olsen, <u>Silences</u> (New York: Dell, 1980) 89.

A book by two or more authors

² Alexander Humez and Keith Fitzgerald Stavely, <u>Family Man:</u>

<u>What Men Feel about Their Wives, Their Children, Their Parents, and</u>

<u>Themselves</u> (Chicago: Contemporary, 1978) 125.

³ Hans A. Linde, et al., <u>Legislative and Administrative Processes</u>

(New York: Foundation, 1981) 33.

An edited book

⁴ George Eliot, <u>Adam Bede,</u> ed. Stephen Gill (Middlesex, England:

Penguin, 1980) 445.

An essay appearing in a book

⁵ Susan Miller, "Classical Practice and Contemporary Basics,"

The Rhetorical Tradition and Modern Writing, ed. James J. Murphy

(New York: MLA, 1982) 46.

An anthology or compilation

[6] James J. Murphy, ed., The Rhetorical Tradition in Modern

Writing (New York: MLA, 1982) 75.

A multivolume work

[7] Norman A. Graebner, et al., A History of the United States, 2

vols. (New York: McGraw, 1970) 2: 783.

The foreword, preface, or afterword of a book

[8] Adrienne Rich, foreword, Working It Out, eds. Sara Ruddick and

Pamela Daniels (New York: Pantheon, 1977) ix.

An article in an encyclopedia

[9] "Panama Canal," New Encyclopaedia Britannica: Macropaedia,

1974 ed.

A reprint

[10] Janet Lewis, The Wife of Martin Guerre (1941; Chicago:

Swallow, 1967) 112.

A pamphlet or bulletin

[11] "Existing–Light Photography" (Rochester: Kodak, 1985)

14–15.

A government publication

[12] Farmers Home Administration, Farm Labor Housing Loans and

Grants (Washington: GPO, 1965) 15.

First References: Articles   Endnotes for articles are similar to those for books. There are differences in form, however, that have to do with the serial nature of publication. First references to articles contain the following information:

1. A number that matches the number in the text
2. Author (name as it appears in the article) — first name, middle name or initial, and last name.
3. Article title (full title in quotation marks)
4. Title of journal or magazine (underlined)
5. Volume number (in Arabic numbers)
6. Date of publication (in parentheses when preceded by volume number)
7. Page reference

Like endnotes for books, endnotes for articles are double-spaced throughout. (Footnotes are single-spaced.)

An article in a scholarly journal with continuous
pagination throughout an annual volume

[1] Marilyn M. Cooper, "The Ecology of Writing," College English
48 (1986) 373.

An article in a scholary journal that has separate pagination in each issue

[2] Elissa Greenwald, "The Ruins of Empire: Reading the Monuments in Hawthorne and James," The CEA Critic 46.3 (1984) 49.

An article in a weekly magazine

[3]Janice Castro, "Bounty from Uncle Sam," Time 18 Aug. 1986: 38.

An unsigned article in a weekly magazine

[4] "Fumbling in Space: The Ariane Fiasco," Newsweek 9 June
1986: 36.

An article in a monthly magazine

[5] Nicholas Lemann, "The Origins of the Underclass," The Atlantic
July 1986: 55.

Emily Card, "New Twists in Banking: What You Can Expect in a
Changing Market," Ms. Sept. 1986: 71.

An article in a daily newspaper

[6] Meg Cox, "Goodness Gracious Snakes Alive! Do People Really
Call Thisss Art?" The Wall Street Journal 21 Nov. 1985, eastern ed.: 33.

An editorial

[7] "Who's Minding the Archives?" editorial, <u>The Boston Globe</u>

22 Aug. 1984, evening ed.: 22.

First References: Nonprint Sources   Nonprint sources must also be documented.

Computer software

[8] <u>Resident Speller</u>, computer software, S and K Technology, 1984.

Material from a computer service

[9] James Marshall and Michael Peters, "New Perspectives on

Piaget's Philosophy," <u>Educational Theory</u> Sept. 1986: 125–36 (ERIC EJ

332 420).

A lecture

[10] Lee Odell, "Crisis and Renewal: A Maturing Discipline,"

Conference on College Composition and Communication, New Orleans,

13 March 1986.

A letter

[11] Anne T. McNeece, letter to the author, 6 Aug. 1986.

An interview

[12] Andrew Wyeth, personal interview, 15 April 1985.

A film

[13] Steven Speilberg, dir., <u>The Color Purple</u>, with Whoopi Goldberg,

Danny Glover, Margaret Avery, and Rae Dawn Chong, Warner Brothers,

1986.

A television or radio program

[14] Among the Wild Chimpanzees," <u>National Geographic</u>, narr.

Jane Goodall, PBS, WQED, Pittsburgh, 10 Aug. 1986.

[15]Traveling Muse, narr. Clarence Washington, WBUR-FM, Boston,

22 Aug 1984.

Subsequent References   After the first reference to a *book,* you no longer have to provide full bibliographic information. The author's last name and the page reference are sufficient.

First reference

[1] Hannah Arendt, The Human Condition (Chicago: U of Chicago

P, 1958) 165.

Subsequent reference

[2] Arendt 231.

If your paper refers to two or more books by the same author, subsequent references to each book should include a shortened form of the title or the full title if it is already short.

[6] Arendt, Human Condition 36.

[7]Arendt, Revolution 279.

Subsequent references to *articles* follow the same format. Here, too, if you use two or more sources by the same author, include titles in your references.

First reference

[16] Marilyn M. Cooper, "The Ecology of Writing," College English

48 (1986) 365.

Subsequent reference

[17] Cooper 373.

The Bibliography   The bibliography is the list of books that you use in your paper. Following the same format as the list of works cited, it appears on a numbered page after the last page of your paper.

The following examples illustrate the differences between bibliography and endnote formats.

Bibliography format

Olsen, Tillie. Silences. New York: Dell, 1980.

Endnote format

¹ Tillie Olsen, <u>Silences</u> (New York: Dell, 1980) 72.

For bibliographic format for the endnotes listed above, see "Listing the Works Cited," p. 625.

APA Format

APA format, which is used extensively in the social sciences, relies on short references — consisting of the last name of the author and the year of publication — inserted within the sentence. As with MLA style, you do not include information that appears in the text in the parenthetical reference.

Parenthetical References in the Text

One author

One study (Kohler, 1925) described the problem-solving behavior of

apes. . . .

Note: APA style calls for a comma between the name and the date, whereas MLA style does not.

Author's name in text

Kohler (1925) described the problem-solving behavior of apes. . . .

Author's name and date in text

In Kohler's 1925 study of the problem-solving behavior of apes. . . .

Two publications by same author(s), same year

An early example can be seen in his early work on insight in learning

(Kohler, 1925a).

Note: If you use two or more publications by the same author that appeared the same year, the first is designated *a*, the second *b* (e.g., Weisberg 1983a and Weisberg 1983b), and so on. These letter designations also appear in the reference list that follows the text of your paper.

Two authors

The procedures of avoidance learning have been used extensively in

recent years (Rescorla & Solomon, 1967).

Note: With two authors, both names are cited. If a work has more than two authors but fewer than six authors, mention all names in the first reference, and in subsequent references cite the first author followed by *et al.* and the year (Sparks et al., 1984.). When a work has six or more authors, cite the name of the first author followed by *et al.* and the year for the first and subsequent references.

Specific parts of a source

Motor learning appears to be an ongoing process (Schmidt, 1975,

p.   168).

Note: When citing a specific part of a source, you should indicate the appropriate point in the text. APA documentation includes an abbreviation for the word *page,* whereas MLA format does not.

Listing of References

The list of all the sources cited in your paper falls at the end on a new page with the heading *References.*

Items are arranged in alphabetical order, with the author's last name spelled out in full and initials only for the author's first and second names. Next comes the date of publication, title, and, for journal entries, volume number and pages. For books, the date of publication, city of publication, and publisher are included.

Capitalize only the first word of the title and subtitle of books. Be sure to underline the title and to enclose in parentheses the date, volume number, and edition number.

A book with one author

Kohler, W.   (1925).   The mentality of apes.   New York: Harcourt,

Brace and World.

A book with more than one author

Rachman, S.J., & Hodgson, R.J.   (1980).   Obsessions and compulsions

(2nd ed.).   Englewood Cliffs, N.J.:   Prentice-Hall.

Note: Both authors are cited last name first.

An edited book.

Mussen, P.H.   (Ed.).   (1970).   Carmichael's manual of child psychol-

ogy.   New York: Wiley.

Capitalize only the first word of the title and subtitle of articles. Do not underline the article or enclose it in quotation marks. Give the journal title in full; underline the title and capitalize all major words. Underline the volume number and include the issue number in parentheses. Give inclusive page numbers.

An article in a scholarly journal with continuous pagination through an annual volume

Chapman, A.J.   (1973).   Social facilitation of laughter in children.

Journal of Experimental Social Psychology, 9, 529–541.

An article in a scholarly journal that has separate pagination in each issue

Williams, S., & Cohen, L.R.   (1984).   Child stress in early learning

situations.   American Psychologist, 21 (10), 1–28.

A magazine article

Chen, E.   (1979, December).   Twins reared apart: A living lab.   Psy-

chology Today, pp.   112–116.

Note: Use *pp.* when referring to page numbers in magazines and newspapers, but not when referring to page numbers in journals.

A newspaper article, no author

Study finds many street people mentally ill.   (1984, June 8).   New

York Times, p.   7.

A newspaper article, author

James, W.B.   (1985, January 3).   The unemployed and the flat tax.

Wall Street Journal, pp.   1, 12.

Note: This article appears on two separate pages.

Number-Reference Format

The number-reference format is used in several of the sciences. Instead of parenthetical name and year citations, numbers in the text refer to a numbered reference list of works in titled *References* at the end of the paper. Works cited appear either in alphabetical order or in the order in which they are cited in the paper.

Reference within text

People attribute the causes of behavior by using three key factors —
distinctiveness, consensus, and consistency — as well as by some
additional basic principles (1).

Reference lists following the paper

1. Kelly, H.H.   The warm-cold variable in freshwater fish.   J. Biol. Sc.
18:431 – 439; 1950.

Acknowledgments

by Charlie Gillett. Copyright © 1983, 1970 by Charlie Gillett. Reprinted by permission of Pantheon Books, a division of Random House, Inc. Canadian rights courtesy of Souvenir Press Limited.

pp. 216–221   Courtesy of John Tytell.

pp. 224–231   From *The Glory and the Dream: A Narrative History of America 1932–1972* by William Manchester. Copyright © 1974, 1973 by William Manchester. Reprinted by permission of Little, Brown and Company.

pp. 236–241   From *The Hero with a Thousand Faces* by Joseph Campbell, Bollingen Series XVII. Copyright 1949. Copyright © 1976 renewed by Princeton University Press. Excerpt pages 30–38 reprinted with permission of Princeton University Press.

pp. 243–251   From *New Larousse Encyclopedia of Mythology.*

pp. 253–258   Reprinted by permission of A & W Publishers, Inc., from *Heroes and Heroines,* introduced and edited by Antonia Fraser. Copyright © 1980 by Weidenfeld and Nicolson.

pp. 261–268   From "The Emerging American Hero" by Marshall W. Fishwick in *American Hero: Myth and Reality.* Reprinted by permission from Public Affairs Press.

pp. 270–278   From *Heroes of the 1920's* by Roderick Nash.

pp. 280–283   Excerpt from *The Great Comic Book Heroes* by Jules Feiffer. Copyright © 1965 by Dial Press, Inc. Reprinted by permission of Doubleday & Company, Inc.

pp. 287–291   Reprinted with permission of Macmillan Publishing

Company from *The Aims of Education* by Alfred North Whitehead. Copyright 1929 by Macmillan Publishing Company, renewed 1957 by Evelyn Whitehead.

pp. 293–298   Reprinted from *The Saturday Evening Post* © 1969 The Curtis Publishing Company, Indianapolis, Indiana.

pp. 300–306   From *The Glory and the Dream: A Narrative History of America 1932–1972* by William Manchester. Copyright © 1974, 1973 by William Manchester. Reprinted by permission of Little, Brown and Company.

pp. 309–313   Copyright © 1985 by The New York Times Company. Reprinted by permission.

pp. 316–323   Excerpts from *Illiterate America* by Jonathan Kozol. Copyright © 1985 by Jonathan Kozol. Reprinted by permission of Doubleday & Company, Inc.

pp. 326–328   Courtesy of Leslie S. P. Brown from "Who Cares About the Renaissance?"

pp. 338–340   Reprinted with permission of The Free Press, a Division of Macmillan, Inc., from *The Morning After: American Successes and Excesses, 1981–1986* by George F. Will. Copyright © 1986 by George F. Will and The Washington Post Company.

pp. 343–351   From *Prison or Paradise?: The New Religious Cults.* Used by permission of the authors. Copyright © 1980 by A. James Rudin and Marcia R. Rudin.

pp. 354–363   Copyright © 1981 by The New York Times Company. Reprinted by permission.

pp. 366–368   Courtesy of Master Books.

pp. 371–373   The Nation Magazine/Nation Insti.

pp. 378–385   From *The Self-Made Man in America: The Myth of Rags to Riches* by Ervin G. Wyllie. Copyright 1955 by the Trustees of Rutgers College, New Brunswick, New Jersey.

pp. 387–395   Excerpt from *Burnout* by Herbert J. Freudenberger and Geraldine Richelson. Copyright © 1980 by Herbert J. Freudenberger, Ph.D. and Geraldine Richelson. Reprinted with permission of Doubleday & Co., Inc.

pp. 397–401   From *Outrageous Acts and Ordinary Rebellions* by Gloria Steinem. Copyright © 1983 by Gloria Steinem. Reprinted by permission of Henry Holt and Company.

pp. 404–408   From *The Work Ethic in Industrial America 1850–1920* by Daniel T. Rodgers, University of Chicago Press.

pp. 410–417   From *Brave New Work-Place* by Robert Howard. Copyright © Robert Howard, 1985. Reprinted by permission of Viking Penguin, Inc.

pp. 420–426   From *Working: People Talk About What They Do All Day and How They Feel About What They Do,* by Studs Terkel. Copyright © 1974, 1972 by Studs Terkel. Reprinted by permission of Pantheon Books, a division of Random House, Inc.

pp. 431–434   From *Connections* by James Burke. Copyright © 1978 by James Burke. Reprinted by permission of Little, Brown and Company.

pp. 437–441   From *The Luddites: Machine Breakers of the Early 19th Century* by Douglas Liversidge. New York, Franklin Watts, Ltd.

pp. 445–452   From *The Social Transformation of American Medicine* by Paul Starr. Copyright © 1982

by Paul Starr. Reprinted by permission of Basic Books, Inc., Publisher.

pp. 454–465   From *Never Done: A History of American Housework* by Susan Strasser. Copyright © 1982 by Susan Strasser. Reprinted by permission of Pantheon Books, a division of Random House, Inc.

pp. 469–472   Copyright © 1975 by Harper's Magazine. All rights reserved. Reprinted from the January 1975 issue by special permission.

pp. 474–477   From *The Soul of a New Machine* by Tracy Kidder. Copyright © 1981 by John Tracy Kidder. Reprinted by permission of Little, Brown and Company.

pp. 484–488   Courtesy of Joyce Howe. Reprinted by permission of the Village Voice. © Joyce Howe.

pp. 489–493   From "From the Subway to the Synagogue" in *A Walker in the City.* Copyright 1979, 1951 by Alfred Kazin. Reprinted by permission of Harcourt Brace Jovanovich, Inc.

pp. 494–499   Copyright © 1983 by Alice Walker. Reprinted from her volume *In Search of Our Mothers' Gardens* by permission of Harcourt Brace Jovanovich, Inc.

pp. 500–504   From *Born on the Fourth of July* by Ron Kovic. Copyright © 1976. Reprinted by permission from McGraw-Hill, the publisher.

pp. 504–512   From *Blooming: A Small Town Girlhood* by Susan Allen Toth. Copyright © 1978, 1981 by Susan Allen Toth. Reprinted by permission of Little, Brown and Company.

pp. 512–518   From *Growing Up* by Russell Baker. Copyright © 1982 by

Russell Baker. Reprinted by permission of Congdon & Weed.

pp. 521–526   From *The Crisis of Confidence: Ideas, Power and Violence in America* by Arthur M. Schlesinger, Jr. Copyright © 1969, 1968, 1967 by Arthur M. Schlesinger, Jr. Reprinted by permission of Houghton Mifflin Company.

pp. 527–531   From *Violence: Our Fastest Growing Public Health Problem* by John Langone. Copyright © 1984 by John Langone. Reprinted by permission of Little, Brown and Company.

pp. 532–537   Reprinted with permission from Psychology Today Magazine. Copyright © 1985 by the American Psychological Association.

pp. 538–543   From *Fanticide* by Maria W. Piers, Ph.D. Reprinted with permission from W. W. Norton Company, Inc. Copyright © 1978 by W. W. Norton Company, Inc.

pp. 543–548   From "War Is Fun, 1954–1975" in *The First Casualty,* Copyright © 1975 by Phillip Knightley. Reprinted by permission of Harcourt Brace Jovanovich, Inc.

pp. 549–555   From *God or Beast: Evolution and Human Nature* by Robert Claiborne. Reprinted by permission from W. W. Norton Company, Inc. Copyright © 1974 by Robert Claiborne.

pp. 558–559   © 1978 American Heritage Publishing Co., Inc. Reprinted by permission from American Heritage, April/May 1978.

pp. 560–565   Copyright © 1973 by Marvin Kaye from the book *The Story of Monopoly, Silly Putty, Bingo, Twister, Frisbee, Scrabble, Et Cetera.* Reprinted with permission of Stein and Day Publishers.

pp. 565–571   From *Never Done: A History of American Housework* by Susan Strasser. Copyright © 1982 by Susan Strasser. Reprinted by permission of Pantheon Books, a division of Random House, Inc.

pp. 572–580   Copyright © 1986 by The New York Times Company. Reprinted by permission.

pp. 581–591   From "Why Americans Love Their Malls," by William Ecenbarger. *Phildelphia Inquirer* (Magazine), Sept. 1, 1985.

pp. 592–605   From "Night as Frontier" by Murray Melbin in the *American Sociology Review,* February 1978, Vol. 43, #1.

Index

Index